Taxation

Taxation

Finance Act 2005

Eleventh edition

Alan Melville
FCA, BSc, Cert. Ed.

FT Prentice Hall
FINANCIAL TIMES

An imprint of Pearson Education
Harlow, England • London • New York • Boston • San Francisco • Toronto • Sydney • Singapore • Hong Kong
Tokyo • Seoul • Taipei • New Delhi • Cape Town • Madrid • Mexico City • Amsterdam • Munich • Paris • Milan

Pearson Education Limited
Edinburgh Gate
Harlow
Essex CM20 2JE
England

and Associated Companies throughout the world

Visit us on the World Wide Web at:
www.pearsoned.co.uk

First published 1995
Eleventh edition published 2006

ISBN: 0 273 70637 3

British Library Cataloguing-in-Publication Data
A catalogue record for this book is available from the British Library

Library of Congress Cataloguing-in-Publication Data
A catalog record for this book is available from the Library of Congress

10 9 8 7 6 5 4 3 2 1
11 10 09 08 07 06

Printed and bound by Bell & Bain Ltd, Glasgow

The publisher's policy is to use paper manufactured from sustainable forests.

Website
A website to accompany the eleventh edition of *Taxation* can be found at:
www.pearsoned.co.uk/melville

Contents

Preface

The main aim of this book is to describe the UK taxation system in sufficient depth and with sufficient clarity to meet the needs of those undertaking a first course of study in taxation. The book has not been written with any specific syllabus in mind but is suitable for students who are preparing for any of the following examinations:

Examining body	*Level*	*Examination title*
Institute of Chartered Accountants in England and Wales	Professional Stage	Taxation
Association of Chartered Certified Accountants	Professional Scheme Part 2	Business Taxation
Chartered Institute of Public Finance and Accountancy	Diploma Stage	Taxation
Association of Taxation Technicians	Associateship	Personal and Business Taxation
Association of Accounting Technicians	Technician Stage	Preparing Personal and Business Taxation Computations
Association of Chartered Certified Accountants	Technician Scheme Advanced Level	Preparing Taxation Computations
Association of International Accountants	Foundation Level	Auditing and Taxation
Institute of Financial Accountants	Technician Level	Personal and Business Taxation

The book will also be of value to those studying taxation as part of a university or college course in accounting, finance or business studies and may be used as an introductory text for a study of taxation at an advanced level.

Every effort has been made to explain the tax system as clearly as possible. There are numerous worked examples and each chapter (except Chapter 1) concludes with a set of exercises which thoroughly test the reader's grasp of the new topics introduced in that chapter. The book also contains four sets of review questions which are drawn from the past examination papers of the professional accounting bodies. The solutions to most of the exercises and review questions are to be found at the back of the book but the solutions to those exercises and questions marked with an asterisk (*) are provided in a separate Lecturer's Guide.

This eleventh edition incorporates the provisions of Finance Act 2005. It does not cover the forthcoming Finance (No. 2) Act 2005, but this second Act is expected to be concerned entirely with technical matters which are beyond the scope of this book.

Alan Melville
June 2005

Acknowledgements

I would like to thank the following accounting bodies for granting me permission to use their past examination questions:

- Institute of Chartered Accountants in England and Wales (ICAEW)
- Association of Chartered Certified Accountants (ACCA)
- Chartered Institute of Management Accountants (CIMA)
- Association of Accounting Technicians (AAT).

I must point out that the answers provided to these questions are entirely my own and are not the responsibility of the accounting body concerned. I would also like to thank the Office for National Statistics for granting me permission to reproduce the table of Retail Price Indexes given in Chapter 17.

Finally, I would like to express my gratitude to Mrs Margaret Cooper who took on the daunting task of checking every calculation in this book and in the accompanying Lecturer's Guide.

Alan Melville
June 2005

Summary of Tax Data

Income Tax

TAX RATES AND BANDS		2005/06 £	2004/05 £
Starting rate	10%	first 2,090	first 2,020
Basic rate	22%	next 30,310	next 29,380
Higher rate	40%	over 32,400	over 31,400

Notes:
(a) Savings income is taxed at 10%, 20% and 40%.
(b) Dividends are taxed at 10% and 32.5%.
(c) Special rates of tax apply to certain trusts.

ALLOWANCES	£	£
Personal allowance		
Age 0 to 64	4,895	4,745
Age 65 to 74	7,090	6,830
Age 75 or over	7,220	6,950
Blind person's allowance	1,610	1,560
Married couple's allowance†		
Age under 75 and born before 6/4/35	5,905	5,725
Age 75 or over	5,975	5,795
Minimum amount	2,280	2,210
Income limit for age-related allowances	19,500	18,900

†*This allowance is relieved at 10%.*

CAR FUEL BENEFIT	£	£
Amount to which the appropriate percentage is applied in order to calculate car fuel benefit	14,400	14,400

Note:
The appropriate percentage depends upon the car's emission rating.

PENSION SCHEMES	£	£
Earnings cap	105,600	102,000

Capital Allowances

Writing Down Allowance (WDA) per annum:	
Plant and machinery	25%
Long-life assets	6%
Industrial buildings and agricultural buildings	4%
First Year Allowance (FYA) on qualifying plant and machinery:	
Acquired on or after 2 July 1998†	40%
Acquired 6 April 2004 to 5 April 2005‡	50%
Energy-saving technology acquired on or after 1 April 2001	100%
Low emission cars acquired 17 April 2002 to 31 March 2008	100%
Water-efficient technology acquired on or after 1 April 2003	100%

† *Small and medium-sized businesses only.*
‡ *Small businesses only. Dates are 1 April 2004 to 31 March 2005 for companies.*

National Insurance Contributions

	2005/06	*2004/05*
CLASS 1 (Not contracted out)		
Primary threshold (weekly)	£94	£91
Upper earnings limit (weekly)	£630	£610
Employee contributions†		
Rate on earnings between threshold and UEL	11%	11%
Rate on earnings beyond UEL	1%	1%
Employer contributions‡		
Secondary threshold (weekly)	£94	£91
Rate on earnings beyond threshold	12.8%	12.8%

† *No employee contributions payable if earnings do not exceed primary threshold.*
‡ *No employer contributions payable if earnings do not exceed secondary threshold.*

CLASS 1A		
Rate	12.8%	12.8%
CLASS 2		
Weekly contribution	£2.10	£2.05
Small earnings exception limit	£4,345	£4,215
CLASS 3		
Weekly contribution	£7.35	£7.15
CLASS 4		
Lower profits limit	£4,895	£4,745
Upper profits limit	£32,760	£31,720
Rate on profits between lower and upper limit	8%	8%
Rate on profits beyond upper limit	1%	1%

Capital Gains Tax

	2005/06	*2004/05*
	£	£
Annual exemption - individuals and disabled trusts	8,500	8,200
- other trusts	4,250	4,100
Chattels exemption	6,000	6,000

Corporation Tax

Financial Year	*FY2005*	*FY2004*	*FY2003*	*FY2002*
Starting rate	0%	0%	0%	0%
Lower limit	£10,000	£10,000	£10,000	£10,000
Upper limit	£50,000	£50,000	£50,000	£50,000
Marginal relief fraction	19/400	19/400	19/400	19/400
Small companies rate	19%	19%	19%	19%
Lower limit	£300,000	£300,000	£300,000	£300,000
Upper limit	£1,500,000	£1,500,000	£1,500,000	£1,500,000
Marginal relief fraction	11/400	11/400	11/400	11/400
Full rate	30%	30%	30%	30%
Non-corporate distribution rate	19%	19%	-	-

Inheritance Tax

Date of transfer	*0% Band*	*Rate on chargeable lifetime transfers*	*Rate on death*
6 April 1998 to 5 April 1999	0 - £223,000	20%	40%
6 April 1999 to 5 April 2000	0 - £231,000	20%	40%
6 April 2000 to 5 April 2001	0 - £234,000	20%	40%
6 April 2001 to 5 April 2002	0 - £242,000	20%	40%
6 April 2002 to 5 April 2003	0 - £250,000	20%	40%
6 April 2003 to 5 April 2004	0 - £255,000	20%	40%
6 April 2004 to 5 April 2005	0 - £263,000	20%	40%
6 April 2005 to 5 April 2006	0 - £275,000	20%	40%

Value Added Tax

Standard rate	17.5%	(from 1 April 1991)
Registration threshold	£60,000	(from 1 April 2005)
Deregistration threshold	£58,000	(from 1 April 2005)

Part 1

INCOME TAX AND NATIONAL INSURANCE

Chapter 1

Introduction to the UK tax system

Introduction

The purpose of this first chapter is to provide an overview of the UK tax system. The principal UK taxes are introduced and classified and the main sources of tax law are explained. This chapter also outlines the structure and functions of Her Majesty's Revenue and Customs (the organisation which is responsible for the administration of the UK tax system) and describes the annual procedure which is used to assess the tax liability of an individual. The chapter concludes by distinguishing between tax evasion and tax avoidance.

UK taxes

The UK taxation system is composed of a number of different taxes, some of which are *direct* taxes and some of which are *indirect* taxes:

(a) Direct taxes are charged on income, profits or other gains and are either deducted at source or paid directly to the tax authorities. The main direct taxes are income tax, capital gains tax and inheritance tax (which are all paid by individuals) and corporation tax (which is paid by companies). Until recently, these taxes were administered by the Inland Revenue. They are now administered by HM Revenue and Customs (HMRC) which was formed in April 2005 by merging the Inland Revenue and HM Customs and Excise. National Insurance contributions, which can also be looked upon as a form of direct taxation, are administered by the National Insurance Contributions Office (NICO) of HMRC.

(b) Indirect taxes are taxes on spending. They are charged when a taxpayer buys an item and are paid to the vendor as part of the purchase price of the item. It is then the vendor's duty to pass the tax on to the tax authorities. Indirect taxes include value added tax (VAT), stamp duty, customs duties and the excise duties levied on alcohol, tobacco and petrol. The only indirect tax considered in this book is VAT, which was administered by HM Customs and Excise until April 2005 but is now administered by HMRC.

Sources of tax law

There is no single source of UK tax law. The basic rules are laid down in Acts of Parliament but it is left to the courts to interpret these Acts and to provide much of the detail of the tax system. In addition, HMRC issues various statements, notices and leaflets which explain how the law is implemented in practice. These statements have no legal backing but they explain the tax authorities' interpretation of the law and will be adhered to unless successfully challenged in the courts.

Statute law

The basic rules of the UK tax system are embodied in a number of tax *statutes* or Acts of Parliament. The main statutes currently in force are as follows:

Tax	*Statute*	*Abbreviation*
Income tax & }	Income and Corporation Taxes Act 1988	ICTA 1988
Corporation tax }	Capital Allowances Act 2001	CAA 2001
Income tax	Income Tax (Earnings and Pensions) Act 2003	ITEPA 2003
	Income Tax (Trading and Other Income) Act 2005	ITTOIA 2005
Capital gains tax & }	Taxation of Chargeable Gains Act 1992	TCGA 1992
Corporation tax }		
Inheritance tax	Inheritance Tax Act 1984	IHTA 1984
National Insurance	Social Security Contributions & Benefits Act 1992	SSCBA 1992
Value added tax	Value Added Tax Act 1994	VATA 1994
Administration of }	Taxes Management Act 1970	TMA 1970
the tax system }	Customs and Excise Management Act 1979	CEMA 1979

These statutes are amended each year by the annual Finance Act, which is based upon the Budget proposals put forward by the Chancellor of the Exchequer. Some of the tax statutes provide for the making of detailed regulations by *statutory instrument*. A statutory instrument (SI) is a document which is laid before Parliament and then automatically becomes law within a stated period unless any objections are raised to it.

Tax Law Rewrite project

The Tax Law Rewrite project was established in 1996 with the aim of rewriting the primary direct tax legislation of the UK in such a way that it is clearer and easier to understand. The first three Acts to arise from this work are:

(a) the Capital Allowances Act 2001

(b) the Income Tax (Earnings and Pensions) Act 2003

(c) the Income Tax (Trading and Other Income) Act 2005.

Other Acts are expected in due course.

European Union law

It is worth noting that membership of the European Union (EU) involves adherence to EU law and that if there is a conflict between EU law and the law of a member state then EU law will take priority. This applies as much to tax law as to any other category of law and the European influence on UK tax law is likely to increase over time. At present, the main impact is on VAT, where the prevailing legislation takes the form of EU Directives. These Directives are binding on the UK and dictate the results which the internal legislation of the UK must bring about.

Case law

Over the years, taxpayers and the tax authorities have frequently disagreed over the interpretation of the tax Acts. As a result, many thousands of tax cases have been brought before the courts. The decisions made by judges in order to resolve these cases form an important part of the tax law of the UK and some of the more significant cases are referred to in this book.

Statements made by the tax authorities

The main statements and other documents produced by HM Revenue and Customs as a guide to the law on taxation are as follows:

(a) **Statements of Practice**. A Statement of Practice (SP) sets out the HMRC interpretation of tax legislation and clarifies the way in which the law will be applied in practice. For example, SP 2/02 (the second SP issued in 2002) deals with the taxation treatment of exchange rate fluctuations.

(b) **Extra-Statutory Concessions**. An Extra-Statutory Concession (ESC) consists of a relaxation which gives taxpayers a reduction in liability to which they are not entitled under the strict letter of the law. In general, concessions are made so as to resolve anomalies or relieve hardship. For example, ESC B10 is concerned with the income of contemplative communities or their members.

(c) **Press releases**. These are issued throughout the year on a wide variety of tax-related subjects. Of especial interest are the Budget press releases which are issued on Budget day and which provide a detailed explanation of the Budget proposals.

(d) **Internal Guidance Manuals**. HMRC produces a comprehensive set of internal tax manuals for the guidance of its own staff. These manuals may be inspected at HMRC Enquiry Offices or via the Internet and are also available for sale.

(e) **Leaflets**. These are aimed at the general public and explain the tax system in non-technical language. For example, leaflet IR121 is a guide to income tax for pensioners.

Most of the information produced by the tax authorities is now available on the HMRC website, the address of which is *www.hmrc.gov.uk*.

The tax year

The proposed amendments to the tax system which are put forward in the annual Budget speech are usually intended to take effect as from the beginning of the next tax year, though some of the proposals may have a more immediate effect. A *tax year*, also known as a *fiscal year* or a *year of assessment*, runs from 6 April to the following 5 April. For example, the tax year referred to as 2004/05 began on 6 April 2004 and ended on 5 April 2005. This book takes into account the provisions of the Finance Act 2005 (based on the March 2005 Budget proposals) and describes the UK tax system for tax year 2005/06.

It is worth noting that the tax year for corporation tax purposes is slightly different from the fiscal year. A corporation tax *financial year* runs from 1 April in one year to 31 March in the following year and is identified by the year in which it begins. This book describes the corporation tax system for Financial Year 2005, which runs from 1 April 2005 to 31 March 2006 inclusive.

Structure of HM Revenue and Customs

HM Revenue and Customs consists of a large body of civil servants headed by the *Commissioners for Revenue and Customs*. The Commissioners are appointed by the Queen in accordance with recommendations made by the *Treasury*. This Government department is managed by the *Chancellor of the Exchequer* and has overall responsibility for the public finances of the UK. The main duties of the Commissioners for Revenue and Customs are as follows:

(a) to implement the law relating to direct and indirect taxation
(b) to provide advice to the Chancellor of the Exchequer on taxation matters
(c) to administer the many divisions and offices into which HMRC is organised.

The routine work of HMRC is carried out by officials known as *Officers of Revenue and Customs*. With regard to direct taxation, the main function of these officials is to calculate or "assess" a taxpayer's tax liability and then to ensure that the correct amount of tax is paid. Under the Self Assessment system (see below) a taxpayer may calculate his or her own tax liability, in which case an HMRC official will check the taxpayer's "self-assessment".

Until fairly recently, tax assessment was the responsibility of *Inspectors of Taxes* whilst tax collection was handled separately by *Collectors of Taxes*. This traditional separation of assessment and collection is now seen as outdated and the two functions have been combined. In consequence, the terms "Inspector" and "Collector" have been dropped in favour of the above-mentioned "Officer of Revenue and Customs".

The functions of HMRC with regard to indirect taxation (and VAT in particular) are explained later in this book (see Chapter 30).

HMRC has specialist offices which deal with such matters as pension schemes, oil taxation, valuations and so forth but most of the day-to-day work relating to direct taxation takes place in a network of local offices. These are of three main types:

(a) **Enquiry Offices**. These offices deal with taxpayers' general queries and carry stocks of tax forms and leaflets.

(b) **Service Offices**. These offices are responsible for most of the routine assessment and collection work.

(c) **District Offices**. These offices concentrate mainly on compliance work (checking that taxpayers have complied with tax regulations).

Administration of the tax system

The remainder of this chapter describes the system which is used each year to assess an individual's liability to income tax and capital gains tax. Later chapters explain the equivalent systems which are used for corporation tax, inheritance tax and VAT.

For tax years up to and including 1995/96, the assessment of an individual's tax liability was entirely the responsibility of the tax authorities and it was possible for taxpayers to delay the assessment (and payment) of tax by withholding information from the authorities for as long as possible. The introduction of Self Assessment in 1996/97 shifted the responsibility for assessment to the taxpayer and made it much more likely that tax is assessed and paid on time.

Self Assessment

If an individual's tax liability for a tax year cannot be collected entirely by deduction at source (see Chapter 2) or via the PAYE system (see Chapter 7), then the tax liability must be the subject of a formal tax assessment. The amount of tax which is due for the year may be calculated by the taxpayer or the taxpayer's accountant and then checked by HMRC. Alternatively, if the taxpayer prefers not to perform the calculation, the amount due is calculated by HMRC. In either case, the first step is the completion of a *tax return*. The annual procedure is as follows:

(a) In early April each year, tax returns are issued to those taxpayers who are likely to need them. The main tax return consists of a basic 10-page form plus a number of supplementary pages, each dealing with a different type of income or gains (e.g. income from employment). Taxpayers are sent only those supplementary pages which are thought to be relevant to their circumstances but can request further supplementary pages if necessary. A 4-page short tax return (STR) is available for taxpayers with simpler tax affairs.

(b) A disk version of the main tax return is available for tax practitioners who wish to complete clients' tax returns with the aid of a computer system and then submit the returns electronically using the "Electronic Lodgement Service". Individual taxpayers can also file main tax returns electronically, via the Internet.

(c) The information requested in a tax return relates to the tax year just ended. For example, the tax returns which were issued in April 2005 required taxpayers to declare their income and gains for tax year 2004/05 and to claim allowances and reliefs (see Chapters 3 and 4) for the same year.

(d) The tax return must be completed in full. It is not permissible to omit figures or to make entries such as "see accounts" or "as submitted by employer". Unless asked to submit accounts or other supporting documentation with the return, a taxpayer is under no obligation to do so. However, it is necessary to retain all supporting documentation in case HMRC enquires into the accuracy of a return.

(e) The main tax return includes an optional tax calculation section in which the taxpayer may calculate his or her own tax liability. If this section is left blank, HMRC will calculate the tax liability on the taxpayer's behalf. The short return does not include a self-calculation facility. If a main return is filed electronically, the tax liability is calculated automatically by computer software. In all cases, the resulting assessment is referred to as a "self-assessment".

(f) A main tax return must be "filed" on or before the following dates:

   (i) 31 January following the end of the tax year to which the return relates (or within three months of the date of issue of the return, if later) for taxpayers who have calculated their own tax liability or submit the return electronically

   (ii) 30 September following the end of the tax year to which the return relates (or within two months of the date of issue of the return, if later) for taxpayers who wish HMRC to calculate their tax liability.

   A short tax return must be filed by 31 January following the end of the tax year, but taxpayers using the short return are encouraged to file by 30 September so as to give HMRC time in which to compute the tax liability before it is due for payment (see below). The 31 January which follows the end of a tax year is known as the "annual filing date" for that year. For example, the annual filing date for tax year 2005/06 is 31 January 2007. A regime of automatic penalties (see Chapter 14) applies if a return is filed late.

(g) HMRC is entitled to reject as incomplete a main tax return which is received after the 30 September deadline unless the tax calculation section of the return has been filled in. In practice, however, returns are not rejected in these circumstances and HMRC will perform the necessary calculations. But HMRC cannot guarantee that it will then be able to notify the taxpayer of the amount payable (if any) in time for this amount to be paid on the due date. This could result in the taxpayer becoming liable to surcharges and interest on overdue tax (see Chapter 14).

(h) HMRC has the right to "repair" a taxpayer's self-assessment (i.e. to correct any obvious mistakes) within nine months of the date on which the return is filed by the taxpayer.

(i) The taxpayer has the right to amend his or her tax return and self-assessment within 12 months of the annual filing date for that return. Taxpayers who believe that an error or mistake in their tax return has resulted in an excessive self-assessment may make an "error or mistake" claim within five years of the annual filing date for the year to which the claim relates.

(j) The tax due in relation to a self-assessment is normally payable as follows:

  (i) A first payment on account (POA) is due on 31 January in the tax year to which the self-assessment relates.

  (ii) A second POA is due on the following 31 July.

  (iii) A final balancing payment is due on the annual filing date (i.e. 31 January following the end of the tax year).

  For example, the tax due in relation to a 2005/06 self-assessment would normally be payable on 31 January 2006 (first POA), 31 July 2006 (second POA) and 31 January 2007 (balancing payment). Further information regarding the payment of tax is given in Chapter 14.

(k) A taxpayer who is entitled to a repayment of tax may make an entry on his or her tax return nominating a charity to receive all or part of that repayment. The taxpayer may also indicate on the tax return that Gift Aid (see Chapter 4) should apply to this charitable donation.

Notification of chargeability to tax

Individuals who have not received a tax return, but have taxable income or gains of which HMRC is not aware, must notify HMRC of their chargeability to tax within six months of the end of the tax year in which the income arises. Penalties are imposed for non-compliance with this requirement (see Chapter 14). Notification of chargeability to tax is *not* required if:

(a) the taxpayer has no capital gains, and

(b) the taxpayer is not a higher rate taxpayer (see Chapter 2), and

(c) all of the taxpayer's income has been subject to deduction of tax at source (see Chapter 2) or has been dealt with via the PAYE system (see Chapter 7).

Enquiries

HMRC adopts a "process now - check later" approach to tax returns filed under the Self Assessment system. The information supplied in tax returns is processed when the returns are filed and any obvious errors in taxpayers' self-assessments are repaired (see above) but no attempt is made at that time to check that the correct amount of income and gains has been declared. However, all returns are eventually checked and some are selected for detailed enquiry. Note that:

(a) Most enquiries arise because HMRC wishes to ask questions about the information given in a tax return, but it is not necessary for an enquiry to be justified and some enquiry cases are chosen entirely at random.

(b) In general, enquiries must begin within 12 months of the annual filing date for the year to which the enquiry relates. This means that a taxpayer who has made full disclosure of all relevant facts in a tax return can be sure that the corresponding self-assessment is final if no enquiry has begun within 12 months of the annual filing date. However, HMRC may raise a "discovery assessment" after these 12 months have elapsed if it is discovered that full disclosure has not been made. The time limits for discovery assessments under the Self Assessment system are as follows:

    (i) 31 January in the sixth tax year following the year to which the assessment relates, in the case of incomplete disclosure of facts without negligence or fraud

    (ii) 31 January in the twenty-first tax year following the year to which the assessment relates, in the case of negligence or fraud.

Determinations

If a taxpayer fails to file a tax return by the required date, an Officer of Revenue and Customs may make a "determination" of the amount of tax due, calculated according to "the best of his information and belief". The taxpayer cannot appeal against this determination and cannot apply for the tax due to be postponed (see below). The determination can be displaced only if the taxpayer files the required return.

Appeals

Under Self Assessment, taxpayers have the right of appeal in relation to certain HMRC decisions. The main classes of appeal are:

(a) an appeal against the imposition of a penalty (see Chapter 14)

(b) an appeal against the imposition of a surcharge (see Chapter 14)

(c) an appeal against a request by HMRC that the taxpayer should submit documents, records etc. in the course of an enquiry

(d) an appeal against amendments made to a self-assessment as a consequence of an enquiry
(e) an appeal to the effect that the relevant conditions for the making of a discovery assessment do not exist
(f) an appeal against a discovery assessment.

The appeals procedure

In general, appeals must be made in writing to HMRC and must be made within 30 days of the relevant HMRC decision. In the case of disputed amendments to self-assessments and disputed discovery assessments, the taxpayer may also apply to postpone payment of all or part of the tax which has been assessed, pending settlement of the appeal. Note that:

(a) Applications to postpone payment are subject to HMRC agreement. Applications for postponement which HMRC refuses to accept may be referred to the appeal Commissioners (see below).

(b) Any non-postponed part of the tax due on a disputed assessment is payable on the due date in the usual way. If the appeal is subsequently determined in the taxpayer's favour, any overpaid tax is refunded.

(c) Most appeals are settled by means of an informal discussion between HMRC and the taxpayer or the taxpayer's agent, culminating in an agreement of the amount of tax which is due. Appeals which cannot be resolved amicably in this way are referred to the appeal Commissioners (who should not be confused with the Commissioners for Revenue and Customs). Appeal Commissioners fall into two categories, the *General Commissioners* and the *Special Commissioners*.

(d) The General Commissioners hear appeals locally. They do not usually possess any formal tax qualifications and are similar in many ways to magistrates, being part-time and unpaid. They are assisted by a paid clerk who is normally a local solicitor or accountant. The appeals brought before the General Commissioners are usually of a fairly straightforward nature.

(e) The Special Commissioners are similar to circuit judges and travel the country hearing appeals which involve complex matters of tax law. They are full-time tax professionals and they are paid for their services.

(f) The appeal Commissioners may confirm, reduce or increase a disputed assessment and their decision on a matter of fact is final. But either HMRC or the taxpayer may express dissatisfaction with the Commissioners' decision on a point of law and take the appeal further, first to the High Court, then to the Court of Appeal and ultimately to the House of Lords.

(g) The costs of bringing an appeal before the appeal Commissioners are usually fairly modest. Each party bears their own costs and the Commissioners cannot normally require the losing party to pay the costs of the victor (although the Special Commissioners may do so if they believe that a taxpayer has acted wholly unreasonably). The costs of taking an appeal to the High Court and beyond can be extremely high and an unsuccessful taxpayer may be required to pay HMRC's costs in defending the appeal as well as his or her own costs.

Record keeping

It is compulsory for taxpayers to keep proper records so that they can make a correct tax return and (if necessary) substantiate the figures entered on the return. A taxpayer who is in business or who lets property must retain these records for five years after the annual filing date for the year concerned. Otherwise, records must be retained for 12 months after the annual filing date. For example, records for tax year 2005/06 (filing date 31 January 2007) must be retained until 31 January 2012 by a taxpayer who is in business or who lets property and until 31 January 2008 otherwise.

The Adjudicator

An independent and impartial Adjudicator (who is not part of the HMRC management structure) considers complaints made by those taxpayers who are not satisfied with the quality of the service which they have received from HMRC. The Adjudicator writes an annual report and makes recommendations for improvements to HMRC procedures and practices. The Adjudicator is not empowered to hear tax appeals.

Taxpayer's Charter

The Taxpayer's Charter sets out the standards of service which a taxpayer has the right to expect from the tax authorities. The Charter also explains the authorities' expectations of the taxpayer. In summary, a taxpayer has the right to expect that the tax authorities will act fairly and impartially, communicate effectively and provide a good quality service. In return, the tax authorities expect taxpayers to keep accurate up-to-date records, provide correct and complete information and pay the correct amount of tax on the correct date. HMRC has published a set of codes of practice in support of the Taxpayer's Charter, each relating to a specific aspect of its work.

Tax evasion

As stated above, HMRC expects taxpayers to provide information which is correct and complete. Dishonest behaviour (such as concealing a source of income) is known as *tax evasion* and is punishable by law. A statutory offence of evading income tax was introduced by the Finance Act 2000. On summary conviction in a magistrate's court, offenders may be sentenced to up to six months in prison and may be fined up to £5,000. On indictment in a higher court, the penalties are increased to a maximum of seven years in prison and/or an unlimited fine.

Tax avoidance

Taxpayers are entitled to organise their financial affairs in any way that they please and may do so in such a way that their tax burden is minimised. This perfectly legal activity is known as *tax avoidance*. For example, a taxpayer might avoid income tax by moving funds from a bank account which pays taxable interest to one which pays tax-free interest (see Chapter 6).

Tax avoidance is acceptable within limits but, over the years, tax advisors have shown great ingenuity in devising complex tax avoidance schemes to exploit "loopholes" in the tax system. These schemes often result in a significant loss of tax revenue until eventually blocked by specific anti-avoidance legislation. A permanent solution to this problem would be to establish a *general anti-avoidance rule* (GAAR). If such a rule existed, an entirely lawful transaction which a taxpayer had performed solely for tax avoidance purposes could be set aside when computing his or her tax liability. The Government has in fact considered the introduction of a GAAR in relation to corporate taxation but has decided not to proceed, at least for the immediate future.

In an attempt to limit the effectiveness of tax avoidance schemes, those who promote and market certain types of scheme are required to provide HMRC with details of each such scheme shortly after it has been sold to the taxpayer who will use it. Promoters must provide a description of the scheme, including details of its tax consequences and the statutory provisions on which it relies. The scheme is then registered by HMRC and allocated a registration number. Taxpayers using such a scheme are required to quote the registration number of the scheme in their tax returns. These disclosure rules are intended to provide HMRC with advance warning of avoidance schemes, so enabling swifter and more effective investigation and counteraction.

Summary

- Direct taxes are charged on income, profits and other gains. The main direct taxes are income tax, capital gains tax, inheritance tax and corporation tax. National Insurance contributions are also a form of direct taxation. Indirect taxes are taxes on spending and are paid as part of the price of a bought item. Indirect taxes include VAT, stamp duty, customs duties and excise duties.
- Taxation law is a combination of statute law and case law. Statements made by the tax authorities have no legal force but provide information on the authorities' interpretation of the law.
- The fiscal year runs from 6 April to the following 5 April. The corporation tax financial year runs from 1 April to the following 31 March.
- HM Revenue and Customs (HMRC) calculates a taxpayer's tax liability or checks the taxpayer's own calculation of the liability. The calculation is based upon the information provided in an annual tax return.
- Taxpayers who complete the main tax return have the option of calculating their own tax liability. The main tax return must normally be filed by 30 September following the end of the tax year if the taxpayer wishes HMRC to calculate the liability. Otherwise, the return must be filed by 31 January following the end of the tax year.
- A taxpayer who has not received a tax return, but has taxable income or gains of which HMRC is not aware, must notify HMRC of his or her chargeability to tax within six months of the end of the tax year in which the income arises.
- HMRC may initiate an enquiry within 12 months of the annual filing date for the year to which the enquiry relates. Discovery assessments may be made after these 12 months have elapsed if it is discovered that the taxpayer has not made full disclosure of all relevant facts.
- In certain circumstances, taxpayers have the right of appeal against HMRC decisions. Appeals are heard initially by the General Commissioners or the Special Commissioners but may progress to the Courts.
- Tax evasion should be distinguished from tax avoidance. The former involves dishonest conduct by the taxpayer and is illegal. The latter involves the sensible arrangement of the taxpayer's affairs so as to minimise the liability to tax and is perfectly legal.

Chapter 2

Introduction to income tax

Introduction

Income tax assessments are computed for a tax year (or "year of assessment") and are based on the taxpayer's aggregate income for that year from all sources, ignoring any income which is exempt from income tax. This chapter explains the main features of an income tax computation, in preparation for the more detailed information which is provided in subsequent chapters.

Current income tax legislation is located mainly in the Income and Corporation Taxes Act 1988, the Income Tax (Earnings and Pensions) Act 2003 and the Income Tax (Trading and Other Income) Act 2005, as amended by subsequent Finance Acts.

Taxable persons

In general, an individual who is resident in the UK for a tax year is liable to pay income tax on all of his or her income for that year, including income arising in the UK and income which is derived from an overseas source. However, there are two main exceptions to this general rule:

(a) Certain forms of income are exempt from income tax altogether (see below).

(b) Income derived from an overseas source by a UK resident who is not domiciled in the UK (i.e. whose permanent home is not the UK) is only subject to income tax to the extent that the income is remitted to the UK.

Individuals who are not UK residents are liable to pay income tax on their UK income only (see Chapter 32). Income tax is payable by:

(a) adults, on their own income and on their share of the income of a partnership

(b) children, if they have sufficient income to pay tax

(c) trustees, on the income of a trust or settlement

(d) personal representatives, on income arising from the estate of a deceased person.

The following persons and organisations are *not* liable to pay income tax, whether or not they are resident in the UK:

(a) companies, which pay corporation tax on their income instead of income tax
(b) registered charities and scientific research associations, except on trading income other than that derived from certain small trading activities
(c) approved pension funds
(d) representatives of foreign countries (e.g. ambassadors)
(e) visiting members of foreign armed forces (on their service pay only)
(f) local authorities
(g) trade unions (on certain types of income).

The schedular system

Since 1803, income has been classified for income tax purposes into categories known as "Schedules", each identified by a letter of the alphabet. There were five Schedules originally (A to E) and each Schedule had its own rules for computing the amount of income of that type arising in a tax year. A sixth Schedule (F) was added in 1965.

This schedular system remained intact until 1988 when Schedule B (income from commercial woodlands) was abolished. Schedule C (income tax deducted by paying and collecting agents) followed in 1996. In 2003, Schedule E, which dealt with income from employment, was also abolished when most of its provisions were transferred into the Income Tax (Earnings and Pensions) Act 2003. This left the following Schedules:

Schedule A		-	Income from property
Schedule D	Case I	-	Profits of a trade
	Case II	-	Profits of a profession or vocation
	Case III	-	UK interest received and certain annual payments
	Case IV	-	Interest on foreign securities
	Case V	-	Income from foreign possessions
	Case VI	-	Income not assessed under any other Schedule or Case
Schedule F		-	Dividends received from UK companies.

In 2005, the Income Tax (Trading and Other Income) Act 2005 repealed Schedules A, D and F and so completed the abolition of the schedular system for income tax.

The tax rules which were enshrined in the Schedules have been preserved (more or less intact) in ITEPA 2003 and ITTOIA 2005 but terms such as "Schedule A" are no longer used. Instead, income is now classified for income tax purposes into categories such as "employment income", "trading income", "property income", "savings and investment income" and "miscellaneous income". However, the schedular system has *not* been abolished for corporation tax purposes (see Chapter 23).

Exempt income

Certain types of income are specifically exempt from income tax and should be completely ignored when preparing an income tax computation. Some of the most important sources of exempt income are:

(a) the first £70 per annum of interest received on a National Savings Bank Ordinary account (see Chapter 6)

(b) income from National Savings Certificates

(c) interest arising from a certified SAYE (Save As You Earn) arrangement

(d) income from Personal Equity Plans (see Chapter 6)

(e) income from Individual Savings Accounts (see Chapter 6)

(f) income from investments held in a Child Trust Fund account (see Chapter 6)

(g) dividends received on shares held in a Venture Capital Trust, so long as certain conditions are satisfied (see Chapter 6)

(h) winnings from betting, competition prizes and premium bond prizes

(i) maintenance payments received from a spouse or ex-spouse after a couple have separated or divorced (see Chapter 4)

(j) income of up to £4,250 per annum received under the "rent-a-room" scheme (see Chapter 5)

(k) certain social security benefits (e.g. child benefit and housing benefit) although some others are taxable (e.g. the state retirement pension)

(l) wound and disability pensions

(m) certain minor benefits provided by employers for their employees (see Chapter 7)

(n) statutory redundancy pay and the first £30,000 of compensation received for loss of employment (see Chapter 7)

(o) income from scholarships

(p) most commissions, discounts and cashbacks received by ordinary retail customers when purchasing goods, investments or services

(q) compensation for mis-sold personal pensions or mis-sold free-standing additional voluntary contribution schemes taken out between certain dates

(r) foster care receipts not exceeding specified limits and financial support provided to adopters by local authorities or adoption agencies.

Structure of an income tax computation

In order to calculate a taxpayer's income tax liability for a tax year it is necessary to bring together *all* of the taxpayer's income into a single tax computation. For reasons which are explained below, income which has already been taxed at source must also be included in this computation. A typical income tax computation for the year 2005/06 might appear as follows:

			£
Business profits			36,640
Income from property			7,469
Building society interest taxed at source (pre-tax equivalent)			700
Total income			44,809
Less: Charges on income			1,000
Statutory total income			43,809
Less: Personal allowance			4,895
Taxable Income			38,914
Income tax			
	2,090	@ 10%	209.00
	30,310	@ 22%	6,668.20
	6,514	@ 40%	2,605.60
	38,914		9,482.80
Less: Tax reducers			0.00
Tax borne			9,482.80
Add: Tax withheld on charges			220.00
Tax liability for the year			9,702.80
Less: Tax paid by deduction at source			140.00
Tax payable			9,562.80

All of the terms used in this computation are explained in great detail in this chapter and in later chapters. For the time being it is sufficient to understand the main features of the computation, which are as follows:

(a) The taxpayer's total income for the year is calculated by adding together income from all sources, including the pre-tax equivalent of any income which has already been taxed but excluding any income which is exempt from income tax.

(b) Certain payments made by the taxpayer known as "charges on income" are deducted from total income, giving statutory total income (STI).

(c) The taxpayer's personal allowance is deducted from STI, giving taxable income. The personal allowance (£4,895 in 2005/06) acts as a tax threshold, ensuring that those on very low incomes do not have to pay income tax.

(d) Income tax is charged on the taxable income, using the rates of tax in force for the year. The amount of tax calculated in this way is then subject to a number of adjustments and the result is the tax payable to HM Revenue and Customs.

(e) The *tax borne* by the taxpayer is the amount of tax suffered for the year. This may be different from the *tax liability*, which is the amount of tax which must be accounted for to HMRC and the *tax payable* which is the tax remaining to be paid after deducting any tax already paid for the year. These distinctions will become clearer in the course of the next two chapters.

A tax computation is not required for every taxpayer. For example, a computation is not usually required for an individual whose income is derived entirely from employment, since the correct amount of tax is deducted automatically by the PAYE system (see Chapter 7). However, the only way to calculate the tax liability in more complex cases is to prepare a computation and this approach should always be adopted when answering examination questions.

Married couples

Married couples are taxed independently, which means that the husband's income and the wife's income are taxed completely separately. If a married couple receive joint income (e.g. interest on a joint bank account), the income is normally divided between them equally for tax purposes. But if the source of income is genuinely held between them in some other proportion, the couple may make a declaration to that effect and the income will then be divided between them as appropriate. As from 5 December 2005, the same treatment applies to the joint income of same-sex "civil partners" who have entered into a legally-recognised civil partnership.

Dividends from jointly owned shares in close companies (see Chapter 27) are always taxed according to the actual proportions of ownership of the shares, rather than automatically being divided equally between the couple concerned.

The rates of income tax

An individual's taxable income is taxed according to the rates of income tax in force for the year in question. For 2005/06, the rates of income tax are as follows:

First £2,090 of taxable income	10% (the "starting rate")
Next £30,310 of taxable income	22% (the "basic rate")
Remainder of taxable income after first £32,400	40% (the "higher rate")

Note that:

(a) The first £2,090 of taxable income is referred to as the "starting rate band" and the next £30,310 of taxable income is referred to as the "basic rate band".

(b) Calculations are made to the nearest pound when calculating taxable income. The amount of tax due on that income is calculated to the nearest penny in this book but HMRC will generally accept calculations made to the nearest pound.

(c) Savings income and dividend income are treated specially, as explained below.

(d) The Scottish Parliament has the power to increase or decrease (by up to 3%) the basic rate of income tax which is set by the UK Parliament. The resulting "Scottish variable rate" applies to the income of Scottish taxpayers only. The examples and exercises in this book all assume that the taxpayers referred to are liable to income tax at unvaried UK rates.

EXAMPLE 1

Calculate the income tax payable in 2005/06 on a taxable income (i.e. income after deducting charges and the personal allowance) of:

(a) £1,250

(b) £20,390

(c) £43,104

(Assume that none of the income is derived from savings or dividends).

Solution

(a) 1,250 @ 10% = £125.00.

(b) 2,090 @ 10% + 18,300 @ 22% = £4,235.00.

(c) 2,090 @ 10% + 30,310 @ 22% + 10,704 @ 40% = £11,158.80.

Income taxed at source

Certain types of income are *taxed at source*, which means that income tax is deducted from the income before the taxpayer receives it. Typical examples are wages and salaries, building society interest and most forms of bank interest. Income which has been taxed at source must still be included in the taxpayer's tax computation, despite the fact that tax has already been paid. This may seem unnecessary but there are two good reasons for including the income in the tax computation:

(a) It is important to derive the correct figures for total income and statutory total income, as will become clearer in later chapters.

(b) The amount of tax which has already been deducted might not be the correct amount. The only way to check this is to aggregate the income concerned with all of the taxpayer's other income in a single tax computation.

In a tax computation, all income must be shown "gross". In other words, the amount shown must be the amount of the income *before* any income tax was deducted at source. When the tax liability has been calculated, tax paid by deduction at source is subtracted and the taxpayer is then required to pay only the balance of the liability. A tax refund is given if tax deducted at source exceeds the tax liability for the year.

Grossing up

If wages and salaries are received net of income tax, the gross pay and the amount of tax deducted can easily be found by examining the end-of-year certificate supplied by the taxpayer's employer. But for other types of income which are received net of tax it is often necessary to deduce the gross figure from the net figure. For reasons which will become clear later in this chapter, some types of income are received net of 20% tax. Some other types of income are received net of basic rate (22%) tax. In each case, the gross income can be calculated by "grossing up" the net income, as follows:

(a) If income is received net of 20% tax, the gross income is equal to the net income multiplied by 100/80. The amount of tax deducted at source is equal to the net income multiplied by 20/80 (or 20% of gross income). The main types of income which are received net of 20% tax are:

    (i) building society interest and most forms of bank interest

    (ii) debenture and other loan interest paid by UK companies

    (iii) the income element of purchased life annuities.

    Interest on most UK Government securities ("gilt-edged" securities or "gilts") used to be received net of 20% tax. But, as from 6 April 1998, anyone receiving such interest may choose whether to receive the interest gross or net. As from that date, new holders of gilts automatically receive their interest gross unless they ask for it to be paid net. Those who held gilts on 6 April 1998 continue to receive their interest net of 20% tax unless they ask for it to be paid gross.

(b) If income is received net of basic rate (22%) tax, the gross income is equal to the net income multiplied by 100/78. The amount of tax deducted at source is equal to the net income multiplied by 22/78 (or 22% of gross income). Patent royalties are an example of income which is received by individuals net of basic rate tax.

EXAMPLE 2

In 2005/06, an individual receives net income of £1,248. Compute the equivalent gross income and the amount of tax deducted at source if the income consists entirely of:

(a) building society interest
(b) patent royalties.

Solution

(a) If the income consists of building society interest then the equivalent gross income is £1,248 x 100/80 = £1,560 and the tax deducted at source is £1,248 x 20/80 = £312.
(b) If the income consists of patent royalties then the equivalent gross income is £1,248 x 100/78 = £1,600 and the tax deducted at source is £1,248 x 22/78 = £352.

Savings income

The tax liability on a taxpayer's "savings income" is calculated differently from the tax liability on non-savings income. The main categories of savings income are:

(a) interest from banks and building societies
(b) interest from gilt-edged securities and corporate bonds (i.e. debentures)
(c) the income element of purchased life annuities
(d) certain foreign income (see Chapter 32).

The crucial difference between savings income and non-savings income is that savings income falling into the basic rate band is taxed at the *lower rate* of 20% (*not* the 22% basic rate). Therefore, if a taxpayer has both savings income and non-savings income, it is necessary to split taxable income between the two categories before calculating the tax liability. Note that:

(a) Non-savings income is regarded as the bottom layer or "slice" of taxable income and savings income is regarded as a higher layer. This means that the starting rate and basic rate bands are made available to non-savings income in priority to savings income.
(b) Charges on income and the personal allowance are set against income in the order which will result in the lowest tax liability. The best approach is to make these deductions from non-savings income in priority to savings income, so that as little income as possible is taxed at 22%.
(c) The effect of these rules is that the tax liability on savings income is generally calculated at the lower rate (20%), sometimes at the starting rate (10%) or higher rate (40%), but *never* at the basic rate (22%). This is why the tax deducted at source (if any) from savings income is calculated at 20%.

(d) Dividends from UK companies used to be regarded as savings income but this ceased to be the case as from 6 April 1999. The special tax regime which now applies to UK dividends is explained later in this chapter.

EXAMPLE 3

In 2005/06, Robert has business profits of £15,360, net bank interest of £360 and no charges on income. He claims the personal allowance of £4,895. Calculate the income tax payable for the year.

Solution

	Total	*Non-savings*	*Savings*
	£	£	£
Business profits	15,360	15,360	
Bank interest £360 x 100/80	450		450
Statutory total income	15,810	15,360	450
Less: Personal allowance	4,895	4,895	
Taxable income	10,915	10,465	450

Income tax due				
Starting rate band	: Non-savings	2,090	@ 10%	209.00
Basic rate band	: Non-savings	8,375	@ 22%	1,842.50
	: Savings	450	@ 20%	90.00
		10,915		
Tax borne				2,141.50
Less: Tax deducted at source				90.00
Tax payable				2,051.50

Non-savings income occupies the whole of the starting rate band and the first £8,375 (£10,465 - £2,090) of the basic rate band. Savings income falls entirely into the basic rate band and is taxed at 20%.

EXAMPLE 4

In 2005/06, Roberta has rental income of £25,195, net bank interest of £6,080 and net building society interest of £4,000. She has no charges on income and she claims the personal allowance of £4,895. Calculate the income tax payable for the year.

Solution

	Total	Non-savings	Savings
	£	£	£
Income from property	25,195	25,195	
Bank interest £6,080 x 100/80	7,600		7,600
BSI £4,000 x 100/80	5,000		5,000
Statutory total income	37,795	25,195	12,600
Less: Personal allowance	4,895	4,895	
Taxable income	32,900	20,300	12,600

Income tax due

Starting rate band	: Non-savings	2,090	@ 10%	209.00
Basic rate band	: Non-savings	18,210	@ 22%	4,006.20
	: Savings	12,100	@ 20%	2,420.00
Higher rate	: Savings	500	@ 40%	200.00
		32,900		
Tax borne				6,835.20
Less: Tax deducted at source				2,520.00
Tax payable				4,315.20

Non-savings income occupies the whole of the starting rate band and the first £18,210 (£20,300 - £2,090) of the basic rate band. This leaves £12,100 (£30,310 - £18,210) of the basic rate band for savings income. The remaining £500 is taxed at the higher rate.

EXAMPLE 5

In 2005/06, Philip has business profits of £40,130 and net bank interest of £4,000. He has no charges on income and he claims the personal allowance of £4,895. Calculate the income tax payable for the year.

Solution

	Total	Non-savings	Savings
	£	£	£
Business profits	40,130	40,130	
Bank interest £4,000 x 100/80	5,000		5,000
Statutory total income	45,130	40,130	5,000
Less: Personal allowance	4,895	4,895	
Taxable income	40,235	35,235	5,000

Income tax due

Starting rate band	: Non-savings	2,090	@ 10%	209.00
Basic rate band	: Non-savings	30,310	@ 22%	6,668.20
Higher rate	: Non-savings	2,835	@ 40%	1,134.00
	: Savings	5,000	@ 40%	2,000.00
		40,235		
Tax borne				10,011.20
Less: Tax deducted at source				1,000.00
Tax payable				9,011.20

Non-savings income occupies the whole of the starting and basic rate bands so savings income (and the balance of non-savings income) is taxed entirely at the higher rate.

EXAMPLE 6

In 2005/06, Philippa has business profits of £3,390, National Savings Bank investment account interest (received gross) of £4,260, net debenture interest of £35,504 and no charges on income. She claims the personal allowance of £4,895. Calculate the income tax payable for the year.

Solution

	Total	Non-savings	Savings
	£	£	£
Business profits	3,390	3,390	
NSB interest	4,260		4,260
Debenture interest £35,504 x 100/80	44,380		44,380
Statutory total income	52,030	3,390	48,640
Less: Personal allowance	4,895	3,390	1,505
Taxable income	47,135	nil	47,135

Income tax due

Starting rate band	: Savings	2,090	@ 10%	209.00
Basic rate band	: Savings	30,310	@ 20%	6,062.00
Higher rate	: Savings	14,735	@ 40%	5,894.00
		47,135		
Tax borne				12,165.00
Less: Tax deducted at source				8,876.00
Tax payable				3,289.00

Dividends from UK companies

Until 6 April 1999, dividends received from UK companies were regarded as savings income and were treated in a similar way to income received net of tax. However, a new tax regime has applied to UK dividends since tax year 1999/00. The main points of this regime are as follows:

(a) UK dividends have an attached "tax credit" which is equal to *one-ninth* of the amount of the dividend. A taxpayer's dividend income for a tax year is equal to the amount of UK dividends received in that year plus the attached tax credits. For example, a taxpayer who receives UK dividends of £720 has dividend income for tax purposes of £800 (£720 plus the tax credits of £80).

(b) UK dividends are not classed as savings income or non-savings income. Dividends constitute a third layer which is treated as the top slice of taxable income, ranking above both non-savings and savings income.

(c) Dividends which fall into the starting rate band or basic rate band are taxed at the "dividend ordinary rate" of 10%. Dividends which lie above these bands are taxed at the "dividend upper rate" of 32.5%.

(d) Charges on income and the personal allowance should be deducted from non-savings income in priority to savings income and from savings income in priority to dividends.

(e) Tax credits relating to dividends which are charged to tax (i.e. dividends forming part of taxable income) may be deducted from the taxpayer's income tax liability on those dividends. However, it is *not* possible to claim payment of any tax credits which exceed this liability. Nor is it possible to deduct tax credits from the tax due on other forms of income. Tax credits relating to dividends which are not charged to tax (because they are covered by charges or the personal allowance) are lost.

The tax treatment of dividends received from overseas companies is described in Chapter 32.

EXAMPLE 7

In 2005/06, Ewan has rental income of £30,245, net bank interest of £3,240 and UK dividends of £3,690. He has no charges on income. He claims the personal allowance of £4,895. Calculate the income tax payable for the year.

Solution

	Total	*Non-savings*	*Savings*	*Dividends*
	£	£	£	£
Income from property	30,245	30,245		
Bank interest £3,240 x 100/80	4,050		4,050	
UK dividends £3,690 + £410	4,100			4,100
Statutory total income	38,395	30,245	4,050	4,100
Less: Personal allowance	4,895	4,895		
Taxable income	33,500	25,350	4,050	4,100

Income tax due

Starting rate band	: Non-savings	2,090	@ 10%	209.00
Basic rate band	: Non-savings	23,260	@ 22%	5,117.20
	: Savings	4,050	@ 20%	810.00
	: Dividends	3,000	@ 10%	300.00
Higher rate	: Dividends	1,100	@ 32.5%	357.50
		33,500		
Tax borne				6,793.70
Less: Tax credits on dividends				410.00
Tax payable				6,383.70
Less: Tax deducted at source				810.00
Tax payable				5,573.70

The dividends are treated as the top slice of income and are taxed at 10% to the extent that they occupy the basic rate band and at 32.5% in the higher rate band. The total tax due on dividends is £657.50, so the tax credits of £410 (i.e. the tax credits relating to dividends which are charged to tax) may be deducted in full.

EXAMPLE 8

Imagine now that Ewan (in the previous example) has no rental income but that all of the other figures remain unchanged. Calculate the income tax payable for the year.

Solution

	Total	Non-savings	Savings	Dividends
	£	£	£	£
Bank interest £3,240 x 100/80	4,050		4,050	
UK dividends £3,690 + £410	4,100			4,100
Statutory total income	8,150		4,050	4,100
Less: Personal allowance	4,895		4,050	845
Taxable income	3,255		-	3,255

Income tax due			
Starting rate band : Dividends	2,090	@ 10%	209.00
Basic rate band : Dividends	1,165	@ 10%	116.50
	3,255		
Tax borne			325.50
Less: Tax credits on dividends			325.50
Tax payable			0.00
Less: Tax deducted at source			810.00
Tax repayable			(810.00)

The dividends all fall into the starting rate and basic rate bands and are taxed at 10%. Tax credits relating to dividends which are charged to tax are £325.50. The tax due on these dividends is also £325.50, so these tax credits may be deducted. However, Ewan cannot claim payment of the remaining £84.50 of tax credits (which relate to the dividends covered by the personal allowance).

Summary

- In general, income tax is chargeable on all of the income of UK residents and on the UK income of non-residents.
- Income is classified into a number of categories, each of which has its own rules for determining the amount of assessable income in a tax year.
- Certain types of income are specifically exempt from income tax.
- To calculate a taxpayer's income tax liability it is necessary to bring together all of the taxpayer's income into a single computation. The gross equivalent of income received net of income tax must be included in the computation.

- Husband and wife are assessed to income tax independently.
- In 2005/06 the rates of income tax are 10% (the starting rate), 22% (the basic rate) and 40% (the higher rate).
- Savings income falling into the basic rate band is taxed at the lower rate of 20%.
- UK dividends are accompanied by tax credits which generally may be set against the tax liability on those dividends. This tax liability is calculated at 10% (the dividend ordinary rate) and 32.5% (the dividend upper rate).
- If the tax credit attached to a UK dividend which is charged to tax exceeds the tax liability with regard to that dividend, the excess tax credit cannot be paid to the recipient under any circumstances.

Exercises

2.1 Calculate the income tax payable in 2005/06 on a taxable income (i.e. income after deducting charges and the personal allowance) of:

(a) £12,690 (b) £40,100 (c) £66,103.

(Assume in each case that none of the income is derived from savings or dividends).

2.2 Calculate the income tax payable in 2005/06 on the following incomes, assuming no charges on income and a personal allowance of £4,895:

(a) Business profits of £20,360 and net bank interest of £720.

(b) Business profits of £25,030, net building society interest of £8,000 and net bank interest of £2,300.

(c) Net building society interest of £30,520.

2.3 Stephanie has the following income in 2005/06:

	£
Income from employment	22,175
Rents received	14,730
Bank interest (net)	160
NSB ordinary account interest, received gross	63
UK dividends	225

Compute the income tax payable by Stephanie for the year (before deducting any tax paid under the PAYE system) assuming that the rents received are not within the "rent-a-room" scheme, there are no charges on income and Stephanie is entitled to the personal allowance of £4,895.

2.4 Ernest has a retirement pension in 2005/06 of £4,285. He also receives net bank interest of £416. Compute the income tax payable by Ernest for the year, assuming a personal allowance of £4,895 and no charges on income.

What difference would it make if Ernest had received UK dividends of £468 instead of the bank interest?

***2.5** Ivan's income for the tax year 2005/06 is as follows:

	£
Salary	17,120
Building society interest (net)	560
Premium bond prize	50
NSB investment account interest, received gross	60

Compute the income tax payable by Ivan for the year (before deducting any tax paid under the PAYE system) assuming a personal allowance of £4,895 and no charges on income.

***2.6** Mary's income for the tax year 2005/06 is as follows:

	£
Business profits	31,575
Rents received	3,750
UK dividends	1,890

Compute the income tax payable by Mary for the year, assuming that the rents received are not within the "rent-a-room" scheme. Mary is entitled to a personal allowance of £4,895 and has no charges on income.

Chapter 3

Personal allowances

Introduction

One of the factors which must be taken into account when preparing an income tax computation is the taxpayer's entitlement to *personal allowances*. Personal allowances are intended to adjust the tax liability of a taxpayer so as to reflect his or her personal circumstances but the number of personal allowances has decreased in recent years. Most taxpayers may now claim only the basic personal allowance. However, there are higher allowances for older people and extra allowances for blind taxpayers and older married couples. The purpose of this chapter is to describe the allowances available in tax year 2005/06 and to explain the way in which relief is given for each allowance.

It is important to appreciate that personal allowances are indeed "personal". If all or part of an allowance cannot be used by the person to whom it is available, then any unused part of the allowance is generally lost. Excess allowances cannot normally be transferred to anyone else and cannot be carried back to previous years or forward to future years. However, some limited provisions exist for transferring excess allowances between husband and wife (see later in this chapter).

Personal allowances for 2005/06

Personal allowances may be claimed by UK residents and by some non-residents. The main classes of non-resident who may claim personal allowances are:

(a) citizens of the UK, the Commonwealth, the Republic of Ireland or the European Economic Area (EEA), which comprises all EU states plus Norway, Iceland and Liechtenstein

(b) residents in the Isle of Man or the Channel Islands and persons who used to reside in the UK but now reside abroad for health reasons

(c) Crown servants, ex-Crown servants and their widows/widowers

(d) missionaries.

The personal allowances for 2005/06 are as follows:

Allowances which are deducted from statutory total income:	£
Personal allowance	
Basic (age 0-64)	4,895
Age 65-74	7,090
Age 75 and over	7,220
Blind person's allowance	1,610
Income limit for age-related allowances	19,500
Allowances which are "tax reducers":	
Married couple's allowance	
Age under 75 and born before 6 April 1935	5,905
Age 75 and over	5,975
Minimum amount	2,280
Income limit for MCA	19,500

The personal allowance (PA)

Anyone who is entitled to claim personal allowances is entitled to at least the basic personal allowance (£4,895 in 2005/06). Relief for this allowance is given by deducting the amount of the allowance from statutory total income. The allowance is given in full in the tax year in which a taxpayer is born or dies.

If an unmarried minor child receives investment income which is derived from a parent then this income is treated for tax purposes as the income of the parent, not the child, unless the amount involved does not exceed £100 (per parent per child) in the tax year. This prevents parents from transferring income-bearing assets to a child so as to utilise the child's personal allowance. Income derived from parental contributions to a Child Trust Fund account (see Chapter 6) does not count towards the £100 limit.

Older taxpayers

As can be seen from the list of allowances given above, the amount of the personal allowance depends upon the taxpayer's age:

(a) A taxpayer who is over 65 years old, or who reaches the age of 65 during the tax year, is entitled to an increased personal allowance (£7,090 in 2005/06), and

(b) the allowance is higher still (£7,220 in 2005/06) for taxpayers who are over 75 years old or who reach the age of 75 during the tax year.

These higher personal allowances are granted *instead* of the usual personal allowance, not in addition to it. A taxpayer who dies in the tax year in which he or she would have reached the age of 65 or 75 is granted the higher allowance for the year of death.

The age-related personal allowances are reduced if the taxpayer's statutory total income exceeds a specified limit (£19,500 in 2005/06). If STI exceeds this limit, then the personal allowance is reduced by one-half of the excess. However, the allowance is never reduced to less than the personal allowance for those aged 0-64.

EXAMPLE 1

Calculate the personal allowance due in 2005/06 to each of the following taxpayers:

(a) Born 31 July 1940, STI £11,800
(b) Born 31 July 1930, STI £11,150
(c) Born 22 November 1937, STI £20,100
(d) Born 2 May 1936, STI £24,500
(e) Born 22 November 1927, STI £19,700
(f) Born 2 May 1926, STI £24,750.

Solution

(a) This taxpayer reaches the age of 65 during 2005/06 and is therefore entitled to a PA of £7,090 for the year.

(b) This taxpayer reaches the age of 75 during 2005/06 and is therefore entitled to a PA of £7,220 for the year.

(c) This taxpayer is in the 65-74 age group and has an STI which exceeds the limit by £600, giving a PA of £6,790 (£7,090 - 1/2 x £600).

(d) This taxpayer is in the 65-74 age group and has an STI which exceeds the income limit by £5,000. This would give a PA of £4,590 (£7,090 - 1/2 x £5,000) but the allowance is never reduced to less than the PA for those aged 0-64 so the taxpayer will claim £4,895.

(e) This taxpayer is over 75 and has an STI which exceeds the limit by £200, giving a PA of £7,120 (£7,220 - 1/2 x £200).

(f) This taxpayer is over 75 and has an STI which exceeds the limit by £5,250. This would give a PA of £4,595 (£7,220 - 1/2 x £5,250) so the taxpayer will claim £4,895.

Blind person's allowance (BPA)

The blind person's allowance (£1,610 in 2005/06) is available to registered blind persons. Relief for this allowance is given by deducting the amount of the allowance from statutory total income. The allowance is given in full in the tax year in which the taxpayer is first registered as a blind person.

If a husband or wife who is granted the blind person's allowance cannot make full use of it, the unused part can be transferred to the other spouse (even if that spouse is not a registered blind person). As from 5 December 2005, surplus BPA may also be transferred between same-sex civil partners who have entered into a legally-recognised civil partnership.

Tax reducers

The personal allowance and the blind person's allowance are deducted from STI when calculating taxable income and so automatically save tax at the taxpayer's highest rate. For instance, the personal allowance for 2005/06 saves a basic rate taxpayer who is under 65 years old the sum of £1,076.90 (£4,895 @ 22%). For higher rate taxpayers the amount saved is £1,958.00 (£4,895 @ 40%).

By contrast, the married couple's allowance (the only other allowance available in 2005/06) is ignored until the amount of tax due on the taxpayer's taxable income has been calculated. The MCA is then relieved by reducing this tax liability by *10% of the amount of the allowance*. For this reason, the MCA is sometimes referred to as a "tax reducer". Note that:

(a) Certain payments made by a taxpayer also act as tax reducers (see Chapter 4).

(b) The amount of tax borne can never be reduced to less than zero as a result of the tax reduction process. If available tax reductions exceed the tax due on taxable income, there is no repayment of the excess. Any unused part of a tax reduction is generally lost (but see later in this chapter for provisions relating to the transfer of married couple's allowance between spouses).

Married couple's allowance (MCA)

The married couple's allowance is available to a legally married couple who live together for at least part of the tax year, *so long as at least one of the spouses was born before 6 April 1935*. For 1999/00 and previous years, the MCA was also available to younger couples but the allowance is now available only to those who were at least 65 years old on 5 April 2000. Note the following points:

(a) The allowance is not available to a married couple who are separated for the whole of the tax year. A couple are regarded as "separated" for tax purposes if they are legally separated or if they are separated in circumstances which make it likely that separation will be permanent.

(b) The amount of the MCA depends upon the age of the older spouse. For 2005/06, the allowance is £5,905 unless the older spouse is aged 75 (or older) at any time during the tax year, in which case the allowance rises to £5,975. If the older spouse dies in the tax year in which he or she would have reached the age of 75, the higher MCA is available for that year.

(c) As from 5 December 2005, MCA is available to same-sex civil partners who have entered into a legally-recognised civil partnership, so long as at least one of the partners was born before 6 April 1935.

(d) In the same way as the age-related personal allowance is reduced for taxpayers whose STI exceeds a specified limit, the MCA for couples who are married before 5 December 2005 is reduced if the *husband's* STI exceeds the same limit (£19,500 in 2005/06). However, the allowance is never reduced to less than a specified minimum amount (£2,280 in 2005/06). It is noteworthy that the *wife's* STI is not taken into account for this purpose, even if the MCA is being given because of her age rather than her husband's age.

(e) For couples who marry on or after 5 December 2005 (and for civil partners) the MCA is reduced if the income of the "higher earner" exceeds the income limit. The higher earner is the spouse or partner with the higher STI.

(f) The procedure which is adopted if a person's STI needs to be taken into account when computing both that person's own PA (because the person is over 65) and the MCA (because of the above rules) is as follows:

  (i) The excess of the person's STI over the income limit is divided by two, giving the required reduction in allowances.

  (ii) The person's own PA is reduced first, but never to an amount which is less than the personal allowance for those aged 0-64.

  (iii) If the reduction made in the personal allowance has not fully achieved the required reduction in allowances, the MCA is reduced next, but never to less than the specified minimum amount.

EXAMPLE 2

Calculate the allowances available in 2005/06 to a husband and wife who were married for the whole of the year, given the following information:

(a) Husband born 1 March 1933 STI £14,600, wife born 5 July 1938 STI £9,300.

(b) Husband born 2 April 1942 STI £nil, wife born 6 August 1934 STI £25,300.

(c) Husband born 3 May 1928 STI £19,650, wife born 7 September 1935 STI £nil.

(d) Husband born 4 June 1932 STI £24,520, wife born 8 October 1927 STI £9,400.

(e) Husband born 5 July 1944 STI £27,500, wife born 9 November 1934 STI £nil.

Solution

(a) Husband and wife are both over 65 and are each entitled to a PA of £7,090. An MCA of £5,905 is also available since the husband was born before 6 April 1935.

(b) The husband is under 65 and is therefore entitled to a PA of £4,895, all of which is unused. His wife is over 65 but her STI exceeds the income limit by £5,800. This would give her a PA of only £4,190 (£7,090 - 1/2 x £5,800) but the allowance is never reduced to less than the PA for those aged 0-64 so she will claim a PA of £4,895.

An MCA of £5,905 is available since the wife was born before 6 April 1935. The MCA is not reduced at all since the husband's STI does not exceed the income limit.

(c) The husband is over 75 but his STI exceeds the limit by £150. This gives him a PA of £7,145 (£7,220 - 1/2 x £150). His wife is over 65 and she is entitled to a PA of £7,090, all of which is unused.

An MCA of £5,975 is available by virtue of the husband's age. This is not reduced at all since the reduction required because of the size of his STI has already been made in full against his own PA.

(d) The husband is over 65 but his STI exceeds the limit by £5,020. Therefore he must lose a total of £2,510 in allowances. His own PA is first reduced from £7,090 to the minimum of £4,895 (a reduction of £2,195). The remaining £315 is deducted from the MCA of £5,975 (available by virtue of the wife's age) giving an MCA of £5,660.

His wife is over 75 and she is entitled to a PA of £7,220.

(e) The husband is under 65 and is therefore entitled to a PA of £4,895. His wife is over 65 and so she is entitled to a PA of £7,090, all of which is unused.

The wife was born before 6 April 1935 so an MCA of £5,905 is available. However, this must be reduced because the husband's STI exceeds the limit by £8,000. None of the required reduction in allowances (£4,000) can be subtracted from his own PA since he is claiming only the basic £4,895. Therefore the whole of the reduction must be set against the MCA. This would give an MCA of £1,905 (£5,905 - £4,000) but the allowance is never reduced to less than the minimum amount (£2,280) so an MCA of £2,280 is available.

Allocation of the MCA

In the case of couples married before 5 December 2005, the tax reduction relating to the MCA is normally set against the husband's tax, but note that:

(a) The husband and wife may elect jointly that the tax reduction relating to the MCA minimum amount (£2,280 for 2005/06) should be set against the wife's tax.

(b) The wife may elect unilaterally that 50% of the tax reduction relating to the MCA minimum amount should be set against her tax.

(c) If either spouse is unable to use their MCA-related tax reduction in full or in part, the unused part may be transferred to the other spouse (assuming that the other spouse can use it).

The elections described in (a) and (b) must normally be made before the start of the tax year to which they relate, but the elections can be made during the tax year if this is the year of marriage. If either of these elections is made, any remaining part of the MCA (above the minimum amount) is dealt with in the husband's tax computation.

The transfer described in (c) may be claimed at any time up to 31 January in the sixth tax year following the year to which it relates. This transfer applies to the whole of the unused MCA, not just to the unused part (if any) of the minimum amount.

In the case of couples married on or after 5 December 2005 (and civil partners) the MCA is normally allocated to the higher earner, but elections similar to those listed above may be used to transfer MCA to the other spouse (or partner).

Year of marriage and year of separation or death

In the tax year in which a marriage occurs (or a civil partnership is registered) MCA is reduced by one-twelfth for each full tax month which elapses between the start of the year and the date of the marriage (or the date of registration). A tax month runs from the 6th of one month to the 5th of the next month, inclusive.

An election to transfer all or 50% of the MCA minimum amount to the other spouse (or partner) in the year of marriage (or registration) applies to that amount reduced in the same proportion as the MCA itself is reduced.

The MCA is available in full in the tax year in which a couple separate or in which one of them dies.

EXAMPLE 3

Calculate the MCA available in 2005/06 to a husband and wife (both born in 1934) who marry on each of the following dates:

(a) 5 April 2005 (b) 9 April 2005 (c) 23 June 2005 (d) 4 April 2006

Assume in each case that neither spouse has an STI exceeding £19,500.

Solution

(a) A couple who marry on 5 April 2005 are already married by the start of tax year 2005/06. Therefore the MCA of £5,905 is available in full.

(b) A couple who marry on 9 April 2005 are not married for the whole of 2005/06 but no full tax months have passed between the start of the tax year and the date of the marriage. Therefore the full MCA of £5,905 is available.

(c) If the marriage takes place on 23 June 2005, two full tax months have passed since the start of the tax year (6 April 2005 to 5 May 2005 and 6 May 2005 to 5 June 2005). The MCA is reduced by two-twelfths, giving an MCA of £5,905 x 10/12 = £4,921.

(d) If the marriage takes place on 4 April 2006, eleven full tax months have passed since the start of the tax year. Therefore the MCA is reduced by eleven-twelfths, giving an MCA of £5,905 x 1/12 = £492.

EXAMPLE 4

Calculate the tax borne in 2005/06 by a husband and wife (both born in 1934) given the information shown below. In each case, an election has been made for 50% of the tax reduction relating to the MCA minimum amount to be set against the wife's tax. None of the income is derived from savings or dividends.

(a) Married all year, husband's STI £20,980, wife's STI £18,040.

(b) Married 1 October 2005, husband's STI £10,075, wife's STI £23,950.

(c) Husband dies 12 October 2005, husband's STI £9,915, wife's STI £18,705.

Solution

					(a) £	(b) £	(c) £
HUSBAND							
Statutory total income					20,980	10,075	9,915
Less: Personal allowance					6,350	7,090	7,090
Taxable income					14,630	2,985	2,825
Income tax							
	(a)	(b)	(c)				
	2,090	2,090	2,090	@ 10%	209.00	209.00	209.00
	12,540	895	735	@ 22%	2,758.80	196.90	161.70
	14,630	2,985	2,825		2,967.80	405.90	370.70
Less: MCA £4,765 @ 10%					476.50		
MCA £2,780 @ 10%						278.00	
MCA £4,765 @ 10% = £476.50							370.70
Tax borne					2,491.30	127.90	nil
WIFE							
Statutory total income					18,040	23,950	18,705
Less: Personal allowance					7,090	4,895	7,090
Taxable income					10,950	19,055	11,615
Income tax							
	(a)	(b)	(c)				
	2,090	2,090	2,090	@ 10%	209.00	209.00	209.00
	8,860	16,965	9,525	@ 22%	1,949.20	3,732.30	2,095.50
	10,950	19,055	11,615		2,158.20	3,941.30	2,304.50
Less: MCA £1,140 @ 10%					114.00		
MCA £665 @ 10%						66.50	
MCA £1,140 @ 10% + £105.80							219.80
Tax borne					2,044.20	3,874.80	2,084.70

Notes:

(i) In case (a), the husband's income is £1,480 over the income limit, therefore his PA is reduced to £6,350 (£7,090 - 1/2 x £1,480). The MCA is available in full. £1,140 (half of the minimum amount) is claimed by the wife, leaving £4,765 for the husband.

(ii) In case (b), the available MCA is 7/12 x £5,905 = £3,445. The wife claims 7/12 x £1,140 = £665, leaving £2,780 for the husband. The wife's income exceeds the income limit by £4,450. The reduced age-related PA would be £4,865 (£7,090 - 1/2 x £4,450) so she claims £4,895.

(iii) In case (c), the MCA is available in full in the year of the husband's death. £1,140 is claimed by the wife, leaving £4,765 for the husband. The tax reduction that he cannot use (£105.80) is transferred to his wife.

Summary

- Everyone is entitled to at least the basic personal allowance. Older taxpayers are entitled to a higher personal allowance but this is reduced if income exceeds a specified limit.
- The blind person's allowance is granted to registered blind persons.
- The married couple's allowance is available to a legally married couple who live together for at least part of the tax year, so long as at least one of the spouses was born before 6 April 1935. As from 5 December 2005, MCA is also available to civil partners.
- For couples married before 5 December 2005, MCA is reduced if the husband's income exceeds a specified limit. For couples married on or after that date (and for civil partners) MCA is reduced if the higher-earner's income exceeds the limit.
- Tax relief for the personal allowance and the blind person's allowance is given by deducting these allowances from the taxpayer's STI. The MCA reduces tax borne by 10% of the amount of the allowance.
- Any part of an allowance that cannot be used by the person to whom it is available is usually lost. However, the married couple's allowance and the blind person's allowance can sometimes be transferred between spouses or civil partners.

Exercises

3.1 Calculate the personal allowance due in 2005/06 to each of the following taxpayers:

(a) Born on 28 August 1938, STI £13,600

(b) Born on 25 May 1929, STI £20,500

(c) Born on 2 February 1941, STI £24,100.

3.2 Calculate the allowances available to a husband and wife in 2005/06 (assuming that the couple are married for the entire tax year) given the following information:

(a) Husband born 1927 STI £14,900, wife born 1933 STI £19,800

(b) Husband born 1934 STI £20,200, wife born 1934 STI £6,500

(c) Husband born 1934 STI £24,060, wife born 1943 STI £17,800.

3.3 Calculate the tax borne in 2005/06 by a husband and wife (both born in 1929), given the information shown below. No elections have been made in relation to the married couple's allowance and none of the income is derived from savings or dividends.

(a) Married all year, husband's STI £13,720, wife's STI £15,020

(b) Married 17 August 2005, husband's STI £6,800, wife's STI £12,445

(c) Husband dies on 16 September 2005, husband's STI to date of death £7,555, wife's STI for the year £14,885.

3.4 Calculate the married couple's allowance available in 2005/06 to a married couple who marry on each of the following dates:

(a) 4 May 2005 (both born 1985)

(b) 14 February 2006 (husband born 1939 STI £13,400, wife born 1933 STI £8,400)

(c) 25 December 2005 (husband born 1942 STI £20,600, wife born 1934 STI £10,000).

3.5 Toby is a widower. He was born in August 1929 and his income for 2005/06 is as follows:

	£
Retirement pension	6,200
Bank interest (net)	912

Calculate the amount of income tax repayable to Toby for 2005/06.

3.6 What personal allowances may be claimed by each of the following taxpayers in 2005/06?

(a) John is single, 45 years old and registered blind.

(b) June is 28 years old. Her husband died in September 2004, leaving her with two young children.

(c) James is 14 years old. He earns about £20 per week from his paper round.

3.7 Richard was born on 5 February 1942. His wife, Patricia, was born on 5 April 1935. They were married in 1967. Their income for 2005/06 is as follows:

	£
Richard:	
Business profits	19,530
Patricia:	
UK dividends	1,800

Calculate their tax borne and tax payable in 2005/06.

***3.8** A married man (born 3 November 1930) died on 8 July 2005. He received a retirement pension of £8,450 between 6 April 2005 and the date of his death. His wife (born 12 August 1940) had no income whilst her husband was alive but received a pension of £14,135 between 8 July 2005 and 5 April 2006.

Calculate their tax borne in 2005/06.

***3.9** Bill was born in 1966. He is married to Hazel who was born in 1970.

In 2005/06, Bill received business profits of £39,350 and UK dividends of £4,680. Hazel received a salary of £18,850 and net bank interest of £2,432. Calculate their tax payable for the year (before deducting any tax paid under the PAYE system).

Chapter 4

Charges on income and other payments

Introduction

Certain types of payment made by a taxpayer are eligible for tax relief. Some of these payments, known as *charges on income*, are relieved by deducting them from the taxpayer's total income when calculating STI. Other payments act as tax reducers and are relieved by reducing the tax due on the taxpayer's taxable income. A special tax regime applies to certain charitable donations.

The purpose of this chapter is to describe the main types of payment (other than pension contributions) which attract tax relief and to explain how relief is given for each type of payment. Tax relief for pension contributions is considered separately in Chapter 13.

Charges on income

The following items are treated as charges on income and are deducted when calculating the taxpayer's statutory total income for the year in which the items occur:

(a) eligible interest payments

(b) patent royalties paid and copyright royalties paid

(c) gifts of listed shares or securities to a charity

(d) gifts of land or buildings to a charity.

Each of these items is explained in more detail later in this chapter. Before 6 April 2000, certain charitable donations were also treated as charges on income but this is no longer the case. The tax regime which now applies to these donations is explained at the end of this chapter.

Tax relief for charges on income is given at the highest rates of tax to which the taxpayer is liable. Deducting charges from total income automatically gives the right amount of relief, since the effect of the deduction is to reduce the amount of taxable income falling into the upper tax bands.

Charges paid gross or net

Some charges are paid gross (without deduction of tax) whilst others are paid net (after deduction of *basic rate* tax). Charges paid gross are deducted from the taxpayer's total income when computing STI, but it is tempting to ignore any charges paid net since the taxpayer has already taken tax relief at source. However, the tax deducted at source is always calculated at the basic rate and this will not give the right amount of relief to a taxpayer whose highest rate of tax is not the basic rate. The only way to be sure that the right amount of tax relief is given for a charge paid net is to:

(a) calculate the gross amount of the charge (net payment × 100/78)

(b) subtract the gross figure from total income when calculating STI (thus giving the correct amount of tax relief)

(c) increase the taxpayer's income tax liability by the amount of basic rate tax which was deducted from the payment when it was made. (In effect, the person making the payment is regarded as having collected basic rate income tax from the recipient on behalf of HM Revenue and Customs and must therefore account to HMRC for this tax as part of his or her income tax liability).

It is worth noting that this treatment of charges paid net is entirely consistent with the treatment of income received net (see Chapter 2). Income received net of tax is shown gross in the taxpayer's computation and the tax deducted at source is subtracted when calculating tax payable. Similarly, charges paid net are shown gross in the taxpayer's computation and the tax deducted at source is added when calculating tax payable.

EXAMPLE 1

Bob has income of £14,700 in 2005/06. None of the income is derived from savings or dividends. He is subject to an annual charge of £200, which he pays gross. Cathy's circumstances are precisely the same as Bob's in all respects except that she pays her charge net (i.e. she pays a net £156 in the year).

Compute Bob and Cathy's tax liabilities for 2005/06. Does it seem to be better to pay charges gross or net?

Solution

	Bob	*Cathy*
	£	£
Total income	14,700	14,700
Less: Charge on income	200	
Charge on income £156 x 100/78		200
Statutory total income	14,500	14,500
Less: Personal allowance	4,895	4,895
Taxable income	9,605	9,605

			£	£
Income tax				
Bob	*Cathy*			
2,090	2,090	@ 10%	209.00	209.00
7,515	7,515	@ 22%	1,653.30	1,653.30
9,605	9,605			
Tax borne			1,862.30	1,862.30
Add: Tax deducted from charge			0.00	44.00
Tax liability			1,862.30	1,906.30

Note:

Bob has paid a charge of £200 and has a tax liability of £1,862.30, a total of £2,062.30. Cathy has paid a charge of £156 and has a tax liability of £1,906.30, again a total of £2,062.30. It makes no difference whether the charge is paid gross or net and this is evidenced by the fact that tax borne is the same for both taxpayers.

Higher rate taxpayers

A charge on income costs a higher rate (or dividend upper rate) taxpayer less than it costs a basic rate taxpayer, since relief is given at the highest rate of tax to which the taxpayer is liable. However, there is no need to adjust the method of computation to deal specially with such taxpayers. The method described above will give the correct result for all taxpayers.

EXAMPLE 2

Derek has income in 2005/06 of £25,880 (none of which is derived from savings or dividends). He pays a net annual charge of £234. Show his income tax computation:

(a) with the annual charge

(b) as it would have been without the annual charge.

How much has the annual charge effectively cost him? How much would it have cost him if his income for the year had been £20,000 higher?

Solution

			Income £25,880 (a)	(b)	Income £45,880 (a)	(b)
			£	£	£	£
Total income			25,880	25,880	45,880	45,880
Less: Charge £234 x 100/78			300		300	
Statutory total income			25,580	25,880	45,580	45,880
Less: Personal allowance			4,895	4,895	4,895	4,895
Taxable income			20,685	20,985	40,685	40,985
Income tax						
(a)	(b)					
2,090	2,090	@ 10%	209.00	209.00		
18,595	18,895	@ 22%	4,090.90	4,156.90		
20,685	20,985					
(a)	(b)					
2,090	2,090	@ 10%			209.00	209.00
30,310	30,310	@ 22%			6,668.20	6,668.20
8,285	8,585	@ 40%			3,314.00	3,434.00
40,685	40,985					
Tax borne			4,299.90	4,365.90	10,191.20	10,311.20
Add: Tax deducted from charge			66.00		66.00	
Tax liability			4,365.90	4,365.90	10,257.20	10,311.20

Notes:

(i) With income of £25,880, Derek's tax liability is the same whether or not he pays the annual charge. This is to be expected since he is a basic rate taxpayer and he has paid the charge net of basic rate tax (giving him the right amount of tax relief at source). The cost of the charge to him is therefore just £234.

(ii) With income of £45,880, Derek becomes a higher rate taxpayer and his tax liability is reduced by £54 if he pays the annual charge. The cost of the charge to him is only £180 (payment £234 less reduction in tax liability £54). In effect, the gross charge of £300 is reduced by tax relief at 40% (£120), leaving £180 as the cost to Derek. An alternative way of looking at the situation is to say that Derek takes 22% tax relief when making the payment but is entitled to 40% tax relief. Therefore the extra 18% is given via Derek's tax computation (18% of £300 = £54).

Starting rate and lower rate taxpayers

A taxpayer whose highest rate of tax is the starting rate or the dividend ordinary rate is entitled to tax relief on charges at that rate only. Similarly, a taxpayer whose highest rate of tax is the lower rate which applies to savings income is entitled to tax relief on charges at that rate only. But there is no need to adjust the method of computation to deal specially with such taxpayers. The method described above will automatically ensure that relief is given at the correct rate.

EXAMPLE 3

Esmé has income of £5,450 in 2005/06 and she is subject to a net annual charge of £124.80. Show her income tax computation:

(a) with the annual charge

(b) as it would have been without the annual charge.

How much has the annual charge effectively cost her?

Solution

	(a)	(b)
	£	£
Total income	5,450	5,450
Less: Charge £124.80 x 100/78	160	
Statutory total income	5,290	5,450
Less: Personal allowance	4,895	4,895
Taxable income	395	555
Income tax		
Tax borne @ 10%	39.50	55.50
Add: Tax deducted from charge	35.20	
Tax liability	74.70	55.50

Notes:

(i) As a starting rate taxpayer, Esmé's tax liability is increased by £19.20 if she pays the annual charge. This is logical since she takes 22% tax relief when making the payment but is entitled to only 10% tax relief. Therefore the difference of 12% is "clawed back" by the tax system (12% of £160 = £19.20). The £19.20 assessment would be raised under Section 350 of ICTA 1988 and assessments of this type are often referred to as "Section 350 assessments".

(ii) The cost of the charge to her is therefore £144 (payment £124.80 plus increase in tax liability £19.20). In effect, the gross charge of £160 is reduced by tax relief at 10% (£16), leaving £144 as the cost to Esmé.

Non-taxpayers

Non-taxpayers (whose taxable income is zero) are not entitled to any tax relief at all on the charges that they pay. Once again, there is no need to adjust the method of computation to deal specially with non-taxpayers. The method described above will automatically ensure that no relief is given.

If charges cannot be relieved in the year in which they are paid, the opportunity for tax relief on those charges is permanently lost. In general, it is not possible to carry the unrelieved charges back to previous years or forward to future years. However, a special rule applies to unrelieved trade charges (see Chapter 11).

EXAMPLE 4

Glenda has income of £4,760 in 2005/06. She is subject to a net annual charge of £39. Show her income tax computation:

(a) with the annual charge

(b) as it would have been without the annual charge.

How much has the annual charge effectively cost her?

Solution

	(a)	(b)
	£	£
Total income	4,760	4,760
Less: Charge £39 x 100/78	50	
Statutory total income	4,710	4,760
Less: Personal allowance (restricted)	4,710	4,760
Taxable income	0	0
Income tax		
Tax borne	0.00	0.00
Add: Tax deducted from charge	11.00	
Tax liability	11.00	0.00

Notes:

(i) As a non-taxpayer, Glenda's tax liability is increased by £11.00 if she pays the annual charge. This is logical since she takes 22% tax relief when making the payment but is entitled to no tax relief. Therefore the tax relief which she deducts at source is clawed back by means of a Section 350 assessment.

(ii) The cost of the charge to her is £50 (payment £39 plus increase in tax liability £11). In effect, she pays the full gross amount of the charge, with no reduction for tax relief.

Eligible interest payments

The interest paid on certain loans is treated as a charge on income. This interest is paid gross. The main types of eligible loan are:

(a) A loan to purchase plant or machinery for use in the taxpayer's employment or for use in the business of a partnership in which the taxpayer is a partner. The interest paid on such a loan is eligible for relief in the tax year in which the loan is taken out and for the next three years.

This relief is not available in relation to the purchase of a mechanically propelled vehicle or a cycle for use in the taxpayer's employment.

(b) A loan to purchase shares in an employee-controlled company or to purchase an interest in a partnership.

(c) A loan to purchase ordinary shares in a close company (see Chapter 27), so long as the taxpayer has a material interest in the company or works for the greater part of his or her time in the management of the company.

(d) A loan to pay inheritance tax. The interest paid on such a loan is eligible for tax relief for 12 months only.

Interest paid wholly and exclusively for business purposes is generally treated as an allowable business expense and is deducted from the business profits assessed to income tax as trading income (see Chapter 8). In this case, the interest is not regarded as a charge on income and it is not necessary for the loan to fall into one of the above categories for relief to be given.

Royalties

Patent royalties paid by an individual are paid net of basic rate tax but copyright royalties are paid gross. These types of payment are most likely to be made in the course of business and are considered more fully in Chapter 8.

Gifts of shares or property

A gift of listed shares and securities made to a charity attracts tax relief as a charge on income. The amount of the charge is taken as the market value of the shares on the date of the gift. This income tax relief is in addition to the relief from capital gains tax which arises when assets are given to charities (see Chapter 16). A similar relief is available in relation to gifts of land or buildings to a charity.

EXAMPLE 5

In 2005/06, a taxpayer who pays both income tax and capital gains tax at 40% gives listed shares with a market value of £20,000 to a charity. A capital gain of £17,000 would have arisen if the shares had been sold. In effect, how much has this gift cost the taxpayer?

Solution

The taxpayer will save income tax of £8,000 (40% x £20,000) and capital gains tax of £6,800 (40% x £17,000). The total tax saving is £14,800. This amounts to tax relief at 74% and the gift has cost the taxpayer only £5,200.

Payments which are tax reducers

The following payments are granted tax relief by means of a reduction in the tax due on the taxpayer's taxable income:

(a) certain maintenance payments made to an ex-spouse (so long as either the payer or the recipient was born before 6 April 1935)

(b) interest on a loan secured on the taxpayer's main residence and used to purchase an annuity (so long as the loan was taken out before 9 March 1999).

If such a payment is made gross, the appropriate tax reduction (see below) is given in the payer's tax computation. This tax reduction takes priority over the tax reduction for the married couple's allowance (see Chapter 3) and no tax refund is available if the available tax reductions exceed the tax due on the payer's taxable income. If the payment is made net, it should be *entirely omitted* from the payer's tax computation. This is because precisely the right amount of tax relief has been given at source and the tax system does *not* claw back excess relief from those whose tax liability is less than the tax deducted at source.

Maintenance payments

Maintenance payments consist of payments to support a spouse or child, made by one spouse to the other after they have separated or divorced. The tax regime which applies to payments made under maintenance agreements is as follows:

(a) Maintenance payments are made gross, without any deduction of tax at source.

(b) Tax relief is available to the person making the payments only if one or both of the spouses was born before 6 April 1935 and the payments are made under a court order or legally binding agreement (or have been assessed by the Child Support Agency). Relief ceases when the *recipient* re-marries.

(c) Maintenance payments made directly to children do not attract tax relief.

(d) In 2005/06, a taxpayer making qualifying maintenance payments is entitled to a tax reduction equal to 10% of the *lower* of:

   (i) the payments falling due and made in the tax year, and

   (ii) the minimum married couple's allowance (£2,280).

(e) The recipient of maintenance payments is not liable to pay income tax on them.

Loans used to purchase an annuity

Tax relief is available in relation to the interest paid on the first £30,000 of a loan taken out *before 9 March 1999* and which was:

(a) made to a taxpayer aged 65 or over at the time that the loan was made, and

(b) used to purchase a life annuity, and

(c) secured on the taxpayer's main residence.

Such arrangements are often referred to as *home income plans*. Relief takes the form of a tax reduction equal to 23% of the qualifying interest. This rate remains at 23% even though the basic rate of income tax has now fallen to 22%. If the interest is paid gross, relief is given in the payer's tax computation. If the interest is paid net it should be entirely omitted from the payer's tax computation (as explained above).

Gift Aid

The Gift Aid scheme was established several years ago as a means of providing a tax incentive for individuals and companies to make charitable donations. The way in which the Gift Aid scheme applies to individuals is explained below. The way in which the scheme applies to companies is explained in Chapter 23.

Gift Aid scheme for individuals

The Gift Aid scheme applies to any charitable donation, however large or small and whether one-off or made regularly under a deed of covenant, so long as:

(a) the donor is either:

   (i) a UK resident, or

   (ii) a Crown servant or member of the UK armed forces working overseas, or

   (iii) a non-resident with income or gains charged to UK tax (see Chapter 32)

(b) the gift is not covered by the payroll giving scheme (see Chapter 7) and is not repayable to the donor

(c) the donor receives no benefit from making the gift, or receives a benefit which does not exceed the following limits:

(i) 25% of the amount of the gift, if the gift does not exceed £100

(ii) £25, if the gift exceeds £100 but does not exceed £1,000

(iii) 2.5% of the amount of the gift, if the gift exceeds £1,000

(d) the donor gives an appropriate declaration to the charity concerned (either orally, in writing, by telephone or via the Internet).

If all of these conditions are satisfied, the gift is treated as if it were made net of basic rate income tax and the charity can then recover the amount of tax which is deemed to have been deducted at source. For instance, a £20 gift would be treated as a gross gift of £25.64 (£20 × 100/78) less tax deducted of £5.64. In this case, the charity would receive £20 from the donor and a further £5.64 from HM Revenue and Customs. The gift is *not* shown in the donor's tax computation, but the following provisions apply:

(a) The donor must pay income tax and capital gains tax equal to at least the amount of tax deemed to have been deducted from the gift. If this is not the case, then the donor's entitlement to personal allowances is restricted to ensure that this amount of tax is in fact paid. If the restriction of personal allowances does not give the required result, the donor is charged to income tax at the basic rate on as much of the gift as is necessary to ensure that the required amount of tax is paid.

(b) The donor's basic rate band is extended by the gross amount of the gift. This extension ensures that relief at the higher rate is automatically given to higher rate taxpayers. If the taxpayer has capital gains, some or all of the relief might be given against capital gains tax (see Chapter 16) rather than income tax.

(c) When determining the donor's entitlement to age-related personal allowances (see Chapter 3) the donor's STI is deemed *for this purpose only* to be reduced by the gross amount of the gift.

(d) The donor may elect that Gift Aid donations made on or before 31 January in a tax year may be treated as if paid in the previous tax year, so long as these donations are made before the tax return for the previous tax year is submitted.

Gift Aid relief is available in relation to donations made to community amateur sports clubs as well as donations to charities.

EXAMPLE 6

In 2005/06, Owen makes qualifying Gift Aid donations totalling £351. He is under 65 and he has no capital gains tax liability for the year. Show his income tax computation if his only income for the year consists of business profits of:

(a) £21,080

(b) £5,010

(c) £39,510.

Solution

	(a)	(b)	(c)
	£	£	£
Business profits	21,080	5,010	39,510
Less: Personal allowance	4,895	4,895	4,895
Taxable income	16,185	115	34,615

Income tax

(a)	(b)	(c)				
2,090	115	2,090	@ 10%	209.00	11.50	209.00
14,095		30,760	@ 22%	3,100.90		6,767.20
		1,765	@ 40%			706.00
16,185	115	34,615				
Tax borne				3,309.90	11.50	7,682.20

Notes:

(i) The donations of £351 are grossed-up to £450 (£351 x 100/78) and are treated as if paid net of 22% tax. Deemed tax deducted is £99.

(ii) In case (a), Owen's income tax liability far exceeds £99 so there is no more to be done.

(iii) In case (b), Owen's income tax liability falls short of £99 by £87.50. Therefore he must pay a further £87.50 of income tax. This is achieved by reducing his personal allowance by £875, so increasing his tax liability by £875 x 10% = £87.50.

(iv) In case (c), Owen's basic rate band is extended by £450 from the normal figure of £30,310 to £30,760. This moves £450 of taxable income from the higher rate to the basic rate and saves tax of £81 (£450 x 18%). Together with the £99 deemed to have been deducted at source, total tax relief is now £180 (i.e. £450 x 40%).

Summary

- Certain payments made by a taxpayer attract tax relief either as a charge on income or as a tax reducer.
- Charges must always be shown gross in the tax computation. Any tax deducted when the payment was made is added to the tax liability of the payer.
- If a payment which ranks as a tax reducer is made gross, the appropriate tax reduction is given in the payer's income tax computation. But payments made net should be omitted from the computation entirely.
- Charges on income comprise eligible interest payments, patent royalties paid and copyright royalties paid. A charitable gift consisting of listed shares or securities (or land and buildings) also ranks as a charge on income.
- Qualifying maintenance payments of up to the amount of the minimum married couple's allowance are relieved at 10%. This relief is available only if either the payer or the recipient was born before 6 April 1935.
- Subject to certain conditions, the interest paid on a home loan which is used to buy a life annuity is relieved at 23%. This relief is available only if the loan was taken out before 9 March 1999.
- The Gift Aid scheme covers one-off donations to charity and regular donations made under the terms of a deed of covenant. Qualifying donations are deemed to have been made net of basic rate tax.
- A taxpayer making a Gift Aid donation must pay income tax and capital gains tax equal to at least the amount of tax deemed to have been deducted from the donation. Higher rate taxpayers obtain higher rate relief on such donations.

Exercises

4.1 Mabel has income of £19,460 in 2005/06, none of which is derived from savings or dividends. During the year she pays a net charge of £195. Show her income tax computation for the year.

4.2 Paul has income of £41,400 in 2005/06, none of which is derived from savings or dividends. During the year he pays a net charge of £1,248. Show his income tax computation:

(a) with the charge (b) as it would have been without the charge.

How much has the charge effectively cost him?

4.3 Rose has income of £4,885 in 2005/06. During the year she pays a net charge of £19.50. Show her income tax computation for the year.

4.4 At what rate of income tax is each of the following types of payment relieved in 2005/06?

(a) interest on a qualifying home loan used to buy an annuity

(b) interest on a loan used to buy an interest in a partnership

(c) qualifying maintenance payments

(d) patent royalties.

4.5 A taxpayer with no capital gains tax liability makes a qualifying Gift Aid donation of £936 in tax year 2005/06. Explain:

(a) why this donation is worth more than £936 to the charity which receives it

(b) why this donation might cost the taxpayer more than £936

(c) why this donation might cost the taxpayer less than £936.

4.6 Raj was born in 1938 and is single. In 2005/06, he has business profits of £20,500 and no other income. He makes a qualifying Gift Aid donation of £273 during the year. Show his 2005/06 income tax computation.

4.7 Geoffrey is aged 48 and lives with his wife (aged 47) and their two children. Geoffrey's income for 2005/06 consists of a salary of £35,875 and UK dividends of £2,880. He makes a qualifying Gift Aid donation of £312 during the year. Show Geoffrey's 2005/06 income tax computation.

***4.8** Pauline (born August 1934) marries Adrian (born June 1941) on 17 October 2005. Their income for 2005/06 is as follows:

	£
Pauline:	
Retirement pension	11,240
Net building society interest	20
Adrian:	
Business profits	22,100
UK dividends	1,575

Adrian pays maintenance of £3,000 per annum to his former wife (born March 1935) as required by a court order.

Show Pauline and Adrian's income tax computations for 2005/06.

***4.9** Matthew dies on 23 December 2005 at the age of 71, leaving a widow aged 63. His only income in 2005/06 is a retirement pension of £20,610. His wife has income from property of £14,550 and no other income. She pays a net charge of £390 during the year and also makes a Gift Aid donation of £100.

Calculate their tax liabilities for 2005/06.

Chapter 5

Income from property

Introduction

For many years, income from property was charged to income tax according to the rules of Schedule A. However, Schedule A was abolished for individuals (though not for companies) as from 6 April 2005 and income from property now falls within the scope of the Income Tax (Trading and Other Income) Act 2005. This Act arose from the work of the Tax Law Rewrite project (see Chapter 2) and made no fundamental changes to the way in which property income is taxed.

The main purpose of this chapter is to explain how a taxpayer's UK property income for a tax year is calculated. Income from property situated overseas is considered separately in Chapter 32.

Definition of property income

Section 268 of ITTOIA 2005 states that income tax is charged on the profits of a property business. The Act also states that a person's UK property business consists of a business which is carried on for generating income from land which is situated in the UK and that "generating income from land" means "*exploiting an estate, interest or right in or over land as a source of rents or other receipts*". This is a broad definition but, in practice, the main classes of property income are:

(a) rents

(b) lease premiums (if the length of the lease does not exceed 50 years)

(c) amounts receivable in respect of rights of way, sporting rights etc.

(d) income from the letting of fixed caravans or permanently moored houseboats.

Despite the use of the word "business" above, income from property is almost always treated as *unearned* income. The only occasion on which property income is treated as earned income is when the income derives from the commercial letting of furnished holiday accommodation (see later in this chapter). The distinction between earned and unearned income may be especially important if the taxpayer is hoping to obtain tax relief on pension contributions (see Chapter 13).

Basis of assessment and allowable expenditure

A taxpayer's property income for a tax year is calculated on the accruals basis, using generally accepted accounting principles, though an exception to this rule occurs in the case of short lease premiums, which are dealt with in a special way (see later in this chapter). Expenditure which is incurred wholly and exclusively for the purposes of the property business is deducted when computing property income. This "wholly and exclusively" rule is copied directly from the rules relating to trading income and is considered more fully in Chapter 8, but the types of expenditure which are likely to be deductible when computing property income include the following:

(a) repairs and maintenance to the property (excluding improvements)

(b) insurance of the property and/or its contents

(c) the cost of providing services to tenants

(d) administrative and management costs, including bad debts incurred

(e) rent paid to a superior landlord (if the property is sub-let)

(f) business rates, water rates or council tax (these are the responsibility of the occupier of premises, not the owner, but may be paid by a landlord on behalf of a tenant and then recouped via an increased rent)

(g) interest paid on a loan to buy or improve the property concerned.

If a property is partly let and partly owner-occupied, it is necessary to apportion the expenditure accordingly.

When a taxpayer derives income from two or more properties it is *not* necessary to calculate the amount of profit (or loss) arising on each property individually. In each tax year, total property expenditure is deducted from total property income, giving a single profit (or loss) figure for the year.

EXAMPLE 1

Ryan owns a house which he lets to a tenant. Rent is payable monthly in advance on the 6th day of each month. For some years the rent has been fixed at £7,200 per annum but this was increased to £7,800 per annum with effect from 6 December 2005. The rent due on 6 March 2006 was not paid until 7 April 2006.

Compute Ryan's property income for 2005/06, given that his allowable expenditure for the year is £2,350.

Solution

The rent relating to 2005/06 is £7,400 (£7,200 x 8/12 + £7,800 x 4/12) so property income for the year is £5,050 (£7,400 - £2,350). The fact that some of the rent was not received until early 2006/07 is irrelevant, since the accruals basis takes into account accrued rent as well as rent actually received.

Capital expenditure

Capital expenditure is never deductible when computing property income but tax relief may be obtained on certain types of capital expenditure as follows:

(a) Allowances for depreciation known as "capital allowances" are available in relation to capital expenditure on:

 (i) plant and machinery which is used in the repair, maintenance or management of let property

 (ii) qualifying industrial buildings let for industrial use

 (iii) the renovation or conversion of vacant or underused space above shops and other commercial premises to provide flats for rent

 (iv) the renovation of business premises in disadvantaged areas.

 Capital allowances are considered in Chapter 10 of this book.

(b) A "wear and tear allowance" may be available in relation to expenditure on furniture and other equipment let to a tenant. The wear and tear allowance is commonly calculated as 10% of the rent for the year, net of any council tax or rates borne by the landlord on behalf of the tenant.

(c) An alternative to the wear and tear allowance is the "renewals basis". If this basis applies, no tax relief is available for the initial cost of providing furniture or equipment, but subsequent expenditure on replacements (not improvements) is allowed as a deduction when computing property income for the year in which the expenditure is incurred.

Also, landlords may claim an allowance for capital expenditure on certain energy-saving items (e.g. loft and wall insulation) in let residential property. The allowance cannot exceed £1,500 per property and no deduction may be claimed for expenditure incurred after 5 April 2009. This allowance is not available to companies which let property.

EXAMPLE 2

Ursula owns a flat which she lets furnished. In 2005/06 the flat was let for 46 weeks at £80 per week. For the remaining 6 weeks of the year, Ursula occupied the flat herself. Her expenditure during the year was as follows:

	£		£
Council tax and water rates	1,240	Cleaning (whilst property let)	592
Minor repairs	270	Painting and decorating	500
Advertising for tenants	76	Insurance	240

Compute Ursula's property income for 2005/06, assuming that the wear and tear allowance is claimed.

Solution

		£	£	£
Rents for the year £80 x 46				3,680
Less: Expenses allowed in full:				
Advertising for tenants			76	
Cleaning			592	
Apportioned expenses:				
Council tax and water rates		1,240		
Minor repairs		270		
Painting and decorating		500		
Insurance		240		
	$\frac{46}{52}$	x 2,250	1,990	
Wear and tear allowance (see note)			258	2,916
Property income				764

Note:

The wear and tear allowance is calculated at 10% of the rents, less any part of those rents which are deemed to reimburse Ursula for expenses incurred by her which are legally the tenants' responsibility (i.e. council tax and water rates). The tenants were in occupation for 46 weeks, so 46/52ths of the council tax and water rates were their responsibility. The wear and tear allowance is therefore 10% of (£3,680 - 46/52 x £1,240) = £258.

Losses

If a taxpayer's total receipts from property for a tax year are exceeded by the allowable expenditure, then the taxpayer has incurred a loss and property income for the year is £nil. The loss is carried forward and relieved against the first available property income arising in subsequent tax years.

Note that any loss incurred on an individual property in a tax year will automatically be set against the profits arising on other properties in the same year, since all property receipts and all property expenses are pooled to give an overall profit or loss figure for the year.

EXAMPLE 3

Sandra's entire income is derived from the letting of property. She has the following income and expenditure in tax years 2003/04 through to 2005/06:

	2003/04	*2004/05*	*2005/06*
	£	£	£
Total rental income	19,320	20,000	21,100
Total allowable expenditure	27,410	15,430	7,540

Compute her property income for each year.

Solution

	2003/04	*2004/05*	*2005/06*
	£	£	£
Total rental income	19,320	20,000	21,100
Total allowable expenditure	27,410	15,430	7,540
Profit/(loss)	(8,090)	4,570	13,560
Assessment before loss relief	0	4,570	13,560
Less: Losses b/f	-	(4,570)	(3,520)
Property income	0	0	10,040

Note:

The 2003/04 loss must be set against the first available property income in subsequent years. This means that Sandra's property income for 2004/05 is reduced to £nil and (since this is her only source of income) her personal allowance for that year is wasted. However, it is not possible to conserve personal allowances by restricting the amount of loss relief claimed in 2004/05.

Lease premiums

A premium is a lump sum payable to a landlord by a tenant on the grant of a lease. The way in which such premiums are taxed depends upon the length of the lease:

(a) If the lease is for more than 50 years (a "long lease") any premium payable to the landlord is not subject to income tax but to capital gains tax (see Chapter 18).

(b) If the lease is for 50 years or less (a "short lease") any premium payable to the landlord on the grant of the lease is charged to income tax in the tax year in which the lease is granted. The amount assessed is equal to the amount of the premium, reduced by 2% for each year of the lease except for the first year.

It should be noted that the above provisions relate only to the *grant* of a lease, not to the *assignment* of a lease. The grant of a lease occurs when a new lease is created, under the terms of which the property will eventually revert to the landlord. The assignment of a lease occurs when an existing lease is sold to a new owner. This distinction is discussed further in Chapter 18.

EXAMPLE 4

In 2005/06, a landlord receives a premium of £36,000 when granting a 25-year lease to a tenant. What is the income tax assessment on this premium?

Solution

For income tax purposes, the premium is reduced by 2% for each year of the lease except for the first year. Therefore 48% (24 x 2%) of the premium is not chargeable to income tax. The remaining 52% is taxable, so the income tax assessment on the premium is £18,720 (52% of £36,000).

Relief for premiums paid

A tenant who pays a premium on being granted a short lease may obtain tax relief on the premium paid in one of two ways:

(a) If the tenant uses the property for business purposes then, throughout the duration of the lease, the tenant may claim an annual deduction from the trading profits which are charged to income tax (see Chapter 8). This annual deduction is equal to the amount of the landlord's income tax assessment on the premium, divided by the number of years of the lease.

(b) If the tenant sub-lets the property to someone else and receives a premium from the sub-lessee, then the assessable amount of the premium received is reduced by virtue of the premium paid. The reduction is equal to:

$$\text{Landlord's income tax assessment on premium paid} \times \frac{\text{Duration of sub-lease}}{\text{Duration of head-lease}}$$

If full relief cannot be given in this way for the premium paid (either because the premium received is too small or because no premium was received at all) the excess is spread evenly over the period of the sub-lease and set against the rents due from the sub-lessee.

EXAMPLE 5

Susan is granted a 20-year lease on a property, paying a premium of £76,000. Explain how tax relief will be given in relation to this premium if:

(a) she uses the property for trading purposes, or

(b) she grants a sub-lease to Timothy for five years, receiving a premium of:

(i) £25,000

(ii) £10,000.

Solution

(a) The amount assessable on Susan's landlord is £47,120 (£76,000 less 38% of £76,000). If Susan uses the premises for trading purposes she will be able to claim an annual deduction of £2,356 from her trading profits for each of the next 20 years (£47,120 divided by 20 = £2,356).

(b)

	(i)	(ii)
	£	£
Premium received	25,000	10,000
Less: 2% x 4 x £25,000	2,000	
2% x 4 x £10,000		800
	23,000	9,200
Less: Premium paid £47,120 x $\frac{5}{20}$	11,780	11,780
Assessable premium	11,220	nil

In case (ii) it is not possible to relieve the whole of the part of the premium paid which relates to the sub-letting period against the premium received for the sub-let. The amount unrelieved is £2,580 (£11,780 - £9,200). No assessment will be raised on the premium received and an deduction of £516 will be made from Susan's property income for each of the five years of the sub-lease (£2,580 divided by 5 = £516).

Reverse premiums

It is not uncommon for a landlord to pay a so-called "reverse premium" to a potential tenant so as to induce that tenant to take out a lease. This arises most frequently when commercial premises are let to business tenants. The amount of any reverse premium paid by a landlord will usually be treated as enhancement expenditure for capital gains tax purposes when the landlord disposes of the property (see Chapter 17). But if the landlord is a property developer or dealer, the premium may be an allowable expense when computing the landlord's trading income (see Chapter 8).

From the point of view of a tenant who receives a reverse premium, this premium is chargeable to income tax (or to corporation tax for a corporate tenant). If the premises are used for business purposes, the amount received is treated as trading income (see Chapter 8). Otherwise the amount received is assessable as property income. In both cases, the timing of the tax charge will usually follow accepted accountancy practice, so that the tax liability arising on the receipt of a reverse premium will probably be spread over the period of the lease.

"Rent-a-room" relief

If an individual lets furnished accommodation which is part of his or her only or main residence, gross annual rents of up to a specified limit (£4,250 for 2005/06) are exempt from income tax. However, the taxpayer concerned may elect to ignore this exemption and to be assessed instead according to the usual property income rules. This might be beneficial if the rents were exceeded by expenses, so that a loss could be claimed.

If gross rents exceed the limit, the exemption does not apply and rents less expenses will be assessed to income tax in the normal way. However, the taxpayer may elect to be assessed instead on the excess of the gross rents over the limit, without deducting expenses of any kind.

Both of the elections referred to above must be made by 31 January in the second tax year following the tax year to which the election relates. The election to ignore the exemption applies only to the year for which it is made. The election to be assessed on the excess of gross rents over the limit applies to all subsequent tax years until a year arises in which gross rents do not exceed the limit (or until the taxpayer withdraws the election).

EXAMPLE 6

In 2005/06, Victor rents out two rooms in his house and receives rents totalling £4,900. He incurs allowable expenses of £820. No elections are currently in force. What elections (if any) should he make?

Solution

The rent-a-room exemption does not apply since gross rents exceed £4,250. If Victor does nothing, he will be assessed on £4,080 (£4,900 - £820). If he elects to be assessed on the excess of gross rents over the rent-a-room relief limit, his assessment will be only £650 (£4,900 - £4,250). He should make this election and he has until 31 January 2008 to do so.

Furnished holiday lettings

If the letting of furnished property satisfies certain conditions, it qualifies as income from the "commercial letting of furnished holiday accommodation" and such income is treated for certain income tax purposes as if it were the income of a trade. The main beneficial effects of this are as follows:

(a) The income is regarded as earned income and qualifies as "net relevant earnings" when determining the extent to which tax relief is available on premiums paid into a retirement annuity or personal pension scheme (see Chapter 13).

(b) Losses are treated as trading losses and may be relieved as such (see Chapter 11).

(c) Capital allowances are available in respect of the furniture (see Chapter 10). The wear and tear allowance and the renewals basis do not apply.

(d) Business-related capital gains tax reliefs may be available (see Chapter 22).

In order that the letting of property should qualify as the commercial letting of furnished holiday accommodation, the property must be let furnished with a view to profit and it must be:

(a) available for letting to the general public as holiday accommodation for at least 140 days in the tax year, and

(b) actually let to the general public as holiday accommodation for at least 70 days in the tax year, and

(c) not normally in the same occupation for more than 31 consecutive days (for at least 155 days in the tax year).

If a taxpayer owns two or more properties each of which satisfies the 140-day rule but which do not all satisfy the 70-day rule, these properties will all be regarded as satisfying the 70-day rule so long as their average number of days let is at least 70.

EXAMPLE 7

Yvonne owns four cottages, all of which she lets furnished with a view to profit. None of the cottages is normally in the same occupation for more than 31 consecutive days. In 2005/06 the number of days for which each cottage was available for letting and the number of days actually let were:

	Days available	*Days actually let*
Cottage A	150	80
Cottage B	170	56
Cottage C	120	113
Cottage D	180	68

Show Yvonne's potential averaging claims.

Solution

Cottage C cannot be regarded as furnished holiday accommodation since it does not pass the 140-day test. Cottages A, B and D all pass this test but only Cottage A also passes the 70-day test. Without any averaging claims, therefore, only Cottage A will be regarded as furnished holiday accommodation. Possible averaging claims are:

(a) Average Cottage A with Cottage B. This is no use since the average number of days let is only 68.

(b) Average Cottage B with Cottage D. This is no use since the average number of days let is only 62.

(c) Average Cottage A with Cottage D. This would be beneficial since the average number of days let is 74.

(d) Average Cottage A with Cottage B and Cottage D. This is no use since the average number of days let is only 68.

Therefore, Yvonne should claim that Cottage A should be averaged with Cottage D, in which case both cottages would qualify as furnished holiday accommodation.

Summary

- Income tax is charged on the profits of a business which is carried on for the purpose of generating income from land situated in the UK.
- Property income is usually treated as unearned income unless it arises from the commercial letting of furnished holiday accommodation.
- A taxpayer's property income for a tax year is calculated in accordance with generally accepted accounting principles. Expenditure incurred wholly and exclusively for the purposes of the property business is deducted when computing property income.
- Capital allowances are available in relation to certain types of capital expenditure incurred in relation to a property business.
- Losses incurred by a property business are carried forward and set against the first available property income arising in subsequent years.
- A premium received on the grant of a lease is charged to income tax if the lease does not exceed 50 years. The assessable amount is the amount of the premium less 2% for each year of the lease except the first.
- A tenant paying a lease premium will receive tax relief on the premium if the property is sub-let or is used for the purposes of a trade.
- Rent-a-room relief is available if a taxpayer receives rents of up to £4,250 p.a. from the letting of furnished rooms in his or her main residence.
- Under certain conditions, the letting of furnished property qualifies as the commercial letting of furnished holiday accommodation. This offers a number of benefits to the taxpayer.

Exercises

5.1 Andrew owns a house which he lets to tenants. Rent is payable quarterly in advance on 1 January, 1 April, 1 July and 1 October. The rent was £8,000 per annum until it was increased to £8,800 per annum with effect from 1 January 2006. Rent received by Andrew during 2005/06 was as follows:

	£
2 July 2005	2,000
30 September 2005	2,000
3 January 2006	2,200
	6,200

Andrew did not receive the payment due on 1 April 2006 until 7 April 2006. Compute his property income for 2005/06, assuming that he incurred no allowable expenditure during the year.

5.2 Simon owns a country cottage which he uses as a holiday home for 4 weeks per year and lets furnished at £120 per week for the remaining 48 weeks of the year. Simon's expenses in relation to the cottage in 2005/06 were as follows:

	£
Council tax	400
Advertising	35
Repairs to furniture (damaged by tenant)	50
Gardener's wages (£10 per week)	520
Insurance	230

Compute Simon's property income for 2005/06.

5.3 In 2005/06, a landlord receives a premium of £12,000 when granting a lease to a tenant. Compute the income tax assessment on this premium if the length of the lease is:

(a) 60 years

(b) 50 years

(c) 20 years

5.4 In 2005/06, Jasper is granted a 10-year lease on a property, paying a premium of £15,000. He uses the property for trading purposes. Compute the tax relief which he will be allowed in respect of the lease premium.

5.5 Georgina owns three holiday flats, all of which she lets furnished with a view to profit. None of the flats is normally in the same occupation for more than 31 consecutive days. In 2005/06 the number of days for which each flat was available for letting, and the number of days actually let, were:

	Days available	*Days actually let*
Flat 1	140	64
Flat 2	150	72
Flat 3	182	74

Show Georgina's potential averaging claims.

***5.6** In 2005/06, Peter is granted a 12-year lease on a property, paying a premium of £40,000. He immediately grants a 4-year sub-lease to Paula, receiving a premium of £14,000. Calculate the income tax assessment on the premium received by Peter.

***5.7** Melissa is single and was born in 1936. She owns a house which she lets unfurnished at a rent of £100 per week. Her allowable expenditure in 2005/06 was £4,100 and she had property losses brought forward from 2004/05 of £1,350. Her other income in 2005/06 was as follows:

	£
Retirement pension	8,334
Net building society interest	9,320

Compute the income tax payable by Melissa for the year.

Chapter 6

Income from savings and investments

Introduction

The main purpose of this chapter is to explain the tax treatment of income arising from savings and investments. The main options available to a taxpayer who wishes to save or invest are to deposit money in bank and building society accounts or to invest in shares and securities. Each of these courses of action has its taxation implications and this chapter explains those implications.

This chapter also briefly considers the taxation of income from trusts and settlements and the tax treatment of certain miscellaneous sources of income.

Interest received

Section 369 of the Income Tax (Trading and Other Income) Act 2005 states that income tax is charged on interest. The Act also states that tax is charged on the full amount of interest arising in the year. Interest "arises" when it is paid to a taxpayer or when it is credited to a taxpayer's account. Therefore, any interest accrued at the end of a tax year but not yet paid or credited to the taxpayer is ignored when computing the income for that year.

Interest ranks as savings income (see Chapter 2) and so any interest falling into the basic rate band is taxed at the lower rate of 20%. No expenses are allowed against this form of income.

Interest received net

Interest is generally received net of 20% income tax. Some investments do pay gross interest but these are comparatively few (see later in this chapter). The main categories of interest taxed at source are:

(a) building society interest

(b) bank interest (other than interest from the National Savings Bank)

(c) debenture and other loan interest from UK companies.

Interest from most Government securities or "gilts" used to be taxed at source but anyone receiving interest on gilts may now choose whether to receive the interest gross or net (see Chapter 2).

The gross equivalent of any interest received net by a taxpayer during a tax year is included in the taxpayer's total income. The tax suffered by deduction at source is then subtracted when calculating tax payable.

Self-certification

Individuals resident in the UK who are unlikely to be liable to income tax for a given tax year may supply a certificate to this effect to their bank or building society. Interest is then paid to such individuals without deduction of tax at source, so avoiding the need for repayment claims at the end of the year. As might be expected, there are penalties for supplying such certificates fraudulently or negligently.

EXAMPLE 1

Alfred is single and 66 years old. He receives the following income in 2005/06:

	£
Retirement pension	6,220
Building society interest (net)	352

Calculate the amount of income tax reclaimed by Alfred at the end of 2005/06. Could the need to make a repayment claim have been avoided?

Solution

Alfred's total income for the year is £6,660 (£6,220 + £352 x 100/80). This is less than his personal allowance of £7,090 (over 65), resulting in a zero income tax liability for the year. He may reclaim the £88 tax deducted at source from the interest.

Since it was probably evident at the beginning of the year that Alfred was going to be a non-taxpayer in 2005/06, he could have supplied his building society with a certificate to that effect. He would then have received his interest without deduction of tax.

Interest received gross

Certain types of interest are received gross (without deduction of tax at source). The amount of any such interest received by a taxpayer during a tax year is included in the taxpayer's total income. The main types of interest received gross are:

(a) National Savings Bank (NSB) ordinary account interest

(b) National Savings Bank investment account interest

(c) interest on gilt-edged securities if the recipient has opted for gross interest.

The first £70 of NSB ordinary account interest arising in a tax year is exempt from income tax (see Chapter 2) but this exemption does not extend to the NSB investment account. It should be noted that it is longer possible to open an NSB ordinary account or to deposit further money into an existing ordinary account. However, any interest received on existing deposits continues to benefit from the £70 exemption.

Accrued income scheme

The accrued income scheme exists in order to prevent a form of tax avoidance known as "bond washing". Bond washing involves selling a security "cum interest" (so that the buyer of the security will receive the next interest payment) just before an interest payment is due. The price paid by the buyer reflects the fact that the sale is cum interest, so the seller is not disadvantaged. However, the effect of the transaction from the tax point of view is that the seller has converted what would have been income into a capital gain. Since capital gains on certain securities are exempt from capital gains tax (see Chapter 19) the seller appears to have avoided tax.

The accrued income scheme overcomes this potential loss of tax by charging the seller income tax on the interest which has accrued up to the date of the sale. The buyer of the securities is entitled to tax relief on the same amount and this is given by deduction from the next interest payment the buyer receives. Similar arrangements apply if securities are transferred "ex interest" (so that the seller will receive the next interest payment). In this case, the buyer is taxed on the interest accruing from the date of the sale to the date of the next interest payment and the seller is entitled to tax relief on the same amount.

The accrued income scheme applies to securities such as gilt-edged stocks, local authority bonds and company debentures. It does not apply to ordinary or preference shares in a company. Transfers made by individuals who have not held securities with a total nominal value exceeding £5,000 in the current tax year or in the preceding tax year are excluded from the scheme.

Dividends received

Section 383 of the Income Tax (Trading and Other Income) Act 2005 states that income tax is charged on dividends received from a UK resident company. The Act also states that tax is charged on the amount of dividends actually received in the tax year (with no adjustment for any accrued dividends). As explained in Chapter 2, UK dividends have an attached tax credit which is equal to one-ninth of the amount of the dividend. A taxpayer's dividend income for a tax year is equal to the UK dividends received in that year plus the attached tax credits.

Dividends are taxed at 10% in the starting rate and basic rate bands. Dividends which lie above these bands are taxed at 32.5% (see Chapter 2). Tax credits relating to dividends which are charged to tax are set against the income tax liability on those dividends. Tax credits exceeding this liability cannot be paid to the taxpayer or set against the tax liability on any other income. Note that:

(a) No expenses are allowed against this form of income.
(b) Any capital gain arising on the disposal of shares or securities is generally subject to capital gains tax (see Chapter 19).

The tax treatment of dividends received from overseas companies is considered in Chapter 32 of this book.

Tax-efficient investments in shares and securities

A taxpayer who is seeking an alternative, tax-efficient means of investing in shares and securities may invest in any of the following:

(a) a Personal Equity Plan (until 6 April 1999)
(b) the Enterprise Investment Scheme
(c) a Venture Capital Trust
(d) a Community Development Finance Institution.

Each of these forms of investment is explained below. A further alternative is to invest in the stocks and shares component of an Individual Savings Account (ISA). ISAs are explained later in this chapter.

Personal Equity Plans

A tax-efficient means of investing in stocks and shares used to be provided by Personal Equity Plans (PEPs) but with the introduction of Individual Savings Accounts (ISAs) as from 6 April 1999 it is no longer possible to set up a new PEP. Investors who held PEPs on 5 April 1999 may continue to hold them if they so wish *and retain the tax exemptions described below*. However, no further investment may now be made in a PEP. The main features of PEPs which are still relevant in tax year 2005/06 are as follows:

(a) The funds invested in a PEP are managed by a plan manager who uses these funds to make qualifying investments. Investments which qualify for inclusion in a PEP are the same as those which qualify for ISAs and include shares listed on a stock exchange anywhere in the world.
(b) Dividends and interest paid on PEP investments are exempt from income tax. Tax deducted at source may be reclaimed by the plan manager.
(c) Disposals of investments in a PEP are exempt from capital gains tax. This means that investors do not have to pay any CGT when disposing of PEP investments which have increased in value but also means that no loss relief is available if investments are sold which have declined in value (see Chapter 16).

Enterprise Investment Scheme

The Enterprise Investment Scheme (EIS) was established in 1994 to provide a means of encouraging investment in industry. The main features of the EIS are as follows:

(a) Income tax relief is available to taxpayers who subscribe for newly-issued shares in certain "qualifying companies". Essentially, these are unlisted UK trading companies whose gross assets are no more than £15 million immediately before the investment is made and no more than £16 million immediately afterwards.

(b) Relief takes the form of a reduction in the amount of tax due on the taxpayer's taxable income, equal to 20% of the amount invested in qualifying companies during the tax year. This reduction takes priority over the tax reductions relating to certain payments made by the taxpayer (see Chapter 4) and the tax reduction relating to the married couple's allowance (see Chapter 3).

(c) A minimum of £500 and a maximum of £200,000 (£150,000 prior to 2004/05) may be invested in each tax year. A taxpayer may claim that up to one-half of the EIS investments made in the first half of a tax year, subject to a limit of £25,000, should be treated as if made in the previous tax year.

(d) The taxpayer must not be connected with the company at any time during the two years prior to the date of the investment and the five years after that date. Broadly speaking, an individual is connected with a company for this purpose if he or she is an employee of the company or, together with associates, owns more than 30% of the company's ordinary shares.

(e) Dividends received on the shares are subject to income tax in the usual way.

(f) Any capital gain arising on the eventual disposal of the shares is exempt from capital gains tax but any loss arising on the disposal is eligible for relief. A loss may be relieved either:

    (i) as a capital loss, in the usual way (see Chapter 16), or

    (ii) under Section 574 of ICTA 1988, against the taxpayer's income of the year in which the loss is incurred or the previous year (see Chapter 11).

    When calculating the gain or loss arising on disposal, the shares are deemed to have been acquired for their issue price, less the tax reduction obtained by the taxpayer when the shares were purchased.

(g) The taxpayer must retain the shares for a minimum holding period of at least three years or both the income tax and capital gains tax reliefs are lost. For shares acquired before 6 April 2000, the minimum holding period is five years.

Venture Capital Trusts

A Venture Capital Trust (VCT) is a company approved as such by HM Revenue and Customs. The main conditions which must be satisfied before HMRC approval can be obtained are:

(a) The company's ordinary shares must be listed on the Stock Exchange.

(b) Its income must be derived wholly or mainly from shares or securities and no more than 15% of this income may be retained by the company.

(c) At least 70% of its total investments must consist of "qualifying holdings" and at least 30% must consist of ordinary shares. Broadly, shares or securities owned by a VCT rank as qualifying holdings if they were newly issued to the VCT and if they consist of shares or securities in unlisted companies carrying on a qualifying trade in the UK.

(d) No holding in any one company (other than in another VCT) can represent more than 15% of a VCT's investments. At least 10% of a VCT's investment in any one company must be held in the form of ordinary shares.

(e) An investment does not count as a qualifying holding unless the company which is issuing shares to the VCT satisfies the same gross assets test as a qualifying company for EIS purposes (see above). If a VCT invests more than £1 million in any one company in the *longer* of the period of six months leading up to a share issue and the period from the start of the tax year up to the date of the issue, the excess over £1 million does not count as a qualifying holding.

An individual who is at least 18 years old can obtain income tax relief in respect of an investment in newly-issued shares of a VCT. For tax years 2004/05 and 2005/06, the relief is equal to 40% of the amount invested, subject to a limit of £200,000 per tax year. Prior to 2004/05 this limit was £100,000. The rate of tax relief was 20% before 2004/05 and will revert to 20% after 2005/06. In order to qualify for relief, the shares must be held for a minimum holding period of at least three years. For shares acquired before 6 April 2000, the minimum holding period is five years.

Dividends on the first £200,000 of VCT shares acquired in each tax year (£100,000 prior to 2004/05) are exempt from income tax and any capital gain or loss arising on the disposal of these shares is exempt from capital gains tax, regardless of whether or not the shares have been held for the minimum holding period.

Community investment tax credit

Community investment tax credits provide tax relief to individuals who make an investment in an accredited Community Development Finance Institution (CDFI). The objective of a CDFI is to provide finance to support enterprises in disadvantaged communities. The main features of this scheme are as follows:

(a) The investment may take the form of a loan to a CDFI or a subscription for the shares or securities of a CDFI. The investor must not control the CDFI or be a partner in it (if it is a partnership).

(b) A loan must be for at least five years. No repayment can be required within the first two years of the loan and required repayments cannot exceed 25% of the loan amount before the end of the third year, 50% before the end of the fourth year and 75% before the end of the fifth year.

(c) Shares or securities must be subscribed for wholly in cash and must not be redeemable within five years of the investment date.

(d) Tax relief may be claimed for the tax year in which the investment is made and for each of the four subsequent tax years. In each year, relief is given by means of a tax reduction equal to the *lower* of:

    (i) 5% of the "invested amount", and

    (ii) the amount which reduces the investor's tax liability to nil.

(e) In the case of a loan the "invested amount" for the tax year in which the loan is made is defined as the average capital balance during the first 12 months of the loan. For subsequent tax years, the invested amount is normally equal to the average capital balance for the 12 months beginning with the anniversary of the investment date which falls into the tax year concerned.

(f) In the case of shares or securities, the invested amount is equal to the amount subscribed by the investor.

(g) If the investment takes the form of a loan, relief is denied for a tax year if the loan is disposed of, or repaid in excess of the permitted amount, before the "qualifying date" for that year. The qualifying date for a tax year is the anniversary of the investment date which falls into the subsequent tax year.

(h) For shares and securities, relief is denied for a tax year if the shares or securities are disposed of before the qualifying date for that year.

A similar relief is available to *companies* which invest in a CDFI.

Individual Savings Accounts

The tax-free Individual Savings Account (ISA) was introduced on 6 April 1999. The main features of this account are:

(a) Individuals who are resident and ordinarily resident in the UK (see Chapter 32) and are at least 16 years old are eligible to hold an ISA. The residence requirement is waived in the case of Crown servants serving overseas and their spouses or (as from 5 December 2005) their civil partners.

(b) An ISA may include three components. These are cash deposits, stocks and shares and life insurance products. A "maxi-ISA" is an ISA which includes a stocks and shares component plus either or both of the other two components. A "mini-ISA" is an ISA which includes only one of the components. Savers under the age of 18 may invest only in a cash mini-ISA or the cash component of a maxi-ISA.

(c) The cash component of an ISA is likely to consist of a bank or building society account or a specially-designed National Savings product. The stocks and shares component can include qualifying shares and securities listed on a stock exchange anywhere in the world. The life insurance component can only include policies on the saver's own life which have been specially designed for ISAs.

(d) Each tax year, a saver may put money into *either* a single maxi-ISA *or* up to three mini-ISAs, one for each component. No more than £7,000 may be invested in each year. This £7,000 limit will be retained until at least 5 April 2010.

(e) Within the overall annual limit of £7,000, there are further annual limits on the amount which can be invested in each component:

Maxi-ISAs	- no more than £3,000 p.a. in cash and £1,000 p.a. in life insurance
Mini-ISAs	- no more than £3,000 p.a. in a stocks and shares mini-ISA
	- no more than £3,000 p.a. in a cash mini-ISA
	- no more than £1,000 p.a. in a life insurance mini-ISA.

(f) There is no cumulative limit on the total amount which an individual can save in ISAs during his or her lifetime. Nor is there a specified minimum level of saving. Savers are able to save as little as they wish in an ISA.

(g) In each tax year, savers may start fresh ISAs (maxi or mini) or may continue to put money into ISAs started in previous years. However, it is not possible to put money into more than one maxi-ISA, or one mini-ISA of each type, in any year.

(h) ISAs are run by ISA managers, typically banks, building societies, insurance companies and some high street stores and supermarkets.

(i) Interest, dividends and bonuses from ISA investments are exempt from income tax. Capital gains (and losses) arising on ISA investments are exempt from capital gains tax.

(j) Withdrawals may be made from an ISA at any time without loss of tax relief. But once the maximum amount has been subscribed to an ISA for a tax year, no further subscriptions will be allowed in that year, regardless of how much is withdrawn from the account.

Child Trust Funds

Tax-free Child Trust Fund (CTF) accounts became available as from April 2005. The intention of these accounts is to build up a stock of assets for a young person to use or reinvest at the age of 18, so giving the young person added security and opportunity in adulthood. The main features of CTF accounts are as follows:

(a) A CTF account is automatically awarded to each child who is born on or after 1 September 2002 and who lives in the UK.

(b) A voucher for £250 is sent to the person who claims Child Benefit in relation to the child (usually the parent) and this person is then responsible for using the voucher to open a CTF account with a provider of their choice.

(c) Children from families with a gross income not exceeding the level at which Child Tax Credit begins to be tapered away receive an additional £250.

(d) The Government will make a further payment into each child's CTF account when the child reaches his or her seventh birthday. The amount of this further payment is yet to be decided.

(e) The child's family and friends (and the child himself or herself, when older) may make additional contributions into the CTF account of up to a total of £1,200 a year between them. These additional contributions do not attract tax relief.

(f) Although income derived from parental gifts is generally treated as that of the parent (not the child) unless the amount of the income does not exceed £100 for the tax year, income derived from parental contributions to a CTF account does not count towards this £100 limit (see Chapter 3).

(g) No money may be withdrawn from a CTF account until the account matures on the child's eighteenth birthday. Income and gains arising from CTF investments are not taxable and there will be no tax liability when the account matures.

(h) There are several different types of CTF account available, including cash deposit accounts, stocks and shares accounts and life policies.

Income from trusts and settlements

A trust or settlement is an arrangement whereby property is held by persons known as *trustees*, for the benefit of other persons known as *beneficiaries*. Trusts fall into two main categories, as follows:

(a) If one or more persons are entitled to receive all of the income generated by the trust property, those persons are "life tenants" and the trust is a "trust with an interest in possession".

(b) If there is no life tenant and the trustees have the discretion to distribute as much or as little of the trust income to the beneficiaries as they see fit, the trust is a "discretionary trust".

Trust taxation is a very complex matter and a full study of the subject is beyond the scope of this book. However, an introduction to trust taxation is given below.

Trusts with an interest in possession

The trustees of a trust with an interest in possession are liable to income tax at the dividend ordinary rate (10%) on the trust's dividend income, the lower rate (20%) on its savings income and the basic rate (22%) on all of its other income. Note that:

(a) The tax liability of the trustees is never calculated at the starting rate, the higher rate or the dividend upper rate.

(b) The expenses of administering the trust are *not* allowed when computing the trustees' liability but expenses which relate to specific items of trust income (e.g. expenses normally deductible from property income) are set against that income.

(c) The trustees' tax liability is calculated without deduction of personal allowances.

(d) Relief is given for income tax deducted at source and tax credits on dividends.

The income which remains after tax and all expenses have been deducted (including administration expenses) is paid to the life tenants and is dealt with in their personal tax computations. In those computations:

(a) trust non-savings income is treated as income received net of basic rate tax

(b) trust savings income is treated as income received net of lower rate tax

(c) trust dividend income is treated as dividend income with an attached tax credit.

The administration expenses of the trust are deemed to have been paid first out of dividend income, then out of savings income and then out of non-savings income.

EXAMPLE 2

An interest in possession trust with one life tenant has the following income in 2005/06:

	£
Rents receivable	30,200
Bank interest (net)	7,200
UK dividends	1,350

Expenses were incurred in the year as follows:

	£
Property expenses	6,900
Administration expenses	1,990

(a) Compute the trustees' income tax liability for 2005/06.

(b) How much income does the life tenant receive from the trust in 2005/06 and how will this be treated in his or her personal tax computation?

Solution

	Total	*Non-Savings*	*Savings*	*Dividends*
	£	£	£	£
Property income £30,200 - £6,900	23,300	23,300		
Bank interest £7,200 x 100/80	9,000		9,000	
UK dividends £1,350 + tax credit £150	1,500			1,500
	33,800	23,300	9,000	1,500
Income tax @ 22%	(5,126)	(5,126)		
Income tax @ 20%	(1,800)		(1,800)	
Income tax @ 10%	(150)			(150)
Income after tax	26,724	18,174	7,200	1,350
Administration expenses	(1,990)		(640)	(1,350)
Income after tax and expenses	24,734	18,174	6,560	0

(a) The trustees' tax liability for the year is £7,076 (£5,126 + £1,800 + £150). The £1,800 of tax deducted at source and the £150 of tax credits are deducted, leaving tax payable by the trustees of £5,126.

(b) The income of the life tenant is:

	Gross	*Tax deducted*
	£	£
Non-savings £18,174 x 100/78	23,300	5,126
Savings £6,560 x 100/80	8,200	1,640
Total	31,500	6,766

This income will be included in the life tenant's tax computation for 2005/06 and the tax deducted at source of £6,766 will be subtracted when computing tax payable for the year.

Discretionary trusts

In general, the income tax liability of the trustees of a discretionary trust is calculated at the "dividend trust rate" (32.5%) on the trust's dividend income and at the "rate applicable to trusts" (40%) on all of its other income. However, these special rates do not apply to income which has been used to fund the expenses of administering the trust. Such income is taxed at the dividend ordinary rate (dividend income), the lower rate (savings income) or the basic rate (non-savings income).

Also, as from 6 April 2005, the first £500 of the income of a discretionary trust is not taxed at the special trust rates but instead is charged to tax at the income tax rate which generally applies to the class of income concerned (i.e. the dividend ordinary rate, the lower rate or the basic rate). When identifying the first £500 of a trust's income, non-savings income is considered first, then savings income, then dividends.

Any payments made to beneficiaries are deemed to have been made net of tax at the rate applicable to trusts and must therefore be grossed-up at 100/60 in their personal income tax computations. The tax which is deemed to have been deducted from such payments is assessable on the trustees, but only to the extent (if any) that the amount of this tax exceeds the trustees' tax liability on the trust income. For this purpose, the tax liability of the trustees is deemed to exclude any tax which is satisfied by deduction of tax credits on dividends.

Trusts with vulnerable beneficiary

The Finance Act 2005 introduced a new tax regime for trusts with a vulnerable beneficiary. This tax regime (which takes effect from 6 April 2004) ensures that the tax liability of such a trust is reduced to the amount of tax that would have been payable if the trust income and gains had accrued directly to the beneficiary concerned.

A "vulnerable beneficiary" may be either a disabled person or (in certain instances) a minor. Trustees who wish to claim the special tax treatment available under the new regime must make an appropriate election to HM Revenue and Customs. Once made, such an election is irrevocable.

EXAMPLE 3

Assume that a discretionary trust has the same income and expenses in 2005/06 as the trust described in the above example. Assume also that a payment of £4,500 was made to a beneficiary during the year.

(a) Compute the trustees' income tax liability for 2005/06.

(b) Show how the £4,500 received by the beneficiary will be treated in his or her personal tax computation.

Solution

	Total	*Non-Savings*	*Savings*	*Dividends*
	£	£	£	£
Property income £30,200 - £6,900	23,300	23,300		
Bank interest £7,200 x 100/80	9,000		9,000	
UK dividends £1,350 + tax credit £150	1,500			1,500
	33,800	23,300	9,000	1,500
First £500 of trust income:				
Income tax at 22% on £500	(110)	(110)		
Remainder of trust income:				
Income tax @ 10% on £1,500	(150)			(150)
Income tax @ 20% on £800	(160)		(160)	
Income tax @ 40% on £8,200	(3,280)		(3,280)	
Income tax @ 40% on £22,800	(9,120)	(9,120)		
Income after tax	20,980	14,070	5,560	1,350
Administration expenses	(1,990)		(640)	(1,350)
Income after tax and expenses	18,990	14,070	4,920	0

Note:

The administration expenses of £1,990 are deemed to have been paid out of the trust's after-tax income, first out of dividends (£1,350) and then out of savings income (£640). As £640 of net savings income has been used for this purpose, gross savings income of £800 is taxed at only 20% and not at the special rate of 40%.

(a) The trustees' tax liability is £12,820 (£110 + £150 + £160 + £3,280 + £9,120). The tax deducted at source of £1,800 and tax credits of £150 are subtracted, leaving tax payable by the trustees of £10,870. This consists of £9,230 payable on the non-savings income and an extra 20% (40% - 20%) on the £8,200 of savings income which is taxed at the trust rate.

(b) The payment of £4,500 is grossed-up at 100/60, giving gross income of £7,500. This income is included in the beneficiary's tax computation for 2005/06 and the £3,000 of tax deducted at source is subtracted when computing tax payable for the year. The trustees' tax liability on the trust income (excluding the £150 which is satisfied by tax credits on dividends) is £12,670. This exceeds £3,000 so there is no further assessment on the trustees in relation to this payment.

Miscellaneous income

Section 574 of the Income Tax (Trading and Other Income) Act 2005 charges income tax on certain items of miscellaneous income (to the extent that these items are not already taxed under another heading). The Act also provides rules for computing the amount of such income arising in the tax year. Examples of miscellaneous income include receipts from the sale of patent rights and income from any source which is not otherwise charged to tax.

Summary

- Income tax is payable on the amount of interest received by a taxpayer during the tax year. Most interest is received net but non-taxpayers may receive their interest gross if they certify themselves as such. The main source of gross interest is the National Savings Bank.
- Income tax is payable on UK dividends received. Such dividends have an attached tax credit. Tax credits relating to dividends which are charged to income tax are set against the tax liability on those dividends.
- Personal Equity Plans used to provide a tax-efficient means of investing in stocks and shares. Because of the introduction of the Individual Savings Account in April 1999, no further investment may now be made in a PEP.
- The Enterprise Investment Scheme provides tax incentives for those subscribing for the newly-issued shares of unlisted UK trading companies.
- Subject to certain conditions, tax relief is available in relation to an investment in a Venture Capital Trust.
- Community investment tax credits provide tax relief for those who make loans to a Community Development Finance Institution (CDFI) or who subscribe for the shares or securities of a CDFI.
- The Individual Savings Account (ISA) provides a tax-free means of saving cash or investing in life insurance products or stocks and shares.
- As from April 2005, Child Trust Fund (CTF) accounts provide a tax-free means of building up a stock of assets for a young person to use or to reinvest at the age of 18.
- Trustees must account for income tax on the income of a trust. The administration expenses of the trust are not allowed when computing the trustees' income tax liability. Special rates of tax apply to the income of a discretionary trust.
- Certain forms of miscellaneous income are charged to income tax.

Exercises

6.1 Edward has the following income in 2005/06:

	£
Building society interest (net)	10,508
UK dividends	27,468

Compute the income tax payable by Edward for the year, assuming that there are no charges on income and that he claims only the basic personal allowance.

6.2 Anne is single and aged 76. She has the following income in 2005/06:

	£
Bank interest:	
Interest on deposit account (net)	384
Interest credited to cash mini-ISA	83
UK dividends	585
Retirement pension	6,606

Compute the income tax payable by (or repayable to) Anne for the year, assuming that she has no charges on income.

6.3 Outline the income tax advantages of investing in:

(a) the Enterprise Investment Scheme

(b) a Venture Capital Trust.

(c) a Community Development Finance Institution.

6.4 Outline the main features of the Individual Savings Account.

6.5 Bernice was born on 1 March 1941 and is a widow. Her income for 2005/06 is as follows:

	£
Retirement pension	14,970
NSB ordinary account interest	78
NSB investment account interest	52
Building society interest (net)	3,784

Compute the income tax payable by Bernice for 2005/06.

***6.6** An interest in possession trust with two life tenants has the following income in 2005/06:

	£
Rents received	12,620
Bank deposit interest (net)	992
Gilt interest received gross	1,800
UK dividends	12,600

Property expenses incurred in the year were £2,220 and general administration expenses amounted to £2,700.

(a) Compute the trustees' income tax liability for 2005/06.

(b) Assuming that the trust income is divided equally between the two life tenants, calculate each life tenant's income from the trust in 2005/06.

Chapter 7

Income from employment

Introduction

For many years, income from employment was taxed according to the rules of Schedule E. However, Schedule E was abolished as from 6 April 2003 and income from employment now falls within the scope of the Income Tax (Earnings and Pensions) Act 2003. As explained in Chapter 2, this Act arose from the work of the Tax Law Rewrite project and made no fundamental changes to the way in which employment income is taxed.

The main purpose of this chapter is to explain how employment income is assessed and to consider the expenses which may be deducted when computing an employee's income for tax purposes. There is also a brief description of the Pay As You Earn (PAYE) system, by means of which most employees pay their income tax. This chapter is concerned with employees whose duties are performed wholly within the UK. The taxation of overseas earnings is considered in Chapter 32.

Employment and self-employment

As will become clear in subsequent chapters, self-employed people enjoy considerable tax advantages when compared with employees. Two of the main advantages of being self-employed are:

(a) A much wider range of expenses is allowed against the income of self-employed people than against the income of employees (see Chapter 8).

(b) Self-employed people pay their income tax by instalments (see Chapter 14) and effectively pay their tax much later than employees, who normally pay income tax under the Pay As You Earn system.

It is usually quite obvious whether someone is employed or self-employed but sometimes there are borderline cases. For example, it may be difficult to distinguish between an employee with a number of part-time jobs and a self-employed person with several clients. In such cases, the taxpayer will usually wish to claim self-employed status, whilst HM Revenue and Customs will often insist that the taxpayer should be treated as an employee.

The key test to be applied when trying to establish a taxpayer's status in cases like these is concerned with the nature of the contract between the taxpayer and the person who is paying for the work done by that taxpayer. There are two possibilities:

(a) If it can be shown that a *contract of service* exists, then the taxpayer is regarded as an employee who is in service to an employer.

(b) If it can be shown that a *contract for services* exists, then the taxpayer is regarded as a self-employed person who is rendering services to a client.

A great deal of case law has accumulated on this subject over the years and several criteria have been established which may be used to distinguish between the two types of contract (and, therefore, between employment and self-employment). The main criteria are as follows:

(a) **Control**. The more control that the person who is paying for the work has over the person who is doing the work, the more likely it is that a contract of service exists. Employees are usually unable to choose whether or not to do certain work, how to do the work, when to do the work or where to do the work. Self-employed people are usually able to decide these matters for themselves.

(b) **Financial risk**. Employees do not usually risk their own capital in the business for which they work and they receive their remuneration regularly, whether or not their employer is making a profit. Self-employed people may make losses as well as profits and may lose their capital if the business fails.

(c) **Equipment**. In general, employees do not provide their own equipment but self-employed people do.

(d) **Work performance and correction**. Employees are usually expected to do their work themselves. If they make mistakes they usually correct the work during working hours and so get paid both for the original work and for the corrections. Self-employed people often delegate their work to staff or to subcontractors. If the work done is unsatisfactory, the client will not expect to have to pay again for it to be corrected.

(e) **Holidays and sickness**. Employees are likely to receive holiday pay and sick pay from their employers. Self-employed people are paid by their clients only for the work that they do and do not get paid when on holiday or when ill.

(f) **Exclusivity**. In general, employees work for a single employer. Self-employed people normally have a number of clients.

There are exceptions to all of the general statements given above and therefore these criteria should be applied with caution. It is vitally important to consider the facts of each case as a whole and not to rely upon just one criterion when trying to decide whether a taxpayer should be regarded as employed or self-employed.

Personal services provided through intermediaries

A specific situation about which the Government has been concerned for some time is the hiring of individuals through their own personal service companies, thus enabling those individuals to exploit the tax (and National Insurance) advantages offered by corporate status. Anti-avoidance legislation designed to thwart this kind of disguised employment took effect as from 6 April 2000. The main points are as follows:

(a) The legislation applies to "relevant engagements" where a worker provides services to a client through an intermediary (usually a company) in circumstances such that the income arising from the engagement would have been treated as income from employment if it had not been for the presence of the intermediary.

(b) The legislation does *not* apply if the worker receives income from the intermediary only in a form which is taxable as employment income and has no other rights to income or capital from the intermediary.

(c) If an intermediary receives income from relevant engagements during a tax year and this income (less allowable expenses) is greater than the worker's employment income from the intermediary in that year, then the excess is treated as a deemed salary payment made on the last day of the year. This deemed payment is subject to both income tax and National Insurance contributions.

(d) The allowable expenses referred to above include all expenses generally allowable against employment income, plus any employer's pension and National Insurance contributions made by the intermediary, plus a further flat-rate 5% of the income arising from relevant engagements (to cover running costs of the intermediary).

(e) To the extent that the deemed salary is paid out to the worker as a dividend, the intermediary may claim that the dividend should not be liable to tax.

Basis of assessment

An individual's employment income for a tax year is the income actually received in that year (the "receipts basis"). Income is deemed to be received on the *earliest* of:

(a) the date that the income is actually received by the employee

(b) the date that the employee becomes entitled to receive the income

and, for a company director only:

(c) the date that the income is credited to the director in the company's records

(d) the end of a period of account, if the amount of the director's income for that period is determined before it ends

(e) the date that the amount of the director's income for a period of account is determined, if this falls after the end of that period.

Note that the income *received* in a tax year is not necessarily the same as the income *earned* during that year.

EXAMPLE 1

Barry is a sales manager. He receives a basic salary plus an annual bonus (received in February) which is based on the sales achieved in the previous calendar year. Compute his total employment income in 2005/06, given that his basic salary for the year was £35,000 and that bonuses for calendar years 2004, 2005 and 2006 are as follows:

	£
year ended 31 December 2004 (received February 2005)	6,250
year ended 31 December 2005 (received February 2006)	7,350
year ended 31 December 2006 (received February 2007)	7,900

Solution

Employment income for 2005/06 is £42,350 (£35,000 + £7,350). The bonus received in February 2006 is assessed in 2005/06, even though part of it was earned in 2004/05.

Employment income

The term "employment income" includes practically anything that could conceivably be received by an employee in respect of an employment e.g. wages, salaries, bonuses, commissions, fees, expense allowances, payments on the termination of employment, pensions arising from an employment and benefits in kind. Also, certain social security benefits are taxed in the same way as employment income, including:

(a) the retirement pension and the widow's pension

(b) the job seeker's allowance

(c) statutory sick pay, maternity pay and paternity pay

(d) incapacity benefit, the carer's allowance and industrial death benefit.

Note that it is not necessary for the employee to receive the income directly from the employer. So long as the income is received as a result of the employment it is taxable as employment income, no matter who has paid it. For example, a waiter's tips are taxable, even though these are paid by customers rather than by the employer.

Soft currency loans

One ingenious way in which employers have sought to remunerate employees in non-taxable form is to make loans to employees in a "soft" currency which rapidly loses value against sterling. When such a loan is repaid (in the same currency) the employee enjoys an exchange gain whilst the employer suffers an exchange loss. The hope is that the employee's gain will not be taxable and that the employer's loss will be tax-deductible. However, HMRC's view is that exchange gains of this type may well be taxable (depending upon the contractual arrangements between the employer and the employee) and that exchange losses incurred in these circumstances are not eligible for tax relief. It seems, therefore that this attempt at tax avoidance is ineffective.

Non-taxable employment income

Certain forms of employment income are exempt from income tax. The main items of exempt income are as follows:

(a) luncheon vouchers provided by an employer of up to 15p per day in value

(b) free or subsidised meals in a staff canteen, if available to all employees

(c) an annual Christmas party or similar function paid for by the employer, so long as the function is open to staff generally and the cost does not exceed £150 per head, but note that:

  (i) if a function costs over £150 per head, the whole cost is taxable

  (ii) if there is more than one function during the year and their total cost exceeds £150 per head, functions totalling £150 per head or less are exempt from tax but any other functions are taxed in full

(d) the provision of a parking space at or near the employee's place of work

(e) the provision of private transport (e.g. a taxi) for the journey home of employees who are occasionally required to work until 9pm or later

(f) the payment by an employer of the costs of an employee's journey home if the employee travels to work in a shared car (in accordance with a regular car-sharing arrangement) and is prevented from travelling home in the shared car because of unforeseen and exceptional circumstances

(g) "green commuting" benefits paid for by the employer and used by employees for travel between home and work, including the provision of:

  - bicycles and cycling safety equipment loaned to employees
  - meals or refreshments for employees taking part in "cycle to work" days
  - works buses with a seating capacity for nine or more passengers
  - subsidies to public bus services, whether employees pay the same fare as other passengers or travel free or at a reduced fare

(h) contributions by an employer towards additional household costs incurred by an employee who works at home (supporting evidence of these costs being required only if the contributions exceed £2 per week)

(i) approved mileage allowances (see below)

(j) the payment by an employer of an employee's personal incidental expenses (e.g. the cost of telephone calls home) when the employee is staying away from home overnight on business, of up to £5 per night for stays within the UK or £10 per night for stays outside the UK

(k) reasonable removal expenses (up to a maximum of £8,000) paid for by an employer when an employee first takes up an employment or transfers to a new location within the organisation

(l) reasonable gifts made by employer to employee in a personal capacity rather than as remuneration for services rendered (e.g. a gift made on an exam success)

(m) non-cash long-service awards, so long as the award is in respect of at least 20 years of service, does not cost the employer more than £50 per year of service and no such award has been made to the employee in the previous 10 years

(n) non-cash gifts received by virtue of the employment from someone other than the employer, so long as the value of the gifts from any one source amounts to no more than £250 in the tax year and the gifts are not made in recognition of the performance of particular services in the course of the employment

(o) awards of up to £5,000 made under a staff suggestion scheme

(p) the cost of work-related training courses for an employee

(q) payments of up to £15,000 per academic year to an employee who is attending a full-time course at a recognised educational establishment

(r) the first £500 per annum of the benefit in kind that would normally arise (see later in this chapter) when computer equipment is loaned to an employee

(s) the provision of a mobile telephone for an employee's use

(t) the provision of job-related living accommodation (see later in this chapter)

(u) the provision of workplace childcare, sports or recreation facilities

(v) up to £50 a week of childcare if the employer contracts directly with an approved childminder or provides vouchers for use in paying an approved childminder

(w) the provision of a low-interest or interest-free loan to an employee if the loan is of a type that qualifies for tax relief (see Chapter 4)

(x) the provision of a welfare counselling service for employees generally

(y) the provision of pensions information and advice if available to all employees and costing less than £150 per employee per year

(z) the private use of equipment or facilities provided to disabled employees to enable them to carry out the duties of their employment.

Approved mileage rates

Employees who use their own vehicles on business may receive mileage allowances from their employers. These allowances are tax-free so long as they do not exceed the HMRC approved mileage allowance payment (AMAP) which is calculated by reference to a table of approved mileage rates. For 2005/06, these rates are:

	first 10,000 miles in the tax year	*each mile over 10,000 miles in the tax year*
Motor cars and vans	40p per mile	25p per mile
Motor cycles	24p per mile	24p per mile
Bicycles	20p per mile	20p per mile

If the mileage allowances paid to an employee exceed the sum calculated using these rates, then the excess is taxable. On the other hand, if the mileage allowances paid to an employee are less than the sum calculated using these rates, the deficit is an allowable expense. Tax relief cannot be claimed for any costs above the AMAP rate.

Employers may also pay employees up to 5p per mile tax-free for each passenger carried on a business trip. However, employees cannot claim tax relief if the employer pays less than this (or pays nothing at all).

EXAMPLE 2

Julie uses her own car when travelling on her employer's business. In 2005/06 she drives 12,000 business miles. Explain the taxation implications if her employer pays her:

(a) 42p per mile (b) 32p per mile (c) None.

Solution

(a) Having driven 12,000 business miles in her own car during the year, Julie may receive a tax-free mileage allowance of up to £4,500 (10,000 @ 40p + 2,000 @ 25p). She actually receives £5,040 (12,000 @ 42p) so her taxable mileage allowance is £540.

(b) If the mileage allowance is 32p per mile, Julie receives only £3,840 from her employer. Therefore she has incurred an allowable expense of £660 (£4,500 - £3,840) which may be set against her income from employment.

(c) If Julie receives nothing, she has an allowable expense of £4,500.

Allowable expenses

If an employee incurs expenses by virtue of his or her employment, then one of two situations may arise:

(a) The employer does not reimburse the employee. In this case the expenses (if allowable) will be deducted from the employee's income for tax purposes.

(b) The employer reimburses the employee. In this case the amount reimbursed by the employer will be treated as part of the employee's income and the expenses (if allowable) will then be deducted from that income. However, reimbursed expenses may be ignored for tax purposes if HMRC grants a dispensation (a "notice of nil liability") to this effect.

Expenses incurred by an employee are allowable for tax purposes only if they fall into one of the following categories:

(a) contributions to an approved occupational pension scheme or premiums paid to secure a retirement annuity (see Chapter 13)

(b) subscriptions to relevant professional bodies

(c) donations made under a payroll giving scheme (see later in this chapter)

(d) travel and subsistence expenses necessarily incurred in the performance of the duties of the employment (see below)
(e) other expenses incurred wholly, exclusively and necessarily in the performance of the duties of the employment.

The "wholly, exclusively and necessarily" rule is applied stringently. In particular, the "necessarily" part of the rule means that an expense will not be allowed unless it can be shown that the duties of the employment could not be performed (by anyone) if the expense were not incurred.

Travel and subsistence expenses

As stated above, travel and subsistence expenses are allowable for tax purposes only if they are necessarily incurred in the performance of the duties of the employment. This means that the cost of travel between home and work is normally disallowed on the grounds that the duties of the employment do not begin until the employee arrives at work. However, the following costs of travel between home and work are allowable:

(a) travel and subsistence costs incurred by a "site-based" employee (i.e. an employee who has no normal place of work) when travelling between home and the site
(b) travel and subsistence costs incurred by an employee who has a normal place of work, when undertaking business journeys which start from home
(c) travel and subsistence costs incurred by an employee who is seconded to a temporary place of work, so long as it is expected that he or she will return to the normal place of work within 24 months.

EXAMPLE 3

In which of the following cases will the expenses described be allowable against the employee's income for tax purposes?

(a) A bank manager voluntarily pays an annual subscription to a London club. He uses the club only for the purpose of meeting the bank's clients.

(b) A workman is required to provide his own tools and protective clothing.

(c) A clerk pays to attend a college course in the evenings, so as to gain qualifications and improve her career prospects.

(d) The finance director of a company pays an annual subscription to the Institute of Chartered Accountants.

(e) A college lecturer teaches at the main college building and then drives to one of the college's annexes to take his next class. He pays his own travel costs.

(f) A barrister living and practising in London is appointed Recorder of Portsmouth. He pays his own travel costs between London and Portsmouth.

Solution

(a) The bank manager uses the club wholly and exclusively for business purposes, but it is not necessary for him to be a member of the club in order to perform his duties. Therefore the cost of the subscription will be disallowed. The facts of this case are similar to those of *Brown* v *Bullock* (1961).

(b) The cost of necessary tools and protective clothing will be allowed. In some cases, HM Revenue and Customs has agreed flat-rate tax allowances with the relevant trade union for such expenses as tools, protective clothing, uniforms and laundry costs.

(c) Whilst attending college, the clerk is not performing the duties of her employment. Therefore the cost of the college course will be disallowed. The facts of this case are similar to those of *Blackwell* v *Mills* (1945).

(d) Relevant professional subscriptions of this nature are specifically allowed by statute. Therefore the cost of the subscription will be allowed.

(e) Travel between the two buildings will be allowed, since the travel is necessary and is incurred in the performance of the duties of the employment.

(f) The duties of the employment are carried out entirely in Portsmouth. Whilst travelling from London, the barrister is not performing those duties so the expense will be disallowed. The facts of this case are similar to those of *Ricketts* v *Colquhoun* (1935).

Entertaining expenses

In general, entertaining expenses are not allowable against employment income and an employee who is obliged to defray such expenses personally cannot claim a deduction for them. However, if an employer either:

(a) reimburses an employee for entertaining expenses incurred, or

(b) pays the employee a specific entertaining allowance

then the entertaining expenses incurred by the employee may be set against the sums received from the employer. This rule is subject to the overriding rule that the entertaining expenses must be incurred wholly, exclusively and necessarily in the performance of the duties of the employment.

Payroll giving scheme

Employees whose employers operate an approved "payroll giving scheme" may make charitable donations by asking that the donations should be deducted from their gross earnings. Income tax is payable on the earnings remaining *after* the donations have been deducted, thus providing tax relief. The employer passes the donations on to an approved charity. A Government grant of up to £500 is payable to small and medium-sized enterprises which set up a payroll giving scheme and then the first £10 per month of each employee's donations are matched pound-for-pound by the Government for a period of six months.

Benefits in kind

The definition of employment income given earlier in this chapter included benefits in kind (which are referred to in ITEPA 2003 simply as "benefits"). Benefits consist of income received in the form of goods or services, rather than money. For the purpose of assessing benefits, employees are divided into two classes, "P11D employees" and "lower-paid employees":

(a) P11D employees comprise those employees who earn at least £8,500 per annum and most company directors. The only exceptions are full-time working directors who earn less than £8,500 p.a. and control no more than 5% of their company's ordinary share capital. Employers must submit a form P11D to HM Revenue and Customs for each such employee for each tax year, listing the employee's benefits and any reimbursed expenses (unless covered by a dispensation).

(b) All other employees are non-P11D employees or "lower-paid employees".

As a general rule, lower-paid employees are taxed only on benefits that are convertible into money, and then only on the amount of money that the employee could obtain in this way. In other words, lower-paid employees are taxed on the *second-hand value* of their benefits. P11D employees are generally taxed on the *cost to the employer* of providing the benefits, whether or not these benefits are convertible into money.

The cost of providing a benefit is the additional cost borne by the employer as a consequence of providing that benefit. This rule was established in the case of *Pepper* v *Hart* (1992) which concerned the provision of school places for the children of masters at the school. It was held that the cost of this provision for tax purposes should consist only of the additional costs borne by the school (e.g. extra food and laundry costs) rather than the average cost per pupil which would be obtained by dividing the total running costs of the school by the total number of pupils.

When comparing an employee's earnings with the watershed figure of £8,500, it is necessary to take into account all earnings, including benefits *valued as if the employee were* a *P11D employee*. No expenses may be deducted from earnings when making this comparison, apart from contributions to an approved superannuation scheme or to a payroll giving scheme. If an employee works for more than one employer and the employers are connected in some way, earnings from the connected employers must be aggregated when deciding the employee's classification for benefits purposes.

EXAMPLE 4

Classify each of the following employees for benefits purposes:

(a) Joan works part-time and has a salary of £7,300 p.a. She also receives benefits which cost her employer £900 but which have a second-hand value of £500.

(b) Kate works part-time and has a salary of £8,320 p.a. She also receives benefits which cost her employer £600 with a second-hand value of £300. Her allowable expenses are £535, including superannuation contributions of £416.

(c) Lawrence is a company director. He has 10% of the company's share capital, works one day per week on company business and receives an annual director's fee of £8,000. Benefits cost his company £250 with a second-hand value of £150.

Solution

(a) Joan's salary, plus the cost of her benefits, total £8,200. This is less than £8,500 and therefore she is a lower-paid employee. She will be taxed on her salary and on the second-hand value of her benefits, a total of £7,800.

(b) Kate's salary, plus the cost of her benefits, total £8,920. Her superannuation contributions of £416 reduce this total to £8,504 but this is not less than £8,500 so she is a P11D employee. She will be taxed on her salary, plus the full cost of her benefits, less her allowable expenses i.e. £8,385 (£8,320 + £600 - £535).

(c) Lawrence is a P11D employee by virtue of being a company director who does not work full-time and who owns more than 5% of his company's share capital. He will be taxed on his fees, plus the full cost of his benefits i.e. £8,250.

Benefits assessable on all employees

The tax treatment of an employee's benefits generally depends upon the employee's classification, as explained above. But certain benefits are assessable in the same way on all employees, regardless of classification. The two main benefits concerned are:

(a) vouchers which may be exchanged for goods or services
(b) living accommodation.

Vouchers for goods or services

All employees are taxed on the cost to their employer of providing vouchers which may be exchanged for goods or services (e.g. gift vouchers,). However, the first 15p per day of luncheon vouchers is exempt from income tax and vouchers for a parking space at or near the employee's workplace are also exempt. Note that:

(a) Entertainment and hospitality vouchers provided by a person other than the employer or someone connected with the employer are exempt from income tax unless provided as a reward for specific services rendered by the employee.

(b) The provision of a cash voucher (i.e. a voucher which may be converted directly into cash) results in an assessable benefit equal to the amount of cash into which the voucher can be converted.

Living accommodation

All employees are taxed in the same way on the value of any living accommodation provided for them by their employer. The rules are as follows:

(a) In the case of accommodation owned by the employer, the employee is assessed on the "annual value" of the accommodation. In practice, this is taken to be the accommodation's rateable value, which was used in the calculation of domestic rates before these were abolished. The rateable value of properties constructed since the abolition of domestic rates has to be estimated.

(b) In the case of accommodation rented by the employer, the employee is assessed on the greater of the rent paid by the employer and the accommodation's annual value.

In either case, the assessable benefit is reduced by any contribution made by the employee. Accommodation costing the employer more than £75,000 is regarded as "expensive" and gives rise to an increase in the assessable benefit. This increase is calculated by applying an appropriate percentage to the amount by which the cost of the accommodation exceeds £75,000. Note the following points:

(a) The "appropriate percentage" used for this purpose is the same as the official rate of interest used in beneficial loan calculations (see later in this chapter) as that rate stood at the beginning of the tax year.

(b) The cost of providing accommodation is equal to the purchase price of the property, plus the cost of any improvements made to the property before the start of the tax year, less any capital contribution made by the employee.

(c) If the property was acquired by the employer more than six years before it was made available to the employee, then the purchase price of the property may be replaced for tax purposes by its market value on the date that it was first occupied by the employee.

EXAMPLE 5

As from 1 January 2005, an employee is provided with the use of a house which has an annual value of £5,300. The employer bought the house in 2002 for £70,000 and spent £35,000 on improvements in 2004. A further £10,000 is spent on improvements in July 2005. The employee pays £1,000 per annum to his employer in relation to this benefit. Calculate the taxable benefit in 2005/06, assuming an official rate of interest of 5% per annum.

Solution

	£
Annual value	5,300
Add: 5% x (£70,000 + £35,000 - £75,000)	1,500
	6,800
Less: Employee contribution	1,000
Assessable benefit	5,800

Job-related accommodation

If accommodation provided by an employer is "job-related" then no taxable benefit arises. Accommodation is job-related if:

(a) it is necessary for the employee to reside in the accommodation for the proper performance of his or her duties (e.g. a caretaker who is required to live in a caretaker's flat on an employer's premises)

(b) the accommodation is provided for the better performance of the employee's duties and it is customary for such accommodation to be provided (e.g. a clergyman living in a vicarage provided by an employer)

(c) the accommodation is provided as part of security arrangements (if there is a special threat to the employee's security).

Special rules for P11D employees

Certain benefits are assessed on P11D employees according to special rules. The main benefits for which special rules exist are:

(a) assets loaned to the employee for private use

(b) ancillary services connected with living accommodation

(c) cars provided for private use

(d) fuel provided for private use

(e) vans provided for private use

(f) beneficial loans.

Lower-paid employees would be taxed on these benefits only if they were capable of being converted into cash in some way, and then only on the amount of cash obtainable.

Assets loaned to the employee for private use

If an employer lends an asset to a P11D employee for his or her own private use, the employee is assessed annually on 20% of the asset's market value on the date of the loan. If the period of the loan exceeds five years, the total of the annual assessments will exceed the total value of the asset. If the asset is subsequently sold or given to the employee, he or she is additionally assessed on the *greater* of:

(a) the market value of the asset when sold or given to the employee, less any amount paid for the asset by the employee, and

(b) the market value of the asset when first loaned to the employee, less the amounts already assessed during the period of the loan, less any amount paid for the asset by the employee.

The loan of a bicycle and cycling safety equipment is exempt from tax if used wholly or mainly for travel between home and work. The first £500 p.a. of the benefit arising when a computer is loaned to an employee is also exempt. If an employee purchases a previously-loaned bicycle or computer from an employer, the benefit arising on this purchase is calculated using method (a) above and not method (b).

EXAMPLE 6

On 6 April 2003, an employer purchases a music system for £400 and immediately lends the system to a P11D employee for his private use. The system remains in the employee's possession until 6 October 2005 when the employee buys it from his employer for £50, its market value on that day being £120. Calculate the assessable benefit for the years 2003/04 to 2005/06 inclusive.

Solution

			£
2003/04	20% of £400		80
2004/05	20% of £400		80
2005/06	20% of £400 x 6/12	40	
	plus, the greater of:		
	(i) £120 - £50 = £70		
	(ii) £400 - £80 - £80 - £40 - £50 = £150	150	190
Total benefit assessed over period of the loan			350

Ancillary services connected with living accommodation

If an employer provides living accommodation for a P11D employee, the employee is taxed not only on the accommodation itself but also on the cost to the employer of providing ancillary services in connection with that accommodation. Ancillary services include such items as heating and lighting, repairs and maintenance and cleaning.

The provision of furniture for the employee's use is also included under the heading of ancillary services and is assessed as an asset loaned for private use (see above). The assessable benefit is reduced by any contribution made by the employee.

However, if the accommodation is job-related, the assessment with regard to ancillary services cannot exceed 10% of the employee's net earnings for the year, less any contribution made by the employee. Net earnings are defined for this purpose as total earnings for the year (apart from the ancillary services) less allowable expenses.

EXAMPLE 7

In 2005/06, an employer provides living accommodation for a P11D employee and also provides the following services in connection with this accommodation:

	£
Cleaning	1,040
Heating and lighting	850
Repairs and maintenance	235
Loan of furniture, cost to the employer	12,000

The employee contributes £100 per month towards the cost of these services. Compute the assessable benefit, given that the employee has net earnings for the year (excluding the ancillary services) of £37,500.

Solution

If the accommodation is not job-related, the assessable benefit is £3,325 (£1,040 + £850 + £235 + 20% of £12,000, less £1,200). If the accommodation is job-related, the assessment is limited to 10% of £37,500, less £1,200 = £2,550.

Cars provided for private use

A P11D employee is assessed on the provision of a motor car unless the car is totally unavailable for the employee's private use. The assessable benefit is based upon the list price of the car when new (even if the employer bought it for less than list price or bought it second-hand) and is adjusted according to the car's level of carbon dioxide emissions. The method of computation is as follows:

(a) The price of the car for the purpose of calculating the taxable benefit is found by taking the *lower* of £80,000 and:

   (i) the list price of the car when new, including standard accessories, plus

   (ii) the cost of all optional accessories (other than mobile telephones) fitted to the car before it is made available to the employee, plus

   (iii) the cost of any optional accessories (other than mobile telephones) costing £100 or more and fitted to the car after it is made available to the employee.

(b) Accessories which are designed for use by a disabled person only are ignored when calculating the price of the car. If the employee holds a disabled person's orange badge, this exemption extends to any accessories required because of the employee's disability (e.g. power steering) and is not limited to accessories designed for use solely by the disabled.

(c) If the car is a "classic car", defined as a car which:

(i) is over 15 years old at the end of the tax year, and

(ii) has a market value at the end of the year exceeding £15,000 and exceeding the price calculated at (a) above

then the car's market value (or £80,000 if lower) is substituted for the car's price when calculating the assessable benefit.

(d) The price calculated at (a) or (c) above is reduced by any capital contribution made by the employee towards the cost of the car or its accessories, up to a maximum of £5,000. If the employee makes a capital contribution exceeding £5,000, the excess over £5,000 is ignored.

(e) The assessable benefit for a tax year is calculated by applying a percentage to the figure calculated at (d) above. The applicable percentage depends upon the car's level of carbon dioxide emissions, rounded down to the nearest 5g/km. For petrol-driven cars this percentage is computed as follows in 2005/06:

Carbon dioxide emissions	*Applicable percentage*
up to 140g/km	15%
each additional 5g/km	1% increase

There is a maximum charge equal to 35% of the car's price. For diesel-driven cars (other than diesels which comply with Euro IV emission standards) the percentage is increased by 3%. However, the maximum charge remains at 35%. As from April 2006, the waiver of the 3% supplement for diesel cars meeting the Euro IV standard will be withdrawn for all cars registered on or after 1 January 2006.

(f) Special rules apply to cars powered by electricity, gas or alternative fuels and to cars which do not have an official emission rating.

(g) The level of carbon dioxide emissions which qualifies for the minimum charge of 15% will remain at 140g/km in 2006/07 and 2007/08.

(h) If a disabled employee is obliged by his or her disability to drive a car with automatic transmission, the applicable percentage is based upon the emission rating of the equivalent car with manual transmission (if lower).

(i) If a car is available to the employee for only part of the year, the assessed benefit in that year is reduced proportionately, depending upon the number of days for which the car is available. This applies if the car is not made available to the employee for the whole of the year or if the car is unusable for a continuous period of at least 30 days during the year.

(j) Finally, the assessable benefit is reduced by any contribution which the employee pays to the employer for private use of the car.

EXAMPLE 8

(a) Throughout the whole of 2005/06, Lucy (a P11D employee) is provided by her employer with a car with a list price of £12,400. She contributed £1,000 towards the car's cost and she pays £300 per annum to her employer for private use of the car. Calculate the benefit assessable in 2005/06 if the car is petrol-driven and has an emission rating of:

(i) 129g/km (ii) 178g/km (iii) 232g/km (iv) 267g/km.

Re-calculate the assessable benefit in each case if the car is diesel-driven.

(b) During 2005/06, Luke (a P11D employee) is provided by his employer with the use of a petrol-driven car first registered in 2002 with a list price at that time of £20,000. His employer bought the car for £15,700 in 2004. The car's emission rating is 186g/km. Calculate the benefit assessable in 2005/06 if:

(i) the car is available to Luke throughout the entire year

(ii) the car is made available to Luke only from 6 November 2005.

Solution

(a) Lucy's capital contribution reduces the price of the car to £11,400 and her annual contribution of £300 reduces the benefit accordingly. If the car is petrol-driven, the assessable benefit in each case is computed as follows:

(i) 15% x £11,400 = £1,710, less £300 = £1,410.

(ii) 15% + 7% = 22% x £11,400 = £2,508, less £300 = £2,208.

(iii) 15% + 18% = 33% x £11,400 = £3,762, less £300 = £3,462.

(iv) 35% x £11,400 = £3,990, less £300 = £3,690.

If the car is diesel-driven, the applicable percentage is increased by 3% (but cannot exceed 35%). The revised assessable benefit in each case is:

(i) 15% + 3% = 18% x £11,400 = £2,052, less £300 = £1,752.

(ii) 15% + 7% + 3% = 25% x £11,400 = £2,850, less £300 = £2,550.

(iii) 35% x £11,400 = £3,990, less £300 = £3,690.

(iv) 35% x £11,400 = £3,990, less £300 = £3,690.

(b) The fact that Luke's employer bought the car for £15,700 is irrelevant. The benefit is based on the list price of the car and the applicable percentage is 24% (15% + 9%).

(i) 24% x £20,000 = £4,800.

(ii) 24% x £20,000 = £4,800 x 5/12 = £2,000.

Pool cars

The above provisions do not apply to "pool cars". A pool car is one which satisfies all of the following criteria:

(a) It is available for use by more than one employee and is not ordinarily used by one employee exclusively.

(b) It is not normally kept at an employee's residence overnight.

(c) It is used for private purposes only incidentally to its use for business purposes.

If all these criteria are satisfied, no assessable benefit will arise.

Fuel provided for private use

The assessable benefit described above is intended to cover the cost of providing the car itself, together with the costs of road fund licence, insurance and maintenance. But a separate benefit arises if any fuel at all is supplied by the employer to the employee for private motoring during the year. The assessable fuel benefit is calculated by applying the same percentage as is used in the calculation of the car benefit to a set figure for the year. For 2005/06 this figure is £14,400. The charge is reduced proportionately if the car is not made available to the employee for the whole tax year and is also reduced if the employee stops receiving free fuel for private motoring part-way through the tax year. However, a full year's tax charge arises if the employee then starts receiving free fuel again later in the same tax year.

It is important to appreciate that the assessed benefit is *not* reduced by any partial contribution which the employee makes towards the cost of private fuel. There is no assessable benefit if the employee pays the full cost of all private fuel. Otherwise, the benefit is calculated as above, ignoring any employee contribution towards fuel costs.

EXAMPLE 9

Miranda (a P11D employee) was supplied throughout 2005/06 with a petrol-engined company car for both business and private use. The car had an emission rating of 204g/km and her employer paid all running costs. The cost of the fuel supplied for private motoring was £1,530. Calculate her assessable fuel benefit in 2005/06 if:

(a) she contributed nothing towards private fuel

(b) she reimbursed her employer for the cost of all private fuel

(c) she reimbursed her employer £1,500 towards the cost of the private fuel.

Solution

(a) 15% + 12% = 27% x £14,400 = £3,888.

(b) £nil, since the employer pays for no private fuel at all.

(c) £3,888. Miranda's contribution is less than 100% and so has no effect on the benefit.

Vans provided for private use

If an employee is provided with a van for private use and the van weighs 3.5 tonnes or less, the assessable benefit in 2005/06 is as follows:

	£
Vans under four years old at the end of the tax year	500
Vans four years old or more at the end of the tax year	350

However, this charge is reduced to £nil in the case of employees who use their vans for journeys between home and work but are allowed no other private use. If a van weighs more than 3.5 tonnes, no assessable benefit arises unless the van is used wholly or mainly for private purposes. There is no separate taxable benefit relating to van fuel provided for private use.

However, as from 6 April 2007, the discount for older vans will be removed and the scale charge for unrestricted private use of a van will rise to £3,000. An additional fuel scale charge of £500 will apply if the employer provides fuel for private use.

Beneficial loans

A beneficial loan is one that is granted by an employer to an employee (or to a member of the employee's family) either interest-free or at a low rate of interest. A loan is deemed to be at a low rate of interest if the rate charged is less than the "official rate" which is set by the Treasury and which is changed from time to time. P11D employees are taxed on the difference between the interest actually payable to the employer and the interest that would have been payable at the official rate. Note that:

(a) Loans made in the ordinary course of the employer's money-lending business and made on the same terms and conditions as loans made to the general public are ignored when calculating the benefit arising in connection with low-interest loans.

(b) "Qualifying loans" are also ignored. Qualifying loans are loans which are eligible for tax relief (see Chapter 4).

(c) No assessable benefit arises if the total amount outstanding on all beneficial loans made to an employee, apart from those covered by (a) and (b) above, does not exceed £5,000 at any time during the tax year.

If a loan is wholly or partly written off by the employer, the amount written off is assessed on the employee in the tax year in which the write-off takes place. This provision applies to all loans, including those made in the ordinary course of a money-lending business. However, no assessable benefit will arise if the loan is written off on the death of the employee or if the loan is to a relative of the employee and it can be shown that the employee has derived no benefit from the write-off.

EXAMPLE 10

Adam (a P11D employee) has the following four loans from his employer:

(a) A £36,000 loan at 3% p.a. interest to enable Adam to buy his own home.

(b) An interest-free season ticket loan of £2,000.

(c) A £2,400 personal loan at 4% p.a. interest.

(d) A £6,000 loan to buy equipment for use in his employment.

The full amount of each loan was outstanding at 6 April 2005 and no repayments were made during 2005/06.

Calculate Adam's assessable benefit in 2005/06 (assuming an official rate of interest of 5% per annum).

Solution

The £6,000 loan is a qualifying loan and is ignored. The remaining loans total more than £5,000 and so give rise to assessable benefits. The amount assessed is:

	£
£36,000 x (5% - 3%)	720
£2,000 x 5%	100
£2,400 x (5% - 4%)	24
	844

Beneficial loans which vary during the year

In the above example, it was assumed that the amount of the loans did not vary during the tax year. However, if the amount of a beneficial loan does vary during the year, the assessable benefit can be calculated in one of two ways:

(a) The amount of the loan outstanding at the start of the tax year and at the end of the tax year are averaged and then multiplied by the average official rate in force during the year. Interest actually paid to the employer is then subtracted, giving the assessable benefit.

(b) Interest at the official rate is calculated precisely on the day-to-day outstanding balance. Interest actually paid is then subtracted, giving the assessable benefit.

Clearly, the first method will be quicker and easier and is generally used. However, either the employee or HM Revenue and Customs may insist that the precise method should be used. The employee will presumably do so if this results in a lower assessment and HMRC may do so if it appears that the "average" method is being deliberately exploited for tax avoidance purposes.

Payments made on termination of employment

Payments received by an employee on the termination of employment fall into three distinct categories:

(a) **Fully exempt**. The following types of termination payment are fully exempt from income tax:

(i) payments made on the death of the employee

(ii) payments made to the employee because of injury or disability

(iii) lump sum payments under approved superannuation schemes.

(b) **Fully taxable**. If an employee receives a termination payment which does not fall into any of the categories listed above (and which is made by way of reward for the employee's services) then the payment is fully taxable in the year in which it is received. This applies if the employee was contractually entitled to the payment or if there was a reasonable expectation that the payment would be made.

(c) **Partially exempt**. Payments made at the employer's discretion to compensate an employee for loss of employment ("ex gratia" payments) are exempt up to £30,000. Any excess over £30,000 is taxable in the year in which it is received. If the employee also receives statutory redundancy pay, the £30,000 exemption is reduced by the amount of SRP received.

The taxable part of a partially exempt termination payment is treated as the top slice of income, ranking above even savings income and dividends. This provision ensures that savings and dividend income are not moved out of the basic rate band (where they are taxed at only 20% and 10% respectively) as a consequence of the taxpayer receiving a partially exempt termination payment.

EXAMPLE 11

Henrietta is made redundant in March 2006. She receives statutory redundancy pay of £2,500 and an ex gratia payment of £40,000 from her employer as compensation for loss of office. Her only other income in 2005/06 consists of her salary of £31,470 and net building society interest of £4,000. Calculate her tax payable for 2005/06, assuming that she claims only the personal allowance.

Solution

	Total	*Non-savings*	*Savings*	*Compensation*
	£	£	£	£
Salary	31,470	31,470		
BSI £4,000 x 100/80	5,000		5,000	
Compensation £40,000 - £27,500	12,500			12,500
Statutory total income	48,970	31,470	5,000	12,500
Less: Personal allowance	4,895	4,895		
Taxable income	44,075	26,575	5,000	12,500

Non-savings income occupies the whole of the starting rate band and the first £24,485 of the basic rate band. Savings income falls entirely into the basic rate band, leaving £825 of this band for the compensation. The remaining compensation is taxed at the higher rate.

Income tax due

Starting rate band	: Non-savings	2,090	@ 10%	209.00
Basic rate band	: Non-savings	24,485	@ 22%	5,386.70
	: Savings	5,000	@ 20%	1,000.00
	: Compensation	825	@ 22%	181.50
Higher rate	: Compensation	11,675	@ 40%	4,670.00
		44,075		
Tax borne				11,447.20
Less: Tax deducted at source				1,000.00
Tax payable				10,447.20

Note:

Any tax paid by means of the PAYE system would also be deducted.

The PAYE system

Under the "Pay As You Earn" (PAYE) system, employers deduct both income tax and National Insurance contributions from their employees when paying them their wages and salaries. The amounts deducted, together with the employer's secondary NICs (see Chapter 15), must be accounted for to HM Revenue and Customs within 14 days of the end of the tax month in which the employees are paid. A tax month runs from the 6th of one month to the 5th of the next month, so employers generally make a payment to HMRC on or before the 19th of each month. But employers whose payments do not exceed an average of £1,500 per month are allowed to make quarterly payments instead of monthly payments. The PAYE system applies to all payments assessable as employment income, including wages, salaries, bonuses, commissions etc. The system also covers:

(a) payments taking the form of assets which are readily convertible into cash, such as shares, gold bars, coffee beans or other similar commodities, but excluding "own company" shares which are provided under an approved share scheme (see later in this chapter)

(b) vouchers exchangeable either for cash or for readily convertible assets

(c) remuneration schemes involving trade debts, whereby employers assign trade debts (amounts owed to them by their customers) to employees, who then receive cash when the debts are settled.

Benefits are usually brought within the scope of PAYE by making an adjustment to the employee's tax code (see below).

Tax codes

The PAYE system is based upon the concept of "tax codes". It is the responsibility of HM Revenue and Customs to issue a tax code for each employee each tax year, representing the amount which the employee may earn in that year before becoming liable to tax. The tax code takes into account a number of factors affecting the employee's income tax liability, including:

(a) the personal allowances to which the employee is entitled

(b) the employee's charges on income

(c) the employee's allowable expenses

(d) adjustments made in order to collect tax on benefits in kind

(e) adjustments for tax overpaid or underpaid in previous years.

The tax code allocated to an employee is equal to one-tenth of the aggregate of the above items, rounded down to a whole number.

EXAMPLE 12

Henry is single and claims only the personal allowance. He pays a gross charge of £100 per annum and an allowable professional subscription of £80 per annum. In 2005/06 he has assessable benefits of £500. Calculate his 2005/06 tax code.

Solution

By virtue of his personal allowance, his charges on income and his allowable expenses, Henry is entitled to earn £5,075 (£4,895 + £100 + £80) in the year before paying tax. But some of this must be set against his benefits of £500, leaving only £4,575 to set against his salary. Therefore Henry's tax code for the year would be 457, which is one-tenth of £4,575, rounded down to a whole number.

The same result would be obtained if the aggregate figure of £4,575 were anywhere in the range £4,570 - £4,579, so tax codes are not absolutely precise. But dividing the aggregate figure by ten results in only one-tenth as many different tax codes as would be obtained otherwise and cuts down the size of the tax tables used by employers (see below).

Tax code suffixes

A tax code also has a suffix, which is generally a letter of the alphabet. The most common suffix is L which stands for "low" and indicates that the employee is entitled to the basic personal allowance only. So Henry's full tax code in the above example would be 457L. Other suffixes in general use include:

P - the employee is entitled to the personal allowance for those aged 65-74

V - the employee is entitled to both the personal allowance for those aged 65-74 and the MCA for those aged less than 75 and born before 6 April 1935.

Code BR instructs the employer to deduct basic rate tax from all payments made to the employee and code NT instructs the employer not to deduct tax from the employee at all. Codes prefixed with the letter K are negative codes, used mainly for employees whose benefits exceed their allowances. Tax on the excess benefits is collected by increasing the amount of tax charged on the employee's wage or salary.

The purpose of tax code suffixes is to facilitate the recoding exercise which is needed whenever personal allowances are increased. When this happens, HMRC instructs employers to increase all L codes by the amount required to reflect the increase in the basic personal allowance, to increase all P codes by the amount required to reflect the increase in the 65-74 personal allowance, and so forth. This avoids the need to individually recode every employee in the country.

Operation of the PAYE system

Employers who operate manual payroll systems are issued with sets of tax tables which enable them to calculate the amount of income tax that should be deducted from an employee in a given week or month. The main tables used are:

Table A This table (also known as the Pay Adjustment Table) contains pages for each week or month of the year and shows, for each tax code, the amount of tax-free pay to which the employee is entitled for the year to date. In effect, the table spreads an employee's allowances evenly over the year, giving 1/12th of the allowances per month or 1/52th of the allowances per week.

Table B This table (also known as the Taxable Pay Table) is used to look up an employee's income tax liability for the year to date, after the entitlement to tax-free pay has been taken into account.

In outline, the procedure followed for each employee in each week or month is:

(a) The employee's tax code is looked up in Table A, which shows the amount of tax-free pay to which the employee is entitled for the year to date.

(b) This is then subtracted from the employee's gross pay for the year to date giving the employee's taxable pay for the year to date.

(c) The employee's taxable pay for the year to date is then looked up in Table B, which shows the tax due for the year to date. Tables C and D are used if the employee is a higher rate taxpayer.

(d) Finally, the tax paid to date by the employee in previous weeks or months is subtracted from the tax due for the year to date, giving the employee's income tax liability for the current week or month.

The entire system is cumulative and requires the employer to keep track of an employee's gross pay and tax paid "to date" (i.e. since the beginning of the tax year on 6 April). Employers are provided with deductions working sheets (form P11) which facilitate the accumulation of the necessary "to date" figures.

In a computer-based payroll system, the tax tables become computer files and the weekly or monthly procedure is carried out by software. However, the operation of the PAYE system does not change in principle when a manual payroll system is replaced by a computer-based system.

PAYE forms

P6 An employee's notice of coding, sent to the employer by HMRC.

P9D An end of year return showing the benefits and expenses of a lower-paid employee. P9Ds must be submitted to HMRC by 6 July following the end of the tax year and the employees concerned must be provided with copies by the same date.

P11 Deductions working sheet (see above).

P11D	An end of year return showing the benefits and expenses of a director or employee earning at least £8,500. P11Ds must be submitted to HMRC by 6 July following the end of the tax year and the employees concerned must be provided with copies by the same date.
P14	An end of year return, sent to HMRC by the employer, showing an individual employee's gross pay, tax paid and National Insurance paid for the year.
P35	An end of year return, sent to HMRC by the employer, showing and summarising all employees' gross pay, tax paid and National Insurance paid for the year. The P35, together with the P14s, must be submitted to HMRC by 19 May following the end of the tax year.
P45	A four-part form used when an employee leaves an employment, showing the employee's tax code, gross pay to date and tax paid to date. Part 1 is sent to HMRC and Parts 2, 3 and 4 are given to the leaving employee. The employee gives Parts 2 and 3 to his or her new employer who retains Part 2 and sends Part 3 to HMRC. The employee retains Part 4.
P60	Certificate of gross pay and tax deducted, given to employees by employers at the end of the tax year. P60s must be provided to employees by 31 May following the end of the tax year.

All employers with 50 or more employees are now required to submit their P35s and P14s to HMRC electronically. Employers with less than 50 employees will have to comply by May 2010 but there are incentive payments of up to £825 (tax-free) for employers who start filing online earlier than this. Employers with 250 or more employees are also required to make electronic PAYE payments to HMRC.

Working Tax Credit

Working people on low incomes may be able to claim a social security benefit known as working tax credit (WTC). Working tax credit is administered by HM Revenue and Customs but (at present) is generally paid by employers to those employees who are entitled to receive it. However, the Government has now decided that the payment of WTC via employers will be phased out between November 2005 and April 2006. In outline, the current system works as follows:

(a) HMRC calculates the amount to be paid to a claimant and notifies the claimant's employer of the required daily rate of payment.

(b) In each pay period, the employer calculates the amount of WTC to be paid to the employee (according to the number of calendar days in the period) and adds this onto the employee's net pay. WTC is shown separately on the employee's payslip.

(c) The amount of PAYE and National Insurance contributions which the employer is required to pay over to HMRC each month or quarter is reduced by the total WTC paid to employees in that month or quarter.

(d) Forms P14, P35 and P60 show WTC separately.

Self-employed people on low incomes may also claim WTC, in which case the amounts to which they are entitled are paid to them directly by HMRC.

Construction industry tax deduction scheme

The construction industry tax deduction scheme applies when payments are made by a contractor to a subcontractor under a contract relating to construction operations. The main features of this scheme are as follows:

(a) Payments made by a contractor to a subcontractor must be made net of tax unless the subcontractor holds a gross payment certificate. Any part of a payment which represents a reimbursement of the cost of materials supplied by the subcontractor may be excluded from the amount which is subject to deduction of tax.

(b) Gross payment certificates are issued only to subcontractors who are carrying on a genuine construction business in the UK with proper premises, equipment etc. The business must have its own bank account and proper accounting records must be maintained. Furthermore, the subcontractor must have complied with all tax and National Insurance obligations throughout the three years prior to the application for a certificate.

(c) A gross payment certificate is not issued unless the subcontractor meets certain minimum turnover requirements. The annual threshold is £30,000 for individuals and £30,000 multiplied by the number of partners or directors for a partnership or company (subject to a maximum requirement of £200,000).

(d) Subcontractors who are ineligible for a gross payment certificate are issued with a registration card. Contractors must deduct tax from such subcontractors and make accurate returns of registration card payments to HM Revenue and Customs.

(e) The amount of tax deducted from subcontractors who do not have gross payment certificates is calculated at a percentage rate which is determined by order of the Treasury (but cannot exceed basic rate). At present, this rate is 18%.

Note that a revised construction industry tax deduction scheme is due to be introduced as from 6 April 2006.

X

Employee incentive schemes

An employee incentive scheme provides financial incentives for employees to improve their work performance. The main types of scheme which currently have income tax implications are:

(a) share incentive plans (SIPs)
(b) approved share option schemes
(c) enterprise management incentives (EMIs).

A brief description of each of these types of scheme is given below.

Share incentive plans

Share incentive plans (SIPs) were introduced during tax year 2000/01. They were originally known as all-employee share ownership plans (AESOPs). The main features of these plans are as follows:

(a) Companies which set up a SIP may offer their employees:

   (i) *free shares* in the company worth up to £3,000 per annum per employee
   (ii) the opportunity to use salary of up to £1,500 per annum to buy *partnership shares* in the company (without having to pay income tax or NICs on the salary used for this purpose)
   (iii) up to two free *matching shares* for each partnership share bought by an employee.

   For a 40% taxpayer, this means that a total of up to £7,500 worth of shares can be acquired per year at a cost of only £900 (60% × £1,500).

(b) The company may offer free shares only, partnership shares only, free shares and partnership shares only, partnership shares and matching shares only, or all three types of shares.

(c) Subject to certain conditions, the plan may link the provision of free shares to the achievement of employee performance targets.

(d) In general, all employees must be eligible to participate in the plan. However, the plan may specify that employees do not become eligible until they have been employed by the company (or by the group, in the case of a group of companies) for a qualifying period of not more than 18 months.

(e) Employees who hold over 25% of the company's ordinary shares (a "material interest") are not eligible to participate in the plan.

(f) The plan may allow (or compel) dividends of up to £1,500 per annum arising on an employee's shares to be reinvested tax-free in further *dividend shares*.

(g) All of an employee's shares leave the plan when he or she ceases to be employed by the company (or group). The plan rules may specify that employees who leave within three years should forfeit their free and matching shares. Additionally, employees may take some or all of their shares out of the plan as follows:

Free/matching shares	:	at any time after the end of the holding period specified by the plan, which must be between three and five years
Partnership shares	:	at any time (though any related matching shares may be forfeited if this occurs within three years)
Dividend shares	:	at any time after three years.

(h) If free, matching or partnership shares leave the plan within three years, a charge to income tax and NICs arises based on the market value of the shares when leaving the plan. If the shares leave the plan after three years but in less than five years, this charge is based upon the *lower* of the market value of the shares when originally awarded and the market value of the shares when leaving the plan.

(i) If dividend shares leave the plan within three years, a tax charge arises on a *notional dividend* equal to the cash dividend which was used to acquire the shares.

(j) No tax charge arises if shares of any type leave the plan after five years (or earlier if this is caused by the employee's death or by injury, disability or redundancy).

(k) Employees who keep their shares in the plan until they sell them incur no liability to capital gains tax. Employees who take their shares out of the plan and sell them later pay CGT on any increase in value since the shares were taken out.

Approved share option schemes

In general, a charge to income tax (and NICs) may arise if an employee who works for a company is granted an option to buy shares in that company. The charge will usually arise only when the option is exercised but if the option can be exercised more than 10 years after it is granted, a charge also arises at the time of grant. The charge is based upon the market value of the shares obtained when the option is exercised, less the amount paid for the shares, less the amount (if any) paid to acquire the option. This charge can, however, be avoided if the option falls within an approved share option scheme. Approved schemes are of two main types:

(a) **Savings-related share option schemes**. Under such a scheme, employees are granted an option to buy shares and then save through a tax-free savings scheme in order to raise funds to exercise the option. The amount saved must be no more than £250 a month and the savings contract may last for three or five years. The scheme must be open to all employees who have worked for the company for a specified qualifying period (which cannot exceed five years). The price at which employees are given the option to buy shares must be at least 80% of the shares' market value at the time that the option is granted.

(b) **Company share option plans**. These schemes are less restrictive than savings-related schemes. The company can select the employees to which it would like to offer share options and can set these employees performance targets which must be achieved before the options are made available. The price at which an option may be exercised must not be manifestly less than the market value of the shares at the time that the option is granted and options must normally be exercised no earlier than three years and no later than 10 years after they are granted. However, options may be exercised within three years by employees whose participation in the scheme ends through injury, disability, redundancy or retirement. There is an upper limit of £30,000 on the value of the shares (at the time of the grant) for which an employee may hold options at any one time.

If a share option is granted under an approved scheme of either type and all necessary conditions are satisfied, then no income tax or NICs are payable on either the grant or the exercise of the option. For capital gains tax purposes (see Chapter 17) the allowable cost of shares acquired under an approved share option scheme is the price actually paid for the shares by the employee.

Enterprise management incentives

Enterprise management incentives (EMIs) offer UK trading companies (listed and unlisted) with gross assets not exceeding £30 million the chance to reward selected employees with tax-free share options. The main features of the EMIs scheme are:

(a) The scheme allows a qualifying company to grant share options to any employee who works at least 25 hours per week for the company or, if less, for at least 75% of his or her working time. The company may select the employees to whom it wishes to grant options and may award different amounts to different employees.

(b) Employees who own more than 30% of the company's ordinary share capital are excluded from the scheme.

(c) If the company so wishes, options may be granted to acquire shares at less than their market value at the time of grant or even at nil cost.

(d) There is an upper limit of £100,000 on the value (at the time of grant) of the shares for which an employee may hold unexercised options granted under the scheme. At any time, the total value of the shares for which options have been granted cannot exceed £3 million.

(e) No charge to income tax (or NICs) arises when an option is granted under the scheme. When the option is exercised, no charge arises if the shares are acquired at not less than their market value at the time of grant. Otherwise, a charge arises based on the *lower* of:

    (i) the excess of the market value of the shares at the time that the option was granted over the amount (if any) paid to acquire them

(ii) the excess of the market value of the shares at the time that the option is exercised over the amount (if any) paid to acquire them.

(f) For capital gains tax purposes (see Chapter 17) the sale of shares acquired under the EMIs scheme is treated as the disposal of a business asset with a qualifying holding period for taper relief purposes beginning on the date that the option was granted (not the date on which it is exercised).

Summary

- Criteria have been established which may be used to distinguish employment from self-employment.
- The basis of assessment for employment income is the income actually received in the year.
- Income tax is payable on all the income received in respect of an employment, including benefits in kind. Certain social security benefits are also taxable.
- In general, an employee's expenses are allowed only if they are incurred wholly, exclusively and necessarily in the performance of the duties of the employment.
- The way in which an employee's benefits are taxed depends upon whether or not the employee is a P11D employee, though some benefits are taxable in the same way on all employees.
- Any amount to which an employee is contractually entitled on the termination of employment is fully taxable. Certain termination payments (e.g. on death or injury) are fully exempt and ex gratia termination payments are partially exempt.
- The PAYE system is used to deduct income tax and National Insurance contributions from employees' wages and salaries.
- Certain employee incentive schemes offer tax advantages. Share incentive plans provide employees with a tax-efficient means of acquiring shares in the companies for which they work. Share options may be granted tax-efficiently to employees by means of approved share option schemes and enterprise management incentives.

Exercises

7.1 List the criteria which might be used to distinguish employment from self-employment.

7.2 Malcolm earns a basic salary of £17,500 in 2005/06. He also receives an annual bonus based on his employer's profits for the accounting year, which ends on 31 March. The bonus for the year ended 31 March 2005 (received 1 June 2005) was £2,350 and the bonus for the year ended 31 March 2006 (received 1 June 2006) was £2,570. Compute Malcolm's employment income for 2005/06.

7.3 Which of the following forms of income from employment would be exempt from income tax?

(a) Luncheon vouchers of £2 per working day.

(b) Free meals in the company canteen.

(c) Removal expenses of £4,500.

(d) A cheque for £1,000 given to an employee on reaching 25 years of service with his employer.

(e) A canteen of cutlery given to an employee on his marriage.

(f) A mileage allowance of 30p per mile given to an employee who drives her own motor car for 2,500 business miles per year.

7.4 Which of the following expenses incurred by an employee would be deductible when computing employment income for tax purposes?

(a) Travel costs between work and home.

(b) Travel costs between employment sites.

(c) Subscriptions to professional bodies.

(d) The cost of protective clothing.

(e) The cost of a suit to wear at the office.

(f) Entertaining expenses.

7.5 Kim is a part-time employee earning a salary of £7,000 per annum, out of which she pays 5% to her employer's superannuation scheme. She has allowable expenses of £1,000 (all of which are reimbursed by her employer) and is provided with a company car on which the assessable benefit if she were a P11D employee would be £1,800. Is she a P11D employee or a lower-paid employee?

7.6 Throughout 2005/06, Niall (a P11D employee) is provided by his employer with a diesel-engined motor car which had a list price of £18,800 when new and has an emission rating of 200g/km. His employer pays all of the car's running expenses including fuel for private use. Compute the assessable benefit in 2005/06.

7.7 On being made redundant by her employer, Penny received statutory redundancy pay of £1,750 and an ex gratia payment from her employer as compensation for the loss of employment. Compute the amount assessable if the ex gratia payment was:

(a) £12,000

(b) £29,000.

***7.8** Emma is the sales director of a company. She earns an annual salary of £40,000 together with a bonus (received in September each year) based on the company's profits for the accounting year ending on the previous 30 June. She also receives a general expenses allowance of £5,000 per annum, which she uses for business travel and entertaining. The company provides her with a new BMW motor car every two years and pays all running costs. She has an interest-free loan from the company of £20,000 and the company pays her annual subscription to a private medical insurance scheme, costing £300. Explain the taxation implications of each of the elements of Emma's remuneration package.

***7.9** Jim is the managing director of a company and earns a basic salary in 2005/06 of £100,000. He receives benefits from the company during the year as follows:

(a) He is provided with the use of a company house which has an annual value of £9,750 and which cost his employer £250,000. Jim makes no contribution towards the cost of the house or towards its running costs which cost the company £2,300 in 2005/06. The company has also furnished the house at a cost of £8,500. Jim's occupation of the house is not job-related.

(b) He is provided with a petrol-engined company car which had a list price when new of £45,000 and which has an emission rating of 193g/km. The company pays all running costs.

(c) He is provided with a company loan of £50,000 on which he pays interest at 2% per annum.

Calculate Jim's assessable benefits in 2005/06 (assuming an official rate of interest of 5%).

Chapter 8

Income from self-employment: Computation of income

Introduction

This is the first of five chapters concerned with income from self-employment. The profits of a self-employed person used to be charged to income tax according to the rules of Schedule D Cases I and II but Schedule D was abolished (for individuals) as from 6 April 2005 and income from self-employment now falls within the scope of the Income Tax (Trading and Other Income) Act 2005. This Act arose from the work of the Tax Law Rewrite project (see Chapter 2) and made no fundamental changes to the way in which income from self-employment is taxed.

A self-employed person may be conducting a trade or may be exercising a profession or vocation. However, the profits of trades, professions and vocations are all taxed in accordance with the same set of rules. Therefore, in this chapter and in subsequent chapters, references to "trades" and "trading" should be assumed to include professions and vocations. Similarly, the terms "trader" and "sole trader" will be used to refer to any self-employed person, regardless of whether that person is actually conducting a trade or is in fact exercising a profession or vocation.

The badges of trade

Section 6 of ITTOIA 2005 states that the trading profits of a person who is resident in the UK are chargeable to income tax wherever the trade is carried on. The trading profits of a non-UK resident are chargeable to income tax only if the trade is carried on wholly or partly in the UK (see Chapter 32). When deciding whether or not a person is trading it is necessary to make two important distinctions:

(a) the distinction between employment and self-employment (see Chapter 7)

(b) for a taxpayer who sells goods or other assets, the distinction between trading activities (which give rise to trading profits) and non-trading activities (which may give rise to income which is charged to income tax under some other heading or which may generate capital gains that are charged to capital gains tax).

Section 832(1) of ICTA 1988 states that a "trade" includes "*every trade, manufacture, adventure or concern in the nature of trade*". This circular definition is of little real help and it has been left largely to the courts to decide whether or not a given activity constitutes trading. The main criteria which have arisen from case law decisions and which may be used to distinguish between trading and non-trading activities are known as the "badges of trade". They are as follows:

(a) **Subject matter of the transaction**

If the taxpayer has sold assets which might normally be acquired for personal enjoyment or as an investment, this may suggest that any profit arising on their sale should be treated as a capital gain rather than a trading profit.

But if the assets concerned do not provide personal enjoyment and would not normally be held as an investment, any profit arising on their sale is more likely to be treated as a trading profit. In *Martin* v *Lowry* (1926) the taxpayer bought and sold 44 million yards of war surplus linen and in *Rutledge* v *CIR* (1929) the taxpayer bought and sold one million toilet rolls. In both of these cases, it was held that the subject matter of the transaction was such that the activity must be construed as trading.

(b) **Length of the period of ownership**

Trading stocks are normally retained for only a short period before being sold, whereas assets acquired for personal use or as an investment are generally retained for much longer. Therefore, if assets are bought and sold within a short space of time it is more likely that any profit made will be treated as a trading profit.

(c) **Frequency of transactions**

The more often that a taxpayer repeats a certain type of transaction, the more likely it is that the activity will be construed as trading. In *Pickford* v *Quirke* (1927) the taxpayer bought a cotton mill and sold off its assets at a profit. This was the fourth time that the taxpayer had carried out this particular type of transaction and therefore he was held to be trading.

(d) **Supplementary work**

A taxpayer who buys an asset, performs work on the asset so as to make it more saleable and then sells the asset is more likely to be regarded as trading than someone who simply buys and sells an asset without performing any supplementary work. In *Cape Brandy Syndicate* v *CIR* (1921) a group of individuals bought a large quantity of brandy which they first blended and then sold. They were held to be trading.

(e) **Reason for the sale**

The circumstances which have prompted the sale of an asset might be taken into account when deciding whether trading has occurred. A sale necessitated by a sudden urgent need for cash is less likely to be regarded as a trading activity than a sale made in the normal course of events.

(f) **Motive**

The presence of a profit motive in the mind of the taxpayer when acquiring an asset provides strong evidence of trading. In *Wisdom* v *Chamberlain* (1969) the taxpayer acquired silver bullion with the intention of selling it at a profit and eventually did so. He was held to be trading.

However, this test is not always conclusive. After all, many investments are bought at least partially with a view to their long-term sale at a profit and yet such profits are generally treated as capital gains. This point emphasises the need to consider the evidence provided by *all* of the badges of trade (not just one) when trying to decide whether or not trading has occurred.

Since trading requires the presence of a profit motive when the asset was acquired, the sale of an asset originally acquired by inheritance or by gift (or in any way otherwise than by purchase) is very unlikely to be construed as trading.

The calculation of trading profits

The computation of a self-employed person's trading profit begins with the net profit shown by that person's accounts. For tax purposes, trading profits must be calculated in accordance with generally accepted accounting practice, which means that income and expenditure must be measured on the accruals basis. Self-employed professionals were allowed at one time to calculate their profits on a cash basis but this concession has now been withdrawn, except for new barristers in their first seven years of practice.

It is usually necessary to make a number of adjustments to the net profit shown by the accounts in order to arrive at the trading profit for tax purposes These adjustments can be summarised as follows:

		£	£
Net profit shown by the accounts			x
Add:	Expenditure shown in the accounts but not deductible for tax purposes	x	
	Trading income not shown in the accounts	x	x
			x
Less:	Expenditure deductible for tax purposes but not shown in the accounts	x	
	Non-trading income shown in the accounts	x	x
Trading profit adjusted for tax purposes			x

Each of these adjustments is explained below.

Deductibility of expenditure

In general, expenditure is deductible (allowable) when computing trading profits only if it is incurred *wholly and exclusively for the purposes of the trade*. This rule is not as restrictive as the "wholly, exclusively and necessarily" rule applied to the expenses of an employee (see Chapter 7) but it does have the following implications:

(a) Expenditure which has no connection with the trade is disallowed (the "remoteness test"). In *Strong & Co of Romsey Ltd* v *Woodifield* (1906), damages paid by a brewery to a hotel guest injured by a falling chimney were disallowed. These damages were incurred by the brewery in its capacity as a property owner, not in its capacity as a trader, and therefore failed the remoteness test.

(b) Expenditure which serves both a business purpose and a private purpose cannot be allowed in full (the "duality test"). If the expenditure can be apportioned with reasonable accuracy, then the private element is disallowed. However, in *Mallalieu* v *Drummond* (1983), the cost of black clothing worn in court by a lady barrister was wholly disallowed, since it was not possible to apportion the cost of the clothing between the part which satisfied professional standards of dress and the part which simply provided warmth and decency.

Even if expenditure passes both the remoteness test and the duality test it may still be disallowed by statute.

Disallowed expenditure

The main classes of expenditure which are disallowed (either statutorily or as a result of case law decisions) when computing trading profits are as follows:

Capital expenditure

Capital expenditure is specifically disallowed by ITTOIA 2005 but the Act does not provide a definition of the term "capital". Consequently, there is a great deal of case law on this subject, much of which is concerned with distinguishing between repairs (allowable) and improvements (disallowed as capital expenditure). In *Atherton* v *British Insulated & Helsby Cables Ltd* (1926), it was stated that capital expenditure is such that it brings an "enduring benefit" to the business, and this test is still widely used. The following capital-related expenses are also disallowed:

(a) legal or professional fees incurred in relation to an item of capital expenditure

(b) depreciation and amortisation charges, though capital allowances may be available instead (see Chapter 10)

(c) losses on the disposal of fixed assets.

Even repairs may be disallowed if they relate to a newly acquired asset and are required in order to put the asset into usable condition. In *Law Shipping Co Ltd* v *CIR* (1923) the cost of putting a newly acquired ship into seaworthy condition was disallowed for this reason. However, repairs to a newly acquired asset which was usable before the repairs were carried out are generally allowed. In *Odeon Associated Theatres Ltd* v *Jones* (1971) repairs to cinemas which had been bought in a state of disrepair (but were nonetheless usable) were allowed.

Appropriations of profit

Appropriations of profit made by the owner of a business (whether these are described as drawings, owner's salary, interest on capital or anything else) are disallowed. The owner's personal income tax payments and NICs are also disallowed.

Provisions

Provisions are allowed so long as they are in respect of revenue expenditure and are made in accordance with generally accepted accounting practice. However, a provision will be disallowed if it cannot be estimated with sufficient accuracy. For this reason, transfers to general provisions (e.g. a general provision for bad and doubtful debts) are usually disallowed.

Charges on income

Payments which are treated as a charge on income (e.g. patent royalties) are relieved against the taxpayer's total income (see Chapter 4) and must therefore be disallowed when computing trading profits. It should be noted that:

(a) the amount disallowed is the amount shown in the accounts, which is usually the amount *accrued* in the period of account, but

(b) the amount relieved as a charge on income for a given tax year is the amount actually *paid* in that year.

Entertainment and gifts

The cost of entertaining customers is disallowed but staff entertaining costs are allowed, though the employees concerned may incur a tax liability if the amount involved is excessive (see Chapter 7). The cost of gifts is also disallowed, other than:

(a) gifts to employees (though the employees may incur a tax liability)

(b) gifts to customers costing no more than £50 per customer per year, displaying a conspicuous advertisement for the business and not consisting of food, drink or tobacco

(c) gifts of trading stock or used plant and machinery to charities, designated UK educational establishments or community amateur sports clubs

(d) reasonably small gifts to local charities, so long as the "wholly and exclusively" test is satisfied (e.g. if the gift attracts favourable publicity and enhances the firm's public image)

(e) contributions made to local enterprise agencies, training and enterprise councils and urban regeneration companies.

Note that charitable donations made within the Gift Aid scheme are given tax relief under the Gift Aid rules and are therefore disallowed when computing trading profits (see Chapter 4).

Political donations and subscriptions are usually not allowed. But political donations which result in a definite benefit to the trade may be allowed. In *Morgan* v *Tate & Lyle Ltd* (1954) the costs of a political campaign against nationalisation were allowed on the grounds that the campaign was waged for the survival of the trade.

Non-trade bad debts

Bad debts incurred in the course of trade are allowable. But employee loans written off are not allowable unless:

(a) the employer is in the business of lending money and the loan was made in the course of trade, or

(b) the written-off loan forms part of the employee's remuneration and is therefore taxable on the employee.

Transfers to a *specific* bad debts provision are allowable but transfers to a general provision are usually disallowed, as stated earlier. Bad debts recovered and reductions in a specific bad debts provision are both treated as trading income.

EXAMPLE 1

A sole trader's nominal ledger contains the following bad and doubtful debts account for the year ended 30 June:

	£	£		£	£
Trade debts w/o		812	Provisions b/f at 1 July:		
Staff loan w/o		50	General	432	
			Specific	312	744
Provisions c/f at 30 June:					
General	459		Trade debt recovered		42
Specific	288	747	P & L Account		823
		1,609			1,609

The staff loan written off was not taxable as employee remuneration. How much of the £823 charged to the profit and loss account for the year should be added back when computing trading profits?

Solution

The figure of £823 charged to the profit and loss account can be analysed as follows:

	£
Trade debts written off, less trade debts recovered (£812 - £42)	770
Staff loan written off	50
Increase in general provision for bad debts (£459 - £432)	27
Decrease in specific provision for bad debts (£312 - £288)	(24)
	823

The £50 staff loan written off and the £27 increase in the general provision are disallowed, so a total of £77 should be added back when calculating the trading profit.

Criminal payments

A payment is disallowed if the making of the payment in itself constitutes a criminal offence (e.g. a bribe). Payments to blackmailers or extortionists are also disallowed.

Fines and penalties

Fines or penalties incurred because of infringements of the law are not regarded as trading expenses and are disallowed. An exception occurs if an employer pays parking fines incurred by employees whilst on their employer's business. Such payments are usually allowed when computing trading profits but may then be assessed on the employees as income from employment.

Allowable expenditure

As explained earlier, expenditure is allowable when computing trading profits if it has been incurred wholly and exclusively for the purposes of the trade and is not specifically disallowed by statute. Apart from the disallowed items listed above, most of the expenditure shown in a typical profit and loss account will probably be allowable but the following points should be noted:

(a) **Interest**. Interest, including credit card and overdraft interest, is allowable if it is incurred for the purposes of the trade. But interest which constitutes a charge on income is disallowed and interest paid on overdue tax is also disallowed.

(b) **Legal and professional fees**. Legal and professional fees relating to capital expenditure are specifically disallowed (see above) but fees incurred for other trade purposes are normally allowable. For example, fees are allowed if incurred in connection with such matters as the collection of trade debts, the raising of loan finance, the renewal of a short lease (a lease of up to 50 years), an action for breach of contract or the preservation of trading rights.

Audit and accountancy fees incurred in relation to the preparation of accounts and the agreement of tax liabilities are normally allowed. Fees incurred in relation to a tax investigation by HMRC are incurred in the role of taxpayer rather than trader and are generally disallowed unless no profit adjustment arises from the investigation. The cost of tax appeals is disallowed, even if successful.

(c) **Short lease premiums**. A premium paid for the grant of a short lease of business premises is discounted according to the length of the lease and is then allowed in equal annual instalments over the period of the lease (see Chapter 5). A reverse premium received by a tenant using premises for business purposes is taxable as trading income.

(d) **Damages**. Damages and compensation payments are allowed if incurred for the purposes of the trade.

(e) **Value added tax**. If a trader pays VAT in relation to an item of expenditure and is unable to reclaim that VAT (see Chapter 30), the amount of VAT suffered will be allowable so long as the item of expenditure is itself allowable.

(f) **Trade subscriptions**. Subscriptions payable to professional and trade associations are generally regarded as having been incurred for the purposes of the trade and are allowable. Political subscriptions are generally disallowed.

(g) **Employees' remuneration**. Remuneration paid to employees is allowable so long as it is genuinely expended for business purposes. In *Copeman* v *Flood (William) & Sons Ltd* (1941) it was held that large salaries paid to family members could be allowed only to the extent that they were expended for trading purposes.

Remuneration which is not actually paid to employees within nine months of the end of the period of account in which it is accrued is disallowed in that period but allowed in the period of payment.

Employers' contributions to approved occupational pension schemes (see Chapter 13) are allowed in the *period of account in which they are paid*.

Redundancy payments and compensation payments for loss of employment are normally allowable, as are lump sum payments made to employees on retirement. On a cessation of trade, contractual redundancy payments, statutory redundancy payments and non-contractual payments of up to three times the statutory amount are all allowed.

The cost of educational courses provided for employees is allowable if incurred for trade purposes. The cost of retraining employees who are about to leave (or have recently left) is allowed subject to certain conditions. The cost of temporarily seconding an employee to a charity or educational establishment is allowable.

(h) **Staff defalcations**. Losses caused by the dishonesty of an employee are normally allowable. But, following the decision in *Curtis* v *J & G Oldfield Ltd* (1925), the defalcations of a person having control over the business (e.g. a business partner or a senior employee) are disallowed.

(i) **Travel expenses**. The cost of business travel is allowable but the cost of travelling between home and work is not. In *Newsom* v *Robertson* (1952) the travelling expenses of a barrister between his home and his chambers were disallowed. But in *Horton* v *Young* (1971) the travelling expenses of a self-employed bricklayer between his home and the building sites at which he worked was allowed, on the grounds that his business was conducted from his home.

Traders whose annual turnover does not exceed the VAT registration threshold (see Chapter 29) may use the HMRC approved mileage rates (Chapter 7) as an alternative to keeping detailed records of their actual motor expenses.

(j) **Car leasing and rental costs**. The costs of hiring, leasing or renting plant and equipment are normally allowable. But in the case of "expensive" cars (defined as those costing more than £12,000) the allowable amount is restricted to:

$$\text{Hire charge} \times \frac{\text{£12,000} + 1/2(\text{Cost of car} - \text{£12,000})}{\text{Cost of car}}$$

For example, if a car costing £18,000 is rented at a cost of £3,600 per annum, then the amount allowed is restricted to:

$$\text{£3,600} \times \frac{\text{£12,000} + 1/2(\text{£18,000} - \text{£12,000})}{\text{£18,000}} = \text{£3,000}.$$

This restriction does *not* apply to the hiring of low-emission cars, so long as the expenditure is incurred on or after 17 April 2002, the car was not first registered before that date and the period of hire begins before 1 April 2008.

(k) **Pre-trading expenditure**. Expenditure incurred during the seven years before starting to trade is treated as if it had been incurred on the first day of trading and is allowable so long as the expenditure is of a type which would normally be allowed when computing trading profits.

(l) **Registration of patents and trademarks**. The cost of registering a patent or trademark is allowable.

Trading income not shown in the accounts

The most common example of trading income not being shown in the accounts of a business occurs when the owner takes goods from stock for personal use, either without paying for them or paying less than their full value. This is referred to as "own consumption".

If own consumption occurs, an amount equal to the normal *selling price* of the goods (less any amount paid for them by the owner) must be added to the net profit shown in the accounts when computing trading profits. This rule was established in the case of *Sharkey* v *Wernher* (1955) in which horses were transferred from a stud farm to the owner's private stables. It was held that the profits of the stud farm should be increased, for tax purposes, by the full market value of the horses.

Non-trading income shown in the accounts

Any non-trading income shown in the accounts of a business must be deducted when computing trading profits. The main categories of non-trading income which might be found in the accounts of a business are:

(a) income which is taxed under another heading (e.g. interest, property income)

(b) profits on the disposal of fixed assets (these are usually depreciation adjustments but a genuine gain may be chargeable to capital gains tax)

(c) decreases in general provisions.

Expenditure not shown in the accounts

The most common example of allowable expenditure not shown in the accounts of a business is the trader's claim (if any) to capital allowances. The types of expenditure which attract capital allowances and the way in which capital allowances are calculated are considered in Chapter 10.

Another instance of allowable expenditure not shown in the accounts is a premium paid for the grant of a short lease of business premises. As explained earlier, part of such a premium is deductible from trading income in equal annual instalments over the period of the lease. If a premium is being amortised in the business accounts, the amortisation charges shown in the accounts are added back and the allowable amount of the premium (according to the rules given in Chapter 5) is deducted instead.

Post-cessation receipts

Post-cessation receipts are sums received after a person permanently ceases trading and which arise from the carrying on of the trade prior to cessation. Post-cessation receipts used to be charged to income tax according to the rules of Schedule D Case VI but such receipts now fall within the scope of ITTOIA 2005 and are treated as trading profits.

Section 242 of ITTOIA 2005 states that income tax is charged on post-cessation receipts arising from a trade. The Act also states that deductions are allowed for any expenses incurred which would have been deductible in calculating the profits of the trade if it had not ceased.

Summary

- A set of criteria known as the "badges of trade" may be used to distinguish between trading activities and non-trading activities.
- The net profit shown in the accounts of a self-employed person has to be adjusted in order to arrive at the trading profit for tax purposes.
- Expenditure is deductible when computing trading profits if it is wholly and exclusively incurred for the purposes of the trade. Expenditure which is not so incurred is disallowed. Certain categories of expenditure are disallowed by statute.
- If the owner of a business takes goods for personal use, the full market value of the goods (less any amount paid by the owner) must be added to the net profit shown by the accounts when computing the trading profit.
- Non-trading income included in the accounts of a business must be deducted from the net profit shown by those accounts when computing the trading profit.
- Any allowable expenditure not shown in the accounts (e.g. the deductible part of a premium paid for the grant of a short lease) must be deducted from the net profit shown by the accounts when computing the trading profit.
- Post-cessation receipts are treated as trading profits for tax purposes.

Exercises

8.1 List the six badges of trade.

8.2 State the general rule which governs whether or not expenditure is deductible when computing trading profits.

8.3 Which of the following items of expenditure would be allowed when computing trading profits?

(a) the salary paid to a sole trader's wife

(b) a Gift Aid donation

(c) a new lathe bought by an engineering business

(d) diaries costing £3 each given to customers

(e) the cost of the annual staff outing to Blackpool

(f) the black suit worn at work by a self-employed undertaker

(g) the legal costs of acquiring new freehold premises

(h) a subscription to the local chamber of commerce

(i) cases of wine costing £49.99 each given to customers at Christmas

(j) the legal costs of suing a trade debtor for non-payment.

8.4 Julian, a self-employed shopkeeper, takes goods costing £30 from his business stock for his own personal use. If he had sold the stock to a customer he would have charged £45. When computing his trading profit, what adjustment would need to be made to the net profit shown by his accounts if:

(a) he pays nothing for the goods?

(b) he puts £30 of his own money into the till so as to pay for the goods?

(c) he puts £45 of his own money into the till?

8.5 (a) A petrol-driven car with an original cost of £21,000 is leased for an annual rental of £5,670. The car is not a low-emission car. How much of the £5,670 should be added back when calculating trading profits?

(b) A sole trader is granted a 15-year lease on premises which he uses for business purposes. He pays a premium of £15,000 and writes off £1,000 per year in his business accounts. How much of the £1,000 should be added back each year when calculating trading profits?

8.6 Linda's profit and loss account for the year ended 31 March 2006 is as follows:

		£	£
Sales			82,500
Less:	Cost of sales		37,200
Gross profit			45,300
Add:	Rents receivable	1,200	
	Bank interest receivable	80	
	Profit on sale of fixed assets	310	1,590
			46,890
Less:	Wages and salaries	22,620	
	Business rates and insurance	1,750	
	Heating and lighting	2,170	
	Repairs and renewals	4,280	
	Telephone	880	
	Motor expenses	3,250	
	Sundry expenses	1,650	
	Bad and doubtful debts	640	
	Credit card interest	120	
	Loss on sale of fixed asset	70	
	Depreciation	2,500	39,930
Net profit for the year			6,960

Notes:

(a) Linda draws a salary of £200 per week from the business. This is included in the wages and salaries figure.

(b) Repairs and renewals are as follows:

	£
Decoration of business premises	400
Installation of new improved heating system	3,800
Minor repair	80
	4,280

(c) It has been agreed with HMRC that one-quarter of telephone costs and one-fifth of motor expenses relate to private use.

(d) Sundry expenses include business entertaining of £520.

(e) Trade debts written off in the year amount to £440 and £200 has been set aside as a general provision for bad and doubtful debts.

Compute Linda's trading profit (before deduction of capital allowances) for the year ended 31 March 2006.

***8.7** A sole trader's bad and doubtful debts account for the year ended 31 March 2006 is as follows:

	£	£		£	£
Trade debts written off		638	Provisions b/f		
Provisions c/f			General	200	
General	150		Specific	231	431
Specific	317	467			
			Staff loan recovered		500
			P & L Account		174
		1,105			1,105

The staff loan recovered was not taxed as employee remuneration when it was originally written off. How much of the £174 charged to the profit and loss account for the year should be added back when calculating trading profit?

***8.8** Imran owns a wholesaling business which operates from rented premises. He has a 10-year lease on the premises and paid a premium of £7,000 in order to obtain the lease. His profit and loss account for the year ended 31 December 2005 is as follows:

	£	£
Gross profit for the year		52,618
Add: Interest receivable	212	
Surplus on sale of office equipment	300	512
		53,130
Less: Wages (see Note 1)	19,280	
Rent, rates and insurance (see Note 2)	6,915	
Electricity	4,328	
Telephone (see Note 3)	1,650	
Repairs (see Note 4)	2,286	
Printing and advertising	1,250	
Motor expenses (see Note 5)	5,712	
Legal and professional expenses (see Note 6)	3,000	
Sundry expenses (see Note 7)	4,777	
Bad and doubtful debts (see Note 8)	860	
Bank charges and interest	2,765	
Lease premium amortisation	700	
Depreciation	8,749	62,272
Net loss for the year		(9,142)

Notes:

1. Wages include £5,800 for Imran's wife (who works part-time for the business) and £1,000 for his son (a student who does not work for the business at all). Also included is Imran's personal income tax of £3,411 and personal National Insurance contributions of £104.

2. Insurance includes Imran's private medical insurance premium of £414.

3. It has been agreed that one-sixth of telephone costs relate to private use.

4. Repairs include £750 for the cost of essential repairs to a newly-acquired second-hand forklift truck which could not be used until the repairs had been carried out.

5. Motor expenses are as follows:

	£
Vehicle servicing and repairs	1,165
Fuel and oil	2,815
Loss on disposal of motor vehicle	422
Road fund licences and insurance	610
Fine for speeding by Imran	700
	5,712

   It has been agreed that one-tenth of motor expenses relate to private use.

6. Legal and professional expenses consist of:

	£
Fees relating to renewal of lease	500
Debt collection	1,500
Accountancy fees	1,000
	3,000

7. Sundry expenses are:

	£
Entertaining UK customers	630
Entertaining overseas customer	150
Staff Christmas dinner	312
Gift to employee on examination success	100
Patent royalties	2,540
Subscription to trade association	250
Donation to political party	200
Miscellaneous small items (all allowable)	595
	4,777

8. Trade debts of £500 were written off during the year. The general provision for bad debts was reduced by £100 and the specific provision for bad debts was increased by £460.

9. During the year, Imran took goods costing £220 from stock for personal use, paying £220 of his own money into the business bank account. His gross profit percentage on turnover is 20%.

Compute Imran's trading profit (before deduction of capital allowances) for the year ended 31 December 2005.

Chapter 9

Income from self-employment: Basis periods

Introduction

Income tax is charged for tax years or "years of assessment", which run from 6 April to the following 5 April. Therefore it would be convenient if all traders were required to choose 5 April as their annual accounting date, so that the trading income for each tax year could be readily identified. However, traders are free to choose any accounting date they wish and so it is necessary to devise some means of establishing a link between the periods of account for which trading profits are calculated and the tax years in which those profits are charged to tax.

The trading profits charged to tax in a tax year are the profits earned during the *basis period* for that year and the purpose of this chapter is to explain the rules which are used to determine the basis period for any given tax year. The basis period rules which are now in use were introduced by Finance Act 1994 and the old rules which these rules replaced are no longer of interest. However, one aspect of the transition to the FA1994 rules which remains relevant is considered towards the end of this chapter.

The current year basis

The main principle of the basis period rules for trading income is that the basis period for a tax year is *the accounting year ending in that tax year*. This is known as the "current year basis" (CYB). However, special rules apply when a business starts trading, ceases trading or changes its accounting date (see below).

EXAMPLE 1

(a) A trader prepares accounts annually to 31 December. Identify the basis period for tax year 2005/06.

(b) A trader prepares accounts annually to 30 April. For which tax year will the accounting year to 30 April 2006 form the basis period?

Assume in both cases that the special rules which are used on commencement, cessation or change of accounting date do not apply in any of the years concerned.

Solution

(a) The accounting year to 31 December 2005 ends during 2005/06 and therefore forms the basis period for tax year 2005/06.

(b) The accounting year to 30 April 2006 ends during 2006/07 and therefore forms the basis period for tax year 2006/07.

Commencement of trade

Special rules are used to determine basis periods for the first three tax years when a business starts trading. *The first tax year in which trading profits are taxed is the tax year in which trade commences.* Basis periods for the opening years are determined in accordance with the following rules:

Tax year			*Basis period*
1			Date of commencement to the following 5 April (the "actual basis")
2	*either*	(a)	12 months to the accounting date in the second tax year (if possible)
	or	(b)	The first 12 months of trading (if the accounting date in the second tax year is less than 12 months after commencement)
	or	(c)	The actual tax year from 6 April to 5 April (if there is no accounting date in the second tax year)
3	*either*	(a)	Current year basis (if possible)
	or	(b)	12 months to the accounting date in the third tax year
4 etc.			Current year basis.

Note the following points:

(a) The basis period for the first tax year may be less than 12 months long but the basis period for each of the remaining opening years will be exactly 12 months long (unless the business ceases trading or changes its accounting date during those opening years).

(b) Basis periods for the opening tax years may overlap to some extent and therefore some of the profits made in the early years of trading may be the subject of more than one tax assessment (see below).

(c) If necessary, the trading profits for early periods of account are apportioned on a time basis in order to compute the amount of profit arising in each basis period.

(d) Section 203 of ITTOIA 2005 states that apportionments should be made by reference to the number of days in the period concerned. However, the Act also states that any other reasonable method of apportionment will be accepted so long as it is applied consistently. In practice, such calculations are usually made to the nearest month and this is the approach adopted in this book. However, *some examining bodies may require exact apportionments*. Therefore the reader is advised to find out whether his or her examining body requires apportionments to be made in days or in months.

EXAMPLE 2

(a) Vera commences trading on 1 January 2004, preparing accounts annually to 31 December. Identify the basis periods for the first four tax years.

(b) Wilbur commences trading on 1 October 2004. He chooses 30 June as his annual accounting date and prepares his first accounts for the 9 months to 30 June 2005. Identify the basis periods for the first four tax years.

(c) Yasmin commences trading on 1 February 2004 and chooses 30 April as her annual accounting date. She prepares her first accounts for the 15 months to 30 April 2005. Identify the basis periods for the first four tax years.

Solution

(a)	2003/04	Actual	1 January 2004 to 5 April 2004
	2004/05	12 months to a/c date in year 2	year to 31 December 2004
	2005/06	CYB	year to 31 December 2005
	2006/07	CYB	year to 31 December 2006
(b)	2004/05	Actual	1 October 2004 to 5 April 2005
	2005/06	First 12 months	1 October 2004 to 30 September 2005
	2006/07	CYB	year to 30 June 2006
	2007/08	CYB	year to 30 June 2007
(c)	2003/04	Actual	1 February 2004 to 5 April 2004
	2004/05	Actual	6 April 2004 to 5 April 2005
	2005/06	12 months to a/c date in year 3	1 May 2004 to 30 April 2005
	2006/07	CYB	year to 30 April 2006

Overlap profits

If a business chooses 5 April as its annual accounting date, the basis periods used in the opening tax years will not overlap at all. In most cases, however, the opening basis periods will overlap and some profits will form the basis of more than one tax assessment. Such profits are known as "overlap profits".

ITTOIA 2005 states that accounts prepared to 31 March or to 1, 2, 3 or 4 April will normally be treated as if prepared to 5 April, so as to avoid very short overlap periods and very small amounts of overlap profits.

EXAMPLE 3

Albert begins trading on 1 May 2004 and has the following results:

	Adjusted trading profit
	£
15 months to 31 July 2005	16,800
year to 31 July 2006	21,600

Compute Albert's trading income for each of the first three tax years and also calculate the amount of any overlap profits.

Solution

Albert's first period of account contains 15 months and his first basis period comprises the 11 months from 1 May 2004 to 5 April 2005. Trading income for the first three tax years is as follows:

Year	*Basis*	*Basis period*	*Workings*	*Trading income*
				£
2004/05	Actual	1/5/04 to 5/4/05	£16,800 x 11/15	12,320
2005/06	12 months to a/c date in year 2	1/8/04 to 31/7/05	£16,800 x 12/15	13,440
2006/07	CYB	y/e 31/7/06		21,600

The overlap period consists of the 8 months from 1 August 2004 to 5 April 2005, which are common to the basis periods for 2004/05 and 2005/06. The overlap profits are therefore £8,960 (£16,800 x 8/15).

Overlap relief

In general, overlap profits which arise in the opening years of a business are relieved by deduction from the trading profits charged to tax in the final tax year when trade ceases. Note the following points regarding "overlap relief":

(a) Overlap relief ensures that, over the entire lifetime of a business, the total of the trading profits which are charged to tax is equal to the total of the adjusted trading profits for each period of account.

(b) Overlap profits are not index-linked. The real value of overlap relief is eroded by inflation, especially in the case of businesses which trade for many years.

(c) If overlap profits exceed the trading profits which are charged to tax in the final tax year, the resulting loss is dealt with in the usual way (see Chapter 11).

However, if a business changes its accounting date at some point during its lifetime, it is possible that some of the overlap profits arising in the opening years may be relieved by deduction from the trading profits which are taxed in the year of the change. It is also possible that further overlap profits might arise on a change of accounting date (see later in this chapter).

Cessation of trade

A cessation of trade occurs when the owner of a business retires, sells the business or dies. The final tax year in which trading profits are taxed is the tax year in which the cessation occurs. The basis period for this final tax year is determined as follows:

(a) If a business commences trading and ceases trading in the same tax year, the basis period for that year consists of the entire lifespan of the business.

(b) If a business ceases trading in its second tax year, the basis period for that year runs from 6 April at the start of the year up to the date of cessation. This rule overrides the usual commencement rules for the second tax year.

(c) Otherwise, the basis period for the final tax year runs from the end of the basis period for the previous tax year up to the date of the cessation. This basis period may be less than, equal to or more than 12 months in length. The usual commencement rules for the third year are overridden if a business ceases trading in its third tax year.

If the final set of accounts prepared for a business covers a period of more than 12 months, it is possible that no accounting date at all falls into the penultimate tax year (the last year but one). This makes it impossible to apply the usual current year basis in that year. In these circumstances, the basis period for the penultimate tax year is the 12 months up to the normal accounting date falling in that year.

It is important to appreciate that income tax is charged on the owner of a business and not on the business itself. Therefore a change in the ownership of a business is treated for tax purposes as a cessation of one business followed by the commencement of another.

EXAMPLE 4

Carmen starts trading on 1 July 2004 and chooses 30 June as her annual accounting date. Identify the basis periods for her last two tax years if she ceases trading as follows:

	Date of cessation	*Final set of accounts*
(a)	31 March 2005	9 months to 31 March 2005
(b)	30 June 2005	year to 30 June 2005
(c)	30 June 2010	year to 30 June 2010
(d)	31 May 2010	11 months to 31 May 2010
(e)	30 April 2010	22 months to 30 April 2010

Solution

(a) Trade both commences and ceases in 2004/05. The basis period for this single tax year is the entire lifespan of the business i.e. 1 July 2004 to 31 March 2005.

(b) The cessation occurs in the second tax year. Basis periods are:

	2004/05	Actual	1 July 2004 to 5 April 2005
	2005/06	6 April to date of cessation	6 April 2005 to 30 June 2005
(c)	2009/10	CYB	y/e 30 June 2009
	2010/11	End of previous basis period up to date of cessation	y/e 30 June 2010
(d)	2009/10	CYB	y/e 30 June 2009
	2010/11	End of previous basis period up to date of cessation	1 July 2009 to 31 May 2010
(e)	2009/10	12 months to normal a/c date	1 July 2008 to 30 June 2009
	2010/11	End of previous basis period up to date of cessation	1 July 2009 to 30 April 2010

EXAMPLE 5

Damien starts trading on 1 July 2000 and chooses 31 December as his annual accounting date. He ceases trading on 30 September 2005 and has the following results:

	Adjusted trading profit
	£
6 months to 31 December 2000	8,400
year to 31 December 2001	9,200
year to 31 December 2002	10,500
year to 31 December 2003	7,500
year to 31 December 2004	6,400
9 months to 30 September 2005	5,800

Compute Damien's trading income for each tax year and show that the total of this income is equal to the total of the adjusted trading profits listed above.

Solution

Year	*Basis period*	*Workings*	*Trading income*
			£
2000/01	1/7/00 to 5/4/01	£8,400 + £9,200 x 3/12	10,700
2001/02	y/e 31/12/01		9,200
2002/03	y/e 31/12/02		10,500
2003/04	y/e 31/12/03		7,500
2004/05	y/e 31/12/04		6,400
2005/06	1/1/05 to 30/9/05	£5,800 - overlap relief £2,300	3,500
			47,800

The overlap period is from 1 January 2001 to 5 April 2001 (3 months) and the overlap profits are £2,300 (£9,200 x 3/12). The total of the trading income which is charged to tax is £47,800, the same as the total of the adjusted trading profits.

Change of accounting date

If a business changes its accounting date from one date (the "old date") to another (the "new date"), special rules are used to determine the basis period for the year of change. The year of change is defined as the first tax year in which accounts are *not* made up to the old date or *are* made up to the new date (or both). There will be a change of basis period for a year of change so long as the following conditions are satisfied:

(a) The first set of accounts made up to the new date does not cover a period of more than 18 months.

(b) Notice of the change of accounting date is given to HM Revenue and Customs in a tax return on or before the due filing date for that return.

(c) Either:

   (i) None of the previous five tax years has been a year of change resulting in a change of basis period, or

   (ii) HMRC is satisfied that the change of accounting date has been made for genuine commercial reasons and not for tax avoidance purposes.

If all of these conditions are satisfied, the basis period for the year of change is determined as follows:

(a) The "relevant period" is identified as the period beginning immediately after the end of the basis period for the previous tax year and ending with the new date in the year of change.

(b) If the length of the relevant period is less than 12 months, the basis period for the year of change is the 12 months to the new date in the year of change.

(c) If the length of the relevant period is not less than 12 months, the basis period for the year of change is the relevant period itself.

(d) In consequence, the basis period for a year of change will always be of at least 12 months' duration.

If all of the required conditions are *not* satisfied, the basis period for the year of change is the 12 months to the old date in that year. However, the following tax year is then regarded as a year of change (the taxpayer being treated as though this were the first year in which the new date had been used) and a change of basis period will occur in that year if all of the conditions are satisfied in relation to that year. A change of accounting date can be carried forward indefinitely in this way until such time as the necessary conditions for a change of basis period are satisfied.

If a taxpayer regularly prepares accounts to a particular *day* in the year (e.g. the last Saturday in June) rather than a particular *date*, the fact that the accounting date will change slightly in each year does not trigger the change of accounting date rules.

EXAMPLE 6

(a) Gary began trading many years ago, preparing accounts to 30 September each year. He decided to change his accounting date to 30 June and the first accounts made up to the new date were for the period from 1 October 2004 to 30 June 2005. The conditions necessary for a change of basis period were all satisfied. Identify the basis periods for years 2003/04 to 2006/07 inclusive.

(b) Audrey began trading on 1 January 2002, preparing accounts to 31 December each year. She decided to change her accounting date to 31 March and the first accounts made up to the new date were for the period from 1 January 2004 to 31 March 2005. The conditions necessary for a change of basis period were all satisfied. Identify the basis periods for years 2001/02 to 2006/07 inclusive.

(c) Grant began trading many years ago, preparing accounts to 30 June each year. He decided to change his accounting date to 31 December and the first accounts made up to the new date were for the period from 1 July 2005 to 31 December 2005. The conditions necessary for a change of basis period were all satisfied. Identify the basis periods for years 2004/05 to 2007/08 inclusive.

(d) Clare began trading on 1 March 2001, preparing accounts to 31 January each year. Her first accounts were for the period to 31 January 2002. She decided to change her accounting date to 30 April and the first accounts made up to the new date were for the period from 1 February 2004 to 30 April 2005. The conditions necessary for a change of basis period were all satisfied. Identify the basis periods for years 2000/01 to 2006/07 inclusive.

Solution

(a) The year of change is 2005/06 (the first year in which the old date was not used and the new date was used). The basis period for 2004/05 ended on 30 September 2004, so the relevant period is from 1 October 2004 to 30 June 2005. This is less than 12 months in length so the basis period for 2005/06 is the 12 months to 30 June 2005. Basis periods for 2003/04 to 2006/07 are:

2003/04	year to 30 September 2003
2004/05	year to 30 September 2004
2005/06	year to 30 June 2005
2006/07	year to 30 June 2006

Note that there is an overlap between the basis periods for 2004/05 and 2005/06. The treatment of overlap profits on a change of accounting date is explained below.

(b) The year of change is 2004/05 (the first year in which the old date was not used and the new date was used). The basis period for 2003/04 ended on 31 December 2003, so the relevant period is from 1 January 2004 to 31 March 2005. This is not less than 12 months in length so the basis period for 2004/05 is the same as the relevant period. Basis periods for 2001/02 to 2006/07 are:

2001/02	1 January 2002 to 5 April 2002
2002/03	year to 31 December 2002
2003/04	year to 31 December 2003
2004/05	1 January 2004 to 31 March 2005
2005/06	year to 31 March 2006
2006/07	year to 31 March 2007

(c) The year of change is 2005/06 (the first year in which the new date was used). The basis period for 2004/05 ended on 30 June 2004, so the relevant period is from 1 July 2004 to 31 December 2005. This is not less than 12 months in length so the basis period for 2005/06 is the same as the relevant period. Basis periods are:

2004/05	year to 30 June 2004
2005/06	1 July 2004 to 31 December 2005
2006/07	year to 31 December 2006
2007/08	year to 31 December 2007

(d) The year of change is 2004/05 (the first year in which the old date was not used). The basis period for 2003/04 ended on 31 January 2004, so the relevant period is from 1 February 2004 to 30 April 2004. This is less than 12 months in length so the basis period for 2004/05 is the 12 months to 30 April 2004, even though this accounting date was not used in 2004/05. Basis periods for 2000/01 to 2006/07 are:

2000/01	1 March 2001 to 5 April 2001
2001/02	1 March 2001 to 28 February 2002
2002/03	year to 31 January 2003
2003/04	year to 31 January 2004
2004/05	year to 30 April 2004
2005/06	year to 30 April 2005
2006/07	year to 30 April 2006

There is an overlap between the basis periods for 2003/04 and 2004/05 (as well as the usual overlap arising on the commencement of trade).

Overlap profits on a change of accounting date

If a change of accounting date results in profits being taxed more than once, these overlap profits are added to any earlier overlap profits (which arose in the opening years or on a previous change of accounting date) and the total is carried forward for relief on cessation or on a subsequent change of accounting date.

Alternatively, if the basis period for a year of change exceeds 12 months, a part of the overlap profits brought forward from previous years may be relieved in the year of change. The amount to be relieved is calculated according to the following formula:

$$\text{Amount relieved} = A \times \frac{(B - C)}{D}$$

where: A = Total overlap profits brought forward and not yet relieved

B = Length of the relevant period

C = 12 (or 365 if daily apportionments are being used)

D = Total length of the overlap period(s) to which the total overlap profits brought forward relate.

EXAMPLE 7

(a) Byron began trading on 1 November 2001, preparing accounts to 31 October each year. He decided to change his accounting date to 31 August and the first accounts made up to the new date were for the period from 1 November 2003 to 31 August 2004. The conditions necessary for a change of basis period were all satisfied. The adjusted trading profits for Byron's first five periods of account were as follows:

	£
Year to 31 October 2002	12,000
Year to 31 October 2003	18,000
Period to 31 August 2004	16,000
Year to 31 August 2005	21,000
Year to 31 August 2006	24,000

Compute Byron's trading income for years 2001/02 to 2006/07.

(b) Michelle began trading on 1 January 2002, preparing accounts to 31 December each year. She decided to change her accounting date to 28 February and the first accounts made up to the new date were for the period from 1 January 2005 to 28 February 2006. The conditions necessary for a change of basis period were all satisfied. The adjusted trading profits for Michelle's first five periods of account were:

	£
Year to 31 December 2002	4,560
Year to 31 December 2003	5,250
Year to 31 December 2004	11,680
Period to 28 February 2006	14,390
Year to 28 February 2007	16,270

Compute Michelle's trading income for years 2001/02 to 2006/07.

Solution

(a) The year of change is 2004/05 (the first year in which the old date was not used and the new date was used). The basis period for 2003/04 ended on 31 October 2003, so the relevant period is from 1 November 2003 to 31 August 2004. This is less than 12 months in length so the basis period for 2004/05 is the 12 months to 31 August 2004. Trading income for 2001/02 to 2006/07 is:

Year	*Basis period*	*Workings*	*Trading income* £
2001/02	1/11/01 to 5/4/02	£12,000 x 5/12	5,000
2002/03	y/e 31/10/02		12,000
2003/04	y/e 31/10/03		18,000
2004/05	y/e 31/8/04	£18,000 x 2/12 + £16,000	19,000
2005/06	y/e 31/8/05		21,000
2006/07	y/e 31/8/06		24,000

There are overlap profits of £5,000 (5 months) on the commencement of trade and a further £3,000 (2 months) on the change of accounting date. Total overlap profits carried forward are £8,000 (7 months).

(b) The year of change is 2005/06 (the first year in which the old date was not used and the new date was used). The basis period for 2004/05 ended on 31 December 2004, so the relevant period is from 1 January 2005 to 28 February 2006. This is not less than 12 months in length so the basis period for 2005/06 is the relevant period itself. Trading income for 2001/02 to 2006/07 is:

Year	*Basis period*	*Workings*	*Trading income* £
2001/02	1/1/02 to 5/4/02	£4,560 x 3/12	1,140
2002/03	y/e 31/12/02		4,560
2003/04	y/e 31/12/03		5,250
2004/05	y/e 31/12/04		11,680
2005/06	1/1/05 to 28/2/06	£14,390 - overlap relief £760	13,630
2006/07	y/e 28/2/07		16,270

There are overlap profits of £1,140 (3 months) on the commencement of trade. The relevant period is 14 months long, which exceeds 12 months by 2 months. Overlap relief in the year of change is calculated as £1,140 x 2/3 = £760. Overlap profits carried forward are £380 (1 month).

Transitional overlap relief

The basis period rules now in use were introduced by Finance Act 1994. Businesses which existed before 6 April 1994 used to be assessed on the *preceding year basis*, which meant that the basis period for a tax year was the accounting year ending in the *previous* tax year. The switch to the current year basis for these businesses occurred as from 1997/98 with a special transitional rule for 1996/97. Broadly, the basis period for 1996/97 was the 24 months to the accounting date in that year and the assessment for the year was computed as 50% of the profits occurring during this 24-month period.

An aspect of this transition which will remain relevant for many years to come is that the period between the end of the basis period for 1996/97 and 5 April 1997 is treated as an overlap period. Ordinary overlap relief is not available to these older businesses but the profits of this special overlap period are eligible for *transitional overlap relief* on a subsequent change of accounting date or cessation of trade.

EXAMPLE 8

Norman began trading in 1975 preparing accounts to 31 October each year. He ceases trading on 31 October 2005. Recent adjusted trading profits have been as follows:

	£
year to 31 October 2004	26,490
year to 31 October 2005	28,100

Adjusted trading profit for the year to 31 October 1997 was £28,560. Compute Norman's trading income for 2005/06.

Solution

Norman's trading income for 1996/97 would have been 50% of the profits for the 24 months to 31 October 1996. Transitional overlap relief is available in relation to the profits of the period from 1 November 1996 to 5 April 1997 (£28,560 x 5/12 = £11,900).

The business ceases in 2005/06 so the basis period for 2005/06 runs from the end of the basis period for 2004/05 to the date of cessation (from 1 November 2004 to 31 October 2005). Trading income for 2005/06 is therefore £16,200 (£28,100 less transitional overlap relief of £11,900).

Averaging of trading profits for farmers, market gardeners and creative artists

Certain trades, professions and vocations are more likely than others to experience profits which fluctuate considerably from one period of account to the next, leading to corresponding fluctuations in the trading income which is charged to tax. In particular, this problem may affect:

(a) farmers and market gardeners (who are at the mercy of the weather)

(b) creative artists.

The income tax system allows farmers, market gardeners and creative artists to smooth out fluctuating profits by making a claim for *averaging*. Trading income for two consecutive tax years may be averaged if the difference between the two income figures is at least 30% of the higher figure. The effect of an averaging claim is to replace the normal trading income for each of these two tax years by the average of the two figures. Note the following points in relation to the averaging process:

(a) If a loss has been incurred in either of the two years involved in an averaging claim, the loss counts as zero in the averaging calculation. The loss is then relieved in the usual way, as described in Chapter 11.

(b) An averaging claim may not be made for the tax year in which trade commences or for the tax year in which trade ceases.

(c) If an averaging claim has been made for two tax years, the revised trading income for the second year may subsequently be used in another averaging claim. For example, if a claim has already been made for 2003/04 and 2004/05, then another claim may be made for 2004/05 and 2005/06. Overlapping claims of this nature must be made in chronological order.

(d) An averaging claim must be made by the first anniversary of the 31 January which follows the end of the second tax year to which the claim relates. For example, an averaging claim which relates to 2004/05 and 2005/06 must be made by 31 January 2008.

EXAMPLE 9

The recent adjusted trading profits of a self-employed farmer who began trading many years ago are as follows:

	£
year to 30 November 2004	46,200
year to 30 November 2005	10,640

He has no other income. May an averaging claim be made and would the farmer benefit from such a claim?

Solution

The tax years in question are 2004/05 and 2005/06. The difference between the trading income of the two years is £35,560, which exceeds 30% of £46,200 so an averaging claim may be made.

If an averaging claim is made, trading income for both 2004/05 and 2005/06 is revised to £28,420 (the average of £46,200 and £10,640). The farmer benefits from this claim in two ways:

(a) the likelihood of paying 40% tax for 2004/05 is removed, so reducing the total tax liability for the two years, and

(b) the farmer's cash flow situation is improved, since the 2004/05 tax liability is reduced and the 2005/06 tax liability is increased.

EXAMPLE 10

A market gardener who began trading many years ago has the following recent results:

	Adjusted trading profit/(loss)
	£
year to 31 December 2001	21,500
year to 31 December 2002	14,200
year to 31 December 2003	(5,400)
year to 31 December 2004	6,900
year to 31 December 2005	10,800

Compute the trading income for 2001/02 to 2005/06 inclusive, assuming that all possible averaging claims are made.

Solution

2001/02 and 2002/03

	£
Original trading income for 2001/02 (y/e 31/12/01)	21,500
Original trading income for 2002/03 (y/e 31/12/02)	14,200
Difference (more than 30% of £21,500)	7,300

Averaging gives revised trading income of £17,850 in 2001/02 and 2002/03.

2002/03 and 2003/04

	£
Revised trading income for 2002/03	17,850
Original trading income for 2003/04 (y/e 31/12/03)	0
Difference (more than 30% of £17,850)	17,850

Averaging gives revised trading income of £8,925 in 2002/03 and 2003/04.

2003/04 and 2004/05

	£
Revised trading income for 2003/04	8,925
Original trading income or 2004/05 (y/e 31/12/04)	6,900
Difference (less than 30% of £8,925)	2,025

No averaging is possible so trading income is unaltered.

2004/05 and 2005/06

	£
Original trading income for 2004/05 (y/e 31/12/04)	6,900
Original trading income for 2005/06 (y/e 31/12/05)	10,800
Difference (more than 30% of £10,800)	3,900

Averaging gives revised trading income of £8,850 in 2004/05 and 2005/06.

The final trading income for all years concerned is as follows:

	£	
2001/02	17,850	
2002/03	8,925	
2003/04	8,925	
2004/05	8,850	
2005/06	8,850	(which may perhaps be averaged with 2006/07).

Marginal relief

As explained above, an averaging claim may not be made if the difference between the trading income figures for the two tax years concerned is less than 30% of the higher income figure. However, if the difference is at least 25% of the higher figure, a form of averaging known as "marginal relief" may be claimed. The effect of marginal relief is to reduce the higher income (H) and to increase the lower income (L) by an amount given by the following formula:

$$3 \times (H - L) - 0.75 \times H$$

If the difference between H and L is exactly 30% of H, this formula has the same effect as an ordinary averaging claim. If the difference between H and L is exactly 25% of H, this formula has no effect at all.

EXAMPLE 11

A farmer's trading income for 2004/05 is £12,000. What averaging claims (if any) can he make if his trading income for 2005/06 is:

(a) £7,600?

(b) £8,600?

(c) £9,600?

Solution

(a) The difference between the two income figures is £4,400, which is more than 30% of £12,000 so a normal averaging claim can be made, revising both of the income figures to £9,800 (the average of £12,000 and £7,600).

(b) The difference between the two income figures is £3,400, which is between 25% and 30% of £12,000 so marginal relief may be claimed. The adjustment to each figure is:

$$3 \times (£12,000 - £8,600) - 0.75 \times £12,000 = £1,200.$$

The income for 2004/05 is reduced to £10,800 and the income for 2005/06 is increased to £9,800.

(c) The difference between the two income figures is £2,400, which is less than 25% of £12,000 so no averaging is possible at all.

Summary

- Trading profits are charged to income tax on the current year basis. Special rules apply in the opening and closing years of a business and on a change of accounting date.
- Overlap profits arising in the opening years of a new business are relieved either on the cessation of trade or on a change of accounting date.
- Further overlap profits may arise on a change of accounting date.
- Transitional overlap relief may be available when a business which commenced before 6 April 1994 ceases trading.
- In certain cases, farmers, market gardeners and creative artists may claim that the trading income of two consecutive tax years should be averaged.

Exercises

9.1 Under the *current year basis*, for which tax years would the following accounting years form the basis period?

(a) year to 31 October 2005 (b) year to 31 March 2006

(c) year to 30 April 2007 (d) year to 5 April 2007

9.2 Frank began trading on 1 July 2003. Identify the basis periods for his first four tax years if he:

(a) chooses 30 June as his annual accounting date and prepares his first accounts for the year to 30 June 2004

(b) chooses 30 April as his annual accounting date and prepares his first accounts for the 22 months to 30 April 2005

(c) chooses 30 April as his annual accounting date and prepares his first accounts for the 10 months to 30 April 2004.

Also identify any overlap periods which arise in each case.

9.3 Greta commences trading on 1 January 2005 and chooses 30 June as her annual accounting date. Her first accounts are made up for the 18 months to 30 June 2006 and show an adjusted trading profit of £27,300. Compute Greta's trading income for the first three tax years and calculate the amount of any overlap profits.

9.4 Hitesh has been trading for many years, preparing accounts to 31 January each year. His last full year of trading is the year to 31 January 2005. Identify the basis periods for the last three tax years in each of the following cases:

	Date of cessation	*Final set of accounts*
(a)	31 May 2005	4 months to 31 May 2005
(b)	31 March 2006	14 months to 31 March 2006
(c)	30 April 2006	15 months to 30 April 2006

9.5 Larry began trading in 1981, preparing accounts to 31 July each year. He ceases trading on 31 July 2005 and his adjusted trading profits in the closing years are as follows:

	£
year to 31 July 2003	14,660
year to 31 July 2004	12,150
year to 31 July 2005	11,200

Adjusted trading profits for the year to 31 July 1997 were £15,900. Compute Larry's trading income for 2005/06.

***9.6** Ivy begins trading as a market gardener on 1 January 2003, making up annual accounts to 31 December. Her adjusted trading profits in the opening years are as follows:

	£
year to 31 December 2003	7,200
year to 31 December 2004	5,010
year to 31 December 2005	4,570

(a) Compute Ivy's trading income for the first four tax years, assuming that no averaging claims are made.

(b) Compute Ivy's revised trading income for the first four tax years, assuming that all possible averaging claims are made.

***9.7** Ken starts trading on 1 October 1999 and chooses 30 April as his accounting date. He ceases trading on 31 January 2005 and has adjusted trading profits as follows:

	£
7 months to 30 April 2000	3,500
year to 30 April 2001	6,480
year to 30 April 2002	7,700
year to 30 April 2003	7,900
year to 30 April 2004	8,200
9 months to 31 January 2005	7,300

Compute Ken's trading income for all tax years.

***9.8** Belinda began trading on 1 March 2001 and chose 31 December as her accounting date. Her first accounts were for the period to 31 December 2001. She eventually decided to change her accounting date to 31 May and the first accounts made up to the new date were for the 17 months to 31 May 2005. The conditions necessary for a change of basis period were all satisfied. The adjusted trading profits for her first five periods of account were as follows:

	Adjusted trading profit
	£
1 March 2001 to 31 December 2001	43,700
year to 31 December 2002	52,590
year to 31 December 2003	54,300
1 January 2004 to 31 May 2005	71,060
year to 31 May 2006	68,200

Compute Belinda's trading income for 2000/01 to 2006/07 inclusive, showing the amounts of any overlap profits or overlap relief.

***9.9** Roger began trading on 1 January 1999, preparing accounts to 30 April each year. His first accounts were for the 16 months to 30 April 2000. In 2002 he decided to change his accounting date to 30 June. The first accounts made up to the new date were for the 14 months to 30 June 2002 and the conditions necessary for a change of basis period were all satisfied. Roger ceased trading on 31 May 2005. His adjusted trading profits were as follows:

	Adjusted trading profit
	£
1 January 1999 to 30 April 2000	33,920
year to 30 April 2001	29,700
1 May 2001 to 30 June 2002	33,300
year to 30 June 2003	41,600
year to 30 June 2004	37,900
1 July 2004 to 31 May 2005	23,500

Compute Roger's trading income for all tax years.

Chapter 10

Income from self-employment: Capital allowances

Introduction

Capital expenditure is not deductible when computing trading income but certain types of capital expenditure do attract tax relief in the form of standardised depreciation allowances known as *capital allowances*. The purpose of this chapter is to define the categories of capital expenditure which are eligible for capital allowances and to explain how capital allowances are calculated.

Eligible expenditure

In order to be eligible for capital allowances, capital expenditure must usually fall into one of the following categories:

(a) plant and machinery

(b) industrial buildings and agricultural buildings

(c) patents, know-how and research and development

(d) mineral extraction, dredging and crematoria.

Each of these categories (other than the last) is considered in this chapter.

Chargeable periods

Capital allowances are granted in respect of *chargeable periods*. For income tax purposes, each period of account generally ranks as a chargeable period and so there is usually one capital allowances computation per period of account. The only exception occurs if a period of account lasts for more than 18 months. In this case, the period of account is divided into one or more 12-month chargeable periods with (possibly) a short chargeable period at the end. Capital allowances are calculated separately for each of these chargeable periods and then aggregated to give the capital allowances due for the whole period of account.

The capital allowances for a period of account are treated as a trading expense and are deducted when computing the adjusted trading profit for that period. The basis period rules described in Chapter 9 are applied to the trading profit *after* deduction of capital allowances.

It is worth noting at this early stage that the chargeable periods of *companies*, which pay corporation tax on their profits rather than income tax, are determined according to a different set of rules (see Chapter 23).

EXAMPLE 1

Lee begins trading on 1 January 2005 preparing accounts to 31 December each year. His adjusted trading profit for the year to 31 December 2005 (before deduction of capital allowances) is £9,000 and capital allowances of £1,200 are claimed for that year. Compute his trading income for 2004/05 and 2005/06.

Solution

The adjusted trading profit for the year to 31 December 2005 (after deduction of capital allowances) is £7,800. Therefore trading income for the first two tax years is as follows:

Year	*Basis*	*Basis period*	*Workings*	*Trading income*
				£
2004/05	Actual	1/1/05 to 5/4/05	£7,800 x 3/12	1,950
2005/06	12 months to a/c date in year 2	y/e 31/12/05		7,800

Plant and machinery

Capital Allowances Act 2001 (the main statute concerned with capital allowances) does not provide a definition of the term "plant and machinery". Therefore it has been left mainly to case law to decide whether or not any given item should qualify as plant and machinery and so attract capital allowances. In *Yarmouth* v *France* (1887) it was stated that plant and machinery includes:

> "whatever apparatus is used by a businessman for carrying on his business, not his stock in trade which he buys or makes for sale, but all goods and chattels, fixed or moveable, live or dead, which he keeps for permanent employment in his business".

It is clear that machinery of all types, motor vehicles and items such as office furniture and equipment all qualify as plant and machinery but difficulties arise in connection with expenditure on buildings and fixtures to buildings. Much case law has been concerned with the distinction between:

(a) assets which perform an *active function* in the carrying on of the business i.e. the apparatus *with which* the business is carried on, and

(b) assets which perform a *passive function* in the carrying on of the business i.e. the setting *in which* the business is carried on.

Assets in the first of these categories qualify as plant and machinery whilst assets in the second category do not, but the distinction between the categories can be a very fine one. Some of the more important case law decisions have been as follows:

Held to be plant and machinery:

(a) a dry dock built for the repair and maintenance of ships, in *CIR* v *Barclay Curle & Co Ltd* (1969)

(b) a swimming and paddling pool, in *Cooke* v *Beach Station Caravans Ltd* (1974)

(c) a concrete grain silo, in *Schofield* v *R & H Hall Ltd* (1975)

(d) decorative screens placed in the window of a building society's offices and incorporating the name of the building society, in *Leeds Permanent Building Society* v *Proctor* (1982)

(e) moveable office partitions, in *Jarrold* v *John Good & Sons Ltd* (1962)

(f) display lighting in a store window, in *Cole Brothers Ltd* v *Phillips* (1982)

(g) light fittings, plaques and pictures on the walls of an hotel, in *IRC* v *Scottish and Newcastle Breweries Ltd* (1982)

(h) storage platforms built in a warehouse, in *Hunt* v *Henry Quick Ltd* (1992)

(i) a barrister's law books, in *Munby* v *Furlong* (1977).

Held *not* to be plant and machinery:

(a) prefabricated school buildings, in *St John's School* v *Ward* (1974)

(b) a moored ship used as a restaurant, in *Benson* v *The Yard Arm Club Ltd* (1979)

(c) a petrol station forecourt canopy, in *Dixon* v *Fitch's Garage Ltd* (1975)

(d) a football stand, in *Brown* v *Burnley Football and Athletic Co Ltd* (1980)

(e) a false ceiling built to hide electrical conduits, in *Hampton* v *Fortes Autogrill Ltd* (1979)

(f) a false ceiling, mezzanine floors, staircases, decorative floor and wall tiles all used to create ambience in a restaurant, in *Wimpey International Ltd* v *Warland* (1988).

In an attempt to clarify the distinction between buildings and plant, Capital Allowances Act 2001 provides a detailed list of types of expenditure on buildings or structures which are statutorily excluded from qualifying as plant. The Act also provides a detailed list of types of expenditure on buildings or structures which are not statutorily excluded from qualifying as plant and may therefore qualify if permitted by case law.

Expenditure statutorily deemed to be plant and machinery

By statute, expenditure of the following types always qualifies as plant and machinery:

(a) expenditure incurred so as to comply with fire regulations

(b) expenditure on the thermal insulation of industrial buildings

(c) expenditure incurred so as to comply with safety regulations at sports grounds

(d) expenditure on assets necessary to safeguard personal security

(e) expenditure on computer software

(f) expenditure incurred on building alterations, incidental to the installation of plant and machinery.

Capital allowances on plant and machinery

Capital allowances are available to a person who incurs capital expenditure on plant and machinery which is provided for the purposes of a trade, profession or vocation carried on by that person.

An item of plant and machinery acquired by hire purchase is treated as if bought for its cash price on the date of the HP agreement. HP interest is an allowable trading expense and may be written off over the life of the HP contract.

Writing down allowance (WDA)

With some exceptions (see later in this chapter) capital allowances are not calculated individually for each item of plant and machinery acquired by a business. Instead, expenditure on plant and machinery is pooled and capital allowances are calculated with reference to the value of the pool. The basic procedure for each chargeable period is as follows:

(a) The written down value (WDV) of the pool at the end of the previous chargeable period is brought forward.

(b) The cost of any plant and machinery acquired during the period but not subject to a claim for first year allowance (see below) is added to the pool. Items of plant and machinery owned by the trader personally and then brought into the business at a later date are treated as if purchased at their market value on that date.

(c) If any items have been disposed of during the chargeable period a disposal value is subtracted from the pool, equal to:

   (i) sale proceeds, if the asset is sold in the open market

   (ii) market value on the date of disposal, if the asset is given away or sold for less than market value (unless the new owner will be claiming capital allowances, in which case the sale proceeds are used)

(iii) scrap value or compensation received, if the asset is scrapped or destroyed.

But if the disposal value exceeds the original cost of the item, only the original cost is subtracted from the pool. The profit on the disposal may give rise to a capital gains tax liability (see Chapter 18).

(d) A *writing down allowance* (WDA) is then given, calculated at 25% per annum on the pool balance.

(e) The WDA given for the chargeable period is subtracted from the pool, leaving a WDV which is carried forward to the next chargeable period. This WDV will then attract WDAs in future chargeable periods (even if all the plant and machinery has now been sold).

(f) It is not mandatory to claim the maximum allowances available for a chargeable period and a trader with low profits (or a loss) may wish to claim less than the maximum amount, usually to avoid wasting personal allowances. This applies to both WDA and FYA (see below). The effect of claiming less than the maximum capital allowances for a chargeable period is to increase the WDV carried forward, thus increasing the allowances available in future chargeable periods.

Note that WDA is calculated at a rate of 25% *per annum*. The "per annum" refers to the length of the chargeable period for which capital allowances are being claimed and WDA is scaled up or down accordingly if the length of this period is not 12 months.

First year allowance (FYA)

Expenditure on plant and machinery incurred *by small and medium-sized businesses* on or after 2 July 1998 qualifies for a first year allowance (FYA) of 40%. This was increased to 50% for expenditure incurred *by small businesses only* between 6 April 2004 and 5 April 2005 inclusive.

If FYA is claimed in relation to an item of plant and machinery, it is generally given *instead* of WDA in the chargeable period in which the item first attracts capital allowances. The remainder of the asset's cost (after deducting FYA) enters the pool and is eligible for WDA in subsequent chargeable periods. Note that:

(a) FYA is not generally available in relation to motor cars, plant and machinery for leasing, sea-going ships or railway assets. However, expenditure incurred *by any business* on a motor car which is electrically-propelled or which has an emission rating not exceeding 120g/km is eligible for a 100% FYA so long as:

(i) the expenditure is incurred between 17 April 2002 and 31 March 2008, and

(ii) the car is first registered on or after 17 April 2002.

Expenditure incurred between 17 April 2002 and 31 March 2008 on plant and machinery for use in connection with refuelling vehicles with gas or hydrogen fuel also attracts a 100% FYA.

(b) Expenditure on certain classes of energy-saving plant and machinery incurred *by any business* on or after 1 April 2001 qualifies for a 100% FYA.

(c) Expenditure on plant and machinery to reduce water use or improve water quality incurred *by any business* on or after 1 April 2003 qualifies for a 100% FYA.

(d) Capital expenditure incurred *by any business* on the renovation of business premises in disadvantaged areas (including expenditure on plant and machinery) may qualify for a 100% FYA (subject to State aid approval). This FYA is known as the Business Premises Renovation Allowance (BPRA).

(e) A business (sole trader, partnership or company) is small or medium-sized for FYA purposes if it meets the company law criteria for small and medium-sized companies. Currently, any two of the following three criteria must be satisfied:

	Small	*Medium*
Balance sheet total	£2.8 million or less	£11.4 million or less
Turnover	£5.6 million or less	£22.8 million or less
Average number of employees	50 or less	250 or less

Most businesses do in fact qualify as small or medium-sized according to these criteria.

(f) A company which is a member of a group (see Chapter 28) does not qualify as small or medium-sized unless the group is small or medium-sized.

Unlike WDA, FYA is not scaled up or down in accordance with the length of the chargeable period in which it is being given. If FYA is available but not claimed in relation to an item of plant and machinery, the item is instead eligible for WDA in the chargeable period in which it is acquired.

EXAMPLE 2

(a) Sharon started a small business on 1 February 2003 and chose 30 April as her annual accounting date. Her first accounts covered the period from 1 February 2003 to 30 April 2004. During this period she bought and sold plant and machinery as follows:

		£
1 February 2003	Bought car (not eligible for 100% FYA)	7,840
1 April 2003	Bought plant	8,000

Prepare a capital allowances computation for the 15 months to 30 April 2004.

(b) Sharon's purchases and sales of plant and machinery during the year to 30 April 2005 were:

		£
1 June 2004	Bought plant	1,240
30 June 2004	Sold plant (original cost £3,500 on 1/4/03)	2,610
28 April 2005	Bought plant	4,750

Prepare a capital allowances computation for the year to 30 April 2005.

Solution

(a) The computation for the 15-month period from 1 February 2003 to 30 April 2004 is as follows:

		Pool	*Allowances*
		£	£
1/2/03 - 30/4/04			
Additions not qualifying for FYA		7,840	
WDA @ 25% x 15/12		2,450	2,450
		5,390	
Additions qualifying for 40% FYA	8,000		
FYA @ 40%	3,200	4,800	3,200
WDV c/f		10,190	
Total allowances			5,650

Capital allowances available for the period are £5,650.

(b) The computation for the year to 30 April 2005 is as follows:

		Pool	*Allowances*
		£	£
y/e 30/4/05			
WDV b/f		10,190	
Disposals		(2,610)	
		7,580	
WDA @ 25%		1,895	1,895
		5,685	
Additions qualifying for 40% FYA	4,750		
FYA @ 40%	1,900	2,850	1,900
Additions qualifying for 50% FYA	1,240		
FYA @ 50%	620	620	620
WDV c/f		9,155	
Total allowances			4,415

Capital allowances available for the year to 30 April 2005 are £4,415.

EXAMPLE 3

Ian started a small business on 1 September 2004, preparing accounts to 31 March each year. His first accounts covered the period from 1 September 2004 to 31 March 2006. Ian bought and sold plant and machinery as follows during this period:

		£
1 September 2004	Bought plant and machinery	12,000
21 August 2005	Bought plant and machinery	16,000
5 September 2005	Bought plant and machinery	8,000
1 January 2006	Sold plant (original cost £3,700 on 1/9/04)	3,000
31 March 2006	Bought plant and machinery	2,000

Prepare a capital allowances computation for the 19 months to 31 March 2006.

Solution

Ian's first period of account covers 19 months. Since this exceeds 18 months it must be divided into two chargeable periods for capital allowances purposes. The first chargeable period is the year to 31 August 2005. The second chargeable period runs from 1 September 2005 to 31 March 2006. The capital allowances computation is as follows:

		Pool	*Allowances*
		£	£
y/e 31/8/05			
Additions qualifying for 40% FYA	16,000		
FYA @ 40%	6,400	9,600	6,400
Additions qualifying for 50% FYA	12,000		
FYA @ 50%	6,000	6,000	6,000
		15,600	
1/9/05 - 31/3/06			
Disposals		(3,000)	
		12,600	
WDA @ 25% x 7/12		1,838	1,838
		10,762	
Additions qualifying for 40% FYA	10,000		
FYA @ 40%	4,000	6,000	4,000
WDV c/f		16,762	
Total allowances			18,238

Capital allowances available for the period are £18,238.

Balancing allowances and charges

If the disposal value of the disposals for a chargeable period exceeds the balance of expenditure in the pool before disposals are deducted, this is evidence that the capital allowances given to date exceed the depreciation which has actually occurred. In these circumstances the written down value of the pool is set to zero and a *balancing charge* is made, equal to the amount of the excess. A balancing charge is a negative capital allowance which is *added* to trading profits for tax purposes.

It may be possible to avoid (or reduce) this balancing charge by not claiming FYA in relation to items of plant and machinery acquired during the chargeable period. Such items then become eligible for WDA in this period and are added to the pool *before* deducting disposal values, thus reducing the likelihood of a balancing charge. A similar effect might be achieved by not making a de-pooling election in relation to a short-life asset acquired during the period (see below).

Balancing adjustments may also be required when a business ceases trading (see later in this chapter) or when a non-pooled asset is disposed of. Non-pooled assets are assets which are treated individually for capital allowances purposes and are not brought into the pool (see below). When a non-pooled asset is disposed of, a balancing adjustment is required to ensure that the total capital allowances granted in relation to the asset are exactly equal to its depreciation. If the asset's disposal value exceeds its WDV brought forward, a *balancing charge* is made, equal to the excess. If WDV brought forward exceeds disposal value, a *balancing allowance* is given, equal to the excess.

Non-pooled assets

The following types of plant and machinery are not brought into the pool:

(a) expensive motor cars

(b) assets with some private use

(c) short-life assets

(d) long-life assets (for certain businesses).

The treatment of each of these types of asset is explained below.

Expensive motor cars

Motor cars costing more than £12,000 do not join the pool but are dealt with on an individual basis and attract a maximum WDA of £3,000 p.a. This rule does not apply to vans and lorries, which join the pool regardless of their cost. Nor does it apply to electrically-propelled or low-emission motor cars acquired between 17 April 2002 and 31 March 2008 which qualify for a 100% FYA (see earlier).

EXAMPLE 4

Bianca began trading on 1 September 2002 and chose 31 December as her annual accounting date. Her first accounts covered the 16 months to 31 December 2003. On 21 October 2002 she bought a motor car (not electrically-propelled and not a low-emission car) costing £17,600. Compute the capital allowances available on this car for the first three chargeable periods.

Solution

Bianca's first accounts cover a 16-month period. The capital allowances computation is:

	Expensive car	*Allowances*
	£	£
1/9/02 - 31/12/03		
Addition	17,600	
WDA restricted to £3,000 x 16/12	4,000	4,000
WDV c/f	13,600	
y/e 31/12/04		
WDA restricted to £3,000	3,000	3,000
WDV c/f	10,600	
y/e 31/12/05		
WDA @ 25% (no restriction necessary)	2,650	2,650
WDV c/f	7,950	

Assets with some private use

An asset which is used partly for private purposes by the *owner* of a business is not pooled but is treated on an individual basis. The capital allowances calculation is carried out in the usual way but the owner of the business may then claim only the business proportion of the allowances which have been calculated.

Note that capital allowances are available in full on assets used for private purposes by an *employee* of the business, but the employee may then be assessed on a benefit in kind (see Chapter 7).

EXAMPLE 5

Allan prepares annual accounts to 31 May. On 1 July 2004 he bought a motor car costing £14,000. The car is not electrically-propelled and is not a low-emission car. Compute the capital allowances available on this car for the first two chargeable periods, assuming 30% private use by Allan.

Solution

	Expensive car (30% private) £		Allowances £
y/e 31/5/05			
Addition	14,000		
WDA restricted to £3,000	3,000	x 70% =	2,100
WDV c/f	11,000		
y/e 31/5/06			
WDA @ 25%	2,750	x 70% =	1,925
WDV c/f	8,250		

Short-life assets

A trader may elect that an asset other than a motor car should be treated as a "short-life asset". Such an election has the following consequences:

(a) The asset does not join the pool but is treated on an individual basis. For this reason, the election is known as a "de-pooling" election.

(b) If the asset is not disposed of within four years of the end of the chargeable period in which it is acquired, it joins the pool at its written down value and the de-pooling election will have had no effect.

(c) If the asset is disposed of within the four-year period, a balancing allowance will be given (or a balancing charge will be made).

De-pooling an asset which is likely to be sold for less than its WDV within four years will generate a balancing allowance on disposal, so ensuring that capital allowances are given as quickly as possible. A de-pooling election in relation to expenditure incurred during a chargeable period must be made by 31 January in the second tax year following the tax year in which the chargeable period ends.

EXAMPLE 6

Anita starts a small business on 1 January 2003, preparing accounts to 31 December. On 1 August 2003 she buys general plant costing £20,000 and a machine costing £4,000. She sells the machine on 31 October 2005 for £800. Compute her capital allowances for the first three chargeable periods if:

(a) she does not make a de-pooling election with regard to the machine

(b) she does make the de-pooling election.

Assume that none of her plant and machinery is eligible for a 100% FYA.

Solution

(a)

	Pool	*Allowances*
	£	£
y/e 31/12/03		
Additions	24,000	
FYA @ 40%	9,600	9,600
WDV c/f	14,400	
y/e 31/12/04		
WDA @ 25%	3,600	3,600
WDV c/f	10,800	
y/e 31/12/05		
Disposal	(800)	
	10,000	
WDA @ 25%	2,500	2,500
WDV c/f	7,500	

(b)

	Pool	*Short-life asset*	*Allowances*
	£	£	£
y/e 31/12/03			
Additions	20,000	4,000	
FYA @ 40%	8,000	1,600	9,600
WDV c/f	12,000	2,400	
y/e 31/12/04			
WDA @ 25%	3,000	600	3,600
WDV c/f	9,000	1,800	
y/e 31/12/05			
Disposal		(800)	
Balancing allowance		1,000	1,000
WDA @ 25%	2,250		2,250
WDV c/f	6,750		
Total allowances			3,250

The de-pooling election increases the capital allowances in the year to 31 December 2005 by £750, at the expense of reducing the WDV c/f (and therefore future capital allowances) by the same amount.

Long-life assets

A long-life asset is defined as one with a working life of 25 years or more. The rate of WDA available in relation to long-life assets acquired by businesses *spending more than £100,000 a year on such assets* is reduced from the usual 25% per annum to 6% per annum. A separate pool of long-life assets is maintained and WDA at 6% per annum is calculated on the balance of expenditure in this pool.

These provisions usually apply only to large businesses but a small or medium-sized business which is affected by the rules on long-life assets cannot claim FYA in relation to such assets acquired on or after 2 July 1998.

Allowances on cessation of trade

When a business ceases trading and all the plant and machinery is disposed of, capital allowances for the final chargeable period are computed as follows:

(a) Items acquired in the final period are added onto the WDV brought forward.

(b) No WDAs or FYAs are given for the final chargeable period.

(c) The disposal value of the pool (and each non-pooled asset) is subtracted from the balance of unrelieved expenditure, giving rise to balancing allowances or balancing charges. Assets taken over personally by the trader are treated as if sold for their market value on the date taken over.

The balancing adjustments normally made on a cessation of trade can be avoided if the business is being taken over by a "connected person" (e.g. the trader's spouse or other relative or a company which the trader controls) so long as an election to this effect is made by both parties. In this case, the final chargeable period is treated in exactly the same way as any other chargeable period (with WDAs and FYAs as appropriate) and the assets are then transferred to the new owner at their WDVs.

EXAMPLE 7

Jake has been trading for many years, preparing accounts to 30 September each year. The written down value of his plant and machinery at 30 September 2004 was:

	£
Pool	11,350
Expensive motor car (20% private use by Jake)	13,200

Jake ceases trading on 30 June 2005. His purchases and sales of plant and machinery in the 9 months to 30 June 2005 are:

		£
15 October 2004	Bought plant	1,150
30 June 2005	Sold all pool items (all for less than original cost)	12,850
30 June 2005	Sold car	12,000

Prepare the capital allowances computation for the 9 months to 30 June 2005.

Solution

	Pool	*Expensive car (20% private)*	*Allowances*
	£	£	£
1/10/04 - 30/6/05			
WDV b/f	11,350	13,200	
Additions	1,150		
	12,500		
Disposals	(12,850)	(12,000)	
Balancing allowance/(charge)	(350)	1,200 x 80% = 960	610

Industrial buildings allowances

Capital allowances known as *industrial buildings allowances* (IBAs) are available in relation to "qualifying buildings", which consist of:

(a) industrial buildings

(b) certain hotels.

Industrial buildings

The term "industrial buildings" includes such buildings as:

(a) factories used for manufacturing purposes or for processing goods and materials in some way

(b) ancillary buildings associated with such factories (e.g. warehouses for the storage of raw materials or finished goods)

(c) staff welfare buildings provided for the welfare of those working in factories and ancillary buildings (e.g. canteens)

(d) sports pavilions provided for the welfare of employees in *any* trade.

The term does *not* include buildings such as dwelling houses, shops, showrooms and offices (other than drawing offices attached to an industrial building). If a building is used partly as a qualifying industrial building and partly for a non-qualifying purpose, the whole building will qualify for IBAs if the cost of the non-qualifying part does not exceed 25% of the cost of the entire building. If the 25% limit is exceeded only the qualifying part of the building attracts IBAs.

Hotels

IBAs may be claimed in relation to an hotel which satisfies the following conditions:

(a) It offers sleeping accommodation consisting wholly or mainly of "letting bedrooms" available to the general public and not normally occupied by the same person for more than one month.

(b) It has at least 10 letting bedrooms.

(c) It offers ancillary services including (at least) breakfast, evening meals, cleaning of rooms and bed-making.

(d) It is open for at least four months between April and October.

Accommodation for hotel staff (either in a separate building or forming part of the hotel itself) is regarded as part of the hotel but accommodation for the proprietor's own use is not. For the remainder of this chapter, references to industrial buildings should be taken to include qualifying hotels.

Qualifying expenditure

The IBAs available in relation to an industrial building are based on the "qualifying expenditure" of the person who first uses the building. This is either:

(a) the cost of constructing the building, if constructed by the user

(b) the price paid for the building, if bought unused from a builder

(c) the lower of the price paid for the building and the building's construction cost, if bought unused from someone other than a builder.

In all cases, the cost of land is excluded but the costs of land preparation are allowed, as are professional fees such as those paid to an architect.

EXAMPLE 8

(a) Smith (who does not trade as a builder) buys a building site for £100,000 and then incurs the following costs on the erection of an industrial building on that site:

	£
Levelling the site and preparing foundations	95,000
Architect's fees	50,000
Building costs	650,000

What is Smith's qualifying expenditure for IBAs purposes?

(b) If the building is sold unused to Brown for £1,000,000 (including £120,000 for the land), what is Brown's qualifying expenditure?

(c) If (instead of buying Smith's building) Brown buys a similar unused building for the same price from a firm of builders, what is Brown's qualifying expenditure?

Solution

(a) The cost of construction (excluding land) amounts to £795,000. This is Smith's qualifying expenditure.

(b) Brown's qualifying expenditure is also £795,000 (the lower of the price paid by Brown and the building's construction cost).

(c) If Brown purchases an industrial building from a firm of builders, the price paid to the builder (which includes the builder's profit) is fully eligible for IBAs. Therefore Brown's qualifying expenditure is £1,000,000 less the part of that price which is allocated to the land.

Initial allowance and first year allowance

At various times in the past, expenditure on industrial buildings has qualified for an *initial allowance* (IA). IA was most recently available (at a rate of 20%) in relation to expenditure incurred between 1 November 1992 and 31 October 1993.

Industrial buildings are usually ineligible for first year allowance. However, capital expenditure on the renovation of business premises in disadvantaged areas (including industrial buildings, agricultural buildings and commercial buildings in general) may qualify for a 100% FYA (subject to State aid approval). As stated earlier, this FYA is known as the Business Premises Renovation Allowance (BPRA).

Writing down allowance

A *writing down allowance* (WDA) is available in relation to an industrial building so long as the building is in industrial use at the end of the chargeable period in which IBAs are claimed. For buildings acquired on or after 6 November 1962, the annual WDA is calculated as 4% of qualifying expenditure. Note that:

(a) WDA is available to the holder of the "relevant interest" in a building. This is the interest of the person who first acquired the building (usually the freehold) and is transferred to the new owner when the building is sold.

(b) The relevant interest is *not* transferred when a building is leased, so that WDA is normally given to the landlord of a leased building, not the tenant. However, the landlord and tenant may jointly elect that the grant of a long lease (a lease of more than 50 years) should be treated as a sale for capital allowances purposes, in which case WDA will be given to the tenant.

(c) Industrial buildings are treated on an individual basis and are not pooled.

(d) WDA is calculated on the straight line basis (as opposed to the reducing balance basis used for plant and machinery) and is given in proportion to the length of the chargeable period for which allowances are claimed.

(e) WDA may be disclaimed wholly or in part for a chargeable period in relation to an industrial building.

(f) IA (if available) and WDA can both be claimed in the same chargeable period.

(g) The total allowances given in relation to an industrial building can never exceed the qualifying expenditure. In general, WDA will be given at 4% per annum for 25 years. However, WDA will cease earlier than this if IA has been claimed and may continue beyond the 25 years if IBAs are disclaimed in some years.

(h) A building has a "tax life" of 25 years, as from the date on which it is first used for any purpose. If a building is used for non-industrial purposes and then later put to industrial use, WDAs may be claimed for the remainder of the building's tax life. In this case, the total WDAs available will be less than 100% of qualifying expenditure. The period between the date on which the building was first used and the date on which it is first used for industrial purposes is covered by "notional allowances" (see below).

(i) Buildings acquired before 6 November 1962 attract an annual WDA of 2% (not 4%) and therefore have a tax life of 50 years (not 25 years).

EXAMPLE 9

Brian began trading on 1 April 2003, preparing accounts annually to 31 December. His first accounts were for the 9 months to 31 December 2003. On 12 May 2003, he bought a new factory building for £250,000 (excluding the cost of land) and immediately put the building to industrial use. Calculate the IBAs available for Brian's first three chargeable periods.

Solution

	Factory	*Allowances*
	£	£
1/4/03 - 31/12/03		
Cost	250,000	
WDA @ 4% of £250,000 x 9/12	7,500	7,500
WDV c/f	242,500	
y/e 31/12/04		
WDA @ 4% of £250,000	10,000	10,000
WDV c/f	232,500	
y/e 31/12/05		
WDA @ 4% of £250,000	10,000	10,000
WDV c/f	222,500	

If Brian keeps the building and uses it for industrial purposes throughout its entire tax life, a WDA of £10,000 per annum will be available up to and including the year to 31 December 2027, with a final WDA of £2,500 in the year to 31 December 2028.

Non-industrial use

A building which is not in industrial use at the end of a chargeable period will either be disused or will be in use for a non-industrial purpose. IBAs may be claimed during a period of temporary disuse following a period of industrial use but IBAs may *not* be claimed if a building is being used for a non-industrial purpose.

A "notional WDA" is calculated for a building which is in non-industrial use at the end of a chargeable period and this notional WDA is deducted from the WDV of the building in the usual way. However, the notional WDA is *not* available to the trader.

EXAMPLE 10

Carole prepares annual accounts to 31 March. On 1 July 2000, she buys a new building for £200,000 (excluding the cost of land) and immediately puts it to industrial use. This use continues until 1 October 2003, when she starts using the building for a non-industrial purpose. The building reverts to industrial use on 1 May 2005. Show the capital allowances computation for all years up to and including the year ending 31 March 2006.

Solution

	Building	*Allowances*
	£	£
y/e 31/3/01, 02 & 03		
Cost	200,000	
WDA @ 4% of £200,000 for 3 years	24,000	24,000
WDV c/f	176,000	
y/e 31/3/04 & y/e 31/3/05		
Notional WDA @ 4% of £200,000 for 2 years	16,000	
WDV c/f	160,000	
y/e 31/3/06		
WDA @ 4% of £200,000	8,000	8,000
WDV c/f	152,000	

Note:

The notional WDAs of £16,000 given in the years to 31 March 2004 and 31 March 2005 serve to reduce the building's WDV but are not available to Carole.

Sale of a building after continuous industrial use

If an industrial building which has been in continuous industrial use is sold during its tax life of 25 (or 50) years, then:

(a) No WDA is given in the final chargeable period and a balancing adjustment is made in the usual way, calculated by comparing the building's WDV with the disposal proceeds (or original cost, if lower).

(b) The second-hand buyer of the building takes over the right to claim a WDA for the remainder of the building's tax life, calculated by dividing the "residue of expenditure" by the number of years remaining of the tax life. The residue of expenditure is equal to the WDV of the building before the sale, plus any balancing charge and less any balancing allowance made on the sale. In effect, the second-hand buyer's WDAs are calculated on the lower of the original cost of the building and the price for which it was sold.

If a building is sold after the expiry of its tax life, no balancing adjustments are made and the second-hand buyer is unable to claim any WDA.

EXAMPLE 11

Christopher prepares annual accounts to 31 December. On 1 January 2002 he bought a new building for £150,000 (excluding land) and started using it immediately for an industrial purpose. Show the capital allowances computation for all affected years if he sells the building to Dean on 1 July 2005 for:

(a) £110,000 (excluding land) (b) £175,000 (excluding land)

Also calculate the WDAs available to Dean, who prepares accounts to 31 March each year.

Solution

(a)	*Building* £	*Allowances* £
y/e 31/12/02, 03 & 04		
Cost	150,000	
WDA @ 4% of £150,000 for 3 years	18,000	18,000
WDV c/f	132,000	
y/e 31/12/05		
Disposal value	110,000	
Balancing allowance	22,000	22,000

The residue of expenditure is £110,000 (£132,000 - £22,000). The tax life of the building ends on 31 December 2026, giving an unexpired life of 21 years 6 months (21.5 years) on the date of the second-hand purchase by Dean. Dean may therefore claim an annual WDA of £110,000/21.5 = £5,116 for each of the 21 years to 31 March 2026 and a final WDA of £2,564 (to bring the total to £110,000) in the year to 31 March 2027.

(b)	*Building*	*Allowances*
	£	£
y/e 31/12/05		
WDV b/f	132,000	
Disposal value (limited to original cost)	150,000	
Balancing charge	(18,000)	(18,000)

The residue of expenditure is £150,000 (£132,000 + £18,000). Therefore Dean may claim an annual WDA of £150,000/21.5 = £6,977 for each of the 21 years to 31 March 2026 and a final WDA of £3,483 in the year to 31 March 2027.

Sale of a building after non-industrial use

As explained above, an industrial building is written down by notional WDAs during a period of non-industrial use. If the building is then sold (within its tax life) the balancing adjustments made on the sale depend upon whether the building is sold for more or less than its original cost.

(a) If the building is sold for *more* than original cost, the balancing charge made on the sale is restricted to the actual allowances given to date (i.e. excluding the notional WDAs).

(b) If the building is sold for *less* than original cost, the required balancing adjustment is calculated as follows:

(i) "Net cost" = original cost - sale proceeds

(ii) "Adjusted net cost" = net cost × $\frac{\text{period of industrial use}}{\text{period of total use}}$

(iii) Balancing adjustment = adjusted net cost - actual allowances given.

(c) The second-hand buyer's WDAs are based on the lower of the residue of expenditure (calculated as before) and the second-hand price paid.

EXAMPLE 12

Rework the above example, assuming that Christopher uses the building for non-industrial purposes between 1 July 2003 and 30 June 2004.

Solution

(a) The period of total use by Christopher is 3 years 6 months (3.5 years), of which 1 year comprises non-industrial use and the remainder comprises industrial use. The building was not in industrial use on 31 December 2003, so only notional WDAs would be calculated for the year to 31 December 2003. The actual allowances given (in the other 2 chargeable periods) are 4% of £150,000 for 2 years = £12,000.

Net cost is £40,000 (£150,000 - £110,000) and adjusted net cost is £28,571 (£40,000 x 2.5/3.5). A balancing allowance of £16,571 (£28,571 - £12,000) would be made.

The residue of expenditure is now £115,429 (£132,000 - £16,571). This exceeds the price paid by Dean so Dean's annual WDAs are equal to £110,000 divided by 21.5.

(b) The balancing charge is limited to the actual allowances given i.e. £12,000. The residue of expenditure is £144,000 (£132,000 + £12,000) and Dean's annual WDAs are equal to this figure divided by 21.5.

Commercial buildings in enterprise zones

Certain areas of the country are designated as "enterprise zones". IBAs are available in relation to *any* commercial building constructed in an enterprise zone, including shops and offices (but not dwellings) so long as the construction expenditure is contracted for within 10 years of the zone's designation and is actually incurred within 20 years of the zone's designation.

An initial allowance of 100% is available for the chargeable period in which the expenditure is incurred. If the full allowance is not claimed, the remaining expenditure is eligible for an annual WDA of 25%, calculated on the straight-line basis on the cost of the building and beginning when the building is first brought into use. For example, if an initial allowance of only 30% is claimed, the remaining 70% of the expenditure is eligible for WDAs equal to 25% of the cost of the building in each of the first two years of use and 20% of the cost in the third year.

Agricultural buildings

Agricultural buildings allowances (ABAs) are available in relation to capital expenditure on the construction of farmhouses, farm cottages, farm buildings, fences and drainage works. However, no more than one-third of the expenditure on a farmhouse is eligible for ABAs. The cost of land is always excluded. The system of granting allowances is similar (but not identical) to that used for industrial buildings:

(a) An annual WDA, calculated at 4% per annum on the straight line basis, is given in relation to qualifying expenditure. WDA begins in the chargeable period in which the expenditure is incurred.

(b) Qualifying expenditure incurred between 1 November 1992 and 31 October 1993 attracted an initial allowance of 20%.

(c) The 25-year tax life of an agricultural building begins on the first day of the chargeable period in which ABAs are first given.

Sale of an agricultural building

If an agricultural building is sold during its tax life and the vendor and buyer do not elect for a balancing adjustment to be made (see below), the buyer simply takes over the right to receive the WDAs that the vendor would have received if the sale had not occurred. The procedure is as follows:

(a) No balancing adjustments are made on the sale and the price paid by the second-hand buyer is totally ignored.

(b) For the chargeable period in which the sale is dealt with, the vendor receives WDA on the building for the last time, calculated at 4% per annum from the start of the chargeable period to the date of the sale.

(c) For the chargeable period in which the purchase is dealt with, the buyer receives WDA for the first time, calculated (on the original cost of the building) at 4% per annum from the date of purchase to the end of the chargeable period.

(d) The buyer then receives WDA of 4% p.a. until the building is fully written off.

If vendor and buyer both elect for the sale of an agricultural building to be treated as a balancing event, the capital allowances computation is exactly the same as that which would be performed on the sale of an industrial building (see above).

EXAMPLE 13

Bill trades as a farmer, preparing accounts to 31 December each year. On 1 December 2003 he constructed a barn at a cost of £50,000 (excluding land). On 1 August 2005 he sells the barn to Ben for £47,000 (excluding land). Ben also trades as a farmer, preparing accounts to 30 June each year. No election is made for the sale to be treated as a balancing event. Calculate the ABAs available to Bill and Ben.

Solution

Bill's allowances are:		£
y/e 31/12/03	£50,000 x 4%	2,000
y/e 31/12/04	£50,000 x 4%	2,000
y/e 31/12/05	£50,000 x 4% x 7/12	1,167
Ben's allowances are:		£
y/e 30/6/06	£50,000 x 4% x 11/12	1,833
y/e 30/6/07 etc.	£50,000 x 4%	2,000

Notes:

(a) Bill's sale is made after 7 months of the chargeable period have elapsed, so his final WDA is calculated at 7/12th of 4%.

(b) Ben's purchase is made with 11 months of the chargeable period remaining, so his first WDA is calculated at 11/12th of 4%.

(c) Ben will receive WDAs of £2,000 per annum until the barn's WDV reaches zero.

EXAMPLE 14

Rework the Bill and Ben example above, given that an election is made for the sale to be treated as a balancing event.

Solution

Bill's allowances in the years to 31 December 2003 and 2004 total £4,000, reducing the WDV of the barn to £46,000. The barn is sold for £47,000, so a balancing charge of £1,000 is made in the year to 31 December 2005.

The tax life of the building began on 1 January 2003 (the first day of the chargeable period in which ABAs were first given) and ends on 31 December 2027, giving an unexpired life of 22 years and 5 months (22.417 years) on the date of the second-hand purchase by Ben. The residue of expenditure is £47,000 (£46,000 + £1,000). Therefore Ben's annual WDA is £2,097 (£47,000/22.417).

Miscellaneous capital allowances

Capital allowances are available in relation to some miscellaneous categories of capital expenditure. These include expenditure on patent rights, know-how and research and development.

Patent rights

Purchased patent rights are treated in a similar way to plant and machinery for capital allowances purposes:

(a) All patent rights are pooled together. The pool is adjusted in each chargeable period for acquisitions and disposals. WDA is then calculated at 25% per annum on the reducing balance.

(b) As with plant and machinery, disposal value is limited to original cost. But whereas a sale of plant and machinery for more than cost may give rise to a capital gains tax liability (see Chapter 18) a sale of patent rights for more than cost gives rise to an income tax liability (see Chapter 6).

(c) If the disposal value of a patent exceeds the balance of unrelieved expenditure in the pool, a balancing charge is made and the pool value is set to zero.

(d) A balancing allowance will arise if there is a cessation of trade and the patents are sold for less than the balance of unrelieved expenditure in the pool. A balancing allowance will also arise if there is no cessation of trade but the last patent in the pool is sold or comes to the end of its term and the disposal value (if any) is less than the balance of unrelieved expenditure in the pool. This treatment is different from that used for plant and machinery.

EXAMPLE 15

Gemma prepares accounts to 31 July each year. At the end of the capital allowances computation for the year to 31 July 2004, the WDV of her patents pool was £3,800.

(a) Calculate the capital allowances due for the year to 31 July 2005 if she acquires no patents during the year but sells for £1,500 a patent which had cost her £2,000.

(b) Rework the computation given that the sold patent is Gemma's last remaining patent.

Solution

(a)

	Patents pool	*Allowances*
	£	£
y/e 31/7/05		
WDV b/f	3,800	
Disposals	(1,500)	
	2,300	
WDA @ 25%	575	575
WDV c/f	1,725	

(b) If the last patent has been sold, then a balancing allowance of £2,300 will be given instead of the £575 WDA and the pool will be closed.

Know-how

"Know-how" is defined as industrial information and techniques of use in either:

(a) manufacturing or the processing of goods or materials

(b) the working of mineral deposits

(c) agricultural, fishing or forestry operations.

All expenditure on know-how is pooled and capital allowances are calculated in much the same way as for patent rights. However, if know-how is sold for more than original cost, the disposal value used in the capital allowances computation is the *full sale proceeds*. Depending upon the balance of unrelieved expenditure in the pool prior to the disposal, this will either create a balancing charge or restrict the value of subsequent WDAs. In either case, the profit made on the disposal is (in effect) treated as trading income.

Research and development

Capital expenditure on research and development related to the claimant's trade attracts a first year allowance of 100%. Any proceeds subsequently received on the disposal of a research and development asset are treated as a trading receipt.

Summary

- Capital allowances are granted for chargeable periods. Each period of account ranks as a chargeable period, except that periods of account exceeding 18 months in length are divided into two or more chargeable periods.
- In order to qualify as plant and machinery, an asset must perform an active function in the trade, not merely provide a setting in which the trade is carried on.
- Writing down allowances on plant and machinery are granted at 25% per annum, calculated on the reducing balance basis.
- A 40% FYA is available in relation to qualifying plant and machinery bought by a small or medium-sized business on or after 2 July 1998. This increased to 50% for expenditure incurred by small businesses between 6 April 2004 and 5 April 2005. A 100% FYA is available to any business which incurs expenditure on energy-saving technology, water-efficient technology or low-emission cars.
- In general, expenditure on plant and machinery is pooled and capital allowances are calculated by reference to the value of the pool. Expensive motor cars (other than low-emission cars) are treated individually, as are assets with private use and short-life assets. Long-life assets acquired by certain businesses are pooled separately and attract an annual WDA of 6%.
- On the cessation of a business, the disposal value of the pool and of each non-pooled asset is subtracted from the balance of unrelieved expenditure, giving rise to balancing adjustments.
- Writing down allowances are available on qualifying industrial buildings, hotels and agricultural buildings at a rate of 4% per annum, calculated on the straight line basis. Notional WDAs are deducted if an industrial building is put to non-industrial use. Commercial buildings constructed in enterprise zones are granted an initial allowance of 100%.
- A 100% FYA known as the Business Premises Renovation Allowance (BPRA) may be available (subject to State aid approval) in relation to capital expenditure on the renovation of business premises in disadvantaged areas.
- Capital allowances are also available in relation to patent rights, know-how and research and development expenditure.

Exercises

10.1 Laura started a small business on 1 June 2004. Her first accounts covered the period from 1 June 2004 to 30 June 2005 and showed an adjusted trading profit (before capital allowances) of £41,780. During this period she bought plant and machinery as follows:

		£
1 June 2004	Bought machinery	8,000
1 June 2004	Bought motor car (not eligible for 100% FYA)	15,000
1 July 2004	Bought machinery	4,000
31 March 2005	Bought machinery	2,400

Compute her trading income for the first two tax years, assuming 40% private use of the car by Laura. Also compute the amount of any overlap profits.

10.2 Maurice is the proprietor of a small business. He prepares accounts to 31 March. The tax written down value of his pool of plant and machinery at 31 March 2005 was £10,300. His transactions during the year to 31 March 2006 were as follows:

		£
1 May 2005	Bought plant	600
11 July 2005	Sold motor car (original cost £7,000)	3,000
11 July 2005	Bought motor car	8,000
1 November 2005	Bought machinery	400
12 January 2006	Sold machinery (original cost £4,000 in 2004)	4,200

The car bought in July 2005 was not electrically-propelled and was not a low-emission car. Compute the capital allowances claimable for the year to 31 March 2006, assuming no private use of any of the assets.

10.3 Norma started a small business on 1 November 2002 and chose 30 June as her annual accounting date. Her first accounts covered the period to 30 June 2004 and showed an adjusted trading profit (before deduction of capital allowances) of £56,200. Her accounts for the year to 30 June 2005 showed an adjusted trading profit (before deduction of capital allowances) of £59,900. Plant and machinery was bought and sold as follows:

		£
1 November 2002	Bought plant	10,000
17 May 2003	Bought plant	17,400
12 October 2003	Bought car (40% private use by Norma)	8,800
3 November 2003	Sold plant (original cost £2,000 in November 2002)	1,750
3 November 2003	Bought plant	4,600
1 February 2004	Bought car	7,200
7 August 2004	Sold plant (original cost £1,500 in November 2003)	1,600
8 August 2004	Bought plant	9,200
31 March 2005	Sold car bought on 12 October 2003	6,300
31 March 2005	Bought car (40% private use by Norma)	14,100

None of the cars qualify for a 100% FYA. Compute Norma's trading income for the first four tax years. Also compute the amount of any overlap profits.

10.4 Oliver prepares accounts to 30 June each year. On 1 May 2004 he acquired a brand new factory for £100,000 and put the factory to immediate industrial use. The cost of £100,000 included land of £20,000 and general offices of £22,500. Calculate the IBAs available for the years to 30 June 2004 and 2005.

10.5 Francesco has traded for many years, preparing accounts to 31 December each year. On 1 December 1997 he buys a new workshop for £56,000 (including land £11,000). He begins using the workshop on 1 January 1998 and it is in continuous industrial use until 1 July 2005, when he sells it to Maria for £45,000 (including land £15,000). Maria immediately begins to use the workshop for an industrial purpose.

(a) Compute the IBAs available to Francesco for all affected years.

(b) Compute the IBAs available to Maria, who starts trading on 1 May 2005, making her first accounts up to 30 November 2005, and then producing accounts annually to 30 November thereafter.

10.6 Giles has traded as a farmer for many years, preparing annual accounts to 31 March. On 1 July 2004 he constructed a barn at a cost (excluding land) of £30,000. On 1 October 2005, he sold the barn to Pam for £35,000 (excluding land). Pam also trades as a farmer and began trading on 1 May 2005. She made up her first accounts for the period from 1 May 2005 to 31 December 2005 and intends to produce accounts for calendar years thereafter. Calculate the ABAs available to Giles and to Pam:

(a) if no election is made for the sale to be treated as a balancing event

(b) if such an election is made.

***10.7** David has traded for many years, preparing accounts to 31 March annually. On 1 July 1998 he buys a new industrial building for £80,000 (excluding land) and puts the building to immediate industrial use. Throughout David's ownership, the building is always in industrial use apart from the period between 1 January 2001 and 31 December 2003 when it is used for a non-industrial purpose. On 1 February 2006, he sells the building to Diana, who started business on 1 July 2005 and makes up accounts to 30 June each year. Calculate the IBAs available to David and to Diana, if the building was sold for:

(a) £60,000 (excluding land) (b) £120,000 (excluding land).

***10.8** Talat prepares accounts to 31 October each year. The written down value of his plant and machinery after deducting capital allowances for the year to 31 October 2002 was as follows:

	£
Pool	13,190
Motor car (30% private use by Talat)	14,500

He had the following transactions during the next three years:

		£
y/e 31/10/03		
10 November 2002	Bought plant	2,000
1 January 2003	Sold plant (original cost £4,200 in 1997)	1,310
y/e 31/10/04		
5 March 2004	Sold car (original cost £7,500)	3,000
5 March 2004	Bought car	8,200
12 June 2004	Bought plant	720
y/e 31/10/05		
5 April 2005	Sold plant (original cost £1,000 in November 2002)	1,150
6 August 2005	Bought plant	750

There were no capital transactions between 1 November 2005 and 31 March 2006, when Talat ceased trading. On 31 March 2006, the plant and machinery was disposed of as follows:

(i) All of the plant and machinery other than cars was sold for £4,000.

(ii) Talat took over his own car. Its market value on 31 March 2006 was £8,000.

(iii) There was only one other car remaining and Talat gave this to his brother, who will be using it for private purposes. The market value of the car on 31 March 2006 was £5,900.

Talat's business is a small business for capital allowances purposes and none of the cars qualify for a 100% FYA.

Prepare the capital allowances computations for the years to 31 October 2003, 2004 and 2005 and for the period from 1 November 2005 to 31 March 2006.

Chapter 11

Income from self-employment: Trading losses

Introduction

If the computation of a self-employed person's adjusted trading profit for a period of account produces a negative result, then a trading loss has been incurred. This has two main consequences:

(a) the person's trading income for the relevant tax year is £nil

(b) tax relief may be claimed in respect of the loss.

Several forms of tax relief are available and each involves offsetting the trading loss against other income or gains of the trader concerned, so reducing the amount of tax payable on that other income or those gains. The purpose of this chapter is to explain the main features of each form of loss relief.

Relief for trading losses

In general, trading losses may be relieved in the following ways:

(a) Under Section 385 of ICTA 1988, a trading loss may be carried forward and set against future profits of the same trade.

(b) Under Section 380 of ICTA 1988, a trading loss may be set against the statutory total income of the trader for a period of up to two years.

(c) Under Section 72 of Finance Act 1991, a Section 380 claim may be extended by a further claim, to the effect that any part of the trading loss which remains un-relieved should be set against the trader's capital gains.

Each of these forms of loss relief is described below. The loss reliefs are usually referred to by their section numbers in ICTA 1988 or Finance Act 1991 and this practice is followed for the remainder of this chapter.

Section 385 relief

Unless a trader claims any other form of loss relief, a trading loss is automatically carried forward under Section 385 and relieved against future trading profits. It is important to note the following points:

(a) Relief under Section 385 is given only against future *trading* profits, not against any other form of income.

(b) Furthermore, relief is given only against future trading profits arising from *the same trade* as that in which the loss was incurred. Therefore, if a trader ceases one trade and commences another, the losses of the old trade cannot be carried forward and relieved against the future profits of the new trade. Similarly, if a trader carries on two trades simultaneously, a loss incurred in one of the trades cannot be carried forward and relieved against the future profits of the other trade.

(c) Relief must be given against the *first available* trading profits arising in the future. The maximum possible amount of relief must be taken in each future year until the loss is fully relieved, even if this leaves insufficient income to absorb personal allowances.

EXAMPLE 1

Carla incurred a trading loss of £10,200 in the year to 30 June 2005. Her projected trading profits for the next three years (adjusted for tax purposes) are as follows:

	£
year to 30 June 2006	4,500
year to 30 June 2007	5,000
year to 30 June 2008	30,000

Carla's only other income consists of interest received of £500 per annum. Assuming that the trading loss is to be carried forward under Section 385, calculate her total income for 2005/06 to 2008/09 inclusive.

Solution

	2005/06	*2006/07*	*2007/08*	*2008/09*
	£	£	£	£
Trading income	nil	4,500	5,000	30,000
Less: S385 relief	-	(4,500)	(5,000)	(700)
	-	-	-	29,300
Interest received	500	500	500	500
Total income	500	500	500	29,800

Notes:

(a) Trading income for 2005/06 is £nil since there is a loss in the basis period for that year.

(b) The trading loss carried forward is relieved only against future trading profits (not against the interest received) and maximum relief must be given in each year. This results in a waste of personal allowances in 2006/07 and 2007/08. Carla would probably prefer to carry forward the loss in its entirety to 2008/09, where it can be put to good use, but this is not possible.

Capital allowances

As explained in Chapter 10, any capital allowances claimed for a period of account are treated as a trading expense of that period. Therefore capital allowances are included automatically in the calculation of a trading loss.

It is important to remember that it is not mandatory to claim the maximum capital allowances available for a chargeable period. If a trading loss has been incurred it may be advisable to claim less than the maximum capital allowances (or even none at all) so as to avoid wasting personal allowances. Disclaimed capital allowances are not lost permanently, since higher WDVs are carried forward than would otherwise have been the case and this results in higher capital allowances in future years (see Chapter 10).

EXAMPLE 2

Colin's adjusted trading profits/(losses) for the years to 31 August 2004 and 2005 are:

	Before capital allowances	*Capital allowances available*	*After capital allowances*
	£	£	£
year to 31 August 2004	(8,300)	1,900	(10,200)
year to 31 August 2005	13,100	2,700	10,400

He has no other income. If the trading loss is carried forward under Section 385, should Colin claim maximum capital allowances in these two years?

Solution

If Colin claims maximum capital allowances in both years, S385 relief in 2005/06 will be £10,200. This will almost entirely absorb the trading profit of £10,400 assessed in that year, leaving only £200 against which to set personal allowances, most of which will therefore be wasted.

It would be better to claim no capital allowances at all for the two years concerned. The loss carried forward under S385 would then be only £8,300 and this would be relieved in 2005/06 against the trading profit of £13,100, leaving income of £4,800 against which to set personal allowances. There would be minimal waste of personal allowances and the capital allowances available to Colin in future years would be increased.

Relief for trade charges

If a trading loss is incurred in the basis period for a tax year, or if a loss is brought forward under Section 385 and set against the year's trading income, it is quite possible that the trader's total income for the year in question will be minimal or even zero. In consequence, the trader may become a non-taxpayer or may pay tax at only 10% or 20% and HMRC might then raise a Section 350 assessment to claw back all or part of the basic rate tax deducted from any charges paid net (see Chapter 4).

In these circumstances, Section 387 of ICTA 1988 allows the amount of any *trade* charges which have been the subject of a Section 350 assessment to be carried forward and set against future trading profits in exactly the same way as trading losses carried forward under Section 385. Trade charges are those which are incurred wholly and exclusively for trade purposes (e.g. patent royalties).

Non-trade charges which have been the subject of a Section 350 assessment *cannot* be carried forward. If a trader has both trade and non-trade charges in a year, any Section 350 assessment can be assumed to refer to trade charges (which can be carried forward) in priority to non-trade charges (which cannot).

EXAMPLE 3

Joyce has been self-employed for many years, producing accounts to 31 December each year. Her recent adjusted trading profits/(losses) are:

	£
year to 31 December 2004	(1,700)
year to 31 December 2005	28,000

She has no other income. In both 2004/05 and 2005/06 she pays trade charges (net) of £1,560 and non-trade charges (net) of £780. Calculate her statutory total income in 2004/05 and 2005/06, assuming that the loss is carried forward under Section 385.

Solution

	2004/05		*2005/06*
	£		£
Trading income	nil		28,000
Less: Section 385 relief	-	1,700	
Section 387 relief	-	2,000	3,700
	-		24,300
Less: Charges (£2,340 x 100/78)	-		3,000
Statutory total income	-		21,300

A Section 350 assessment would be raised for 2004/05 to recover the basic rate tax deducted from the charges of £3,000 (gross). To the extent that this assessment relates to trade charges (£1,560 x 100/78 = £2,000) it is carried forward with the trading loss.

Section 380 relief

As illustrated earlier, carrying trading losses forward under Section 385 does not always provide the most satisfactory form of loss relief. Problems associated with Section 385 relief include:

(a) Relief is delayed until sufficient profits arise from the same trade in future years (if, indeed, they ever do).

(b) The trader has no control over the amount of relief given in each year and therefore personal allowances may be wasted.

(c) If tax rates are falling, relief may be given at a lower rate than the rates which were in force when the loss was incurred.

An alternative form of loss relief which overcomes some of these problems is provided by Section 380, under which trading losses may be set against the trader's *statutory total income* (total income from all sources, less charges) for a period of up to two years. It is important to note that:

(a) The trader is under no obligation to make a Section 380 claim. If no such claim is made, trading losses are automatically carried forward under Section 385.

(b) Any unrelieved losses remaining after a Section 380 claim has been made are automatically carried forward under Section 385.

(c) Section 380 relief is available only if the business is being carried on on a commercial basis with a view to making profits. If this is not the case then only Section 385 relief is available.

(d) In the case of *farmers*, a loss is usually not eligible for Section 380 relief if losses have also been incurred in each of the previous five tax years.

(e) Section 380 relief is set against income in the order which will result in the lowest tax liability. The best approach is to deduct the relief first from non-savings income, then from savings income and finally from dividends.

Relieving a trading loss under Section 380

Section 380 relief is available in respect of the trading loss "incurred in a year of assessment". In most cases, the loss incurred in a year of assessment (or tax year) is the loss incurred in the basis period for that year. However, a special rule applies to trading losses incurred in an overlap period (see later in this chapter). A trading loss incurred in a tax year may be set against the statutory total income of:

(a) the tax year in which the loss is incurred, or

(b) the previous tax year, or

(c) both of these years (if the loss is large enough for this).

A claim for Section 380 relief must be made by 31 January in the second tax year following the tax year in which the loss was incurred. For example, a Section 380 claim in relation to a loss incurred in 2005/06 must be made by 31 January 2008.

The trader can decide whether to make a Section 380 claim for one of the available years, for both of these years, or for neither year. But partial claims are not allowed. A Section 380 claim must be for as much of the loss as can be relieved, even if this leaves insufficient income to absorb personal allowances. However, if a claim is made for both years and the combined STI of the two years exceeds the amount of the loss, the trader can decide whether to claim maximum relief in the year of the loss (relieving the remainder of the loss in the previous year) or vice versa. A trading loss may be set against the STI of the previous tax year whether or not the loss-making trade was being carried on in that year.

If two Section 380 claims are made for the same tax year (one for a loss incurred in that year and another for a loss incurred in the following tax year) the claim in respect of the current year's loss takes priority.

EXAMPLE 4

Ashok has been trading for many years, preparing annual accounts to 30 June. Recent trading profits/(losses), adjusted for tax purposes, are as follows:

	£
year to 30 June 2003	12,400
year to 30 June 2004	9,450
year to 30 June 2005	(9,500)

He has other income amounting to £4,000 per annum and claims only the personal allowance. Show his possible Section 380 claims. Which of these claims (if any) should be recommended?

Solution

Ashok's trading income is:

Year	*Basis period*	*Trading income*
		£
2003/04	y/e 30/6/03	12,400
2004/05	y/e 30/6/04	9,450
2005/06	y/e 30/6/05	nil

He could make a Section 380 claim for 2005/06 only, for 2004/05 only, for both of these years, or for neither year:

(a) A claim for 2005/06 only would relieve £4,000 of the loss against his other income, leaving no tax liability for the year and losses of £5,500 to carry forward under Section 385. This would be a waste, since the other income of £4,000 would have been covered by personal allowances anyway.

(b) A claim for 2004/05 only would relieve the entire loss against that year's STI of £13,450 (£9,450 + £4,000), leaving income of £3,950 (£13,450 - £9,500) against which to set personal allowances. There would be some wastage of personal allowances but the tax liability for 2004/05 would become zero. This seems to be a fairly efficient way of relieving the loss.

(c) A claim for both years is pointless, since:

  (i) a claim giving maximum relief in 2004/05 would leave no losses to relieve in 2005/06, and

  (ii) a claim giving maximum relief in 2005/06 leads to a waste of personal allowances in that year (see above).

(d) A claim for neither year would result in the entire loss being carried forward under Section 385. This would mean that loss relief would be delayed until such time as sufficient profits of the same trade arose in future years.

On balance, a Section 380 claim for 2004/05 might be recommended. This claim combines early relief of the loss with a fairly small wastage of personal allowances. The claim would have to be made by 31 January 2008.

Section 72 relief

If a Section 380 claim is made for a tax year and the effect of that claim is to reduce the trader's total income for the year to nil, a claim may also be made under Section 72 of the Finance Act 1991 for any unrelieved part of the loss to be set against the trader's capital gains for the year. The time limit for making such a claim is the same as for Section 380 relief. Section 72 relief is considered further in Chapter 16.

Losses on commencement of trade

Losses incurred in the opening years of trading may, just like any other trading losses, be carried forward under Section 385 or set against statutory total income under Section 380. But, in addition to these forms of relief, Section 381 of ICTA 1988 allows trading losses incurred in any of the first four tax years to be set against the statutory total income of the three previous years. Note that:

(a) Section 381 relieves the trading loss incurred in a tax year against the STI of the three previous tax years, beginning with the earliest year. For example, a trading loss incurred in 2005/06 could be set against the STI of 2002/03, 2003/04 and 2004/05, in that order.

(b) A Section 381 claim, if made, applies to *all* of the three years previous to the loss-making year. The trader cannot specify the years in which relief is to be given or the amount of relief to be given in each year. The maximum possible relief is given in each year and this may result in a wastage of personal allowances.

(c) Relief is given against income in the order which results in the lowest tax liability.

(d) Claims under Section 381 must be made by 31 January in the second tax year following the loss-making tax year.

(e) Unlike a Section 380 claim, a claim under Section 381 cannot be extended so as to set unrelieved trading losses against capital gains.

(f) A loss incurred in an overlap period is treated as *a loss of the earlier tax year only.* This rule ensures that a loss is relieved only once.

EXAMPLE 5

Carl begins trading on 1 July 2003 and chooses 30 June as his accounting date. His adjusted trading profits/(losses) for the first two accounting years are as follows:

	£
year to 30 June 2004	(43,200)
year to 30 June 2005	(12,400)

Now that he is self-employed, Carl has no other income. Prior to becoming self-employed his only income was from employment, as follows:

	£
2000/01	23,900
2001/02	18,760
2002/03	16,120
2003/04 (to 30 June 2003)	4,180

Assuming that Carl makes all possible Section 381 claims, calculate his total income for years 2000/01 to 2003/04 inclusive.

Solution

The losses which are eligible for Section 381 relief are:

Year	*Basis period*	*Workings*	*Trading loss* £	*Years for S381 claim*
2003/04	1/7/03 to 5/4/04	£(43,200) x 9/12	(32,400)	00/01-02/03
2004/05	y/e 30/6/04	£(43,200) - overlap £(32,400)	(10,800)	01/02-03/04
2005/06	y/e 30/6/05		(12,400)	02/03-04/05

Trading income for 2003/04 through to 2005/06 is of course £nil. If all possible Section 381 claims are made, total income for years 2000/01 to 2003/04 is:

	2000/01 £	*2001/02* £	*2002/03* £	*2003/04* £
Employment income	23,900	18,760	16,120	4,180
Less: Section 381 relief:				
2003/04 loss	(23,900)	(8,500)		
2004/05 loss		(10,260)	(540)	
2005/06 loss			(12,400)	
Total income (after loss reliefs)	-	-	3,180	4,180

Losses on cessation of trade

In normal circumstances, a trader has a choice between carrying forward trading losses under Section 385 or relieving such losses against total income under Section 380. But if a loss is incurred in the final year of trading the first of these alternatives is not available since there can be no future profits against which to set the loss. In order to remedy this situation, Section 388 of ICTA 1988 provides a relief known as "terminal loss relief" which allows a trading loss incurred in the last 12 months of trading to be set against the trading profits of the tax year in which the cessation occurs and the previous three tax years.

In effect, terminal loss relief is a form of Section 385 relief which works backwards rather than forwards.

Calculating the terminal loss

The "terminal loss" eligible for relief is the trading loss incurred in the final 12 months of trading, excluding any part of the loss which is relieved under Section 380. The terminal loss is calculated by adding together the following components:

(a) *Losses*:

   (i) the actual trading loss incurred from 6 April to the date of the cessation

   (ii) the actual trading loss incurred from a date 12 months before the cessation to the following 5 April

(b) *Trade charges*:

   (i) any trade charges of the final tax year on which a Section 350 assessment has been raised

   (ii) any trade charges of the previous tax year on which a Section 350 assessment has been raised (restricted so that only trade charges of the final 12 months are included in the calculation altogether).

If either (a)(i) or (a)(ii) yields a profit, this profit counts as zero in the calculation of the terminal loss. Any available overlap relief is added to the terminal loss.

EXAMPLE 6

Andrea ceases trading on 31 October 2005. Her adjusted trading profits/(losses) for the closing periods of account are as follows:

	£
year to 31 December 2003	6,600
year to 31 December 2004	2,400
10 months to 31 October 2005	(22,500)

Her trade charges and her other income are as follows:

	2004/05	*2005/06*
	£	£
Trade charges paid net (gross amounts)	6,000	3,000
Other income	nil	nil

Overlap profits of £3,200 arose when Andrea began trading. Calculate the amount of the terminal loss, assuming that no Section 380 claims are made.

Solution

			£
(a) *Losses*:			
(i)	6/4/05 to 31/10/05	£(22,500) x 7/10	(15,750)
	Overlap relief		(3,200)
(ii)	1/11/04 to 5/4/05	£2,400 x 2/12 + £(22,500) x 3/10	(6,350)
(b) *Trade charges*:			
(i)	S350 assessment in 2005/06		(3,000)
(ii)	S350 assessment in 2004/05 £6,000, restricted to £6,000 x 5/12		(2,500)
Terminal loss			(30,800)

Notes:

1. Taxable income for 2004/05 is £nil (profits of £2,400 are covered by the personal allowance). Taxable income for 2005/06 is also £nil. Section 350 assessments would be raised in both years to recover the basic rate tax deducted from charges.
2. Trade charges for 2005/06 cover 7 months (6 April 2005 to 31 October 2005) so only 5 months' worth of the trade charges for 2004/05 are taken into account when calculating the terminal loss.

Relieving the terminal loss

As stated above, the terminal loss may be relieved against the trading profits of the year of cessation and the three tax years preceding the year of cessation. Note that:

(a) Relief is given in later years first. For example, a terminal loss arising as a consequence of a business ceasing to trade during 2005/06 would be set against the trading profits of 2005/06, 2004/05, 2003/04 and 2002/03, in that order.

(b) The trader cannot specify how much relief is given in each year. The maximum possible relief must be given in each year even if this results in a wastage of personal allowances.

(c) Relief is given after the deduction from trading profits of any charges paid net which are not covered by other income.

EXAMPLE 7

Brendan ceases trading on 30 June 2005. His recent trading profits/(losses) are as follows:

	£
year to 31 January 2003	24,700
year to 31 January 2004	12,500
year to 31 January 2005	10,560
5 months to 30 June 2005	(27,300)

He pays charges (net of income tax) and receives other income as follows:

	2002/03	*2003/04*	*2004/05*	*2005/06*
	£	£	£	£
Trade charges (gross amounts)	2,000	2,000	2,000	2,000
Non-trade charges (gross amounts)	500	500	500	500
Other income	nil	nil	nil	nil

Overlap profits of £2,700 arose when Brendan began trading. Calculate the amount of the terminal loss (assuming that no Section 380 claims are made) and show how this may be relieved.

Solution

The calculation of the terminal loss is as follows:

			£
(a) *Losses*:			
	(i) 6/4/05 to 30/6/05	£(27,300) x 3/5	(16,380)
	Overlap relief		(2,700)
	(ii) 1/7/04 to 5/4/05	£10,560 x 7/12 + £(27,300) x 2/5	(4,760)
(b) *Trade charges*:			
	(i) Section 350 assessment in 2005/06		(2,000)
	(ii) Section 350 assessment in 2004/05		nil
Terminal loss			(25,840)

The loss may be relieved as follows:

	2002/03 £	*2003/04* £	*2004/05* £	*2005/06* £
Trading income	24,700	12,500	10,560	nil
Less: Charges	2,500	2,500	2,500	-
	22,200	10,000	8,060	-
Less: Terminal loss relief:				
(i) 2004/05			(8,060)	
(ii) 2003/04		(10,000)		
(iii) 2002/03	(7,780)			
Total income	14,420	-	-	-

Post-cessation expenditure

As a general rule, post-cessation expenditure which was not provided for in the final accounts of a business is relieved against any post-cessation receipts (which are taxed as trading income). If post-cessation receipts are insufficient to absorb post-cessation expenditure, the excess expenditure is normally unrelieved.

However, certain categories of unrelieved post-cessation expenditure may be set against the taxpayer's income and capital gains for the year of assessment in which the expenditure is incurred. The main categories of post-cessation expenditure which may be relieved in this way are:

(a) the costs of remedying defective work done whilst the business was operating, together with associated legal costs and insurance premiums

(b) bad debts which were not provided for in the accounts of the business, together with associated debt collection costs.

Transfer of a business to a company

If the owner of a business transfers that business to a limited company, there is a change in the legal ownership of the business and the vendor is deemed to have ceased trading. As a consequence, any trading losses sustained by the vendor before the date of the transfer cannot be carried forward and set against the company's trading profits.

Relief for these losses might be sought under Section 380 or (if the losses were incurred in the final 12 months of trading) in the form of terminal loss relief, but an alternative is provided by Section 386 of ICTA 1988. Section 386 provides that:

(a) if a business is transferred to a limited company wholly or mainly in exchange for shares in that company, and

(b) the vendor of the business continues to hold those shares, and

(c) the company continues to carry on the transferred business

then the vendor may set unrelieved trading losses against the first available income that he or she receives from the company. The offset is against earned income (e.g. salaries and directors' fees) in priority to dividends.

Losses on shares in unlisted trading companies

An individual who subscribes for shares in an unlisted UK trading company and then incurs a capital loss on the disposal of those shares may claim that this loss should be set against his or her total income as if it were a trading loss being relieved under Section 380. This relief is provided by Section 574 of ICTA 1988 and a Section 574 claim in a year of assessment takes priority over any Section 380 or Section 381 claims made for the same year.

Tax relief under Section 574 is available only if the trading company concerned is of a type which would qualify for the purposes of the Enterprise Investment Scheme (see Chapter 6).

Summary

- Under Section 385 of ICTA 1988, a trading loss may be carried forward and relieved against future profits of the same trade.
- Under Section 380 of ICTA 1988, trading losses may be relieved against the statutory total income of the trader for a specified two-year period.
- Under Section 72 of the Finance Act 1991, any losses remaining unrelieved after a Section 380 claim has been made for a tax year may be set against the trader's capital gains for that year.
- Trade charges which have been the subject of a Section 350 assessment may be carried forward as if they were trading losses.
- On a commencement of trade, a loss incurred in any of the first four tax years may be set against the STI of the previous three tax years.
- On a cessation of trade, a trading loss incurred during the final 12 months of trading may be set against the trading profits of the tax year in which trade ceases and the previous three tax years.
- If a business is transferred to a company, the unrelieved trading losses of the vendor may (subject to certain conditions) be set against the first available income which the vendor receives from the company.

Exercises

11.1 Sally, who has been trading for many years, incurs an adjusted trading loss of £10,000 in the year to 31 December 2005.

(a) What is her trading income for 2005/06?

(b) If she makes no claim under Section 380, how will the loss be relieved?

(c) How will the loss be relieved if she does make a Section 380 claim?

11.2 Jane is self-employed. Her recent adjusted trading profits/(losses) are:

	£
year to 31 May 2002	(18,860)
year to 31 May 2003	4,710
year to 31 May 2004	6,210
year to 31 May 2005	14,810

Jane has other income of £5,000 per annum. Assuming that the trading loss is carried forward under Section 385, calculate her total income for tax years 2002/03 through to 2005/06.

11.3 Marcus begins trading on 1 January 2004 and has the following results:

	Adjusted trading profits/(losses) before capital allowances	*Capital allowances claimed*
	£	£
year to 31 December 2004	12,720	2,460
year to 31 December 2005	(8,480)	1,320

(a) Compute the trading income (before any loss relief) for 2003/04 to 2005/06.

(b) Assuming that Marcus has no other income, show his possible Section 380 claims. Which (if any) of these claims should be recommended?

11.4 Nathan begins trading on 1 October 2003, making up accounts to 31 December each year. His first two sets of accounts show the following adjusted trading losses:

	£
15 months to 31 December 2004	(26,850)
year to 31 December 2005	(25,660)

He has had no other income since becoming self-employed but his income before he started trading was as follows:

	£
2000/01	15,100
2001/02	15,250
2002/03	16,400
2003/04 (to 30 September 2003)	8,450

Assuming that all possible Section 381 claims are made, calculate Nathan's total income for years 2000/01 to 2003/04.

***11.5** Olive ceases trading on 31 May 2005. Her recent adjusted trading profits/(losses) are:

	£
year to 30 June 2001	37,450
year to 30 June 2002	39,190
year to 30 June 2003	16,120
year to 30 June 2004	(6,840)
11 months to 31 May 2005	(36,300)

Her charges (paid net) are as follows:

	2002/03	*2003/04*	*2004/05*	*2005/06*
	£	£	£	£
Trade charges (gross amounts)	1,500	1,500	1,500	1,500
Non-trade charges (gross amounts)	6,750	-	-	-

She had no other income in any of these years. Overlap relief of £4,390 is available. Calculate the terminal loss and show how this would be relieved (assuming that no Section 380 claims are made).

***11.6** Craig began trading on 1 August 2003 and has the following results:

	Adjusted trading profits/(losses) before capital allowances	*Capital allowances claimed*
	£	£
year to 31 July 2004	5,460	1,140
year to 31 July 2005	(17,400)	1,920

Before commencing to trade, Craig had only investment income. He sold all of his investments in July 2004 (realising a large capital gain) so as to raise extra working capital for his own business. His income from investments in recent years has been:

	£
2001/02	3,150
2002/03	3,040
2003/04	1,390
2004/05 (to July 2004)	510

(a) Compute the trading income for 2003/04 to 2005/06.

(b) Explain the loss reliefs available to Craig. Which would you recommend?

Chapter 12

Income from self-employment: Partnerships

Introduction

The purpose of this chapter is to explain the taxation treatment of partnerships. In many ways, a partnership is treated for tax purposes in the same way as a sole trader and the rules given in Chapters 8 to 11 as regards computation of adjusted trading profit, basis periods, capital allowances and trading losses apply to partnerships as well as sole traders. The important new problem which arises when considering partnership taxation is that of calculating each partner's share of the partnership profit and much of this chapter is devoted to that problem.

Limited Liability Partnerships (LLPs) which are regulated by the Limited Liability Partnership Act 2000 and which carry on a trade or profession are generally taxed as a partnership rather than as a company.

Principles of partnership taxation

Under the partnership tax rules, a partnership is not regarded as a separate entity for taxation purposes and the partnership itself is not charged to tax. Instead, the profits of the partnership are allocated between the partners and then each partner is taxed as an individual. In detail, the procedure for each tax year is as follows:

(a) The partnership submits a tax return to HM Revenue and Customs. This return provides information on the profit or loss for the period of account ending in the tax year and gives details of the profit-sharing agreement in force during that period. The return is also used to:

   (i) claim capital allowances for the period of account, both on partnership assets and on individual partners' assets

   (ii) claim relief for any business expenses which have been incurred by partners personally.

(b) The adjusted trading profit or loss of the partnership is calculated in the usual way. Any drawings or other appropriations of profit made by the partners are disallowed. Capital allowances on partnership assets are treated as a trading expense.

(c) The adjusted trading profit or loss is then allocated between the partners according to the profit-sharing agreement in force during the period of account. If the agreement changes during the period, it is necessary to time-apportion the profit or loss, applying the old agreement to the pre-change profit or loss and the new agreement to the post-change profit or loss.

(d) Any capital allowances claimed on an individual partner's assets and any expenses incurred personally by a partner are deducted from the relevant partner's share of the adjusted trading profit or added to that partner's share of the adjusted trading loss.

(e) Partners are then assessed to tax individually, as if each partner's share of the partnership's trading profit or loss had arisen from a trade carried on by that partner alone. In effect, each partner is treated as a sole trader who:

   (i) begins trading when joining the partnership

   (ii) has the same periods of account as the partnership (except that a partner who joins or leaves the partnership part-way through a period of account will have an individual period of account which begins or ends part-way through a partnership period of account)

   (iii) ceases trading when leaving the partnership.

(f) Each partner is solely responsible for the tax due on his or her share of the partnership profit. Partners must include their share of the partnership profit or loss in their own tax returns and in their self-assessment calculations.

EXAMPLE 1

Tom, Dick and Harry begin trading as a partnership on 1 January 2004, sharing profits in the ratio 3:2:1. With effect from 1 January 2005, they agree that Harry should receive a salary of £4,000 per annum, that partners should be entitled to 4% per annum interest on capital and that remaining profits should be shared in the ratio 5:3:2. The adjusted trading profits of the partnership are:

	£
y/e 31/12/04	18,000
y/e 31/12/05	22,000

Fixed capitals are Tom £10,000, Dick £12,000, Harry £16,000. Compute each partner's trading income for 2003/04, 2004/05 and 2005/06.

Solution

The allocation of trading profit for each period of account is:

	Tom	*Dick*	*Harry*	*Total*
	£	£	£	£
y/e 31/12/04				
Profit (shared 3:2:1)	9,000	6,000	3,000	18,000
y/e 31/12/05				
Salary	-	-	4,000	4,000
Interest on capital	400	480	640	1,520
Remainder of profit (shared 5:3:2)	8,240	4,944	3,296	16,480
	8,640	5,424	7,936	22,000

Each partner is treated as a sole trader, commencing trade on 1 January 2004, making up accounts to 31 December and with trading profits for the first two accounting years as shown above. The trading income of each partner is:

Tom

Year	*Basis period*	*Workings*	*Trading income*
			£
2003/04	1/1/04 to 5/4/04	£9,000 x 3/12	2,250
2004/05	y/e 31/12/04		9,000
2005/06	y/e 31/12/05		8,640

Dick

Year	*Basis period*	*Workings*	*Trading income*
			£
2003/04	1/1/04 to 5/4/04	£6,000 x 3/12	1,500
2004/05	y/e 31/12/04		6,000
2005/06	y/e 31/12/05		5,424

Harry

Year	*Basis period*	*Workings*	*Trading income*
			£
2003/04	1/1/04 to 5/4/04	£3,000 x 3/12	750
2004/05	y/e 31/12/04		3,000
2005/06	y/e 31/12/05		7,936

Note:

In each case, the overlap period is from 1 January 2004 to 5 April 2004. Overlap profits are Tom £2,250, Dick £1,500 and Harry £750. These overlap profits will be relieved when the relevant partner leaves the partnership (or on a change of accounting date).

Notional profits and losses

Occasionally, the effect of taking into account partners' salaries and/or interest on capital is to allocate a trading loss to an individual partner, even though the partnership as a whole has made a trading profit. In these circumstances, that partner's share of the trading profit is set to £nil and then his or her "notional loss" is allocated between the remaining partners in proportion to their original profit allocations. A similar procedure is followed if a partner is allocated a "notional profit" in a year in which the partnership as a whole has sustained a trading loss.

EXAMPLE 2

(a) Lock, Stock and Barrel are in partnership, making up accounts to 30 June each year. Their profit-sharing agreement specifies that Lock and Barrel should receive annual salaries of £20,000 and £24,000 respectively and that remaining profits or losses should be divided equally. The partnership has an adjusted trading profit of £26,000 in the year to 30 June 2005. Show how this will be allocated between the partners.

(b) Rod, Pole and Perch are in partnership, also making up accounts to 30 June each year. Their profit-sharing agreement specifies that Perch should receive an annual salary of £25,000 and that remaining profits or losses should be shared in the ratio 3:2:1. The partnership has an adjusted trading loss of £5,000 in the year to 30 June 2005. Show how this will be allocated between the partners.

Solution

(a)

	Lock	*Stock*	*Barrel*	*Total*
	£	£	£	£
Salaries	20,000	-	24,000	44,000
Remainder (£26,000 - £44,000)	(6,000)	(6,000)	(6,000)	(18,000)
	14,000	(6,000)	18,000	26,000
Stock's notional loss divided in the ratio 14,000:18,000	(2,625)	6,000	(3,375)	-
Allocation of trading profit	11,375	-	14,625	26,000

(b)

	Rod	*Pole*	*Perch*	*Total*
	£	£	£	£
Salaries	-	-	25,000	25,000
Remainder (£5,000 + £25,000)	(15,000)	(10,000)	(5,000)	(30,000)
	(15,000)	(10,000)	20,000	(5,000)
Perch's notional profit divided 15,000:10,000	12,000	8,000	(20,000)	-
Allocation of trading loss	(3,000)	(2,000)	-	(5,000)

Change in partnership composition

A change in partnership composition occurs if a new partner joins the partnership or if an existing partner dies or leaves the partnership. Such a change has no effect on those persons who were carrying on the trade before the change (either alone or in partnership) and who continue to carry on the trade after the change (either alone or in partnership). Such persons are taxed on the current year basis as if the change had not taken place. But new partners have commenced trading and are subject to the commencement rules, whilst leaving partners have ceased trading and are subject to the cessation rules.

EXAMPLE 3

Red and White begin trading as a partnership on 1 October 2002, sharing profits equally. On 1 January 2004, they agree to admit Blue as a partner and to share profits in the ratio 3:2:1. The adjusted trading profits of the partnership are:

	£
y/e 30/9/03	21,000
y/e 30/9/04	24,000
y/e 30/9/05	27,000

Compute each partner's trading income for the years 2002/03 through to 2005/06.

Solution

The allocation of trading profit for each period of account is:

	Red	*White*	*Blue*	*Total*
	£	£	£	£
y/e 30/9/03 (shared equally)	10,500	10,500	-	21,000
y/e 30/9/04				
1/10/03 - 31/12/03				
£24,000 x 3/12 (shared equally)	3,000	3,000	-	6,000
1/1/04 - 30/9/04				
£24,000 x 9/12 (shared 3:2:1)	9,000	6,000	3,000	18,000
	12,000	9,000	3,000	24,000
y/e 30/9/05 (shared 3:2:1)	13,500	9,000	4,500	27,000

For tax purposes, each partner is now treated as a sole trader and is assessed on his or her share of the partnership trading profit. The position of each partner is as follows:

(a) Red began trading on 1 October 2002, preparing accounts to 30 September. Each period of account is 12 months long. Profits are £10,500 for the year to 30/9/03, £12,000 for the year to 30/9/04 and £13,500 for the year to 30/9/05.

(b) White began trading on 1 October 2002, preparing accounts to 30 September. Each period of account is 12 months long. Profits are £10,500 for the year to 30/9/03, £9,000 for the year to 30/9/04 and £9,000 for the year to 30/9/05.

(c) Blue began trading on 1 January 2004, preparing accounts to 30 September. The first accounts cover the 9-month period from 1/1/04 to 30/9/04 with profits of £3,000. Profits are £4,500 for the year to 30/9/05.

Each partner's trading income is as follows:

Red

Year	*Basis period*	*Workings*	*Trading income*
			£
2002/03	1/10/02 to 5/4/03	£10,500 x 6/12	5,250
2003/04	y/e 30/9/03		10,500
2004/05	y/e 30/9/04		12,000
2005/06	y/e 30/9/05		13,500

White

Year	*Basis period*	*Workings*	*Trading income*
			£
2002/03	1/10/02 to 5/4/03	£10,500 x 6/12	5,250
2003/04	y/e 30/9/03		10,500
2004/05	y/e 30/9/04		9,000
2005/06	y/e 30/9/05		9,000

Blue

Year	*Basis period*	*Workings*	*Trading income*
			£
2003/04	1/1/04 to 5/4/04	£3,000 x 3/9	1,000
2004/05	1/1/04 to 31/12/04	£3,000 + £4,500 x 3/12	4,125
2005/06	y/e 30/9/05		4,500

Note:

In the case of Red and White, the overlap period is from 1 October 2002 to 5 April 2003 and each partner has overlap profits of £5,250. In the case of Blue, there is an overlap period from 1 January 2004 to 5 April 2004 and another overlap period from 1 October 2004 to 31 December 2004. Blue's overlap profits are £1,000 + £4,500 x 3/12 = £2,125.

Non-trading income

A partnership which has trading income may also have non-trading income. For partnership tax purposes, non-trading income falls into two categories:

(a) **Taxed income**

For this purpose, "taxed income" is defined as income from which tax has been deducted at source (e.g. most interest) and dividends. The amount of any taxed income arising in a period of account is divided between the partners in profit-sharing ratio and then each partner's share is apportioned between tax years and assessed to tax on the actual basis.

It is acceptable to allocate taxed income between tax years on the receipts basis if this would be more appropriate than time-apportionment.

(b) **Untaxed income**

For this purpose, "untaxed income" is defined as non-trading income which is not taxed income (e.g. income from property or interest received gross). The amount of any untaxed income arising in a period of account is allocated between the partners in profit-sharing ratio and is then assessed to tax using *the same basis periods as those used for the trading income*. The basis periods that would normally be applied if the income were received by an individual rather than a partnership are totally ignored. If this treatment results in non-trading income being taxed twice when a partner starts trading, overlap relief is available.

If a partnership does not carry on a trade or profession, the treatment described at (a) above applies to *all* of the partnership's non-trading income.

EXAMPLE 4

Hook, Line and Sinker begin trading as a partnership on 1 July 2003, sharing profits equally. The chosen accounting date is 30 June and the first accounts are made up for the year to 30 June 2004. In addition to its trading income, the partnership has non-trading income as follows:

	y/e 30/6/04	*y/e 30/6/05*
	£	£
Income from property	1,500	1,800
Net bank interest	2,400	3,600

(a) Compute each partner's income from property for tax years 2003/04, 2004/05 and 2005/06.

(b) Compute the gross amount of bank interest on which each partner is taxed in tax years 2003/04 and 2004/05.

Solution

(a) Each partner is allocated property income of £500 in the year to 30 June 2004 and £600 in the year to 30 June 2005. Property income per partner for each tax year is as follows:

Year	*Basis period*	*Workings*	*Property income*
			£
2003/04	1/7/03 to 5/4/04	£500 x 9/12	375
2004/05	y/e 30/6/04		500
2005/06	y/e 30/6/05		600

Each partner is entitled to overlap relief of £375.

(b) Each partner is allocated net bank interest of £800 in the year to 30 June 2004 and £1,200 in the year to 30 June 2005. When grossed-up at 100/80, these figures become £1,000 and £1,500 respectively. The gross amount of bank interest on which each partner is taxed (assuming time-apportionment between the tax years) is as follows:

Year	*Workings*	*Savings income*
		£
2003/04	£1,000 x 9/12	750
2004/05	£1,000 x 3/12 + £1,500 x 9/12	1,375

The remaining 3/12ths of the bank interest received during the year to 30 June 2005 will be taxed in 2005/06, along with the first 9/12ths of any bank interest received in the year to 30 June 2006.

Trading losses

As explained above, a trading loss is allocated between the partners in the same way as a trading profit. Each partner is then entitled to precisely the same loss reliefs as a sole trader (see Chapter 11) with regard to his or her share of the loss.

EXAMPLE 5

Game, Set and Match begin trading in partnership on 1 August 2003, preparing accounts to 31 January each year and sharing profits equally. With effect from 1 March 2004, they agree to share profits in the ratio 1:2:2. The adjusted trading profits/(losses) of the partnership are as follows:

	£
period to 31/1/04	8,610
y/e 31/1/05	4,320
y/e 31/1/06	(7,420)

Compute each partner's trading income for tax years 2003/04, 2004/05 and 2005/06 and explain how the trading loss incurred in the year to 31 January 2006 will be treated.

Solution

The allocation of trading profit or loss for each period of account is:

	Game	*Set*	*Match*	*Total*
	£	£	£	£
period to 31/1/04 (shared equally)	2,870	2,870	2,870	8,610
y/e 31/1/05				
1/2/04 - 28/2/04				
£4,320 x 1/12 (shared equally)	120	120	120	360
1/3/04 - 31/1/05				
£4,320 x 11/12 (shared 1:2:2)	792	1,584	1,584	3,960
	912	1,704	1,704	4,320
y/e 31/1/06 (shared 1:2:2)	(1,484)	(2,968)	(2,968)	(7,420)

Each partner's trading income is as follows:

Game

Year	*Basis period*	*Workings*	*Trading income*
			£
2003/04	1/8/03 to 5/4/04	£2,870 + £912 x 2/12	3,022
2004/05	y/e 31/1/05		912
2005/06	y/e 31/1/06		nil

Set

Year	*Basis period*	*Workings*	*Trading income*
			£
2003/04	1/8/03 to 5/4/04	£2,870 + £1,704 x 2/12	3,154
2004/05	y/e 31/1/05		1,704
2005/06	y/e 31/1/06		nil

Match

Year	*Basis period*	*Workings*	*Trading income*
			£
2003/04	1/8/03 to 5/4/04	£2,870 + £1,704 x 2/12	3,154
2004/05	y/e 31/1/05		1,704
2005/06	y/e 31/1/06		nil

Notes:

(i) The basis period for 2003/04 for each partner includes two months out of the year to 31 January 2005. The profit for these two months is calculated by taking 2/12ths of the partner's profit for that year. In the case of Game (for example) it would be wrong to take £120 + 1/11 x £792 as the profit of the period from 1/2/04 to 5/4/04.

(ii) Each partner has overlap profits, calculated in the usual way.

(iii) Each partner may choose individually how to relieve his or her share of the trading loss incurred in the basis period for 2005/06. Possibilities include carrying the loss forward under S385, a S380 claim for 2005/06 and/or 2004/05 and a S381 claim for 2002/03, 2003/04 and 2004/05.

Summary

- Under the partnership tax rules, each partner is taxed individually on his or her share of the partnership profit. Each partner is solely responsible for his or her tax liability.
- The adjusted trading profit of a partnership is allocated between the partners in accordance with the profit-sharing agreement for the period of account in which the profit arises. Notional profits and losses allocated to a partner are redistributed among the remaining partners.
- In effect, each partner is treated as a sole trader who begins trading when joining the partnership, has the same accounting dates as the partnership and ceases trading when leaving the partnership.
- The tax treatment of the non-trading income of a partnership depends upon whether the income ranks as taxed income or untaxed income and whether or not the partnership also has trading income.
- The trading losses of a partnership are allocated between the partners in the same way as trading profits. Each partner may then choose individually how to relieve his or her share of the loss.

Exercises

12.1 Nickleby, Copperfield and Drood have traded as equal partners for many years, making up accounts to 31 December each year. As from 1 April 2005 they agree to share profits in the ratio 1:2:2. The adjusted trading profit for the year to 31 December 2005 is £18,300. Show how this profit is allocated between the partners.

12.2 Pickwick, Snodgrass and Tupman are in partnership, making up accounts to 31 March annually. Each partner receives 6% interest on fixed capital, Pickwick and Tupman each receive an annual salary of £8,000 and remaining profits or losses are divided equally. Fixed capitals are Pickwick £12,000, Snodgrass £20,000 and Tupman £10,000. The adjusted trading profit for the year to 31 March 2006 is £14,500. Show how this profit is allocated between the partners.

12.3 Dodson and Fogg began trading in equal partnership on 1 July 2002. On 1 July 2003, they admitted Jackson as a partner and agreed to share profits in the ratio 5:4:1. The adjusted trading profits of the partnership are:

	£
year to 30 June 2003	17,000
year to 30 June 2004	22,000
year to 30 June 2005	29,000

Compute each partner's trading income for 2002/03 through to 2005/06.

12.4 Wardle, Jingle and Trotter began trading on 1 October 2003, preparing accounts to 30 September each year and sharing profits in the ratio 7:2:1. Results for the first two years of trading are as follows:

	y/e 30/9/04	*y/e 30/9/05*
	£	£
Trading profit	23,490	27,310
Interest received gross	2,000	2,200
Interest received net (net amount received)	1,000	1,088

(a) Compute each partner's trading income for 2003/04, 2004/05 and 2005/06.

(b) Compute each partner's interest received gross for 2003/04, 2004/05 and 2005/06.

(c) Compute the gross amount of taxed interest on which each partner is charged to tax in 2004/05.

***12.5** Cluppins and Raddle form a partnership on 1 November 2001, preparing accounts to 31 May each year. Bardell is admitted as a partner on 1 January 2003. Cluppins leaves the partnership on 28 February 2004 and Winkle is admitted as a partner on 1 March 2004.

Profits and losses are shared as follows:

Cluppins and Raddle	1:2
Cluppins, Raddle and Bardell	7:8:5
Raddle, Bardell and Winkle	4:3:1

Adjusted trading profits are:

	£
1 November 2001 to 31 May 2002	6,000
year to 31 May 2003	12,000
year to 31 May 2004	3,000
year to 31 May 2005	8,000

Calculate each partner's trading income for 2001/02 through to 2005/06, identifying any overlap periods and profits.

Chapter 13

Pension schemes

Introduction

The most tax-efficient way of providing for a pension is to make contributions into an approved pension scheme. Employees might join an occupational pension scheme or a personal pension scheme. Self-employed people might join a personal pension scheme or may have a retirement annuity contract. The purpose of this chapter is to explain the tax reliefs available in relation to each of these ways of providing for a pension.

This chapter explains the current tax treatment of pension contributions. However, the Government has announced that the present system will be replaced by a new set of rules as from 6 April 2006. A very brief introduction to the new rules is given at the end of this chapter.

Occupational pension schemes

An occupational pension (or "superannuation") scheme is a pension scheme set up by an employer for the benefit of employees. The employer makes contributions to the scheme and employees usually also make contributions calculated as a percentage of their earnings, though some employers operate non-contributory schemes.

Occupational pension schemes may be "defined benefit" or "defined contribution" schemes. In a defined benefit scheme, the pension payable on retirement is based upon the employee's final salary. In a defined contribution ("money purchase") scheme, the contributions made during an employee's working life are used to build up a fund which is then used to provide a pension on retirement. The size of the pension depends upon the size of this fund and is not linked to the employee's final salary.

In order for an occupational pension scheme to be approved by HM Revenue and Customs it is necessary that the following conditions should be satisfied:

(a) The sole purpose of the scheme must be to provide benefits on retirement (or death) to employees or to their widows, widowers and dependants.

(b) Employees' pensions must normally start at some time between the ages of 60 and 75, with no distinction made between men and women.

(c) The employer must make contributions into the scheme.

(d) Any contributions made by employees must be non-returnable.

(e) The maximum pension payable to an employee on retirement must not exceed the product of the number of years of service worked by the employee (up to a maximum of 40) and 1/60th of the employee's average annual remuneration over the final three years of service. This gives a maximum pension equal to two-thirds of final remuneration.

(f) A lump sum may be payable on retirement of no greater than 3/80ths of final remuneration for each year of service up to 40 years, giving a maximum lump sum equal to 150% of final remuneration.

If a scheme satisfies these criteria then the *tax consequences* are as follows:

(a) An employee may contribute up to 15% of earnings into the scheme and these contributions are deductible when computing the employee's income from employment (see Chapter 7). For this purpose, earnings include benefits in kind.

(b) The employer's contributions on behalf of an employee are not treated as part of the employee's earnings.

(c) The contributions *actually paid* by the employer during a period of account are allowable when computing the employer's trading income which is charged to income tax (see Chapter 8) or corporation tax (see Chapter 23).

(d) The scheme may enable employees to be "contracted out" of the State Second Pension (S2P) which was formerly known as the State Earnings-Related Pension Scheme (SERPS). In this case, the employee's and employer's National Insurance contributions are both reduced (see Chapter 15).

For approved schemes established after 13 March 1989 and for employees joining older schemes after 31 May 1989, the maximum contributions which an employee can make in a tax year are restricted by reference to the "earnings cap". Maximum contributions are calculated according to the employee's actual earnings for the year or the earnings cap, whichever is the lower. For 2005/06 the earnings cap is £105,600.

EXAMPLE 1

Gordon joined his employer's approved occupational pension scheme in 1996. Calculate the maximum pension contributions which he could make in 2005/06 if his earnings for the year were:

(a) £50,000 (b) £250,000.

Solution

(a) Gordon could contribute no more than 15% of £50,000 = £7,500.

(b) Gordon could contribute no more than 15% of £105,600 = £15,840.

Retirement annuities and personal pensions

Subject to certain conditions (see below) tax relief is available on premiums paid in respect of a *retirement annuity contract* or a *personal pension scheme*.

Retirement annuity contracts

Retirement annuities were for many years the main means by which the self-employed and certain employees were able to provide for their retirement. The following persons were eligible to take out a retirement annuity contract:

(a) the self-employed
(b) employees in non-pensionable employment
(c) employees who chose to opt out of their employer's occupational pension scheme (if this was permitted by the employer).

Individuals taking out a retirement annuity contract agreed to pay regular premiums in order to provide for a pension which would commence at some time between the ages of 60 and 75. The premiums paid attracted tax relief.

With effect from 1 July 1988 (the date on which personal pension schemes were introduced) no new retirement annuity contracts can be taken out. However, there are many such contracts still in existence which were taken out on or before 30 June 1988 and the premiums paid in relation to such contracts continue to attract tax relief.

Personal pension schemes

Personal pension schemes were introduced on 1 July 1988 and are similar in some ways to retirement annuities. As before, premiums may be paid by the self-employed or by employees in order to provide for a pension in later life and these premiums attract tax relief. The main differences between retirement annuity contracts and personal pension schemes are as follows:

(a) Benefits under a personal pension scheme may be taken from the age of 50.

(b) Employees are now legally entitled to opt out of their employer's occupational scheme if they so wish and join a personal pension scheme instead.

(c) If an employee joins a personal pension scheme, the employer may also make contributions to this scheme and these contributions do not rank as part of the employee's taxable earnings. (It was not possible for employers to contribute towards an employee's retirement annuity).

(d) An employee who belongs to an occupational scheme may concurrently make contributions to a personal pension scheme, so long as he/she is not a controlling director and does not earn more than £30,000 per annum. In these circumstances, the maximum annual contributions which can be made to the personal pension scheme by employee and employer combined cannot exceed £3,600.

(e) An individual who is neither employed nor self-employed may join a personal pension scheme and obtain tax relief (within limits) on the premiums paid.

Stakeholder pension schemes

A new type of personal pension known as a "stakeholder pension" was introduced on 6 April 2001. Stakeholder pension schemes are designed to be simple, low-cost schemes intended primarily for individuals on low to middle incomes who have no access to an occupational scheme. Stakeholder pensions are available either through employers or directly from pension scheme providers. Employers with five or more employees who do not offer an occupational pension scheme are required to facilitate access to stakeholder pensions for their employees by designating a scheme, deducting contributions from pay for the employees who join the scheme and forwarding those contributions to the scheme provider.

The tax regime which applies to personal pension schemes in general (see below) applies also to stakeholder schemes. In fact, this tax regime applies to money purchase occupational pension schemes as well, if employers opt into the regime.

Relief for premiums paid

Tax relief on premiums paid in relation to an approved retirement annuity contract or personal pension scheme is given as follows:

(a) **Retirement annuity contracts**. The premiums paid by an individual in a tax year attract tax relief by deduction from the individual's "net relevant earnings" (see below) for that year. The premiums are paid gross. The premiums which attract tax relief cannot exceed an annual maximum which depends upon the individual's age and net relevant earnings (see below).

(b) **Personal pension schemes**. Premiums paid into a personal pension scheme by an individual are paid net of basic rate tax. The individual's basic rate band is then extended by the gross amount of the premiums paid in the tax year, so providing relief at the higher rate to higher rate taxpayers. The basic rate tax deducted from premiums at source is *not* clawed back from those who do not pay tax at the basic rate. The premiums which attract tax relief (including any employer contributions in the case of an employee) cannot exceed an annual maximum which depends to some extent upon the individual's age and net relevant earnings (see below).

When determining a taxpayer's entitlement to age-related personal allowances (see Chapter 3) the taxpayer's statutory total income is deemed *for this purpose only* to be reduced by the gross amount of any personal pension contributions made by the taxpayer.

Net relevant earnings

An employee's "net relevant earnings" (NRE) for a tax year are equal to the employee's earnings from non-pensionable employment for that year (including benefits in kind) less allowable expenses.

A self-employed person's net relevant earnings for a tax year are defined as that person's trading income for the year, plus any income arising from furnished holiday lettings (see Chapter 5) and less:

(a) loss reliefs claimed in the year and set against trading income

(b) trade charges paid in the year (e.g. patent royalties) to the extent that they cannot be set against the individual's unearned income.

If, in a given tax year, a trading loss is relieved against non-trading income (usually by virtue of a Section 380 claim) the amount relieved against non-trading income has no effect on that year's NRE but reduces the NRE of the following year instead. If the following year's earnings are insufficient to absorb the whole of the loss, any balance is carried forward to subsequent years.

EXAMPLE 2

Wesley is self-employed. His trading income for 2005/06 is £32,700. He has losses brought forward under Section 385 of £15,200 and pays trade charges during the year of £500. His only other income for 2005/06 is £200 of interest arising on a National Savings Bank investment account. Calculate his net relevant earnings for 2005/06.

Solution

	£	£
Trading income		32,700
Less: Loss relief	15,200	
Excess of trade charges over unearned income (£500 - £200)	300	15,500
Net relevant earnings for 2005/06		17,200

Maximum premiums allowable

As mentioned earlier, there is an upper limit on the amount of retirement annuity or personal pension premiums which can attract tax relief in a tax year.

(a) **Retirement annuity contracts**. The maximum contributions which can attract tax relief in a tax year are equal to a percentage of NRE which depends upon the individual's age at the start of the year, according to the following table:

Age at start of tax year	*% of NRE*
Up to 50	17.5
51-55	20
56-60	22.5
Over 60	27.5

The earnings cap which applies to occupational pension schemes and to personal pension schemes (see below) does not apply to retirement annuity contracts.

(b) **Personal pension schemes**. The maximum contributions which can attract tax relief in a tax year are equal to *the greater of £3,600 and a percentage of NRE* as given by the following table:

Age at start of tax year	*% of NRE*
Up to 35	17.5
36-45	20
46-50	25
51-55	30
56-60	35
Over 60	40

The NRE figure to which these percentages are applied is *the highest NRE of the current year and the previous five years*. If earnings cease, any contributions made in the year of cessation and the next five years continue to attract tax relief, based upon the highest NRE for the year of cessation and for the previous five years.

The maximum NRE to which the relevant percentage can be applied in any tax year is equal to the earnings cap (£105,600 for 2005/06).

EXAMPLE 3

Calculate the maximum relief available to each of the following individuals in respect of their retirement annuity or personal pension premiums in 2005/06. Assume in each case that the NRE for each of the previous five years was less than the NRE for 2005/06.

(a) Alana was born on 4 May 1969. She is a member of a personal pension scheme and her net relevant earnings for 2005/06 are £27,000.

(b) Bruce was born on 14 August 1947. He is a member of a personal pension scheme and his net relevant earnings for 2005/06 are £10,000.

(c) Charlotte was born on 24 December 1943. She is a member of a personal pension scheme and her net relevant earnings for 2005/06 are £110,000.

(d) Diane was born on 12 January 1953. She has a retirement annuity contract and her net relevant earnings for 2005/06 are £120,000.

Solution

(a) Alana is aged 35 at the start of tax year 2005/06. The maximum relief to which she is entitled is £4,725 (17.5% of £27,000).

(b) Bruce is aged 57 at the start of tax year 2005/06. The maximum relief to which he is entitled is £3,600 (greater than 35% of £10,000).

(c) Charlotte is aged 61 at the start of tax year 2005/06. Her net relevant earnings exceed the earnings cap, so the maximum relief to which she is entitled is £42,240 (40% of £105,600).

(d) Diane is aged 52 at the start of tax year 2005/06. The earnings cap does not apply to retirement annuities so the maximum relief to which she is entitled is £24,000 (20% of £120,000).

Premiums carried back

An individual may elect that retirement annuity or personal pension premiums should be treated as if they had been paid in an earlier tax year, as follows:

(a) **Retirement annuity contracts**. Retirement annuity premiums paid in a tax year may be carried back wholly or partly to the previous tax year or (if there are no net relevant earnings in that year) to the year before that. An election to this effect must be made by 31 January following the end of the tax year in which the premiums are paid.

(b) **Personal pension schemes**. Personal pension premiums paid by 31 January in a tax year may be carried back wholly or partly to the previous tax year. An election to this effect must be made on or before the date that the premiums are paid.

A "carry-back" election might be made if the premiums paid in a tax year exceed the allowable maximum for that year whilst the premiums paid in the previous year were less than the maximum. An election might also be made if the individual's marginal rate of income tax was higher in the previous tax year than in the current year, so that carrying back premiums to the previous year will save tax.

EXAMPLE 4

Jill was born in March 1965. She is a member of a personal pension scheme, paying net premiums of £3,822 in 2004/05 and £4,368 in 2005/06. Her net relevant earnings (which have risen every year since 1999/00) were £26,400 in 2004/05 and £27,100 in 2005/06. Can she use the carry-back election to obtain tax relief on all of her 2005/06 personal pension premiums?

Solution

In 2004/05 Jill's maximum allowable premiums are £5,280 (20% of £26,400) and so her premiums for that year of £4,900 (£3,822 x 100/78) are allowable in full.

In 2005/06 her maximum allowable premiums are £5,420 (20% of £27,100) and so her premiums for that year of £5,600 (£4,368 x 100/78) exceed the maximum by £180. This £180 cannot be relieved in 2005/06.

However, so long as at least £180 of her 2005/06 premiums are paid by 31 January 2006 and she makes the carry-back election on or before the date of payment, she can elect to treat the £180 as if it had been paid in 2004/05. This gives relief on £5,080 in 2004/05 (still within the maximum allowable for that year) and on £5,420 in 2005/06. In this way tax relief can be obtained on the entire £10,500 of premiums paid in 2004/05 and 2005/06.

EXAMPLE 5

Eric was born on 1 January 1972. His net relevant earnings were £50,000 in 2004/05 (this was higher than in any of the previous five tax years) and £18,000 in 2005/06. He pays £1,404 per annum (net) into a personal pension scheme. Show the alternative ways in which tax relief may be given on the premiums paid in 2004/05 and 2005/06.

Solution

Eric's allowable percentage in 2004/05 and 2005/06 is 17.5%. The maximum premiums allowable are therefore £8,750 (17.5% of £50,000) in each year, since the NRE figure which is used to calculate the allowable maximum for a year is the highest of the current year and the previous five years. The premiums of £1,800 (£1,404 x 100/78) paid in each year are beneath each year's maximum, so Eric does not need to make a carry-back election in order to obtain tax relief on both years' premiums.

However, he could elect that any premiums paid between 6 April 2005 and 31 January 2006 inclusive should be treated as if they were paid in 2004/05. Since he is presumably a 40% taxpayer in 2004/05 (but not in 2005/06) this would provide a tax saving.

Retirement annuity relief carried forward

If the retirement annuity premiums paid by an individual in a tax year are less than the allowable maximum for that year, there is "unused relief" equal to the difference between the premiums actually paid and the maximum premiums that could have been allowed. Unused relief represents a wasted opportunity to obtain tax relief but it may not be lost irretrievably. In general, unused relief can be carried forward for up to six tax years and used to relieve excess premiums paid during those six years. Note that:

(a) *The carry-forward of unused relief applies only to retirement annuity contracts, not to personal pension schemes.*

(b) Unused relief brought forward from previous years can only be used if the current year's maximum relief has already been used in full.

(c) Unused relief brought forward from earlier years is used in preference to unused relief brought forward from later years (a first-in, first-out basis).

(d) With the introduction of a new tax regime for pension schemes as from 6 April 2006 (see later in this chapter) it is not possible to carry forward unused retirement annuity relief to tax year 2006/07 or later years.

EXAMPLE 6

Freda was born in June 1962 and has a retirement annuity contract. Her net relevant earnings for 2004/05 were £15,000. Calculate the amount of Freda's unused relief in 2004/05 if premiums paid in the year were:

(a) £1,500

(b) £2,625

(c) £3,000.

Solution

Freda's allowable percentage in 2004/05 was 17.5%. The maximum premiums allowable in 2004/05 were therefore £2,625 (17.5% of £15,000).

(a) If Freda paid premiums in the year of £1,500 then the entire £1,500 was allowable for tax purposes and she had unused relief of £1,125 (£2,625 - £1,500).

(b) If Freda paid premiums of £2,625 then she paid precisely the maximum allowable premiums. The entire £2,625 was allowable for tax purposes and she had no unused relief.

(c) If Freda paid premiums of £3,000 then she paid more than the allowable maximum. Only £2,625 was allowable and she had no unused relief for the year. (She might have elected to carry back the excess premiums of £375 to 2003/04).

EXAMPLE 7

Sharon is 58 years old and pays retirement annuity premiums of £2,380 in 2005/06. Her net relevant earnings for the year are £9,600. She has unused relief of £250 brought forward from 1999/00 and £400 brought forward from 2002/03. Compute the allowable premiums in 2005/06.

Solution

Sharon's maximum allowable premiums for 2005/06 are £2,160 (22.5% of £9,600). Since the premiums paid exceed this maximum by £220 she would normally have excess premiums of £220 which would not attract tax relief (unless they could be carried back to the previous year).

However, £220 of the unused relief brought forward from 1999/00 (used in preference to the more recent unused relief from 2002/03) may be used to relieve this shortfall, so ensuring that the full £2,380 is allowed in 2005/06.

The remaining £30 of the 1999/00 unused relief is now too old to carry forward and the opportunity to use this relief is lost forever. The £400 of unused relief arising in 2002/03 is also lost, since unused relief cannot be carried forward to 2006/07 or a later year.

Choice between carry-back and carry-forward

An individual with a retirement annuity contract may be faced with a choice between:

(a) carrying excess premiums back to the previous tax year
(b) relieving excess premiums by means of unused relief brought forward from the previous six tax years.

In this situation it is necessary to consider the consequences of each choice and to select the most tax-effective alternative.

EXAMPLE 8

Stuart was born in March 1952 and had net relevant earnings of £46,000 in 2004/05. He paid retirement annuity premiums of £2,350 in the year and he had no unused relief brought forward from previous years.

(a) How much unused relief did Stuart have in 2004/05?

(b) If his net relevant earnings for 2005/06 decrease to £7,200 and the premiums paid remain the same as in 2004/05, calculate his allowable premiums in that year (ignore for a moment the possibility of carrying back premiums from 2005/06 to 2004/05).

(c) Would the carry-back provisions be of any use to Stuart?

Solution

(a) Maximum allowable premiums in 2004/05 for a taxpayer of Stuart's age were 20% of NRE i.e. £9,200. He paid only £2,350 in the year, so the full £2,350 was allowable and there was unused relief of £6,850.

(b) 20% of Stuart's NRE in 2005/06 amounts to only £1,440, leaving excess premiums of £910. However, he has unused relief of £6,850 to bring forward from 2004/05 so £910 of this can be used to relieve the excess premiums. The remainder of the unused relief (£5,940) is lost. The situation in 2004/05 and 2005/06 is as follows:

	2004/05	*2005/06*
	£	£
NRE	46,000	7,200
Less: allowable premiums	2,350	2,350
Taxable earnings	43,650	4,850

(c) As an alternative to carrying forward unused relief from 2004/05 and using it to relieve excess premiums paid in 2005/06, Stuart could elect to treat £910 of his premiums paid in 2005/06 as if they had been paid in 2004/05. If he did this, the situation would be as follows:

	2004/05	*2005/06*
	£	£
NRE	46,000	7,200
Less: allowable premiums	3,260	1,440
Taxable earnings	42,740	5,760

As before, the total of the taxable earnings in the two years is £48,500. However, the way in which the £48,500 is split between the two years is different and, in particular, the carry-back alternative reduces Stuart's taxable earnings in 2004/05, a year in which he was probably a higher rate taxpayer. In fact it would be beneficial for Stuart to carry back the whole of the £2,350 paid in 2005/06, not just the excess premium of £910.

Additional voluntary contributions

Employees who belong to an occupational pension scheme can obtain tax relief on contributions made to a form of pension scheme known as a "free standing additional voluntary contributions" (FSAVC) scheme. An employee would contribute to such a scheme in order to provide for an extra pension, additional to the pension payable from the employer's scheme. Contributions are limited to a maximum of 15% of earnings up to the earnings cap (£105,600 for 2005/06) less any contributions made to the occupational pension scheme.

New pension scheme rules from April 2006

At present, there are eight different tax regimes governing pension schemes of various types, each with its own complex set of rules regarding the amounts that individuals may contribute and the benefits that may be obtained on retirement. The main features of some of these regimes are explained above. However, as from 6 April 2006, these complex rules will be replaced by a simplified tax regime which will apply to all tax-registered pension schemes. Very briefly, the key elements of the new regime are as follows:

(a) The pension contributions made by an individual will no longer be limited to a percentage of capped earnings. An individual will be able to make unlimited pension contributions. Tax relief will be given on contributions of up to the higher of 100% of relevant earnings and £3,600. Employers will also be able to make unlimited contributions to an employee's pension scheme and will be given tax relief on the full amount paid.

(b) However, there will be an annual limit on tax-privileged contributions to defined contribution schemes and increases in the value of defined benefit schemes. The individual will be taxed at 40% on contributions or increases in excess of the annual allowance (set initially at £215,000). Contributions made by an individual in excess of 100% of earnings will not attract tax relief and so will not count towards the annual allowance.

(c) Furthermore, there will be a lifetime limit (set initially at £1.5 million) on the amount of pension savings that can benefit from tax relief. If this limit is exceeded, there will be a 25% tax charge on the excess. This tax charge will rise to 55% if the excess is taken by the individual as a lump sum.

(d) The minimum pension age will rise from 50 to 55 by 2010.

Summary

- Contributions of up to 15% of earnings made by an employee to an approved occupational pension scheme are allowable against employment income.
- Subject to certain conditions, tax relief is available on premiums paid to secure a retirement annuity or personal pension. The maximum allowable premium in any tax year generally depends upon the taxpayer's age at the start of the year and earnings during the year. In the case of personal pension schemes, premiums of up to £3,600 per year are allowable regardless of age and earnings.
- Subject to certain conditions, retirement annuity or personal pension premiums paid in a tax year may be treated as if paid in the previous year.
- If the retirement annuity premiums paid in a tax year are less than the maximum amount that could have been relieved, the unused relief may be carried forward and used to relieve excess premiums for up to six years. However, unused relief may not be carried forward to 2006/07 or later years.
- An employee belonging to an occupational pension scheme may obtain tax relief on premiums paid to a free standing additional voluntary contributions scheme.
- As from 6 April 2006, a new simplified tax regime will apply to all tax-registered pension schemes.

Exercises

13.1 List the main conditions which must be satisfied in order for an occupational pension scheme to be approved by HM Revenue and Customs and explain the taxation consequences of a scheme being approved.

13.2 Calculate the maximum contribution which could normally be made to an occupational pension scheme in 2005/06 by an employee with earnings in the year of:

(a) £20,000 (b) £120,000.

13.3 Explain the meaning of the term "net relevant earnings".

13.4 Karen is self-employed and was born on 7 April 1944. Her trading income for 2005/06 is £22,450. She has losses brought forward under Section 385 of £1,200 and trade charges for the year of £250. She has no other income. Assuming that her net relevant earnings in the previous five years are less than those in 2005/06, calculate the maximum allowable personal pension premium which Karen could pay in 2005/06.

13.5 Damon is self-employed and was born on 10 July 1953. He has net relevant earnings and retirement annuity premiums as follows:

	NRE	*Premiums paid*
	£	£
2003/04	17,200	2,500
2004/05	18,400	2,600
2005/06	5,600	2,600

He has unused relief from 1998/99 of £400. Assuming that no carry-back elections are made, show how relief would be given for the retirement annuity premiums.

***13.6** Irma is self-employed and was born in 1947. Her trading income for 2005/06 is £21,400 and she pays a trade charge of £300. During the year she also pays personal pension premiums of £6,240 (net). Her only other income in 2005/06 comprises bank interest (net) of £27,208.

Calculate Irma's 2005/06 income tax liability, assuming that her net relevant earnings in the previous five years are less than those in 2005/06.

Chapter 14

Payment of income tax, surcharges, interest and penalties

Introduction

Interest is charged on income tax which is paid late. Conversely, interest may be added to repayments of income tax. The main purpose of this chapter is to identify the dates on which income tax is payable and to explain how the interest due on underpaid or overpaid tax is calculated. This chapter also considers financial penalties to which a taxpayer may become liable as a consequence of non-compliance with tax law.

Payment of income tax

Under the Self Assessment system (see Chapter 1) income tax which is not deducted at source is payable as follows:

(a) The taxpayer's income tax liability for the year in relation to all sources of income is aggregated. This liability is increased by the amount of any Class 4 National Insurance contributions which are due for the year (see Chapter 15).

(b) Payments on account of the total liability (POAs) are due on 31 January in the tax year and on 31 July following the end of the tax year. For example, the POAs for 2005/06 are due on 31 January 2006 and 31 July 2006. Each POA is normally equal to 50% of the taxpayer's liability to income tax and Class 4 NICs for the *previous* tax year, less any tax paid by deduction at source. For this purpose, the term "deduction at source" includes tax paid via the PAYE system and any tax satisfied by the set-off of tax credits, as well as tax deducted at source from bank interest etc. Note that:

   (i) POAs are not required if the taxpayer's total liability to income tax and Class 4 NICs for the preceding year (less tax deducted at source) was beneath a specified "de minimis" limit, currently set at £500.

(ii) POAs are also not required if more than 80% of the taxpayer's liability to income tax and Class 4 NICs for the previous year was satisfied by deduction of tax at source.

(iii) The taxpayer may make a claim to reduce (or cancel) POAs by contacting HM Revenue and Customs and stating the grounds for the claim. Suitable grounds for a claim to reduce or cancel POAs would be the taxpayer's belief that the liability for the year in question will be less than in the previous year. HMRC cannot reject such a claim but there are penalties for making a claim fraudulently or negligently (see below).

(c) A balancing payment (or repayment) is due on 31 January following the end of the tax year. For example, the balancing payment for 2005/06 is due on 31 January 2007. But note that:

(i) If a tax return is issued late (i.e. after 31 October following the end of the tax year to which it relates) and this has not been caused by the taxpayer's failure to notify his or her chargeability to tax, the balancing payment is due three months after the issue date of the return.

(ii) If a self-assessment is amended by the taxpayer or by HMRC (or if a discovery assessment is raised) any additional amount payable is due 30 days after the date of its notification to the taxpayer or on 31 January following the end of the tax year, whichever is the later. However, this rule does *not* defer the date from which interest accrues on the additional tax.

Interest is always charged if a payment is late and surcharges may also be imposed (see below). Taxpayers receive regular statements of account from HMRC showing the amounts of tax and Class 4 NICs payable, the amounts paid to date and the amounts of any interest and surcharges.

EXAMPLE 1

Warren's total liability to income tax and Class 4 NICs for 2004/05 was £17,200, of which £14,500 was paid by deduction at source. His total liability for 2005/06 is £19,300, of which £16,100 is paid by deduction at source. State the dates on which Warren is required to pay his 2005/06 income tax and Class 4 NICs and compute the amount payable on each date.

Solution

Over 80% of Warren's total liability for 2004/05 was paid by deduction at source and so no POAs are required for 2005/06. His 2005/06 liability of £3,200 (£19,300 - £16,100) is payable on 31 January 2007.

EXAMPLE 2

In 2004/05, Barbara's total liability to income tax and Class 4 NICs was £26,000, of which £4,000 was paid by deduction at source. Her total liability for 2005/06 is £34,000, of which £5,000 is paid by deduction at source. State the dates on which Barbara is required to pay her 2005/06 income tax and Class 4 NICs and compute the amount payable on each date.

Solution

(i) 31 January 2006, POA £11,000 (50% of (£26,000 - £4,000))

(ii) 31 July 2006, POA £11,000

(iii) 31 January 2007, balancing payment £7,000 (£34,000 - £5,000 - POAs £22,000).

Surcharges

In addition to any interest due on tax paid late (see below), the taxpayer may also be required to pay a "surcharge". The surcharges scheme operates as follows:

(a) If all or part of a balancing payment remains unpaid more than 28 days after the due date, a surcharge arises equal to 5% of the amount unpaid.

(b) If a self-assessment is amended (or a discovery assessment is raised) and any of the additional amount which becomes payable remains unpaid more than 28 days after the due date, a surcharge arises equal to 5% of the amount unpaid.

(c) Any amount that remains unpaid more than six months after the due date is subject to a further 5% surcharge.

(d) Surcharges are payable 30 days after the date on which they are imposed.

Note that the surcharges scheme does *not* apply to POAs.

EXAMPLE 3

Continuing the above example, Barbara made the following payments for 2005/06:

	£
31 January 2006	11,000
1 September 2006	11,000
31 January 2007	6,000
1 September 2007	1,000

Compute the surcharges (if any) which would be imposed.

Solution

(i) The first POA is paid in full and on time.

(ii) The second POA is paid in full but 32 days late. However, late POAs do not attract surcharges.

(iii) £1,000 of the balancing payment is paid over six months late. A first surcharge of £50 (£1,000 x 5%) will be imposed on 1 March 2007 (payable 31 March 2007) and another surcharge of £50 will be imposed on 1 August 2007 (payable 31 August 2007).

Interest on income tax

Under the Self Assessment system, interest is charged on all late payments of income tax and Class 4 NICs. Interest is also charged if a surcharge is paid late. On the other hand, interest is paid to the taxpayer when repayments of overpaid income tax and Class 4 NICs are made.

Interest on overdue income tax

Interest charged on overdue income tax and Class 4 NICs is calculated as follows:

(a) In the case of late POAs and balancing payments, interest runs from the due date of payment up to the date on which the tax is actually paid.

(b) In the case of discovery assessments and amendments to self-assessments, interest normally runs from the *annual filing date* for the relevant tax year (i.e. 31 January following the tax year) even though the tax itself might not be due for payment until a later date.

(c) Interest on a surcharge runs from the due date of payment of the surcharge (i.e. 30 days after its imposition).

(d) If a taxpayer submits a tax return by the 30 September deadline (see Chapter 1) and asks HM Revenue and Customs to calculate the tax due, but HMRC fails to issue a statement of account in time for the first POA to be made on the usual due date (31 January), interest on this POA starts to run 30 days after the issue date of the statement of account.

(e) Interest is calculated on a daily basis. Apparently it is HMRC practice to use a denominator of 366 in such calculations, whether or not a leap year is involved.

EXAMPLE 4

Again continuing the above example, calculate the total interest payable by Barbara for 2005/06, assuming that the two surcharges are both paid on 29 September 2007 and that interest is charged at 7.5% per annum.

Solution

(i) Interest on the second POA is £72.13 (£11,000 x 7.5% x 32/366).

(ii) Interest on the final £1,000 of the balancing payment (paid 213 days late) is £43.65 (£1,000 x 7.5% x 213/366).

(iii) Interest on the first surcharge (paid 182 days late) is £1.86 (£50 x 7.5% x 182/366).

(iv) Interest on the second surcharge (paid 29 days late) is £0.30 (£50 x 7.5% x 29/366).

Total interest due is £117.94 (£72.13 + £43.65 + £1.86 + £0.30).

Interest on overpaid income tax

Repayments of overpaid income tax and Class 4 NICs attract interest. This is calculated at a lower rate than the rate of interest charged on overdue income tax but is itself exempt from income tax. Interest on overpaid income tax and Class 4 NICs (known as "repayment supplement") runs from the "relevant time" to the date on which repayment is made to the taxpayer. The relevant time is:

(a) as regards POAs and any other payments of income tax and Class 4 NICs (other than tax deducted at source), the date of payment

(b) as regards income tax deducted at source, 31 January following the tax year for which the tax is deducted.

Repayments of income tax and Class 4 NICs for a year are attributed first to the balancing payment made for that year, secondly in two equal parts to the POAs for that year and finally to tax deducted at source for the year. Note that:

(a) If a repayment is triggered by a claim to carry back a loss or payment from a later year to an earlier year (e.g. if a trading loss is carried back under Section 380 or if a personal pension contribution is carried back) interest on this repayment runs from 31 January following the later year, *not* the earlier year.

(b) Surcharges and penalties repaid to a taxpayer also attract interest, running from the date of payment to the date of repayment.

(c) Apparently it is HMRC practice to use a denominator of 365 when computing interest on a repayment, whether or not a leap year is involved.

Penalties

A taxpayer who fails to comply with statutory requirements may become liable to a number of financial penalties, the most important of which are listed below. Some of these penalties are fixed in amount but the law often specifies only the *maximum* amount of a penalty and HM Revenue and Customs has the power to "mitigate" (i.e. reduce) the amount charged if it sees fit to do so. Whether or not a penalty is mitigated will usually depend upon the seriousness of the taxpayer's offence and the degree to which the taxpayer has co-operated with HMRC.

(a) **Failure to notify chargeability to tax**. An individual must notify HMRC if he or she is liable to tax for a tax year, even if a return has not been issued for that year. Failure to do so within six months of the end of the tax year could render the individual liable to a maximum penalty equal in amount to the tax remaining unpaid on 31 January following the end of the tax year.

(b) **Late submission of a tax return**. A £100 fixed penalty is imposed if a tax return is submitted late and a further £100 fixed penalty is imposed if the return is more than six months late. If the return is more than 12 months late, an additional penalty may be imposed of up to 100% of the tax liability for the year.

Furthermore, the General or Special Commissioners may direct that a penalty of up to £60 per day should be imposed on the taxpayer, running from the date of the Commissioners' direction to the date on which the tax return is finally submitted.

(c) **Submission of an incorrect tax return**. If a taxpayer, fraudulently or negligently, submits an incorrect tax return (or submits incorrect information in support of a tax return) a penalty may be imposed of up to 100% of the amount of tax underpaid as a consequence of the incorrect return.

(d) **Fraud or negligence when claiming reduced POAs**. A taxpayer who makes a claim for reduced POAs and does so fraudulently or negligently may be subject to a maximum penalty equal to the difference between the POAs actually made and the POAs that should have been made.

(e) **Failure to keep required records**. A taxpayer who fails to maintain or retain adequate records in support of the year's tax return may be subject to a penalty of up to £3,000.

In every case, the penalty is *in addition* both to the tax itself and to any surcharges or interest charged in relation to that tax.

Summary

- Under the Self Assessment system, income tax not collected at source or via the PAYE system is usually payable by means of two payments on account, followed by a balancing payment.
- Surcharges may be levied if a balancing payment is paid late and interest is payable on any tax paid late. Interest usually runs from the due date of payment up to the actual date of payment.
- Repayments of overpaid tax also attract interest, usually running from the date on which the tax was paid up to the date of repayment.
- Financial penalties may be imposed for various breaches of the tax law.

Exercises

14.1 For each of the following taxpayers, state the dates on which the 2005/06 income tax is due to be paid and calculate the amount payable on each date. (Ignore Class 4 NICs).

(a) Guy's 2004/05 income tax liability was £1,600, of which £1,150 was paid via the PAYE system and £50 was deducted at source from investment income. His 2005/06 liability is £1,750, of which £1,250 is paid via PAYE and £60 is deducted at source.

(b) Marie's 2004/05 income tax liability was £6,730, of which £4,370 was paid via PAYE and £20 was deducted at source. Her 2005/06 liability is £6,580, of which £4,810 is paid via PAYE and £35 is deducted at source.

(c) Majid's 2004/05 income tax liability was £14,850, of which £11,990 was paid via PAYE and £110 was deducted at source. His 2005/06 liability is £16,110, of which £12,370 is paid via PAYE and £140 is deducted at source.

14.2 Dorothy's income tax and Class 4 NICs liability for 2004/05 was £30,000, of which £6,000 was deducted at source. Her liability for 2005/06 is £35,000, of which £7,000 is deducted at source. She made a first POA for 2005/06 on 27 February 2006 and a second POA on 12 September 2006. She also made a balancing payment for the year on 21 February 2007. All of her payments were for the correct amount.

(a) Calculate the amount of any surcharges payable by Dorothy in relation to 2005/06.

(b) Assuming an interest rate of 7.5% per annum, calculate the amount of any interest payable by Dorothy in relation to 2005/06.

14.3 Jabran did not receive a tax return for 2005/06 but he was aware that he had income which had not been assessed to tax. He notified HMRC of this fact on 2 October 2006 and a return was issued to him on 15 November 2006. He completed the return and sent it back with the necessary payment on 7 April 2007.

Explain the penalties, surcharges and interest which Jabran might be required to pay.

***14.4** Frances paid income tax and Class 4 NICs of £43,000 in 2004/05, of which £19,000 was deducted at source. Her total liability for 2005/06 is £63,000, of which £21,000 is deducted at source. Her payments for 2005/06 are as follows:

	£
15 February 2006	12,000
14 September 2006	12,000
3 February 2007	14,000
15 December 2007	4,000

Calculate the surcharges and interest payable for the year, assuming that any surcharges are paid on 15 December 2007 and that interest is charged at 7.5% per annum.

Chapter 15

National Insurance contributions

Introduction

National Insurance contributions (NICs) are payable by employees, by employers and by those who are self-employed. Contributions are collected by the National Insurance Contributions Office (NICO) of HM Revenue and Customs and paid into a National Insurance Fund. This fund, supplemented by a grant from the Treasury, is then used to provide contributory social security benefits such as the state retirement pension. The purpose of this chapter is to explain the circumstances in which NICs are payable and the way in which NICs are calculated.

Class 1 National Insurance contributions

Class 1 NICs are payable in relation to employees aged 16 or over. The employees themselves pay *primary* Class 1 NICs whilst employers pay *secondary* Class 1 NICs on their employees' behalf. Employees who continue to work after reaching state pension age pay no further primary contributions but employers must still pay secondary contributions for such employees.

The amount of Class 1 NICs payable in relation to an employee depends upon the employee's earnings. For this purpose, an employee's earnings consist of his or her gross pay *before* deducting pension contributions, donations made under the terms of a payroll giving scheme or any other expenses borne by the employee. An employee's earnings for this purpose do *not* include:

(a) tips received directly from customers
(b) mileage allowances received from the employer (see Chapter 7) if calculated at a rate which does not exceed the approved rate for the first 10,000 miles (regardless of the number of miles actually driven by the employee) although any excess forms part of the employee's earnings chargeable to Class 1 NICs
(c) redundancy pay and pensions
(d) employer contributions to an approved pension scheme

(e) certain items paid for or provided by the employer to the extent that these items are exempt from income tax, including relocation expenses, personal incidental expenses, workplace car parking, suggestion scheme awards, works buses, the loan of bicycles, up to £50 per week of childcare vouchers etc. (see Chapter 7)

(f) business expenses paid for or reimbursed by the employer, including reasonable travel and subsistence expenses.

Benefits in kind which are not convertible into cash are generally not subject to Class 1 NICs. However, such benefits may give rise to a Class 1A liability (see below). If an employee's remuneration is paid in the form of non-cash assets such as gold bars, coffee beans, fine wines or assigned trade debts, a liability to Class 1 NICs will arise if the assets are readily convertible into cash. Payments made in shares are also liable to Class 1 NICs unless they are "own company" shares provided under an approved share scheme or share option scheme (see Chapter 7).

Contribution periods

The main principles of the Class 1 National Insurance system are as follows:

(a) Primary and secondary Class 1 NICs are calculated according to the amount of an employee's earnings in a "contribution period". For those paid weekly or monthly, each week or month usually constitutes a contribution period. However, special rules apply to company directors (see later in this chapter).

(b) The liability to Class 1 NICs in a given contribution period is governed solely by the employee's earnings in that period and is totally unaffected by earnings in other periods. This is in contrast to the income tax PAYE system (see Chapter 7) which accumulates earnings over the year and calculates a tax liability each week or month based on the employee's total earnings for the tax year to date.

(c) If an employee has two or more employments in a contribution period, each of these employments is considered separately for the purposes of calculating the liability to Class 1 NICs. Earnings from two or more employments are aggregated only if the employments are with the same employer or associated employers.

(d) The rate at which Class 1 NICs are calculated depends upon whether the employee is contracted out of the State Second Pension (S2P), which was formerly known as the State Earnings Related Pension Scheme (SERPS). Those who are not contracted out pay higher Class 1 NICs in return for an earnings-related increase in some of their social security benefits.

    Some contracted-out employees are members of their employer's contracted-out salary-related (COSR) occupational pension scheme. Others belong to contracted-out money-purchase (COMP) schemes or pay contributions into an appropriate personal pension scheme. The primary and secondary Class 1 NICs payable in relation to a contracted-out employee depend upon the type of scheme to which the employee belongs. Only members of COSR schemes are considered here.

Primary Class 1 NICs

The primary Class 1 NICs payable by an employee for a contribution period falling during 2005/06 are calculated as follows:

(a) The employee's earnings in the period are compared with the *primary threshold*, which is equal to the weekly or monthly equivalent of the income tax personal allowance for the year, rounded to the nearest pound. The primary threshold for 2005/06 is £94 per week (£4,895 ÷ 52) or £408 per month (£4,895 ÷ 12). No primary contributions are payable if earnings in a contribution period do not exceed this threshold.

(b) If earnings in the period exceed the primary threshold, primary Class 1 NICs are payable at the following rates:

	Not contracted out	*Contracted out (COSR)*
Weekly-paid:		
On the first £94	nil	nil
On the next £536	11%	9.4%
On remaining earnings above £630	1%	1%
Monthly-paid:		
On the first £408	nil	nil
On the next £2,322	11%	9.4%
On remaining earnings above £2,730	1%	1%

(c) The figure of £630 per week (£2,730 per month) is known as the *upper earnings limit* (UEL). Until 6 April 2003, no primary contributions were due on earnings above the UEL. However, as from that date, earnings above the UEL attract primary contributions at the rate of 1%, as indicated above.

EXAMPLE 1

(a) Compute the primary Class 1 NICs payable by the following weekly-paid employees for the week ending 6 August 2005:

(i) Employee A has earnings for the week of £90 and is not contracted out.

(ii) Employee B has earnings for the week of £224 and is not contracted out.

(iii) Employee C has earnings for the week of £645 and is contracted out.

(b) Compute the primary Class 1 NICs payable by the following monthly-paid employees for the month of August 2005:

(i) Employee D has earnings for the month of £400 and is not contracted out.

(ii) Employee E has earnings for the month of £1,148 and is contracted out.

(iii) Employee F has earnings for the month of £2,767 and is not contracted out.

Solution

(a) (i) £nil (earnings do not exceed the primary threshold).

(ii) 11% x (£224 - £94) = £14.30.

(iii) 9.4% x (£630 - £94) + 1% x (£645 - £630) = £50.53.

(b) (i) £nil (earnings do not exceed the primary threshold).

(ii) 9.4% x (£1,148 - £408) = £69.56.

(iii) 11% x (£2,730 - £408) + 1% x (£2,767 - £2,730) = £255.79.

Secondary Class 1 NICs

The secondary Class 1 NICs payable by an employer in relation to an employee for a contribution period falling during 2005/06 are calculated as follows:

(a) The employee's earnings in the period are compared with the *secondary threshold*. This is currently the same as the primary threshold and is therefore £94 for weekly-paid employees and £408 for monthly-paid employees. No secondary contributions are payable if an employee's earnings in a contribution period do not exceed this threshold.

(b) If earnings in the period exceed the secondary threshold, secondary Class 1 NICs are payable at the following rates:

	Not contracted out	*Contracted out (COSR)*
Weekly-paid:		
On the first £94	nil	nil
On the next £536	12.8%	9.3%
On earnings beyond £630 (UEL)	12.8%	12.8%
Monthly-paid:		
On the first £408	nil	nil
On the next £2,322	12.8%	9.3%
On earnings beyond £2,730 (UEL)	12.8%	12.8%

(c) Whereas primary contributions were not payable on earnings beyond the upper earnings limit (UEL) until 6 April 2003, secondary contributions have always been payable on all earnings beyond the secondary threshold.

EXAMPLE 2

Refer back to the previous example in this chapter and compute the secondary Class 1 NICs payable in relation to each employee.

Solution

(a) (i) £nil (earnings do not exceed the secondary threshold).

(ii) 12.8% x (£224 - £94) = £16.64.

(iii) 9.3% x (£630 - £94) + 12.8% x (£645 - £630) = £51.77.

(b) (i) £nil (earnings do not exceed the secondary threshold).

(ii) 9.3% x (£1,148 - £408) = £68.82.

(iii) 12.8% x (£2,767 - £408) = £301.95.

Directors' Class 1 NICs

The fact that NICs are calculated for each contribution period separately, without reference to earnings in other contribution periods, means that employees with identical annual earnings may pay very different amounts of primary contributions in the year, depending upon the distribution of their earnings over that year. Consider the following (rather extreme) example:

EXAMPLE 3

During 2005/06, an employee (not contracted out) earns a total of £33,000, paid at the rate of £2,750 each month.

(a) Calculate the total primary Class 1 NICs payable for the year.

(b) What would the total primary contributions be for the year if the employee received £33,000 in one month and nothing in the remaining 11 months?

Solution

(a) Primary contributions each month are equal to 11% x (£2,730 - £408) + 1% x (£2,750 - £2,730) = £255.62. This gives a total of £3,067.44 for the year.

(b) Primary contributions for the month in which the employee was paid £33,000 would be equal to 11% x (£2,730 - £408) + 1% x (£33,000 - £2,730) = £558.12, with nothing payable for the rest of the year.

Therefore the employee would save £2,509.32 in primary contributions (£3,067.44 - £558.12) if the entire year's salary were received in a single month.

Employees are not normally able to arrange for all of their year's earnings to be paid in one contribution period so as to avoid primary Class 1 NICs, but company directors may well have sufficient influence to make such an arrangement. To counter this, the Class 1 NICs of company directors are calculated on an *annual* basis, regardless of the distribution of their earnings over the tax year. In effect, the entire year becomes a single contribution period. For 2005/06, the Class 1 NICs of a company director are payable according to the following rules:

(a) The primary threshold and the upper earnings limit for the year are £4,895 and £32,760 respectively.

(b) The total primary contributions payable for the year by a director with earnings which exceed £4,895 are calculated as follows:

	Not contracted out	*Contracted out (COSR)*
Annual earnings:		
On the first £4,895	nil	nil
On the next £27,865	11%	9.4%
On earnings beyond £32,760	1%	1%

(c) The secondary threshold for the year is £4,895. The total secondary contributions payable for the year in relation to a director with earnings which exceed £4,895 are calculated as follows:

	Not contracted out	*Contracted out (COSR)*
Annual earnings:		
On the first £4,895	nil	nil
On the next £27,865	12.8%	9.3%
On earnings beyond £32,760	12.8%	12.8%

EXAMPLE 4

Rework the previous example, given that the employee in question is a company director.

Solution

Regardless of the distribution of the director's earnings over the tax year, primary contributions would be equal to 11% x (£32,760 - £4,895) + 1% x (£33,000 - £32,760) = £3,067.55.

Class 1A National Insurance contributions

Benefits in kind which are not convertible into cash are generally exempt from Class 1 NICs. However, these benefits give rise to a Class 1A contribution instead, *payable by the employer only* (not by the employee). For 2005/06, this contribution is calculated as 12.8% of the amount of the benefit in kind which is assessed on the employee for income tax purposes (see Chapter 7).

EXAMPLE 5

In 2005/06, George (a P11D employee) is provided with a petrol-engined motor car by his employer who pays for all fuel and other running costs. The car had a list price when new of £11,700 and has an emission rating of 194g/km. George's employer also pays his private medical insurance premium of £600 per annum.

Calculate the Class 1A contribution payable by George's employer for the year.

Solution

The employee benefits assessed on George for income tax purposes are:

	£
Car (15% + 10% = 25% x £11,700)	2,925
Fuel (25% x £14,400)	3,600
Medical insurance premium	600
	7,125

Therefore the Class 1A contribution payable by George's employer is 12.8% x £7,125 = £912.

Class 1B National Insurance contributions

On occasion, an employer may enter into a PAYE Settlement Agreement (PSA) with HM Revenue and Customs. The effect of such an agreement is that the employer pays the income tax liability of employees in relation to minor or irregular benefits in kind. In these circumstances, the employer is liable to make a Class 1B National Insurance contribution calculated (in 2005/06) as 12.8% of the sum of the benefits in kind and the associated tax which is payable under the terms of the PSA.

Class 2 National Insurance contributions

Class 2 NICs are payable by self-employed people who are over 16 and under pensionable age. Contributions are payable at a flat rate (for 2005/06) of £2.10 per week. A self-employed person whose earnings from self-employment in a tax year are less than the "small earnings exception" limit (£4,345 for 2005/06) is not required to pay Class 2 NICs for that year but may do so voluntarily in order to maintain a full contributions record. Note that:

(a) For Class 2 purposes, a self-employed person's earnings in a tax year are equal to the net profit, *before* adjustment for tax purposes, shown by the person's accounts for the year. The required figure is the actual net profit from 6 April to the following 5 April. Unless accounts are drawn up to 5 April, it will be necessary to apportion the net profits shown in two years' accounts to obtain this figure.

(b) If a self-employed person has two or more businesses, the profits of all of them are aggregated and a Class 2 liability arises unless the aggregate profits are less than the exception limit.

EXAMPLE 6

(a) Alison is self-employed. Her accounts for the year to 5 April 2006 show a net profit of £4,290. Is she liable to pay Class 2 NICs for 2005/06?

(b) Amanda is also self-employed. Her accounts for the year to 31 December 2005 show a net profit of £4,150 and her accounts for the year to 31 December 2006 show a net profit of £5,350. Is she liable to pay Class 2 NICs for 2005/06?

Solution

(a) Alison's accounts (which coincide with tax year 2005/06) show a net profit which is less than the small earnings exception limit. Therefore she is not required to pay Class 2 NICs for 2005/06.

(b) Amanda's accounts do not coincide with the tax year so some apportionment is necessary. Her actual net profit in 2005/06 is £4,450 (£4,150 x 9/12 + £5,350 x 3/12). This is not less than the small earnings exception limit so she will be required to pay Class 2 NICs for 2005/06.

Class 3 National Insurance contributions

Any individual (employed or self-employed) whose earnings are too low in a contribution period to require a National Insurance contribution may make a voluntary Class 3 contribution so as to maintain a full contributions record. For 2005/06, the amount of the Class 3 contribution is £7.35 per week.

Class 4 National Insurance contributions

In addition to the flat rate Class 2 liability described above, self-employed people who are over 16 and under pensionable age may also be liable to pay earnings-related Class 4 NICs. A self-employed person's Class 4 liability for a given tax year is based on the amount of trading income which is charged to income tax for that year. The Class 4 contributions are collected along with the income tax liability. Note that:

(a) The Class 4 liability is based on the person's trading income for the tax year *after* adjusting for capital allowances, trade charges and trading losses but *before* adjusting for retirement annuity or personal pension premiums.

(b) If a self-employed person has more than one business, the earnings from all businesses for the year are aggregated.

(c) There is no liability to Class 4 NICs if profits do not exceed the *lower profits limit* (£4,895 for 2005/06).

(d) If profits exceed the lower profits limit, Class 4 NICs (for 2005/06) are payable at the following rates:

On the first £4,895	nil
On the next £27,865	8%
On profits beyond £32,760	1%

(e) The figure of £32,760 is known as the *upper profits limit*. Until 6 April 2003, no Class 4 NICs were due on profits above this limit. As from that date, however, profits above the upper profits limit attract Class 4 contributions at the rate of 1%, as indicated above.

EXAMPLE 7

Calculate the Class 4 NICs payable for 2005/06 in each of the following cases:

(a) Shawn has trading income for 2005/06 of £13,680.

(b) Catherine has trading income for 2005/06 of £42,040.

(c) Paul has trading income for 2005/06 of £4,580.

Solution

(a) 8% x (£13,680 - £4,895) = £702.80.

(b) 8% x (£32,760 - £4,895) + 1% x (£42,040 - £32,760) = £2,322.00.

(c) Paul's profits are less than the lower profits limit so his Class 4 liability for the year is nil.

Annual maximum contributions

An employee who has more than one employment will normally be required to make Class 1 contributions in respect of each employment. Similarly, an individual who is both employed and self-employed will normally be required to make Class 1 contributions in respect of the employment and Class 2 and Class 4 contributions in respect of the self-employment. In these circumstances, the total NICs payable could become onerous but relief is available in the form of limits on the amount of NICs payable by any one person in any one year. In practice, the calculation of these limits can be very complex but a brief summary of the rules is as follows:

(a) **Maximum Class 1 and 2 contributions**. In any one year, the total of the Class 1 contributions payable by an individual *at the main rate* (currently 11%) plus any Class 2 contributions is limited to the amount of the Class 1 contributions which would be payable by a weekly-paid employee with 53 weeks of earnings equal to the UEL. For 2005/06, this gives a maximum contribution of £3,124.88 (53 × 11% × (£630 - £94)). A refund is made if this limit is exceeded, but the refund calculation takes into account the fact that earnings above the primary threshold which do not attract 11% contributions should attract 1% contributions instead.

(b) **Maximum Class 1, 2 and 4 contributions**. A refund of *Class 4 contributions only* is made if the total main rate (11%) Class 1 contributions, Class 2 contributions and main rate (8%) Class 4 contributions paid by an individual in any one year exceed the amount obtained by adding 53 Class 2 contributions to the maximum main rate Class 4 contribution for the year. For 2005/06 this limit is equal to £2,340.50 (53 @ £2.10 + 8% × (£32,760 - £4,895)). The refund calculation takes into account the fact that profits above the lower profits limit which do not attract Class 4 contributions at 8% should attract Class 4 contributions at 1% instead.

If an employee is contracted out, Class 1 contributions paid in the year are recalculated at the not-contracted-out rate before comparison is made with the above limits.

EXAMPLE 8

(a) Sabrina has two employments throughout 2005/06. Calculate the refund of NICs due for the year if she is not contracted out and her regular monthly earnings from the two employments are as follows:

(i) £823 and £1,223 (ii) £1,523 and £2,023 (iii) £3,000 and £4,000.

(b) Stephanie is employed at a monthly salary of £2,800. She is not contracted out. She also has a small business and pays 53 weekly Class 2 NICs in 2005/06. Calculate the refund of NICs due for the year.

(c) Stewart is self-employed and pays 53 weekly Class 2 NICs in 2005/06. His trading income for 2005/06 is £22,530. He also receives directors' fees of £12,860 in the year. He is not contracted out. Calculate the refund of NICs due for the year.

Solution

(a) Sabrina will have paid main rate Class 1 NICs as follows:

	(i)	(ii)	(iii)
	£	£	£
First employment:			
12 x 11% x (£823 - £408)	547.80		
12 x 11% x (£1,523 - £408)		1,471.80	
12 x 11% x (£2,730 - £408)			3,065.04
Second employment:			
12 x 11% x (£1,223 - £408)	1,075.80		
12 x 11% x (£2,023 - £408)		2,131.80	
12 x 11% x (£2,730 - £408)			3,065.04
	1,623.60	3,603.60	6,130.08

In case (i), total contributions do not exceed the maximum, so no refund is due.

In case (ii), contributions exceed the maximum by £478.72 (£3,603.60 - £3,124.88) so Sabrina is entitled to a refund. However, the earnings which have given rise to the excess contributions are still subject to 1% contributions, so the refund is reduced by one-eleventh to £435.20.

In case (iii), Sabrina's contributions exceed the maximum by £3,005.20 (£6,130.08 - £3,124.88) so she is entitled to a refund of 10/11 x £3,005.20 = £2,732.00.

(b) Stephanie will have paid main rate Class 1 NICs and Class 2 NICs as follows:

	£
Class 1 (12 x 11% x (£2,730 - £408))	3,065.04
Class 2 (53 @ £2.10)	111.30
	3,176.34

This exceeds the maximum by £51.46 (£3,176.34 - £3,124.88). The refund can be made entirely out of Class 2 contributions so there will be no need to collect further 1% contributions on refunded main rate Class 1 contributions. The refund is £51.46.

(c) Stewart will have paid NICs as follows:

	£
Class 1 (11% x (£12,860 - £4,895))	876.15
Class 2 (53 @ £2.10)	111.30
Class 4 (8% x (£22,530 - £4,895))	1,410.80
	2,398.25

The total main rate Class 1 and Class 2 contributions are well within the maximum of £3,124.88. But the total of the main rate Class 1 contributions, Class 2 contributions and main rate Class 4 contributions exceeds the maximum of £2,340.50 by £57.75. Therefore Stewart is entitled to a refund of Class 4 contributions. However, the profits which have given rise to the excess contributions are still subject to 1% contributions, so the refund is reduced by one-eighth to £50.53.

Summary

- Class 1 NICs are payable by employees (primary contributions) and by their employers (secondary contributions). Both primary and secondary contributions are reduced if the employee is contracted out.
- Class 1 NICs are calculated with respect to earnings in a contribution period and each contribution period is considered independently.
- Until 6 April 2003, no primary Class 1 contributions were payable on earnings beyond the upper earnings limit. As from that date, primary contributions are payable at 1% on earnings beyond the UEL.
- The Class 1 NICs of company directors are assessed on an annual basis and are unaffected by the distribution of the director's earnings over the year.
- Class 1A NICs are payable by employers in relation to benefits in kind which are not convertible into cash. Class 1B NICs are payable by employers in relation to PAYE Settlement Agreements.
- Class 2 NICs are payable at a flat rate by self-employed people whose profits exceed the small earnings exception limit.
- Class 4 NICs are paid by self-employed people and are earnings-related. Until 6 April 2003, no Class 4 contributions were payable on profits beyond the upper profits limit. As from that date, Class 4 contributions are payable at 1% on profits beyond the upper limit.
- Class 3 NICs are paid voluntarily in order to maintain a full contributions record.
- There are annual maximum limits on the amount of NICs payable by an individual.

Exercises

15.1 Compute the primary and secondary Class 1 NICs payable in relation to the following employees (none of whom are contracted out):

(a) A earns £98 for the week ending 18 June 2005.

(b) B earns £208 for the week ending 18 June 2005.

(c) C earns £665 for the week ending 18 June 2005.

(d) D earns £390 for the month of September 2005.

(e) E earns £495 for the month of September 2005.

(f) F earns £2,894 for the month of September 2005.

15.2 Rework your answer to Exercise 15.1, assuming now that each of the employees is a member of a COSR scheme.

15.3 Mark is self-employed and makes up his accounts annually to 30 November. His accounts for the year ended 30 November 2005 show a net profit of £6,890 and his accounts for the year ended 30 November 2006 show a net profit of £3,120. His 2005/06 trading income is £8,080. Calculate the NICs payable by Mark for 2005/06.

***15.4** Brenda is a company director and earns a regular monthly salary of £3,000. In December 2005 she received a £5,000 bonus. She is provided with a diesel-engined company car which has an emission rating of 237g/km and which had a list price when new of £16,000. The company pays all the running costs of the car, including fuel. Her BUPA subscription of £750 per year is paid by the company.

Calculate the NICs payable in respect of Brenda for 2005/06 (she is a member of a COSR scheme).

***15.5** Leonard is employed and receives a salary of £2,230 per month. He is not contracted out. He also has a small business and pays 53 weekly Class 2 NICs for 2005/06. His trading income for 2005/06 is £9,180. Calculate the refund of NICs due to Leonard for the year.

Review questions (Set A)

A 1 Tom Tulliver has been appointed sales director of Pembridge plc, a large company in the building industry. In addition to a basic salary of £50,000, he has been offered a comprehensive benefits package. The proposed deal is:

(i) The company will provide him with a new car which, together with accessories, will cost £19,500. The car has an emission rating of 240g/km. Petrol for private use will be provided but Mr Tulliver must make a contribution of £400 per year towards its cost.

(ii) An interest-free loan of £5,250 will be made to him on appointment and need only be repaid on his leaving the company. The loan will be used to purchase various household items.

(iii) He has a choice of meals in the company canteen, which is open to all staff free of charge, or luncheon vouchers worth £5 per day, an amount equivalent to the normal cost of the meals. He has decided to accept the luncheon vouchers. The normal working year is 200 working days.

(iv) His son, aged three, is presently attending a nursery (which does not have approved childminder status) at a cost of £3,286 per year. Pembridge plc has offered to give his son a free place in their own day nursery but Mr Tulliver would like to continue the existing arrangement and for Pembridge to pay the fees to the existing nursery.

Mrs Tulliver's wife earns £14,000 per year. She pays pension contributions to her employer's pension scheme of 6% of her salary. Both Mr and Mrs Tulliver have building society accounts which will yield net interest of £6,400 and £2,392 respectively in 2005/06. Mr Tulliver receives UK preference dividends of £4,680 annually.

Mr Tulliver's appointment will begin on 1 April 2005 and he wishes to examine his and his wife's tax position before the start of fiscal year 2005/06.

Required:

(a) Advise Mr Tulliver on the taxation implications of his employment package.

(b) Advise him of any changes you consider that he should make to maximise the tax efficiency of the proposed package.

(c) Using your answer in (a) as to the amount of Mr Tulliver's income, advise him of the likely income tax borne by him and his wife for 2005/06 and, again, suggest how the tax position might be improved. (*Note*: Assume that the official rate of interest is 5%). *(AAT)*

A 2 Jeremy, who is married, is 77 years old and receives a state retirement pension of £12,720 per annum. He also receives dividend income of £6,750 per annum. In 2001 he purchased a life annuity from which a monthly income of £325 (gross) is paid. The capital element of each payment was agreed with HM Revenue and Customs at £300. Income tax is being deducted from the income element.

Jeremy owns a furnished cottage which he rents to holidaymakers. In tax year 2005/06 it was let for 20 weeks at a weekly rental of £250.

The following expenditure was incurred:

	£
Insurance (see note)	400
Water rates	200
Council tax	300

Note: The £400 was paid on 1 January 2006. The insurance paid on 1 January 2005 was £360.

You are required:

To calculate the income tax payable by Jeremy for the year 2005/06. *(ACCA)*

A 3 The system of Self Assessment for income tax has applied since 6 April 1996.

You are required:

(a) To state the latest date by which a taxpayer should submit a tax return if:

  (i) he or she wishes HM Revenue and Customs to calculate the tax liability, and

  (ii) he or she wishes to calculate the liability.

(b) To state:

  (i) the normal dates of payment of income tax for a sole trader in respect of fiscal year 2005/06, and

  (ii) how the amounts of these payments are arrived at.

(c) To state:

  (i) the fixed penalties for late submission of tax returns and when they apply,

  (ii) the circumstances in which these penalties will be reduced, and

  (iii) the further penalties which may be imposed where HMRC believes that the fixed penalties will not result in the submission of the return.

(ACCA)

A 4 In each of the following situations, show the tax position assuming that the maximum potential reliefs are claimed as soon as possible. Then advise your client of any alternatives that might be available.

(i) Mr de Praet - a married man - began trading on 1 January 2000, preparing accounts to 31 December annually. Recent results are:

	£	
Year to 31 December 2004	20,000	Profit
Year to 31 December 2005	(30,000)	Loss

He receives rents of £5,000 annually. His wife is employed part-time at a salary of £4,920 per year. It is estimated that the trading profits for the year to 31 December 2006 are likely to be £68,000.

(ii) Henry Percy started a small business on 1 July 2001 and makes up accounts to 30 June annually. His adjusted trading results (before capital allowances) for the last two years have been:

	£	
Year to 30 June 2004	18,000	Profit
Year to 30 June 2005	(10,000)	Loss

Up to 31 December 2004 he always leased his plant and machinery but on 1 January 2005 he purchased a new machine for £14,720. He has no income other than his business profits. *(AAT)*

A 5 In May 2005 Bernard, a self-employed plumber, and his son Gerald, a self-employed electrician, purchased 1,000 empty barrels from a Scottish whisky distillery. The barrels were over 100 years old and of no further use to the distillery. Bernard and Gerald sawed the barrels into halves and sold them to several local garden centres for use as ornamental flower tubs. Bernard and Gerald paid £10 per barrel to the distillery and sold a half-barrel for £8. Three-quarters of the barrels were sold by Bernard and Gerald in the summer of 2005 and the remainder in the summer of 2006.

You are required:

To prepare a list of points for consideration prior to writing a report to Bernard and Gerald on the liability to income tax of the profit generated by the venture. *(ACCA)*

***A 6** Your directors are considering paying substantial cash bonuses to a number of senior employees, including some directors.

You are required:

To draft a report to the board setting out the regulations for taxing these bonuses, indicating when the tax and National Insurance contributions on them would be payable. *(CIMA)*

***A7** Claud Chapperon is a self-employed wholesale clothing distributor who began trading on 1 July 2000. His summarised accounts for the year to 30 June 2005 are shown below (figures in brackets refer to notes).

	£	£
Sales (1)		400,000
Opening stock (2)	40,000	
Purchases	224,000	
	264,000	
Closing stock (2)	32,000	232,000
Gross profit		168,000
Wages and national insurance (3)	52,600	
Rent and rates	29,100	
Repairs and renewals (4)	3,490	
Miscellaneous expenses (5)	665	
Taxation (Claud's income tax)	17,554	
Bad debts (6)	820	
Legal expenses (7)	1,060	
Depreciation	570	
Lease rental on Claud's car (8)	8,400	
Loss on sale of office furniture	60	
Gift Aid donations (9)	195	
Transport costs	4,136	
Interest (10)	990	
Running expenses of Claud's car (11)	2,000	
Premium on lease (12)	6,000	
Lighting and heating	1,250	
Sundry expenses (all allowable)	710	
Relocation expenditure (13)	2,400	132,000
Net profit		36,000

Notes:

1. Sales include £500 reimbursed by Claud's family for clothing taken from stock. The reimbursement represented cost price.

2. The basis of both the opening and closing stock valuations was "lower of cost or market value", less a contingency reserve of 50%.

3. Included in wages are Claud's drawings of £50 per week, his NICs of £107 for the year and his wife's wages and NICs totalling £11,750. His wife works full-time in the business as a secretary.

4. The charge for repairs and renewals includes £3,120 for fitting protective covers over the factory windows and doors to prevent burglary.

5. Miscellaneous expenses comprise:

	£
Theft of money by employee	65
Political donation to Green Party	100
Gifts of 100 "Chapperon" calendars	500
	665

6. Bad debts comprise:

	£
Trade debt written off	720
Loan to former employee written off (not taxable as employee remuneration)	250
Reduction in general provision	(150)
	820

7. Legal expenses comprise:

	£
Defending action re alleged faulty goods	330
Costs re lease of new larger premises	250
Unsuccessful appeal against previous year's income tax assessment	200
Defending Claud in connection with speeding offence	190
Debt collection	90
	1,060

8. Claud's leased car was a BMW costing £20,000. The car is petrol-driven and has an emission rating exceeding 120g/km.

9. Gift Aid donations consist of £120 paid to the local children's hospital and £75 paid to Oxfam. Both payments were made on 30 April 2005.

10. Interest is as follows:

	£
Bank overdraft interest (business account)	1,020
Interest on overdue tax	130
Interest credited on NSB ordinary a/c (see note 14)	(160)
	990

11. HM Revenue and Customs has agreed that one-third of Claud's mileage is private. Included in the charge for motor running expenses is £65 for a speeding fine incurred by Claud whilst delivering goods to a customer.

12. The premium was for a lease of six years.

13. The relocation expenditure was incurred in transferring the business to new and larger premises.

14. Interest recently credited to the NSB ordinary account is as follows:

	£
31 December 2004	160
31 December 2005	140

The following information is also provided:

(i) Capital allowances for the year to 30 June 2005 are £480.

(ii) Claud was born on 10 April 1949 and he always pays the maximum permitted personal pension contribution. His net relevant earnings for pension purposes are greater in 2005/06 than in any of the previous five years. His wife was also born in 1949.

You are required:

(a) To prepare a profit adjustment statement in respect of the period of account to 30 June 2005, showing the trading income for 2005/06.

(b) To calculate the Class 4 NICs payable by Claud for 2005/06.

(c) To prepare an estimate of Claud's income tax borne for 2005/06. *(ACCA)*

***A8** When submitting a business's annual accounts to HM Revenue and Customs, it is usual to send schedules under the following expenditure headings:

(i) Gifts and entertainment

(ii) Major repairs

(iii) Redundancy payments to employees.

You are required:

To state the information which should be included under each of the above headings, explaining why such information will be required. *(CIMA)*

***A9** Joseph Kent started business on 1 October 2002 as a joiner making conservatories. His tax-adjusted profits (before deduction of capital allowances) were as follows:

	£
Period to 31 December 2003	35,000
Year ended 31 December 2004	24,000
Year ended 31 December 2005	42,000

Capital additions and disposals were as follows:

		£
Additions		
1 October 2002	Car (at valuation)	12,200
1 October 2002	Trailer	2,000
1 October 2002	Plant and machinery	8,000
1 December 2004	Car	13,000
1 December 2005	Plant and machinery	6,000

			£
Disposals			
	1 December 2004	Car acquired 1/10/02	7,000
	1 January 2005	Plant and machinery (at less than cost)	2,000

Neither of the cars is a low-emission car. Private use of both cars has been agreed with HM Revenue and Customs at 20%. No claim is made to treat any of the assets as short-life assets. The business ranks as a small business for capital allowances purposes.

Joseph manufactured the conservatories in rented premises until 1 January 2005, when he purchased a new factory unit on an industrial estate for £20,000 (not in an enterprise zone). All assets were brought into use immediately upon acquisition.

Joseph's wife Sephora is a solicitor employed by a practising firm at a salary of £41,150 per annum. The following additional information is provided for 2005/06:

(i) A new petrol-engined car was provided for Sephora's use in August 2004. The list price at that time was £25,000. Of this amount, £4,000 was contributed by Sephora so that a better car could be provided. She was required to pay £25 per month towards the private use of the car but not towards the private fuel, all of which was provided by her employers. The car's emission rating is 192g/km.

(ii) Sephora has received a loan of £60,000 on the matrimonial home from her employers on which she pays interest at 1.75%.

(iii) Sephora made a qualifying donation to the Oxfam charity on 1 July 2005 of £390 under the Gift Aid scheme.

(iv) Both Joseph and Sephora are under 65 years old.

You are required:

(a) To calculate Joseph's trading income for 2002/03 to 2005/06 inclusive.

(b) To calculate Sephora's income tax liability for 2005/06 (assuming an official rate of interest of 5% per annum). *(ACCA)*

***A10** Thomas Pilkington bought an existing business, Marcus Fashionwear, a gentlemen's outfitters, on 1 December 2004. The summarised trading profit and loss account for the year to 30 November 2005 is set out below:

		£	£
Sales			201,600
Cost of sales			53,900
			147,700
Investment income			9,100
			156,800
Rent and rates		25,400	
Lighting and heating		3,200	
Wages and salaries		22,500	
Insurances		1,100	
Motor vehicle expenses		5,200	
Postage, stationery and telephone		800	
Repairs to premises		4,900	
Advertising		3,200	
Bad debts		2,100	
Subscriptions and donations		500	
Depreciation:	Motor vehicles	3,900	
	Fixtures and fittings	2,000	
	Office machinery	3,000	
Legal and professional charges		3,300	81,100
Net profit			75,700

You are required:

To state what further information you would require to enable you to calculate the income which is chargeable to income tax. *(ACCA)*

Part 2

CAPITAL GAINS TAX

Chapter 16

Introduction to capital gains tax

Introduction

The next seven chapters of this book deal with capital gains tax (CGT), which was introduced in 1965 with the aim of taxing gains arising on the disposal of capital assets. CGT has undergone many changes since its inception and the changes made between 1965 and 1992 were consolidated into the Taxation of Chargeable Gains Act 1992. This Act has since been amended by subsequent Finance Acts.

Chargeable persons

A liability to CGT may arise when a "chargeable person" makes a "chargeable disposal" of a "chargeable asset". The main categories of chargeable person are as follows:

(a) individuals who are resident or ordinarily resident in the UK

(b) business partners, who are each responsible for their share of the CGT due on the capital gains of a partnership

(c) trustees and personal representatives.

Husbands and wives are assessed independently for CGT purposes, as are same-sex civil partners. The following are *not* chargeable persons for CGT purposes and therefore cannot incur a CGT liability:

(a) companies, which pay corporation tax on their chargeable gains, not CGT

(b) registered charities and friendly societies, community amateur sports clubs, local authorities, approved superannuation funds, unit trusts, investment trusts and approved scientific research associations, all of which are exempt from CGT.

Chargeable assets

All assets are regarded as chargeable assets except for those which are specifically exempted from CGT. The main exemptions are as follows:

(a) a taxpayer's principal private residence (see Chapter 21)

(b) motor cars, including vintage and veteran motor cars

(c) items of tangible, movable property ("chattels") disposed of for £6,000 or less (see Chapter 18)

(d) chattels with a predictable useful life of 50 years or less ("wasting chattels") unless used in business and eligible for capital allowances (see Chapter 18)

(e) gilt-edged securities and qualifying corporate bonds (see Chapter 19)

(f) works of art and collections of scientific interest if donated for the benefit of the nation

(g) National Savings Certificates, Premium Bonds and British Savings Bonds

(h) foreign currency if acquired for private use

(i) winnings from pools, lotteries, betting etc.

(j) decorations for valour (unless acquired by purchase)

(k) compensation received for personal or professional injury and compensation for mis-sold personal pensions or (by concession) mis-sold free standing additional voluntary contribution schemes taken out between certain dates

(l) life assurance policies (unless purchased from a third party)

(m) Personal Equity Plans, shares in a Venture Capital Trust and investments held in an Individual Savings Account or Child Trust Fund (see Chapter 6).

If an asset is not a chargeable asset, then neither a chargeable gain nor an allowable loss can arise on its disposal.

Chargeable disposals

The main (and the most obvious) instance of a chargeable disposal occurs when a chargeable asset is sold. However, the sale of an asset in the course of trade (i.e. the sale of trading stock) does *not* constitute a chargeable disposal for CGT purposes since trading profits are assessed to income tax instead.

Before CGT was introduced in 1965 there was a great incentive for taxpayers to show that the gain arising on the sale of an asset was a capital gain (and so not taxable at all) rather than a trading profit (and so subject to income tax). With the introduction of CGT this incentive was diminished but it is still important to distinguish between capital gains and trading profits since the rules of computation for CGT and income tax are different.

As well as the sale of a chargeable asset, the following are also chargeable disposals:

(a) the sale of *part* of a chargeable asset
(b) the gift of all or part of a chargeable asset
(c) the loss or destruction of a chargeable asset
(d) the receipt of a capital sum derived from a chargeable asset (e.g. compensation received from an insurance company if an asset is damaged).

With regard to gifts, it is important to realise that CGT is basically a tax on the increase in value of an asset whilst owned by the taxpayer. This increase in value is chargeable to tax even if the taxpayer gives the asset away and receives nothing in return.

In general, the date on which a chargeable disposal is deemed to occur is the date on which ownership of the asset changes hands, regardless of the date on which payment (if any) takes place.

Non-chargeable disposals

The following types of disposal are *not* chargeable disposals and therefore any gains or losses arising on such disposals are exempt from CGT:

(a) gifts to charities, art galleries, museums etc.
(b) disposals caused by the death of the taxpayer.

Disposals between a husband and wife who live together at any time during the tax year in which the disposal occurs *are* chargeable disposals. However, such disposals are deemed to occur at a disposal value such that neither a chargeable gain nor an allowable loss arises (see Chapter 17). As from 5 December 2005, this rule also applies to same-sex civil partners who have entered into a legally-recognised civil partnership.

Basis of assessment

A person's CGT liability for a tax year is based upon the chargeable disposals made by that person during the tax year. For example, the 2005/06 CGT assessment is based upon chargeable disposals made between 6 April 2005 and 5 April 2006 inclusive. No liability to CGT arises until an asset is disposed of, so the mere fact that an asset has appreciated in value will not of itself trigger a CGT assessment. The amount of the CGT assessment for a tax year is calculated as follows:

(a) The gain or loss arising on each disposal made during the year is calculated separately (the method of calculation is described in great detail in subsequent chapters of this book).

(b) If total gains exceed total losses, the losses are subtracted from the gains to give the "net gains" for the year. If total losses exceed total gains, the gains are subtracted from the losses to give the "net losses" for the year.

(c) If there are net gains for the year, these are reduced first by any unrelieved losses brought forward from previous years or carried back on the death of the taxpayer (see later in this chapter) and then by any "taper relief" available. Taper relief is calculated separately for each gain arising in the year, according to:

(i) the length of time for which the asset was held before disposal

(ii) whether or not the asset qualifies as a "business asset"

(iii) the extent to which the gain has been reduced by losses of the year or losses brought forward or carried back.

These results are then aggregated to give total taper relief for the year. (A much more detailed explanation of taper relief is given in Chapter 17.)

(d) The net gains left after deduction of taper relief are then further reduced by the amount of the "annual exemption" (£8,500 for 2005/06) and the remainder is the CGT assessment for the year. If net gains (after taper relief) are less than the annual exemption in any year, the CGT assessment for that year is £nil and the balance of the annual exemption is lost.

(e) If there are net losses for the year, the CGT assessment for that year is £nil and the whole of the annual exemption is lost. The net losses may then be carried forward for relief in future years, as described later in this chapter.

Husbands and wives are each entitled to the full annual exemption. This exemption is also available to the trustees of a trust established for a mentally disabled person or for certain other infirm or disabled persons. For trustees of other settlements the annual exemption is lower (£4,250 for 2005/06). The personal representatives of a deceased person are entitled to the full annual exemption for the year of death and for the following two years.

EXAMPLE 1

Four taxpayers each make three chargeable disposals during 2005/06. Compute their CGT assessments for the year (assuming that there are no unrelieved losses brought forward or carried back and that no taper relief is available) if these disposals give rise to the following gains and losses:

(a) Taxpayer A has gains of £2,500, £2,700 and £5,550.

(b) Taxpayer B has gains of £4,800, £5,840 and a loss of £1,250.

(c) Taxpayer C has gains of £950, £7,630 and a loss of £2,950.

(d) Taxpayer D has a gain of £8,950 and losses of £9,500 and £800.

Solution

(a) Taxpayer A has total gains of £10,750 and no losses. Therefore net gains are £10,750. Subtracting the annual exemption of £8,500 gives a CGT assessment for the year of £2,250.

(b) Taxpayer B has total gains of £10,640 and total losses of £1,250. Therefore net gains are £9,390. Subtracting the annual exemption of £8,500 gives a CGT assessment for the year of £890.

(c) Taxpayer C has total gains of £8,580 and total losses of £2,950. Therefore net gains are £5,630. This is less than the annual exemption of £8,500, so the CGT assessment for the year is £nil. The unused part of the annual exemption (£2,870) is lost.

(d) Taxpayer D has total gains of £8,950 and total losses of £10,300. Therefore net losses are £1,350. The CGT assessment for the year is £nil and the whole of the annual exemption is lost.

Rates of CGT

The rates of CGT for individuals are aligned with the rates of income tax payable on savings income (see Chapter 2). The rules for calculating the amount of capital gains tax due on an individual's CGT assessment for 2005/06 are as follows:

(a) If any part of the individual's income is charged to income tax at the higher rate (40%) or at the dividend upper rate (32.5%), the whole of the CGT assessment is charged to capital gains tax at the higher rate (40%).

(b) If none of the individual's income is charged to income tax at the higher rate or at the dividend upper rate, then:

   (i) capital gains of up to the amount of any unused part of the starting rate band are taxed at the starting rate (10%)

   (ii) remaining gains of up to the amount of any unused part of the basic rate band (which is extended if the taxpayer makes a Gift Aid donation or pays a personal pension premium in the year, as indicated in Chapters 4 and 13) are taxed at the lower rate (20%)

   (iii) any further remaining gains are taxed at the higher rate (40%).

It is important to note that individuals with no income tax liability are *not* allowed to offset any unrelieved charges or unused personal allowances against their capital gains. Similarly, tax reducers may be used only to reduce a taxpayer's income tax liability, not his or her CGT liability.

The CGT rate applicable to trustees and personal representatives is equivalent to the special rate of income tax applicable to certain trusts, currently 40% (see Chapter 6).

EXAMPLE 2

Alan has a capital gains tax assessment of £7,400 in 2005/06. Calculate the amount of CGT payable for 2005/06 if his taxable income for the year (i.e. his total income after deduction of charges and the personal allowance) is:

(a) £22,570 (b) £28,500 (c) £33,500 (d) £870.

Alan makes no Gift Aid donations and pays no personal pension premiums in 2005/06.

Solution

(a) Taxable income uses the whole of the starting rate band and £20,480 (£22,570 - £2,090) of the basic rate band, leaving £9,830 (£30,310 - £20,480) of the basic rate band unused. Alan's CGT assessment is less than this. Therefore the amount of CGT payable is £7,400 @ 20% = £1,480.

(b) Taxable income uses the whole of the starting rate band and £26,410 (£28,500 - £2,090) of the basic rate band, leaving £3,900 (£30,310 - £26,410) of the basic rate band unused. Therefore the amount of CGT payable is £3,900 @ 20% + £3,500 @ 40% = £2,180.

(c) Alan's taxable income uses the whole of the starting rate and basic rate bands and he pays income tax at 40% (or 32.5%) on the last £1,100 of his income. Therefore the whole of his CGT assessment is charged to capital gains tax at 40%. The amount of CGT payable is £7,400 @ 40% = £2,960.

(d) The unused part of the starting rate band is £1,220 (£2,090 - £870) and the whole of the basic rate band (£30,310) is also unused. Therefore the amount of CGT payable is £1,220 @ 10% + £6,180 @ 20% = £1,358.

Relief for capital losses

If a taxpayer has net losses for a year, the CGT assessment for that year is £nil and the annual exemption is lost. The amount of the net losses may then be carried forward without time limit and set against the net gains of future years.

Losses carried forward must be offset against the first available net gains, but are offset only to the extent that net gains (before taper relief) exceed the annual exemption for the year in which they arise, so preventing the annual exemption from being wasted. Any losses remaining unrelieved are carried forward again to subsequent years. This method of preserving the annual exemption applies *only* to losses brought forward from a previous year. It is *not* possible to preserve the annual exemption by restricting the set-off of current year losses. Since married couples (and same-sex civil partners) are taxed independently, the losses of one spouse (or partner) cannot be offset against the gains of the other spouse (or partner).

EXAMPLE 3

Four taxpayers each have £3,000 of capital losses brought forward from previous years. Calculate their 2005/06 CGT assessments if their total gains and losses in 2005/06 are as follows (and no taper relief is available):

(a) Taxpayer A has gains of £6,400 and losses of £1,300.

(b) Taxpayer B has gains of £9,100 and losses of £600.

(c) Taxpayer C has gains of £10,700 and losses of £500.

(d) Taxpayer D has gains of £14,600 and losses of £1,200.

Solution

(a) Taxpayer A's net gains for the year are £5,100. This is less than the annual exemption of £8,500 so the CGT assessment for the year is £nil and the balance of the annual exemption is lost. There is no scope for relieving losses brought forward, so the entire £3,000 is carried forward to 2006/07.

(b) Taxpayer B's net gains for the year are £8,500. This is exactly equal to the annual exemption so the CGT assessment for the year is £nil. There is no scope for relieving losses brought forward, so the entire £3,000 is carried forward to 2006/07.

(c) Taxpayer C's net gains for the year are £10,200. This exceeds the annual exemption by £1,700 so £1,700 of the losses brought forward are relieved in 2005/06, giving a CGT assessment for the year of £nil. The remaining £1,300 of the losses are unrelieved and are therefore carried forward to 2006/07.

(d) Taxpayer D's net gains for the year are £13,400. This exceeds the annual exemption by £4,900 so the entire £3,000 of losses brought forward are relieved in 2005/06, giving a CGT assessment for the year of £1,900. There are no unrelieved losses to carry forward.

Losses in the year of death

As stated above, disposals caused by the death of a taxpayer are exempt from CGT, though such disposals may give rise to an inheritance tax liability. But disposals made in the year of death (i.e. from 6 April up to the date of death) are *not* exempt from CGT and are taxed in the usual way, with a full annual exemption given for the year.

If a taxpayer suffers net losses in the year of death, such losses cannot (for obvious reasons) be carried forward for relief in future years. However, a measure of relief is available in that net losses incurred in the year of death may be carried back and set off against the net gains of the previous three years (most recent years first). As is the case with losses carried forward, losses carried back are set against a year's net gains only to the extent that net gains before taper relief exceed the annual exemption for the year in which they arise.

EXAMPLE 4

Sarah dies on 16 December 2005, having made net capital losses of £7,300 between 6 April 2005 and the date of her death. Her net gains in the previous three years are:

	£
2002/03	8,850
2003/04	1,800
2004/05	12,550

Calculate her CGT assessments for 2002/03 to 2005/06 inclusive, given that the annual exemption was £7,700 in 2002/03, £7,900 in 2003/04 and £8,200 in 2004/05. No taper relief is available in any year.

Solution

Since losses in the year of death are carried back to the most recent year first, it is easier to begin with the year of death and then work backwards.

(a) In 2005/06, Sarah has net losses. Her CGT assessment for the year is therefore £nil and the annual exemption (available in full) is lost. The net losses of £7,300 may be carried back to 2004/05, 2003/04 and 2002/03, in that order.

(b) In 2004/05, Sarah's net gains of £12,550 exceed the annual exemption by £4,350 so £4,350 of the losses carried back are relieved in 2004/05, giving a CGT assessment for the year of £nil. The remaining £2,950 of the losses are carried back to 2003/04.

(c) In 2003/04, Sarah's net gains of £1,800 are less than the annual exemption of £7,900. Therefore the CGT assessment for the year is £nil and the balance of the annual exemption is lost. There is no scope for relieving losses carried back, so the £2,950 is now carried back to 2002/03.

(d) In 2002/03, Sarah's net gains of £8,850 exceed the annual exemption by £1,150 so £1,150 of the losses carried back are relieved in 2002/03, giving a CGT assessment for the year of £nil. The remaining £1,800 of the losses incurred in the year of death cannot be carried back any further and therefore cannot be relieved in any way.

Assuming that CGT assessments have already been made for 2002/03 and 2004/05, it will be necessary to revise these assessments to take into account the relief for losses carried back and to refund any CGT already paid for those years.

Losses on disposals to connected persons

A taxpayer is deemed to be connected with a number of persons, mainly relatives and business associates (see Chapter 17). As an anti-avoidance measure, the Taxation of Chargeable Gains Act 1992 states that losses incurred on a disposal to a connected person can be offset only against gains made on disposals to the *same connected person*, in the same or future years.

Relief for trading losses

Under Section 72 of the Finance Act 1991, a taxpayer's trading losses may in certain circumstances be offset against that taxpayer's net capital gains (see Chapter 11). If a Section 72 claim is made for a tax year, the amount of the claim must be for the *lower* of:

(a) the amount of the trading loss which is available for relief in that year

(b) the "maximum amount", which is the amount of the CGT assessment, *disregarding the annual exemption*, that would have been raised for that year if a Section 72 claim had not been made

It is important to realise that the "maximum amount" is calculated as if the annual exemption simply did not exist. Not only is the annual exemption itself ignored in this calculation but so is the fact that capital losses brought forward might be restricted so as to preserve the exemption. The situation becomes more complex if the taxpayer is entitled to taper relief for the year in question (see Chapter 17).

A Section 72 claim is treated as a capital loss incurred in the year of the claim and is therefore relieved *before* giving relief for capital losses brought forward.

EXAMPLE 5

(a) Richard is a sole trader and is considering making a Section 72 claim for 2005/06. His net gains for the year are £14,700 and he has capital losses brought forward of £3,300. Calculate his CGT assessment for 2005/06 (ignoring any Section 72 claim).

(b) Richard's unrelieved trading losses (eligible for a Section 72 claim in 2005/06) amount to £12,500. Calculate his CGT assessment for 2005/06 if he decides to make a Section 72 claim for the year.

(c) Now calculate the CGT assessment for 2005/06 if Richard's capital losses brought forward are £7,300 instead of £3,300.

Assume in all cases that no taper relief is available in 2005/06.

Solution

(a) Without a Section 72 claim for 2005/06, the CGT assessment for the year will be:

	£
Net gains	14,700
Less: Capital losses b/f	3,300
	11,400
Less: Annual exemption	8,500
CGT assessment	2,900

There will be no unrelieved capital losses to carry forward.

(b) A Section 72 claim would have to be for the lower of:

(i) the trading loss (£12,500)

(ii) the CGT assessment (disregarding the annual exemption) that would be raised if a Section 72 claim were not made (£11,400).

Therefore the Section 72 claim would be £11,400. This would be relieved in priority to capital losses brought forward. The CGT assessment would be:

	£
Net gains	14,700
Less: Section 72 claim	11,400
	3,300
Less: Annual exemption (restricted)	3,300
CGT assessment	nil

The remainder of the annual exemption (£5,200) would be lost. There would be no scope for relieving any of the capital losses brought forward, so the entire £3,300 would be carried forward to 2006/07. This Section 72 claim would seem to be quite wasteful, since trading losses of £11,400 are sacrificed in order to reduce the CGT assessment by £2,900 and preserve capital losses of £3,300 (a total of £6,200).

(c) Without a Section 72 claim, the CGT assessment would be calculated as follows:

	£
Net gains	14,700
Less: Capital losses b/f (restricted)	6,200
	8,500
Less: Annual exemption	8,500
CGT assessment	nil

There would be unrelieved capital losses of £1,100 carried forward. The maximum amount for Section 72 purposes is £7,400 (£14,700 - £7,300) so a Section 72 claim would have to be for £7,400 and the CGT assessment would be:

	£
Net gains	14,700
Less: Section 72 claim	7,400
	7,300
Less: Annual exemption (restricted)	7,300
CGT assessment	nil

The remainder of the annual exemption (£1,200) would be lost and the capital losses of £7,300 would be carried forward to 2006/07 in their entirety. The effect of the claim would be to preserve capital losses of £6,200 at the expense of sacrificing trading losses of £7,400. This might be worthwhile if Richard believes that he will have more chance of relieving capital losses than trading losses in future years.

Administration of CGT

The administration system which was described in Chapter 1 applies to CGT as well as to income tax. Note that:

(a) Taxpayers are normally not required to fill in the capital gains tax pages of their tax returns if both of the following conditions are satisfied:

  (i) total disposal proceeds for the year do not exceed four times the amount of the annual exemption (£34,000 for 2005/06)

  (ii) total chargeable gains for the year do not exceed the amount of the annual exemption (£8,500 for 2005/06),

  For this purpose, the meaning of the term "total chargeable gains" depends upon whether there are any allowable losses (either current year losses or losses brought forward) to be deducted from the year's chargeable gains. If there are no such losses, then the total chargeable gains for the year are computed *after* deduction of taper relief. But if there are any allowable losses, then the total chargeable gains are computed *before* deduction of losses and *before* deduction of taper relief.

(b) A capital loss is not an allowable loss unless its amount is quantified and notified to HM Revenue and Customs. If the taxpayer receives a tax return for the year in which a loss is incurred, then notification must be made in that return. Otherwise, notification may be made in a later year's tax return or by sending a separate notice to HMRC. Losses are not allowed unless notified to HMRC by 31 January in the sixth year of assessment following the year in which the losses are incurred. For example, the latest date by which capital losses incurred in 2005/06 must be notified to HMRC is 31 January 2012.

(c) Acquisitions of chargeable assets do not need to be entered on the tax return.

Payment of CGT

CGT is normally payable on 31 January following the end of the tax year to which the tax relates. For instance, the normal due date for the 2005/06 CGT liability is 31 January 2007. An important difference between the payment of CGT and the payment of income tax is that payments on account of the CGT liability are *not* required.

If the proceeds of a disposal are received by the taxpayer in instalments over a period of more than 18 months, the taxpayer may make a claim for the CGT due in relation to the disposal to be payable over the period of the instalments or over an 8-year period, whichever is the shorter.

Interest, surcharges and penalties

The regime of interest, surcharges and penalties which was described in Chapter 14 applies to both CGT and income tax.

Summary

- A liability to CGT may arise when a chargeable person makes a chargeable disposal of a chargeable asset. Individuals resident or ordinarily resident in the UK are chargeable persons. Companies are not chargeable persons.
- All assets are chargeable assets unless specifically exempted.
- A chargeable disposal occurs when all or part of a chargeable asset is sold other than in the course of trade, given away, lost or destroyed.
- An individual's CGT liability for a tax year is based upon the chargeable disposals made by that individual during the tax year. For 2005/06, the first £8,500 of net gains is exempt from CGT.
- Capital gains tax is payable at the same rates as the rates of income tax which apply to savings income.
- Net losses may be carried forward and set against the net gains of subsequent years. Net losses incurred in the year of death of a taxpayer may be carried back for up to three years. Losses incurred on a disposal to a connected person may be offset only against gains made on disposals to the same connected person.
- In certain circumstances, trading losses may be set against net gains.
- CGT is normally payable on 31 January following the end of the tax year.

Exercises

16.1 Which of the following disposals might give rise to a CGT liability?

(a) the sale of freehold property by a UK company

(b) the gift of shares from husband to wife (assuming that the couple live together)

(c) the gift of an oil painting to a charity

(d) the sale of an oil painting by a charity

(e) the sale of an oil painting by an art dealer

(f) the sale of leasehold property by a partnership.

16.2 Which of the following are chargeable assets for CGT purposes?

(a) shares in British Telecom plc

(b) gilt-edged securities

(c) an antique table worth £20,000

(d) an antique chair worth £5,000

(e) a taxpayer's home

(f) a vintage Bentley.

16.3 A taxpayer has capital losses of £2,500 in 2005/06. Compute the CGT assessment for 2005/06 if capital gains for the year are as follows (assuming that there are no unrelieved losses brought forward or carried back and that no taper relief is available):

either (a) £nil
or (b) £1,500
or (c) £6,150
or (d) £12,450.

16.4 A single man's only income in 2005/06 consists of a salary of £33,570. His CGT assessment for the year is £5,400. Calculate his CGT liability, assuming that he makes no Gift Aid donations and pays no personal pension premiums in the year.

16.5 A taxpayer has capital losses brought forward from previous years amounting to £4,800. Compute the CGT assessment for 2005/06 if total gains and losses for the year are as follows (and no taper relief is available):

either (a) gains £8,600, losses £2,000
or (b) gains £9,900, losses £800
or (c) gains £14,500, losses £nil.

16.6 John dies on 3 March 2006. Between 6 April 2005 and 3 March 2006, he has total gains of £1,200 and total losses of £15,400. His net gains in recent years have been as follows:

	£
2001/02	52,100
2002/03	14,200
2003/04	10,700
2004/05	1,750

Show how the losses incurred in the year of John's death may be relieved, given that the annual exemption was £7,500 in 2001/02, £7,700 in 2002/03, £7,900 in 2003/04 and £8,200 in 2004/05. (No taper relief is available in any year.)

16.7 On what date is CGT for 2005/06 normally due for payment?

***16.8** Rosemary has the following capital gains and losses:

	Gains	*Losses*
	£	£
2002/03	6,200	12,700
2003/04	7,700	2,350
2004/05	11,000	nil
2005/06	17,600	7,500

There were no unrelieved losses to bring forward from 2001/02 or earlier years. Compute her CGT assessments for the years 2002/03 to 2005/06, given that the annual exemption was £7,700 in 2002/03, £7,900 in 2003/04 and £8,200 in 2004/05. (No taper relief is available in any year.)

***16.9** In 2004/05, Ahmed incurred a capital loss of £3,750 on the disposal of an asset to his father. He also had capital gains in that year of £11,200. In 2005/06, Ahmed has capital gains of £38,000 and no losses. The capital gains in 2005/06 include gains of £2,000 on a disposal to his father and £3,500 on a disposal to his mother.

Compute Ahmed's CGT assessments for the years 2004/05 and 2005/06 given that the annual exemption was £8,200 in 2004/05. (No taper relief is available in either year.)

***16.10** Melissa is a sole trader. She has trading losses eligible for a Section 72 claim in 2005/06 of £13,500. Her capital gains and capital losses for 2005/06 are £24,800 and £1,000 respectively. She has capital losses brought forward from 2004/05 of £13,700.

Show Melissa's CGT assessment for 2005/06, assuming that:

(a) the Section 72 claim is not made

(b) the Section 72 claim is made.

No taper relief is available in 2005/06.

Chapter 17

Computation of gains and losses

Introduction

The computation of the gain arising on the disposal of a chargeable asset begins by subtracting the acquisition cost of the asset from its disposal value. It may then be necessary to adjust the gain to take account of inflation and it may also be necessary to deduct taper relief. The computation becomes more complex if the asset was acquired on or before 31 March 1982.

The main purpose of this chapter is to explain the basic method of computation and to show how this method is modified for disposals of older assets.

Layout of a CGT computation

The computation of the chargeable gain or allowable loss arising on a chargeable disposal is laid out as follows:

	£	£
Disposal value		x
Less: Incidental costs of disposal		x
		x
Less: *Allowable expenditure*:		
Acquisition cost of asset	x	
Incidental costs of acquisition	x	
Enhancement expenditure	x	
Cost of defending the owner's title to the asset	x	
Valuation fees	x	x
Unindexed gain or loss		x
Less: Indexation allowance		x
Chargeable gain (before taper relief) or allowable loss		x

Each of the terms used in this layout is explained below.

Disposal value

If a disposal consists of the sale of an asset, disposal value is generally taken to be the proceeds of the sale. But if a sale does not constitute a bargain made at arm's length, the sale proceeds are ignored and disposal value is taken to be the market value of the asset on the date of the sale. This rule applies particularly to transactions between "connected persons". For CGT purposes, a taxpayer is connected to his or her:

(a) spouse (husband or wife)

(b) relatives (brothers, sisters, ancestors, direct descendants) and their spouses

(c) spouse's relatives and their spouses

(d) business partners and their spouses and relatives.

As from 5 December 2005, all references above to "spouse" should be taken to include same-sex civil partners who have entered into a legally-recognised civil partnership.

Market value is also used as disposal value if a disposal takes the form of a gift. But disposals between spouses (or civil partners) who live together are deemed to occur at a disposal value such that neither a gain nor a loss arises (see Chapter 16). This rule takes precedence over the usual rules concerning sales to connected persons and gifts.

In general, the market value of an asset is the amount which the asset would fetch if sold on the open market. Shares and securities which are listed on a recognised stock exchange ("listed" or "quoted" shares or securities) are valued for CGT purposes in the same way as they are valued for inheritance tax purposes (see Chapter 31).

The incidental costs of disposal which may be deducted when calculating a gain or loss include legal fees, estate agents' and auctioneers' fees, advertising costs etc.

Allowable expenditure

The following expenditure may be set against disposal value when calculating the gain or loss arising on a disposal:

(a) the acquisition cost of the asset (or its market value on the date of acquisition if it was acquired by gift or otherwise than by way of a bargain made at arm's length)

(b) incidental costs of acquisition (e.g. legal fees)

(c) "enhancement expenditure", which is expenditure on making improvements to the asset, so long as that expenditure is still reflected in the state of the asset at the time of disposal (but the costs of mere repairs and maintenance are disallowed)

(d) costs incurred in defending the owner's title to the asset (generally legal costs)

(e) valuation fees necessarily incurred for CGT purposes.

If an asset is acquired as the result of a disposal between spouses (or civil partners) who live together, the deemed acquisition cost for the spouse or partner receiving the asset is equal to the deemed disposal value for the spouse or partner who makes the disposal (see above).

Indexation allowance

The object of indexation allowance is to ensure that any gains which have been caused solely by the effects of inflation are not charged to tax. The allowance was originally introduced in 1982 but was "frozen" at April 1998. In consequence, no indexation allowance is available in relation to inflation occurring after April 1998.

Indexation allowance is calculated separately for each item of allowable expenditure shown in a computation. The indexation allowance available on an item of expenditure is equal to the amount of that expenditure multiplied by an *indexation factor*, which is computed according to the following formula and rounded to three decimal places:

$$\frac{RD - RI}{RI}$$

where: RD is the Retail Prices Index (RPI) for the month of disposal or for April 1998, whichever is the earlier, and

RI is the RPI for the month in which the expenditure was incurred.

A table of RPIs is given at the end of this chapter. It is very important to note that:

(a) No indexation allowance is given in relation to allowable expenditure incurred on or after 1 April 1998.

(b) Special rules apply to expenditure incurred before 31 March 1982 (see later in this chapter).

(c) Although companies are not chargeable persons for CGT purposes, their capital gains are computed in a similar way to those of individuals and are then charged to corporation tax. However, the freezing of indexation allowance at April 1998 does *not* apply to companies (see Chapter 23).

EXAMPLE 1

An asset was bought in June 1989 (RPI 115.4) for £1,200 and was sold in August 2005 (RPI 193.0) for £3,350. The RPI for April 1998 was 162.6. Compute the chargeable gain.

Solution

	£
Sale proceeds	3,350
Less: Acquisition cost	1,200
Unindexed gain	2,150
Less: Indexation allowance	
$\frac{162.6 - 115.4}{115.4}$ = 0.409 x £1,200	491
Chargeable gain (before taper relief)	1,659

(Note that the RPI for August 2005 was not used in this computation).

EXAMPLE 2

An asset was bought for £15,000 in August 1990 (RPI 128.1). Enhancement expenditure was £2,000 in January 1991 (RPI 130.2) and £3,000 in June 2000. The asset was sold in July 2005 for £28,000. The RPI for April 1998 was 162.6. Compute the chargeable gain.

Solution

		£	£
Sale proceeds			28,000
Less:	Acquisition cost	15,000	
	Enhancement expenditure (£2,000 + £3,000)	5,000	20,000
Unindexed gain			8,000
Less:	Indexation allowance:		
	(i) on acquisition cost		
	$\frac{162.6 - 128.1}{128.1}$ = 0.269 x £15,000	4,035	
	(ii) on enhancement expenditure		
	$\frac{162.6 - 130.2}{130.2}$ = 0.249 x £2,000	498	4,533
Chargeable gain (before taper relief)			3,467

(Indexation allowance is not available on the expenditure incurred in June 2000).

Restrictions on indexation allowance

Note the following points about the indexation allowance:

(a) If RPI goes *down* between the month in which expenditure is incurred and the month of disposal (or April 1998), the indexation allowance available in relation to that expenditure is nil.

(b) No indexation allowance is available in respect of the incidental costs of disposal, even if they were incurred prior to the month of disposal.

(c) Indexation allowance cannot be used to convert a gain into a loss. Therefore, if the indexation allowance (calculated in the normal way) exceeds the unindexed gain, the indexation allowance is restricted so as to give neither a gain nor a loss.

(d) Indexation allowance cannot be used to increase an unindexed loss. If there is an unindexed loss on a disposal then the indexation allowance is nil.

EXAMPLE 3

An asset was acquired in February 1987 (RPI 100.4) at a cost of £5,000. The asset was sold in January 2006. The RPI for April 1998 was 162.6. Compute the chargeable gain or allowable loss if the sale proceeds were:

(a) £9,000 (b) £6,500 (c) £4,800

Solution

	(a) £	(b) £	(c) £
Sale proceeds	9,000	6,500	4,800
<u>Less</u>: Acquisition cost	5,000	5,000	5,000
Unindexed gain or loss	4,000	1,500	(200)
<u>Less</u>: Indexation allowance			
$\frac{162.6 - 100.4}{100.4} = 0.620 \times £5,000$	3,100	1,500	nil
Chargeable gain (before taper relief) or allowable loss	900	nil	(200)

Notes:

(i) In case (a), the indexation allowance can be given in full.

(ii) In case (b), the full indexation allowance would convert an unindexed gain of £1,500 into a loss of £1,600. Indexation allowance is restricted to £1,500 to prevent this.

(iii) In case (c) there is an unindexed loss, so indexation allowance is restricted to £nil.

Taper relief

To compensate for the freezing of indexation allowance at April 1998, the gain arising on a disposal occurring on or after 6 April 1998 may be reduced by taper relief, which is calculated according to:

(a) the number of *complete* years in the "qualifying holding period" of the asset (i.e. the period for which the asset has been held after 5 April 1998)

(b) whether the asset is classed as a "business asset" or a "non-business asset"

(c) the extent to which the gain has been reduced by losses of the same year or losses brought forward or carried back (see later in this chapter).

For disposals occurring on or after 6 April 2002, taper relief is calculated by reference to the following tables:

No of years held after 5/4/98	*% of gain chargeable (business assets)*
0	100
1	50
2 or more	25

No of years held after 5/4/98	*% of gain chargeable (non-business assets)*
2 or less	100
3	95
4	90
5	85
6	80
7	75
8	70
9	65
10 or more	60

Note that:

(a) A *non-business* asset acquired before 17 March 1998 qualifies for an addition of one year to its qualifying holding period (often referred to as the "bonus year").

(b) If enhancement expenditure has been incurred in relation to an asset, the date of that expenditure is not relevant for taper relief purposes. Taper relief on the whole of the gain arising on disposal is calculated according to the date on which the asset was originally acquired.

(c) If an asset is transferred between spouses (or same-sex civil partners) who live together, taper relief on a subsequent disposal is based on the combined period of holding by both of the spouses (or partners).

(d) Taper relief is *not* available to companies (which pay corporation tax on their chargeable gains).

EXAMPLE 4

Assuming that a gain arises on each of the following disposals (and that no losses are to be set against that gain), state the percentage of the gain which will be chargeable to CGT:

(a) A business asset is acquired on 1 January 2005 and disposed of on 17 March 2006.

(b) A non-business asset is acquired on 23 June 1996 and disposed of on 9 April 2005.

(c) A non-business asset is acquired on 27 March 1998 and disposed of on 8 May 2007.

(d) A business asset is acquired on 1 March 1998 and disposed of on 3 April 2005.

Solution

(a) 50% (business asset, qualifying holding period 1 year)

(b) 70% (non-business asset, qualifying holding period 8 years including bonus year)

(c) 65% (non-business asset, qualifying holding period 9 years)

(d) 25% (business asset, qualifying holding period 6 years).

Business assets and non-business assets

For taper relief purposes, a gain is a gain on the disposal of a business asset if the asset was a business asset throughout the "relevant period". This period is the shorter of:

(a) the period after 5 April 1998 for which the asset was held before disposal

(b) the period of 10 years ending on the date of disposal.

If an asset was a business asset for only *part* of the relevant period, the gain is time-apportioned accordingly into two gains. These two gains are then treated as if they had arisen on the disposal of two separate assets (one business asset and one non-business asset) each held for the *whole* of the qualifying holding period. A similar approach is adopted if an asset is used partly for business purposes and partly for private purposes throughout the relevant period.

The definition of "business asset" has changed several times since taper relief was introduced. As from 6 April 2004, business assets are defined broadly as follows:

(a) assets used for trade purposes by any individual or partnership (whether or not the taxpayer who owns the asset is involved in the carrying on of the trade)

(b) assets used for the purposes of the taxpayer's employment, so long as the taxpayer is employed by a person who is carrying on a trade

(c) assets used for trade purposes by a "qualifying company" or shares in a qualifying company (see below).

Qualifying companies

For taper relief purposes, a *trading* company is a qualifying company with respect to a taxpayer if *one or more* of the following conditions are met:

(a) the company's shares are not listed on a recognised stock exchange (the company is "unlisted" or "unquoted")

(b) the taxpayer is an officer or employee of the company

(c) the taxpayer has at least 5% of the voting rights in the company.

A *non-trading* company is a qualifying company with respect to a taxpayer only if the taxpayer is an officer or employee of that company and does not have a "material interest" in the company. A taxpayer has a material interest in a company if he or she holds more than 10% of any class of shares in the company or holds more than 10% of the company's voting rights.

Most business activities are treated as trades for taper relief purposes. However, share investment and property investment are not trades. If a company has both trading and non-trading activities, it will be treated as a trading company so long as the non-trading activities are not "substantial". It is the practice of HM Revenue and Customs to treat a company as a trading company if the company derives no more than 20% of its income from non-trading activities.

Interaction of taper relief and losses

Taper relief is applied only to those gains which remain after deducting:

(a) allowable losses for the year

(b) allowable losses brought forward from previous years

(c) allowable losses carried back from the year of death.

The allocation of losses to gains for this purpose is to be done on the basis which produces the lowest charge to tax. This means that losses should be deducted from gains which have a high chargeable percentage in priority to gains which have a low chargeable percentage.

EXAMPLE 5

A taxpayer has the following chargeable gains (before taper relief) in 2005/06:

(a) a gain of £12,000 on a business asset, qualifying holding period 1 year (Gain A)

(b) a gain of £10,000 on a non-business asset, qualifying holding period 4 years (Gain B)

(c) a gain of £3,000 on a non-business asset, qualifying holding period 2 years (Gain C).

The taxpayer also has a single allowable loss of £8,000 in the year. Compute the CGT assessment for the year.

Solution

	Total	*Gain A (50%)*	*Gain B (90%)*	*Gain C (100%)*
	£	£	£	£
Chargeable gains	25,000	12,000	10,000	3,000
Less: Allowable losses	8,000		5,000	3,000
	17,000	12,000	5,000	nil
Less: Taper relief	6,500	6,000	500	nil
Tapered gains	10,500	6,000	4,500	nil
Less: Annual exemption	8,500			
CGT assessment	2,000			

The allowable loss is set first against Gain C (which attracts no taper relief) and then against Gain B (which attracts a lower rate of taper relief than Gain A). In this way, the gains which remain after deduction of taper relief are held to a minimum.

Trading losses and taper relief

If trading losses sustained in 2004/05 or subsequent years are set against capital gains under Section 72 of Finance Act 1991 (see Chapter 16) the "maximum amount" of the Section 72 claim is equal to the amount of the CGT assessment that would have been raised for the year if a Section 72 claim had not been made, disregarding the annual exemption and *before deduction of taper relief*.

For trading losses sustained in 2003/04 or earlier years, the maximum amount of a Section 72 claim was generally equal to the CGT assessment that would have been raised for the year if the claim had not been made, disregarding the annual exemption and *after* deduction of taper relief. However, a taxpayer who made a Section 72 claim in respect of a trading loss incurred in 2002/03 or 2003/04 could elect that the maximum amount should be computed before deduction of taper relief.

EXAMPLE 6

Charlie's only disposal in 2005/06 is a business asset disposed of in May 2005. The asset was purchased in July 2003 and the chargeable gain on the disposal (before taper relief) is £20,000. Charlie also has trading losses of £21,500 which are available for relief under Section 72 of Finance Act 1991. Compute Charlie's CGT assessment for 2005/06, if:

(a) he has no capital losses b/f and does not make a Section 72 claim

(b) he has £15,000 of capital losses b/f and does not make a Section 72 claim

(c) he has £15,000 of capital losses b/f and makes a Section 72 claim

(d) he has £2,000 of capital losses b/f and does not make a Section 72 claim

(e) he has £2,000 of capital losses b/f and makes a Section 72 claim.

Solution

The asset disposed of is a business asset with a qualifying holding period of 1 year, so the chargeable percentage is 50%. The computations are as follows:

	(a)	(b)	(c)	(d)	(e)
	£	£	£	£	£
Chargeable gains	20,000	20,000	20,000	20,000	20,000
Less: Section 72 relief	-	-	5,000	-	18,000
	20,000	20,000	15,000	20,000	2,000
Less: Capital losses b/f	-	11,500	6,500	2,000	-
	20,000	8,500	8,500	18,000	2,000
Less: Taper relief	10,000	4,250	4,250	9,000	1,000
	10,000	4,250	4,250	9,000	1,000
Less: Annual exemption	8,500	4,250	4,250	8,500	1,000
CGT assessment	1,500	nil	nil	500	nil

Notes:

(i) In case (b), capital losses b/f must be used to the extent that net gains (before taper relief) exceed the annual exemption.

(ii) In case (c), the maximum amount of a Section 72 claim is £5,000 (£20,000 - £15,000). This displaces £5,000 of capital losses b/f and therefore conserves capital losses at the expense of trading losses.

(iii) In case (e), the maximum amount of a Section 72 claim is £18,000. The effect of this claim is to conserve all £2,000 of capital losses b/f and to reduce the CGT assessment by £500. However, taper relief of £8,000 is lost, as is £7,500 of the annual exemption. This is a very inefficient claim.

Part disposals

If only *part* of a chargeable asset is disposed of, only part of its cost can be allowed when computing the gain or loss. The allowable part cost is the full cost of the asset multiplied by the following fraction:

$$\frac{A}{A+B}$$

where: A is the value of the part disposed of (i.e. the disposal value), and

B is the value of the part remaining in the taxpayer's ownership.

This part disposal fraction applies not only to the acquisition cost of the asset but also to any other items of allowable expenditure which relate to the whole asset. But any item of expenditure which relates only to the part of the asset which has been disposed of should be allowed in full.

EXAMPLE 7

Peter buys a chargeable asset for £26,000 in October 1995 (RPI 149.8). He sells a one-quarter interest in the asset for £12,000 in August 2005, incurring incidental costs of disposal of £500. The value of the other three-quarters interest in the asset in August 2005 is £40,000. The RPI for April 1998 was 162.6. Calculate the chargeable gain.

Solution

	£
Sale proceeds	12,000
Less: Incidental costs of disposal	500
	11,500
Less: Part cost:	
$\frac{£12,000}{£12,000 + £40,000}$ x £26,000	6,000
Unindexed gain	5,500
Less: Indexation allowance	
$\frac{162.6 - 149.8}{149.8}$ = 0.085 x £6,000	510
Chargeable gain (before taper relief)	4,990

Notes:

(i) The fact that Peter has sold a one-quarter interest in the asset is irrelevant. What is relevant is that he has sold £12,000 worth out of an asset currently worth £52,000, as indicated by the part disposal fraction.

(ii) The incidental costs of disposal clearly relate only to the part of the asset that has been disposed of, not to the whole asset. Therefore these costs are allowed in full.

(iii) If Peter disposes of the remaining three-quarters of the asset at some future time, the remainder of the cost i.e. £20,000 (£26,000 - £6,000) will be allowable in the computation of the gain arising on that disposal.

Small part disposals of land

An exception to the usual part disposal rules occurs when a taxpayer makes a "small" part disposal of land. For this purpose a disposal of land is regarded as "small" so long as the following conditions are met:

(a) The land in question must be freehold or long leasehold (i.e. held on a lease with more than 50 years left to run).

(b) If the disposal is caused by a compulsory purchase order, the disposal proceeds must be no more than 5% of the value of the whole piece of land.

(c) If the disposal is not caused by a compulsory purchase order, the disposal proceeds must be no more than 20% of the value of the whole piece of land and the total proceeds of all disposals of land in the year of assessment (excluding small disposals caused by compulsory purchases) must be no more than £20,000.

In these circumstances, the taxpayer may claim that there should be no chargeable gain and that, instead, the disposal proceeds should be subtracted from the original cost of the land for CGT purposes. This has the effect of increasing the chargeable gain arising on a subsequent disposal of the remainder of the land and therefore, in effect, the gain arising on the small part disposal is deferred. Obviously, the taxpayer will not make such a claim if the gain arising on the small part disposal is covered by the annual exemption for the year.

On a subsequent disposal of the remainder of the land, it would be unfair to calculate indexation allowance on the reduced cost only. Instead, indexation allowance is first calculated on the full original cost of the land and is then reduced by a negative indexation allowance, calculated on the proceeds of the small part disposal.

It is very important to appreciate that these small part disposal rules apply only to land, whereas the more general part disposal rules explained earlier apply to all types of chargeable asset.

EXAMPLE 8

In July 1989 (RPI 115.5), Malcolm bought a piece of land for £40,000. In June 1993 (RPI 141.0) he sold part of the land for £11,000 (this being his only disposal of land in 1993/94). The value of the remainder of the land at the time of the part disposal was £50,000. Malcolm had substantial capital gains in 1993/94, sufficient to absorb his annual exemption for the year, and therefore decided to make the small part disposal claim.

Calculate the chargeable gain arising in January 2006 when Malcolm sells the remainder of the land for £60,000. The RPI for April 1998 was 162.6.

Solution

The small part disposal claim in 1993/94 was valid since the total value of the land immediately prior to the disposal was £61,000 (£11,000 + £50,000) and the disposal raised £11,000 which is less than 20% of £61,000. Also, the disposal proceeds of all land disposals in the year did not exceed £20,000. The gain on the January 2006 disposal is as follows:

			£
Sale proceeds			60,000
Less: Reduced cost (£40,000 - £11,000)			29,000
Unindexed gain			31,000
Less: Indexation allowance:			
(i) on full original cost			
$\frac{162.6 - 115.5}{115.5}$	= 0.408 x £40,000	16,320	
(ii) on proceeds of small part disposal			
$\frac{162.6 - 141.0}{141.0}$	= 0.153 x £11,000	(1,683)	14,637
Chargeable gain (before taper relief)			16,363

Assets with negligible value

If the value of a chargeable asset has become negligible, the owner of the asset may make a "negligible value" claim. If this claim is accepted, the asset is treated as if it had been disposed of at its current, negligible value (giving rise to an allowable loss) and then immediately re-acquired at that value.

Assets held on 31 March 1982

CGT was originally introduced in 1965 and applied to disposals made on or after 6 April 1965 (the "base date" for CGT). Gains accruing before 6 April 1965 were not taxable. Therefore, if an asset was acquired before 6 April 1965 and disposed of after that date, only the part of the gain accruing after 6 April 1965 was taxable.

The Finance Act 1988 changed the CGT base date to 31 March 1982. Therefore, if an asset is now disposed of which was acquired before 31 March 1982, only the part of the gain accruing since 31 March 1982 is taxable. The calculation of the taxable part of the gain is achieved by means of a technique known as "rebasing" whereby the market value of the asset at 31 March 1982 is substituted for its original acquisition cost in the CGT calculation. However, rebasing does *not* apply if the rebasing calculation results in a greater gain than the calculation based on original cost.

EXAMPLE 9

A chargeable asset was acquired in April 1980 for £2,000 and sold in January 2006 for £9,500. Compute the unindexed gain if the asset's market value at 31 March 1982 was:

(a) £4,200 (b) £1,500

Solution

(a) The unindexed gain over the entire period of ownership, based on the original cost of the asset, is £7,500 (£9,500 - £2,000). But the rebasing calculation gives an unindexed gain of only £5,300 (£9,500 - £4,200). This is less than the gain based on original cost so rebasing applies and the unindexed gain is £5,300.

(b) The rebasing calculation gives an unindexed gain of £8,000 (£9,500 - £1,500). This is more than the gain based on original cost so rebasing does not apply and the unindexed gain is £7,500.

Indexation allowance for pre-31 March 1982 assets

The rules for calculating the indexation allowance available on the disposal of an asset held on 31 March 1982 are as follows:

(a) Indexation allowance is based on the change in RPI between March 1982 and the month of disposal (or April 1998, if earlier). No further indexation allowance is available to compensate for the effects of pre-March 1982 inflation (which is why the table of RPIs at the end of this chapter begins with the RPI for March 1982).

(b) In *both* the rebasing calculation and the calculation based on original cost, indexation allowance is calculated with reference to the *greater* of original cost and market value at 31 March 1982 i.e. the same indexation allowance is given in both calculations.

EXAMPLE 10

Calculate the chargeable gain arising on the disposal described in the above example. RPI for March 1982 was 79.44 and RPI for April 1998 was 162.6.

Solution

(a)

		Original cost	Rebasing
		£	£
Sale proceeds		9,500	9,500
Less: Original cost		2,000	
Market value 31/3/82			4,200
Unindexed gain		7,500	5,300
Less: Indexation allowance			
$\frac{162.6 - 79.44}{79.44}$	= 1.047 x £4,200	4,397	4,397
Chargeable gain (before taper relief)		3,103	903

The rebasing calculation gives the lower gain, so rebasing applies and the chargeable gain (before taper relief) is £903.

(b)

		Original cost	Rebasing
		£	£
Sale proceeds		9,500	9,500
Less: Original cost		2,000	
Market value 31/3/82			1,500
Unindexed gain		7,500	8,000
Less: Indexation allowance			
$\frac{162.6 - 79.44}{79.44}$	= 1.047 x £2,000	2,094	2,094
Chargeable gain (before taper relief)		5,406	5,906

The rebasing calculation gives the higher gain, so rebasing does not apply and the chargeable gain (before taper relief) is £5,406.

EXAMPLE 11

In May 1979, Margaret bought a chargeable asset for £10,000. Enhancement expenditure was incurred of £2,000 in June 1980 and £3,000 in June 1984 (RPI 89.20). The asset had a market value of £16,000 on 31 March 1982 (RPI 79.44) and was sold in July 2005 for £40,000. The RPI for April 1998 was 162.6. Compute the chargeable gain.

Solution

		Original cost	*Rebasing*
	£	£	£
Sale proceeds		40,000	40,000
Less: Cost up to 31 March 1982:			
Acquisition cost	10,000		
Enhancement expenditure June 1980	2,000	(12,000)	
Market value 31 March 1982			(16,000)
Enhancement expenditure June 1984		(3,000)	(3,000)
Unindexed gain		25,000	21,000
Less: Indexation allowance:			
(i) on MV at 31 March 1982 $\frac{162.6 - 79.44}{79.44}$ = 1.047 x £16,000	16,752		
(ii) on enhancement June 1984 $\frac{162.6 - 89.20}{89.20}$ = 0.823 x £3,000	2,469	19,221	19,221
Chargeable gain (before taper relief)		5,779	1,779

The rebasing calculation gives the lower gain, so rebasing applies and the chargeable gain (before taper relief) is £1,779.

Notes:

(i) Margaret has spent a total of £15,000 (£10,000 + £2,000 + £3,000) on buying and enhancing the asset. Therefore the calculation based on original cost takes into account total allowable expenditure of £15,000.

(ii) The market value at 31 March 1982 is the value of the asset as it stood on that date (i.e. the value of the asset including the June 1980 enhancement). But this valuation did not take into account the second enhancement, which did not occur until June 1984. Therefore the rebasing calculation takes into account both the market value at 31 March 1982 and the cost of the second enhancement.

(iii) Indexation allowance based on the change in RPI from March 1982 to April 1998 is given on *the greater of total cost up to 31 March 1982 and market value at 31 March 1982*. Indexation allowance is also given on the second enhancement, based on the change in RPI from June 1984 to April 1998.

Losses on disposal of pre-31 March 1982 assets

As shown above, if the rebasing calculation gives a gain and the original cost calculation also gives a gain, the chargeable gain is the *smaller* of these two gains. Similarly, if the rebasing calculation gives a loss and the original cost calculation also gives a loss, the allowable loss is the *smaller* of these two losses. Finally, if the rebasing calculation gives a loss and the original cost calculation gives a gain (or vice versa), or if either of the calculations gives a nil result, the situation is "no gain, no loss" i.e. there is no chargeable gain and no allowable loss.

EXAMPLE 12

Neil acquired a chargeable asset in 1978. The asset was sold in May 2005 for £2,200. The RPI for April 1998 was 162.6. Compute the chargeable gain or allowable loss if the original cost of the asset and its market value on 31 March 1982 (RPI 79.44) were:

	Original cost	*MV 31 March 1982*
	£	£
(a)	750	850
(b)	3,500	4,000
(c)	10	2,050

Solution

(a)

	Original cost	*Rebasing*
	£	£
Sale proceeds	2,200	2,200
Less: Original cost	750	
Market value 31/3/82		850
Unindexed gain	1,450	1,350
Less: Indexation allowance		
$\frac{162.6 - 79.44}{79.44}$ = 1.047 x £850	890	890
Chargeable gain (before taper relief)	560	460

The rebasing calculation gives the lower gain, so rebasing applies and the chargeable gain (before taper relief) is £460.

(b)

	Original cost	*Rebasing*
	£	£
Sale proceeds	2,200	2,200
Less: Original cost	3,500	
Market value 31/3/82		4,000
Allowable loss	(1,300)	(1,800)

The rebasing calculation gives the higher loss, so rebasing does not apply and the allowable loss is £1,300. Indexation allowance was £nil in both calculations, since indexation allowance cannot be used to increase an unindexed loss.

(c)	Original cost	Rebasing
	£	£
Sale proceeds	2,200	2,200
Less: Original cost	10	
Market value 31/3/82		2,050
Unindexed gain	2,190	150
Less: Indexation allowance		
$\frac{162.6 - 79.44}{79.44} = 1.047 \times £2,050$	2,146	150
Chargeable gain (before taper relief)	44	nil

The rebasing calculation gives a nil result, whilst the calculation based on original cost gives a gain. Therefore the situation is "no gain, no loss". Indexation allowance was restricted to £150 in the rebasing calculation, since indexation allowance cannot be used to convert a gain into a loss.

Part disposals of pre-31 March 1982 assets

When a part disposal is made of an asset which was owned on 31 March 1982, the part disposal fraction which is applied to the original cost of the asset (see earlier in this chapter) is also applied to the market value at 31 March 1982 for the purposes of the rebasing calculation.

EXAMPLE 13

A chargeable asset was purchased in November 1976 for £2,000. The asset had a market value on 31 March 1982 (RPI 79.44) of £5,000. Part of the asset was disposed of for £8,000 in November 2005 at which time the remainder of the asset was valued at £12,000. The RPI for April 1998 was 162.6. Compute the chargeable gain.

Solution

The part disposal fraction to be used in this case is:

$$\frac{£8,000}{£8,000 + £12,000}$$

The computation of the chargeable gain is therefore as follows:

	Original cost	*Rebasing*
	£	£
Sale proceeds	8,000	8,000
Less: Part cost:		
$\frac{£8,000}{£8,000 + £12,000} \times £2,000$	800	
Part market value 31/3/82:		
$\frac{£8,000}{£8,000 + £12,000} \times £5,000$		2,000
Unindexed gain	7,200	6,000
Less: Indexation allowance		
$\frac{162.6 - 79.44}{79.44} = 1.047 \times £2,000$	2,094	2,094
Chargeable gain (before taper relief)	5,106	3,906

The rebasing calculation gives the lower gain, so rebasing applies and the chargeable gain (before taper relief) is £3,906.

The rebasing election

A taxpayer may make an *irrevocable* election to the effect that gains and losses arising on all future disposals of assets held on 31 March 1982 should be calculated by the rebasing method, with no reference whatsoever to the costs incurred before 31 March 1982. Such an election must be made on or before 31 January in the second tax year following the year in which the first disposal of a pre-31 March 1982 asset occurs after 5 April 1988. For example, if the first such disposal occurs during tax year 2005/06, the election must be made by 31 January 2008.

If this election is made, costs incurred before 31 March 1982 are completely ignored for all purposes, including calculation of the indexation allowance. Therefore indexation allowance will always be based upon market value at 31 March 1982, even if this is lower than the costs incurred before 31 March 1982.

Assets acquired before 6 April 1965

When CGT was first introduced, special rules were devised for the calculation of the gain arising on the disposal of an asset acquired before 6 April 1965. These rules are now falling into disuse as it becomes increasingly uncommon for a disposal to involve an asset acquired before 6 April 1965. Furthermore, from the perspective of disposals made in the 21st century, the disposal of an asset acquired before 6 April 1965 must also be the disposal of an asset held on 31 March 1982. Therefore rebasing is available in relation to such disposals and rebasing will generally give a lower gain than the gain calculated according to the special rules referred to above. However, these rules are still used if they give the lower gain.

In summary, the calculation of the chargeable gain arising on the disposal of an asset acquired before 6 April 1965 is as follows:

(a) The gain is first calculated by the "time apportionment" method. This method calculates the total gain arising since the asset was acquired and then apportions the gain between the period before 6 April 1965 (which is not taxable) and the period after 6 April 1965 (which is taxable). For the purposes of this method, indexation allowance is based on the higher of original cost and market value at 31 March 1982. If the asset was acquired before 6 April 1945 it is assumed to have been acquired on that date for time apportionment purposes.

(b) Alternatively, the taxpayer may elect for the "6 April 1965 market value" method (and will presumably do so if this produces a lower gain). This method calculates the gain by comparing disposal proceeds with the market value of the asset on 6 April 1965. For the purposes of this method, indexation allowance is based on the higher of market value at 6 April 1965 and market value at 31 March 1982.

(c) Finally, the gain produced by the above rules is compared with the gain produced by the rebasing rules and the lower gain is taken as the chargeable gain. The indexation allowance used in the rebasing calculation is based on either:

   (i) the greater of original cost and market value at 31 March 1982 (if the time apportionment method is being used), or

   (ii) the greater of market value at 6 April 1965 and market value at 31 March 1982 (if the taxpayer has elected for the 6 April 1965 market value method).

EXAMPLE 14

A chargeable asset was purchased on 6 October 1957 for £50,000 and sold on 6 October 2005 for £250,000. The market value of the asset was £25,000 on 6 April 1965 and £75,000 on 31 March 1982 (RPI 79.44). The RPI for April 1998 was 162.6. Compute the chargeable gain (performing apportionment calculations to the nearest month).

Solution

	Time apportionment	MV 6/4/65
	£	£
Sale proceeds	250,000	250,000
Less: Original cost	50,000	
Market value 6/4/65		25,000
Unindexed gain	200,000	225,000
Less: Indexation allowance		
$\frac{162.6 - 79.44}{79.44}$ = 1.047 x £75,000	78,525	78,525
Chargeable gain	121,475	146,475
Time apportioned $\frac{40.5}{48.0}$ x £121,475	102,495	

The gain produced by the time apportionment method is lower than the gain produced by the 6 April 1965 market value method. Therefore the taxpayer will not elect for the 6 April 1965 market value method and the gain (before considering rebasing) is £102,495. The gain produced by the rebasing calculation is £96,475 (£250,000 - £75,000 - £78,525). This is lower than the gain based on cost, so rebasing will apply and the chargeable gain (before taper relief) is £96,475.

Notes:

(i) Indexation allowance was based on 31 March 1982 market value in each case, since this was greater than original cost or 6 April 1965 market value.

(ii) The asset was owned for 48 years and disposal took place 40 years and 6 months after 6 April 1965, hence the time apportionment fraction used above.

Losses on disposal of pre-6 April 1965 assets

If all three of the computations required on the disposal of an asset held on 6 April 1965 result in a gain (as in the above example), the chargeable gain is the lowest of these three gains. But the situation is more complex if any of the computations result in a loss. If this happens, the following rules apply:

(a) If time apportionment gives a loss and market value at 6 April 1965 gives a gain or a smaller loss, the taxpayer will not elect (and cannot be forced to elect) for the 6 April 1965 market value method of calculation. The time apportioned loss is then compared with the outcome of the rebasing calculation in the usual way.

(b) If time apportionment gives a gain and market value at 6 April 1965 gives a loss, the situation is "no gain, no loss" and there is no need for a rebasing calculation.

(c) If time apportionment gives a loss and market value at 6 April 1965 gives a greater loss, the allowable loss is restricted to the amount of the loss based on original cost, *ignoring time apportionment*. This loss is then compared with the outcome of the rebasing calculation in the usual way.

EXAMPLE 15

A chargeable asset was purchased on 6 April 1963 for £24,000 and sold on 6 April 2005 for £18,000. RPI for April 1998 was 162.6. The market value of the asset was £26,000 on 6 April 1965 and £30,000 on 31 March 1982 (RPI 79.44). Compute the allowable loss.

Solution

	Time apportionment	*MV 6/4/65*
	£	£
Sale proceeds	18,000	18,000
Less: Original cost	24,000	
Market value 6/4/65		26,000
Unindexed loss	(6,000)	(8,000)
Less: Indexation allowance		
$\frac{162.6 - 79.44}{79.44}$ = 1.047 x £30,000	nil	nil
Allowable loss	(6,000)	(8,000)
Time apportioned $\frac{40}{42}$ x £6,000	(5,714)	

Time apportionment gives a loss and market value at 6 April 1965 gives a greater loss. Therefore the allowable loss is restricted to the amount of the loss based on original cost, ignoring time apportionment (£6,000). This loss is then compared with the loss produced by the rebasing calculation, which is £12,000 (£18,000 - £30,000). The allowable loss is the lower of these figures (£6,000).

Summary

- The disposal value of an asset is normally equal to sale proceeds, but if an asset is given away or is sold other than by way of a bargain at arm's length, the disposal value is deemed to be the market value of the asset on the date of disposal.
- Allowable costs include acquisition cost of the asset, costs of acquisition and disposal, enhancement expenditure, costs of defending the owner's title and valuation fees.
- Indexation allowance is calculated for each allowable cost (apart from the costs of disposal) and is based on the change in RPI between the month in which the cost was incurred and the month of the disposal (or April 1998, if earlier). Indexation allowance is not available for expenditure incurred on or after 1 April 1998.
- Indexation allowance cannot be used to create or increase a loss.
- Taper relief may be used to reduce a chargeable gain, depending upon the length of the qualifying holding period and the type of asset involved (business or non-business). This relief applies only to those gains remaining after losses have been relieved. Losses are allocated to gains on the basis which produces the lowest tax charge.
- On a part disposal, the allowable part cost is calculated by multiplying the full cost by the part disposal fraction.
- A taxpayer may claim that an asset has negligible value, so triggering a disposal which gives rise to an allowable loss.
- If an asset is disposed of which was owned on 31 March 1982, it is necessary to perform a calculation based on original cost and a "rebasing" calculation based on market value at 31 March 1982. The chargeable gain (allowable loss) is the lower of the gains (losses) given by these two calculations. If one calculation gives a gain and the other gives a loss (or either calculation gives a nil result) the situation is "no gain, no loss".
- A taxpayer may make a once-and-for-all election for the rebasing method to be used on all disposals of pre-31 March 1982 assets.
- Special rules apply to the disposal of assets owned on 6 April 1965.

Retail Prices Index (RPI)

(*Source*: Office for National Statistics)

	Jan	Feb	Mar	Apr	May	Jun	Jul	Aug	Sep	Oct	Nov	Dec
1982			79.44	81.04	81.62	81.85	81.88	81.90	81.85	82.26	82.66	82.51
1983	82.61	82.97	83.12	84.28	84.64	84.84	85.30	85.68	86.06	86.36	86.67	86.89
1984	86.84	87.20	87.48	88.64	88.97	89.20	89.10	89.94	90.11	90.67	90.95	90.87
1985	91.20	91.94	92.80	94.78	95.21	95.41	95.23	95.49	95.44	95.59	95.92	96.05
1986	96.25	96.60	96.73	97.67	97.85	97.79	97.52	97.82	98.30	98.45	99.29	99.62
1987	100.0	100.4	100.6	101.8	101.9	101.9	101.8	102.1	102.4	102.9	103.4	103.3
1988	103.3	103.7	104.1	105.8	106.2	106.6	106.7	107.9	108.4	109.5	110.0	110.3
1989	111.0	111.8	112.3	114.3	115.0	115.4	115.5	115.8	116.6	117.5	118.5	118.8
1990	119.5	120.2	121.4	125.1	126.2	126.7	126.8	128.1	129.3	130.3	130.0	129.9
1991	130.2	130.9	131.4	133.1	133.5	134.1	133.8	134.1	134.6	135.1	135.6	135.7
1992	135.6	136.3	136.7	138.8	139.3	139.3	138.8	138.9	139.4	139.9	139.7	139.2
1993	137.9	138.8	139.3	140.6	141.1	141.0	140.7	141.3	141.9	141.8	141.6	141.9
1994	141.3	142.1	142.5	144.2	144.7	144.7	144.0	144.7	145.0	145.2	145.3	146.0
1995	146.0	146.9	147.5	149.0	149.6	149.8	149.1	149.9	150.6	149.8	149.8	150.7
1996	150.2	150.9	151.5	152.6	152.9	153.0	152.4	153.1	153.8	153.8	153.9	154.4
1997	154.4	155.0	155.4	156.3	156.9	157.5	157.5	158.5	159.3	159.5	159.6	160.0
1998	159.5	160.3	160.8	162.6	163.5	163.4	163.0	163.7	164.4	164.5	164.4	164.4
1999	163.4	163.7	164.1	165.2	165.6	165.6	165.1	165.5	166.2	166.5	166.7	167.3
2000	166.6	167.5	168.4	170.1	170.7	171.1	170.5	170.5	171.7	171.6	172.1	172.2
2001	171.1	172.0	172.2	173.1	174.2	174.4	173.3	174.0	174.6	174.3	173.6	173.4
2002	173.3	173.8	174.5	175.7	176.2	176.2	175.9	176.4	177.6	177.9	178.2	178.5
2003	178.4	179.3	179.9	181.2	181.5	181.3	181.3	181.6	182.5	182.6	182.7	183.5
2004	183.1	183.8	184.6	185.7	186.5	186.8	186.8	187.4	188.1	188.6	189.0	189.9
2005	188.9	189.6	190.5	*191.0*	*191.5*	*192.0*	*192.5*	*193.0*	*193.5*	*194.0*	*194.5*	*195.0*
2006	*195.5*	*196.0*	*196.5*									

Notes:

(i) Indexation allowance is frozen at April 1998 for individuals. The RPIs for May 1998 onwards are used only when computing the chargeable gains of companies.

(ii) RPIs for April 2005 and later months have been estimated by the author.

Exercises

17.1 Carol purchased a holiday flat in December 1987 (RPI 103.3) for £35,000. She spent £3,000 on installing central heating in February 1988 (RPI 103.7) and a further £650 on repainting the interior of the flat in March 1992 (RPI 136.7). The flat was never Carol's main residence. She sold the flat at auction in February 2006 (RPI 196.0) for £172,000, paying a 5% fee to the auctioneer. The RPI for April 1998 was 162.6. Compute the chargeable gain (before taper relief).

17.2 David was given a chargeable asset in November 1991 (RPI 135.6) at which time the asset had a market value of £4,500. He sold the asset in January 2006 (RPI 195.5). The RPI for April 1998 was 162.6. Compute the chargeable gain (before taper relief) or the allowable loss if the sale proceeds were:

(a) £4,950

(b) £4,350

(c) £5,780.

How would the computation differ if David had been given the asset in 2001 (instead of 1991) assuming that it was still worth £4,500 when given to him?

17.3 Brenda has the following chargeable gains (before taper relief) in a year of assessment:

(i) a gain of £17,000 (Gain A) on a non-business asset with a qualifying holding period of 5 years

(ii) a gain of £4,000 (Gain B) on a business asset with a qualifying holding period of 1 year

(iii) a gain of £20,000 (Gain C) on an asset with a qualifying holding period of more than 10 years and a relevant period of exactly 10 years, during which time the asset has been used as a business asset for 3 years.

Brenda also has allowable losses for the year of £22,000. Compute her CGT assessment for the year, assuming an annual exemption of £8,500.

17.4 Edwina bought a chargeable asset in August 1991 (RPI 134.1) for £240,000, paying acquisition costs of £12,000. In June 2001 she sold a one-quarter interest in the asset for £100,000, incurring disposal costs of £5,000. The remaining three-quarter interest in the asset was valued at £500,000 in June 2001. RPI for April 1998 was 162.6. Compute the chargeable gain (before taper relief).

In January 2006, Edwina sold her remaining three-quarter interest in the asset for £520,000. Compute the chargeable gain (before taper relief).

17.5 Francis acquired an oil painting for £12,500 in March 1978. He sold the painting for £37,500 in March 2006. RPI for April 1998 was 162.6. Compute the chargeable gain (before taper relief) if the painting's market value on 31 March 1982 (RPI 79.44) was:

(a) £10,000 (b) £15,000.

17.6 In June 1998 (RPI 163.4) Gillian was given a chargeable asset with a market value at that time of £6,000. In November 2005 (RPI 194.5) she made a successful claim to the effect that the asset now had a negligible value of only £80.

(a) Compute the allowable loss.

(b) Compute the chargeable gain (before taper relief) arising in March 2006 (RPI 196.5) when Gillian sold the asset for £120.

17.7 Henry acquired a chargeable asset in August 1975 at a cost of £100. He sold the asset in August 2005 for £8,450. RPI for April 1998 was 162.6. Compute the chargeable gain (before taper relief) or the allowable loss if the asset had a market value on 31 March 1982 (RPI 79.44) of:

(a) £7,000

(b) £12,500.

***17.8** Iris bought a chargeable asset on 6 April 1960 for £400. The asset had a market value of £600 on 6 April 1965 and £850 on 31 March 1982 (RPI 79.44). She sold the asset on 6 April 2005 for £4,200. The RPI for April 1998 was 162.6. Compute the chargeable gain (before taper relief).

***17.9** Jon (who is self-employed) bought a chargeable asset in 1975 for £23,000. He incurred enhancement expenditure of £10,000 in 1979 and a further £4,000 in June 1998 (RPI 163.4). The asset was valued at £33,500 on 31 March 1982 (RPI 79.44) and was sold for £85,000 in February 2006 (RPI 196.0). RPI for April 1998 was 162.6.

(a) Compute the tapered gain, assuming that the asset was used for the purposes of Jon's trade throughout his period of ownership. Jon has no allowable losses in tax year 2005/06 and no allowable losses to bring forward from previous years.

(b) Now re-compute the gain, assuming that the person who bought the asset from Jon in February 2006 was his wife (who lives with him).

***17.10** Karen bought a house in 1979 for £30,000. The house was valued at £32,000 on 31 March 1982 (RPI 79.44). In November 1986 (RPI 99.29) she spent £18,000 on dividing the house into two self-contained flats and in May 2005 (RPI 191.5) she sold one of the flats for £95,000, at which time the other flat was valued at £105,000. In January 2006 (RPI 195.5) she sold the second flat for £110,000. Karen never lived in either of the flats. The RPI for April 1998 was 162.6.

Compute the tapered gains arising on the two disposals, given that the flats do not rank as business assets. Karen has no allowable losses in 2005/06 and no allowable losses to bring forward from previous years.

Chapter 18

Chattels and wasting assets

Introduction

A "chattel" is an item of tangible, movable property. A "wasting asset" is one with an expected useful life not exceeding 50 years at the time of disposal. If an asset is both a chattel and a wasting asset (e.g. a TV set) it is a "wasting chattel". Special CGT rules apply to the disposal of chattels, wasting assets and wasting chattels. The purpose of this chapter is to explain these rules.

Please note that the RPI for April 1998 (which is used in many of the examples in this chapter) is 162.6.

The chattels exemption

If a chattel is disposed of for £6,000 or less, the disposal is exempt from CGT. This provision removes from charge a great many trivial disposals and ensures that CGT is levied only if the disposal is material. The following points relate to the chattels exemption:

(a) This exemption applies only to chattels, not to assets in general.

(b) The exemption means that gains arising on the disposal of a chattel for £6,000 or less are not chargeable to CGT. It also means that losses arising on such disposals are not generally allowable. However, special rules apply to chattels acquired for more than £6,000 and disposed of for £6,000 or less (see later in this chapter).

(c) The £6,000 figure relates to the *gross* disposal proceeds. These are the proceeds before deducting incidental costs of disposal.

(d) If the gross disposal proceeds of a chattel exceed £6,000, the chargeable gain (before taper relief) cannot exceed five-thirds of the amount by which disposal proceeds exceed £6,000. This "marginal relief" ensures that taxpayers who dispose of chattels for slightly more than £6,000 are not unduly penalised by the tax system.

EXAMPLE 1

In 2005/06, a taxpayer makes a number of disposals, as listed below. Which of these disposals would be exempt from CGT?

(a) An antique table sold for £5,000.

(b) A watercolour painting sold at auction. The auctioneer deducted his 10% commission from the selling price and sent the taxpayer a cheque for the remaining £5,670.

(c) A holding of shares sold for £4,500.

Solution

(a) The antique table is a chattel disposed of for £6,000 or less. Therefore the disposal is exempt from CGT.

(b) A watercolour painting is a chattel. The gross disposal proceeds must have been £6,300, since £6,300 less 10% = £5,670. The chattels exemption will not apply but the chargeable gain (before taper relief) cannot exceed five-thirds of £300 i.e. £500.

(c) A shareholding is not a chattel. Therefore the £6,000 exemption does not apply and the disposal will be chargeable to CGT.

EXAMPLE 2

In December 2005, Michael sells a piece of antique furniture for £6,360. He pays incidental disposal costs of £320. He had acquired the furniture as a gift from his mother in January 1991 (RPI 130.2). Compute the chargeable gain if the market value of the furniture in January 1991 was:

(a) £4,800 (b) £4,300

Solution

	(a)	(b)
	£	£
Sale proceeds	6,360	6,360
Less: Incidental costs of disposal	320	320
	6,040	6,040
Less: Deemed acquisition cost	4,800	4,300
Unindexed gain	1,240	1,740
Less: Indexation allowance		
$\frac{162.6 - 130.2}{130.2}$ = 0.249 x £4,800	1,195	
$\frac{162.6 - 130.2}{130.2}$ = 0.249 x £4,300		1,071
Chargeable gain (before taper relief)	45	669

Notes:

(a) The maximum gain is £360 x 5/3 = £600. £45 is less than this, so the chargeable gain (before taper relief) is £45.

(b) £669 exceeds £600, so the gain is restricted to £600.

Chattels disposed of at a loss

If a chattel is disposed of at a loss, there are two possibilities. Either:

(a) the disposal proceeds are more than £6,000, in which case the allowable loss is calculated in the usual way, or

(b) the disposal proceeds are £6,000 or less, in which case the chattels exemption applies and it appears that no allowable loss could arise.

However, if a chattel is acquired for more than £6,000 and then disposed of for less than £6,000, the chattels exemption is overruled and an allowable loss is given. But the amount of the loss is restricted to the amount that would arise if the disposal proceeds were exactly £6,000.

EXAMPLE 3

In March 2006, Naomi sells an oil painting which she had acquired some years previously for £10,000. Compute the allowable loss if she sells the painting for:

(a) £7,200 (b) £5,700

Solution

(a) Naomi has disposed of a chattel for more than £6,000, so the disposal is not exempt from CGT. The allowable loss is calculated in the usual way as £10,000 - £7,200 = £2,800. There is of course no indexation allowance to consider, since indexation allowance cannot be used to increase a loss.

(b) Naomi has disposed of a chattel for less than £6,000 and normally this disposal would be exempt from CGT. However, since the asset was acquired for more than £6,000 a loss is allowed, calculated by substituting £6,000 for the disposal proceeds. The allowable loss is £10,000 - £6,000 = £4,000. Again, there is no point in calculating indexation allowance.

Part disposals of chattels

A part disposal of a chattel may be made in one of two ways. Either:

(a) a part interest in a chattel may be disposed of, or

(b) for chattels forming a set, one or more of the items in the set may be disposed of.

Each of these forms of part disposal is considered below.

Disposal of a part interest in a chattel

If a disposal is made of a part interest in a chattel, this part disposal will be exempt from CGT only if the value of the *whole* chattel immediately prior to the part disposal is £6,000 or less.

If the value of the whole chattel exceeds £6,000 the disposal is not exempt from CGT and the usual part disposal calculation is performed. However, the chargeable gain on the part disposal (before taper relief) is limited to five-thirds of the amount by which the value of the whole chattel exceeds £6,000, multiplied by the usual part disposal fraction.

EXAMPLE 4

In October 1999 Jackie bought a statuette for £3,500. In October 2005 she sells a one-third interest in the statuette for £2,000. Compute the chargeable gain if the value of the remaining two-thirds interest in October 2005 is:

(a) £4,000 (b) £5,000.

Solution

(a) The value of the whole chattel on the date of the part disposal is £6,000. Since this value does not exceed £6,000 the part disposal is exempt from CGT.

(b) The value of the whole chattel on the date of the part disposal is £7,000. Since this value exceeds £6,000 the part disposal is not exempt from CGT. The computation of the chargeable gain is as follows:

	£
Sale proceeds	2,000
Less: Part cost:	
$\frac{£2,000}{£2,000 + £5,000}$ x £3,500	1,000
Chargeable gain (before taper relief)	1,000

The part disposal fraction cancels down to 2/7ths, so the gain is restricted to (£7,000 - £6,000) x 5/3 x 2/7 = £476. No indexation allowance is available since the asset was acquired on or after 1 April 1998.

Disposal of part of a set

If a taxpayer acquires a set of chattels (e.g. a set of dining chairs) and then disposes of them individually, each disposal is regarded as a part disposal and will in general be chargeable to CGT only if the disposal proceeds of an individual item exceed £6,000.

However, a taxpayer who wished to dispose of a set of chattels with a total value exceeding £6,000 could use this rule to avoid CGT by disposing of the items one by one (with each disposal raising less than £6,000). In order to prevent such avoidance, a series of disposals of chattels which form part of a set *to the same person or to persons connected with each other or acting together* are treated as a single transaction for CGT purposes.

EXAMPLE 5

Andrew acquired a set of six dining chairs in January 1987 (RPI 100.0) for £4,300. In June 2005 he sold three of the chairs to a friend for £3,500 (the other three chairs also being valued at £3,500). In August 2005 he sold the remaining chairs to the friend's brother for £3,700. Compute the chargeable gain arising on these disposals.

Solution

If it were not for the rule introduced above, neither of these disposals would be chargeable to CGT since neither of them raises more than £6,000. However, the two disposals are made to connected persons and are therefore to be regarded as a single transaction for CGT purposes. The total disposal proceeds are £7,200 (£3,500 + £3,700). This exceeds £6,000 so the disposals are chargeable. The computation is as follows:

	£
Sale proceeds	7,200
Less: Cost	4,300
Unindexed gain	2,900
Less: Indexation allowance	
$\frac{162.6 - 100.0}{100.0} = 0.626 \times £4,300$	2,692
Chargeable gain (before taper relief)	208

The maximum gain is (£7,200 - £6,000) x 5/3 = £2,000. £208 is less than this, so the chargeable gain (before taper relief) is £208.

Wasting chattels

Wasting chattels (chattels with an expected useful life of 50 years or less at the time of disposal) are generally exempt from CGT. Therefore the disposal of a wasting chattel will usually give rise to neither a chargeable gain nor an allowable loss.

The only exception to this rule relates to movable plant and machinery used in business and eligible for capital allowances. Plant and machinery is always regarded as a wasting asset for CGT purposes and therefore movable plant and machinery is a wasting chattel. Unless disposal proceeds are £6,000 or less, disposals of movable plant and machinery used in business and eligible for capital allowances are *not* exempt from CGT. One of two situations may arise on such a disposal:

(a) Disposal proceeds may be less than original cost. In this (the most likely) case, the unindexed loss is reduced by the total capital allowances which have been available on the asset. This will reduce the loss to £nil and since no indexation allowance is available on assets sold at a loss, the allowable loss will also be £nil.

(b) Disposal proceeds may be greater than original cost. In this case, the total of available capital allowances on the asset is £nil and therefore capital allowances have no effect on the computation which will proceed in the usual way.

In fact, these rules (other than the £6,000 exemption) also apply to fixed plant and machinery used in business and eligible for capital allowances.

EXAMPLE 6

An item of movable plant and machinery is bought in February 2003 for £8,000 and used solely for trade purposes. Capital allowances are available in relation to this item. Compute the chargeable gain arising if the item is sold in July 2005 and the sale proceeds are:

(a) £4,500 (b) £6,500 (c) £8,500 (d) £10,500.

Solution

In case (a), sale proceeds do not exceed £6,000 so the disposal is exempt from CGT. In cases (b), (c) and (d), the sale proceeds exceed £6,000 so there is no exemption. The computations are as follows:

	(b)	(c)	(d)
	£	£	£
Sale proceeds	6,500	8,500	10,500
Less: Acquisition cost	8,000	8,000	8,000
	(1,500)	500	2,500
Less: Available capital allowances	1,500	0	0
Chargeable gain (before taper relief)	nil	500	2,500

Notes:

(i) In case (c), the maximum gain is £4,167 (£2,500 x 5/3). £500 is less than this, so the chargeable gain (before taper relief) is £500.

(ii) In case (d), the maximum gain is £7,500 (£4,500 x 5/3). £2,500 is less than this, so the chargeable gain (before taper relief) is £2,500.

(iii) No indexation allowance is available since the item was acquired on or after 1 April 1998.

Wasting assets

A wasting asset which is not a chattel is *not* exempt from CGT. Typical examples of such wasting assets include:

(a) intangible assets such as copyrights, patents and options with less than 50 years' life remaining

(b) leases with less than 50 years' life remaining.

In general, the original cost of a wasting asset is deemed to waste away on a straight line basis over the asset's predictable life. The computation of the gain or loss arising on the disposal of such an asset is achieved by comparing disposal proceeds with the unexpired portion of the asset's cost at the time of disposal. However, special rules apply to the disposal of a lease (see later in this chapter).

EXAMPLE 7

In January 1997 (RPI 154.4), Fiona acquired a 20-year copyright at a cost of £30,000. In January 2006 she sold the copyright for £35,500. Compute the chargeable gain.

Solution

When the copyright was bought it had a 20-year life. When it was sold there were 11 years remaining. Therefore the computation is as follows:

		£
Sale proceeds		35,500
Less: Unexpired portion of cost		
	$\frac{11}{20}$ x £30,000	16,500
Unindexed gain		19,000
Less: Indexation allowance		
	$\frac{162.6 - 154.4}{154.4}$ = 0.053 x £16,500	875
Chargeable gain (before taper relief)		18,125

EXAMPLE 8

In March 1981, Philip acquired a 30-year copyright at a cost of £50,000. The copyright was valued at £63,000 on 31 March 1982 (RPI 79.44). In March 2006 Philip sold the copyright for £47,000. Compute the chargeable gain.

Solution

When the copyright was bought it had a 30-year life and when it was valued on 31 March 1982 it had a 29-year life. When it was sold there were 5 years remaining. Therefore the computation is as follows:

		Original cost	*Rebasing*
		£	£
Sale proceeds		47,000	47,000
Less: Unexpired portion of cost			
	$\frac{5}{30}$ x £50,000	8,333	
	Unexpired portion of MV 31/3/82		
	$\frac{5}{29}$ x £63,000		10,862
Unindexed gain		38,667	36,138
Less: Indexation allowance			
	$\frac{162.6 - 79.44}{79.44}$ = 1.047 x £10,862	11,373	11,373
Chargeable gain (before taper relief)		27,294	24,765

The rebasing calculation gives the lower gain, so rebasing applies and the chargeable gain (before taper relief) is £24,765.

Leases

For CGT purposes, leases are classified into long leases (those with more than 50 years to run) and short leases (those with 50 years or less to run). A chargeable disposal may occur in connection with a lease in any of the following ways:

(a) A taxpayer who has a long lease on a piece of property assigns that long lease to someone else.

(b) A taxpayer who has a short lease on a piece of property assigns that short lease to someone else.

(c) A taxpayer who has the freehold (or a long head-lease) grants a long lease (or sub-lease) on the property to someone else, the property eventually reverting to the taxpayer.

(d) A taxpayer who has the freehold (or a long head-lease) grants a short lease (or sub-lease) on the property to someone else, the property eventually reverting to the taxpayer.

(e) A taxpayer who has a short head-lease grants a shorter sub-lease on the property to someone else, the property eventually reverting to the taxpayer.

Each of these cases is considered below. Note that if a property is or has been the taxpayer's main residence, the gain arising on the disposal of a lease on the property may be subject to the principal private residence exemption described in Chapter 21.

Assignment of a long lease

The assignment of a long lease is treated as a disposal of the whole asset and therefore causes no CGT difficulties at all. The computation proceeds in precisely the same way as the computation on the disposal of any other whole asset.

EXAMPLE 9

In 2001, Jim acquired a 99-year lease on a flat for £70,000. In 2006, he assigned the lease to a third party for £92,000. The flat was never Jim's residence. Compute the chargeable gain.

Solution

The chargeable gain (before taper relief) is £22,000. No indexation allowance is available since the lease was acquired on or after 1 April 1998.

Assignment of a short lease

A short lease is, by definition, a wasting asset. Therefore the computation of the gain arising on the disposal of a short lease should be achieved by comparing disposal proceeds with the unexpired portion of the lease's cost at the time of disposal.

However, unlike other wasting assets, the cost of a short lease is not deemed to waste away on a straight line basis. Instead, the cost of a short lease is deemed to waste away according to a table of percentages given in Schedule 8 of the Taxation of Chargeable Gains Act 1992. The effect of this table is to write off the cost of a short lease slowly in the early years and more quickly in the closing years. The table is reproduced at the end of this chapter.

The proportion of the cost of a short lease which is allowed in the CGT computation on its disposal is:

$$\frac{\text{\% relating to number of years lease has left to run on disposal}}{\text{\% relating to original length of lease}}$$

If the lease was originally a long lease but the taxpayer has owned the lease for some years so that the lease now being assigned is a short lease, the denominator in the above fraction is taken as 100%, corresponding to "50 or more" in the Schedule 8 table.

EXAMPLE 10

Jean acquired a 30-year lease on a property in July 1995 (RPI 149.1) for £32,000. In July 2005 she assigned the lease to a third party for £45,000. The property was never Jean's residence. Compute the chargeable gain.

Solution

When the lease was acquired it had a 30-year life (Sch 8 percentage 87.330%). When it was assigned there were 20 years remaining (Sch 8 percentage 72.770%). Therefore the computation is as follows:

	£
Sale proceeds	45,000
Less: Unexpired portion of cost	
$\frac{72.770}{87.330}$ x £32,000	26,665
Unindexed gain	18,335
Less: Indexation allowance	
$\frac{162.6 - 149.1}{149.1}$ = 0.091 x £26,665	2,427
Chargeable gain (before taper relief)	15,908

Schedule 8 gives percentages only for whole numbers of years. If the duration of a lease is not a whole number of years, then the appropriate percentage is calculated from the table on a pro rata basis.

EXAMPLE 11

A taxpayer assigns a lease of duration 12 years and 5 months. Calculate the appropriate percentage for use in the CGT computation on the disposal.

Solution

The percentage for 12 years is 53.191%. The percentage for 13 years is 56.167%. The difference between these percentages is 2.976%. Therefore the appropriate percentage for a lease of duration 12 years and 5 months is 53.191 + (2.976 x 5/12) = 54.431%.

EXAMPLE 12

Joan acquired a 40-year lease on a property on 31 May 1981 for £38,000. The market value of the lease on 31 March 1982 (RPI 79.44) was £35,000. On 30 November 2005 she assigned the lease to a third party for £65,000. The property was never Joan's residence. Compute the chargeable gain.

Solution

When the lease was acquired it had a 40-year life (Sch 8 percentage 95.457%). On 31 March 1982 there were 39 years and 2 months remaining (Sch 8 percentage 94.842 + 0.615 x 2/12 = 94.945%). When it was assigned there were 15 years and 6 months remaining (Sch 8 percentage = 61.617 + (2.499 x 6/12) = 62.867%). The computation is as follows:

	Original cost	*Rebasing*
	£	£
Sale proceeds	65,000	65,000
Less: Unexpired portion of cost		
$\frac{62.867}{95.457}$ x £38,000	25,026	
Unexpired portion of MV 31/3/82		
$\frac{62.867}{94.945}$ x £35,000		23,175
Unindexed gain	39,974	41,825
Less: Indexation allowance		
$\frac{162.6 - 79.44}{79.44}$ = 1.047 x £25,026	26,202	26,202
Chargeable gain (before taper relief)	13,772	15,623

The rebasing calculation gives the higher gain, so rebasing does not apply and the chargeable gain (before taper relief) is £13,772.

Grant of a long lease

The grant of a long lease (or sub-lease) out of a freehold (or a long head-lease) is treated as a part disposal for CGT purposes and the normal part disposal rules apply. The value of the part disposed of is clearly the proceeds of the disposal. The value of the part remaining takes into account both:

(a) the right of the taxpayer making the disposal to receive rents from the tenant, and

(b) the taxpayer's "reversionary interest", which is the right to take back the property when the lease (or sub-lease) finishes.

Grant of a short lease

The grant of a short lease (or sub-lease) out of a freehold (or a long head-lease) is also treated as a part disposal for CGT purposes and once again the part disposal rules apply. However, the premium received on the grant of a short lease (or sub-lease) will be assessable to income tax as property income (see Chapter 5) and therefore, in order to avoid double taxation, the disposal proceeds are reduced by the amount of the income tax assessment.

EXAMPLE 13

Jeffrey acquired a freehold property in 1995 for £117,000. In 2005 he granted Jill a lease on the property for £80,000. The market value of the freehold after the lease had been granted was £100,000. The property was never Jeffrey's residence. Compute the chargeable gain, given that the lease granted to Jill was of duration:

(a) 99 years (b) 40 years.

Assume an indexation factor of 10%.

Solution

(a) This is a part disposal with A = £80,000 and B = £100,000. The computation is as follows:

	£
Sale proceeds	80,000
<u>Less</u>: Part cost:	
$\frac{£80,000}{£80,000 + £100,000} \times £117,000$	52,000
Unindexed gain	28,000

	£
Unindexed gain	28,000
Less: Indexation allowance	
10% of £52,000	5,200
Chargeable gain (before taper relief)	22,800

(b) This is also a part disposal but the disposal proceeds will be subject to an income tax assessment of £17,600 (£80,000 - (2% x £80,000 x 39)) and this must be taken into account in the CGT computation. The computation is as follows:

	£
Sale proceeds (£80,000 - £17,600)	62,400
Less: Part cost:	
$\frac{£62,400}{£80,000 + £100,000} \times £117,000$	40,560
Unindexed gain	21,840
Less: Indexation allowance	
10% of £40,560	4,056
Chargeable gain (before taper relief)	17,784

Note that the numerator of the part disposal fraction is taken as the disposal proceeds *after* deducting the income tax assessment, whilst the denominator takes into account the disposal proceeds *before* deducting the income tax assessment.

Grant of a short sub-lease out of a short head-lease

In essence, the grant of a short sub-lease out of a short head-lease is treated in a similar fashion to the assignment of a short lease, as discussed earlier in this chapter. Once again, the Schedule 8 table of percentages is called into use to determine the part cost that should be deducted in the CGT computation. But since the property will be returning to the original tenant when the sub-lease finishes, the proportion of the cost of the short head-lease which is allowed in the CGT computation on the granting of the sub-lease is equal to:

$$\frac{P1 - P2}{P3}$$

where:

P1 = % relating to the number of years left of the short head-lease when the sub-lease begins

P2 = % relating to the number of years left of the short head-lease when the sub-lease ends

P3 = % relating to original length of the short head-lease.

Since the premium received by the taxpayer on the grant of a short sub-lease will be assessable to income tax as property income, the gain arising is reduced by the amount of the income tax assessment. However, this reduction cannot be used to convert a gain into a loss or to increase a loss.

EXAMPLE 14

Joanna acquired a 15-year lease on a property in September 1999 for £45,000. In September 2005 she granted a 4-year sub-lease to a third party for £20,000. The property was never Joanna's residence. Compute the chargeable gain.

Solution

The computation of the chargeable gain is as follows:

	£
Sale proceeds	20,000
Less: Proportion of cost	
$\frac{43.154 - 26.722}{61.617}$ x £45,000	12,001
	7,999
Less: Income tax assessment (£10,160)	7,999
Chargeable gain	nil

Notes:

(i) P1 = 43.154 (9 years), P2 = 26.722 (5 years) and P3 = 61.617 (15 years)

(ii) No indexation allowance is available since the lease was acquired on or after 1 April 1998.

(iii) The income tax assessment (see Chapter 5) is:

	£
Premium received	20,000
Less: £20,000 x (4 - 1) x 2%	1,200
	18,800
Less: Relief for premium paid:	
$\frac{4}{15}$ x (£45,000 - (£45,000 x (15 - 1) x 2%))	8,640
	10,160

(iv) The relief given for the income tax assessment is restricted to £7,999 so as not to turn a gain into a loss.

Summary

- A chattel is an item of tangible, movable property. A wasting asset is one with an expected useful life of 50 years or less at the time of disposal. A wasting asset that is also a chattel is a wasting chattel.
- Chattels disposed of for £6,000 or less are exempt from CGT.
- The allowable loss on chattels acquired for more than £6,000 and disposed of for less than £6,000 is restricted by substituting £6,000 for the disposal proceeds.
- Disposals of a part interest in a chattel are exempt from CGT if the value of the whole chattel is £6,000 or less.
- A series of disposals of chattels forming a set will be treated as a single transaction for CGT purposes if the disposals are to connected persons.
- Wasting chattels are exempt from CGT apart from movable plant and machinery used in business on which capital allowances are available.
- Wasting assets are not exempt from CGT. In general, the original cost of a wasting asset is written off over its predictable life using the straight line method. However, special rules apply to leases.
- An assignment of a long lease is regarded as the disposal of a whole asset.
- An assignment of a short lease is a disposal of a wasting asset. The original cost of a short lease is written off over its predictable life, using a table of percentages contained in Schedule 8, TCGA 1992.
- The grant of a long lease is treated as a part disposal.
- The grant of a short lease (or sub-lease) out of a freehold (or long head-lease) is treated as a part disposal. The income tax assessment raised on the premium received is deducted from disposal proceeds in the CGT computation.
- The grant of a short sub-lease out of a short head-lease is a part disposal of a wasting asset. The Schedule 8 table is used to determine the allowable cost used in the CGT computation. The income tax assessment raised on the premium received is deducted from the gain arising but cannot be used to convert a gain into a loss or to increase a loss.

Short lease amortisation table

(Schedule 8 of TCGA 1992)

Years	*Percentage*	*Years*	*Percentage*	*Years*	*Percentage*
50 or more	100	33	90.280	16	64.116
49	99.657	32	89.354	15	61.617
48	99.289	31	88.371	14	58.971
47	98.902	30	87.330	13	56.167
46	98.490	29	86.226	12	53.191
45	98.059	28	85.053	11	50.038
44	97.595	27	83.816	10	46.695
43	97.107	26	82.496	9	43.154
42	96.593	25	81.100	8	39.399
41	96.041	24	79.622	7	35.414
40	95.457	23	78.055	6	31.195
39	94.842	22	76.399	5	26.722
38	94.189	21	74.635	4	21.983
37	93.497	20	72.770	3	16.959
36	92.761	19	70.791	2	11.629
35	91.981	18	68.697	1	5.983
34	91.156	17	66.470	0	0

Exercises

Please note that the RPI for April 1998 is 162.6.

18.1 Classify each of the following assets as either chattels, wasting assets or wasting chattels:

(a) A domestic washing machine.

(b) A gold ring.

(c) A personal computer.

(d) A 20-year lease on a building.

(e) A suit of clothes.

(f) An antique vase.

18.2 In October 2005 Keith sells an antique cabinet for £7,200. He incurs incidental costs of disposal amounting to £200. The cabinet cost £2,000 in July 1989 (RPI 115.5). Compute the chargeable gain (before taper relief).

18.3 In September 2005 Kevin sells a drawing for £2,000. He bought the drawing in February 1997 (RPI 155.0) for £50,000 when it was thought (incorrectly) to be by a famous artist. Compute the allowable loss.

18.4 In January 2006 Karl sells a one-quarter interest in a painting for £25,000. The remaining three-quarter interest is valued at £85,000. The painting had cost Karl £38,500 in January 1994 (RPI 141.3). Compute the chargeable gain (before taper relief).

18.5 In January 2003 Katrina buys an item of movable plant and machinery for use in her business. The plant costs her £50,000 and capital allowances are claimed. Compute the chargeable gain (before taper relief) arising in March 2006 when she sells the plant, assuming that sale proceeds are:

(a) £65,000

(b) £35,000.

18.6 In June 2003 (RPI 181.3), Katie acquired a 5-year option to buy a piece of land. The option cost her £10,000. In June 2005 she sold the option for £8,000. Compute the chargeable gain (before taper relief).

18.7 Katherine acquired a 30-year lease on a property on 31 August 1980 for £12,500. The lease was valued at £15,000 on 31 March 1982 (RPI 79.44). On 31 August 2005 she assigned the lease to a third party for £20,000. The property was never Katherine's residence. Compute the chargeable gain (before taper relief).

***18.8** In March 1996 (RPI 151.5), Sean acquired a pair of matching antique silver candlesticks at a cost of £4,000. In August 2005 he sold one of the candlesticks to James for £6,750. At that time the other candlestick was valued at £5,750. In September 2005 he sold the other candlestick to Julia for £5,800. Calculate the chargeable gain (before taper relief) arising on these two disposals if:

(a) James and Julia are unconnected.

(b) James and Julia are a married couple.

***18.9** On 31 March 1980, Estelle acquired a patent with a 30-year life at a cost of £21,000. The patent was valued at £20,000 on 31 March 1982 (RPI 79.44) and Estelle sold the patent on 31 March 2006 for £13,000. Compute the chargeable gain (before taper relief).

***18.10** Edward bought a 20-year lease on a flat in May 1997 (RPI 156.9) at a cost of £35,000. In November 2005 he granted a 5-year sub-lease to a third party for £15,000. The flat was never Edward's principal private residence. Compute the chargeable gain (before taper relief).

Chapter 19

Shares and securities (1)

Introduction

A disposal of shares or securities causes no CGT problems unless a taxpayer disposes of part of a shareholding which was originally acquired over a period of time in several separate transactions. If this happens, it is not possible to identify the shares which have been disposed of. But the calculation of the gain or loss arising on the disposal cannot proceed until the cost and acquisition date of the shares concerned have been established. It is necessary, therefore, to devise a set of *share identification* or *share matching* rules which may be used to match disposals against acquisitions in these circumstances. The purpose of this chapter is to explain these rules and to show how they are used to calculate the gain or loss arising on a disposal of shares.

Please note that the RPI for April 1998 (which is used in many of the examples in this chapter) is 162.6.

The share matching rules

With effect from 6 April 1998, disposals of shares or securities are matched for CGT purposes against acquisitions of *the same class of shares in the same company* in the following order:

(a) First, against any acquisitions made on the same day as the day of the disposal.

(b) Next, against any acquisitions made during the following 30 days, matching with shares acquired earlier rather than later within that 30-day period. This rule is intended to counter the practice known as "bed and breakfasting", whereby shares are sold and then almost immediately re-acquired so as to trigger gains or losses for tax avoidance purposes.

(c) Next, against previous acquisitions made after 5 April 1998, matching the most recent acquisitions first (a last-in, first-out basis).

(d) Next, against shares forming the "Section 104 holding". This is a pool of shares acquired between 6 April 1982 and 5 April 1998 inclusive.

(e) Next, against shares forming the "1982 holding". This is a pool of shares acquired between 6 April 1965 and 5 April 1982 inclusive.

(f) Next, against shares acquired before 6 April 1965 (on a last-in, first-out basis).

(g) Finally, if the above rules fail to exhaust a disposal of shares, the remainder of the disposal is matched with subsequent acquisitions made beyond the 30-day period mentioned above in rule (b).

These matching rules were introduced by Finance Act 1998 and replaced an older set of rules. However, it is important to note that the new rules do *not* apply to companies and that the gain or loss arising on a disposal of shares by a company is still computed in accordance with the old, pre-FA1998 matching rules (see Chapter 23).

EXAMPLE 1

Paul made the following acquisitions and disposals of ordinary shares in Crimson plc:

Date			*Date*		
11 May 1962	acquisition	1,000	1 October 1998	acquisition	100
15 January 1965	acquisition	100	1 October 1998	disposal	(450)
9 June 1979	acquisition	170	7 December 1998	acquisition	500
14 February 1990	acquisition	350	11 January 2002	disposal	(750)
4 July 1998	acquisition	200	18 February 2002	acquisition	400
31 August 1998	acquisition	300	28 March 2006	disposal	(960)

No further shares were acquired before the end of April 2006. Against which acquisitions will the disposals be matched?

Solution

(a) The 450 shares disposed of on 1 October 1998 are matched first against the 100 shares acquired on the same day, leaving 350 shares still to be matched. No shares were acquired in the next 30 days so the next step is to match against acquisitions made after 5 April 1998 on a LIFO basis. 300 of the shares disposed of are matched against those acquired on 31 August 1998 and the remaining 50 are matched against 50 of the shares acquired on 4 July 1998.

(b) The disposal of 750 shares on 11 January 2002 cannot be matched against any acquisitions on the same day or during the next 30 days. The only shares acquired after 5 April 1998 (on a LIFO basis) are the 500 acquired on 7 December 1998 and 150 acquired on 4 July 1998 (200, less 50 already matched with a disposal) so 650 of the shares disposed of on 11 January 2002 are matched with these acquisitions, leaving 100 shares still to be matched.

The next step is to match against the Section 104 holding, which is the pool of shares acquired between 6 April 1982 and 5 April 1998 inclusive. This pool contains only the 350 shares acquired on 14 February 1990, so the remaining 100 shares in the disposal are matched against 100 of these shares.

(c) The disposal of 960 shares on 28 March 2006 cannot be matched against any acquisitions made on the same day or during the next 30 days. The disposal is matched first against the 400 shares acquired on 18 February 2002, leaving 560 shares still to be matched. The Section 104 holding now contains 250 of the shares which were acquired on 14 February 1990 (350, less 100 already matched) so 250 of the shares disposed of on 28 March 2006 are matched with this acquisition, leaving 310 shares still to be matched.

The next step is to match against the 1982 holding, which is the pool of shares acquired between 6 April 1965 and 5 April 1982 inclusive. This pool contains only the 170 shares acquired on 9 June 1979 so 170 of the shares disposed of on 28 March 2006 are matched with this acquisition, leaving 140 shares still to be matched.

The remaining 140 shares are matched first against the 100 shares acquired on 15 January 1965 and finally against 40 of the 1,000 shares acquired on 11 May 1962.

The Section 104 holding

A taxpayer's "Section 104 holding" of shares of a certain class in a certain company consists of the pool of shares which were acquired between 6 April 1982 and 5 April 1998 inclusive. The pool's name is derived from Section 104 of TCGA 1992, which provides the legal basis for its existence, but it is important to note that this name was introduced comparatively recently (by the Finance Act 1998) and that the pool might also be referred to as either:

(a) the "new holding", or

(b) the "Finance Act 1985 pool" (since share pooling was introduced by that Act).

The distinguishing characteristic of shares acquired between 6 April 1982 and 5 April 1998 is that the indexation factor used on their disposal will differ according to the date of acquisition. This is not true for shares acquired before 6 April 1982 (which all attract the same rate of indexation allowance, as explained later in this chapter) or for shares acquired after 5 April 1998 (which do not attract indexation allowance at all).

If it were not for the provisions of Section 104, it would be necessary to keep detailed records of the date and cost of each individual share acquisition made between 6 April 1982 and 5 April 1998, so that indexation allowance could be calculated correctly on a disposal. However, the pooling arrangement provided by Section 104 eliminates the need to keep these records. Instead, all that is required is a record of:

(a) the total number of shares in the pool

(b) their total cost

(c) their total *indexed cost*, which consists of total cost plus all indexation allowance due up to the date of the most recent "operative event". An operative event occurs whenever shares enter or leave the pool.

Shares acquired after 5 April 1998 cannot join this pool since it is necessary to retain the date and cost of each such acquisition for taper relief purposes.

EXAMPLE 2

Pauline makes the following purchases of preference shares in Violet plc:

Date	*No of shares*	*Cost*
		£
23 June 1990	1,000	1,100
14 May 1992	2,000	2,300
8 July 1997	3,000	3,150

Assuming an indexation factor of 10% between June 1990 and May 1992, and a further 13% between May 1992 and July 1997, calculate the cost and indexed cost of the S104 holding at:

(a) 14 May 1992 (b) 8 July 1997.

Solution

(a) The S104 holding commences on 23 June 1990 with the purchase of 1,000 shares at a cost of £1,100. On 14 May 1992, an operative event occurs, i.e. the purchase of a further 2,000 shares. Before adding these shares to the pool it is necessary to index the pool up to May 1992. The calculation is as follows:

	No of shares	*Cost*	*Indexed cost*
		£	£
Bought 23 June 1990	1,000	1,100	1,100
Add: Indexation to May 1992			
10% x £1,100			110
			1,210
Bought 14 May 1992	2,000	2,300	2,300
S104 holding c/f at 14 May 1992	3,000	3,400	3,510

The total of the indexed cost column represents the cost *in May 1992 terms* of the S104 holding and includes all indexation allowance due up to that date.

(b) The next operative event is the purchase of 3,000 shares in July 1997. Before adding these shares to the pool it is necessary to index the pool from May 1992 (when the previous indexation calculation took place) to July 1997. The calculation is:

	No of shares	*Cost*	*Indexed cost*
		£	£
S104 holding b/f at 14 May 1992	3,000	3,400	3,510
Add: Indexation to July 1997			
13% x £3,510			456
			3,966
Bought 8 July 1997	3,000	3,150	3,150
S104 holding c/f at 8 July 1997	6,000	6,550	7,116

The three acquisitions forming the S104 holding have now been combined into a single pool of 6,000 shares, costing £6,550 but with an indexed cost (including all indexation allowance due to July 1997) of £7,116. It is now necessary to carry forward only these three "bottom line" figures, rather than the details of each individual acquisition.

Calculation of the indexed cost of the S104 holding

The example given above was a slight simplification of the way in which the indexed cost of the S104 holding is calculated. The full method of calculation is as follows:

(a) The number of shares in the pool at 5 April 1985 (if any) is totalled and the cost of these shares is also totalled. The indexed cost of the pool at 5 April 1985 is calculated as total cost, plus an indexation allowance for each acquisition forming part of the pool, based on the change in RPI between the date of the acquisition and April 1985.

(b) On the occurrence of a subsequent operative event, the indexed cost of the pool is increased by reference to the change in RPI since the previous operative event (if any) or since April 1985 (if the previous event was before April 1985). *TCGA 1992 does not require the indexation factor used in this calculation to be rounded to 3 decimal places*. No further indexation adjustments are required once the pool has been indexed up to April 1998. The pool is then adjusted to take account of the operative event as follows:

   (i) If the event is an acquisition, the number of shares acquired is added to the number of shares in the pool and their cost is added to the cost and to the indexed cost of the pool.

   (ii) If the event is a disposal, the number of shares disposed of is subtracted from the number of shares in the pool. It is then necessary to deduct a proportion of the cost and indexed cost of the pool. Strictly speaking, this proportion should be calculated using the part disposal fraction (see Chapter 17) which takes into account the value of the shares disposed of and the value of the shares remaining. In most cases, however, the value per share of the shares disposed of will be the same as the value per share of the shares remaining, so that the proportion to be deducted from the cost and indexed cost of the pool can be based upon the *number* of shares disposed of. This is assumed to be the case for the remainder of this book.

The unindexed gain (or loss) arising on a disposal from the pool is calculated as the difference between the disposal proceeds and the amount which has been subtracted from the cost of the pool as a consequence of the disposal. The indexation allowance due on the disposal is the difference between the amount subtracted from the cost of the pool and the amount subtracted from the indexed cost of the pool. As usual, indexation allowance cannot be used to create a loss or to increase a loss.

If a S104 holding first came into being before 17 March 1998 (and the shares rank as a non-business asset) *all* of the shares in the holding are eligible for the taper relief "bonus year", including any shares acquired between 17 March and 5 April 1998.

EXAMPLE 3

Paula makes the following acquisitions of ordinary shares in Indigo plc:

Date	*No of shares*	*Cost* £	*RPI*
1 July 1983	5,000	6,300	85.30
2 August 1984	2,000	2,500	89.94
3 February 1987	1,200	2,300	100.4
4 June 1993	1,800	3,400	141.0

She sells 500 shares on 8 July 2005. No shares are acquired within the next 30 days.

(a) Calculate the cost and indexed cost of the S104 holding on 8 July 2005, just prior to and just after the above disposal (RPI for April 1985 is 94.78).

(b) Compute the chargeable gain or allowable loss on the disposal if sale proceeds are:

(i) £1,300 (ii) £1,000 (iii) £700

Solution

(a) The cost and indexed cost of the S104 holding on 8 July 2005 are calculated as follows:

	No of shares	*Cost* £	*Indexed cost* £
Bought 1 July 1983	5,000	6,300	6,300
Bought 2 August 1984	2,000	2,500	2,500
Add: Indexation to April 1985			
(a) $\frac{94.78 - 85.30}{85.30} = 0.111$			
0.111 x £6,300			699
(b) $\frac{94.78 - 89.94}{89.94} = 0.054$			
0.054 x £2,500			135
S104 holding at 5 April 1985	7,000	8,800	9,634
Add: Indexation to February 1987			
$\frac{100.4 - 94.78}{94.78}$ x £9,634			571
			10,205
Bought 3 February 1987	1,200	2,300	2,300
S104 holding at 3 February 1987	8,200	11,100	12,505

	No of shares	*Cost* £	*Indexed cost* £
S104 holding at 3 February 1987	8,200	11,100	12,505
Add: Indexation to June 1993 $\frac{141.0 - 100.4}{100.4}$ x £12,505			5,057
			17,562
Bought 4 June 1993	1,800	3,400	3,400
S104 holding at 4 June 1993	10,000	14,500	20,962
Add: Indexation to April 1998 $\frac{162.6 - 141.0}{141.0}$ x £20,962			3,211
			24,173
Sold 8 July 2005 (500/10,000ths)	(500)	(725)	(1,209)
S104 holding c/f at 8 July 2005	9,500	13,775	22,964

Notes:

1. The indexation allowance calculated on operative events occurring after 5 April 1985 has not been rounded off to 3 decimal places.
2. The disposal in July 2005 must have come from the S104 holding since it cannot be matched against shares acquired on the same day, during the next 30 days or after 5 April 1998.
3. The pool has been indexed up to April 1998 and no further, since indexation allowance is not available in relation to increases in the RPI after April 1998.
4. The disposal is 500 shares out of a holding of 10,000. Therefore 500/10,000ths or 1/20th of the pool has been sold and so 1/20th of the cost and indexed cost are subtracted from the pool.
5. The cost of the shares disposed of is £725. Since the equivalent indexed cost is £1,209, the maximum indexation allowance due on the disposal is £484 (£1,209 - £725).

(b)

	(i) £	(ii) £	(iii) £
Sale proceeds	1,300	1,000	700
Less: Cost	725	725	725
Unindexed gain or loss	575	275	(25)
Less: Indexation allowance	484	275	nil
Chargeable gain (before taper relief) or allowable loss	91	nil	(25)

The qualifying holding period for taper relief purposes is seven years (plus the bonus year if the shares do not rank as a business asset).

The 1982 holding

The 1982 holding is a pool of shares acquired between 6 April 1965 and 5 April 1982 inclusive. All of the shares in this pool (including those acquired during the first five days of April 1982) attract the same rate of indexation allowance, based on the change in RPI between March 1982 and the date of disposal (or April 1998, if earlier). This means that the calculation of this pool's value is much simpler than the calculation of the value of the Section 104 holding. All that is needed is a record of:

(a) the number of shares in the pool

(b) the total cost of these shares

(c) their market value at 31 March 1982.

When a disposal occurs, the number of shares in the pool is reduced and proportionate amounts are deducted from the pool's cost and from its market value at 31 March 1982. The gain or loss arising on the disposal is then calculated in the usual way, as for any disposal of a pre-31 March 1982 asset.

EXAMPLE 4

Patrick made the following acquisitions of ordinary shares in Cornflower plc:

Date	*No of shares*	*Cost*
		£
1 June 1970	1,000	3,000
30 October 1975	800	2,500
15 August 1981	900	3,100

The shares had a market value of £3.10 per share on 31 March 1982 (RPI 79.44). Patrick sold 750 of the shares on 18 January 2006 for £6,500. No shares were acquired within the next 30 days. Compute the chargeable gain.

Solution

The sale of 750 shares on 18 January 2006 cannot be matched against any acquisitions on the same day, during the next 30 days, after 5 April 1998 or between 6 April 1982 and 5 April 1998. The next step is to match against the 1982 holding, as follows:

	No of shares	*Cost*	*MV 31/3/82*
		£	£
Acquired 1 June 1970	1,000	3,000	3,100
Acquired 30 October 1975	800	2,500	2,480
Acquired 15 August 1981	900	3,100	2,790
	2,700	8,600	8,370
Sold 18 January 2006 (750/2,700ths)	(750)	(2,389)	(2,325)
1982 holding c/f	1,950	6,211	6,045

The sold shares are deemed to have cost £2,389 and their market value at 31 March 1982 was £2,325. The calculation of the gain arising on the disposal is:

	Original cost	Rebasing
	£	£
Sale proceeds	6,500	6,500
Less: Original cost	2,389	
Market value 31/3/82		2,325
Unindexed gain	4,111	4,175
Less: Indexation allowance		
$\frac{162.6 - 79.44}{79.44}$ = 1.047 x £2,389	2,501	2,501
Chargeable gain (before taper relief)	1,610	1,674

The rebasing calculation gives the higher gain, so rebasing does not apply and the chargeable gain before taper relief is £1,610. The qualifying holding period is seven years (plus the bonus year if the shares do not rank as a business asset).

Shares acquired before 6 April 1965

Special rules apply to the disposal of shares which were originally acquired before 6 April 1965. However, these rules are now falling into disuse as it becomes increasingly uncommon for a disposal to involve shares acquired before that date. The CGT treatment of shares acquired before 6 April 1965 depends upon whether the shares are listed or unlisted. Each of these categories is considered briefly below.

Listed shares - the pooling election

A taxpayer who owns listed shares acquired before 6 April 1965 may elect *irrevocably* for these shares to be incorporated into the 1982 holding at their market value on 6 April 1965. This is known as the "pooling election". If the election is made, the shares acquired before 6 April 1965 present no new difficulties and the gains or losses arising on subsequent disposals can be calculated as described earlier in this chapter.

The pooling election was first made available in 1968 and could be made either for equities or for fixed interest shares and securities (or for both). The election had to be made within two years of the end of the tax year in which the first disposal of such shares took place after 19 March 1968. Another opportunity to make the election is provided by TCGA 1992. This Act allows taxpayers to make the election (this time, for *all* types of listed shares and securities) by 31 January in the second year of assessment following the year in which the first disposal of such shares takes place after 5 April 1985.

EXAMPLE 5

Roseanne made the following acquisitions of ordinary shares in Magenta plc (a listed company):

Date	*No of shares*	*Cost*	*RPI*
		£	
12 October 1960	100	1,100	
17 March 1963	120	1,400	
18 March 1979	80	800	
23 July 1988	150	1,800	106.7

The shares had a market value of £9 per share on 6 April 1965 and £11 per share on 31 March 1982 (RPI 79.44). Roseanne sold 200 shares on 9 October 2005 for £21 each. Compute the chargeable gain, assuming that no shares were acquired within the next 30 days and that an election has been made to incorporate pre-6 April 1965 shares into the 1982 holding.

Solution

The sale of 200 shares on 9 October 2005 cannot be matched against acquisitions made on the same day, during the next 30 days or after 5 April 1998. The next step is to match against the S104 holding. This pool consists only of the shares acquired in July 1988, so only 150 shares can be matched. The S104 holding is as follows:

	No of shares	*Cost*	*Indexed cost*
		£	£
Bought 23 July 1988	150	1,800	1,800
Add: Indexation to April 1998 $\frac{162.6 - 106.7}{106.7}$ x £1,800			943
			2,743
Sold 9 October 2005	(150)	(1,800)	(2,743)
S104 holding c/f	nil	nil	nil

The gain arising on the disposal of these 150 shares is:

	£
Sale proceeds (150 @ £21)	3,150
Less: Cost	1,800
Unindexed gain	1,350
Less: Indexation allowance (£2,743 - £1,800)	943
Chargeable gain (before taper relief)	407

The 50 remaining shares must be matched against the 1982 holding, which incorporates the pre-6 April 1965 shares (included at 6 April 1965 market value, *not* at original cost). The 1982 holding is:

	No of shares	Cost	MV 31/3/82
		£	£
Acquired 12 October 1960 (@ £9)	100	900	1,100
Acquired 17 March 1963 (@ £9)	120	1,080	1,320
Acquired 18 March 1979	80	800	880
	300	2,780	3,300
Sold 9 October 2005 (50/300ths)	(50)	(463)	(550)
1982 holding c/f	250	2,317	2,750

The gain arising on the disposal of these 50 shares is:

	Original cost	Rebasing
	£	£
Sale proceeds (50 @ £21)	1,050	1,050
Less: Original cost	463	
Market value 31/3/82		550
Unindexed gain	587	500
Less: Indexation allowance		
$\frac{162.6 - 79.44}{79.44}$ = 1.047 x £550	576	500
Chargeable gain (before taper relief)	11	nil

The rebasing calculation gives a nil result, so this is a no-gain, no-loss situation. The total gain on the disposal of the entire 200 shares is therefore £407.

Listed shares - no pooling election made

Without a pooling election, the disposal of listed shares acquired before 6 April 1965 is treated in a broadly similar way to the disposal of any other pre-6 April 1965 asset (see Chapter 17). Basically, the gain produced by a calculation based on original cost is compared with the gain produced by a calculation based on market value at 6 April 1965 and the lower of these two gains is then compared with the gain produced by a rebasing calculation. But there are some significant differences between a disposal of listed shares and a disposal of other types of asset. These differences are:

(a) The calculation based on original cost is performed *without* time apportionment.

(b) The comparison of the calculation based on original cost and the calculation based on market value at 6 April 1965 is mandatory, rather than depending on an election by the taxpayer.

(c) The treatment of losses is as follows:

(i) If the calculation based on original cost gives a loss and the calculation based on market value at 6 April 1965 also gives a loss, then the lower of these two losses is compared with the outcome of the rebasing calculation in order to arrive at the allowable loss.

(ii) If the calculation based on original cost gives a gain and the calculation based on market value at 6 April 1965 gives a loss (or vice versa), then the situation is no gain, no loss. In these circumstances there is no need to perform a rebasing calculation.

EXAMPLE 6

In June 1964, Samuel acquired 1,000 shares in Purple plc (a listed company) at a cost of £500. The shares had a market value of £2 each on 6 April 1965 and £1 each on 31 March 1982. Samuel made no further acquisitions of shares in the company and no election was made to incorporate pre-6 April 1965 shares into the 1982 holding. He sold his entire shareholding in January 2006. Compute the chargeable gain if sale proceeds were:

(a) £10 per share (b) £1.80 per share.

Solution

(a)

		Cost	*MV 6/4/65*	*MV 31/3/82*
		£	£	£
Sale proceeds		10,000	10,000	10,000
Less: Original cost		500		
Market value 6/4/65			2,000	
Market value 31/3/82				1,000
Unindexed gain		9,500	8,000	9,000
Less: Indexation allowance				
$\frac{162.6 - 79.44}{79.44}$	= 1.047 x £1,000	1,047		
$\frac{162.6 - 79.44}{79.44}$	= 1.047 x £2,000		2,094	2,094
Chargeable gain (before taper relief)		8,453	5,906	6,906

Comparing the gains based on cost and on market value at 6 April 1965 gives a gain of £5,906. This gain is lower than the gain produced by the rebasing calculation, so rebasing will not apply and the chargeable gain (before taper relief) is £5,906.

Notes:

(i) The indexation allowance in the original cost calculation is based on the greater of original cost (£500) and market value at 31 March 1982 (£1,000).

(ii) The indexation allowance in the 6 April 1965 market value calculation is based on the greater of market value at 6 April 1965 (£2,000) and market value at 31 March 1982 (£1,000).

(iii) The indexation allowance in the rebasing calculation is also based on the greater of market value at 6 April 1965 (£2,000) and market value at 31 March 1982 (£1,000), since the rebasing calculation is being compared with the 6 April 1965 market value calculation (see Chapter 17).

(b)

	Cost	*MV 6/4/65*
	£	£
Sale proceeds	1,800	1,800
Less: Original cost	500	
Market value 6/4/65		2,000
Unindexed gain or loss	1,300	(200)
Less: Indexation allowance	1,047	nil
Chargeable gain (before taper relief) or allowable loss	253	(200)

The situation is no gain, no loss. There is no need to perform a rebasing calculation.

Unlisted shares acquired before 6 April 1965

None of the rules described above for listed shares apply to unlisted shares. There is no pooling election available in respect of unlisted shares and the computation of the gain or loss arising on a disposal of unlisted shares acquired before 6 April 1965 is performed in the same way as for any other pre-6 April 1965 asset.

Gilts and qualifying corporate bonds

Gilt-edged securities and "qualifying corporate bonds" are not chargeable assets for CGT purposes. Therefore neither a chargeable gain nor an allowable loss can arise on their disposal. Note that:

(a) Gilt-edged securities are British Government securities such as Treasury Stock, Exchequer Stock, War Loan etc.

(b) Qualifying corporate bonds consist of company debentures and other fixed-interest securities which are expressed in sterling and which comprise a normal commercial loan.

(c) Gains and losses arising on the disposal of gilts or corporate bonds by a *company* are assessed under the "loan relationships" rules for corporation tax purposes (see Chapter 23).

Summary

- Special matching rules are used to match disposals of shares and securities against acquisitions.
- Disposals are matched first against shares acquired on the same day as the disposal, then against shares acquired in the next 30 days, then against shares acquired after 5 April 1998, then against the S104 holding, then against the 1982 holding and then against shares acquired before 6 April 1965.
- The S104 holding consists of a pool of shares acquired between 6 April 1982 and 5 April 1998 inclusive. It is necessary to keep a record of the number of shares in this pool, their total cost and their total indexed cost.
- The 1982 holding consists of a pool of shares acquired between 6 April 1965 and 5 April 1982 inclusive. It is necessary to keep a record of the number of shares in this pool, their total cost and their market value at 31 March 1982.
- Listed shares acquired before 6 April 1965 may join the 1982 holding at their 6 April 1965 market value if the taxpayer makes a pooling election to this effect.
- In the absence of a pooling election, disposals of listed shares acquired before 6 April 1965 are dealt with according to a special set of rules which differ in some respects from the usual rules for dealing with pre-6 April 1965 assets.
- Disposals of unlisted shares acquired before 6 April 1965 are dealt with according to the usual rules for dealing with pre-6 April 1965 assets.
- Gilt-edged securities and qualifying corporate bonds are not chargeable assets for CGT purposes.

Exercises

Please note that the RPI for April 1998 is 162.6.

19.1 A taxpayer makes the following acquisitions of preference shares in Mauve Ltd (an unlisted company):

Date	*No of shares purchased*
1 August 1959	200
10 September 1962	500
4 August 1981	1,000
23 February 1990	250
17 October 1999	100
20 October 2004	200
1 December 2004	150

No further shares are acquired during 2004 or 2005. How will the following disposals be matched against these acquisitions?

(a) 250 shares sold on 20 October 2004

(b) 500 shares sold on 25 January 2005

(c) 1,200 shares sold on 1 November 2005.

19.2 Sandra acquired the following ordinary shares in Pink plc:

Date	*No of shares*	*Cost*	*RPI*
		£	
29 June 1982	1,000	3,000	81.85
5 May 1984	1,000	3,500	88.97
13 August 1987	1,350	6,500	102.1
7 September 1990	2,650	14,150	129.3
4 October 1995	2,000	22,500	149.8

Calculate the cost and indexed cost of the S104 holding at 4 October 1995 (RPI for April 1985 was 94.78).

19.3 In June 2005 Sandra (in exercise 19.2 above) sold 2,000 of her shares in Pink plc. She acquired no further shares in the company. Calculate the chargeable gain (before taper relief) or allowable loss if the sale proceeds are:

(a) £14,000

(b) £12,000

(c) £17,000.

19.4 Dennis acquired the following ordinary shares in Bronze plc:

Date	*No of shares*	*Cost*
		£
5 August 1978	300	2,400
12 May 1980	200	1,700
11 July 1981	250	2,000

Dennis made no other acquisitions and the shares had a market value of £10 per share on 31 March 1982 (RPI 79.44). Calculate the chargeable gain (before taper relief) arising in August 2005 when Dennis sold 150 shares for £3,500.

19.5 Denise acquired the following ordinary shares in Turquoise plc:

Date	*No of shares*	*Cost*	*RPI*
		£	
28 December 1980	10,000	5,000	
21 June 1990	10,000	9,000	126.7
3 March 1993	10,000	11,000	139.3

The shares were valued at 60p each on 31 March 1982 (RPI 79.44). In December 2005, Denise sold 25,000 shares for £1.25 per share. She made no further acquisitions of the shares. Calculate the chargeable gain (before taper relief) arising in December 2005 and state the length of the qualifying holding period for taper relief purposes. The shares do not rank as a business asset.

19.6 Raymond acquired the following ordinary shares in Buff plc (which are listed on the Stock Exchange):

Date	*No of shares*	*Cost*
		£
17 February 1963	500	4,000
8 January 1980	700	8,500

The shares were valued at £9 each on 6 April 1965 and £15 each on 31 March 1982. Raymond elected to incorporate pre-6 April 1965 shares into the 1982 holding and made no further acquisitions of the shares. In September 2005 he sold 1,000 shares for £40 each. Compute the chargeable gain (before taper relief) arising on this disposal and state the length of the qualifying holding period. The shares rank as a business asset.

19.7 Rework exercise 19.6, assuming now that Raymond had *not* elected to incorporate pre-6 April 1965 shares into the 1982 holding.

***19.8** Suzanne acquired the following ordinary shares in Aquamarine plc:

Date	*No of shares*	*Cost*	*RPI*
		£	
2 October 1979	100	300	
10 January 1981	150	500	
5 December 1983	200	700	86.89
8 November 1984	250	1,000	90.95
4 July 1991	300	1,400	133.8
20 May 2002	400	2,500	176.2

She made no further acquisitions. The shares were valued at £3.25 each on 31 March 1982 (RPI 79.44). RPI for April 1985 was 94.78. On 5 October 2005 Suzanne sold 1,200 shares for £7 per share. Compute the chargeable gains (before taper relief) arising on this disposal and state the qualifying holding period for each gain. The shares do not rank as a business asset.

***19.9** Stephen acquired the following ordinary shares in Olive plc (a listed company):

Date	*No of shares*	*Cost*
		£
1 June 1958	10	100
1 January 1960	90	9,000

The shares had a market value of £85 each on 6 April 1965 and £120 each on 31 March 1982 (RPI 79.44). Stephen acquired no further shares in the company and sold all his shares in January 2006 at £80 each. Compute the chargeable gain (before taper relief) or allowable loss, given that no pooling election had been (or will be) made in relation to shares acquired before 6 April 1965.

Chapter 20

Shares and securities (2)

Introduction

A company may reorganise its share capital by making bonus issues or rights issues or by repaying shareholders part of their share capital (to the extent that this is permitted by company law). This chapter considers the CGT impact of a reorganisation of share capital and also describes the treatment of disposals occurring on the takeover of one company by another.

Please note that the RPI for April 1998 (which is used in many of the examples in this chapter) is 162.6.

Bonus issues

A bonus issue occurs when a company issues free extra shares to its shareholders. The number of bonus shares received by a shareholder is generally in proportion to his or her existing shareholding. For instance, a "1 for 5" bonus issue would give each shareholder one free extra share for every five shares previously held.

For CGT purposes, the making of a bonus issue is regarded as a reorganisation of the company's share capital, rather than an issue of new shares. Accordingly, the CGT treatment of a bonus issue is as follows:

(a) Any bonus shares received by a taxpayer are *not* treated as an acquisition in the usual way. Instead, the bonus shares serve to increase the number of shares in each of the taxpayer's holdings as they stood immediately prior to the issue. The cost of those holdings is not affected, since bonus shares are issued free of charge.

(b) On a subsequent disposal, the qualifying holding period for taper relief purposes begins on the date that the taxpayer's original holdings were acquired and not on the date that the bonus shares were issued.

(c) If a bonus issue is made after 31 March 1982, the market value of the company's shares at 31 March 1982 is adjusted to reflect the issue.

EXAMPLE 1

Sherjeel made the following acquisitions of ordinary shares in Triangle plc:

Date	*No of shares*	*Cost*	*RPI*
		£	
22 January 1978	1,000	2,000	
27 September 1981	200	500	
28 July 1986	800	2,800	97.52
3 February 1993	500	2,200	138.8
5 July 2000	300	1,500	

The market value of the company's shares on 31 March 1982 (RPI 79.44) was £3.19 per share. On 1 September 2004, the company made a 1 for 10 bonus issue. Show each of Sherjeel's holdings immediately after this bonus issue.

Solution

Prior to the bonus issue, Sherjeel owned 2,800 shares in Triangle plc, of which 1,200 comprised the 1982 holding, 1,300 comprised the S104 holding and 300 were acquired on 5 July 2000 (and were not pooled). He received a further 280 shares as a consequence of the bonus issue. 120 of these shares join the 1982 holding, 130 shares join the S104 holding and 30 shares are attached to the acquisition made on 5 July 2000. The holdings immediately after the bonus issue are as follows:

The 1982 holding:

	No of shares	*Cost*	*MV 31/3/82*
		£	£
Acquired 22 January 1978	1,000	2,000	3,190
Acquired 27 September 1981	200	500	638
	1,200	2,500	3,828
Bonus issue 1 September 2004	120	nil	nil
1982 holding c/f	1,320	2,500	3,828

Notice that the market value of this holding at 31 March 1982 remains at £3,828 but the number of shares in the holding has increased to 1,320. In effect, the market value per share at 31 March 1982 has been reduced to £2.90 (£3,828 divided by 1,320) to reflect the fact that 11 shares now exist for every 10 that existed on 31 March 1982. The revised market value per share (£2.90) is 10/11ths of the original market value (£3.19).

The S104 holding:

	No of shares	*Cost*	*Indexed cost*
		£	£
Bought 28 July 1986	800	2,800	2,800
Add: Indexation to February 1993			
$\frac{138.8 - 97.52}{97.52} \times £2,800$			1,185
c/f	800	2,800	3,985

	No of shares	Cost	Indexed cost
		£	£
b/f	800	2,800	3,985
Bought 3 February 1993	500	2,200	2,200
S104 holding at 3 February 1993	1,300	5,000	6,185
Add: Indexation to April 1998			
$\frac{162.6 - 138.8}{138.8}$ x £6,185			1,061
			7,246
Bonus issue 1 September 2004	130	nil	nil
S104 holding at 1 September 2004	1,430	5,000	7,246

In summary, Sherjeel now has a 1982 holding containing 1320 shares, a S104 holding containing 1,430 shares and a holding of 330 shares acquired on 5 July 2000.

EXAMPLE 2

Calculate the chargeable gain arising in March 2006 when Sherjeel (in the above example) sells 1,830 shares for £6 each, assuming that he makes no further acquisitions within the next 30 days.

Solution

The disposal is matched first against the holding of 330 shares acquired on 5 July 2000. These shares were sold for £1,980 (330 x £6) and have a cost of £1,500 so the chargeable gain is £480 (with a qualifying holding period of five years). The remainder of the disposal is matched against the S104 holding and the 1982 holding, as follows:

S104 holding (1,430 shares sold):

	No of shares	Cost	Indexed cost
		£	£
S104 holding at 1 September 2004	1,430	5,000	7,246
Sold March 2006	(1,430)	(5,000)	(7,246)
S104 holding c/f	nil	nil	nil

The gain arising on the disposal of the S104 holding is:

	£
Sale proceeds (1,430 @ £6)	8,580
Less: Cost	5,000
Unindexed gain	3,580
Less: Indexation allowance (£7,246 - £5,000)	2,246
Chargeable gain (before taper relief)	1,334

1982 holding (70 shares sold):

	No of shares	*Cost*	*MV 31/3/82*
		£	£
b/f	1,320	2,500	3,828
Sold March 2006 (70/1,320ths)	(70)	(133)	(203)
1982 holding c/f	1,250	2,367	3,625

The gain arising on the disposal from the 1982 holding is:

	Original cost	*Rebasing*
	£	£
Sale proceeds (70 @ £6)	420	420
Less: Original cost	133	
Market value 31/3/82		203
Unindexed gain	287	217
Less: Indexation allowance		
$\frac{162.6 - 79.44}{79.44}$ = 1.047 x £203	213	213
Chargeable gain (before taper relief)	74	4

The gain is £4. In summary, the gains arising on the disposal are £480 with a qualifying holding period of five years and £1,338 (£1,334 + £4) with a qualifying holding period of seven years (plus the bonus year if the shares are a non-business asset).

Rights issues

A rights issue occurs when a company offers its shareholders the right to buy extra shares. Rights issues are similar to bonus issues in that the number of shares offered to each shareholder is generally in proportion to his or her existing shareholding. But rights shares are not issued free of charge. Shareholders who are offered rights shares may either:

(a) ignore the rights issue (in which case there is no CGT impact)

(b) sell their "rights" (see later in this chapter)

(c) buy the shares which they are offered.

For CGT purposes, the making of a rights issue is regarded as a reorganisation of the company's share capital and therefore shares acquired as the result of such an issue are not treated as an acquisition in the usual way. The CGT treatment of a rights issue is as follows:

(a) Any rights shares acquired by a taxpayer serve to increase the number of shares in each of the taxpayer's holdings immediately prior to the rights issue. The cost of the rights shares increases the cost of these holdings.

(b) If rights shares join the 1982 holding after 31 March 1982, then:

- (i) it is necessary (for indexation purposes) to keep a separate record of the original cost of the 1982 holding and the cost of the rights shares
- (ii) the cost of the rights shares is treated as enhancement expenditure incurred in relation to a pre-31 March 1982 asset (see Chapter 17).

(c) On a subsequent disposal, the qualifying holding period for taper relief purposes begins on the date that the taxpayer's original holdings were acquired and not on the date that the rights shares were acquired.

EXAMPLE 3

Tina made the following acquisitions of ordinary shares in Rhombus plc:

Date	*No of shares*	*Cost*	*RPI*
		£	
15 August 1980	500	1,000	
23 January 1987	600	2,500	100.0

The market value of the company's shares on 31 March 1982 (RPI 79.44) was £2.50 per share. In June 1997 (RPI 157.5), the company made a 1 for 20 rights issue at £8 per share and Tina decided to buy the shares which she was offered. Show the S104 holding and the 1982 holding immediately after the rights issue.

Solution

The 1982 holding:

	No of shares	*Cost (original)*	*Cost (rights)*	*MV 31/3/82*
		£	£	£
Acquired 15 August 1980	500	1,000		1,250
Rights issue June 1997 (1 for 20)	25		200	
1982 holding c/f	525	1,000	200	1,250

The S104 holding:

	No of shares	*Cost*	*Indexed cost*
		£	£
Bought 23 January 1987	600	2,500	2,500
Add: Indexation to June 1997 $\frac{157.5 - 100.0}{100.0} \times £2,500$			1,438
			3,938
Rights issue June 1997 (1 for 20)	30	240	240
S104 holding c/f	630	2,740	4,178

EXAMPLE 4

Calculate the chargeable gain arising in November 2005 when Tina (in the above example) sells 840 shares for £7 each, assuming that she makes no further acquisitions within the next 30 days.

Solution

S104 holding (630 shares sold):

	No of shares	Cost £	Indexed cost £
b/f at June 1997	630	2,740	4,178
Add: Indexation to April 1998 $\frac{162.6 - 157.5}{157.5} \times £4,178$			135
			4,313
Sold November 2005	(630)	(2,740)	(4,313)
S104 holding c/f	nil	nil	nil

The gain arising on the disposal of the S104 holding is:

	£
Sale proceeds (630 @ £7)	4,410
Less: Cost	2,740
Unindexed gain	1,670
Less: Indexation allowance (£4,313 - £2,740)	1,573
Chargeable gain (before taper relief)	97

1982 holding (210 shares sold):

	No of shares	Cost (original) £	Cost (rights) £	MV 31/3/82 £
b/f	525	1,000	200	1,250
Sold November 2005 (210/525ths)	(210)	(400)	(80)	(500)
1982 holding c/f	315	600	120	750

The gain arising on the disposal from the 1982 holding is:

		Original cost	Rebasing
		£	£
Sale proceeds (210 @ £7)		1,470	1,470
Less: Cost up to 31 March 1982		(400)	
Market value 31/3/82			(500)
Cost June 1997		(80)	(80)
Unindexed gain		990	890
Less: Indexation allowance			
$\frac{162.6 - 79.44}{79.44}$	= 1.047 x £500	(524)	(524)
$\frac{162.6 - 157.5}{157.5}$	= 0.032 x £80	(3)	(3)
Chargeable gain (before taper relief)		463	363

The rebasing calculation gives the lower gain, so rebasing applies and the gain is £363. The total chargeable gain on the entire disposal of 840 shares is therefore £460 (£97 + £363) with a qualifying holding period of seven years (plus the bonus year if the shares are a non-business asset).

Capital distributions

A capital distribution occurs when shareholders are repaid part of their share capital, usually when a company goes into liquidation. Unless the amount of the distribution is small (see later in this chapter) a capital distribution is regarded as a part disposal for CGT purposes.

EXAMPLE 5

In March 1990 (RPI 121.4), Vincent bought 10,000 ordinary shares in Trapezium plc for £44,000. In June 2005, the company went into liquidation and Vincent received a first distribution of £0.50 per share. The market value of an ordinary share in Trapezium plc just after this distribution was £0.75. Compute the allowable loss arising in June 2005.

Solution

The value of the part disposed of is £5,000 (10,000 @ £0.50) and the value of the part remaining is £7,500 (10,000 @ £0.75). The part disposal fraction is 5,000/12,500 which is equivalent to 2/5ths.

S104 holding:

	No of shares	Cost	Indexed cost
		£	£
Bought March 1990	10,000	44,000	44,000
Add: Indexation to April 1998 $\frac{162.6 - 121.4}{121.4}$ x £44,000			14,932
			58,932
Distribution June 2005 (2/5ths)	-	(17,600)	(23,573)
S104 holding c/f	10,000	26,400	35,359

The computation of the allowable loss is as follows:

	£
Disposal proceeds	5,000
Less: Part cost	(17,600)
Unindexed loss	(12,600)
Less: Indexation allowance (£23,573 - £17,600)	nil
Allowable loss	(12,600)

Sale of rights nil paid

Another example of a capital distribution occurs when a company makes a rights issue and a shareholder decides not to buy the shares concerned but instead to sell his or her rights to someone else (a "sale of rights nil paid"). When shareholders sell their rights they are *not* selling shares. What they are selling is the right to buy shares, often at an attractive price. The proceeds of such a sale are treated as a capital distribution. If the amount of money involved is small (see below) the amount received will be treated as a small capital distribution.

Small capital distributions

If the amount of a capital distribution is small when compared with the value of the shares concerned, the distribution is not treated as a disposal. Instead, the proceeds of the distribution are subtracted from the acquisition cost of the shares. The effect of this is that the gain which would have been chargeable on the distribution is deferred until a subsequent disposal takes place. This is very similar to the treatment of small part disposals of land (see Chapter 17). Note that:

(a) A capital distribution is generally regarded as small if it consists of no more than 5% of the value of the company's shares just before the distribution. It is also the practice of HM Revenue and Customs to regard an amount of £3,000 or less as small for this purpose, even if the 5% test is not satisfied.

(b) HM Revenue and Customs will usually allow a small capital distribution to be treated as a disposal if this is to the taxpayer's advantage (e.g. if the gain arising is covered by the annual exemption).

EXAMPLE 6

In April 1996 (RPI 152.6), Vanessa bought 100 shares in Pentagon plc at a cost of £5 per share. The company went into liquidation and Vanessa received a first distribution of 40p per share in July 2004. The shares had a market value of £9.75 immediately after the distribution.

(a) Show how the distribution will be dealt with for CGT purposes.

(b) Calculate the chargeable gain arising in March 2006, when Vanessa received a second and final distribution of £9.82 per share.

Solution

(a) The value of the shares immediately prior to the distribution must have been £10.15 (£9.75 + £0.40). 40p is 3.9% of £10.15 so the distribution ranks as a small capital distribution. The £40 received by Vanessa may be deducted from the £500 that she paid for her shares, reducing the allowable cost on a future disposal to £460.

(b) Assuming that the small capital distribution is not treated as a disposal, the S104 holding is:

	No of shares	*Cost*	*Indexed cost*
		£	£
Bought April 1996	100	500	500
Add: Indexation to April 1998 $\frac{162.6 - 152.6}{152.6} \times £500$			33
			533
Distribution July 2004	-	(40)	(40)
	100	460	493
Disposal March 2006	(100)	(460)	(493)
S104 holding c/f	nil	nil	nil

The gain arising on the disposal is:

	£
Disposal proceeds (100 @ £9.82)	982
Less: Indexed cost	493
Chargeable gain (before taper relief)	489

Small capital distributions and the 1982 holding

If a small capital distribution which is not treated as a disposal is made after 31 March 1982 and the taxpayer has a 1982 holding, the part of the distribution which relates to the shares in that holding will be subtracted from its cost. Note that:

(a) It is necessary (for indexation purposes) to keep a separate record of the original cost of the 1982 holding and the amount of the small capital distribution

(b) In effect, the amount of the distribution is dealt with as *negative* enhancement expenditure incurred in relation to a pre-31 March 1982 asset.

EXAMPLE 7

In January 1980, Wendy bought 2,000 shares in Square plc for £2.50 per share. On 31 March 1982 (RPI 79.44) the shares had a market value of £3.00 each. In July 1997 (RPI 157.5) when the shares had a market value of £12 each, the company made a rights issue but Wendy decided to sell her rights, realising £100. Compute the chargeable gain arising in December 2005, when Wendy sold all her shares for £25,000 (assuming that she made no further acquisitions within the next 30 days).

Solution

The value of Wendy's shares immediately prior to the sale of rights was £24,000 (2,000 @ £12). Wendy realised £100, which is 0.4% of £24,000. Therefore the sale of rights ranks as a small capital distribution. Assuming that the distribution is not treated as a disposal, the 1982 holding is:

	No of shares	*Cost (original)* £	*Small capital distribution* £	*MV 31/3/82* £
Bought January 1980	2,000	5,000		6,000
Distribution July 1997	-		(100)	
1982 holding c/f	2,000	5,000	(100)	6,000
Sold December 2005	(2,000)	(5,000)	100	(6,000)
1982 holding c/f	nil	nil	nil	nil

The computation of the gain arising in December 2005 is as follows:

	Original cost £	*Rebasing* £
Sale proceeds	25,000	25,000
Less: Cost up to 31 March 1982	(5,000)	
Market value 31/3/82		(6,000)
Small capital distribution July 1997	100	100
Unindexed gain	20,100	19,100

		Original cost	Rebasing
		£	£
Unindexed gain		20,100	19,100
Less: Indexation allowance:			
$\frac{162.6 - 79.44}{79.44}$	= 1.047 x £6,000	(6,282)	(6,282)
$\frac{162.6 - 157.5}{157.5}$	= 0.032 x £100	3	3
Chargeable gain (before taper relief)		13,821	12,821

The rebasing calculation gives the lower gain, so rebasing applies and the chargeable gain (before taper relief) is £12,821.

Takeovers

A takeover occurs when one company acquires the shares of another company. Shareholders of the "target" company exchange their shares in return for cash, or shares of the acquiring company, or a combination of both cash and shares. The CGT treatment of such disposals is as follows:

(a) If a takeover is entirely for cash, the shareholders of the target company have sold their shares and have made chargeable disposals. The fact that shares have been sold as a consequence of a takeover is irrelevant and the gain or loss is computed in the usual way.

(b) If a takeover is entirely for shares (a "paper for paper" takeover), no chargeable disposals have taken place. A shareholder's newly-acquired shares in the acquiring company replace the shares originally held in the target company and are deemed for all CGT purposes (including taper relief) to have been acquired on the same date and at the same cost as the original holding.

(c) If a takeover is partly for cash and partly for shares, a part disposal has taken place and a part disposal calculation is usually required. The value of the part disposed of is the amount of cash received and the value of the part remaining is the value of the shares received. However, if the amount of cash received by a taxpayer is no more than 5% of the total consideration (or no more than £3,000) the cash received may be treated as a small capital distribution.

EXAMPLE 8

In October 1992 (RPI 139.9), Winston bought 8,000 shares in Hexagon plc at a cost of £3 per share. In October 2005 Circle plc made a takeover bid for Hexagon plc, offering the Hexagon shareholders three Circle shares plus £1 in cash for every two Hexagon shares. The offer was accepted on 29 October 2005 when the market value of shares in Circle plc was £5 per share. Compute Winston's chargeable gain.

Solution

Winston received 12,000 shares in Circle plc, worth £60,000, plus £4,000 in cash, a total of £64,000. The amount received in cash is 6.25% of the total and exceeds £3,000, so this cannot be treated as a small capital distribution. The S104 holding is:

	No of shares	*Cost*	*Indexed cost*
		£	£
Bought (Hexagon plc) October 1992	8,000	24,000	24,000
Add: Indexation to April 1998			
$\frac{162.6 - 139.9}{139.9} \times £24,000$			3,894
			27,894
Distribution October 2005 (6.25%)	-	(1,500)	(1,743)
S104 holding after distribution	8,000	22,500	26,151
S104 holding (Circle plc) c/f	12,000	22,500	26,151

The gain arising on the disposal is:

	£
Disposal proceeds	4,000
Less: Cost	1,500
Unindexed gain	2,500
Less: Indexation allowance (£1,743 - £1,500)	243
Chargeable gain (before taper relief)	2,257

Summary

- The CGT effect of a bonus issue is to increase the number of shares in each of the taxpayer's holdings prior to the issue. The cost of the holdings is not affected.
- The CGT effect of a rights issue which is taken up is to increase both the number and the cost of the shares in each of the taxpayer's holdings prior to the issue.
- A sale of rights nil paid is regarded as a capital distribution.
- A capital distribution is treated for CGT purposes as a part disposal unless it ranks as a small capital distribution, in which case the amount of the distribution is deducted from the acquisition cost of the shares concerned.
- A small capital distribution is one which consists of no more than 5% of the value of the company's shares immediately prior to the distribution. A distribution which fails the 5% test is still regarded as small if the amount of money received by a taxpayer does not exceed £3,000.
- If a takeover is entirely for cash, the shareholders of the target company have made chargeable disposals.
- If a takeover is entirely for shares, no chargeable disposals have taken place.
- If a takeover is partly for cash and partly for shares, a part disposal has occurred unless the amount of cash can be treated as a small capital distribution.

Exercises

Please note that the RPI for April 1998 is 162.6.

20.1 William made the following acquisitions of preference shares in Heptagon plc:

Date	*No of shares*	*Cost*	*RPI*
		£	
17 February 1980	600	900	
13 November 1988	200	400	110.0
9 October 2003	100	300	

The market value of the shares at 31 March 1982 (RPI 79.44) was £1.70 per share. In January 2006 the company made a 1 for 4 bonus issue.

Show William's holdings as they stand immediately after this bonus issue.

20.2 In February 2006, William (in exercise 20.1) sells 425 shares for £4 per share. Calculate the chargeable gain before taper relief, assuming that he makes no acquisitions in the following 30 days.

20.3 Yvonne made the following acquisitions of ordinary shares in Rectangle plc:

Date	*No of shares*	*Cost*	*RPI*
		£	
30 September 1979	2,000	1,200	
1 December 1992	3,000	3,600	139.2

The market value of the shares on 31 March 1982 (RPI 79.44) was 75p each. In January 1998 (RPI 159.5), the company made a 1 for 8 rights issue at £1 per share and Yvonne decided to buy the shares which she was offered. Show the S104 holding and the 1982 holding as they stand immediately after the rights issue.

20.4 In March 2006, Yvonne (in exercise 20.3) sells all her shares in Rectangle plc for £1.80 per share. Calculate the chargeable gain before taper relief arising in March 2006, given that no further shares are acquired within the following 30 days.

20.5 In November 1997 (RPI 159.6), Yorick bought 6,000 ordinary shares in Octagon plc for £30,000. In May 2005, the company went into liquidation and Yorick received a first distribution of £1 per share. The market value of an ordinary share in Octagon plc just after this distribution was £2. Compute the allowable loss arising in May 2005.

20.6 In January 1998 (RPI 159.5), Yolande bought 300 ordinary shares in Ellipse plc at a cost of £1.20 per share. In March 2004, when shares in Ellipse plc had a market value of £2 each, the company made a rights issue. Yolande sold her rights, realising £25. Compute the chargeable gain (before taper relief) arising in November 2005 when Yolande sold all her shares for £780, assuming that no further shares were acquired within the following 30 days.

20.7 In April 2002, Walter bought 12,000 shares in Oval plc at a cost of £5.85 per share. In September 2005, Round plc made a takeover bid for Oval plc, offering the Oval shareholders eight Round shares plus £2.50 in cash for every five Oval shares. The offer was accepted on 2 September 2005 when the market value of shares in Round plc was £4.30 per share. Compute Walter's chargeable gain (before taper relief).

***20.8** Saeed made the following purchases of ordinary shares in Hyperbola plc:

Date	*No of shares*	*Cost*	*RPI*
		£	
24 August 1975	800	800	
25 November 1980	1,200	1,350	
26 February 1985	1,600	2,400	91.94
11 October 1993	400	800	141.8

The company's shares had a market value of £1.20 each on 31 March 1982 (RPI 79.44). In March 1994 (RPI 142.5), the company made a 1 for 40 rights issue at £1.50 per share and Saeed took up the shares which he was offered.

Calculate the chargeable gain (before taper relief) arising in November 2005, when Saeed sold 2,870 shares at £3 each. Assume that no further shares were acquired within the following 30 days. (RPI for April 1985 was 94.78.)

***20.9** Susan made the following purchases of ordinary shares in Semicircle plc:

Date	*No of shares*	*Cost*
		£
11 January 1981	1,500	4,800
20 January 1982	1,140	5,700

The market value of the company's shares on 31 March 1982 (RPI 79.44) was £4. In January 2006, the company went into liquidation and Susan received a first distribution of £2 per share. The market value of an ordinary share in Semicircle plc just after this distribution was £1. Compute the allowable loss arising in January 2006.

***20.10** Steven made the following purchases of ordinary shares in Convex plc:

Date	*No of shares*	*Cost*
		£
9 May 1998	2,000	8,000
28 November 2001	500	2,500

In February 2006, Concave plc made a takeover bid for Convex plc, offering the Convex shareholders two Concave shares plus £2 in cash for every Convex share. The offer was accepted on 21 February 2006 when the market value of shares in Concave plc was £4 per share. Compute Steven's chargeable gain (before taper relief) or allowable loss.

Chapter 21

Principal private residences

Introduction

This chapter examines the CGT consequences of the disposal of a taxpayer's principal private residence. Although a principal private residence is not a chargeable asset for CGT purposes, a CGT liability may arise when a property is disposed of which has been used as a residence for only part of the period of ownership or which has been used partly as a residence and partly for other purposes.

Please note that the RPI for April 1998 (which is used in many of the examples in this chapter) is 162.6.

Principal private residence

A dwelling which is a taxpayer's only or main residence is known as that taxpayer's principal private residence (PPR). A taxpayer's PPR is not a chargeable asset for CGT purposes. Therefore any gain which arises on the disposal of a PPR is not chargeable to tax and any loss which arises is not allowable. For a property to be regarded as a PPR, the taxpayer must actually occupy the property as a residence. Mere ownership is not sufficient. Furthermore, the term "residence" implies a degree of permanency and it is unlikely that the PPR exemption will apply to a property which has been used only as temporary accommodation. In *Goodwin* v *Curtis* (1998) a property which had been occupied by the taxpayer for only 32 days did not qualify as a residence.

The large majority of taxpayers own (at most) a single property and reside in that property, so that it is obvious that the property is the taxpayer's PPR. However, the following points may be relevant in more complex cases:

(a) A taxpayer may have only one PPR at any given time.

(b) A taxpayer who owns and lives in two (or more) properties may make an election to determine which property is to be regarded as the PPR. Such an election must be made within two years of the date from which it is to take effect.

(c) A married couple who live together may have only one PPR between them. As from 5 December 2005, this rule extends to same-sex civil partners who live together and who have entered into a legally-recognised civil partnership.

(d) The PPR exemption covers the residence itself together with grounds or gardens of up to half a hectare (5,000 square metres) in area. Larger areas may be included in the exemption if they are warranted by the size of the residence.

(e) The requirement that there must be actual residence in the property is relaxed if the taxpayer is required to live in job-related accommodation (see Chapter 7). In these circumstances, the PPR exemption is extended to any property which the taxpayer owns so long as he or she intends to occupy the property in the future.

Partial exemption

If a property has been occupied as a PPR for only a part of the period of ownership, only a part of the gain realised on disposal will be exempt from CGT. The exempt part of the gain is equal to:

$$\frac{\text{length of period of residence}}{\text{length of period of ownership}} \times \text{whole gain}$$

The lengths of the periods of residence and ownership are usually calculated to the nearest month. Note the following important points:

(a) If the property was acquired before 31 March 1982, the period of ownership prior to that date and any period of residence prior to that date are ignored.

(b) If a property has been the taxpayer's PPR at some time, the last 36 months of ownership always count as a period of residence, whether or not the taxpayer was actually resident then (so helping taxpayers who move house and have difficulty in selling their previous residence). This rule applies even if the taxpayer claims another property to be his or her PPR during the 36 months.

EXAMPLE 1

Allan bought a house in January 1979 for £20,000. The market value of the house on 31 March 1982 (RPI 79.44) was £29,000. Allan lived in the house until 1 May 2002 on which date he bought another house and made this his principal private residence. The house he had bought in January 1979 was sold on 31 January 2006 for £145,000. Compute the chargeable gain.

Solution

In examples of this type it is necessary first to calculate the gain arising (ignoring any PPR exemption) and then to consider the PPR exemption as a second stage. The gain arising is as follows:

	Original cost	Rebasing
	£	£
Sale proceeds	145,000	145,000
Less: Original cost	20,000	
Market value 31/3/82		29,000
Unindexed gain	125,000	116,000
Less: Indexation allowance		
$\frac{162.6 - 79.44}{79.44}$ = 1.047 x £29,000	30,363	30,363
Chargeable gain (before PPR exemption)	94,637	85,637

The rebasing calculation gives the lower gain, so rebasing applies and the chargeable gain (before considering the PPR exemption) is £85,637.

After 31 March 1982, Allan owned the house for 23 years and 10 months (286 months). He was actually resident for 20 years and 1 month (241 months) and the last 36 months of ownership also count as a period of residence, making a total of 277 months during which the PPR exemption applies. The chargeable gain is therefore as follows:

	£
Total gain (as above)	85,637
Less: $\frac{277}{286}$ x £85,637	82,942
Chargeable gain (before taper relief)	2,695

Deemed residence

The period of residence in a property is deemed to include certain periods when the taxpayer was not actually resident, so long as:

(a) there is a period of actual residence both at some time before the period of absence and at some time after the period of absence, and

(b) the taxpayer claims no other property to be a PPR during the period of absence.

These periods of "deemed residence" are as follows:

(a) any periods of absence during which the taxpayer is working abroad

(b) a total of up to four years of absence during which the taxpayer is working elsewhere in the UK

(c) a total of up to three years of absence for any reason.

By concession, the requirement that the taxpayer must reside in the property at some time after the period of absence is waived if the absence is work-related and the terms of the taxpayer's employment prevent him or her from returning to the residence.

EXAMPLE 2

On 1 June 1985 (RPI 95.41), Alice bought a house in Derby for £35,000. She occupied the house as her PPR until 1 May 1987 when she left to work in Exeter, living in rented accommodation. She returned to the house in Derby on 1 November 1988 and stayed until 1 July 1991 when she left to take up a post in the USA, again living in rented accommodation. She returned to Derby on 1 February 1994 and stayed until 1 December 2001 when she bought another house in Nottingham and made this her principal private residence. On 1 February 2006 she sold the house in Derby for £154,000. Compute the chargeable gain.

Solution

	£
Sale proceeds	154,000
Less: Acquisition cost	35,000
Unindexed gain	119,000
Less: Indexation allowance	
$\frac{162.6 - 95.41}{95.41} = 0.704 \times £35,000$	24,640
Chargeable gain (before PPR exemption)	94,360

Alice's period of ownership of the house in Derby (a total of 248 months) can be broken down into the following periods:

(i)	1 June 1985 to 30 April 1987	23 months	Actual residence
(ii)	1 May 1987 to 31 October 1988	18 months	Working in UK
(iii)	1 November 1988 to 30 June 1991	32 months	Actual residence
(iv)	1 July 1991 to 31 January 1994	31 months	Working abroad
(v)	1 February 1994 to 30 November 2001	94 months	Actual residence
(vi)	1 December 2001 to 31 January 2006	50 months	Living in new PPR

Periods (i), (iii) and (v) are exempt since Alice was actually resident in the property during those periods. Period (ii) is exempt since Alice was working elsewhere in the UK, the four-year time limit has not been exceeded and she was resident in the property both before and after the absence. Similarly, period (iv) is exempt. The last 36 months of ownership are always exempt, which leaves the first 14 months of period (vi) to consider. During these 14 months Alice was claiming another property to be her PPR, so the period cannot count as a period of deemed residence and the gain arising during these 14 months is chargeable. The remaining 234 months benefit from the PPR exemption. The chargeable gain is therefore as follows:

	£
Total gain (as above)	94,360
Less: $\frac{234}{248} \times £94,360$	89,033
Chargeable gain (before taper relief)	5,327

Letting relief

An extension to the PPR exemption, known as "letting relief", applies if a PPR has been let to tenants as residential accommodation. There are two situations to consider:

(a) A property might have been used entirely as a residence for part of the period of ownership but let to tenants during periods of absence by the owner. A chargeable gain will arise if the periods of absence are not entirely covered by the exemptions already described in this chapter, but letting relief will then be available in relation to this gain.

(b) Part of a property might have been used as a residence whilst the other part has been let. In this case, the PPR exemption will cover:

   (i) the gain arising on the whole property during the last 36 months of ownership, and

   (ii) the remainder of the gain, to the extent that this is attributable to the part of the property which was occupied by the owner.

   The balance of the gain will be chargeable to CGT, but letting relief may then be available. In general, letting relief will *not* be granted if the part that has been let forms a dwelling which is entirely separate from the accommodation which forms the owner's residence (e.g. a self-contained flat with its own access from the road). Relief *will* normally be granted if the let accommodation forms part of the owner's dwelling and the owner previously resided in the entire premises.

Letting relief is calculated as the *lowest* of:

(a) the part of the gain which relates to the let part of the property or to the letting period
(b) the part of the gain which is exempt because of the PPR exemptions
(c) £40,000.

EXAMPLE 3

In relation to the previous example in this chapter, assume now that Alice always let her Derby house when she was not resident there. Compute the chargeable gain.

Solution

The only chargeable period was a period of 14 months during which a gain of £5,327 arose and during which the property was let. Letting relief is available as the lowest of:

(a) The part of the gain which relates to the letting period (£5,327)
(b) The part of the gain which is exempt because of the PPR exemptions (£89,033)
(c) £40,000.

The lowest of these is £5,327. Therefore letting relief of £5,327 is available and the chargeable gain is reduced to £nil.

EXAMPLE 4

Alistair bought a house in 1978 for £97,500 and occupied the entire house until 1 May 1994 when he rented the top floor (comprising one-half of the house) to tenants, retaining the ground floor as his own residence. This arrangement continued until 1 October 2005 when he sold the house for £615,000. The house had a market value of £125,000 on 31 March 1982 (RPI 79.44). Compute the chargeable gain.

Solution

	Original cost	*Rebasing*
	£	£
Sale proceeds	615,000	615,000
Less: Original cost	97,500	
Market value 31/3/82		125,000
Unindexed gain	517,500	490,000
Less: Indexation allowance		
$\frac{162.6 - 79.44}{79.44}$ = 1.047 x £125,000	130,875	130,875
Chargeable gain (before PPR exemption)	386,625	359,125

The rebasing calculation gives the lower gain, so rebasing applies and the chargeable gain (before considering exemptions) is £359,125.

After 31 March 1982, Alistair owned the house for 23 years and 6 months (282 months). Exemption is available for the 145 months during which he occupied the whole property and for the last 36 months (a total of 181 months). He was resident in half of the property for the remaining 101 months, so 50% of the gain arising during these 101 months is also exempt. The other 50% is chargeable but letting relief is available. The chargeable gain is calculated as follows:

	£	£
Total gain (as above)		359,125
Less: PPR exemption:		
£359,125 x 181/282	230,502	
£359,125 x 101/282 x 1/2	64,312	294,814
		64,311
Less: Letting relief, lowest of:		
(a) £64,311		
(b) £294,814		
(c) £40,000		40,000
Chargeable gain (before taper relief)		24,311

Business use

If a property is used partly as a residence and partly for business purposes, the gain which is attributable to the part used for business purposes is chargeable to CGT. No reliefs are available in relation to this gain. The usual exemption for the last 36 months of ownership does not apply to the part of the property which has been used for business purposes.

EXAMPLE 5

Ava bought a house on 1 July 1987 (RPI 101.8) for £32,000. She occupied the entire property as her PPR until 1 August 1994 when she began using one-quarter of the house for business purposes. This continued until 1 November 2005 when she sold the house for £177,000. Compute the chargeable gain.

Solution

		£
Sale proceeds		177,000
Less: Acquisition cost		32,000
Unindexed gain		145,000
Less: Indexation allowance		
$\frac{162.6 - 101.8}{101.8}$	= 0.597 x £32,000	19,104
Chargeable gain (before PPR exemption)		125,896

Ava owned the house for 18 years and 4 months (220 months). For the first 7 years and 1 month (85 months) she occupied the entire house as her PPR. For the remaining 135 months she occupied three-quarters of the house. The chargeable gain is as follows:

	£	£
Total gain (as above)		125,896
Less: PPR exemption:		
£125,896 x 85/220	48,642	
£125,896 x 135/220 x 3/4	57,941	106,583
Chargeable gain (before taper relief)		19,313

Summary

- A taxpayer's principal private residence (PPR) is exempt from CGT.
- Taxpayers with two or more residences may elect which property is to be regarded as the PPR.
- A married couple (or civil partners) who live together may have only one PPR between them.
- If a property has been occupied as a PPR for only a part of the period of ownership, only a part of the gain realised on disposal will be exempt from CGT.
- The last 36 months of ownership of a PPR always count as a period of residence.
- Certain periods of absence are deemed to be periods of residence.
- Letting relief may be available if a residence has been let to tenants as residential accommodation.
- If a residence is used partly for business purposes, the gain relating to the part used for business purposes is chargeable to CGT.

Exercises

Please note that the RPI for April 1998 is 162.6.

21.1 Mohammed owns two properties - a flat in Central London and a country cottage in Sussex. In general he lives in his London flat during the week and spends the weekends in his Sussex cottage. Which of his two properties will be regarded as his principal private residence?

21.2 Melanie bought a house in November 1979 for £18,000. The house had a market value of £21,000 on 31 March 1982 (RPI 79.44) and was sold on 31 October 2005 for £163,000. Compute the chargeable gain (before taper relief) arising in each of the following cases:

(a) Melanie occupied the house as her principal private residence throughout the period of ownership.

(b) Melanie occupied the house throughout her period of ownership with the exception of the period between 1 June 1985 and 31 May 1989 when she lived with a friend. During this time the house stood empty.

(c) As (b) except that the house was let as residential accommodation during Melanie's absence.

21.3 Rupert bought a house in Manchester on 1 November 1985 (RPI 95.92) for £55,000. He occupied the house until 1 November 1989 when he left to work abroad for a year, moving back into the house on 1 November 1990. He stayed until 1 February 1993 when he left again, this time to work in Aberdeen, where he stayed until his return on 1 May 1997. This time he stayed for only a month, leaving on 1 June 1997 to go to live with a friend. He never returned to the house and it was sold on 1 March 2006 for £172,000. During his absences, Rupert always let his house and he claimed no other property to be his principal private residence. Compute the chargeable gain (before taper relief) arising on the disposal.

21.4 Samantha bought a house for £37,500 on 1 August 1986 (RPI 97.82) and occupied the house as her principal private residence. On 1 June 1988 she began to use one-fifth of the house for business purposes. Unfortunately her business eventually failed and on 1 June 1994 she ceased trading. From that date onwards she resided in the entire house until it was sold on 1 August 2005 for £155,000. Compute the chargeable gain (before taper relief).

***21.5** Terry bought a house for £65,000 on 1 June 1987 (RPI 101.9) and occupied the house as his principal private residence. He lived in the house until 1 June 1991 when he went to stay with relatives in Australia, letting the house in his absence. He did not return until 1 June 1995, when he began using one-quarter of the house for business purposes and the other three-quarters as his residence. This arrangement continued until 1 June 2005 when he sold the house for £190,000. Compute the chargeable gain (before taper relief).

Chapter 22

CGT reliefs

Introduction

A taxpayer's capital gains tax liability may sometimes be reduced or deferred by taking advantage of various CGT reliefs. The purpose of this chapter is to explain, for each of these reliefs, the circumstances in which the relief is available and the way in which the amount of relief is calculated.

Please note that the RPI for April 1998 (which is used in many of the examples in this chapter) is 162.6.

Damaged assets

If an asset has been damaged and insurance money or other compensation is received in consequence, the situation is usually treated as a part disposal. The value of the part disposed of (A) is the amount of money received and the value of the part remaining (B) is the value of the asset on the date that the money is received. Any money spent on restoration is treated as enhancement expenditure.

However, in certain circumstances, the taxpayer may elect that the situation should *not* be treated as a part disposal and that the amount of money received should instead be deducted from the allowable expenditure relating to the asset. This has the effect of increasing the gain arising on a subsequent disposal and is very similar to the CGT treatment of small capital distributions (see Chapter 20). The circumstances in which a part disposal may be avoided are as follows:

(a) All of the money received is applied to restoring the asset, or

(b) The asset is not a wasting asset and all the money received is applied to restoring the asset except for an amount which is small in comparison with the amount received and which is not reasonably required for restoration purposes, or

(c) The asset is not a wasting asset and the amount of money received is small in comparison with the value of the asset.

For this purpose, a sum is regarded as "small" if it does not exceed £3,000 or 5% of the amount with which it is being compared, whichever is the higher.

A part disposal calculation is unavoidable if only part of the money received is spent on restoring the asset and neither of the "small" tests is satisfied. However, the taxpayer may elect that the calculation should relate only to the amount which is received but not spent on restoration. If this election is made, the remainder of the money received is deducted from the allowable expenditure relating to the asset (so increasing the gain arising on a subsequent disposal).

EXAMPLE 1

In July 1997 (RPI 157.5), Laura bought an oil painting for £120,000. In October 2005, the painting was damaged by fire. In February 2006, Laura received compensation from her insurance company of £30,000. Compute the chargeable gain or allowable loss arising in each of the following circumstances:

(a) Laura spent none of the insurance money on restoration and the damaged painting was valued at £170,000 in February 2006.

(b) Laura spent £30,000 on restoring the painting in November 2005 and elected that the situation should not be treated as a part disposal.

(c) Laura spent £29,000 on restoring the painting in November 2005 and elected that the situation should not be treated as a part disposal.

(d) Laura spent £20,000 on restoring the painting in November 2005 and elected that the part disposal should relate only to the retained £10,000. The restored painting was valued at £200,000 in February 2006.

Solution

(a) This is a part disposal, with A = £30,000 and B = £170,000. The computation is:

	£
Disposal proceeds	30,000
Less: Part cost:	
$\frac{£30,000}{£30,000 + £170,000}$ x £120,000	18,000
Unindexed gain	12,000
Less: Indexation allowance	
$\frac{162.6 - 157.5}{157.5}$ = 0.032 x £18,000	576
Chargeable gain (before taper relief)	11,424

The balance of allowable expenditure carried forward and used in the calculation of the gain arising on a subsequent disposal of the painting is £102,000 (£120,000 - £18,000).

(b) The entire amount received is spent on restoration so the election to avoid a part disposal is valid. The balance of allowable expenditure carried forward is:

	£
Incurred July 1997	120,000
Incurred November 2005	30,000
	150,000
Less: Received February 2006 (and not treated as a disposal)	30,000
	120,000

(c) The £1,000 retained is small in comparison with the amount received and therefore the election to avoid a part disposal is valid (so long as the £1,000 is not required for restoration purposes). The balance of allowable expenditure carried forward is:

	£
Incurred July 1997	120,000
Incurred November 2005	29,000
	149,000
Less: Received February 2006 (and not treated as a disposal)	30,000
	119,000

(d) The amount retained is not small in comparison with the amount received and so a part disposal is unavoidable. However, by virtue of Laura's election, this will relate only to the retained £10,000, not to the entire £30,000 received. The computation is:

	£	£
Disposal proceeds		10,000
Less: Part original expenditure:		
$\frac{£10,000}{£10,000 + £200,000} \times £120,000$	5,714	
Part restoration expenditure:		
$\frac{£10,000}{£10,000 + £200,000} \times £20,000$	952	6,666
Unindexed gain		3,334
Less: Indexation allowance		
$\frac{162.6 - 157.5}{157.5} = 0.032 \times £5,714$		183
Chargeable gain (before taper relief)		3,151

The balance of allowable expenditure carried forward in this case is:

	£
Incurred July 1997 (£120,000 - £5,714)	114,286
Incurred November 2005 (£20,000 - £952)	19,048
	133,334
Less: Received February 2006 (and not treated as a disposal)	20,000
	113,334

Destroyed assets

The loss or destruction of an asset is a chargeable disposal and usually results in a CGT computation in which disposal value is equal to the amount of any insurance money or other compensation received. However, if *all* of the money received is spent (within 12 months) on the purchase of a replacement asset, the taxpayer may claim that the disposal of the original asset should give rise to neither a gain nor a loss. The cost of the replacement asset is then reduced by the gain which would have been chargeable on the disposal of the original asset if this claim had not been made.

If only *part* of the money received is spent on the purchase of a replacement asset, the taxpayer may claim that the chargeable gain on the disposal of the original asset should be restricted to the amount of money retained (so long as this is less than the gain). The cost of the replacement asset is then reduced by the balance of the gain that would have been chargeable if the claim had not been made.

Taper relief

Taper relief is available only if gains are chargeable to tax. This means that the effect of making the first of the claims described above is that any taper relief which might have been available in connection with the original asset is lost. The effect of making the other claim is that taper relief is available only in relation to the restricted amount of the gain which remains chargeable to tax. In both cases, taper relief on the disposal of the replacement asset is calculated according to the qualifying holding period of that asset only. The holding period of the original asset is ignored.

EXAMPLE 2

Maurice bought an item of jewellery in November 1996 (RPI 153.9) for £125,000. In 1999 the jewellery was stolen. As a result, Maurice's insurance company paid him £141,500 in October 1999. In December 1999 he spent £150,000 on the purchase of replacement jewellery and claimed that neither a gain nor a loss should arise on the disposal of the original jewellery.

(a) Compute the chargeable gain arising in March 2006 when the replacement jewellery was sold for £180,000.

(b) How would this computation alter if the jewellery bought in December 1999 had cost only £140,000 and Maurice had made an appropriate claim?

Solution

(a) Without a claim, the gain arising on the loss of the original jewellery would be:

		£
Disposal proceeds		141,500
Less: Acquisition cost		125,000
Unindexed gain		16,500
Less: Indexation allowance		
$\frac{162.6 - 153.9}{153.9}$	= 0.057 x £125,000	7,125
Chargeable gain		9,375

The entire proceeds were spent on a replacement asset within 12 months so Maurice is entitled to make the claim. This reduces the acquisition cost of the new jewellery to £140,625 (£150,000 - £9,375). The gain arising on the subsequent sale of this jewellery is as follows:

	£
Disposal proceeds	180,000
Less: Deemed acquisition cost	140,625
Chargeable gain (before taper relief)	39,375

No indexation allowance is available as the replacement jewellery was acquired on or after 1 April 1998. This gain has a qualifying holding period of six years. The holding period of the original jewellery is ignored.

(b) £1,500 of the insurance money was retained and so £1,500 of the gain arising on the stolen jewellery is immediately chargeable. The remaining £7,875 of the gain may be deducted from the acquisition cost of the new jewellery, reducing this cost to £132,125 (£140,000 - £7,875). The chargeable gain arising on the March 2006 disposal becomes £47,875 (£180,000 - £132,125).

Replacement of business assets

Subject to certain conditions, a taxpayer may claim that the gain arising on the disposal of a business asset (the "old asset") may be "rolled-over" against the cost of acquiring a replacement business asset (the "new asset"). The main effects of a claim for roll-over relief are as follows:

(a) The disposal of the old asset is deemed to give rise to neither a gain nor a loss.

(b) The cost of the new asset is reduced by the gain which would have been chargeable on the disposal of the old asset if the claim for roll-over relief had not been made.

Full relief is available only if the disposal proceeds of the old asset are *wholly* applied in acquiring the new asset. If only *part* of the disposal proceeds are used to acquire the new asset, the effect of a claim for roll-over relief is that the chargeable gain on the disposal of the old asset is restricted to the amount of money retained (so long as this is less than the gain). The cost of the new asset is then reduced by the balance of the gain that would have been chargeable if the claim had not been made. The conditions which must be satisfied if a roll-over claim is to be accepted are:

(a) Both the old asset and the new asset must be drawn from the following list (though they need not both be the same type of asset):

    (i) land, buildings and fixed plant and machinery

    (ii) goodwill

    (iii) ships, aircraft, hovercraft, satellites, space stations and spacecraft

    (iv) milk, potato and fish quotas and certain EU agricultural quotas

    (v) Lloyd's syndicate rights.

(b) The old asset must have been used only for trade purposes throughout the period of ownership and the new asset must be used only for trade purposes.

(c) The new asset must be acquired during the period beginning one year before and ending three years after the date of disposal of the old asset.

(d) The taxpayer must claim the relief by 31 January in the sixth tax year following the *later* of the year in which the old asset is disposed of and the year in which the new asset is acquired.

Note that a similar relief is available to companies (which pay corporation tax on their chargeable gains) when a business asset is disposed of and a replacement business asset is acquired. For companies, however, the list of assets which are eligible for this relief excludes goodwill and quotas. These assets fall instead within the scope of the corporation tax intangible assets regime (see Chapter 23).

Taper relief

As mentioned earlier in this chapter, taper relief is available only if gains become chargeable to tax. Therefore one effect of making a roll-over claim is that any taper relief which might have been available on the disposal of the old asset is either lost completely or restricted according to the amount of the gain which remains chargeable after the claim has been made. Taper relief on the eventual disposal of the new asset is calculated according to the qualifying holding period of that asset only. The holding period of the old asset is ignored.

EXAMPLE 3

Janine bought a building for use in her business in May 1992 (RPI 139.3) for £75,000. In July 2005 she sold the building for £160,000 and, in the same month, bought another building for use in her business. Assuming that Janine claims roll-over relief, calculate the chargeable gain arising on the July 2005 disposal if the replacement building has a cost of:

(a) £170,000 (b) £140,000 (c) £85,000.

Solution

The gain on the disposal of the original building is computed as follows:

	£
Sale proceeds	160,000
Less: Acquisition cost	75,000
Unindexed gain	85,000
Less: Indexation allowance	
$\frac{162.6 - 139.3}{139.3}$ = 0.167 x £75,000	12,525
Chargeable gain (before taper relief)	72,475

(a) The entire sale proceeds have been spent on a replacement building. Therefore none of the gain is immediately chargeable and the entire gain may be rolled-over against the cost of the new building, reducing its allowable cost to £97,525 (£170,000 - £72,475).

(b) £20,000 of the sale proceeds have been retained. Therefore £20,000 of the gain is immediately chargeable. The remaining £52,475 may be rolled-over against the cost of the new building, reducing its allowable cost to £87,525 (£140,000 - £52,475).

(c) £75,000 of the sale proceeds have been retained. This exceeds the amount of the gain. Therefore the whole gain is immediately chargeable and no part of the gain may be rolled-over. The allowable cost of the new building is the full £85,000.

Replacement with a depreciating asset

If the new asset is a "depreciating asset" (an asset with an expected life of 60 years or less at the time of acquisition) the gain arising on the disposal of the old asset cannot be rolled-over and is *not* deducted from the cost of the new asset. Instead, the gain is temporarily deferred or "held-over" until it crystallises (becomes chargeable) on the *earliest* of the following three dates:

(a) the date on which the new asset is disposed of

(b) the date on which the new asset ceases to be used for trade purposes

(c) the 10th anniversary of the acquisition of the new asset.

Clearly, a gain which is held-over in these circumstances will become chargeable no more than ten years after the date of acquisition of the depreciating asset. However, if a suitable non-depreciating asset is acquired at any time before the end of this 10-year period, the held-over gain may be transferred to this new asset, so converting a temporarily held-over gain into a permanently rolled-over gain.

Taper relief

Taper relief in relation to a held-over gain which has become chargeable is calculated according to the qualifying holding period of the old asset on which the held-over gain arose. The period of up to thirteen years which may have passed since that asset was disposed of (up to three years until the depreciating asset was acquired and then a further ten years until crystallisation) is ignored.

EXAMPLE 4

In June 2005, Ian sells a freehold building for £100,000, realising a chargeable gain (before taper relief) of £25,000. The building was acquired in 1997 and used only for trade purposes. In the same month he acquires fixed plant and machinery costing £120,000 and elects to hold-over the gain on the building against the plant and machinery. Explain the way in which the held-over gain will be treated in each of the following situations:

(a) Ian sells the plant and machinery in July 2009.

(b) Ian sells the plant and machinery in March 2017.

Solution

(a) The replacement asset is sold before the 10th anniversary of its acquisition and so the deferred gain becomes chargeable in 2009/10.

(b) The replacement asset is still in Ian's possession ten years after its acquisition, so the held-over gain of £25,000 crystallises in June 2015 and forms part of Ian's chargeable gains in 2015/16.

In both cases, taper relief will be calculated with reference to a qualifying holding period of seven years (April 1998 to June 2005).

EXAMPLE 5

Imagine now that Ian (in the above example) buys another freehold building for business use in November 2008 and elects to transfer the held-over gain on the plant and machinery to the new freehold building. Explain the treatment of the held-over gain if the new building costs:

(a) £150,000 (b) £90,000.

Solution

(a) The entire proceeds of the sale of the original building have been invested in a new building so the whole held-over gain of £25,000 can be converted into a rolled-over gain, reducing the allowable cost of the new building to £125,000.

(b) £10,000 out of the sale proceeds of the original building have not been invested in the new building and therefore cannot be rolled-over against its cost. This £10,000 will continue to be held-over against the plant and machinery and will become chargeable no later than June 2015. However, the remaining £15,000 is converted into a rolled-over gain, reducing the allowable cost of the new building to £75,000.

Gains rolled over between 1 April 1982 and 5 April 1988

Special provisions apply to a claim for roll-over relief on the replacement of a business asset which was originally acquired before 31 March 1982 and replaced between 1 April 1982 and 5 April 1988. In these circumstances, some part of the rolled-over gain relates to the period before 31 March 1982 and it would now be unfair to bring such gains to charge when the replacement asset is sold, since gains arising before 31 March 1982 have been exempt from CGT since 6 April 1988.

So as to avoid detailed calculations of the amount of the rolled-over gain which relates to the period before 31 March 1982, the Finance Act 1988 provides that such rolled-over gains are to be reduced by a flat-rate 50%.

Gift of business assets

The gift of an asset is a chargeable disposal and this is the case whether or not the asset is used in business. However, subject to certain conditions, a claim may be made for the gain arising on a gift of business assets to be held-over until the transferee disposes of the assets concerned. If such a claim is made, the transferor's gain on the disposal is reduced to zero and the transferee's deemed acquisition cost is reduced by the amount of the gain that would have been chargeable on the transferor if the claim had not been made. The conditions which must be satisfied are as follows:

(a) Both the transferor and the transferee must elect for the gain arising on the gift to be held-over. This election must be made by 31 January in the sixth tax year following the year in which the gift is made.

(b) The gifted assets must consist of either:

  (i) assets used in a business carried on by the transferor or by the transferor's *personal trading company* (a trading company in which the transferor has at least 5% of the voting rights), or

  (ii) shares or securities of an unlisted trading company or of the transferor's personal trading company (so long as the transferee is not a company).

If the gift is of shares, rather than of individual business assets, the gain arising on the disposal is apportioned between the amount which relates to chargeable business assets owned by the company on the date of the gift and the amount which relates to other chargeable assets (e.g. investments). Only the part of the gain relating to chargeable business assets is eligible for hold-over relief.

Sale for less than market value

Gift relief is also available if an asset is sold for less than market value (typically to a connected person). But if the actual consideration received by the transferor exceeds the original cost of the asset (so that part of the unindexed gain has been realised) the amount of the gain which may be held-over is reduced by the excess of the actual consideration over the asset's cost.

Taper relief

Any taper relief to which the transferor might have been entitled is lost if a hold-over claim is made. Taper relief available to the transferee on a subsequent disposal of the gifted assets is calculated according to the qualifying holding period of the transferee only. The holding period of the transferor is completely ignored.

EXAMPLE 6

In March 2006, Jonathan gives the goodwill of his business to his daughter. Jonathan acquired the goodwill for £25,000 in May 2000 and its market value on the date of the gift is £60,000. Both Jonathan and his daughter elect that the gain arising should be held-over.

(a) Compute the gain arising on the gift and the amount which may be held-over.

(b) How would the computation differ if Jonathan's daughter had paid him £30,000 for the goodwill?

Solution

(a) The chargeable gain (before taper relief) is £35,000 (£60,000 - £25,000). The whole of this gain may be held-over, reducing Jonathan's daughter's deemed acquisition cost to £25,000 (£60,000 - £35,000).

(b) The chargeable gain is still £35,000, since this is not a bargain made at arm's length and therefore disposal value is taken to be the market value of the asset on the date of disposal. However, £5,000 of the gain (£30,000 - £25,000) has been realised in cash, so the amount of the gain which may be held-over is reduced to £30,000. The remaining £5,000 of the gain is immediately chargeable and has a qualifying holding period of five years. The daughter's deemed acquisition cost is £30,000 (£60,000 - £30,000).

EXAMPLE 7

Kathy is the managing director of Kathy Ltd (an unlisted trading company). She bought 90% of the voting share capital of the company for £70,000 in July 1985 (RPI 95.23). In August 1993 (RPI 141.3) she gave all her shares to her son and both Kathy and her son elected that the gain arising on this gift should (as far as possible) be held-over. The net assets of the company on the date of the gift (at market value) were as follows:

	£
Goodwill	100,000
Freehold building (used only for business purposes)	150,000
Listed investments	50,000
Net current assets (none of which are chargeable)	40,000
Total net assets	340,000

(a) Compute the gain arising on the gift and the amount which may be held-over.

(b) Compute the gain arising in December 2005 when Kathy's son sells the shares for £350,000.

Solution

(a) Presumably, the value of the shares on the date of the gift was 90% of £340,000 = £306,000. The gain arising on the gift was therefore as follows:

		£
Deemed disposal proceeds		306,000
Less: Acquisition cost		70,000
Unindexed gain		236,000
Less: Indexation allowance		
$\frac{141.3 - 95.23}{95.23}$	= 0.484 x £70,000	33,880
Chargeable gain		202,120

The company's chargeable assets on the date of the gift were £300,000 of which £250,000 were chargeable business assets. So £202,120 x 250,000/300,000 = £168,433 of the gain was held-over whilst the remaining £33,687 was chargeable.

(b) The gain arising in December 2005 is as follows:

		£
Sale proceeds		350,000
Less: Deemed acquisition cost (£306,000 - £168,433)		137,567
Unindexed gain		212,433
Less: Indexation allowance		
$\frac{162.6 - 141.3}{141.3}$	= 0.151 x £137,567	20,773
Chargeable gain (before taper relief)		191,660

So long as the company's non-trading activities (e.g. the making of investments) are not substantial, the company's shares will rank as a business asset for taper relief purposes and the gain will have a qualifying holding period of seven years.

Gifts between 1 April 1982 and 5 April 1988

Special provisions apply to a claim for hold-over relief on the gift of a business asset which was originally acquired before 31 March 1982 and gifted between 1 April 1982 and 5 April 1988. These special provisions are identical to those described above for roll-over relief on the replacement of business assets (i.e. the held-over gain is reduced by a flat-rate 50%).

Transfer of a business to a limited company

Subject to certain conditions, the gain arising on the transfer of a business to a limited company in return for shares in that company is held-over until the transferor disposes of the shares. If this relief applies, the gain arising on the disposal of the business is deducted from the deemed acquisition cost of the shares. The required conditions are:

(a) The business is transferred as a going concern.

(b) All of the assets of the business (other than cash) are transferred to the company.

(c) The consideration received by the transferor consists wholly or partly of shares in the company.

This relief (known as "incorporation relief") applies automatically, so there is no need for the transferor to claim that the gain should be held-over. However, the transferor may elect that incorporation relief should *not* apply. Such an election might be made if the transferor intends to dispose of the shares in the fairly near future and wishes to preserve his or her entitlement to taper relief (see below). If incorporation relief applies and the consideration for a transfer consists only partly of shares, then only part of the chargeable gain is held-over. The held-over gain is calculated as follows:

$$\frac{\text{value of the shares received}}{\text{total consideration received}} \times \text{whole gain}$$

If a transfer of a business to a limited company occurred between 1 April 1982 and 5 April 1988 and at least some of the assets transferred were acquired before 31 March 1982, the held-over gain is reduced by a flat-rate 50%.

Taper relief

Taper relief is not available in relation to the held-over gain. On a subsequent disposal of the shares, taper relief is calculated according to the qualifying holding period of the shares only.

EXAMPLE 8

In July 2005, Leroy transferred his business to a limited company in exchange for £5,000 in cash and shares valued at £60,000. The gain arising on the transfer (before taper relief) was £26,000. Leroy does not elect that incorporation relief should not apply. Calculate the amount of the gain which is immediately chargeable and the amount which is held-over.

Solution

The held-over gain is £26,000 x 60,000/65,000 = £24,000. The remaining £2,000 of the gain is immediately chargeable and is eligible for taper relief. The acquisition cost of the shares is reduced to £36,000 (£60,000 - £24,000).

Reinvestment into EIS or VCT shares

The gain arising on the disposal of *any* asset may be deferred if an amount of money equal to the gain is used to subscribe for shares which are eligible under the rules of the Enterprise Investment Scheme (see Chapter 6). Note the following points:

(a) The shares must be subscribed for during the period starting one year before and finishing three years after the disposal concerned.

(b) A gain may be deferred if an amount equal to that gain is invested in eligible shares. It is *not* necessary to invest the entire disposal proceeds.

(c) There is no requirement that income tax relief should be available in relation to the investment. It follows that the taxpayer does not have to be unconnected with the company concerned and that the amount of a deferred gain can exceed the maximum amount on which income tax relief is granted.

(d) A taxpayer claiming this relief may restrict the amount of relief claimed so as to avoid wasting the annual exemption.

(e) The deferred gain usually becomes chargeable on the disposal of the EIS shares, but further deferral is possible if further EIS shares are then subscribed for.

(f) When the deferred gain becomes chargeable, taper relief is calculated by reference to the qualifying holding period of the asset on which the deferred gain arose.

Until 6 April 2004, a similar relief was available if the amount of a gain was used to subscribe for shares in a Venture Capital Trust, so long as the VCT investment attracted income tax relief (see Chapter 6). However, deferral relief is not available for investments in VCT shares issued on or after 6 April 2004.

Serial EIS investment

If a chargeable gain arises on the disposal of EIS shares which have been the subject of income tax relief or CGT deferral relief, this gain (like any other gain) can be deferred by reinvesting it in new EIS shares. The gain on the disposal of the original EIS shares will then become chargeable when the new EIS shares are disposed of. In order to encourage investors to move from one EIS investment to another, taper relief on this type of deferred gain is calculated *as though the holding period of the original EIS shares began when they were acquired and ended when the new EIS shares were disposed of.*

The qualifying holding period of the original EIS shares can be further extended if a third holding of EIS shares is acquired (and so forth). In effect, the qualifying holding period of each successive holding of EIS shares runs from the date that those shares were acquired until the date that the final holding of EIS shares is disposed of.

Loans to traders

If a taxpayer lends money to a trader and then finds that all or part of the loan is irrecoverable, the loss incurred may be treated as a capital loss and set against the taxpayer's capital gains. This relief is subject to the following conditions:

(a) the trader who has borrowed the money must be resident in the UK

(b) the money must have been borrowed for trade purposes (but not for the trade of money-lending)

(c) the debt must be unsecured.

Subject to these conditions, the amount lost is treated as a capital loss of the year in which the taxpayer makes the claim for relief, though a claim may be backdated for up to two years if it can be shown that the debt was irrecoverable then. If relief is given and then all or part of the loan is recovered, the amount recovered is treated as a capital gain of the year in which recovery takes place.

Summary

- If the compensation received on the loss or destruction of an asset is spent on the purchase of a replacement, the taxpayer may claim that the disposal should give rise to neither a gain nor a loss. The gain which would have been chargeable is then subtracted from the cost of the replacement asset.
- The gain arising on the disposal of a business asset may be rolled-over against the cost of acquiring a replacement.
- If a business asset is replaced by a depreciating asset, the gain arising cannot be permanently rolled-over but may be temporarily held-over instead. This gain will become chargeable no later than 10 years after the replacement asset was acquired (unless the gain is transferred to a non-depreciating asset in the meantime).
- The gain arising on the gift of a business asset may be held-over until the transferee disposes of the asset.
- The gain arising on the transfer of a business to a limited company is held-over until the transferor disposes of the shares which were received in exchange for the assets of the business. The transferor may elect that this relief should not apply.
- The gain arising on the disposal of any asset may be deferred if the amount of the gain is used to subscribe for shares eligible under the rules of the EIS.

Exercises

Please note that the RPI for April 1998 is 162.6.

22.1 In March 1996 (RPI 151.5) Matthew bought a piece of rare porcelain for £10,000. The porcelain was damaged in early 2003 and in March of that year Matthew spent £3,850 on restoration work. In July 2003, Matthew's insurance company paid him £4,000 and Matthew successfully claimed that this should not be treated as a part disposal. He sold the porcelain in March 2006 for £23,500. Compute the chargeable gain (before taper relief).

22.2 In February 1988 (RPI 103.7) Maria bought a diamond necklace for £13,500. In 1993 the necklace was stolen and, as a result, an insurance payment of £19,000 was received in February 1994 (RPI 142.1). In the same month, Maria spent £19,500 on the purchase of a replacement necklace and claimed that the disposal of the original necklace should give rise to neither a gain nor a loss. Compute the chargeable gain (before taper relief) arising in January 2006 when the replacement necklace was sold for £24,000.

22.3 In September 1990 (RPI 129.3) Pamela bought a building for business use at a cost of £50,000. In September 2005 she sold the building for £174,300 and immediately bought another building, again for business use. Assuming that Pamela claims roll-over relief, calculate the chargeable gain (before taper relief) arising in September 2005 if the cost of the new building is:

(a) £171,800

(b) £62,700

(c) £176,800.

22.4 In July 2005, Phillip (a sole trader) gave his entire business to his grandson. Both Phillip and his grandson elected that the gains arising on this gift should be held-over. The chargeable gains arising (before taper relief) were as follows:

	£
Freehold buildings	23,500
Goodwill	40,000
Listed investments	10,600

State the amount of the gains which could be held-over.

22.5 In August 2005, Susannah (a sole trader) gave her business premises to her son. The premises had been bought by Susannah for £91,500 in July 1995 (RPI 149.1) and extended in May 1998 at a cost of £34,500. Their market value in August 2005 was £215,000. Both Susannah and her son elected that the gain arising should be held-over.

Compute the amount of the held-over gain and explain how the situation would differ if Susannah's son had paid her £150,000 for the premises.

***22.6** In January 1981, Norman bought a freehold building for use in his business at a cost of £120,000. The building had a market value on 31 March 1982 (RPI 79.44) of £125,000. In June 1990 (RPI 126.7) he sold the building for £275,000 and in August 1990 (RPI 128.1) he spent £270,000 on buying another building for use in his business. This building was sold in December 2005 for £330,000. Compute the gains arising on the disposal of each building (assuming that Norman claims roll-over relief).

***22.7** In May 2000, Ruth sold a freehold building which she had used exclusively for business purposes. The building was sold for £120,000, realising a chargeable gain of £42,500. In the following month, Ruth acquired fixed plant for £120,000 and elected to hold-over the gain on the freehold property against this plant and machinery. In August 2005, she acquired another freehold building for £105,000 and elected to transfer the held-over gain to this new building. Explain the treatment of the £42,500 gain.

***22.8** In October 2005, Roger sold the goodwill of his business for £100,000. He had acquired the goodwill in the form of a gift from his brother in January 1986 (RPI 96.25) when it was valued at £50,000. Roger's brother had purchased the goodwill in 1980 and the gain arising on the gift to Roger was £37,350. Both Roger and his brother elected that this gain should be held-over. Compute the gain arising in October 2005.

***22.9** In 1981, Shaun bought a 20% stake in the ordinary shares of a trading company. The shares cost £80,000 and in March 1982 (RPI 79.44) had a market value of £75,000. In January 2006 he gave all the shares to a friend. On the date of the gift, the shares had a market value of £500,000 and the company's assets were valued as follows:

	£
Freehold land and buildings	1,700,000
Goodwill	500,000
Investments	100,000
Motor cars	40,000
Plant and machinery	60,000
Net current assets	100,000

The plant and machinery consisted entirely of small movable items each costing less than £6,000 and each with a market value of less than £6,000.

Calculate Shaun's chargeable gain (before taper relief) and state the qualifying holding period for this gain, assuming that:

(a) both Shaun and his friend elected that the gain arising should (as far as possible) be held-over, and

(b) the presence of investments on the company's balance sheet does not preclude the company from being treated as a trading company for taper relief purposes.

Review questions (Set B)

B1 In March 2006, Vasco sold at auction an antique dressing-table. He received £11,960 after auctioneer's commission of 8%. He had purchased the table in January 1988 for £500. The table was not a business asset. The indexation factor from January 1988 to April 1998 is 0.574.

Columbus sold one of his factories on 30 April 2005 for £900,000. The factory had been purchased in September 1983 for £300,000. In March 2006, Columbus purchased another factory for £700,000 and claimed roll-over relief in relation to the gain arising on the factory sold in April 2005. The indexation factor from September 1983 to April 1998 is 0.889.

You are required to:

(i) Calculate Vasco's chargeable gain (before taper relief) and state the length of the qualifying holding period for taper relief purposes.

(ii) Calculate the chargeable gain (before taper relief) arising on the disposal made by Columbus in April 2005. Also calculate the base cost of the factory acquired in March 2006. *(ACCA)*

B2 Yvonne had the following transactions in the shares of Scotia plc:

			£
18 August 1995	Bought	3,000 shares	6,000
19 September 2000	Bought	2,000 shares	5,000
13 March 2006	Sold	5,000 shares	23,000
28 March 2006	Bought	1,000 shares	4,400

The indexation factor from August 1995 to April 1998 was 0.085.

Sally's capital gains tax position in 2005/06 was as follows:

	£
Capital gain on an asset qualifying for 15% taper relief	20,000
Capital gain on an asset qualifying for no taper relief	10,000
Capital losses arising in the year	6,000
Capital losses brought forward	12,000

You are required to:

(i) Calculate Yvonne's chargeable gain (before taper relief).

(ii) Calculate Sally's CGT assessment for 2005/06. *(ACCA)*

B3 Ranek sold a factory in November 2005 for £250,000 and moved his business into rented premises. The factory was purchased in April 1994 (RPI 144.2) for £100,000. Ranek purchased fixed plant in December 2004 costing £240,000 and elected to "hold-over" any gain on the sale of the building against the cost of the plant.

You are required to:

(i) Calculate the chargeable gain on the sale of the factory (before taper relief) and the effect of the "hold-over" claim on that gain. (RPI April 1998 was 162.6).

(ii) State the earliest time that the "hold-over" would cease to be effective. *(ACCA)*

B4 Consider each of the following situations:

(a) Marlene has chargeable gains for the year 2005/06 of £12,000 and capital losses for the year 2005/06 of £8,000.

(b) Moira has chargeable gains for the year 2005/06 of £12,000 and capital losses brought forward of £8,000.

(c) Marina has chargeable gains for the year 2005/06 of £3,000 and capital losses brought forward of £8,000.

(d) Melissa has chargeable gains for the year 2005/06 of £12,000, capital losses for the year 2005/06 of £8,000 and capital losses brought forward of £4,000.

You are required to:

For each situation, calculate the capital gains assessable for 2005/06 (assuming that no taper relief is available) and state the amount of any losses carried forward. *(ACCA)*

B5 In the year to 5 April 2006, Thomas More made the following disposals:

(i) A flat in a house that he had purchased on 1 December 1981 for £29,000. It had never been occupied as the main residence and had been consistently let during his period of ownership. The property had been converted into two flats in September 1984 at a cost of £18,000. The flat was sold for £71,000 on 1 December 2005 and out of this legal fees of £2,000 were paid. It was agreed that the value of the other flat was £65,000 in December 2005 and that the entire house was valued at £40,000 in March 1982.

(ii) 20,000 shares in ICI plc which cost £60,000 in December 1983 and which were sold for £150,000 in December 2005. (No shares were acquired within the next 30 days).

Assume that the Retail Prices Index has the following values:

March 1982	79.44	December 1983	86.89
September 1984	90.11	April 1985	94.78
April 1998	162.6		

Required:

(a) Calculate the capital gains tax payable on the sale of the flat and the shares in ICI plc (neither of which are business assets) assuming that Thomas is married and has taxable income of £23,000 after the personal allowance for 2005/06. There were no other chargeable disposals in the year and no capital losses brought forward from previous years. Thomas made no Gift Aid donations and paid no personal pension premiums in the year.

(b) If you were told at the start of 2005/06 that Mr More intended making the above disposals and that Mrs More had capital losses of £26,000 brought forward (and did not intend to make any disposals in 2005/06) would there be any advice that you would consider giving to Thomas? *(AAT)*

***B6** Mrs Laura Stapleton, a widow, has decided to dispose of her residence and retire to Canada, where she will live with her son, Danny.

She acquired her house on 1 June 1988 and lived there until 31 March 1989 when she left the UK in order to care for Danny and his wife who had been injured in a serious car accident in Canada. Liking it there, she extended her stay and on 1 November 1989 she took a job at a local hospital until 31 December 1990 when she returned to the UK and resumed residence in her property.

She remained living in her house until 31 December 2000, when she left it permanently in order to live in a flat. Contracts were exchanged for the sale of the house on 31 May 2005.

The house originally cost £50,000 and an extension was completed in December 1991 at a cost of £20,000. The agreed sale proceeds are £300,000 and the expenses of sale are £5,200. Throughout the periods of Mrs Stapleton's absence, the property was let at a market rent.

Assume that the Retail Prices Index has the following values:

June 1988	106.6	December 1991	135.7
April 1998	162.6		

Required:

Calculate the chargeable gain (before taper relief) arising on the disposal of Mrs Laura Stapleton's residence. *(AAT)*

***B7** You have been consulted by Mr Christopher Rodrigues on two matters relating to capital gains tax. Extracts from his letter to you are:

"On 31 January 2006, I sold my shares in Fledgeby plc, a listed company. I had acquired them as follows:

1 January 1983	1,000	shares cost £4,200
19 June 1984	700	shares cost £2,950
31 December 1986	1,200	shares cost £5,620
11 August 1988	400	shares cost £2,100

I also took up a 1 for 4 rights issue at £3.50 per share on 31 May 1987. The shares were all sold for £38,000 on 31 January 2006 and I do not intend to buy any shares in the company in the future.

Also on 31 January 2006, I sold for £100,000 a plot of land that I acquired in January 1970 for £10,000. A friend has told me that the gain might be either a capital gain or a trading gain but, as capital gains are broadly charged at income tax rates, it doesn't really matter which way it is dealt with."

Assume that the Retail Prices Index has the following values:

January 1983	82.61	June 1984	89.20
April 1985	94.78	December 1986	99.62
May 1987	101.9	August 1988	107.9
April 1998	162.6		

Required:

(a) Calculate the chargeable gain (before taper relief) arising on the sale of the shares in Fledgeby plc.

(b) Do you agree with the statement of the other taxation practitioner? Draft brief notes that will form the basis of the letter that you will write to Mr Rodrigues.

(AAT)

***B8** On 1 May 1991 (RPI 133.5), Nigel acquired a 30-year lease for £20,000. He assigned the lease on 1 November 2005 for £75,000. The RPI for April 1998 was 162.6.

Kay purchased 20 acres of land in February 1995 (RPI 146.9) for £40,000. She sold part of the land for £18,000 in March 2006 when the value of the remainder of the land was £60,000. The RPI for April 1998 was 162.6. Kay made no other capital disposals in 2005/06.

Shirley had the following dealings in the shares of Wingfield plc, a listed company:

			£	RPI
January 1981	Bought	4,000 shares	18,000	
March 1993	1 for 4 rights issue	1,000 shares	7,000	139.3
November 1995	Bought	3,000 shares	24,000	149.8
January 1998	1 for 2 bonus issue	4,000 shares	-	159.5
March 2006	Sold	7,000 shares	56,000	

On 31 March 1982 (RPI 79.44) the shares had a market value of £8 per share. This value has not been adjusted to reflect the subsequent bonus issue. No election has been made to re-base the cost of all assets held on 31 March 1982 to their value on that date. The RPI for April 1998 was 162.6. No further shares were acquired during 2006.

You are required to:

(i) Calculate Nigel's chargeable gain (before taper relief).

(ii) Calculate Kay's tapered gain, assuming no losses brought forward from previous years. The land is a business asset for taper relief purposes.

(iii) Calculate Shirley's chargeable gain (before taper relief). *(ACCA)*

***B9** Gillian purchased 10,000 ordinary shares in Downtown plc in January 1995 (RPI 146.0) for £20,000. In October 2005, Upmarket plc acquired the whole of the share capital of Downtown plc following a take-over bid. The terms of the take-over offer were:

One ordinary share in Upmarket plc, and

Two preference shares in Upmarket plc, and

£3 cash

for every five shares held in Downtown plc. The share prices of Upmarket plc immediately after the take-over were:

Ordinary shares £10 each, and

Preference shares £3 each.

The RPI for April 1998 was 162.6.

You are required to:

Calculate the chargeable gain (before taper relief) arising in 2005/06. *(ACCA)*

***B10** Joan, who is 55, has been a full-time working director of Sunnybank Pursuits Ltd since 1988 and has owned 10% of the company's ordinary shares since 1990. She retired in February 2006 and gave all of her shares in the company to her daughter, Sylvia. The capital gain on the gift was £750,000 after indexation allowance but before other reliefs. Joan and Sylvia have jointly elected to have the capital gain held-over.

The market values of the assets in the company's balance sheet at the time that the shares were gifted were:

	£
Land and buildings	4,000,000
Plant and machinery	2,000,000
Goodwill	1,000,000
Quoted shares	1,000,000

All items of plant and machinery cost more than £6,000.

The quoted shares do not preclude the company from being treated as a trading company for the purposes of taper relief.

You are required to:

Calculate Joan's assessable capital gain for 2005/06. *(ACCA)*

Part 3

CORPORATION TAX

Chapter 23

Introduction to corporation tax

Introduction

The next six chapters of this book deal with corporation tax, which was introduced in 1965 as the tax payable on the profits of companies. Prior to 1965, companies paid income tax on their profits. The purpose of this first chapter is to provide an introduction to the basic principles of corporation tax. Corporation tax legislation is to be found in the Income and Corporation Taxes Act 1988 and in the Taxation of Chargeable Gains Act 1992, as amended by subsequent Finance Acts.

Scope of corporation tax

UK resident companies are liable to corporation tax on their "chargeable profits", no matter where in the world those profits arise. Companies which are not UK resident but which trade in the UK through a permanent establishment are liable to corporation tax on the income and chargeable gains arising from that establishment (see Chapter 32).

A company's chargeable profits consist of its income plus its capital gains, less any charges on income. The schedular system which has now been abolished for income tax purposes (see Chapter 2) continues to apply to corporation tax, so (for example) a company's trading income is referred to as its Schedule D Case I income. Despite this difference in terminology, a company's income and gains are computed in a similar way to the income and gains of an individual. However, there are some important distinctions between the assessment of an individual's income and the assessment of a company's income. These distinctions are explained later in this chapter.

For corporation tax purposes, the word "company" is taken to mean any corporate body or unincorporated association, excluding partnerships, local authorities and local authority associations. As well as limited companies, the main types of organisation which are liable to corporation tax include clubs and societies, political associations, building societies and nationalised corporations.

Charities are generally exempt from corporation tax. Other exempt organisations (subject to various conditions and limits) include agricultural societies, scientific research associations, friendly societies, trade unions, approved pension schemes and community amateur sports clubs.

Accounting periods

Corporation tax is charged in respect of "accounting periods". It is very important to distinguish between an *accounting period* (i.e. a period for which corporation tax is charged) and a *period of account* (i.e. a period for which a company prepares a set of accounts). Although accounting periods and periods of account are often the same thing, this is not always the case. An accounting period *begins* when:

(a) the company starts to trade or otherwise comes within the charge to corporation tax, or

(b) when the previous accounting period ends, so long as the company remains within the charge to corporation tax.

An accounting period *ends* on the *earliest* occurrence of any of the following events:

(a) the expiration of 12 months from the beginning of the accounting period

(b) the end of a period of account

(c) the commencement of winding-up proceedings

(d) the company ceasing to be UK resident

(e) the company ceasing to be within the charge to corporation tax.

These rules have the following consequences:

(a) The length of an accounting period can never exceed 12 months.

(b) If a set of accounts covers a period of 12 months or less, the period covered by the accounts is regarded as an accounting period in its own right and a corporation tax assessment is raised for this period.

(c) If a set of accounts covers a period exceeding 12 months, the period covered by the accounts is broken down into two or more accounting periods, each giving rise to a separate corporation tax assessment. The first accounting period consists of the first 12 months of the period of account. The second accounting period consists of the next 12 months and so forth. If the period covered by the accounts is not an exact multiple of 12 months, the final accounting period will be of less than 12 months' duration.

EXAMPLE 1

Identify the accounting periods which relate to the following periods of account:

(a) A Ltd prepares accounts for the year to 31 December 2005.

(b) B Ltd prepares accounts for the six months to 31 October 2005.

(c) C Ltd prepares accounts for the sixteen months to 31 December 2005.

(d) D Ltd prepares accounts for the thirty months to 31 March 2006.

Solution

(a) The year to 31 December 2005 is an accounting period in its own right.

(b) The six months to 31 October 2005 is an accounting period in its own right.

(c) The sixteen months to 31 December 2005 is divided into two accounting periods - the 12 months to 31 August 2005 and the 4 months to 31 December 2005.

(d) The thirty months to 31 March 2006 is divided into three accounting periods. These are the 12 months to 30 September 2004, the 12 months to 30 September 2005 and the 6 months to 31 March 2006.

Chargeable profits

The main elements which are taken into account when computing a company's chargeable profits for an accounting period may be summarised as follows:

	£	£
Schedule D Case I (trading income)	x	
Less: Trading losses brought forward	x	x
Schedule D Case III (mainly income from non-trading loans)		x
Schedule D Case V (income from foreign possessions)		x
Schedule D Case VI (miscellaneous income)		x
Schedule A (income from property)		x
Chargeable gains	x	
Less: Allowable losses brought forward	x	x
		x
Less: Schedule A losses	x	
Deficits on non-trading loans	x	
Trading losses relieved under S393A(1)	x	
Charges on income	x	x
Profits chargeable to corporation tax (PCTCT)		x

Most of the factors listed above are explained in this chapter but a company's losses and deficits are considered in Chapter 26 and the tax treatment of foreign income is described in Chapter 32. Note that:

(a) In general, a company's income under each Schedule and Case is computed in accordance with income tax principles and its chargeable gains are computed in accordance with CGT principles. However, this general rule is overridden by special corporation tax provisions in some instances (see below).

(b) A company cannot be an employee and so cannot have employment income.

(c) A company is not a "person" and is not entitled to claim personal allowances.

Schedule D Case I (trading income)

A company's Schedule D Case I trading income for an accounting period consists of its trading profit for that period, adjusted for tax purposes. There are no special rules relating to commencement of trade, cessation of trade or change of accounting date. Each accounting period is a single chargeable period for capital allowances purposes. Note that:

(a) When calculating a company's trading income, there will be no need to disallow the private proportion of expenses shown in the profit and loss account or to restrict capital allowances because of the private use of assets. This is because a company does not have a private existence. Any private use *by employees* is treated simply as an allowable cost of employing staff (who may then be assessed to income tax on a benefit in kind).

(b) Accounts drawn up in accordance with International Accounting Standards are valid for UK tax purposes.

(c) A special corporation tax regime applies to a company's income and expenditure in relation to intangible fixed assets (see below).

(d) Small or medium-sized companies which incur research and development expenditure may, subject to certain conditions, claim tax relief on 150% of the amount of that expenditure. The main conditions which must be satisfied are:

    (i) The expenditure must not be of a capital nature and must be relevant to the company's trade. Qualifying expenditure includes staffing costs, consumables, payments to subcontractors and expenditure on power, fuel and water.

    (ii) The company must have incurred at least £10,000 of qualifying research and development expenditure in the accounting period (or proportionately less if the accounting period is less than 12 months in length).

    For this purpose, the definition of a "small or medium-sized company" is given by EU recommendations. Currently, companies qualify as small or medium-sized if they have less than 250 employees and *either* annual turnover not exceeding 40 million Euros *or* a balance sheet total not exceeding 27 million Euros.

    In general, tax relief is given by deducting 150% of the qualifying expenditure when computing the company's trading income.

(e) Large companies may deduct 125% of their qualifying research and development expenditure when computing trading income.

(f) Expenditure incurred *by small companies* on plant and machinery between 1 April 2004 and 31 March 2005 qualified for a first year allowance of 50%. For small unincorporated businesses the expenditure had to be incurred between 6 April 2004 and 5 April 2005 (see Chapter 10).

(g) The provisions whereby farmers may average their profits (see Chapter 9) do not apply to farming companies.

Intangible fixed assets

Since April 2002, a special corporation tax regime has applied to a company's income and expenditure in relation to intangible fixed assets (IFAs) such as patents, trade-marks, copyrights and goodwill. In summary, the system is as follows:

(a) Companies may obtain tax relief for the cost of IFAs created or acquired on or after 1 April 2002. In most cases, the amount of relief is equal to the amortisation charged in the company's accounts. If an asset is not amortised in the accounts or is amortised over a very long period, the company may elect for the asset to be subject to a fixed rate tax allowance calculated at 4% p.a.

(b) Capital allowances are no longer available to companies in respect of patent rights or know-how acquired on or after 1 April 2002. Computer software falls within the IFAs regime unless the company elects for capital allowances to apply.

(c) A loss on the disposal of an IFA which was created or acquired on or after 1 April 2002 is eligible for tax relief. Similarly, a profit on the disposal of such an asset is taxable income. But if an IFA is disposed of for more than original cost and the disposal proceeds are re-invested in newly-acquired IFAs, the amount by which disposal proceeds exceed original cost may be rolled-over against the cost of the new assets. The company is then taxed as if:

(i) the disposal proceeds of the old asset, and
(ii) the acquisition cost of the new asset (or assets)

were both reduced by the excess of disposal proceeds over original cost.

(d) Royalties payable or receivable for the use of IFAs (e.g. patent royalties) are within the scope of the IFAs regime. The tax treatment of royalties follows their accounting treatment, so that accruals and prepayments are taken into account.

(e) If royalties are paid net of basic rate income tax (see Chapter 25) the company must account to HM Revenue and Customs for the amount of tax deducted. Similarly, a company can reclaim any income tax suffered on royalties received. In both cases, the company's corporation tax computation will take into account the *gross* amount of royalties accrued in the accounting period.

(f) If IFAs are held for trade purposes, the related income and expenditure is taken into account when computing trading income. If IFAs are held for non-trade purposes, the income and expenditure is aggregated to produce an overall non-trading gain or loss. A gain is taxable under Schedule D Case VI (miscellaneous income). A loss may be relieved in a number of ways (see Chapter 26).

(g) Gains or losses on the disposal of IFAs acquired before 1 April 2002 continue to be dealt with as chargeable gains or allowable losses. However, chargeable gains roll-over relief (see Chapter 22) is no longer available in relation to the replacement of an IFA by a company. Under transitional rules, gains arising on the disposal of an "old" IFA are eligible for the rollover relief described above.

Schedule D Case III (income from non-trading loans)

The main classes of income assessed under Schedule D Case III for a company are:

(a) profits and gains arising from "non-trading loan relationships"

(b) any annuity or other annual payment which is not chargeable as property income and which does not fall within the loan relationships regime.

Income from non-trading loan relationships consists mainly of bank interest, building society interest and other interest receivable by a company. Such interest is assessed on the *accruals* basis. The loan relationships rules are explained in detail later in this chapter. Note that:

(a) Unlike individuals, companies receive all bank and building society interest gross.

(b) Interest received by a UK company from another UK company is received gross.

(c) If a company receives interest from an individual net of lower rate income tax (see Chapter 25) the company may reclaim the income tax deducted at source and is then assessed on the gross amount of interest accrued in the accounting period.

(d) The first £70 p.a. of National Savings Bank ordinary account interest received by a company is *not* exempt from corporation tax.

Schedule A (income from property)

A company's property income is assessed in much the same way as an individual's property income (see Chapter 5). However, the following important distinctions should be noted:

(a) Interest payable on a loan taken out by a company for the purpose of buying or improving let property is dealt with under the loan relationships rules and is therefore disallowed when computing property income.

(b) The loss reliefs available to a company which suffers a loss in relation to a property business are different from those available to an individual (see Chapter 26).

(c) The landlord's allowance for expenditure on loft and wall insulation in let residential property (see Chapter 5) is not available to companies which let property.

Franked investment income

Dividends received from other UK companies are paid out of profits which have already been subject to corporation tax. Therefore, to avoid double taxation, such dividends are not included in the chargeable profits of the receiving company. The term "franked investment income" (FII) is used to refer to the UK dividends received by a company, together with the attached tax credits. For example, a company which receives a UK dividend of £9,000 has FII of £10,000 (£9,000 + tax credit £1,000). FII does *not* form part of a company's chargeable profits.

Chargeable gains

A company's chargeable profits for an accounting period include any chargeable gains arising in respect of disposals made in that period. The chargeable gains of a company are computed in a similar way to those of an individual but the following important distinctions should be noted:

(a) The CGT reforms which were introduced by the Finance Act 1998 do *not* apply when computing the chargeable gains of companies. Therefore, for the purposes of corporation tax:

   (i) Indexation allowance is not frozen at April 1998.

   (ii) Taper relief does not apply.

   (iii) The matching rules used on a disposal of shares or securities are the old, pre-FA98 rules (see below).

(b) When a company makes a disposal of shares or securities, the disposal is matched against acquisitions in the following order:

   (i) first, against acquisitions made on the same day

   (ii) next, against acquisitions made in the previous nine days (on a FIFO basis)

   (iii) next, against shares taken from the S104 holding, which is the pool of shares acquired on or after 1 April 1982 and which is *not* frozen at April 1998

   (iv) next, against the 1982 holding, which is the pool of shares acquired between 6 April 1965 and 31 March 1982 inclusive

   (v) finally, against shares acquired before 6 April 1965 (on a LIFO basis).

(c) A gain arising on the disposal of all or part of a "substantial shareholding" by a trading company or a member of a trading group is exempt from corporation tax so long as certain conditions are satisfied. Similarly, any loss arising on such a disposal is not an allowable loss. The main conditions which must be satisfied are:

   (i) The company making the disposal must have held a substantial shareholding in the investee company throughout a 12-month period beginning not more than two years before the disposal takes place.

   (ii) The investee company must be a trading company or the holding company of a trading group.

   For this purpose, a company holds a substantial shareholding in another company if it holds at least 10% of that company's ordinary share capital and is entitled to at least 10% of that company's profits and assets.

(d) With the introduction of the special intangible fixed assets regime, goodwill and quotas acquired by a company are removed from the list of assets qualifying for chargeable gains rollover relief (see Chapter 22).

(e) Companies are not entitled to the annual exemption.

Charges on income

For corporation tax purposes, the main types of payment which are classed as charges on income are:

(a) qualifying donations under the Gift Aid scheme (see Chapter 4)

(b) gifts of listed shares or securities to a charity

(c) gifts of land and buildings to a charity.

Until 1 April 2002, patent royalties paid by a company were classified as a charge on income, but such royalties are now covered by the intangible fixed assets regime. Note the following points:

(a) The amount of charges deducted when computing a company's chargeable profits for an accounting period is the amount of the charges actually *paid* during the period. Accruals and prepayments are ignored.

(b) A company may obtain tax relief on its charitable donations as follows:

  (i) Gift Aid donations are relieved as a charge on income.

  (ii) Charitable donations incurred for trade purposes and not within the Gift Aid scheme are deductible when computing the company's trading income.

(c) Gift Aid donations made by a company are paid gross.

(d) The extension of the Gift Aid scheme to cover donations to community amateur sports clubs does not apply to companies.

Loan relationships

A company has a "loan relationship" if it is a debtor or creditor with regard to any debt which is a loan under general law. The main classes of debt to which the term refers are bank and building society deposits, bank overdrafts, Government securities (gilts), corporate bonds (e.g. debentures) and other corporate debt. The tax treatment of income and expenditure relating to a loan relationship depends upon whether the relationship has been entered into for trade purposes:

(a) **Trading loan relationships**. If a company has entered into a loan relationship for trade purposes, then:

  (i) Any interest payable (and any other cost relating to the debt) is treated as a trading expense.

  (ii) Any interest receivable (and other income relating to the debt) is treated as trading income. This will usually apply only if the company's trade is that of lending money.

(b) **Non-trading loan relationships**. If a company has entered into one or more loan relationships for non-trading purposes, then all of the "debits" and "credits" (costs and income) relating to such relationships are aggregated. Then:

  (i) If total credits exceed total debits, the net credits are assessable under Schedule D Case III.

  (ii) If total debits exceed total credits, the net debits may be relieved in a variety of ways (see Chapter 26).

  Interest payable on underpaid corporation tax is treated as a non-trading debit. Similarly, interest receivable on a repayment of overpaid corporation tax is treated as a non-trading credit (see Chapter 24).

It is important to appreciate that the above treatment of costs and income relating to loan relationships applies to all such costs and income, *whether of a revenue or capital nature*. This means that the profit (or loss) arising on a disposal of Government securities or corporate bonds by a company is taxable (or allowable) even though such assets would not be chargeable assets for CGT purposes if held by individuals.

Accounting methods for loan relationships

In most cases, the amount of income and expenditure brought into account for a loan relationship is calculated on the *accruals basis*. If receipts or payments are made net of income tax (at the lower rate) they must be grossed-up. Any income tax deducted from the income received in an accounting period may be reclaimed from HM Revenue and Customs and any income tax deducted from the payments made in an accounting period must be accounted for to HMRC (see Chapter 25).

An alternative accounting method which may be used is the *mark to market* basis. If this method is used, the fair value of the loan relationship must be determined at the end of each accounting period. The income or expenditure which is brought into account for an accounting period then comprises the receipts and payments of that period, together with the change in the fair value of the loan relationship between the start and end of the period.

EXAMPLE 2

A manufacturing company has the following results for the year to 31 March 2006:

	£
Trading income	883,000
Income from property	14,200
Bank interest (gross amount received)	6,200
Interest on Government securities (gross amount received)	28,000
Dividends from UK companies	18,450
Chargeable gains	123,000
Gift Aid donation	24,000

The following information is also relevant:

(a) Bank interest of £2,100 was owing to the company at the end of the year. The corresponding amount at the start of the year was zero.

(b) The Government securities were acquired on 1 July 2005. Interest of £28,000 (gross) is payable to the company on 30 June and 31 December each year.

Compute the company's chargeable profits for the year to 31 March 2006.

Solution

		£
Schedule D Case I	(trading income)	883,000
Schedule A	(property income)	14,200
Schedule D Case III	(income from non-trading loans)	50,300
Chargeable gains		123,000
		1,070,500
Less: Charges on income		24,000
Chargeable profits		1,046,500

Notes:

(i) The bank interest is income from a non-trading loan relationship and is assessed under Schedule D Case III on the accruals basis. The amount assessable for the year is £8,300 (£6,200 received + £2,100 accrued).

(ii) The interest on Government securities is income from a non-trading loan relationship and is assessed under Schedule D Case III on the accruals basis. The gross income accrued in the year of £42,000 (£28,000 + £14,000) forms part of the company's chargeable profits for corporation tax purposes.

(iii) The dividends received from UK companies (plus the attached tax credits) are franked investment income and do not form part of the company's chargeable profits for corporation tax purposes.

(iv) The Gift Aid donation of £24,000 is a charge on income.

EXAMPLE 3

A company produces the following profit and loss account for the year to 31 March 2006:

	£	£
Gross profit brought down from trading account		758,950
Add: Rental income (Note 1)	5,000	
Loan interest receivable (Note 2)	2,600	
Dividends received (Note 3)	18,750	
Bank interest receivable (Note 4)	4,789	
Patent royalties receivable (Note 5)	6,500	
Profit on sale of building (Note 6)	6,000	43,639
		802,589
Less: Operating expenses (Note 7)		568,912
Net profit for the year		233,677

Notes:

1. The property was let on 1 January 2006 at a rent of £20,000 per annum, payable annually in advance. The figure shown in the profit and loss account represents the rent for the period 1 January 2006 to 31 March 2006. No allowable expenditure has been incurred in relation to the let property.
2. Gross loan interest of £1,950 was received during the year and a further £650 was owing to the company at the end of the year. None was owed to the company at the start of the year. The profit and loss account shows the total of £2,600.
3. Dividends of £18,750 were received from other UK companies during the year.
4. Bank interest received in the year was £4,684. Of this, £1,000 was owed to the company at the start of the year. A further £1,105 was owing to the company at the end of the year but was not received until April 2006.
5. Patent royalties of £6,000 (gross) were received in the year and a further £500 was owing to the company at the end of the year. None was owed to the company at the start of the year. The profit and loss account shows the total of £6,500. The patents are held for trade purposes.
6. The chargeable gain on the sale of the building is £2,350.
7. Operating expenses include:

	£
Directors' fees	100,000
Debenture interest (gross amounts):	
Paid 1 January 2006	4,000
Accrued at 31 March 2006	2,000
Depreciation of tangible fixed assets	102,500
Customer entertaining expenses	2,400
Gift Aid donation paid in the year	750

All of the remaining operating expenses are allowable as trading expenses. The debentures were issued on 1 July 2005 for trade purposes. The company claims capital allowances for the year of £87,450.

Required:

(a) Compute the company's Schedule D Case I trading income for the year to 31 March 2006.

(b) Compute the company's chargeable profit for the year to 31 March 2006.

Solution

(a) The Schedule D Case I trading income is as follows:

		£	£
Net profit per accounts			233,677
Less: *Non-trading income*:			
	Income from property	5,000	
	Loan interest receivable	2,600	
	Dividends received	18,750	
	Bank interest receivable	4,789	
	Profit on sale of building	6,000	37,139
			196,538
Add: *Disallowed expenses*:			
	Depreciation	102,500	
	Customer entertaining	2,400	
	Gift Aid donation	750	105,650
			302,188
Less: Capital allowances			87,450
Trading income			214,738

(b) The chargeable profits for the year are:

		£
Schedule D Case I	(trading income)	214,738
Schedule A	(property income)	5,000
Schedule D Case III	(income from non-trading loans)	7,389
Chargeable gain		2,350
		229,477
Less: Charges on income		750
Chargeable profits		228,727

Notes:

(i) The computation of the company's Schedule D Case I trading income is performed in the same way as that of an individual. The starting point is the net profit shown by the accounts. Non-trading income included in this net profit is subtracted and disallowed expenses are added back. The aim is to separate out the company's trading profit from the total net profit shown in the accounts. The debenture interest is an allowable expense since the debentures were issued for trade purposes. The patent royalties receivable are trading income since the patents are held for trade purposes.

It is extremely important to classify the company's profits correctly and to arrive at a separate figure for each category of profit (e.g. trading income, rents, interest, chargeable gains etc.). This analysis is necessary because different rules of assessment apply to each category of profit and is especially vital if the company has incurred any losses (see Chapter 26).

(ii) Property income is computed on the accruals basis.

(iii) The amount of accrued loan interest forms part of the company's income from non-trading loans (assuming that the loan was not made for trade purposes). The remainder of the Schedule D Case III figure is bank interest, received gross and assessed on the accruals basis.

(iv) FII is not chargeable to corporation tax and does not form part of the chargeable profit.

(v) The chargeable gain on the sale of the building is fully chargeable to corporation tax since the company is not entitled to the annual exemption.

(vi) The Gift Aid donation is treated as a charge on income.

Long periods of account

As stated above, a period of account exceeding 12 months must be divided into two or more accounting periods, each of which will give rise to a separate corporation tax assessment. A company's profit for a long period of account is allocated between accounting periods as follows:

(a) Adjusted trading profits (before deduction of capital allowances) are usually time-apportioned. Capital allowances are then computed separately for each accounting period.

(b) Property income is also usually time-apportioned.

(c) A net credit on non-trading loan relationships is allocated between accounting periods on the accruals basis.

(d) Capital gains are allocated to the accounting period in which the disposals occur.

(e) Charges on income are allocated to the accounting period in which they are paid.

(f) Dividends received from other UK companies are allocated to the accounting period in which they are received. Although a company's FII does not form part of its chargeable profits, this allocation may be important when determining the rate of corporation tax which must be paid by the company (see Chapter 24).

In practice, the time-apportionment method which is normally used for trading profits and property income may be replaced by a more accurate method of allocation if one is available. For instance, if trading profits have been earned as a result of a small number of transactions and the profit arising on each transaction can be calculated individually, trading profits may be allocated between accounting periods according to the transactions occurring in each period.

EXAMPLE 4

A company makes up accounts for the 21 months to 30 September 2005. The company's results for this period of account are as follows (all figures are shown gross):

	£
Adjusted trading profits (before capital allowances)	630,000
Non-trade loan interest receivable:	
Received 31 October 2004	600
Received 30 April 2005	600
Accrued to 30 September 2005	500
Chargeable gains:	
Disposal on 25 May 2004	2,300
Disposal on 12 December 2004	700
Disposal on 15 February 2005	10,500
Charges on income:	
Paid 31 December 2004	4,000
Accrued to 30 September 2005	3,000

The loan interest receivable relates to a £12,000 loan made on 1 May 2004 at 10%. Show how the period of account will be divided into accounting periods and compute the company's chargeable profits for each accounting period (ignoring capital allowances).

Solution

There are two accounting periods - the year to 31 December 2004 and the 9 months to 30 September 2005. The chargeable profits for each accounting period are as follows:

	12 months to 31/12/04	*9 months to 30/9/05*
	£	£
Trading income (12:9)	360,000	270,000
Loan interest receivable	800	900
Chargeable gains	3,000	10,500
	363,800	281,400
Less: Charges on income	4,000	nil
Chargeable profits	359,800	281,400

Notes:

(i) The loan interest is allocated on the accruals basis. Interest on the loan accrues at £100 per month so the interest for the period from 1 May 2004 to 31 December 2004 (eight months) is £800 and the interest for the period from 1 January 2005 to 30 September 2005 (nine months) is £900.

(ii) The chargeable gains are allocated according to the date of disposal and the charges on income are allocated according to the date of payment. The charges accrued at 30 September 2005 are ignored for now but will be taken into account when computing the chargeable profits of the subsequent accounting period in which they are paid.

Summary

- Corporation tax is charged on the profits of UK resident companies. The term "company" includes clubs, societies and other unincorporated associations.
- Corporation tax is charged in respect of accounting periods. The length of an accounting period can never exceed 12 months. A period of account which is longer than this is divided into two or more accounting periods.
- A company's chargeable profits consist of its income and capital gains, less any charges on income.
- A company's Schedule D Case III income consists mainly of net credits on non-trading loan relationships. Income and expenditure relating to loan relationships entered into for trade purposes is taken into account when computing Schedule D Case I trading income.
- A company's Schedule A property income is assessed in a similar way to the property income of an individual. However, interest payable on a loan for the purchase or improvement of property is dealt with under the loan relationships rules. The reliefs available to a company which incurs a loss in relation to a property business are different from those available to an individual.
- Dividends received from other UK companies (plus the attached tax credits) are referred to as franked investment income and are not part of the chargeable profits of the receiving company.
- The CGT reforms which were introduced by the Finance Act 1998 do not apply to corporation tax.
- A company's charges on income consist mainly of Gift Aid donations. Charges are relieved on the payments basis.

Exercises

23.1 Identify the accounting periods relating to the following periods of account:

(a) year to 30 November 2005
(b) 1 October 2004 to 31 July 2005
(c) 1 January 2006 to 31 January 2006
(d) 33 months to 31 August 2005
(e) 1 April 2004 to 30 September 2005.

23.2 On 1 January 2006, a company receives gross debenture interest of £1,600 from another UK company and pays net debenture interest of £8,640 to individuals.

(a) Outline the corporation tax treatment of each of these items.
(b) Explain how each of these items would appear in the company's accounts.

23.3 During the year to 31 March 2006, a company receives gross interest of £1,500 on its holding of Government securities. Describe the corporation tax treatment of this item.

23.4 A company's accounts for the 17 months to 30 June 2005 include:

	£
Trading income	425,000
Debenture interest (gross amounts):	
Received 31 October 2004	2,400
Received 30 April 2005	2,400
Accrued to 30 June 2005	800
Income from property (let in 2001)	9,010
Chargeable gains:	
Disposal on 31 January 2005	28,700
Disposal on 1 February 2005	49,760
Dividend received from UK company	10,000
Gift Aid donations:	
Paid 31 July 2004	6,000
Paid 31 January 2005	6,000

The debentures were acquired (not for trade purposes) on 1 May 2004. Interest is payable half-yearly on 30 April and 31 October. Show how the company's period of account will be divided into accounting periods and compute the chargeable profits for each accounting period.

23.5 A company has the following results for the year to 31 March 2006:

	£	£
Trading profits, after capital allowances		1,561,400
Bank deposit interest (account opened 1/4/05):		
Received 30 June 2005		19,820
Received 31 December 2005		44,670
Accrued to 31 March 2006		23,980
Chargeable gain on sale of factory		531,000
Dividends received from UK companies		132,000
Deed of covenant payable annually to a charity:		
Paid 1 October 2005, for year to 30 September 2006	9,000	
Less: Prepayment	4,500	4,500

The charitable covenant began on 1 October 2005 and falls within the Gift Aid scheme. Compute the company's chargeable profits for the year.

***23.6** A company's profit and loss account for the year to 31 March 2006 is as follows:

	£	£
Gross trading profit		373,870
Receivable from other UK companies:		
Dividends		4,000
Debenture interest (Note 1)		6,000
Bank interest receivable (Note 2)		12,600
Income from property (Note 3)		4,000
Profit on sale of investments (Note 4)		22,490
		422,960
Less:		
Distribution costs (all allowable)	97,500	
Administrative expenses (all allowable)	101,150	
Directors' fees	50,000	
Interest on bank overdraft	23,780	
Debenture interest payable (Notes 5, 8)	50,000	
Patent royalties payable (Notes 6, 8)	7,500	
Depreciation of tangible fixed assets	108,300	438,230
Net loss for the year		15,270

Notes:

1. The company acquired £240,000 of 10% debentures (for non-trade purposes) on 1 January 2006. Interest is receivable half-yearly on 30 June and 31 December. No interest was received during the year to 31 March 2006.
2. Bank interest receivable includes interest of £1,450 which had accrued at 31 March 2006 but which was not received until April 2006. There was no accrued interest at 31 March 2005.
3. The property was let on 1 December 2005 at a rent of £1,000 per month payable quarterly in advance on 1 December, 1 March, 1 June and 1 September. There were no allowable expenses in the year to 31 March 2006.
4. The agreed chargeable gain on the sale of the investments was £8,450.
5. £500,000 of 10% debentures were issued (for trade purposes) on 1 April 2005. The interest is payable (net of income tax) on 1 January each year.
6. As from 1 July 2005, the company is required to pay patent royalties of £10,000 per annum, deducting basic rate income tax at source. The net amount paid in the year to 31 March 2006 was £3,900. The royalties are payable for trade purposes.
7. Capital allowances of £32,700 are claimed for the year.
8. All figures given in the profit and loss account are gross.

Compute the company's chargeable profits for the year.

Chapter 24

Computation and payment of the corporation tax liability

Introduction

Having ascertained a company's chargeable profits for an accounting period, the next step is to compute the corporation tax liability arising in that period. The purpose of this chapter is to describe the way in which the corporation tax liability is computed and to explain the system by means of which the tax is collected.

Corporation tax financial years

A corporation tax financial year (FY) runs from 1 April to the following 31 March and is identified by the year in which it *begins*. For example, FY2004 ran from 1 April 2004 to 31 March 2005 and FY2005 runs from 1 April 2005 to 31 March 2006. The income tax year (from 6 April to the following 5 April) is irrelevant when dealing with corporation tax matters.

The rates of corporation tax are fixed for each financial year, so if an accounting period coincides with an FY (the year to 31 March) or is entirely contained within an FY (e.g. the six months to 31 December) the computation of the tax liability for the period is very straightforward. The appropriate rate of corporation tax for the FY in question is applied to the chargeable profits for the accounting period, giving the corporation tax liability.

If an accounting period straddles 31 March, the chargeable profits for the period are time-apportioned between the two FYs involved and then charged to tax at the rates applicable to each FY. It may seem obvious that this apportionment will be required only if corporation tax rates have changed from one FY to the next. In practice, however, the amount of tax payable for each FY has to be calculated separately in order to ascertain the figures required for the company's tax return. It is important to note that a simple time-apportionment is always made in these circumstances. This differs from the method described in Chapter 23 for the apportionment between accounting periods of the income, gains and charges of long periods of account.

EXAMPLE 1

A company has chargeable profits of £5,000,000 for an accounting period. Explain how the corporation tax liability for this period will be calculated if:

(a) the accounting period is the 12 months to 31 March 2006

(b) the accounting period is the 9 months to 31 January 2006

(c) the accounting period is the 10 months to 31 October 2005.

Solution

(a) The 12 months to 31 March 2006 coincide with FY2005, so the chargeable profits of £5,000,000 will be charged to corporation tax at the rates applicable to FY2005.

(b) The 9 months to 31 January 2006 are entirely contained within FY2005, so the chargeable profits of £5,000,000 will be charged to corporation tax at the rates applicable to FY2005.

(c) The 10 months to 31 October 2005 are contained partly within FY2004 (3 months) and partly within FY2005 (7 months). The chargeable profits of £5,000,000 will be apportioned between FYs as follows:

FY2004	1 Jan 2005 to 31 March 2005	£5,000,000 x 3/10 = £1,500,000
FY2005	1 April 2005 to 31 Oct 2005	£5,000,000 x 7/10 = £3,500,000

The profits of £1,500,000 falling into FY2004 will be taxed at FY2004 rates whilst the profits of £3,500,000 falling into FY2005 will be taxed at FY2005 rates.

Rates of corporation tax

There are currently three main rates of corporation tax, known as the *starting rate*, the *small companies rate* and the *full rate*. For FY2005, these are 0%, 19% and 30%. The rate which applies to a company for an accounting period depends upon the amount of the company's profits for that period and is determined as follows:

(a) The starting rate applies to companies with profits not exceeding the *starting rate lower limit* (£10,000 for FY2005).

(b) The small companies rate applies to companies with profits which lie between the *starting rate lower limit* and the *small companies rate lower limit* (£300,000 for FY2005). But the tax liability is reduced by an amount known as "marginal relief" if profits do not exceed the *starting rate upper limit* (£50,000 for FY2005). The marginal relief calculation is explained later in this chapter.

(c) The full rate applies to companies with profits which exceed the *small companies rate lower limit*. But the tax liability is reduced by marginal relief if profits do not exceed the *small companies rate upper limit* (£1,500,000 for FY2005).

These apparently complex rules for determining the applicable rate of corporation tax can in fact be summarised into a fairly simple table, as follows:

Profit for the period (£)	*Applicable rate of tax*
0 - 10,000	0%
10,000 - 50,000	19% less marginal relief
50,000 - 300,000	19%
300,000 - 1,500,000	30% less marginal relief
1,500,000 -	30%

It is important to appreciate that the applicable rate of corporation tax is applied to the *whole* of a company's chargeable profits. This differs from the income tax system, in which each band of income is taxed at a different rate. Recent corporation tax rates and limits have been as follows:

	Starting rate	*Small companies rate*	*Full rate*	*Starting rate limits*		*Small companies rate limits*	
				Lower	*Upper*	*Lower*	*Upper*
				£	£	£	£
FY2001	10%	20%	30%	10,000	50,000	300,000	1,500,000
FY2002	0%	19%	30%	10,000	50,000	300,000	1,500,000
FY2003	0%	19%	30%	10,000	50,000	300,000	1,500,000
FY2004	0%	19%	30%	10,000	50,000	300,000	1,500,000

Note that:

(a) The upper and lower limits are reduced pro rata if the accounting period (or the part of the period that falls into the FY) is of less than 12 months' duration.

(b) It has been announced that the full rate of corporation tax will remain at 30% for FY2006.

(c) Special rules apply to companies which have profits not exceeding the starting rate upper limit (£50,000 for FY2005) and which pay dividends to individual shareholders. These rules are explained later in this chapter.

Profits and chargeable profits

The profits which are compared with the upper and lower limits in order to determine the applicable rate of corporation tax are *not* the company's chargeable profits. For this purpose alone, the term "profits" is defined as the company's chargeable profits plus its franked investment income. Even though FII is not charged to corporation tax, the FII received by a company *is* taken into account when determining the rate of tax which the company should pay. The process of calculating a company's corporation tax liability for an accounting period involves the following steps:

(a) The chargeable profits (or "basic profits") for the period are calculated.

(b) The "profits" figure is calculated by adding on any FII for the period.

(c) The profits figure calculated at (b) is used to determine the applicable rate of corporation tax. That rate is then applied to the company's chargeable profits.

(d) If the accounting period straddles 31 March, chargeable profits and profits should both be time-apportioned between the two FYs involved and a separate computation performed for each FY. The results of these two tax computations should then be aggregated to give the corporation tax liability for the period. However, this apportionment is not needed (other than to provide the figures required for the company's tax return) if corporation tax rates and limits have not changed from one FY to the next.

EXAMPLE 2

Four companies each prepare a set of accounts for the year to 31 March 2006. Calculate the corporation tax liability of each company, given that:

(a) A Ltd has chargeable profits of £2,000,000 and has received no UK dividends

(b) B Ltd has chargeable profits of £143,000 and UK dividends of £9,000

(c) C Ltd has chargeable profits of £282,500 and UK dividends of £1,125,000

(d) D Ltd has chargeable profits of £7,500 and UK dividends of £270. The company has paid no dividends during the year.

Solution

	(a)	(b)	(c)	(d)
	£	£	£	£
Chargeable profits	2,000,000	143,000	282,500	7,500
FII (UK dividends + tax credits)	0	10,000	1,250,000	300
Profits	2,000,000	153,000	1,532,500	7,800
Applicable rate of corporation tax	30%	19%	30%	0%
Corporation tax liability:				
£2,000,000 @ 30%	£600,000			
£143,000 @ 19%		£27,170		
£282,500 @ 30%			£84,750	
£7,500 @ 0%				£nil

Notes:

(i) Each company's accounting period coincides with FY2005. Therefore the limits and rates of tax used are those for FY2005.

(ii) All of the dividends have an attached tax credit of 1/9th (see Chapter 2).

(iii) In each case, the profits figure is used to determine the applicable rate of tax but this rate is then applied to the chargeable profits.

EXAMPLE 3

This example is set in 2002 so as to illustrate the situation in which corporation tax rates change partway through an accounting period.

E Ltd has chargeable profits of £227,040 for the 11 months to 30 November 2002 and received a UK dividend of £9,900 on 30 June 2002. Calculate the corporation tax liability for this period.

Solution

Chargeable profits are £227,040. FII is £11,000 (£9,900 + tax credit £1,100) so profits are £238,040. Three months of the accounting period fall into FY2001 and the remaining eight months fall into FY2002. Chargeable profits, profits, the lower limits and the upper limits are apportioned between the two FYs as follows:

	FY2001 (1/1/02 to 31/3/02)	*FY2002 (1/4/02 to 30/11/02)*
PCTCT	£227,040 x 3/11 = £61,920	£227,040 x 8/11 = £165,120
Profits	£238,040 x 3/11 = £64,920	£238,040 x 8/11 = £173,120
SR limits:		
Lower limit	£10,000 x 3/12 = £2,500	£10,000 x 8/12 = £6,667
Upper limit	£50,000 x 3/12 = £12,500	£50,000 x 8/12 = £33,333
SCR limits:		
Lower limit	£300,000 x 3/12 = £75,000	£300,000 x 8/12 = £200,000
Upper limit	£1,500,000 x 3/12 = £375,000	£1,500,000 x 8/12 = £1,000,000

Notes:

(i) The date on which the FII was received is irrelevant to the apportionment process.

(ii) Profits are between the SR upper limit and the SCR lower limit in both FYs.

(iii) The corporation tax liability is (20% x £61,920) + (19% x £165,120) = £43,756.80.

(iv) From the size of the company's profits for the 11 months, it was fairly obvious that the small companies rate would apply in both financial years. Realising this would have saved the effort of apportioning the lower and upper limits between the two FYs.

Marginal relief

As explained earlier, a company's corporation tax liability is reduced by an amount known as "marginal relief" (or "taper relief") if either:

(a) profits fall between the starting rate lower and upper limits, in which case the tax liability is calculated at the small companies rate less marginal relief, or

(b) profits fall between the small companies rate lower and upper limits, in which case the tax liability is calculated at the full rate less marginal relief.

In each case, marginal relief is calculated according to the following formula:

$$\text{fraction} \times (M - P) \times \frac{I}{P}$$

where: M = the relevant upper limit
P = profits
I = chargeable profits.

Since FY2002, the marginal relief fraction has been 19/400 if profits lie between the starting rate lower and upper limits and 11/400 if profits lie between the small companies rate lower and upper limits.

EXAMPLE 4

(a) F Ltd makes up accounts annually to 31 March. In the year to 31 March 2006, the company has chargeable profits of £30,000 and neither pays nor receives any dividends. Compute the corporation tax liability for the year.

(b) G Ltd has chargeable profits of £975,000 for the year to 31 March 2006 and FII of £50,000. Compute the corporation tax liability for the year.

(c) H Ltd has chargeable profits of £240,000 and FII of £10,000 for the eight months to 31 January 2006. Compute the corporation tax liability for the period.

Solution

(a) The company's profits are £30,000, a figure which lies between the starting rate lower limit and the starting rate upper limit for FY2005. Therefore the chargeable profits (also £30,000) are taxed at the small companies rate and marginal relief is available. The computation is as follows:

	£
Corporation tax on £30,000 @ 19%	5,700.00
Less: Marginal relief:	
$\frac{19}{400} \times (£50{,}000 - £30{,}000) \times \frac{£30{,}000}{£30{,}000}$	950.00
Corporation tax liability	4,750.00

(b) The company's profits are £1,025,000 (£975,000 + £50,000), which lie between the small companies rate lower and upper limits for FY2005. The chargeable profits (£975,000) are taxed at the full rate and marginal relief is available. The computation is as follows:

	£
Corporation tax on £975,000 @ 30%	292,500.00
Less: Marginal relief:	
$\frac{11}{400} \times (£1{,}500{,}000 - £1{,}025{,}000) \times \frac{£975{,}000}{£1{,}025{,}000}$	12,425.30
Corporation tax liability	280,074.70

(c) The accounting period falls wholly within FY2005. The scaled-down small companies rate lower and upper limits for an eight-month period are £200,000 (8/12 x £300,000) and £1,000,000 (8/12 x £1,500,000) respectively. Profits of £250,000 (£240,000 + £10,000) lie between these limits. Therefore chargeable profits are taxed at the full rate and marginal relief is available. The computation is as follows:

	£
Corporation tax on £240,000 @ 30%	72,000.00
<u>Less</u>: Marginal relief:	
$\frac{11}{400}$ x (£1,000,000 - £250,000) x $\frac{£240,000}{£250,000}$	19,800.00
Corporation tax liability	52,200.00

Marginal rate

The above example shows that the marginal relief formula seems to be achieving its object. This is to set a corporation tax rate (in FY2005) of somewhere between 0% and 19% for companies whose profits lie between the starting rate lower and upper limits and somewhere between 19% and 30% for companies whose profits lie between the small companies rate lower and upper limits. In the first part of the example, tax of £4,750 on chargeable profits of £30,000 gives a tax rate of 15.83%. In the second part, tax of £280,074.70 on chargeable profits of £975,000 gives a tax rate of 28.73%.

However, if a company's profits lie between the starting rate lower and upper limits, each extra £1 of chargeable profits gives rise to an extra 23.75p in corporation tax. For instance, if the first company in the above example had a further £4 of chargeable profits, its tax liability would increase by 95p (the calculation is left to the reader). So a *marginal rate* of 23.75% applies in these circumstances, higher than the small companies rate of 19%. Similarly, a company with profits which lie between the small companies rate lower and upper limits is subject to a marginal rate of 32.75%, which is higher than the full rate of 30%.

Marginal rates are particularly significant when a company is trying to determine the most tax-efficient way of relieving a loss (see Chapters 26 and 28).

Non-corporate distribution rate

As from 1 April 2004, companies which pay dividends to individuals (rather than to other companies) must pay at least a minimum amount of corporation tax on the profits which are used to pay those dividends. This minimum amount is calculated at the "non-corporate distribution rate" which is currently set at 19%. The effect of this rule is that a company which would normally pay tax at 0% or at 19% less marginal relief must pay additional tax if any part of its profits are distributed to individual shareholders. The method of calculation is illustrated below. Note that:

(a) Transitional rules apply to accounting periods which straddle 1 April 2004.

(b) If dividends paid to individual shareholders in an accounting period exceed the company's chargeable profits for that period, the excess is carried forward and treated as a dividend paid in the following accounting period.

EXAMPLE 5

In the year to 31 March 2006, a company has profits chargeable to corporation tax of £7,500 and no FII. Compute the company's corporation tax liability if dividends paid during the year to individual shareholders are:

(a) £nil (b) £5,000 (c) £7,500.

Solution

The "underlying rate" for the accounting period (i.e. the rate that would be charged if there were no dividends to individual shareholders) is 0%. But the company must pay at least the NCD rate (19%) on profits which are distributed to individual shareholders. Therefore the corporation tax liability in each case is as follows:

(a) £7,500 @ 0% = £7,500.

(b) £5,000 @ 19% + £2,500 @ 0% = £950.

(c) £7,500 @ 19% = £1,425.

EXAMPLE 6

In the year to 31 March 2006, a company with no FII pays dividends of £15,000 to other companies and pays dividends of £10,000 to individuals. Compute the corporation tax liability if chargeable profits for the accounting period are:

(a) £30,000 (b) £75,000 (c) £20,000.

Solution

(a) If there were no dividends to individual shareholders, the corporation tax liability would be £30,000 @ 19%, less marginal relief of 19/400 x (£50,000 - £30,000) = £4,750, giving an underlying rate of 15.83%.

The dividends to corporate shareholders are irrelevant but £10,000 of the profits were distributed to individuals and must be taxed at the NCD rate. The remaining £20,000 is taxed at the underlying rate.

Therefore the tax liability is £10,000 @ 19% + £20,000 @ 15.83% = £5,066.67.

(b) Since profits fall between £50,000 and £300,000, the underlying rate is 19%. The NCD rate can be ignored since it does not exceed the underlying rate. Therefore the tax liability is £75,000 @ 19% = £14,250.

(c) If there were no dividends to individual shareholders, the corporation tax liability would be £20,000 @ 19%, less marginal relief of 19/400 x (£50,000 - £20,000) = £2,375, giving an underlying rate of 11.875%.

Dividends paid exceed chargeable profits and the proportion of dividends paid to individuals is 10/25ths. Therefore profits of 10/25 x £20,000 = £8,000 are deemed to have been paid to individual shareholders and are taxed at the NCD rate.

The corporation tax liability is £8,000 @ 19% + £12,000 @ 11.875% = £2,945.

The remaining £2,000 of dividends paid to individual shareholders is carried forward and treated as a dividend paid in the following accounting period.

Corporate Venturing Scheme

One way in which a company might reduce its corporation tax liability is by making an investment under the Corporate Venturing Scheme. Under the terms of this scheme, a company (the "investing company") which subscribes for new ordinary shares in a small unlisted trading company (the "issuing company") may qualify for a number of tax reliefs. These are:

(a) relief against corporation tax ("investment relief") equal to 20% of the amount invested, so long as the shares are held for at least three years

(b) deferral of the tax due on any gain made on a subsequent disposal of the shares, so long as the amount of the gain is reinvested in another shareholding which qualifies under the scheme

(c) relief against income for any capital loss which arises on a disposal of the shares.

For these tax reliefs to be available, the issuing company must satisfy certain criteria. These are similar to those which apply for the purposes of the Enterprise Investment Scheme (see Chapter 6). Additionally, at least 20% of the issuing company's ordinary shares must be held by individuals and the investing company's stake in the issuing company must not exceed 30%.

Due date of payment

A company's corporation tax liability for an accounting period is generally payable by means of a single payment which is due nine months and one day after the end of the period. However, certain large companies are required to pay their corporation tax by instalments.

EXAMPLE 7

(a) A company's period of account is the year to 31 July 2005. When is the corporation tax liability for this period due for payment?

(b) A company's period of account is the 18 months to 31 December 2005. When is the corporation tax liability for this period due for payment?

Assume in both cases that the company is not required to pay by instalments.

Solution

(a) The year to 31 July 2005 is a single accounting period. Tax is payable on 1 May 2006.

(b) This period of account breaks down into two accounting periods. The corporation tax for the year to 30 June 2005 is due on 1 April 2006. The corporation tax for the six months to 31 December 2005 is due on 1 October 2006.

Payment by instalments

As mentioned above, large companies are generally required to pay their corporation tax by instalments. The main features of the instalments system are as follows:

(a) A "large company" for this purpose is defined as one which pays corporation tax at the full rate, without deduction of marginal relief. However, a large company is *not* required to pay tax by instalments for an accounting period if:

   (i) it has chargeable profits of £10 million or less for the accounting period and was not a large company in the 12 months preceding that period, or

   (ii) it has a tax liability of less than £10,000 for the period but pays tax at the full rate, either because it has substantial amounts of dividend income or because it has a number of associated companies (see Chapter 28).

(b) Instalment payments are based on the company's own estimate of its corporation tax liability for the accounting period. When the tax liability for the year is finalised, the company is charged interest on any underpaid instalments and is paid interest on any overpaid instalments.

(c) For a 12-month accounting period there are four equal instalments. The first instalment falls due six months and 14 days from the start of the accounting period. The remaining three instalments then fall due at quarterly intervals. For instance, if the accounting period is the year to 31 December 2005, instalments fall due on 14 July 2005, 14 October 2005, 14 January 2006 and 14 April 2006.

If an accounting period is of less than 12 months' duration, the final instalment is always due three months and 14 days after the end of the period. Earlier instalments are due on the usual quarterly dates but only to the extent that those dates fall before the date of the final instalment. For instance, if an accounting period consists of the eight months to 30 September 2005, corporation tax is due in three equal instalments on 14 August 2005, 14 November 2005 and 14 January 2006.

In order to calculate the amount of each instalment, it is first necessary to multiply the corporation tax liability by 3/n, where n is the number of months in the accounting period. Each instalment is then equal to this figure, except that the final instalment may be lower than this in order to bring the total of the instalments to the correct amount.

EXAMPLE 8

A large company has a corporation tax liability of £720,000 for an accounting period. State the dates on which instalments are payable and compute the amount of each instalment if the accounting period is:

(a) the year to 31 March 2006

(b) the five months to 31 May 2005.

Solution

(a) Instalments are due on 14 October 2005, 14 January 2006, 14 April 2006 and 14 July 2006. Each instalment is equal to £720,000 x 3/12 = £180,000.

(b) Instalments are due on 14 July 2005 and 14 September 2005. The first instalment is equal to £720,000 x 3/5 = £432,000. The second and final instalment is £288,000, bringing the total to £720,000.

Self Assessment

The system of Self Assessment for companies is similar in many ways to the equivalent system for individuals (see Chapter 1). The main features of Corporation Tax Self Assessment (CTSA) are as follows:

(a) On the issue of a notice by HM Revenue and Customs, a company must file a corporation tax return (form CT600) for the period specified in the notice, with supporting accounts and computations. The return is made up of a basic form together with relevant supplementary pages and must normally be filed with HMRC by the *latest* of the following dates:

   (i) 12 months after the end of the period specified in the notice

   (ii) 12 months after the end of the period of account in which the last day of the specified period falls (but periods of account which last for more than 18 months are treated for this purpose as ending after 18 months)

   (iii) 3 months after issue of the notice.

   Most companies prepare their accounts to the same date each year and notices are usually issued within a few weeks of the end of each period of account, so that the required filing date is normally 12 months after the end of the period of account. There is nothing to prevent a company from submitting an early return.

(b) The CT600 return includes a formal self-assessment of the company's tax liability for the accounting period covered by the return. Unlike individuals, a company is *not* able to ask HMRC to calculate the tax liability.

(c) A company which is chargeable to corporation tax for an accounting period but has not received a notice requiring submission of a return must notify HMRC of its chargeability to tax within 12 months of the end of the period. Companies must also notify HMRC of their chargeability to tax within three months of the start of their first accounting period.

(d) HMRC has the right to repair a company's self-assessment (to correct any obvious errors or omissions) within nine months of the date on which the company files the return. Similarly, the company has the right to amend its return and self-assessment within 12 months of the required filing date for that return. A company which detects an error in its tax return after these 12 months have expired may make an "error or mistake" claim to recover any overpaid tax within six years of the end of the relevant accounting period.

(e) In general, if HMRC wishes to open an enquiry into a company's tax return, then this must be done by the first anniversary of the required filing date for that return. However, if a return is late or if a company amends its return, this deadline is extended to the quarter date (31 January, 30 April, 31 July or 31 October) which follows the first anniversary of the date that the return or the amendment was submitted.

(f) Unless HMRC opens an enquiry into a company's tax return, the company's tax position for the accounting period may usually be regarded as finalised 12 months after the required filing date for that return. However, HMRC may raise a "discovery assessment" after these 12 months have elapsed if it is discovered that insufficient tax has been assessed. In general, no such assessment can be made later than six years after the end of the accounting period to which it relates, but this period is extended to 21 years in the case of fraud or negligence on the part of the company or a person acting for the company.

(g) If a company fails to file a return by the required date, HMRC may make a determination of the amount of tax due. A determination can be displaced only if the company delivers the required return. There is no right of appeal against a determination.

(h) A company is required to keep and preserve adequate records to substantiate the information entered on its tax return. These records must be retained for at least six years after the end of the accounting period concerned.

(i) Appeals are heard by the General or Special Commissioners (see Chapter 1) and may then progress to the courts.

Interest and penalties

Interest on underpaid corporation tax runs from the date on which the tax should have been paid until the date on which it is actually paid. The rate at which the interest is calculated rises and falls in line with base rates. Interest on overpaid corporation tax is calculated at a lower rate than interest on underpaid tax and runs from the "material date" until the date of the repayment. The material date is the date on which the tax was originally paid or (if later) the date on which it was due to be paid. Note that:

(a) Apparently it is HMRC practice to use a denominator of 366 when calculating interest on underpaid tax and a denominator of 365 when calculating interest on overpaid tax, whether or not a leap year is involved.

(b) Interest receivable on a repayment of overpaid corporation tax is taxable as a credit arising from a non-trading loan relationship. Similarly, interest payable on underpaid corporation tax is deductible as a non-trading debit.

(c) If a company makes instalment payments on the assumption that it is a large company and this assumption later proves to be false, interest on any repaid instalments runs from the date on which a truly large company would have paid those instalments (or from the actual date of payment, if later).

(d) The interest rates applicable to underpaid and overpaid instalments are lower than the normal rates during the period from the due date of the first instalment to the date which falls nine months and one day after the end of the accounting period.

EXAMPLE 9

(a) Hay Ltd calculates its corporation tax liability for the year to 30 September 2005 as £250,000 and pays this amount on the due date. The correct liability for the year eventually turns out to be £274,000 and the company pays a further £24,000 on 12 September 2006. Calculate the interest payable by Hay Ltd (assuming an interest rate of 7.5% per annum).

(b) Bee Ltd also calculates its corporation tax liability for the year to 30 September 2005 as £250,000 and also pays this amount on the due date. The correct liability for the year eventually turns out to be only £193,000. The necessary repayment is made on 18 December 2006. Calculate the interest payable to Bee Ltd (assuming an interest rate of 4% per annum).

Neither company is a large company for the purposes of payment by instalments.

Solution

(a) The due date is 1 July 2006 (9 months and 1 day after 30 September 2005). Most of the corporation tax was paid on this date but the final £24,000 was paid on 12 September 2006, 73 days late. The interest payable by the company is:

$$£24{,}000 \times 7.5\% \times \frac{73}{366} = £359.02.$$

(b) The overpaid tax of £57,000 was paid on the due date of 1 July 2006 and repaid on 18 December 2006, 170 days later. The interest payable to the company is:

$$£57{,}000 \times 4\% \times \frac{170}{365} = £1{,}061.92.$$

Penalties

Penalties are charged if a company does not file its tax return, together with supporting accounts and computations, by the required date. These penalties are as follows:

(a) If the return is up to three months late, a fixed penalty is charged of £100. This is increased to £500 for a third consecutive late return.

(b) If the return is over three months late, a fixed penalty is charged of £200. This is increased to £1,000 for a third consecutive late return.

(c) In addition to the above penalties, a further tax-geared penalty is charged if the return is submitted more than six months late. In these circumstances the penalty is expressed as a percentage of the amount of tax outstanding at the end of the six months, as follows:

  (i) If the return is made between six and 12 months late, the penalty is 10% of the tax outstanding six months after the return was due.

  (ii) If the return is made more than 12 months late, the penalty rises to 20% of the tax outstanding six months after the return was due.

Penalties may also arise in the following circumstances:

(a) If a company which has neither filed a return nor been issued with a notice fails to notify HM Revenue and Customs of its chargeability to corporation tax within 12 months of the end of the accounting period, a penalty may be charged of up to 100% of the tax which remains unpaid 12 months after the end of the period.

(b) If a company fraudulently or negligently submits an incorrect return (or fails to rectify an error which it has detected in a return) a penalty may be charged of up to 100% of the tax lost.

(c) A company which fails to keep and preserve adequate records is liable to a penalty of up to £3,000.

EXAMPLE 10

A company makes up accounts to 31 July. It calculates its corporation tax liability for the year to 31 July 2004 at £180,000 and pays this sum on 1 May 2005. Despite being issued with a notice by HM Revenue and Customs in August 2004, the company fails to submit its return for the year to 31 July 2004 until 31 March 2006. The corporation tax liability for the year was finally assessed at £206,000. Calculate the penalties that would be charged.

Solution

The return was made eight months late and tax of £26,000 was still outstanding six months after the return was due. Assuming that the company is not a persistent offender, a fixed penalty of £200 would be charged, together with a tax-geared penalty of £2,600 (10% of £26,000). Interest would also be charged on the unpaid tax.

Summary

- A corporation tax financial year runs from 1 April to the following 31 March.
- There are currently three rates of corporation tax. These are the starting rate, the small companies rate and the full rate. The rate which applies to a company for a given accounting period depends upon the company's profits (including FII) for that period.
- Marginal relief eases the transition from the starting rate to the small companies rate and from the small companies rate to the full rate.
- A company must pay at least the non-corporate distribution rate on profits which are distributed to individual shareholders.
- A company which subscribes for new ordinary shares in a small unlisted trading company under the terms of the Corporate Venturing Scheme may qualify for a reduction in its corporation tax liability.

- The due date of payment for corporation tax is normally nine months and one day after the end of the accounting period. Large companies are required to pay their tax by instalments. Interest is charged on underpaid tax and is paid on refunds of overpaid tax.
- The system of Self Assessment for companies is similar in many ways to Self Assessment for individuals.
- Companies are usually required to file a CT600 return within 12 months of the end of each period of account. Late submission results in a penalty fine and there are penalties for various other infringements of the Self Assessment regulations.

Exercises

24.1 A company has chargeable profits of £30,000 for the year to 30 June 2005. Show how these profits will be apportioned between corporation tax financial years.

24.2 Four companies each have an accounting year ending on 31 March 2006. Compute the corporation tax liability of each company, given the following information:

(a) Company A has chargeable profits of £267,000 and UK dividends of £18,450.

(b) Company B has chargeable profits of £1,450,000 and UK dividends of £49,500.

(c) Company C has chargeable profits of £10,000,000 and no UK dividends.

(d) Company D has chargeable profits of £1,000 and no UK dividends. The company also pays no dividends during the year.

24.3 A company has chargeable profits of £536,000 for the year to 31 March 2006 and UK dividends of £36,900 received in June 2005. Compute the corporation tax liability.

24.4 Compute the corporation tax liability of each of the following companies:

(a) For the year to 28 February 2006, Company X has chargeable profits of £875,983 and FII of £32,800.

(b) For the six months to 31 December 2005, Company Y has chargeable profits of £12,500 and no FII. The company pays no dividends during the period.

(c) For the year to 31 March 2006, Company Z has chargeable profits of £28,000 and no FII. During the year, the company pays dividends to individual shareholders amounting to £8,000.

24.5 A company calculates its corporation tax liability for the year to 31 August 2004 as £120,000 and pays this amount on 1 June 2005. The company's CT600 return is submitted during August 2005 and the tax liability for the year is finalised at £124,650. The balance of £4,650 is paid on 3 October 2005. The company is not a large company for the purposes of payment by instalments. Calculate the interest payable (assuming an interest rate of 7.5% per annum).

***24.6** A company has the following results for the year to 31 March 2006:

	£
Adjusted trading profit, after deduction of capital allowances	360,282
Bank deposit interest (a/c opened 1 July 2005):	
Received 31 December 2005	9,957
Accrued to 31 March 2006	3,000
UK dividend received in January 2006	24,300
Chargeable gains	295,327
Charges payable (gross amounts):	
Paid 30 November 2005	24,600
Accrued to 31 March 2006	8,200

Compute the company's corporation tax liability for the year.

***24.7** A company has the following results for the 14 months to 31 December 2005:

	£
Adjusted trading profit, before deduction of capital allowances	1,413,508
Capital allowances claimed:	
Year to 31 October 2005	222,650
2 months to 31 December 2005	37,210
Capital gains:	
Disposal 12 May 2005	16,575
Disposal 6 November 2005	21,692
Building society interest:	
Received 31 December 2004	3,500
Received 31 December 2005	4,300
UK dividend received on 25 September 2005	3,150

Accrued building society interest was £3,000 on 31 October 2004, £4,000 on 31 October 2005 and £nil on 31 December 2005.

Compute the company's total corporation tax liability for the 14-month period.

Chapter 25

Income tax and advance corporation tax

Introduction

Companies are liable to corporation tax, not income tax. Therefore, companies which suffer income tax by deduction at source from any of their income are entitled to a repayment of the income tax suffered. Similarly, companies which deduct income tax at source from any of their payments must account for this income tax to HM Revenue and Customs. The first purpose of this chapter is to explain how the necessary repayments and payments of income tax are made.

Until 6 April 1999, companies were required to pay Advance Corporation Tax (ACT) when paying dividends or making other qualifying distributions. Subject to certain conditions, the ACT paid for an accounting period was generally treated as an advance payment of the corporation tax liability for that period, so reducing the amount of tax payable on the normal due date. ACT has been abolished with effect from 6 April 1999 but some aspects of the ACT system will linger on for many years to come. The second purpose of this chapter is to provide a brief description of the way in which the ACT system operated before abolition and then to explain the situation which applies as from 6 April 1999.

Income received net of income tax

As explained in Chapter 23, certain types of income received by a company are received net of income tax. A company receiving such income is able to reclaim the income tax deducted at source but the grossed-up amount of the income is then liable to corporation tax. The main sources of taxed income are as follows:

Type of income		*Rate of income tax deducted at source*
Patent royalties }	*unless received from*	basic rate (22%)
Loan interest }	*other UK companies*	lower rate (20%)
Gilt interest (if net interest opted for)		lower rate (20%)

Patent royalties, loan interest and interest on gilts are generally assessed to corporation tax on the accruals basis (see Chapter 23). But the income tax which may be reclaimed for an accounting period is the amount of income tax suffered on the income actually *received* in that period. Note that:

(a) Patent royalties and loan interest received from another UK company are received gross. Patent royalties and loan interest received from an individual are subject to deduction of income tax at source.

(b) As stated in Chapter 23, companies (unlike individuals) receive their bank deposit interest and building society interest gross.

(c) The holders of gilt-edged securities may now choose whether to receive their interest gross or net (see Chapter 2). Most companies opt to receive such interest gross.

Payments made net of income tax

Certain types of payment made by a company are made net of income tax. A company making such a payment must account to HM Revenue and Customs for the income tax deducted at source but the grossed-up amount of the payment is then granted relief in the company's corporation tax computation. The main types of payment made net of income tax are:

Type of income		*Rate of income tax deducted at source*
Patent royalties }	*unless paid to other*	basic rate (22%)
Loan interest }	*UK companies*	lower rate (20%)

Patent royalties and loan interest are generally relieved on the accruals basis in the paying company's corporation tax computation (see Chapter 23). But the income tax which must be accounted for to HMRC for an accounting period is the income tax deducted from the amounts actually *paid* in that period. Note that:

(a) As stated above, patent royalties and loan interest are paid gross if paid to another UK company. Patent royalties and loan interest paid to an individual are subject to deduction of income tax at source.

(b) Companies are not required to deduct income tax from royalties and interest paid to certain tax-exempt bodies such as charities and local authorities.

(c) Royalties and interest paid by a UK company to an EU company are paid gross if the two companies are "associated". For this purpose, two companies are associated if one holds at least 25% of the other's share capital or if a third company holds at least 25% of the share capital of each of them.

The quarterly accounting system

Companies are required to make periodic (usually quarterly) returns to HM Revenue and Customs of the income tax deducted from payments and the income tax suffered on taxed income. A return, on form CT61, is required for:

(a) each of the four quarters ending on 31 March, 30 June, 30 September and 31 December which fall completely into an accounting period, and

(b) each part of an accounting period which does not comprise a complete quarter.

A company with an annual accounting date which coincides with one of the above four dates will make four returns each year but companies with any other accounting date will need to submit a fifth return each year. Each return must be submitted (and any tax due must be paid) within 14 days of the end of the period to which the return relates. Nil returns are not required.

EXAMPLE 1

(a) A company prepares accounts to 30 June each year. Identify the income tax return periods for the year to 30 June 2005.

(b) A company prepares accounts to 31 January each year. Identify the income tax return periods for the year to 31 January 2006.

Solution

(a) The company's accounting date coincides with one of the four standard dates, so there will be four return periods each year. The return periods for the year to 30 June 2005 are 1 July 2004 to 30 September 2004, 1 October 2004 to 31 December 2004, 1 January 2005 to 31 March 2005 and 1 April 2005 to 30 June 2005.

(b) The company's accounting date does not coincide with one of the four standard dates, so there will be five return periods each year. The return periods for the year to 31 January 2006 are 1 February 2005 to 31 March 2005, 1 April 2005 to 30 June 2005, 1 July 2005 to 30 September 2005, 1 October 2005 to 31 December 2005 and 1 January 2006 to 31 January 2006.

The quarterly procedure

The procedure adopted for each return period is as follows:

(a) The income tax suffered on taxed income received during the return period is subtracted from the income tax deducted from payments made during the return period. The result of this calculation is the excess of income tax deducted over income tax suffered (or vice versa).

(b) The cumulative excess of income tax deducted over income tax suffered (or vice versa) for the accounting period to date is then calculated.

(c) If there is a cumulative excess of income tax deducted over income tax suffered, this excess is compared with the total of the income tax payments made to HMRC in previous return periods during the same accounting period (if any) and the difference is payable by the company or repayable to the company.

(d) If there is a cumulative excess of income tax suffered over income tax deducted, then no income tax payment is required for the current return period and any payments made to HMRC in previous return periods during the same accounting period may be reclaimed. However, the excess itself is *not* repayable to the company but is carried forward to the next return period.

EXAMPLE 2

A company has the following payments made net of income tax and income received net of income tax for the year to 31 March 2006 (amounts are stated net):

		Payments	*Income*
		£	£
1 May 2005	Debenture interest paid	4,000	
5 July 2005	Patent royalties paid	780	
1 September 2005	Loan interest received		6,000
1 November 2005	Debenture interest paid	4,000	
12 January 2006	Patent royalties paid	9,360	
31 March 2006	Loan interest received		1,600

Compute the amounts of income tax payable or repayable in each return period.

Solution

Return period	*Tax deducted*	*Tax suffered*	*Tax deducted less tax suffered*	*Cumulative*	*Income tax payable (repayable)*
	£	£	£	£	£
1/4/05 - 30/6/05	1,000		1,000	1,000	1,000
1/7/05 - 30/9/05	220	1,500	(1,280)	(280)	(1,000)
1/10/05 - 31/12/05	1,000		1,000	720	720
1/1/06 - 31/3/06	2,640	400	2,240	2,960	2,240
	4,860	1,900	2,960		2,960

Notes:

(i) The net payments and the net income in each return period are grossed up at the appropriate rate to give the amounts of income tax deducted and suffered, as shown in the first two columns of the table. For each return period, the excess of tax deducted over tax suffered is shown in the third column. If tax suffered exceeds tax deducted, the figure is shown in parentheses. The cumulative total of tax deducted less tax suffered is shown in the fourth column.

(ii) At the end of the first return period, tax deducted exceeds tax suffered by £1,000, so £1,000 is due for payment on 14 July 2005.

(iii) At the end of the second return period, there is a cumulative excess of tax suffered over tax deducted of £280. The company now has no income tax liability for the accounting period to date and may reclaim the £1,000 paid in the previous return period. The excess tax suffered of £280 is *not* repayable to the company but the cumulative nature of the system ensures that this excess will automatically be taken into account in future return periods.

(iv) At the end of the third return period, there is a cumulative excess of tax deducted over tax suffered of £720. Since the tax paid in previous return periods is £nil (£1,000 paid less £1,000 reclaimed), income tax of £720 is due for payment on 14 January 2006.

(v) At the end of the fourth return period, there is a cumulative excess of tax deducted over tax suffered of £2,960. Since the tax paid in previous return periods is £720, income tax of £2,240 is due for payment on 14 April 2006.

Tax suffered in excess of tax deducted

At the end of an accounting period, one of two possible situations will apply:

(a) The income tax deducted from payments made in the accounting period exceeds the income tax suffered on income received during that period. In this case, the excess will have been paid over to HMRC by virtue of the system described above and no further action is required.

(b) The income tax suffered on income received during the accounting period exceeds the income tax deducted from payments made in that period. In this case the quarterly system will not have provided the necessary income tax repayment.

EXAMPLE 3

A company has the following net payments and net income for the year to 31 March 2006 (amounts are stated net):

		Payments	*Income*
		£	£
1 April 2005	Debenture interest paid	8,000	
1 July 2005	Loan interest received		9,600
1 October 2005	Debenture interest paid	8,000	
1 January 2006	Loan interest received		9,600

Compute the amounts of income tax payable or repayable in each return period.

Solution

Return period	*Tax deducted*	*Tax suffered*	*Tax deducted less tax suffered*	*Cumulative*	*Income tax payable (repayable)*
	£	£	£	£	£
1/4/05 - 30/6/05	2,000		2,000	2,000	2,000
1/7/05 - 30/9/05		2,400	(2,400)	(400)	(2,000)
1/10/05 - 31/12/05	2,000		2,000	1,600	1,600
1/1/06 - 31/3/06		2,400	(2,400)	(800)	(1,600)
	4,000	4,800	(800)		0

Note:

The income tax suffered exceeds the income tax deducted by £800 but the operation of the quarterly accounting system has not resulted in repayment of this income tax.

Set-off against corporation tax liability

If the amount of income tax suffered during an accounting period exceeds the amount of income tax deducted from payments, the required repayment of income tax is made by means of a reduction in the company's corporation tax liability for the accounting period in which the surplus arises. If this liability is less than the required repayment, the balance is repaid in cash.

EXAMPLE 4

In the year to 31 March 2006, a company receives net loan interest of £40,000 and makes no payments net of income tax. Calculate the required income tax repayment and show how this repayment will be made if the company's corporation tax liability for the year is:

(a) £100,000

(b) £7,000.

The company is not a large company for the purposes of payment by instalments.

Solution

(a) The required repayment is £40,000 x 20/80 = £10,000. This will be offset against the company's corporation tax liability payable on 1 January 2007, reducing this liability from £100,000 to £90,000.

(b) If the company's corporation tax liability for the year is only £7,000, this liability will be reduced to £nil and the remaining £3,000 will be repaid to the company in cash.

ACT before 6 April 1999

A company which made a "qualifying distribution" before 6 April 1999 was required to make a payment of Advance Corporation Tax (ACT) to the Inland Revenue (as it then was). By far the most common example of a qualifying distribution was the payment of a dividend.

The ACT payable in relation to a dividend was calculated as a fraction of the amount of the dividend. The *ACT fraction* was linked to the lower rate of income tax and was most recently set at 20/80. In other words, the amount of ACT payable was equal to one-quarter of the amount of the dividend. The amount of a dividend plus the related ACT was known as a "franked payment". Note that:

(a) The franked payment was equal to the dividend paid multiplied by 100/80.

(b) The ACT attributable to a dividend could be expressed as 20% of the franked payment. Thus the *rate of ACT* was 20%.

EXAMPLE 5

On 3 April 1999, a company with an issued share capital of ten million £1 ordinary shares paid a dividend of 40p per share.

(a) Compute the amount of ACT payable in relation to this dividend.

(b) Compute the amount of the franked payment.

Solution

(a) The amount of the dividend was £4,000,000. The ACT fraction was 20/80. Therefore the ACT payable in relation to the dividend was £4,000,000 x 20/80 = £1,000,000.

(b) The franked payment was £5,000,000 (i.e. the dividend plus the attributable ACT). The ACT payable could be expressed as 20% of £5,000,000 = £1,000,000.

Franked investment income

As explained in Chapter 23, the term "franked investment income" (FII) refers to the UK dividends received by a company, together with the attached tax credits. These tax credits cannot be paid to the company but, before 6 April 1999, they *could* be used to reduce the amount of ACT payable by the company. In essence, the FII for an accounting period was set against the franked payments made in that period and ACT was then payable only on the excess. Note the following points:

(a) The tax credit attached to a dividend received before 6 April 1999 was *not* equal to one-ninth of the amount of the dividend (as is now the case) but was instead equal to *one-quarter* of the amount of the dividend.

(b) If there was an excess of FII over franked payments for an accounting period then the company had "surplus FII". There was no ACT liability in such an accounting period. Surplus FII was carried forward to the next accounting period and treated as if it were FII received on the first day of that period.

EXAMPLE 6

In the year to 31 March 1999, a company paid dividends totalling £6,000 and received UK dividends totalling £5,300. Compute the amount of ACT payable for the year.

Solution

(i) Dividends paid were £6,000, so franked payments were £7,500 (£6,000 x 100/80).

(ii) Dividends received were £5,300, so FII was £6,625 (£5,300 + £1,325).

(iii) The excess of franked payments over FII was £875. Therefore the amount of ACT payable for the year was £175 (20% x £875).

EXAMPLE 7

In the year to 31 March 1998, a company paid dividends of £5,000 and received dividends (all from UK companies) of £9,000. In the year to 31 March 1999, the company paid dividends of £4,800 and received none. Compute the amounts of ACT payable for each year.

Solution

In the year to 31 March 1998, franked payments were £6,250 (£5,000 x 100/80) and FII was £11,250 (£9,000 + £2,250). Therefore there was surplus FII of £5,000. There was no ACT liability for the year and surplus FII of £5,000 was carried forward to the following year.

In the year to 31 March 1999, the surplus FII brought forward was treated as if received on the first day of the year. Therefore FII for the year was £5,000. Franked payments were £6,000 (£4,800 x 100/80). The excess of franked payments over FII was £1,000, so ACT of £200 (20% x £1,000) was payable for the year.

Set-off of ACT

In general, the ACT paid for an accounting period ending before 6 April 1999 was treated as a payment on account of the company's tax liability for the period. However, there was an upper limit on the amount of ACT which could be set against the company's corporation tax liability. The *maximum ACT set-off* was equal to the amount of ACT which would be attributable to a franked payment equal in size to the company's entire chargeable profits. If the amount of ACT paid by a company in relation to an accounting period exceeded the maximum set-off allowed, the company had "surplus ACT" equal to the excess.

EXAMPLE 8

A company had chargeable profits of £100,000 for the year to 31 March 1999 and paid a dividend of £28,000 on 1 January 1999. No other dividends were paid or received during the year.

(a) Calculate the ACT payable for the year and the amount of any surplus ACT.

(b) Repeat the calculation, now assuming that the amount of the dividend was £88,000 rather than £28,000.

Solution

(a) ACT payable for the year was £7,000 (£28,000 x 20/80). This is within the maximum ACT set-off of £20,000 (20% of £100,000) so there was no surplus ACT. The whole of the £7,000 could be set against the corporation tax liability for the year.

(b) ACT payable for the year was £22,000 (£88,000 x 20/80), exceeding the maximum ACT set-off. Only £20,000 of the £22,000 could be set against the corporation tax liability for the year and there was surplus ACT of £2,000.

Relief of surplus ACT

Prior to 6 April 1999, surplus ACT could be carried forward and relieved against the company's corporation tax liability for the next accounting period. To the extent that it could not be relieved in that accounting period it could be carried forward again, without time limit, until it could eventually be relieved.

It is important to note that the total amount of ACT relieved in any accounting period (including surplus ACT brought forward) could not exceed the maximum ACT set-off for that accounting period, calculated as described above.

Surplus ACT on a change of ownership

A company which incurred losses (or made fairly low profits) over a number of years prior to 6 April 1999 and yet managed to maintain dividend payments during those years may have accumulated a substantial amount of surplus ACT. Such a company could be a desirable acquisition, since a new owner could use the company to operate a profitable business and then set the pre-acquisition surplus ACT against the tax payable on the post-acquisition profits, so avoiding liability to corporation tax.

Before 6 April 1999, this manoeuvre was prevented from succeeding by anti-avoidance legislation. If there was a change in the ownership of a company and certain conditions were satisfied, surplus ACT arising before the change in ownership could not be set against a corporation tax liability arising after the change.

Abolition of ACT

As was stated at the beginning of this chapter, ACT has been abolished with effect from 6 April 1999. The main consequences of this abolition are as follows:

(a) No ACT is payable on a dividend (or other qualifying distribution) which is paid after 5 April 1999 and therefore no ACT liability can arise in connection with accounting periods which begin after that date.

(b) If a company has unrelieved surplus ACT at 6 April 1999, the extent to which the surplus may be relieved against future corporation tax liabilities is determined by the "shadow ACT" regulations (see below).

Shadow ACT

The legislation which allows surplus ACT to be carried forward has been repealed with effect from 6 April 1999. However, unrelieved surplus ACT existing on that date is dealt with by the "shadow ACT" system, which substantially preserves previous rights with regard to the carry-forward of surplus ACT. The main features of this system are as follows:

(a) The previous limit on the set-off of ACT is retained, so that a company may use ACT of up to 20% of chargeable profits to satisfy its corporation tax liability for an accounting period.

(b) The capacity for relieving ACT in an accounting period must first be filled by "shadow ACT", which is calculated in the way that real ACT would have been calculated on the dividends paid in the period if ACT had not been abolished but had continued at the rate of 20%. However, *shadow ACT does not result in any reduction in the corporation tax liability* for the period. All that it does is to reduce the scope for set-off of surplus ACT brought forward.

(c) When calculating the shadow ACT arising in an accounting period, the FII for that period must be multiplied by nine-eighths before being used in the computation. This is because the rate of tax credits on dividends was reduced from one-quarter to one-ninth as from 6 April 1999. For example, a UK dividend of £720 received before 6 April 1999 was equivalent to FII of £900. The same dividend received on or after that date is equivalent to FII of only £800. Therefore it is necessary to multiply the post-6 April 1999 FII by nine-eighths to convert the FII figure to a pre-6 April 1999 equivalent (£800 × 9/8 = £900).

(d) If there is still capacity for relieving ACT in an accounting period after shadow ACT has been deducted, this capacity may be used to relieve surplus ACT brought forward from before 6 April 1999. Subtracting surplus ACT results in an actual reduction in the corporation tax liability for the period.

(e) If the amount of shadow ACT for an accounting period exceeds the maximum ACT set-off for that period, then the company has "surplus shadow ACT". The consequences of this are as follows:

   (i) There is no scope for relieving real surplus ACT in such a period.

   (ii) The surplus shadow ACT is first carried back to any accounting periods beginning in the previous six years (but not before 6 April 1999) in which shadow ACT has not filled the capacity available for relieving it. The carry-back is to more recent years in priority to earlier years.

   (iii) Carried-back surplus shadow ACT displaces any real surplus ACT relieved in periods beginning in the 24 months before the end of the period in which the surplus shadow ACT arose. Any real surplus ACT which is displaced by surplus shadow ACT in this way is payable to HMRC.

   (iv) Any remaining surplus shadow ACT is carried forward and regarded as shadow ACT of the next accounting period.

(f) The process continues (for as many accounting periods as required) until all of the surplus ACT brought forward from before 6 April 1999 is relieved. However, companies may opt out of the shadow ACT system if they wish (so avoiding all of the computations involved) and simply write off their surplus ACT instead.

(g) The shadow ACT regulations contain certain anti-avoidance provisions. These are very similar to the surplus ACT anti-avoidance legislation which was repealed as from 6 April 1999 (see above).

EXAMPLE 9

A company has unrelieved surplus ACT of £70,000 brought forward from before 6 April 1999. In the year to 31 March 2006, the company has chargeable profits of £200,000, pays dividends of £80,000 and receives UK dividends of £36,000. Calculate the amount of surplus ACT which will be relieved in the year.

Solution

The maximum ACT set-off for the year is £40,000 (20% x £200,000). If ACT had not been abolished on 6 April 1999, franked payments for the year would have been £100,000 (£80,000 x 100/80). The company has FII of £40,000 (£36,000 + £4,000) so the amount of FII taken into account in ACT calculations is £45,000 (£40,000 x 9/8).

The excess of franked payments over uplifted FII is £55,000 so there is shadow ACT of £11,000 (20% x £55,000). This reduces the scope for relieving surplus ACT brought forward to £29,000 (£40,000 - £11,000). Therefore the company's corporation tax liability for the year is reduced by £29,000 and the remaining £41,000 of surplus ACT is carried forward.

Summary

- Companies receive certain types of income net of income tax at either the basic rate or the lower rate, depending upon the type of income.
- Companies make certain types of payment net of income tax at either the basic rate or the lower rate, depending upon the type of payment.
- Companies must submit quarterly returns of the income tax suffered on taxed income and deducted from relevant payments. From the information given in these returns, the amount of income tax payable/repayable for each return period can be calculated.
- If the income tax suffered in an accounting period exceeds the income tax deducted from payments made in that period, the excess is deducted from the company's corporation tax liability.
- Until 6 April 1999 (when ACT was abolished) ACT was payable when a company made a qualifying distribution. The most common example of a qualifying distribution was the payment of a dividend.
- The amount of a dividend paid, plus its associated ACT, was known as a franked payment. The ACT liability for an accounting period was based upon the excess of franked payments over franked investment income for the period.
- Surplus FII could be carried forward to subsequent accounting periods and used to reduce the company's ACT liability in those accounting periods.
- The maximum ACT set-off for an accounting period was the ACT which would be attributable to a franked payment equal to the entire chargeable profits for that accounting period.
- Unrelieved surplus ACT on 6 April 1999 is dealt with by the shadow ACT system.

Exercises

25.1 Classify each of the following as paid/received by companies net of income tax or paid/received by companies gross:

(a) debenture interest paid to an individual

(b) debenture interest received from another UK company

(c) patent royalties received from an individual

(d) Gift Aid donations

(e) interest received from a UK bank.

Also specify the rate at which income tax (if any) is deducted or suffered in each case.

25.2 A company has the following payments made net of income tax and income received net of income tax for the year to 31 March 2006 (amounts are stated net):

		Payments	*Income*
		£	£
1 May 2005	Debenture interest paid	16,000	
30 June 2005	Patent royalties received		7,800
1 November 2005	Debenture interest paid	16,000	
1 January 2006	Loan interest received		5,200

Compute the amounts of income tax payable or repayable in each return period.

25.3 A company has chargeable profits of £240,000 for the year to 31 March 2006. No dividends were paid or received during the year. Payments made net of income tax and income received net of income tax during the year (net amounts) were as follows:

		Payments	*Income*
		£	£
30 June 2005	Loan interest received		28,000
17 August 2005	Debenture interest paid	36,000	
1 January 2006	Loan interest received		28,000

Compute the corporation tax payable on 1 January 2007.

25.4 (a) Outline the main features of the ACT system as it operated until 6 April 1999.

(b) Outline the main features of the shadow ACT system as it now operates.

***25.5** A company's profit and loss account for the year to 31 March 2006 is as follows:

		£	£
Sales			254,628
Less:	Cost of sales		112,876
Gross profit			141,752
Add:	Profit on sale of tangible fixed asset	542	
	Income from investments	15,000	15,542
			157,294
Less:	Distribution costs	32,189	
	Administrative expenses	42,974	
	Interest payable	22,876	98,039
Net profit			59,255

Notes:

(i) The sale of the fixed asset gave rise to a chargeable gain of £212.

(ii) Income from investments consists of:

	£
UK dividends received	9,000
Loan interest received (gross amount)	4,000
Loan interest accrued (gross amount)	2,000
	15,000

(iii) Administrative expenses include:

	£
Directors' fees	20,000
Depreciation of tangible fixed assets	5,764
Audit fee	1,000

(iv) Interest payable consists of:

	£
Debenture interest paid (gross amount)	2,000
Debenture interest accrued (gross amount)	1,000
Bank overdraft interest	19,876
	22,876

(v) The loan on which the company receives interest (with income tax deducted at source) was not made for trade purposes. The debentures on which the company pays interest (deducting income tax at source) were issued for trade purposes.

(vi) Capital allowances of £5,318 are claimed for the year.

Calculate the corporation tax payable on 1 January 2007.

***25.6** On 1 October 2004, a company had surplus ACT brought forward of £2,000. The company's chargeable profits for the year to 30 September 2005 were £32,000. In that year, the company paid dividends and received dividends (all from UK companies) as follows:

	Paid	*Received*
	£	£
31 July 2005		9,000
30 September 2005	30,000	

Calculate the amount of ACT set against the company's corporation tax liability for the year and state the amount of any surplus ACT carried forward at the end of the year.

Chapter 26

Corporation tax losses

Introduction

The loss reliefs which are available to a company incurring a trading loss are similar to those available to individuals (see Chapter 11) and generally involve either carrying the loss forward against future trading profits or setting the loss against the company's total profits for a specified period. The main purpose of this chapter is to describe these loss reliefs and to explain the factors which might influence a company when choosing between them. The tax treatment of a company's non-trading losses is also considered in this chapter.

Relief for trading losses

A company's trading losses may be relieved in any of the following ways:

(a) Under Section 393(1) of ICTA 1988, trading losses may be carried forward and relieved against future trading profits.

(b) Under Section 393A(1)(a) of ICTA 1988, trading losses may be relieved against the total profits of the accounting period in which the loss arises.

(c) Under Section 393A(1)(b) of ICTA 1988, trading losses may be relieved against the total profits of the 12 months prior to the accounting period in which the loss arises.

Each of these loss reliefs is described below. The loss reliefs are usually referred to by their section numbers in the Income and Corporation Taxes Act 1988 and this practice is followed for the remainder of this chapter.

Section 393(1) relief

Unless a company claims any other form of loss relief, trading losses are carried forward under S393(1) and relieved against the company's future trading profits. It is important to note the following points:

(a) Relief under S393(1) is given only against future *trading* profits, not against any other form of profits.

(b) Furthermore, relief is given only against future trading profits arising from *the same trade* as that in which the loss was incurred. If a company ceases one trade and commences another, the losses of the old trade cannot be carried forward and relieved against the future profits of the new trade. Similarly, if a company carries on two trades simultaneously, a loss incurred in one of the trades cannot be carried forward and relieved against the future profits of the other trade.

(c) Relief must be given against the *first available* trading profits of future accounting periods.

(d) There are restrictions on the carry-forward of trading losses when there is a change in the ownership of a company (see later in this chapter).

EXAMPLE 1

In the year to 31 March 2004, a company incurred a trading loss of £140,000 which was carried forward under S393(1). The company's results for the next two years were:

	y/e 31 March 2005	*y/e 31 March 2006*
	£	£
Trading profits	110,000	1,850,000
Bank interest receivable	50,000	60,000
Chargeable gains	125,000	572,000
Franked investment income	nil	nil

Compute the company's chargeable profits for the years to 31 March 2005 and 2006.

Solution

	y/e 31 March 2005	*y/e 31 March 2006*
	£	£
Schedule D Case I	110,000	1,850,000
Less: S393(1) relief	110,000	30,000
	0	1,820,000
Schedule D Case III	50,000	60,000
Chargeable gains	125,000	572,000
Chargeable profits	175,000	2,452,000

Notes:

(i) In the year to 31 March 2005, the trading losses brought forward are relieved to the fullest possible extent against the trading profits of the year. The trading losses of £30,000 which remain unrelieved cannot be offset against the bank interest or chargeable gains but must instead be carried forward and relieved against the trading profits of the following year.

(ii) In the year to 31 March 2005 the company pays corporation tax at only 19% (the small companies rate for FY2004). But in the year to 31 March 2006 it pays corporation tax at 30% (the full rate for FY2005). If the company could defer the whole £140,000 of S393(1) relief until the year to 31 March 2006 it would make a tax saving. But S393(1) relief must be given at the first available opportunity and so the company cannot prevent relief being given to the fullest possible extent in the year to 31 March 2005.

Unrelieved charges on income

Charges on income fall into two categories:

(a) *Trade charges* are charges incurred for trade purposes. Patent royalties used to be the main example of trade charges paid by a company, but these are now dealt with by the intangible fixed assets regime (see Chapter 23) and are no longer treated as charges. In consequence, trade charges are now rarely encountered in corporation tax computations.

Furthermore, it seems likely that the few remaining items that could be treated as trade charges when paid by a company will shortly be reclassified as management expenses. This will leave only non-trade charges.

(b) *Non-trade charges* are those charges which are not incurred for trade purposes (e.g. Gift Aid donations).

If a company's total profits are insufficient to cover the charges paid during an accounting period (perhaps because the company has incurred a trading loss) some or all of the charges will be unrelieved. Unrelieved charges are dealt with as follows:

(a) Under Section 393(9) of ICTA 1988, unrelieved *trade* charges (if any) are carried forward in the same way as trading losses and set against future trading profits. But non-trade charges cannot be carried forward in this way and will remain permanently unrelieved to the extent that they cannot be relieved in the accounting period in which they are incurred.

(b) In an accounting period in which charges exceed total profits, non-trade charges are relieved in priority to trade charges (if any) so that non-trade charges are given the greatest possible chance of relief.

EXAMPLE 2

A company has the following results for the three years to 31 March 2006:

	y/e 31/3/04	*y/e 31/3/05*	*y/e 31/3/06*
	£	£	£
Trading profits/(losses)	(78,900)	36,300	64,900
Bank interest receivable	21,500	-	-
Gift Aid donations	1,000	1,000	1,000

Assuming that the trading loss of £78,900 is to be carried forward under S393(1), calculate the company's chargeable profits for each of the three years.

Solution

	y/e 31/3/04	*y/e 31/3/05*	*y/e 31/3/06*
	£	£	£
Schedule D Case I	-	36,300	64,900
Less: S393(1) relief	-	36,300	42,600
	-	0	22,300
Schedule D Case III	21,500	-	-
Less: Non-trade charges	1,000	-	1,000
Chargeable profits	20,500	0	21,300
Trading losses c/f	78,900	42,600	-
Non-trade charges unrelieved	-	1,000	-

Notes:

(i) In the year to 31 March 2004, the £1,000 of non-trade charges are relieved against the bank interest receivable. The £78,900 of trading losses are carried forward.

(ii) In the year to 31 March 2005, the trading profit of £36,300 is used to relieve part of the losses brought forward, leaving £42,600 to carry forward. The non-trade charges for the year are completely unrelieved.

(iii) In the year to 31 March 2006, the losses brought forward are fully relieved. The remaining profits of £22,300 are then reduced by the non-trade charges, leaving chargeable profits of £21,300 for the year.

Section 393A(1) relief

As indicated earlier in this chapter, Section 393A(1) relief is available in two parts:

(a) Under S393A(1)(a), a company may claim that a trading loss incurred during an accounting period should be relieved against the total profits of that accounting period. For this purpose, the term "total profits" means the income and gains of the company, *before* deducting any charges on income.

(b) Under S393A(1)(b), the company may further claim that any part of the trading loss which remains unrelieved after a claim has been made under S393A(1)(a) should be relieved against the total profits of accounting periods falling wholly or partly within the 12 months prior to the loss-making period. Note the following points:

   (i) For S393A(1)(b) purposes, "total profits" means the income and gains of the company *after* deducting trade charges but *before* deducting non-trade charges. Since trade charges are now rarely encountered and seem likely to disappear totally in the near future, the effect of this rule is that total profits for the purposes of S393A(1)(b) are generally computed in the same way as for S393A(1)(a). In both cases, total profits consist of the company's income and gains *before* deducting charges.

   (ii) If more than one accounting period falls wholly or partly into the 12 months preceding a loss-making period, S393A(1)(b) relief is given in later accounting periods in priority to earlier accounting periods.

   (iii) If an accounting period falls only partly into the 12 months preceding a loss-making period, the profits of that accounting period are time-apportioned and S393A(1)(b) relief is available against only the profits which fall into the specified 12 months.

S393A(1) relief is voluntary in its operation and a company wishing to relieve a trading loss in this way must make the appropriate claim within two years of the end of the accounting period in which the trading loss arises. A claim may be made under S393A(1)(a) without a further S393A(1)(b) claim but a claim under S393A(1)(b) cannot be made without a prior S393A(1)(a) claim.

A company may not specify how much of its trading loss should be relieved under S393A(1). The effect of a claim is to relieve trading losses to the fullest possible extent in each affected accounting period. Any part of the trading loss which remains unrelieved after a S393A(1) claim has been made is automatically carried forward under S393(1). If no claim at all is made under S393A(1) then the entire trading loss is carried forward under S393(1).

EXAMPLE 3

A company has the following results for the year to 31 December 2005:

	£
Trading loss	(92,500)
Building society interest receivable	14,000
Chargeable gains	103,000
Non-trade charges	28,700

Assuming that a claim is made for the trading loss to be relieved under S393A(1)(a), compute the company's chargeable profits for the year.

Solution

	£
Schedule D Case I	-
Schedule D Case III	14,000
Chargeable gains	103,000
	117,000
Less: S393A(1)(a) relief	92,500
	24,500
Less: Non-trade charges	24,500
Chargeable profits	0

Note:

Only £24,500 of the non-trade charges can be relieved. The remaining £4,200 is lost.

EXAMPLE 4

A company has the following results for the three years to 31 March 2006:

	y/e 31/3/04	*y/e 31/3/05*	*y/e 31/3/06*
	£	£	£
Trading profits/(losses)	112,500	110,700	(136,500)
Income from property	3,300	8,400	8,800
Non-trade charges	2,000	2,000	2,000

Assuming that a claim is made under both S393A(1)(a) and S393A(1)(b) in relation to the trading loss incurred in the year to 31 March 2006, calculate the company's chargeable profits for each of the three years.

Solution

	y/e 31/3/04	*y/e 31/3/05*	*y/e 31/3/06*
	£	£	£
Schedule D Case I	112,500	110,700	-
Schedule A	3,300	8,400	8,800
	115,800	119,100	8,800
Less: S393A(1)(a) relief	-	-	8,800
	115,800	119,100	0
Less: S393A(1)(b) relief	-	119,100	-
	115,800	0	0
Less: Non-trade charges	2,000	-	-
Chargeable profits	113,800	0	0
Trading loss c/f	-	-	8,600
Non-trade charges unrelieved	-	2,000	2,000

Notes:

(i) In the year to 31 March 2006, the claim under S393A(1)(a) must be for the maximum possible amount of £8,800. This leaves nothing against which to relieve the non-trade charges and therefore they are lost.

(ii) The remaining £127,700 of the trading loss is eligible for S393A(1)(b) relief in the year to 31 March 2005. The claim must be for the maximum possible amount of £119,100. This leaves nothing against which to relieve the non-trade charges, which are lost.

(iii) The loss may not be carried back any further. The computation for the year to 31 March 2004 is therefore completely unaffected by loss reliefs.

(iv) A total of £127,900 (£8,800 + £119,100) of the trading loss has been relieved under S393A(1)(a) and S393A(1)(b). The remaining £8,600 is carried forward under S393(1).

EXAMPLE 5

A company has the following results for the three accounting periods to 31 March 2006:

	y/e 30/6/04	*9 months to 31/3/05*	*y/e 31/3/06*
	£	£	£
Trading profits/(losses)	13,400	69,900	(122,800)
Chargeable gains	1,200	3,500	38,600

Assuming that a claim is made under both S393A(1)(a) and S393A(1)(b) in relation to the trading loss incurred in the year to 31 March 2006, calculate the company's chargeable profits for each of the three accounting periods.

Solution

		y/e 30/6/04	*9 months to 31/3/05*	*y/e 31/3/06*
		£	£	£
Schedule D Case I		13,400	69,900	-
Chargeable gains		1,200	3,500	38,600
		14,600	73,400	38,600
Less: S393A(1)(a) relief		-	-	38,600
		14,600	73,400	0
Less: S393A(1)(b) relief	(1)		73,400	
	(2)	3,650		
Chargeable profits		10,950	0	0
Trading losses c/f		-	-	7,150

Notes:

(i) £38,600 of the trading losses incurred in the year to 31 March 2006 are relieved under S393A(1)(a). This leaves losses of £84,200 which are eligible for S393A(1)(b) relief in the previous 12 months.

(ii) The 9-month accounting period to 31 March 2005 is entirely contained within the specified 12 months and so losses of £73,400 are relieved under S393A(1)(b). Losses relieved so far now total £112,000, leaving £10,800 still to be relieved.

(iii) Only 3 months of the year to 30 June 2004 fall into the specified 12-month period (i.e. 1 April 2004 to 30 June 2004). The maximum S393A(1)(b) relief available is therefore £3,650 (£14,600 x 3/12). The remaining £7,150 of the trading loss is carried forward under S393(1).

Further points relating to S393A(1) relief

(a) A trading loss can be carried back under S393A(1)(b) only to accounting periods in which the loss-making trade was being carried on.

(b) If more than one loss is eligible for relief against the profits of a given accounting period, earlier losses are relieved before later losses.

(c) Trading losses incurred by a company in the 12 months before the loss-making trade ceases, together with unrelieved trade charges of those 12 months (if any), may be carried back and set against the profits of *the preceding three years*.

(d) Relief under S393A(1) is available only if the loss-making trade is being carried on on a commercial basis with a view to profit.

(e) In the case of *farming companies*, a loss is usually not eligible for relief under S393A(1) if losses have also been incurred for the previous five years.

(f) There are restrictions on the carry-back of trading losses under S393A(1)(b) when there is a change in the ownership of a company (see below).

Anti-avoidance legislation

Specific anti-avoidance legislation exists to prevent the following manoeuvre, which would otherwise be very tax-efficient:

(a) Acquire a company with substantial amounts of unrelieved trading losses.

(b) Revive the loss-making trade.

(c) Use S393(1) relief to set the company's pre-acquisition trading losses against its post-acquisition trading profits, so avoiding liability to corporation tax.

The legislation referred to above provides that if there is a change in the ownership of a company and certain conditions are satisfied, trading losses arising before the change cannot be set against trading profits arising after the change. Nor can trading losses arising after the change be set (by virtue of S393A) against profits arising before the change. The required conditions are that:

(a) a change in ownership has occurred at a time when the company's business has become negligible and then (at any time after the change) there has been a revival of the company's business, or

(b) a change in ownership and a major change in the nature or conduct of the company's business have both occurred within the same three-year period.

For this purpose, a change in ownership is deemed to occur if over half of the company's ordinary share capital is acquired either by one person or by a group of people, each acquiring at least a 5% shareholding.

Losses and surplus ACT

If a trading loss is set against the profits of an accounting period under S393A(1)(a) or S393A(1)(b), the chargeable profits of that period are reduced. This also reduces the maximum ACT set-off allowed in that period (see Chapter 25) and so reduces the scope for relieving surplus ACT brought forward from before 6 April 1999. The expected beneficial effects of the S393A(1) claim might therefore be diminished or even eliminated and it is evident that the potential ACT consequences of making S393A(1) claims should be considered before such claims are made.

Repayments of corporation tax

If a claim under S393A(1)(b) results in a repayment of corporation tax for an earlier accounting period, this repayment will attract interest. The interest is calculated in the usual way (see Chapter 24) unless the accounting period for which repayment is being made began more than 12 months before the loss-making accounting period. In these circumstances, the interest is calculated as if the repayment were a repayment of tax for the loss-making accounting period itself.

EXAMPLE 6

A company has the following results for the three accounting periods to 31 March 2006:

	y/e 30/9/04	*6 months to 31/3/05*	*y/e 31/3/06*
	£	£	£
Chargeable profits	180,000	120,000	nil
Franked investment income	nil	nil	nil

A claim is made under S393A(1)(b) in relation to trading losses of £250,000 incurred in the year to 31 March 2006. All corporation tax was originally paid on the due date and the necessary repayment of corporation tax is made on 1 February 2007. Calculate the amount of the repayment and the amount of interest which will accompany this repayment, assuming an interest rate of 4% per annum.

Solution

The trading loss for the year to 31 March 2006 may be relieved against the company's profits of the previous 12 months. The whole of the £120,000 profit for the 6 months to 31 March 2005 is available, together with the £90,000 profit (6/12 x £180,000) for the 6 months to 30 September 2004. The remaining loss of £40,000 is carried forward under S393(1). The S393A(1)(b) claim will generate the following repayment:

		£
6 months to 31 March 2005	120,000 @ 19%	22,800
y/e 30 September 2004	90,000 @ 19%	17,100
Total repayment		39,900

Notes:

(i) The small companies rate was 19% in FY2003 and in FY2004.

(ii) The 6 months to 31 March 2005 did not begin more than 12 months before the loss-making period so interest on the £22,800 will run from 1 January 2006 (the due date of payment for the 6 months to 31 March 2005).

(iii) The year to 30 September 2004 began more than 12 months before the loss-making period so interest on the £17,100 will run only from 1 January 2007 (the due date of payment for the loss-making period itself).

(iv) The repayment takes place on 1 February 2007, which is 396 days after 1 January 2006 and 31 days after 1 January 2007. Therefore the interest due is:

$$(\pounds 22{,}800 \times 4\% \times \frac{396}{365}) + (\pounds 17{,}100 \times 4\% \times \frac{31}{365}) = \pounds 1{,}047.55.$$

Choice of loss relief

A company which incurs a trading loss must choose between carrying the loss forward against future trading profits or relieving the loss against the total profits of the current period and (possibly) the total profits of the previous 12 months. Some of the main criteria which will influence this choice are as follows:

(a) the likelihood and expected amount of future profits arising from the same trade as that in which the loss was incurred

(b) the company's cash flow situation (a cash shortage may dictate that loss relief should be obtained as soon as possible)

(c) the rates of corporation tax in earlier accounting periods and the expected rates in future periods

(d) the possibility that relief for trading losses may reduce the chargeable profits of an accounting period to such an extent that the rate of corporation tax payable for that period is reduced

(e) the possibility that non-trade charges may be unrelieved

(f) the possibility of reducing the scope for relieving surplus ACT brought forward from before 6 April 1999

(g) in general, the desire to maximise the tax saved as a result of loss relief claims.

Non-trading losses

A company may incur non-trading losses in any of the following ways:

(a) **Schedule A losses**. A loss incurred by a company on its property business is set against the company's total profits for the accounting period in which the loss occurs. To the extent that the loss cannot be relieved in this way, it is either:

(i) carried forward and set against the total profits of succeeding accounting periods (so long as the property business is still being carried on in those accounting periods), or

(ii) relieved by means of group relief (see Chapter 28).

These reliefs are much more generous than their income tax equivalents (see Chapter 5). Note that there are restrictions on the carry-forward of Schedule A losses when there is a change in the ownership of a company. These restrictions are similar to those relating to trading losses (see earlier in this chapter).

(b) **Schedule D Case VI losses**. A Schedule D Case VI loss is relieved first against any other Schedule D Case VI (miscellaneous) income of the same accounting period and then against the Schedule D Case VI income of subsequent periods.

(c) **Net debits on non-trading loan relationships**. If a company incurs a deficit on its non-trading loan relationships (see Chapter 23), a claim may be made for the deficit to be relieved in any of the following ways:

(i) by set-off against the company's total profits for the accounting period in which the deficit occurs (*after* deducting any trading losses brought forward and relieved under S393(1) but *before* deducting any trading losses relieved under S393A(1) and *before* deducting charges)

(ii) by group relief (see Chapter 28)

(iii) by set-off against the company's income from non-trading loan relationships in the previous 12 months

(iv) by set-off against non-trading profits of the next accounting period.

Part of the deficit may be relieved in one way and part in another, if the company so wishes. Claims must be made within two years of the end of the accounting period in which the deficit occurs. Any part of the deficit which is not subject to such a claim is carried forward automatically and regarded as a non-trading debit of the next accounting period.

(d) **Non-trading losses on intangible fixed assets**. A company which incurs a non-trading loss on intangible fixed assets in an accounting period (see Chapter 23) may claim that all or part of the loss should be set against the company's total profits for that period. Any part of the loss which is not subject to such a claim and which is not relieved by means of group relief (see Chapter 28) is carried forward and treated as non-trading expenditure of the next accounting period.

(e) **Capital losses**. A company's capital losses are treated in a similar way to those of an individual (see Chapter 16). Capital losses are relieved first against capital gains of the same accounting period and then against the capital gains of subsequent accounting periods. Since companies are not entitled to the annual exemption, there is no need to restrict capital losses brought forward so as to conserve the exemption. Capital losses cannot be relieved against any other form of income.

Summary

- A company's trading losses are carried forward under S393(1) and relieved against the first available profits of the same trade, unless the company makes a claim under S393A(1).
- Unrelieved trade charges (which are now rarely encountered) may be carried forward under S393(9) but unrelieved non-trade charges are lost.
- Under S393A(1)(a), a trading loss may be relieved against the total profits of the loss-making accounting period.
- Under S393A(1)(b), a trading loss may be further relieved against the total profits of the 12 months prior to the loss-making accounting period.
- Trading losses relieved in an accounting period under S393A(1) may reduce the scope in that period for relieving surplus ACT brought forward from before 6 April 1999.
- If a claim under S393A(1)(b) results in a repayment of corporation tax for an earlier accounting period, this repayment will attract interest.
- Loss reliefs are also available in relation to Schedule A losses, Schedule D Case VI losses, net debits on non-trading loan relationships, capital losses and non-trading losses on intangible fixed assets.

Exercises

26.1 A Ltd has the following results for the three years to 31 May 2005:

	y/e 31/5/03	*y/e 31/5/04*	*y/e 31/5/05*
	£	£	£
Trading profits/(losses)	(32,200)	23,800	40,300
Gift Aid donations	400	500	600

Assuming that the trading loss is to be carried forward under S393(1), calculate the company's chargeable profits for each of the three years, showing the amount of the losses carried forward at the end of each year.

26.2 B Ltd has the following results for the year to 31 October 2005:

	£
Trading loss	(232,300)
Income from property	210,200
Chargeable gains	45,540
Non-trade charges	24,000

Assuming that a loss relief claim is made under S393A(1)(a), calculate the chargeable profits for the year.

26.3 Which of the following statements is true?

(a) Capital losses may be carried forward and relieved against future trading profits.

(b) Trading losses may be carried forward and relieved against future capital gains.

(c) Trading losses may be relieved against capital gains of the same period.

(d) Capital losses may be relieved against trading profits of the same period.

26.4 C Ltd has the following results for the three years to 31 January 2006:

	y/e 31/1/04	*y/e 31/1/05*	*y/e 31/1/06*
	£	£	£
Trading profits/(losses)	22,700	73,600	(155,700)
Capital gains	-	-	48,700
Non-trade charges	1,000	1,000	1,000

Assuming that a claim is made under both S393A(1)(a) and S393A(1)(b) in relation to the trading loss incurred in the year to 31 January 2006, calculate the company's chargeable profits for each of the three years.

26.5 In the year to 31 March 2005, D Ltd has chargeable profits of £800,000. In the nine months to 31 December 2005, the company incurs a trading loss of £600,000 and has no other income or gains. There is no franked investment income and there are no charges in either period. The company has a substantial amount of unrelieved surplus ACT brought forward from before 6 April 1999.

Describe the corporation tax effects of a claim under S393A(1)(b) in relation to the trading loss (detailed computations are not required).

***26.6** E Ltd has the following results for the four years to 31 March 2006:

	y/e 31/3/03	*y/e 31/3/04*	*y/e 31/3/05*	*y/e 31/3/06*
	£	£	£	£
Trading profits/(losses)	61,900	77,400	64,200	(172,500)
Capital gains/(losses)	(7,500)	4,300	2,700	5,700
Non-trade charges	3,400	3,400	3,400	3,400

Calculate the total repayment of corporation tax (with interest) to which the company is entitled, assuming that:

(a) claims under S393A(1)(a) and S393A(1)(b) are made in relation to the trading loss for the year to 31 March 2006

(b) any repayment of corporation tax which is generated by these claims is made on 15 January 2007

(c) corporation tax for the three years to 31 March 2005 was all paid on the due dates

(d) the company has neither paid nor received any dividends in any of the four years

(e) the rate of interest paid on repayments of corporation tax is 4%.

Also explain how the situation would differ if the company had ceased trading on 31 March 2006 (computations are not required).

Chapter 27

Close companies and companies with investment business

Introduction

In general terms, a "close company" is one which is controlled by a small number of people and a "company with investment business" is one whose business consists at least partly of making investments. Special corporation tax rules apply to each of these types of company and the main purpose of this chapter is to explain the nature of these rules. The tax implications of incorporation are also considered in this chapter.

Close companies

The essence of a close company is that its affairs can be controlled and manipulated by a small group of people, possibly for tax-avoidance purposes. In fact, most companies in the UK are close companies. A body of anti-avoidance legislation has grown up over the years in relation to close companies and the main points of this legislation are explained later in this chapter. The first step, however, is to provide a precise definition of the term "close company".

Definition of a close company

A close company is defined as a UK resident company which is under the *control* of:

(a) five or fewer *participators*, or

(b) any number of participators who are also *directors* of the company.

The rights of a participator's *associates* are aggregated with that participator's own rights for the purpose of determining whether a company is a close company. Some important terms used in this definition are explained below.

Control

Persons are deemed to have "control" over a company if, taken together, they:

(a) own over 50% of the company's issued share capital, or

(b) have over 50% of the company's voting power, or

(c) would receive over 50% of the company's income, if it were all distributed, or

(d) would receive over 50% of the company's assets, if the company were wound up.

Participators

A "participator" is defined as someone who has a share or interest in the capital or income of the company. In most cases, a company's only participators are its shareholders, but other persons (e.g. option holders) might also rank as participators.

Directors

A "director", for this purpose, is any person:

(a) who occupies the position of director (whether called a director or not), or

(b) whose directions or instructions are normally obeyed by the directors, or

(c) who is a manager of the company and (possibly together with associates) controls at least 20% of the company's ordinary share capital.

Associates

The "associates" of a participator are defined as:

(a) the participator's business partners

(b) the participator's relatives (which, for this purpose, consist of spouses, parents or remoter ancestors, children or remoter issue, brothers and sisters)

(c) the trustees of a settlement established by the participator or by his/her relatives.

As from 5 December 2005, this definition extends to same-sex civil partners who have entered into a legally-recognised civil partnership.

EXAMPLE 1

A company's issued share capital consists of 1,000 £1 ordinary shares, held as follows:

	No of shares		*No of shares*
David	200	Helen	50
Emma	50	Ian	30
Frederick	100	Jacqueline	40
George	50	Others (1 share each)	480

None of the shareholders are associated in any way and no shareholder is also a director.

(a) Is the company a close company?

(b) Would the company be a close company:

   (i) if David were Jacqueline's brother, or

   (ii) if Emma married Ian, or

   (iii) if David were Jacqueline's brother and Emma married Ian?

Solution

(a) The five largest shareholders own 45% of the share capital, so the company is not under the control of five or fewer participators. The company is also not under the control of its directors. Therefore the company is not a close company.

(b) (i) If David were Jacqueline's brother, her 4% holding would be aggregated with his and the five largest shareholders would control 49% (45% + 4%) of the share capital. The company would not be a close company.

   (ii) If Emma married Ian, his 3% would be aggregated with hers and the five largest shareholders would control 48% (45% + 3%) of the share capital. The company would still not be a close company.

   (iii) If David were Jacqueline's brother and Emma married Ian, the five largest shareholders would control 52% (45% + 4% + 3%) of the share capital. The company would then be a close company.

EXAMPLE 2

A company's issued share capital consists entirely of ordinary shares, held as follows:

	% holding	*Director*
Keith	7	Yes
Leonora	7	Yes
Martin	7	Yes
Norma	7	Yes
Oliver	7	Yes
Penny	16	No
Richard	4	No
Others (all non-directors owning under 1%)	45	
Total	100	

None of the shareholders are associated in any way.

(a) Is the company a close company?

(b) Would the company be a close company:

   (i) if Penny were a manager, or

   (ii) if Penny were Richard's daughter, or

   (iii) if Penny were both a manager and Richard's daughter?

Solution

(a) The five largest shareholders own 44% of the share capital, so the company is not under the control of five or fewer participators. The company is also not under the control of its directors, who own 35% of the share capital. Therefore the company is not a close company.

(b) (i) If Penny were a manager, she would not rank as a director since her shareholding is less than 20%. The situation would be unaltered and the company would not be a close company.

(ii) If Penny were Richard's daughter, then his 4% holding would be aggregated with hers and the five largest shareholders would control 48% (44% + 4%) of the share capital. The company would still not be a close company.

(iii) If Penny were both a manager and Richard's daughter, then her deemed 20% holding (16% + 4%) would make her a director. The six directors would control 55% of the share capital and the company would then be a close company.

Exceptions

Certain types of company are statutorily excepted from close company status, even if they are controlled by five or fewer participators or by the participator-directors. The main exception consists of listed companies with a substantial public interest. In order for this exception to apply, a company must satisfy all of the following conditions:

(a) The company's voting shares must have been both dealt in and listed on a recognised stock exchange within the 12 months prior to the date on which the company's status is being determined.

(b) The total voting power possessed by the *principal members* of the company must not exceed 85% of the total voting power.

(c) At least 35% of the company's voting power must be in the hands of the public.

For this purpose, a "principal member" is a shareholder who (possibly with associates) has more than 5% of the voting power of the company and is also one of the top five shareholders. If two or more shareholders, each holding more than 5%, tie for fifth place, there will be more than five principal members.

The "public" excludes the company's directors, their associates and most principal members. But principal members which are themselves either non-close companies or occupational pension schemes (other than schemes established for the benefit of the company's own employees) are included within the definition of the public.

EXAMPLE 3

The issued share capital of XYZ plc consists entirely of ordinary shares. For many years, these shares have been listed on the London Stock Exchange and there have been frequent dealings in these shares within the last 12 months. The company's shares are owned as follows:

	% holding	*Director*
ABC Ltd (a non-close company)	13	-
DEF Ltd (a close company)	7	-
Terry	8	Yes
Ursula	10	Yes
Vincent (a manager)	33	No
Wendy	4	No
Others (all non-directors owning under 1%)	25	
Total	100	

None of the shareholders are associated in any way. Is the company a close company?

Solution

At first sight, XYZ plc seems to be a close company. It is under the control of its directors (since Vincent ranks as a director) and it is also under the control of five or fewer participators. However, the company is listed on a recognised stock exchange and its shares have been dealt in within the past 12 months. Furthermore, its principal members (the top five shareholders, each owning more than 5% of the voting shares) hold only 71% of the company's voting power and the public (ABC Ltd, Wendy and the others) hold 42%. Therefore the company is excepted from being a close company.

Consequences of close company status

There are two main tax consequences of being a close company. These are:

(a) Benefits in kind provided by the company to participators or their associates are generally treated as distributions.

(b) Loans made to participators or their associates are assessed to tax.

Each of these consequences is explained below.

Benefits in kind provided to participators

Benefits in kind provided by a close company to its participators (or their associates) are generally regarded as distributions. The taxation effects of this are as follows:

(a) The cost to the company of providing the benefit is disallowed when computing its corporation tax liability.

(b) The company is deemed to have made a distribution equal to the amount which would be assessed on a director or employee earning at least £8,500 per annum if the benefit had been received by such a employee (see Chapter 7).

(c) The person receiving the benefit is taxed as if he or she had received a dividend of the same amount as the deemed distribution.

A benefit in kind provided to a participator is *not* treated as a distribution if it is already assessable as employment income. This will be the case if the participator is a director of the company or an employee earning at least £8,500 p.a. (see Chapter 7).

EXAMPLE 4

On 31 August 2005, a close company which prepares accounts to 31 March each year provides the brother of one of its major shareholders with a free holiday abroad. The cost of the holiday is £3,600 and this amount is charged to the profit and loss account for the year to 31 March 2006. Explain the tax treatment of this item.

Solution

The £3,600 is disallowed in the company's tax computation for the year to 31 March 2006. The company is deemed to have made a distribution of £3,600 and the shareholder's brother is taxed as if he had received a UK dividend of £3,600 (tax credit £400).

Loans made to participators

If a close company makes a loan to a participator (or associate), the tax consequences are as follows:

(a) The company is required to pay an amount of tax which is calculated at 25% of the amount of the loan. This tax is payable nine months and one day after the end of the accounting period in which the loan is made. However, no tax is payable in relation to any part of a loan which is repaid to the company before the date on which the tax falls due.

(b) The tax paid when the loan was made is repaid to the company if the participator repays the loan or if the loan is written off. This tax repayment is made nine months and one day after the end of the accounting period in which the loan is repaid or written off.

(c) If a loan to a participator is wholly or partly written off, the participator is deemed to have received net income equal to the amount written off. This income is grossed-up at the dividend ordinary rate (currently 10%).

The tax which is deemed to have been deducted at source from this income is not repayable to the participator, even if he or she is a non-taxpayer. However, further tax at the dividend upper rate (currently 32.5%) is payable on any part of the grossed-up income which, when added to the participator's other income, falls beyond the basic rate limit.

(d) Certain loans are excluded from the treatment described above. These include loans made to a participator in the normal course of the company's business and loans not exceeding £15,000 made to a participator who is a full-time employee or director of the company, so long as that participator (with associates) has no more than a 5% interest in the company.

EXAMPLE 5

On 1 May 2005, a close company which prepares accounts to 30 June each year lends £30,000 to Ravi, who is one of its directors. No interest is charged on this loan. Ravi owns 25% of the company's ordinary share capital. Explain the tax treatment of the loan if:

(a) it is repaid in full on 30 April 2006

(b) £12,000 is repaid on 30 April 2006 and the remainder of the loan is written off on the same day.

Solution

Tax of £7,500 (25% of £30,000) is payable by the company on 1 April 2006. Since the loan is made interest-free, it is treated as a beneficial loan and Ravi is subject to income tax on the related benefit in kind. As regards the eventual repayment or write-off of the loan:

(a) The tax of £7,500 is repaid to the company on 1 April 2007.

(b) The tax of £7,500 is repaid to the company on 1 April 2007. Ravi is taxed as if he had received net income in 2006/07 of £18,000 (tax deducted at source £2,000).

Companies with investment business

A "company with investment business" is defined by ICTA 1988 as "any company whose business consists wholly or partly in the making of investments". The investment income of such a company will normally consist of:

(a) income from property

(b) net credits on non-trading loan relationships

(c) chargeable gains.

The company may also receive franked investment income but of course this is not chargeable to corporation tax. The expenses incurred by a company in relation to its investment business fall into two categories:

(a) expenses which are directly related to one of the company's sources of income and which may be set against that income (e.g. property expenses offset against property income, debits on non-trading loan relationships set against credits)

(b) management expenses, which are not related to any particular source of income but which may be set against the company's total income.

Note that only genuine management expenses are allowed. For example, in *L G Berry Investments Ltd* v *Attwooll* (1964), excessive directors' remuneration included in management expenses was disallowed.

To the extent that management expenses cannot be relieved in the accounting period in which they are incurred they may be carried forward (without time limit) to future periods. There are restrictions on the carry-forward of management expenses when there is a change in the ownership of a company. These restrictions are similar to those relating to the carry-forward of trading losses (see Chapter 26).

Close investment-holding companies

A close company is also a close investment-holding company (CIC) unless it exists wholly or mainly for one or more of a number of purposes defined by statute. The main purposes which except a company from CIC status are:

(a) the carrying on of a trade on a commercial basis, or

(b) the letting of property (other than to connected persons).

A close investment-holding company is subject to all of the close company rules which are described above, but is also subject to further provisions. The most important of these is that a CIC is not entitled to the starting rate or the small companies rate of corporation tax, no matter how small its chargeable profits. Nor can it benefit from marginal relief. A CIC always pays corporation tax at the full rate (30% for FY2005).

Unincorporated business vs close company

An individual who starts trading is faced with a choice between two alternatives:

(a) To trade as an unincorporated business, either as a sole trader or in partnership with others. In this case the individual is self-employed and the business profits are assessed to income tax as trading income.

(b) To trade as a limited company (probably a close company) with the individual concerned being a director and/or shareholder of the company. In this case, the company's profits are assessed to corporation tax and the individual's earnings and dividends from the company are assessed to income tax.

The choice between these two alternatives will be determined partly (though not solely) by taxation considerations. A full analysis of these considerations is beyond the scope of this book but some of the main factors which should be taken into account when deciding whether to trade as an unincorporated business or as a company include:

(a) the rates of income tax and corporation tax
(b) the NI contributions which are payable by the self-employed and by employees and employers
(c) the tax effects of distributing profits to the owner of the business
(d) the tax reliefs available on pension contributions
(e) the dates on which tax and NI contributions are due for payment
(f) the tax reliefs available in relation to trading losses
(g) the taxation of chargeable gains
(h) the tax treatment of loans made to the owner of the business.

Each of these factors is discussed below.

Rates of tax

The entire profits of an unincorporated business are charged to income tax, regardless of whether or not the profits are drawn out of the business. The rate of tax in 2005/06 is 10%, 22% or 40%, depending upon the owner's taxable income. A marginal rate of 40% applies if the owner's taxable income exceeds £32,400 (a relatively small sum).

By contrast, the profits of a company for FY2005 are charged to corporation tax at 0%, 19% or 30% with marginal rates of 23.75% and 32.75% if profits lie between the starting rate limits or small companies rate limits. The marginal rate of 32.75% does not apply until profits reach £300,000 and the 30% rate does not apply until profits reach £1,500,000. Furthermore, the owners of a company can determine the amount of profits to be paid out as directors' remuneration and can therefore control the extent to which profits are assessed to personal income tax rather than corporation tax.

Note, however, that retaining profits in a company so as to minimise the tax liability in the short term will serve to increase the value of the company's shares. This may result in an increased CGT liability in the longer term when shareholders dispose of their shares, though the gains made on disposal might be eligible for business assets taper relief and/or other CGT reliefs.

National Insurance

In 2005/06, the self-employed pay flat-rate Class 2 NICs of £2.10 per week. Class 4 contributions are also payable, calculated as 8% of profits between £4,895 and £32,760 and 1% of profits beyond £32,760.

The total amount of Class 1 NICs payable in respect of directors' remuneration can be much higher than this. A director who is not contracted out pays primary contributions at 11% on earnings between £4,895 and £32,760 and at 1% on further earnings. In addition, the company pays 12.8% secondary contributions on all earnings in excess of £4,895. However, these secondary contributions are deductible in the company's corporation tax computation.

Distribution of profits

The amount of income tax payable on the profits of an unincorporated business is entirely unaffected by the level of the owner's drawings. But the distribution of profits by a company (either as directors' remuneration or as dividends) has tax implications:

(a) The payment of directors' remuneration reduces the company's corporation tax liability at the expense of increasing the income tax liability of the directors concerned and creating a liability to both primary and secondary NICs.

(b) The payment of a dividend avoids the NI liability and a dividend has an attached tax credit. But dividends are an appropriation of profit and are not allowed in the company's corporation tax computation. Furthermore, the payment of a dividend to an individual shareholder may trigger a corporation tax liability at the non-corporate distribution rate (see Chapter 24).

The decision as to whether to pay out a company's profits as directors' remuneration or dividends (or a mixture of both) is a complex one and should take into account the personal circumstances of the shareholders and directors as well as all of the factors listed above. A constraint which should be borne in mind is the need to pay sufficient directors' remuneration to comply with National Minimum Wage regulations.

EXAMPLE 6

A close company which prepares accounts to 31 March each year is owned and managed by a single shareholder/director who is paid a salary of £5,000 per month. In addition to this salary, the company's owner intends to withdraw £20,000 from the company on 31 March 2006. Two approaches are being considered:

(a) that the company should make an extra salary payment to the owner, such that the total of this payment and the related secondary NICs will equal £20,000

(b) that the company should pay a dividend to the owner, such that the total of this dividend and the company's extra corporation tax liability (when compared with the other approach) will equal £20,000.

Consider the tax-effectiveness of each of these two approaches. For the approach which involves the payment of a dividend, show separately the situation which will apply if the company's marginal rate of corporation tax for the year is 19%, 30% or 32.75%. (Perform all calculations to the nearest £.)

Solution

	Extra salary £	*Dividend (19%)* £	*Dividend (30%)* £	*Dividend (32.75%)* £
Payments made by company:				
Salary	17,730			
Secondary Class 1 NICs @ 12.8%	2,270			
Corporation tax on £20,000		3,800	6,000	6,550
Dividend		16,200	14,000	13,450
Total payments	20,000	20,000	20,000	20,000
Amount received by owner:				
Gross salary	17,730			
Dividend + tax credit (1/9th)		18,000	15,556	14,944
Primary Class 1 NICs @ 1%	177			
Income tax @ 40%	7,092			
Income tax @ 32.5%		5,850	5,056	4,857
Income remaining after tax	10,461	12,150	10,500	10,087

Notes:

(i) The owner's regular salary is sufficient to ensure that any further income is subject to primary Class 1 NICs at 1% and income tax at the higher rate or at the dividend upper rate.

(ii) If the company's marginal rate of corporation tax is 19% or 30%, payment of a dividend seems to be more tax-effective than payment of extra salary. The situation is reversed if the company's marginal rate is 32.75%.

Pension contributions

In 2005/06, a self-employed person may contribute the greater of £3,600 and 17.5% of net relevant earnings (more for older taxpayers) into a personal pension scheme and obtain tax relief on these contributions. A company director may obtain tax relief on payments into an occupational pension scheme of up to 15% of earnings and the company may make further substantial contributions on the director's behalf, these payments being deductible in the company's corporation tax computation.

In general, the total of the tax-deductible contributions which may be made is greater for a company director than for a self-employed person but this depends upon profits being paid out in the form of remuneration (which is earned income and therefore relevant for pension contributions relief purposes) rather than as dividends (which are unearned income).

Dates of payment of tax and NICs

A self-employed person must make payments on account of his or her liability to income tax and Class 4 NICs. These payments are due on 31 January in the tax year and on the following 31 July. The balance of the liability (if any) is payable on the following 31 January. Note that:

(a) Choosing an accounting date early in the tax year (e.g. 30 April) maximises the delay between earning profits and paying tax on them. For example, the tax on profits for the year to 30 April 2005 (basis period for 2005/06) is payable on 31 January 2006 and 31 July 2006 with a balancing payment on 31 January 2007.

(b) However, choosing an accounting date early in the tax year has the adverse effect of maximising the amount of overlap profits which are assessed twice on the commencement of trade.

(c) Class 2 NICs of £2.10 per week are payable throughout the tax year.

In general, close companies will pay their corporation tax nine months and one day after the end of the accounting period. Income tax and Class 1 NICs in relation to directors' remuneration must be accounted for via the PAYE system.

Relief for trading losses

For both individuals (Section 385) and companies (Section 393(1)) trading losses may be carried forward and set against future trading profits. The main distinctions between trading loss reliefs for individuals and companies are concerned with the opportunities to set such losses against total income:

(a) Section 380 of ICTA 1988 allows the trading losses of a self-employed person to be set against that person's total income for the year of the loss, the previous year or both of these years.

In the case of a company, a Section 393A(1)(b) claim to set trading losses against profits of the previous year cannot be made unless a Section 393A(1)(a) claim has already been made, to set losses against profits of the current accounting period.

(b) Section 72 of FA1991 allows the trading losses of an individual to be set against capital gains. A company receives a similar relief by virtue of the fact that a company's capital gains are automatically included in its total income.

(c) Trading losses of an individual incurred in the opening years of a business may be relieved against total income of the previous three years. There is no equivalent relief for companies.

Note that a company's losses can be relieved only against the company's own income and gains, not against the income and gains of individual shareholders.

Chargeable gains

If an unincorporated business disposes of a chargeable asset, the resulting gain is calculated in accordance with the reformed rules of computation introduced by the Finance Act 1998 and is assessed to CGT on the owner of the business. The rates of CGT (for 2005/06) are 10%, 20% and 40% and the annual exemption is available.

If a company makes a chargeable disposal, the gain is calculated in accordance with the rules of computation which applied before FA1998 and is subject to corporation tax (in FY2005) at either 0%, 19%, 23.75%, 30% or 32.75%. No annual exemption is available. Gains retained in the company increase the value of the company's shares, so resulting in an increased CGT liability when shareholders eventually dispose of their shares. In effect a gain may be taxed twice, first to corporation tax and then to CGT.

Close company loans to participators

As explained earlier in this chapter, close companies must pay tax when making loans to participators. A tax charge of this type can sometimes be triggered accidentally if a director overdraws his or her current account with the company. These provisions have no relevance to unincorporated businesses.

Incorporation

If the initial choice is to trade as an unincorporated business, the trader may still consider incorporation at some future time. Some of the main consequences of incorporation are as follows:

(a) The transfer of the assets of a business to a company might give rise to a CGT liability. However, subject to certain conditions, the gains arising may be held-over until the shares which were acquired in exchange for the business assets are disposed of (see Chapter 22).

(b) If the company is under the control of the person who was previously the owner of the unincorporated business, assets which are eligible for capital allowances can be transferred at their written down values for capital allowances purposes, so avoiding the need for balancing adjustments (see Chapter 10).

(c) The transfer of assets to the company will not be treated as a supply for VAT purposes so long as the business is transferred as a going concern and the company is a taxable person at the time of the transfer (see Chapter 29).

(d) If the proprietor of the unincorporated business has unrelieved trade losses, these cannot be carried forward and used by the company but may, subject to certain conditions, be relieved against the proprietor's income from the company (see Chapter 11).

Summary

- A close company is one which is under the control of five or fewer participators or any number of participator-directors. The rights of the associates of a participator are aggregated with that participator's own rights when determining whether or not a company is a close company.
- Certain types of company (mainly listed companies with a substantial public interest) are excepted from close company status.
- Benefits in kind provided to the participators of a close company are treated as distributions. Loans to the participators are charged to tax.
- A company with investment business is a company whose business consists wholly or partly of the making of investments.
- A close company is also a close investment-holding company unless it exists wholly or mainly for the purposes of trading or the letting of property. A close investment-holding company always pays corporation tax at the full rate.

Exercises

27.1 Andrew Pearson is a shareholder of A Pearson (Nottingham) Ltd. Which of the following (if any) are his associates for the purposes of deciding whether the company is a close company?

(a) his sister
(b) his brother-in-law
(c) his nephew
(d) his father
(e) his partner in a firm of solicitors.

27.2 The share capital of Romans Ltd consists of 5,000 ordinary shares, held as follows:

	Number of shares
Sejanus (a manager)	900
Claudius (a director)	400
Agrippa (a director)	300
Cleopatra (a director)	300
Tiberius (a director)	200
Gaius (a director)	200
Ptolemy	190
Livia (the grandmother of Claudius)	190
Apicata (the wife of Sejanus)	120
Others (all non-directors owning 10 shares or less)	2,200
Total	5,000

Is the company a close company?

27.3 On 31 October 2005, a close company which prepares accounts to 31 March each year provides one of its full-time working directors with:

(a) an interest-free loan of £12,000 (the company does not provide loans in the ordinary course of its business)

(b) a season ticket for the opera, costing the company £1,800.

Explain the tax treatment of these two items, assuming that the director in question owns 10% of the company's ordinary share capital.

***27.4** On 19 April 2004, a close company (which makes up accounts to 31 March annually) lends £100,000 to Siobhan, who is a director of the company and who owns 30% of its ordinary share capital. The company does not provide loans in the ordinary course of its business. Siobhan pays a commercial rate of interest on this loan until 1 October 2005, when she repays £55,000. She then continues to pay a commercial rate of interest on the remainder of the loan until it is written off by the company on 31 March 2006. Explain the tax implications of these transactions.

***27.5** A close company has the following results for the year to 31 March 2006:

	£
Income from letting property	89,000
Chargeable gains	600
Franked investment income	1,200

(a) Compute the corporation tax payable for the year.

(b) Would it make any difference if the property income were trading income instead?

(c) Would it make any difference if the property income were a net credit on non-trading loan relationships instead?

Chapter 28

Groups of companies and reorganisations

Introduction

For corporation tax purposes, groups of companies are divided into a number of categories and each category enjoys certain tax advantages. These advantages may include:

(a) the transfer of trading losses and certain other deficits from one group member to another

(b) the transfer of chargeable assets from one group member to another in such a way that no chargeable gain arises on the transfer.

However, group companies also incur certain tax disadvantages, principally a reduction in the starting rate and small companies rate upper and lower limits. The main purpose of this chapter is to describe the categories of group which exist and the extent to which these advantages and disadvantages apply to each category. The tax implications of company reorganisations are also briefly considered in this chapter.

Associated companies

For taxation purposes, two companies are associated if one of the companies is under the control of the other or if they are both under the control of a third party, which may be an individual, a partnership or a company. In this context, the word "control" means the same as it does with regard to close companies (see Chapter 27). Control over a company is deemed to accompany:

(a) ownership of over 50% of the company's issued share capital, or

(b) ownership of over 50% of the company's voting power, or

(c) entitlement to over 50% of the company's income, if it were all distributed, or

(d) entitlement to over 50% of the company's assets, if the company were wound up.

The main consequence of two or more companies being associated with one another is that the starting rate and small companies rate upper and lower limits are divided equally between the companies concerned. This is an anti-avoidance measure, designed to block the practice of breaking large companies into several smaller ones in order to take advantage of the starting rate or the small companies rate. The following points should be noted:

(a) Companies which are associated for only part of an accounting period are deemed to be associated for the entire period. However, if an accounting period straddles two FYs and the upper and lower limits have changed between those two FYs, the accounting period is treated as two separate "notional accounting periods" for this purpose.

(b) Associated companies which are dormant are ignored.

(c) Associated companies are counted whether or not they are resident in the UK. For instance, if a UK company has nine overseas subsidiaries, the upper and lower limits will be divided between all ten of the companies concerned, even though the overseas subsidiaries are outside the charge to UK corporation tax.

(d) If a company controls a second company which in turn controls a third company, then (for this purpose) the first company also controls the third company, even though it may own (indirectly) less than 50% of the third company's issued share capital.

EXAMPLE 1

A Ltd owns 100% of the issued share capital of B Ltd and 70% of the issued share capital of C Ltd. C Ltd owns 70% of the issued share capital of D Ltd. Which of these companies are associated with one another?

Solution

A Ltd clearly controls B Ltd and C Ltd. Even though A Ltd (indirectly) owns only 49% of the issued share capital of D Ltd (70% x 70%) D Ltd is controlled by C Ltd which is controlled by A Ltd. Therefore A Ltd controls D Ltd as well and all four companies are associated.

EXAMPLE 2

S Ltd has chargeable profits of £120,000 for the six months to 30 September 2005 and no franked investment income. Until 1 July 2005 the company had no associated companies but, on that date, its entire share capital was acquired by H Ltd. H Ltd has five other wholly-owned subsidiaries, two of which are dormant. Compute S Ltd's corporation tax liability for the period.

Solution

S Ltd is deemed to have had four associated companies (H Ltd and its three active subsidiaries) throughout the entire accounting period. Therefore the small companies rate lower and upper limits are reduced to £60,000 and £300,000 respectively (one-fifth of their usual values). These are annual figures, which are multiplied by 6/12 for a six-month accounting period, giving £30,000 and £150,000. Profits of £120,000 fall between these limits, so marginal relief is available. The corporation tax computation is:

FY2005	£
£120,000 @ 30%	36,000.00
Less: Marginal relief:	
$\frac{11}{400}$ x (£150,000 - £120,000) x $\frac{£120,000}{£120,000}$	825.00
Corporation tax liability	35,175.00

Of course, the starting rate limits are also reduced to one-fifth of their usual values but the company's profits are too high for this to be relevant.

Transfer pricing

For many years, the UK tax system has contained "transfer pricing" rules which prevent UK companies from gaining a tax advantage by carrying out transactions at artificial prices with connected companies overseas (see Chapter 32). The transfer pricing rules require companies to compute their profits for corporation tax purposes as if the transactions in question had been carried out at "arm's length" (i.e. at the prices which would have applied between unconnected parties).

The original transfer pricing rules applied only to transactions with connected companies overseas, but these rules have now been extended to cover transactions between connected UK companies. Broadly, companies are connected for this purpose if one controls the other or they are under common control. The rules require an adjustment for tax purposes to the profits of the company which gains a potential tax advantage from the transactions concerned and a corresponding adjustment to the profits of the other company.

Small and medium-sized companies are generally exempt from all of the transfer pricing legislation.

51% groups

Company B is said to be a 51% subsidiary of Company A if *all* of the following conditions are satisfied:

(a) Company A owns (directly or indirectly) over 50% of Company B's ordinary share capital, ignoring shares that are held indirectly through a non-UK resident company.

(b) Company A is entitled to more than 50% of the profits available to the ordinary shareholders of Company B.

(c) Company A would be entitled to more than 50% of the assets available to the ordinary shareholders of Company B if Company B were to be wound-up.

Two companies are members of a 51% group if they are both UK resident and either one company is a 51% subsidiary of the other or they are both 51% subsidiaries of a third UK resident company.

By definition, members of a 51% group are also associated companies. Therefore such companies suffer from the reductions in the starting rate and small companies rate limits described above. On the other hand, 51% groups used to enjoy certain tax advantages. Most of these advantages have now ceased to exist but there are still some tax provisions which relate specifically to 51% groups. These are as follows:

(a) Dividends received from a 51% subsidiary or from a fellow 51% subsidiary are disregarded when computing the profits of the receiving company for the purpose of determining the applicable rate of corporation tax (see Chapter 24).

(b) If a company which is a member of a group has an excess of non-corporate distributions (NCDs) over chargeable profits for an accounting period (see Chapter 24) then the excess must be allocated as far as possible to other companies in the group. Broadly, excess NCDs are allocated to recipient companies which have chargeable profits exceeding their own NCDs. A company which is allocated an amount of excess NCDs is treated as if it had made an NCD of that amount itself. Excess NCDs which cannot be allocated to other group members in this way are carried forward by the company which has made the excess distributions.

    For this purpose, a "group" consists of a parent company together with its 51% subsidiaries and their 51% subsidiaries and so on.

(c) If at least one of the companies in a 51% group is liable to pay corporation tax by instalments (see Chapter 24) one of the group members may be nominated to pay all of the corporation tax due from all of the group members. In these circumstances, instalments are based upon the estimated tax liability of the group as a whole. When the total liability of each group member is finally determined, the instalments already paid may be allocated between the group members in such a way as to minimise any interest payable on underpaid instalments.

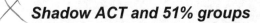

Shadow ACT and 51% groups

As explained in Chapter 25, any surplus ACT existing on 6 April 1999 is dealt with by means of the shadow ACT system. The shadow ACT regulations contain the following rules relating to 51% groups:

(a) If a member of a 51% group has surplus shadow ACT in an accounting period and that surplus cannot be carried back to accounting periods beginning on or after 6 April 1999 and during the previous six years, the surplus *must* be allocated (so far as is possible) to other companies in the group. This reduces the capacity of those other companies to relieve surplus ACT.

(b) The allocation should be performed by the parent company of the group. Failing this, the allocation will be done by HM Revenue and Customs.

(c) If the surplus to be allocated exceeds the total amount which can be utilised by all of the companies in the group, the excess is retained by the company in which the surplus arose and is carried forward to the next accounting period.

(d) Intra-group dividends are not treated as distributions when computing the shadow ACT of the paying company. Similarly, such dividends are not treated as FII when computing the shadow ACT of the receiving company.

(e) If a group company receives FII from outside the group, it may elect to pay an intra-group dividend of an equivalent amount and treat this dividend as a distribution. This election has the effect of transferring FII from one group company to another and allows the company which receives the intra-group dividend to reduce the shadow ACT arising on its own dividends.

75% groups

Company B is said to be a 75% subsidiary of Company A if *all* of the following conditions are satisfied:

(a) Company A owns (directly or indirectly) at least 75% of the ordinary share capital of Company B.

(b) Company A is entitled to at least 75% of the profits available to the ordinary shareholders of Company B.

(c) Company A would be entitled to at least 75% of the assets available to the ordinary shareholders of Company B if Company B were to be wound-up.

Two companies are members of a 75% group if they are both UK resident and either one company is a 75% subsidiary of the other or they are both 75% subsidiaries of a third company (which might or might not be UK resident).

The members of a 75% group benefit from two main tax reliefs. These are the right to transfer trading losses and certain other items between group members ("group relief") and the transfer of chargeable assets between group members in such a way that no chargeable gain arises on the transfer. These reliefs are described below.

EXAMPLE 3

P Ltd is the holding company of a small group. All companies in the group are UK resident and all of the issued shares of each company are ordinary shares. Shareholdings within the group are as follows:

(a) P Ltd owns 80% of Q Ltd, 100% of R Ltd and 60% of S Ltd.

(b) Q Ltd owns 90% of T Ltd.

(c) S Ltd owns 70% of W Ltd.

Identify associated companies, 51% subsidiaries and 75% subsidiaries within this group structure.

Solution

P Ltd controls Q Ltd (which controls T Ltd) , R Ltd and S Ltd (which controls W Ltd), so all six companies are associated.

P Ltd owns (indirectly) 72% of the ordinary share capital of T Ltd (80% x 90%) and 42% of the ordinary share capital of W Ltd (60% x 70%). Therefore:

(i) Q Ltd and R Ltd are 75% subsidiaries (and 51% subsidiaries) of P Ltd.

(ii) S Ltd and T Ltd are 51% subsidiaries of P Ltd.

(iii) T Ltd is a 75% subsidiary (and a 51% subsidiary) of Q Ltd.

(iv) W Ltd is a 51% subsidiary of S Ltd.

Group relief

Group relief consists of the surrender of trading losses and/or certain other items by one member of a 75% group (the "surrendering company") to another member of the group (the "claimant company"). The main items which may be surrendered are:

(a) trading losses and deficits on non-trading loan relationships

(b) charges, Schedule A losses and non-trading losses on intangible fixed assets.

Capital losses cannot be surrendered under the group relief rules, but a capital loss can in effect be transferred from one group company to another by a different means (see later in this chapter). Note the following points with regard to group relief:

(a) The surrender may be in whole or in part as best meets the requirements of the surrendering company and the claimant company. Trading losses and deficits on non-trading loan relationships may be surrendered even if they could instead be set against the profits of the accounting period in which they are incurred. The remaining items are available for surrender only to the extent that (in aggregate) they exceed the surrendering company's gross profits for the period in which they are incurred. For this purpose, a company's "gross profits" are its profits before deducting amounts which are eligible for group relief and before deducting losses or other amounts carried forward or back from any other period.

(b) A surrender may be made from subsidiary to parent, from parent to subsidiary or from subsidiary to fellow subsidiary.

(c) Only current-period losses (or other items) are eligible for group relief and these must be set against the claimant company's profits for a *corresponding* accounting period. If the accounting periods of the surrendering company and the claimant company do not correspond exactly, group relief is available only in respect of the period of overlap between the two periods. The losses of the surrendering company and the profits of the claimant company are time-apportioned so as to determine the amounts which fall into the overlap period.

(d) A similar time-apportionment is required when a company joins or leaves a group part-way through an accounting period.

(e) The amount surrendered to a claimant company cannot exceed that company's profits for the corresponding accounting period, *before* deduction of any reliefs derived from a subsequent accounting period but *after* deduction of any other relief from tax, including:

- trading losses brought forward under Section 393(1)
- current-period trading losses which are relieved (or which could have been relieved) under S393A(1)(a)
- Schedule A losses of the current period or previous periods

- deficits on non-trading loan relationships which are set against profits of the current period or brought forward from previous periods
- non-trading losses on intangible fixed assets which are set against profits of the current period or brought forward from previous periods
- charges for the accounting period.

The reference to "reliefs derived from a subsequent accounting period" means that group relief is given before relief for trading losses carried back and before relief for deficits on non-trading loan relationships carried back.

(f) A group relief claim must normally be made within two years of the end of the claimant company's accounting period.

(g) Any amount of money paid to the surrendering company by the claimant company as consideration for the surrendered items is ignored for tax purposes so long as the payment does not exceed the amount of the surrendered items.

EXAMPLE 4

Low Ltd is a wholly-owned subsidiary of High Ltd. Both companies are UK resident and prepare accounts to 31 March each year. Results for the year to 31 March 2006 are:

	High Ltd	*Low Ltd*
	£	£
Trading profit/(loss)	100,000	(180,000)
Chargeable gains	5,000	75,000
Charges	12,000	-

Show how the trading loss sustained by Low Ltd may be relieved.

Solution

High Ltd has chargeable profits of £93,000 (£100,000 + £5,000 - £12,000). This sets an upper limit on the amount of group relief which may be claimed. The trading loss sustained by Low Ltd may be relieved in a number of ways. For example:

(a) The entire loss could be carried forward under S393(1).

(b) £75,000 of the loss could be relieved against the company's chargeable gains under S393A(1)(a) and the balance of £105,000 carried forward.

(c) The claim under S393A(1)(a) could be supplemented by a further claim under S393A(1)(b) to set the remaining £105,000 of the loss against the profits of Low Ltd for the previous 12 months.

(d) Group relief of anything up to £93,000 could be claimed and the balance of the loss then dealt with as above.

EXAMPLE 5

L Ltd prepares accounts annually to 31 March and is a 75% subsidiary of H Ltd, which prepares accounts annually to 31 December. Both companies are UK resident. Recent results are as follows:

	H Ltd	*L Ltd*
	£	£
Trading loss for year to 31 March 2005		(40,000)
Chargeable profits year to 31 December 2004	35,000	
Chargeable profits year to 31 December 2005	56,000	

Compute the amount of group relief that may be claimed.

Solution

The accounting periods of H Ltd and L Ltd do not correspond, so it is necessary to time-apportion profits and losses, as follows:

	1/4/04 - 31/12/04 (9 months)	*1/1/05 - 31/3/05 (3 months)*
	£	£
(i) H Ltd profit	26,250	14,000
(ii) L Ltd loss	(30,000)	(10,000)

The group relief available in each period is the lower of (i) and (ii). Therefore, H Ltd may claim that group relief of up to £26,250 should be set against its 2004 profits and that group relief of up to £10,000 should be set against its 2005 profits. The remaining £3,750 of the loss is not eligible for group relief.

Using group relief effectively

Group relief should be used to ensure that trading losses are relieved as tax-effectively as possible and that the group's overall tax liability is minimised. Points to bear in mind are:

(a) Surrendering companies should surrender trading losses first to claimant companies which pay corporation tax at the marginal rate of 32.75% and then to those companies paying tax at 30%, 23.75% and 19% (in that order). There is no point in surrendering a loss to a claimant company which pays tax at 0%.

(b) Claimant companies should consider claiming less than the full amount of capital allowances available for an accounting period, so maximising the profits available for group relief set-off.

(c) A company with a trading loss should use the loss itself in a claim under S393A(1)(a) and S393A(1)(b) if this would save more tax than surrendering the loss to another group company.

Transfer of chargeable assets within a group

If a chargeable asset is transferred from one member of a 75% group to another, the transfer is deemed to have occurred at a value giving rise to neither a gain nor a loss. When an asset which has been transferred between group members in this way is finally disposed of outside the group, the chargeable gain arising on the disposal is then (in effect) calculated with reference to the original cost of the asset to the group.

The definition of a 75% group for this purpose is less rigorous than the definition given above in relation to group relief. A *capital gains group* consists of a principal company plus its 75% subsidiaries (as previously defined) plus the subsidiaries' 75% subsidiaries and so forth, subject to the overriding requirement that the principal company must have more than a 50% interest in each member of the group.

EXAMPLE 6

J Ltd owns 80% of the ordinary share capital of K Ltd, which owns 80% of the share capital of L Ltd, which owns 80% of the share capital of M Ltd, which owns 80% of the share capital of N Ltd. All of these companies are UK resident. Which of the companies belongs to a capital gains group with J Ltd as the principal company?

Solution

At first sight, all five companies seem to belong to the capital gains group which has J Ltd at its head. However, J Ltd must have more than a 50% interest in each member of the group. J Ltd's actual interests in each member are as follows:

K Ltd	80%
L Ltd	80% x 80% = 64%
M Ltd	80% x 80% x 80% = 51.2%
N Ltd	80% x 80% x 80% x 80% = 40.96%

Therefore, N Ltd is not a member of this capital gains group.

Degrouping charge

A chargeable gain may arise in relation to an intra-group transfer if a company has a chargeable asset transferred to it from another group member and then leaves the group within six years of the date of the transfer. The company leaving the group is deemed to have sold the asset on the date of the intra-group transfer for its market value on that date (perhaps giving rise to a chargeable gain) and then immediately to have re-acquired the asset on the same date and for the same amount.

Any chargeable gain arising from this treatment is chargeable in the accounting period in which the company leaves the group. However, such a gain may be treated as if it had accrued to another company in the group (subject to a joint election) and is also eligible for roll-over relief.

EXAMPLE 7

SubOne Ltd and SubTwo Ltd are members of a capital gains group. In January 2001, SubOne Ltd transferred a chargeable asset to SubTwo Ltd. The asset had originally cost £10,000 and its market value in January 2001 was £25,000. If the asset had been sold outside the group in January 2001, indexation allowance of £1,350 would have been available. In March 2005, SubTwo Ltd (which prepares accounts to 31 December each year) leaves the group. Calculate the chargeable gain arising on SubTwo Ltd's departure.

Solution

SubTwo Ltd is deemed to have sold the asset for £25,000 in January 2001 and then to have immediately re-acquired it for the same amount. The sale would have given rise to a chargeable gain of £13,650 (£25,000 - £10,000 - £1,350) so a chargeable gain of £13,650 arises in SubTwo Ltd's accounting period for the year to 31 December 2005.

Roll-over relief for capital gains groups

For the purposes of roll-over relief on the replacement of a business asset (see Chapter 22) all of the companies in a capital gains group are treated as a single company. This means that a gain arising on the disposal of a business asset by one member of a group can be rolled-over against the cost of a qualifying business asset acquired by any other member of that group.

It is important to note that the qualifying business asset against which a gain is rolled-over must be an asset which has been newly acquired *by the group as a whole*. It is not possible to roll-over a gain against an asset which has been acquired by one group member from another.

Capital losses

Capital losses cannot be surrendered to another group member. This is in contrast to the treatment of trading losses and certain other items which can be surrendered (see above). At one time, the only way around this problem was to transfer assets between group members in such a way that capital gains and capital losses arose in the same company. Imagine that Company L and Company G were both members of a capital gains group, that Company L had capital losses and that Company G was about to dispose of an asset and realise a capital gain. Company L's capital losses could be set against this gain in the following way:

(a) Company G could transfer its asset to Company L (on a no gain/no loss basis).

(b) Company L could then dispose of the asset. The gain arising would in this way be realised by Company L rather than Company G, so allowing Company L's losses to be set against it.

However a simpler procedure is now available. Two members of a 75% group may now jointly elect that an asset which has been disposed of outside the group by one of them should be treated as if it had been transferred between them immediately before that disposal. This election allows gains and losses to be brought together in the same company without having to transfer assets between group members. The election must be made within two years of the end of the accounting period in which the disposal outside the group takes place.

X

Pre-entry capital losses

A group which anticipates making disposals which will give rise to substantial capital gains might try to shelter those gains by acquiring a "capital loss company". This is a company which has capital losses brought forward or assets which would realise capital losses on disposal. The intention of the acquisition would be to set these capital losses against the group's capital gains (by means of the procedure outlined above) and so reduce the group's overall corporation tax liability.

This tax-avoidance manoeuvre is prevented by TCGA 1992, which allows a group company's *pre-entry capital losses* to be set only against gains arising on the following types of disposal:

(a) disposals of assets which the company owned before it joined the group

(b) disposals of assets acquired by the company *from outside the group* since becoming a group member.

The pre-entry capital losses of a company are defined as:

(a) any capital losses incurred by the company before joining the group, and

(b) the pre-entry part of any capital losses incurred by the company after joining the group on the disposal of pre-entry assets.

When a company joins a group and subsequently disposes of a pre-entry asset at a loss, the pre-entry part of that loss is obtained by applying a formula to each item of allowable expenditure in the computation and then aggregating the results. The formula used is:

$$A \times \frac{B}{C} \times \frac{D}{E}$$

where: A = the total amount of the allowable loss

B = the amount of the item of allowable expenditure

C = the sum of the amounts of all the items of allowable expenditure

D = the length of time between the date of the expenditure (or 1 April 1982 if later) and the date of joining the group

E = the length of time between the date of the expenditure (or 1 April 1982 if later) and the date of disposal.

EXAMPLE 8

A company acquired a chargeable asset on 1 January 1996 at a cost of £200,000 and incurred enhancement expenditure of a further £50,000 on 1 January 2000. The company joined a capital gains group on 1 April 2005 and the asset was sold on 1 September 2005 for £130,000. Calculate the total loss arising on this disposal and the amount of the pre-entry loss (working to the nearest whole month).

Solution

	£	£
Sale proceeds		130,000
Less: Cost	200,000	
Enhancement	50,000	250,000
Allowable loss		(120,000)

Notes:

(i) Indexation allowance is £nil, since indexation allowance cannot be used to increase a loss.

(ii) The asset was originally acquired 111 months before joining the group and 116 months before disposal. The enhancement expenditure was incurred 63 months before joining the group and 68 months before disposal.

(iii) The pre-entry loss is:

$$(£120,000 \times \frac{£200,000}{£250,000} \times \frac{111}{116}) + (£120,000 \times \frac{£50,000}{£250,000} \times \frac{63}{68}) = £114,097.$$

Pre-entry capital gains

Anti-avoidance legislation applies when a company joins a group part-way through an accounting period and has realised capital gains between the start of its accounting period and the date of joining the group. In these circumstances, the only losses which may be set against those earlier gains are losses which arose before the company joined the group and losses which arose after that date on assets which the company owned before it joined the group.

Pre-entry surplus ACT

In Chapter 25, it was stated that there are restrictions on the carry-forward of a company's surplus ACT when the ownership of the company changes and there is a major change in the nature of the company's business. Another restriction on the relief of surplus ACT arises when a company joins a group, but this time there is no need for there to be a major change in the nature of the company's business. The restriction is that the company's *pre-entry surplus ACT* cannot be set against the corporation tax due in relation to disposals of chargeable assets which:

(a) are acquired from other group members on a no-gain, no-loss basis, and
(b) are then disposed of within three years of the company joining the group.

This provision is intended to prevent groups from acquiring companies with the sole intention of using their surplus ACT (arising from before 6 April 1999) to avoid paying corporation tax on the group's capital gains.

Consortia

A company is owned by a consortium and is known as a *consortium company* if at least 75% of its ordinary share capital is owned by other companies (who are known as *consortium members*) each of which:

(a) owns at least 5% but less than 75% of the consortium company's ordinary share capital, and
(b) is entitled to at least 5% of the profits available to the consortium company's ordinary shareholders, and
(c) would be entitled to at least 5% of the assets available to the consortium company's ordinary shareholders on a winding-up.

A 90% subsidiary of a consortium company is also a consortium company.

Group relief for a consortium

Group relief is available in either direction between a consortium member and a consortium company, so long as both companies are UK resident and the consortium company is either a trading company or a company whose business consists wholly or mainly of holding shares in trading companies which are its 90% subsidiaries. Note the following points with regard to group relief for a consortium:

(a) The relief is restricted in proportion to the consortium member's shareholding in the consortium company. For instance, if CC Ltd is a consortium company and CM Ltd is a consortium member which owns x% of CC Ltd, CM Ltd may claim up to x% of CC Ltd's losses. Alternatively, CM Ltd may surrender to CC Ltd losses of up to x% of CC Ltd's profits.

(b) A group relief claim must be agreed by all the consortium members.

(c) The amount of a consortium company's trading loss which is available for group relief is the amount of the loss less any potential claim for loss relief under S393A(1)(a), whether or not such a claim is actually made.

EXAMPLE 9

The ordinary share capital of W Ltd (a UK trading company) is owned 30% by X Ltd, 25% by Y Ltd and 45% by Z Ltd. All companies are UK resident and prepare accounts to 31 March annually. Results for the year to 31 March 2006 are as follows:

	W Ltd	*X Ltd*	*Y Ltd*	*Z Ltd*
	£	£	£	£
Trading profit/(loss)	(62,000)	41,000	11,000	38,000
Chargeable gains	10,000	-	-	-

What are the maximum possible group relief claims which may be made?

Solution

The amount of W Ltd's loss which is available for group relief is £52,000 (£62,000 less a potential S393A(1)(a) claim of £10,000, whether or not that claim is actually made). This is shared between the consortium members in proportion to their shares in the consortium, as follows:

	X Ltd	*Y Ltd*	*Z Ltd*
	£	£	£
Share of W Ltd's available loss	15,600	13,000	23,400
Chargeable profits	41,000	11,000	38,000
Maximum group relief claim	15,600	11,000	23,400

Reorganisations

If a company transfers a trade to another company, this ranks as a cessation of that trade and any unrelieved trading losses incurred before the date of the transfer cannot normally be carried forward under S393(1) and set against the subsequent profits of the transferred trade. But if a trade is transferred between two companies (both within the charge to UK corporation tax in respect of that trade) and at least 75% of the trade is effectively owned by the same persons both:

(a) at some time within the year before the date of the transfer, and

(b) at some time within the two years after the date of the transfer

then unrelieved trading losses of the transferor company may be carried forward and set against subsequent profits (from the same trade) of the transferee company. For instance, this "succession of trade" relief would apply if a company created a new 75% subsidiary and then transferred a trade to that subsidiary. Note the following points in relation to such a transfer:

(a) For capital allowances purposes, assets are transferred at their tax-written down values, with no balancing adjustments.

(b) Chargeable business assets are transferred to the transferee company on a no-gain, no-loss basis, so long as the transferor company receives no consideration for the assets and the assets remain within the scope of UK corporation tax.

(c) Only trading losses may be carried forward as described above. The relief does not extend to non-trading losses, capital losses or surplus ACT, none of which can be carried forward.

Summary

- Two companies are associated if one of the companies is under the control of the other, or if they are both under the control of a third party.
- The starting rate and small companies rate upper and lower limits are shared equally between associated companies.
- Transfer pricing rules apply to transactions carried out an artificial prices between group companies.
- Trading losses and certain other items may be surrendered between members of a 75% group. This is known as "group relief".
- Chargeable assets may be transferred between members of a capital gains group without giving rise to a chargeable gain.
- Subject to certain conditions, group relief is available between consortium members and consortium companies.
- If a trade is transferred between two companies, the unrelieved trading losses of the transferor company may (subject to certain conditions) be carried forward and set against the subsequent trading profits of the transferee company.

Exercises

28.1 Arm Ltd and Foot Ltd are both 100% subsidiaries of Head Ltd, which has no other subsidiaries. They are all UK resident. How will the relationship of the three companies affect the way in which they are taxed?

28.2 Alpha Ltd is a wholly-owned subsidiary of Beta Ltd, which has two other wholly-owned subsidiaries (one of which is dormant). In the year to 31 March 2006, Alpha Ltd has the following results:

	£
Trading profits	220,000
Bank deposit interest	6,000
Income from property	4,000
UK dividend received from non-group company on 1 May 2005	27,000
Charges paid	17,000

Compute the corporation tax liability for the year.

28.3 Base Ltd is a wholly-owned subsidiary of Apex Ltd. Both companies are UK resident and prepare accounts annually to 31 March. The results for the year to 31 March 2006 are as follows:

	Apex Ltd	*Base Ltd*
	£	£
Trading profit/(loss)	120,000	(90,000)
Trading losses b/f under S393(1)	(42,000)	(19,000)
Schedule A income	7,000	3,000
Charges paid	12,000	4,000

Calculate the maximum group relief that may be claimed for the year by Apex Ltd.

28.4 A1 Ltd owns 90% of the ordinary share capital of A2 Ltd. A2 Ltd owns 80% of the ordinary share capital of A3 Ltd and 70% of the ordinary share capital of A4 Ltd. Which of these companies (all UK resident) form a capital gains group with A1 Ltd as its principal company?

28.5 The ordinary share capital of PP Ltd (a UK trading company) is owned 32% by QQ Ltd, 35% by RR Ltd, 23% by SS Ltd. The remaining 10% is owned by various individuals, none of whom own more than 1%. All companies are UK resident and prepare accounts to 31 July annually. Results for the year to 31 July 2005 are as follows:

	PP Ltd	*QQ Ltd*	*RR Ltd*	*SS Ltd*
	£	£	£	£
Trading profit/(loss)	(96,000)	41,000	38,000	11,000
Chargeable gains	-	15,000	-	-
Schedule D Case III income	12,000	6,000	11,000	4,000
Charges paid	-	(3,000)	(2,000)	(1,000)

Compute the maximum possible group relief claims.

***28.6** T Ltd owns 90% of the ordinary share capital of B Ltd. Both are UK resident. Recent results for the two companies are as follows:

	T Ltd	*T Ltd*	*B Ltd*
	y/e 31/3/05	*y/e 31/3/06*	*y/e 30/11/05*
	£	£	£
Trading profit/(loss)	190,000	130,000	(174,000)
Chargeable gains	25,000	13,000	4,000
Charges paid	5,000	5,000	-

No dividends have been paid or received by either company in any of these accounting periods and maximum group relief is claimed. Calculate the corporation tax payable by each company for each accounting period, making and stating any necessary assumptions.

Review questions (Set C)

C1 Tolbooth Ltd is a small manufacturing company. It commenced trading on 1 April 2004 and prepared its first set of accounts for the 18 month period to 30 September 2005. As the accounting technician responsible for preparing the tax computation, you have extracted the following information from the audit file:

		£
(i)	Trading profits (before capital allowances)	390,000
(ii)	Rental income:	
	£20,000 per year from property rented on 1 April 2004.	
	Rent received annually in advance on 1 April.	
(iii)	Bank deposit interest:	
	Received 30 June 2004	2,000
	Received 31 December 2004	2,000
	Accrued to 31 March 2005	1,000
	Received 30 June 2005	12,000
	Accrued to 30 September 2005	4,000
(iv)	Plant and machinery was purchased on 30 June 2004, costing	120,000
(v)	Charges paid (gross amounts):	
	Paid 31 December 2004	5,000
	Accrued to 31 March 2005	2,500
	Paid 30 June 2005	5,000
	Accrued to 30 September 2005	2,500
(vi)	Chargeable gain on disposal 1 August 2005	10,000

Required:

(a) State how the first period of account to 30 September 2005 will be divided into accounting periods.

(b) Calculate the corporation tax liability for each accounting period. *(AAT)*

C 2 P Ltd is in receipt of periodic payments in respect of patent royalties and pays debenture interest twice in each accounting period. Income tax is deducted at source from both the royalties and the debenture interest. The following is a list, in date order, of the various transactions of these types during the year to 31 March 2006 (amounts are shown net):

		£
10/5/05	Patent royalties received	24,960
12/7/05	Debenture interest paid	36,000
30/8/05	Patent royalties received	15,600
24/11/05	Debenture interest paid	41,600
15/1/06	Patent royalties received	21,840

The directors wish to have information on the cash inflows and outflows arising from the taxation associated with each transaction.

You are required:

To calculate, by means of quarterly settlement statements for income tax, the amounts which became payable and/or recoverable in each case, stating the date (or approximate date) concerned. *(CIMA)*

C 3 Poynton Producers Ltd, who make up annual accounts to 30 September, purchased a new industrial building for £150,000 on 1 April 1998. The building was not in an enterprise zone and was brought into industrial use immediately. On 31 August 2000, production ceased and the building was leased to a national charity as a collection centre. Production in the factory re-commenced on 1 February 2002. On 1 April 2005 the building was sold to Sale Switches Ltd, who make up annual accounts to 31 December, for £140,000. It was brought into industrial use immediately.

You are required to calculate:

(a) the Industrial Buildings Allowances for all accounting periods when the building was owned by Poynton Producers Ltd

(b) the balancing adjustment on the sale of the building in 2005

(c) the Industrial Buildings Allowances claimable by Sale Switches Ltd in respect of the building in future years. *(ACCA)*

C4 Unusual Urns Limited is a UK resident company. It has no associated companies. Recent results are as follows:

	Year to 31 July 2004	*6 months to 31 January 2005*
	£	£
Schedule D Case I profit/(loss)	210,000	(150,000)
Non-trade charges	1,500	750

The company's chargeable profits for the year to 31 January 2006 are expected to be approximately £700,000, derived mostly from trading income. The company receives no dividends.

You are required:

(a) to state the alternative methods by which the company can obtain relief for the loss of £150,000 sustained in the period to 31 January 2005, and

(b) to state, with your reasons, which of these alternatives you would choose so as to obtain the maximum tax advantage when claiming relief in respect of the £150,000 loss. You should also state the effect that your proposed treatment will have on the charges on income paid by the company. *(ACCA)*

C5 Antietam Ltd makes up accounts to 31 March annually. Results for the 12 months to 31 March 2006 are as follows:

	£
Trading profits (before capital allowances)	170,000
Capital allowances	32,000
Rental income	46,000
Capital gains	6,400

The company has capital losses brought forward from previous accounting periods of £1,400 and made a Gift Aid donation of £20,000 on 31 March 2006. It also received a dividend from ICI plc on 16 December 2005 of £14,400.

Required:

(a) Calculate the corporation tax liability of Antietam Ltd for the year to 31 March 2006.

(b) Recalculate the liability if you are told that the company has one subsidiary company. *(AAT)*

***C6** Undulating Uplands Ltd is a UK resident manufacturing company with no associated companies. It had always made up accounts to 30 November but decided to change the year end from November to February. The company's results for the period from 1 December 2004 to 28 February 2006 are as follows:

	Notes	£
Adjusted trading profit		750,000
Dividends received from UK companies	1	45,000
Bank interest received	2,5	13,500
Building society interest received	3,5	8,400
Gift Aid donations	4	16,000
Capital allowances on plant and machinery	10	65,000

The following additional information is available:

1. Dividends were received from UK companies as follows:

	£
30/12/04	7,200
30/3/05	10,800
30/9/05	9,000
30/1/06	18,000

2. Bank interest was credited by Natland Bank plc as follows:

	£
21/12/04	4,900
20/6/05	3,800
21/12/05	4,800

   Accrued interest amounted to £4,500 on 30/11/04, £4,300 on 30/11/05 and £4,000 on 28/2/06.

3. Building society interest was credited by Northshires Building Society as follows:

	£
31/3/05	4,000
30/9/05	4,400

   The account was opened on 1/12/04 and closed on 30/9/05.

4. The Gift Aid donations were paid as follows:

	£
15/5/05	8,000
15/11/05	8,000

5. The amounts shown for bank and building society interest received are the actual amounts received.
6. The company had trading losses brought forward of £400,000 on 1 December 2004.
7. The company had capital losses brought forward of £15,000 on 1 December 2004.

8. On 1 March 2005, the company bought a factory which qualifies for Industrial Buildings Allowance from the original owner for £450,000. The factory was first brought into qualifying use by the original owner on 1 March 1986. It had cost £250,000 and a 25% initial allowance had been claimed. It was not in an Enterprise Zone. There had been no non-qualifying use before 1 March 2005.

9. The company had purchased a new factory, which qualified for Industrial Buildings Allowance, on 1 January 2000 for £150,000. It was brought into use immediately. The factory was sold on 1 January 2006 for £350,000. An appropriate claim to minimise the chargeable capital gain was made. The building was not in an Enterprise Zone. (Assume RPIs of 166.6 in January 2000 and 195.5 in January 2006.)

10. The capital allowances figure of £65,000 comprised:

	£
12 months to 30/11/05	39,000
3 months to 28/2/06	26,000

You are required:

To calculate the corporation tax payable for the accounting periods ended 28 February 2006 and to state when this is payable. *(ACCA)*

***C7** R Ltd is a small company engaged in the manufacture and distribution of plumbing equipment. Following a period of poor trading results, its taxable income in recent years has been approximately £180,000. Early in 2005 the directors estimated that the taxable profit would be £220,000 for the year to 31 March 2006.

In March 2005, the directors were considering the possibility of R Ltd acquiring a controlling interest in two other small companies in the same trade - S Ltd and T Ltd. The taxable profit of each of these companies for the year to 31 March 2006 was estimated at £20,000.

You are required:

To advise the directors of the differing aggregate corporation tax liabilities which will arise for the year to 31 March 2006 if:

(i) the above plan is adopted

(ii) R Ltd acquires the businesses of S Ltd and T Ltd - taking over their assets, trades and workforces, but not acquiring a shareholding. S Ltd and T Ltd would be wound up. *(CIMA)*

***C8** On 1 August 2002 X Ltd granted a 20-year lease to Y Ltd on the following terms:

- An annual rental of £20,000, payable quarterly in advance on 1 August, 1 November, 1 February and 1 May each year.
- A premium of £80,000 payable by Y Ltd on 1 August 2002.

On 1 April 2005, Y Ltd intends sub-letting the premises to Z Ltd on the following terms:

- A term of five years, at the end of which Y Ltd will resume occupancy.
- An annual rental of £28,000, payable in advance each year on 1 April.
- A premium of £45,000 payable by Z Ltd on 1 April 2005.

You are required:

(a) To compute, for the year ended 31 March 2003, the amount assessed to corporation tax under Schedule A on X Ltd and the amount of the premium which Y Ltd may deduct in arriving at its trading profits chargeable to corporation tax. (Assume that both companies make up accounts annually to 31 March.)

(b) To compute the amount assessed to corporation tax under Schedule A on Y Ltd for its year ended 31 March 2006.

(c) To comment briefly on the capital gains implications of the above transactions.

(CIMA)

***C9** Mr B has been production manager in a large engineering firm for several years, earning approximately £40,000 p.a. He has recently decided to start up his own business and seeks your advice on all of the differences, from a taxation point of view, between trading as a sole trader or as a limited company. It is possible that his wife will become involved in the running of the business.

He has estimated that during the first year, while the business is developing, it is unlikely that any profit will result. Indeed, it is possible that a loss will arise. Thereafter he anticipates that profits will rise rapidly to approximately £70,000 p.a. His living expenses amount to about £20,000 per year and initially this will be provided from his savings.

You are required:

To prepare a list of headings which would be contained in a report designed to highlight these differences. Under each heading, you should give a brief description of the difference between trading as a sole trader or as a company. You are not required to write the complete report. *(CIMA)*

***C10** HD Ltd owns 80% of the ordinary share capital of SD Ltd. These shares were acquired during 1991. Both companies are UK resident for tax purposes and neither has any other associated companies. Their most recent results have been:

	HD Ltd	*SD Ltd*
	y/e 31/12/05	*9 months to 31/3/06*
	£	£
INCOME		
Trading profit	890,000	-
Trading loss	-	(102,000)
Bank interest	6,000	4,000
Schedule A	2,000	8,000
Capital gains	-	20,000
Capital losses	(15,000)	-
Dividend from SD Ltd	27,000	
Dividends from UK companies		32,000
CHARGES PAID		
Non-trade charge (gross amount)	4,000	5,000
DIVIDEND PAID	327,000	33,750

You are required:

(a) To compute the corporation tax payable by each company for the above accounting periods, assuming that maximum group relief is claimed by HD Ltd.

(b) To suggest a more tax-efficient way in which HD Ltd might have arranged the sales of the assets which gave rise to the capital gains and losses shown above.

(CIMA)

Part 4

MISCELLANEOUS

Chapter 29

Value added tax (1)

Introduction

This is the first of two chapters concerned with value added tax (VAT). VAT is an indirect tax charged on the supply of a wide variety of goods and services. The tax was introduced in 1973 but current legislation is to be found in the VAT Act 1994, as amended by subsequent Finance Acts.

VAT was administered by HM Customs and Excise until the merger of the Inland Revenue and HM Customs and Excise in April 2005. The tax is now administered by HM Revenue and Customs (HMRC).

The principle of VAT

The basic principle of VAT is that tax should be charged at each stage of the production and distribution process but that the total tax due should be borne by the final consumer of the product. This is achieved as follows:

(a) Traders who are registered for VAT (see below) are required to charge VAT on their sales and must account for this *output tax* to HM Revenue and Customs, but

(b) such traders are allowed to recover from HM Revenue and Customs the *input tax* which they pay to their own suppliers, so that

(c) in effect, registered traders suffer no VAT and the total VAT is borne by the consumer at the end of the distribution chain.

EXAMPLE 1

A Ltd owns a quarry. It extracts stone from this quarry and sells the stone to B Ltd for £10,000 plus VAT. B Ltd converts all the stone into paving slabs and sells these slabs to C Ltd for £18,000, plus VAT. C Ltd owns and runs a garden centre, where the slabs are sold to the general public for a total of £32,000, plus VAT. Show how VAT is charged and collected at each stage of this process. (Assume that VAT is to be calculated at 17.5% throughout.)

Solution

	Cost price before VAT	Input tax	Selling price before VAT	Output tax	Paid to HMRC
	£	£	£	£	£
A Ltd	-	-	10,000	1,750	1,750
B Ltd	10,000	1,750	18,000	3,150	1,400
C Ltd	18,000	3,150	32,000	5,600	2,450
Total VAT charged					5,600

Note:

None of the three companies involved suffers any net VAT. In each case, the total of input tax paid to suppliers and the amount due to HMRC is precisely equal to the output tax received from customers. The final consumers, who are unable to reclaim the VAT which they pay, bear the total VAT of £5,600.

Taxable persons

Formally, VAT is chargeable when a *taxable supply* of goods or services is made in the UK by a *taxable person* in the course of business. The term "person" can refer to an individual, partnership or company, as well as to any other body which supplies goods or services in the course of business. There is no need for a profit motive to exist, just that goods or services are supplied for a consideration, so the term "person" can also refer to a charity, a club etc. A *taxable person* is a person making taxable supplies who is, or should be, registered for VAT. Persons must register if their turnover of taxable items exceeds a prescribed threshold and might register voluntarily even if turnover is below the threshold (see later in this chapter).

A taxable person charges VAT to customers when making taxable supplies, must account for this output tax to HM Revenue and Customs and may reclaim the tax suffered on inputs. A person who is not a taxable person can neither charge VAT to customers nor reclaim input tax. The main national museums and art galleries are an exception to this rule, in that they are allowed to reclaim input tax even though they provide free admission to the public and so do not operate a business.

Taxable supplies

A *taxable supply* is any supply of goods or services in the UK other than a supply which is specifically exempted from VAT. VAT is charged on a taxable supply at the standard rate (17.5%) unless the supply attracts VAT at the lower rate (5%) or the zero rate (0%). The lower (or "reduced") rate applies to:

(a) fuel and power supplied for domestic or charity use

(b) the domestic installation of certain energy-saving equipment and materials

(c) the grant-funded installation, repair or maintenance of certain heating or security equipment in the homes of qualifying pensioners or the less well-off
(d) women's sanitary products
(e) children's car seats
(f) certain urban regeneration building works and residential conversions and grant-funded maintenance to places of worship that are listed buildings
(g) the provision of advice or information regarding the welfare of children or elderly or disabled people (unless the supply is otherwise exempt from VAT).

The types of supply which are taxable at the zero rate and the types of supply which are exempted from VAT altogether are described later in this chapter.

Supply of goods

A supply of goods is deemed to occur when the ownership of goods passes from one person to another. In general, a supply of goods will fall within the scope of VAT only if it is made for a consideration (i.e. in return for money or payment in kind) but the following are also deemed to be supplies of goods for VAT purposes:

(a) gifts of business assets other than:
   (i) gifts made to any one person in any rolling 12-month period costing in total no more than £50
   (ii) gifts consisting of samples (but if two or more identical samples are given to the same person, only one of these samples is deemed not to be a supply)
(b) goods permanently taken out of a business for private use by the owner or an employee of the business, in respect of which input tax has been paid.

The sale of goods on hire purchase is deemed to be a supply of goods even though, strictly speaking, ownership of the goods does not transfer until the end of the HP contract. VAT is charged on the cash price of the goods, not the HP price.

Supply of services

Any supply which is made for a consideration but which is not a supply of goods is deemed to be a supply of services. However, a gift of services is not a taxable supply. The hiring of goods to a customer is a supply of services, not a supply of goods, since the ownership of the goods does not pass to the customer. A supply of services is also deemed to occur if the owner or an employee of a business:

(a) temporarily makes private use of goods owned by the business, in respect of which input tax has been paid, or
(b) makes private use of services which have been supplied to the business, in respect of which input tax has been paid.

By concession, the private use of a business motor car is not a taxable supply.

Exempt supplies

A supply of goods or services is an exempt supply if it falls within one of fifteen exemption groups. In summary, these exemption groups are as follows:

Group 1 The sale or lease of land and buildings, other than:

- (i) the sale (or lease for more than 21 years) of new and certain second-hand buildings for residential or charitable use (zero-rated)
- (ii) the sale of new or uncompleted commercial buildings or of land to be used for their construction (standard-rated)
- (iii) the supply of used commercial buildings, if the vendor elects to treat the supply as taxable at the standard rate (the "option to tax")
- (iv) the grant of gaming or fishing rights; the provision of hotel or holiday accommodation or seasonal caravan and camping pitches; the grant of timber rights; the provision of parking facilities or facilities for the storage or mooring of aircraft, ships etc.; the grant of the right to occupy a box or a seat at a theatre, sports ground etc.; the letting of sports facilities (all standard-rated)

Group 2 Insurance

Group 3 Postal services provided by the Post Office

Group 4 Betting, gaming and lotteries

Group 5 Financial services (e.g. bank charges, stockbroking, underwriting)

Group 6 Education provided by schools, universities and further education colleges

Group 7 Health and welfare services

Group 8 Burial and cremation services

Group 9 Supplies made to members of trade unions and professional bodies in return for a membership subscription

Group 10 Sports competition entry fees paid to non-profit making bodies

Group 11 Disposals of works of art to approved bodies (e.g. the National Gallery)

Group 12 Certain fund-raising events organised by charities

Group 13 Cultural services

Group 14 Supplies of goods where input tax cannot be recovered

Group 15 Investment gold.

The tax implications of a supply of goods or services being exempt are as follows:

(a) VAT cannot be charged on an exempt supply.

(b) A person who makes only exempt supplies cannot register for VAT, charges no output tax, is not a taxable person and, most importantly, cannot reclaim input tax.

(c) In effect, a person making only exempt supplies is in the same position as the final consumer at the end of a distribution chain.

It is this inability to reclaim input tax which might lead the vendor of a used commercial building to elect for the "option to tax" (see above). If the election is made, the vendor charges output tax on the sale or rent of the building, becomes a taxable person and may reclaim input tax. Of course, the buyer of the building will have to pay VAT, but if the buyer is also a taxable person then he or she will be able to reclaim the tax paid and therefore may not object to the arrangement.

Zero-rated supplies

Supplies which are made by a taxable person and which are not specifically exempted from VAT are taxed at the standard rate of 17.5% (or at the lower rate of 5%) unless they fall within one of sixteen zero-rated groups. These are listed below.

Group 1	Food, but certain luxury foods (e.g. chocolates) and food supplied in the course of catering are standard-rated
Group 2	Sewerage services and water (other than for industrial use)
Group 3	Books, newspapers, journals etc. (but stationery is standard-rated)
Group 4	Talking books, radios etc. for the blind
Group 5	The sale by builders of new buildings for residential or charitable use and of second-hand buildings which were previously non-residential but which have been converted for residential use. Zero-rating also applies to the amount payable by a tenant on the grant of a lease of more than 21 years on such a building. Also the sale of renovated houses that have been empty for 10 years or more.
Group 6	The sale by builders of substantially reconstructed "protected buildings" (i.e. listed buildings) to be used for residential or charitable purposes. As for Group 5, zero-rating also applies to leases of more than 21 years on such buildings.
Group 7	International services (e.g. making arrangements for services which are to be performed outside the European Union)
Group 8	Passenger transport, but pleasure transport and transport in vehicles seating less than 10 people (e.g. taxis) are standard-rated
Group 9	Certain caravans and houseboats
Group 10	Gold supplied by a central bank to another central bank or to a member of the London Gold Market
Group 11	Bank notes
Group 12	Drugs, medicines etc. prescribed by a medical practitioner and certain aids for the handicapped

Group 13	Certain exports (see later in this chapter)
Group 14	Sales in tax-free shops
Group 15	The sale by a charity of donated goods and certain types of supply made to a charity (e.g. advertising)
Group 16	Children's clothing and footwear and certain protective clothing (e.g. crash helmets and pedal cycle helmets).

The tax implications of a supply of goods or services being zero-rated are as follows:

(a) The supply is a taxable supply but the VAT due is calculated at 0% so, in effect, no tax is charged.

(b) A person who makes only zero-rated supplies is nonetheless making taxable supplies and must register as a taxable person if taxable turnover exceeds the prescribed threshold. Having registered (and this may be done voluntarily, even if taxable turnover is less than the threshold, as explained below) the person will then be able to reclaim input tax.

The value of a supply

The *value* of a taxable supply is the amount on which the VAT charge is based and this is normally equal to the price (before VAT) charged by the supplier. For example, if a standard-rated supply is made at a price of £1,000, plus VAT at 17.5%, the value of the supply is £1,000 and the consideration given for the supply is £1,175.

The VAT component of the consideration (for standard-rated supplies) can be found by multiplying the consideration by the *VAT fraction* which is currently 17.5/117.5 = 7/47ths. Note the following points regarding the value of a supply:

(a) If a supply consists of a gift of business assets, the value of the supply is deemed to be the price (excluding VAT) which the person receiving the gift would have to pay to purchase goods identical in every respect to the goods concerned. This rule also applies if assets are taken permanently out of a business for private use by the owner or an employee of the business.

(b) If the owner or an employee temporarily makes private use of business assets, the value of the resulting supply of services is the cost of providing the services. This cost is based on the amount by which the assets have depreciated whilst being used for private purposes.

(c) If private use is made of services which have been supplied to the business, the value of the resulting supply of services is equal to an appropriate proportion of the value of the supply which was made to the business.

(d) If the consideration for a supply is paid in kind or if the supply is made to a connected person for less than market value, the value of the supply is taken to be the market value of the goods or services supplied.

EXAMPLE 2

(a) A standard-rated supply is made with a value of £180. Calculate the VAT charged and the total consideration for the supply.

(b) A standard-rated supply is made for a total consideration of £1,739. Calculate the VAT element and the value of the supply.

Solution

(a) The VAT charged is £31.50 (£180 x 17.5%) and the total consideration is £211.50.

(b) The VAT element is £259 (£1,739 x 7/47) and the value of the supply is £1,480.

Cash discounts

If a customer is offered a cash discount in return for prompt payment, the value of the supply is the price charged by the supplier (before VAT), less the maximum cash discount which the customer might receive. This is the case whether or not the customer actually takes advantage of the discount.

Note that the VAT fraction cannot be used to calculate the VAT component of the consideration if a cash discount is offered but not taken.

EXAMPLE 3

A standard-rated supply is made at a price of £4,000, plus VAT. The customer is offered a 3% discount if payment is made within 30 days. Calculate the value of the supply and the VAT charged on the supply.

Solution

The value of the supply is £3,880 (£4,000, less 3%) and the VAT charged is £679 (£3,880 x 17.5%). If the customer pays within 30 days, the consideration will be £4,559. If the customer pays after 30 days, the consideration will be £4,679 (£4,000 + £679).

Mixed supplies

A "mixed supply" occurs if a mixture of goods and/or services is invoiced together at a single inclusive price. If all of the items in the mixture are chargeable to VAT at the same rate, the value of the supply and the related output tax can be calculated in the usual way. Otherwise, it will be necessary to apportion the price charged between the various elements of the mixture in order to calculate the output tax due. There is no standard way of achieving this apportionment but the method used must be fair and justifiable.

EXAMPLE 4

A VAT-exclusive price of £320 is charged for a mixed supply of goods. The goods concerned consist of standard-rated goods which cost the supplier £141 (excluding VAT) and zero-rated goods which cost the supplier £19. Calculate the output tax due.

Solution

From the information given, the only way of apportioning the price of the mixed supply into the standard-rated element and the zero-rated element is to split the price according to the cost of each element to the supplier. On this basis, the value of the supply represented by standard-rated goods is £320 x 141/160 = £282. VAT at 17.5% of this figure gives £49.35. Therefore the total price charged should be £369.35.

Composite supplies

A "composite supply" occurs if a mixture of goods and/or services is supplied together in such a way that it is not possible to split the supply into its component parts. In this case, the supply as a whole must be considered in order to determine the rate of tax due (if any). For example, in the case of *Mander Laundries Ltd* (1973) it was held that the services of a launderette consist of a single, standard-rated supply of services, not a mixed supply of water, heat, hire of washing machines etc.

Self-supply

A "self-supply" occurs when a taxable person makes a supply to himself or herself. For example, a self-supply of a motor car occurs if a motor manufacturer produces a car and then uses it instead of supplying it to a customer. The Treasury is empowered to order that, for VAT purposes, self-supplied goods or services are regarded as both:

(a) a taxable supply made *by* the business, and

(b) a taxable supply made *to* the business.

The effect of such an order is that output tax must be accounted for in relation to the supply but that an equal amount of input tax is deemed to have been suffered. This input tax may then be irrecoverable in whole or part (see Chapter 30).

Imports and exports

The VAT treatment of imports and exports depends upon two main factors:

(a) whether the transactions involve goods or services, and

(b) whether the transactions are between the UK and a country which is not a member of the European Union (EU) or between the UK and another EU member.

A brief summary of this complex area is given below.

Imports of goods to the UK from non-EU countries

VAT is charged on the import of goods to the UK from outside the EU at the same rate as if the goods had been supplied in the UK and must be paid by the person to whom the goods are supplied, whether or not that person is a taxable person. Note the following points:

(a) The VAT on imported goods is normally payable at the point of entry to the UK, but importers who are taxable persons may defer immediate payment and pay by direct debit once a month. HM Revenue and Customs will usually require a guarantee from an approved bank or insurance company before allowing an importer to defer payments in this way.

(b) For importers who are taxable persons, the VAT due on postal imports with a value not exceeding £2,000 may be deferred until the VAT return is submitted for the tax period which includes the date of importation.

(c) The VAT suffered by taxable persons on imported goods may be treated as input tax.

Exports of goods from the UK to non-EU countries

Exports of goods from the UK to non-EU countries are zero-rated.

Goods traded between EU countries

If a registered person in one EU country supplies goods to a registered person in another EU country and the customer's VAT registration number is obtained and shown on the sales invoice, then:

(a) The supply is zero-rated in the country of origin, so the supplier does not have to account for any output tax in relation to the supply.

(b) The customer must account for VAT on the "acquisition" (the term "import" is not used in this context) at whatever rate is applicable to those goods in the destination country.

(c) The VAT suffered by the customer may then be treated as input tax.

If the purchaser's VAT registration number is not known, or if the purchaser is not a registered person, the supplier will charge VAT at the rate applicable in the country of origin.

International services

If certain services are supplied in the UK by an overseas supplier then the person *receiving* the services is treated as if he or she were the supplier and is required to account for output tax in relation to them. This is known as the "reverse charge" procedure. The VAT suffered by taxable persons on imported services as a result of this procedure may be treated as input tax. The reverse charge procedure applies to the following types of services (excluding any services which are exempt from VAT):

(a) certain advertising, professional, financial, insurance etc. services which are used by the recipient for business purposes (whether or not the recipient is a registered person)

(b) services of any kind which are supplied to a registered person and which are used for business purposes.

Subject to the normal registration rules, an overseas supplier may register in the UK and charge UK VAT on the supply of services in the UK. In this case, the reverse charge procedure does not apply.

Exports of services are largely outside the scope of UK VAT.

Registration

The total value of the taxable supplies made by a person in a year is known as that person's *taxable turnover*. A person whose taxable turnover exceeds the registration threshold (£60,000 from 1 April 2005) *must* register with HM Revenue and Customs. Form VAT1 is used for this purpose. A VAT registration number is issued, which must be quoted on the person's tax invoices (see next chapter).

A person who is liable to register but who fails to do so is still a taxable person and is personally responsible for the output tax due in relation to supplies made since the date on which registration should have occurred.

When deciding whether or not the registration threshold has been exceeded, it is necessary to aggregate the taxable turnover from all of a person's business activities. The registration relates to the person, *not* to an individual business. It is important to bear in mind the definition of the word "person" for VAT purposes (see above) and to aggregate taxable supplies only if they are made by the same person.

EXAMPLE 5

(a) Jim is a sole trader with a taxable turnover of £53,000 p.a. Is he required to register with HM Revenue and Customs?

(b) Pearl and Dean are in partnership, operating a business with a taxable turnover of £65,000 p.a. Is anyone required to register?

(c) Julia is a sole trader with a taxable turnover of £26,000 p.a. She is also in partnership with Julie, operating a business with a taxable turnover of £45,000 p.a. Is anyone required to register?

Solution

(a) No. Jim's taxable turnover does not exceed the registration threshold.

(b) Yes. The partnership of Pearl and Dean is one "person" for VAT purposes and has a taxable turnover exceeding the registration threshold. Therefore the partnership must register.

(c) No. Julia as a sole trader is one "person", whilst the partnership of Julia and Julie is another, quite separate, "person". Neither of these persons has a taxable turnover exceeding the registration threshold so neither of them is required to register.

Business splitting

"Business splitting" or "disaggregation" occurs when a business with a taxable turnover exceeding the registration threshold is divided into two or more smaller businesses, each operated by a different person and each with a taxable turnover not exceeding the registration threshold, in the hope of avoiding registration.

If this type of manoeuvre were successful, supplies could be made to customers without charging VAT and the administrative costs associated with making VAT returns and maintaining VAT records (see next chapter) could be avoided. The only disadvantage would be that input tax could not be reclaimed but in the case of a business with mainly exempt or zero-rated inputs this disadvantage would be slight.

However, if a business has been split artificially, HM Revenue and Customs may direct that the persons conducting the split businesses should be treated as a single taxable person for VAT purposes. This direction may be made even if the split businesses have never been operated as a single unit, so long as HMRC is satisfied that only one business really exists.

When to register

A person is required to register for VAT if, at the end of any month, the value of that person's taxable supplies for the year ended on the last day of the month exceeds the registration threshold (£60,000 from 1 April 2005). HM Revenue and Customs must be notified within 30 days of the end of the relevant month. Registration will then usually take effect after the end of the month following the relevant month. However, registration is not required if HMRC is satisfied that the person's taxable turnover for the following 12 months will not exceed the deregistration threshold (£58,000 from 1 April 2005).

Registration is also required if there are reasonable grounds for believing that taxable turnover during the next 30 days alone will exceed the registration threshold. In this case, HMRC must be notified by the end of the 30-day period and registration will take effect from the beginning of that period.

For the purpose of deciding whether the registration threshold has been or will be exceeded, supplies consisting of the capital assets of the business are excluded from taxable turnover. However, such supplies normally receive no special treatment, so that the sale of a fixed asset will be a taxable supply unless the asset falls into one of the exemption groups.

EXAMPLE 6

Kevin begins trading on 1 January 2004. Taxable turnover during the first 18 months of trading is as follows:

2004	£	*2005*	£
January	1,800	January	6,300
February	2,100	February	4,900
March	2,800	March	5,400
April	2,600	April	5,900
May	2,400	May	7,400
June	2,900	June	7,200
July	3,300		
August	3,500		
September	4,200		
October	5,500		
November	6,900		
December	6,200		

The turnover in January 2005 includes £2,000 relating to the sale of machinery previously used in the trade. The VAT registration threshold was £56,000 until 1 April 2004 and £58,000 until 1 April 2005. State the date on which Kevin must register for VAT.

Solution

At the end of each month, cumulative taxable turnover during the previous 12 months (or since the start of trade, if less) are as follows:

2004	£	*2005*	£
January	1,800	January	46,700
February	3,900	February	49,500
March	6,700	March	52,100
April	9,300	April	55,400
May	11,700	May	60,400
June	14,600	June	64,700
July	17,900		
August	21,400		
September	25,600		
October	31,100		
November	38,000		
December	44,200		

The registration threshold is passed at the end of May 2005. Kevin must notify HMRC by 30 June 2005 and registration will probably take effect as from 1 July 2005.

Note:

The cumulative figure at the end of January 2005 is turnover for the months of February 2004 to January 2005 inclusive, less the £2,000 relating to the sale of a capital asset.

Transfer of a business to an unregistered person

If a registered person transfers a business as a going concern to an unregistered person, supplies made by the business before the transfer date are deemed (for the purpose of deciding whether or not the transferee should register for VAT) to have been made by the transferee. So if the transferred business, together with any other business operated by the transferee, had a taxable turnover exceeding the registration threshold in the 12 months prior to the transfer, the transferee must register for VAT immediately.

Voluntary registration

A person making taxable supplies which do not exceed the registration threshold may nonetheless register for VAT voluntarily. This enables the person concerned to recover input tax but means that output tax must be charged when taxable supplies are made to customers. However, if the supplies are all zero-rated, or consist of standard-rate or reduced-rate supplies made wholly or mainly to customers who are themselves taxable persons, the fact that output tax must be charged will probably not deter customers.

Being registered for VAT will add to the administrative costs of running the business but this consideration may be outweighed by the benefit of being able to recover input tax.

EXAMPLE 7

Lindsey is not registered for VAT. In the year to 31 December 2005, she has inputs costing £10,000 plus VAT at 17.5%. Her outputs total £32,000.

(a) How much profit does she make for the year?

(b) If she had registered for VAT voluntarily, how much profit would she have made for the year?

(c) Does it matter whether the supplies that she makes are all:

- (i) zero-rated?
- (ii) standard-rated supplies made to VAT-registered businesses?
- (iii) standard-rated supplies made to the general public?

Solution

(a) Her profit is £20,250 (£32,000 - £11,750).

(b) If she had registered for VAT (and her outputs had remained at £32,000) she would have been able to reclaim her input tax, giving her a profit of £22,000 (£32,000 - £10,000).

(c) (i) If she makes only zero-rated supplies, voluntary registration has no effect on her selling prices and, therefore, no effect on her sales.

(ii) If she makes only standard-rated supplies to VAT-registered businesses, her prices will increase by 17.5% but her customers will be able to reclaim the extra tax paid and so there will be no effect on her sales.

(iii) If she makes only standard-rated supplies to the general public, increasing her prices by 17.5% may well entail a loss of custom. In these circumstances she may prefer not to register.

Exemption from registration

HM Revenue and Customs may grant exemption from registration to a person making supplies which exceed the registration threshold, so long as these supplies are all zero-rated. Such an application might be made if the amount of input tax which could be reclaimed if the person concerned were registered is small when contrasted with the increased administrative costs associated with VAT registration.

Pre-registration input tax

VAT incurred before registration is not input tax. Nonetheless, it can be treated as input tax so long as certain conditions are satisfied. These conditions vary according to whether the VAT is incurred on a supply of goods or a supply of services:

(a) **Goods**. VAT suffered on a pre-registration supply of goods may be treated as input tax so long as the goods were supplied to the taxable person for business purposes within the three years prior to the date of registration and were not sold or consumed before that date.

(b) **Services**. VAT suffered on a pre-registration supply of services may be treated as input tax so long as the services were supplied to the taxable person for business purposes no more than six months before the date of registration.

Group registration

A group of associated companies (see Chapter 28) may apply for the group to be registered as a single taxable person, rather than each company in the group being registered individually. Group registration has the following consequences:

(a) The input tax suffered by the group as a whole is set against the output tax charged by the group as a whole.

(b) One of the companies in the group is nominated as the "representative member" and this company takes responsibility for submitting VAT returns and accounting for VAT on behalf of the entire group. However, if the representative member fails to pay any amount of VAT which is due to HM Revenue and Customs, any other company in the group can be held liable for the debt.

(c) Supplies between group members are not regarded as taxable supplies and are ignored for VAT purposes.

Individual group companies may register separately if they wish and choose not to join the VAT group. This may improve the cash flow position of a company which makes mainly zero-rated supplies and which has chosen to make monthly VAT returns (see next chapter). It is also possible for a group of associated companies to form two or more VAT groups, with some of the companies belonging to one VAT group and some belonging to another.

It is worth noting that the group registration rules offer tax avoidance opportunities to certain companies and that HM Revenue and Customs may remove a company from a VAT group if avoidance is suspected.

Deregistration

Deregistration may be either voluntary or compulsory:

(a) A registered person may deregister voluntarily if HMRC is satisfied that taxable turnover, excluding supplies of capital assets, will not exceed the deregistration threshold (£58,000 from 1 April 2005) in the next 12 months.

(b) Compulsory deregistration is triggered when a registered person entirely ceases to make taxable supplies. The person must notify HMRC within 30 days that this has occurred and deregistration will normally take effect as from the date on which taxable supplies ceased.

(c) Deregistration is also compulsory on a change of legal status (e.g. when a sole trader admits a partner or when the business of a partnership is taken over by a company).

On deregistration, the person concerned is deemed to make a supply of all the tangible assets of the business and output tax is charged accordingly. However, assets on which no input tax was incurred are excluded from this deemed supply and the output tax due is not collected if it does not exceed £1,000 in total. The deemed supply does *not* take place if the business is sold as a going concern to another taxable person.

Summary

- VAT is chargeable when a taxable person makes a taxable supply of goods or services in the course of business.
- A taxable supply is any supply of goods or services other than an exempt supply and may be charged to value added tax at either the standard rate, the lower rate or the zero rate.
- A taxable person is a person who is making taxable supplies and who is (or should be) VAT registered. A taxable person may be an individual, a partnership, a company, a charity, a club or an association.
- A person making taxable supplies which exceed the registration threshold must register with HM Revenue and Customs. A person making taxable supplies which do not exceed the threshold may register voluntarily.
- A taxable person must account to HM Revenue and Customs for the output tax charged to customers but may recover some or all of the input tax paid to suppliers.
- A person making only exempt supplies cannot charge VAT to customers and is unable to recover input tax.

Exercises

29.1 A standard-rated supply is made at a price of £340, plus VAT. Calculate the VAT chargeable and the consideration for the supply if:

(a) no discount is offered

(b) a 2% discount is offered for prompt payment and the customer takes advantage of this discount

(c) a 2% discount is offered for prompt payment and the customer does not take advantage of this discount.

29.2 In each of the following cases, is anyone required to register with HM Revenue and Customs? If so, who?

(a) Lorna is a sole trader, making taxable supplies of £68,000 p.a.

(b) Mike owns two distinct businesses. One has a taxable turnover of £30,000 p.a. and the other has a taxable turnover of £35,000 p.a.

(c) Pat and Phil are in partnership. Their taxable turnover is £44,000 p.a. Phil also owns another business with a taxable turnover of £38,000 p.a.

(d) JS Ltd has a taxable turnover of £250,000 p.a. The company's shares are owned entirely by John Smith and his wife.

29.3 Rosemary owns a business which has an annual turnover (excluding any VAT) of £77,000. Describe her VAT position if:

(a) she makes wholly exempt supplies

(b) she makes wholly standard-rated supplies

(c) she makes wholly zero-rated supplies.

29.4 Explain the VAT consequences of making a "self-supply".

***29.5** Answer the following questions:

(a) who should register for VAT?

(b) when should registration occur?

(c) what are the consequences of failing to register?

(d) when may a taxable person deregister?

(e) why might someone choose to register voluntarily?

Chapter 30

Value added tax (2)

Introduction

The previous chapter outlined the main principles of value added tax and explained the processes of registration and deregistration. This second VAT chapter is concerned with the procedures used to account for VAT to HM Revenue and Customs and the way in which the tax is administered. Other matters considered in this chapter include non-recoverable input tax and the VAT position of persons who supply a mixture of exempt and taxable goods or services. The chapter also explains a number of VAT schemes which exist in order to simplify the workings of the VAT system.

Accounting for VAT

At regular intervals (usually quarterly) registered persons must submit a return to HM Revenue and Customs, showing the input tax and output tax for the period covered by the return. Any excess of output tax over input tax is payable to HMRC, whilst any excess of input tax over output tax is repayable by HMRC.

The return is made on form VAT100 and must be submitted within one month of the end of the "tax period" to which it relates, together with any tax due. VAT returns may now be submitted via the Internet.

Monthly accounting

A registered person making supplies which are wholly or mainly zero-rated will be entitled to a VAT repayment in most tax periods. Such a person may opt to submit VAT returns monthly rather than quarterly, so speeding up tax repayments at the expense of making twelve returns per year rather than four.

Annual accounting

A person who has been VAT-registered for at least 12 months and who has a taxable turnover which is not expected to exceed £660,000 in the next 12 months may opt to join the "annual accounting scheme" and submit only one VAT return per year. The scheme operates as follows:

(a) During the year the person makes nine interim payments to HM Revenue and Customs, each equal to 10% of the VAT liability for the previous year. These payments must be made by direct debit or by other electronic means and begin in the fourth month of the year.

(b) Optionally, the person may choose to make three interim payments in months four, seven and ten rather than the nine payments referred to above. In this case, each payment is equal to 25% of the VAT liability for the previous year.

(c) At the end of the year the annual return is submitted together with a final payment consisting of the balance of the VAT due for the year. The return and payment must be made within two months of the end of the year.

A person with a taxable turnover which is not expected to exceed £150,000 per annum may join the annual accounting scheme without having to wait for 12 months after the date of registration. The interim payments in such a case are based upon the expected VAT liability for the year. Registered persons must withdraw from the scheme if their taxable turnover exceeds £825,000 for the previous year.

Monthly payments on account

A registered person who makes quarterly returns and whose annual VAT liability exceeds £2,000,000 is obliged to make monthly payments on account (POAs) to HM Revenue and Customs. The first payment is due one month before the end of the quarter, the second payment is due at the end of the quarter and a balancing payment is due one month after the end of the quarter. All of these payments must be made electronically, e.g. through the Bankers Automated Clearing System (BACS).

Each of the two payments on account is usually calculated as 1/24th of the person's total VAT liability for the previous year. However, the person concerned may choose to pay the actual VAT liability for each month rather than the set POAs.

The tax point

The date on which a supply is deemed to occur is known as the "tax point" of that supply. The tax point of a supply determines:

(a) for outputs, the tax period in which the tax on that supply must be accounted for

(b) for inputs, the tax period in which the tax on that supply may be reclaimed

(c) the rate of VAT applicable to the supply (if VAT rates change).

For a supply of goods the "basic tax point" is the date on which the goods are removed or made available to the customer. For a supply of services the basic tax point is the date on which the services are performed. However, the actual tax point of a supply will differ from the basic tax point in the following circumstances:

(a) If the supplier issues a tax invoice or receives payment on a date which is earlier than the basic tax point, then that date becomes the actual tax point.

(b) Otherwise, if the supplier issues a tax invoice within 14 days after the basic tax point, then the invoice date becomes the actual tax point.

HM Revenue and Customs may extend the 14-day rule mentioned above if asked to do so by a registered person. For example, a person who normally issues invoices at the end of each month might request that the invoice date should always be used as the tax point, even though this date will be more than 14 days after the basic tax point for supplies made in the first half of the month.

Cash accounting

A registered person whose taxable turnover is not expected to exceed £660,000 in the next 12 months may opt to join the "cash accounting scheme". Those who belong to this scheme account for output tax in the tax period in which *payment is received* from the customer and reclaim input tax in the tax period in which *payment is made* to the supplier. The tax point is ignored when allocating inputs and outputs to tax periods.

Joining this scheme allows a registered person to delay the payment of output tax to HM Revenue and Customs until the tax has actually been received from customers, which is of benefit if customers are given extended credit. The scheme also provides automatic relief for bad debts (see below). On the other hand, input tax cannot be reclaimed until that input tax has actually been paid to suppliers. A registered person may not join the cash accounting scheme unless:

(a) the person's taxable turnover (excluding sales of capital items) is not expected to exceed £660,000 in the next 12 months

(b) the person's VAT returns are up to date

(c) all amounts of VAT due to be paid to HMRC (including any penalties and interest) have in fact been paid, or the person has come to an arrangement for such payments to be made by instalments

(d) within the previous 12 months, the person has not been convicted of a VAT offence or assessed to a penalty for VAT evasion involving dishonest conduct.

A person operating the cash accounting scheme must withdraw from the scheme at the end of a tax period if the value of his or her taxable turnover for the last 12 months has exceeded £825,000. HM Revenue and Customs will allow such a person to remain in the scheme only if it can be demonstrated that the high turnover was caused by a large "one-off" sale which is not expected to recur and that the expected value of taxable turnover for the next 12 months will be no more than £660,000.

The cash accounting scheme cannot be used for supplies of goods and services which are invoiced before the supply is made, or for supplies where payment is not due for more than six months after the date of the invoice.

Tax invoices

If a taxable person makes a taxable supply to another taxable person, a "tax invoice" must be issued. The purpose of this invoice is to provide documentary evidence of the transaction, so allowing the person receiving the supply to reclaim the input tax related to that supply. The required contents of a valid tax invoice (which may be on paper or issued electronically) are:

(a) the invoice number, date and tax point
(b) the name, address and VAT registration number of the supplier
(c) the name and address of the customer
(d) for each invoice item, a description of the goods or services supplied
(e) for each description, the quantity of the goods or the extent of the services, the unit price, the amount payable (before VAT) and the rate of VAT applicable.
(f) the total amount due, before VAT
(g) the rate of any cash discount available
(h) the total amount of VAT chargeable.

The issue of a tax invoice is optional if a supply is made to a customer who is not a taxable person. Retailers are not required to issue a tax invoice unless asked for one by the customer and may then issue a less detailed tax invoice if the consideration for the supply does not exceed £250. A less detailed tax invoice need show only the following information:

(a) the name, address and VAT registration number of the retailer
(b) the tax point
(c) a description of the goods or services supplied
(d) the total amount payable by the customer, including VAT
(e) the rate of tax applicable to the supply.

Accounting records

Every taxable person must keep such records as are required by HM Revenue and Customs. The main records which must be kept are as follows:

(a) the usual business and accounting records (e.g. cashbooks, till rolls, paying-in slips, bank statements, purchases and sales books, orders and delivery notes, business correspondence, annual accounts etc.)
(b) a VAT account

(c) a copy of each tax invoice issued
(d) all tax invoices received, though tax invoices are not required for payments of £25 or less relating to telephone calls, parking fees or purchases made through coin-operated machines
(e) documentation relating to imports and exports.

These records must be retained for at least six years and are open to inspection by HMRC, who may make "control visits" to registered persons.

Bad debts

If a taxable person makes use of the cash accounting scheme, the output tax relating to a supply is not accounted for until the consideration for that supply has been received and so automatic relief is given for bad debts. But persons who do not use the cash accounting scheme might account for the output tax relating to a supply before the consideration for that supply is received and then find that a bad debt has occurred. In these circumstances, a claim may be made for a refund of the VAT lost, so long as:

(a) goods or services have been supplied for a consideration in money and the related output tax has been accounted for to HM Revenue and Customs
(b) the value of the supply was no more than its open market value
(c) the debt has been written off in the books of account
(d) at least six months have elapsed since both the date of the supply and the date that payment was due
(e) the claim for bad debt relief is made within three years and six months from the later of the date of the supply and the date that payment was due.

Any business that has made a claim to recover the input tax relating to a supply but has not paid the supplier within six months of the date of that supply (or the date on which payment was due, if later) must repay the input tax to HMRC.

Non-deductible input tax

In general, a taxable person can reclaim the input tax relating to a supply so long as the supply is evidenced by a tax invoice and the goods or services involved are for use in the person's business. However, input tax is not reclaimable on certain types of supply, even though the supply is received in the course of business. The main examples of such "non-deductible input tax" are:

(a) VAT on business entertaining, if the entertaining is not allowable when computing trading profits for income tax or corporation tax purposes.
(b) VAT on costs incurred by a company in relation to the provision of domestic accommodation for a director of the company.

(c) VAT on the purchase of motor cars, apart from:

   (i) cars acquired by a car dealer, as stock in trade
   (ii) cars acquired for use by a driving school, car rental business or taxi business
   (iii) cars acquired *wholly* for business use (primarily for leasing purposes).

   If the input tax on the purchase of a car cannot be reclaimed, the subsequent sale of that car should be treated as an exempt supply.

(d) VAT on second-hand goods bought from a dealer operating the margin scheme (see later in this chapter).

The VAT on goods or services which are not used at all for business purposes cannot be reclaimed. If goods or services are used partly for business purposes and partly for private purposes, then there are two possible treatments. Either:

(a) the input tax on the supply is apportioned and the business element of the tax is then reclaimed, or
(b) the whole of the input tax on the supply is reclaimed, but output tax is then accounted for in relation to the element of private use.

The first treatment may be applied to a supply of either goods or services. The second treatment may be applied to a supply of goods but not to a supply of services (except in certain limited circumstances).

Fuel for private motoring

If the owner or an employee of a business is provided with fuel for private motoring, all of the input tax relating to purchases of fuel by the business is reclaimable but output tax (in accordance with fixed scale charges) must be accounted for in relation to the supply of fuel for private use. As from 1 May 2005, the amount of VAT due per car per quarter is as follows:

	Petrol engines	*Diesel engines*
up to 1,400cc	£36.64	£35.15
up to 2,000cc	£46.32	£35.15
2,001cc or more	£68.06	£44.68

Note the following points:

(a) These charges can be avoided if no input tax is reclaimed in relation to car fuel.
(b) The Government has proposed that the fuel scale charge system should be reformed so that charges are based on the car's level of carbon dioxide emissions rather than on engine size and fuel type.
(c) The input tax suffered in relation to car repairs and maintenance is reclaimable in full (without any adjustment for private use) so long as the car is used for business purposes to some extent.
(d) Only 50% of the input tax relating to car leasing charges is reclaimable if there is any private use of the car.

EXAMPLE 1

Malcolm is self-employed and owns a 1,300cc petrol-engined car which he uses for business and private motoring. During the year to 30 April 2006, the total cost of the fuel used by the car is £1,410. Should he reclaim the input tax paid in relation to this fuel?

Solution

The input tax in question is £1,410 x 7/47 = £210.00. If this is reclaimed, Malcolm will have to account for output tax amounting to 4 x £36.64 = £146.56. This is less than £210.00 and so Malcolm should reclaim the input tax.

Partial exemption

As explained in the previous chapter, a taxable person making wholly taxable supplies may reclaim all input tax suffered (with the exceptions listed above). A person making wholly exempt supplies is not a taxable person and may reclaim no input tax at all.

A taxable person making partly taxable and partly exempt supplies is "partially exempt" and may reclaim only part of the input tax suffered. The amount of input tax which may be reclaimed for a tax period is the amount which is "attributed to taxable supplies". This amount is usually calculated as follows:

(a) Input tax suffered in the period on goods and services which are used exclusively for the purpose of making taxable supplies is attributed to taxable supplies and is reclaimable in full.

(b) Input tax suffered in the period on goods and services which are used exclusively for the purpose of making exempt supplies is attributed to exempt supplies and cannot be reclaimed at all.

(c) A proportion of any unattributed or "residual" input tax suffered in the period (on goods and services used for making both taxable supplies and exempt supplies) is attributed to taxable supplies and may be reclaimed. This proportion is equal to:

$$\text{Residual input tax} \times \frac{\text{Value of taxable supplies}}{\text{Value of all supplies}}$$

The ratio of taxable supplies to all supplies is expressed as a percentage rounded up to the nearest whole number unless residual input tax exceeds £400,000 per month on average, in which case the percentage is rounded to two decimal places. When computing this ratio, certain supplies made by the taxable person are omitted from the calculation, including self-supplies and supplies consisting of the capital assets of the business.

(d) If the total amount of input tax not attributed to taxable supplies for a tax period does not exceed a "de minimis" limit of £625 per month (on average) and is also no more than 50% of all the input tax for the period, then it is treated as being attributed to taxable supplies and is reclaimable in full.

It is important to note that the calculation of reclaimable input tax for a tax period is only provisional. The calculation is performed again at the end of each year, taking into account input tax for the whole year and using a de minimis limit of £7,500 (12 × £625). Any difference between the amount of reclaimable input tax for the year and the amount which was calculated provisionally is an underpayment or overpayment of VAT and this must be accounted for to HM Revenue and Customs. Note also that (subject to HMRC approval) alternative methods may be used to calculate the amount of input tax which is reclaimable by a partially exempt taxable person.

EXAMPLE 2

During the quarter to 31 March 2006, Nancy makes supplies as follows:

	£
Standard-rated supplies (excluding VAT)	120,000
Zero-rated supplies	80,000
Exempt supplies	50,000

She suffers input tax as follows:

	£
Attributed to taxable supplies	7,500
Attributed to exempt supplies	8,500
Unattributed	12,000

Compute the VAT provisionally payable to HMRC for the quarter.

Solution

	£	£
Output tax		
Standard-rated supplies £120,000 @ 17.5%		21,000
Zero-rated supplies £80,000 @ 0%		0
		21,000
Input tax		
Attributed to taxable supplies	7,500	
Unattributed:		
$\frac{£120,000 + £80,000}{£120,000 + £80,000 + £50,000}$ = 80% x £12,000	9,600	17,100
Payable to HMRC		3,900

The input tax not attributed to taxable supplies for the quarter is £10,900 (£8,500 + 20% x £12,000). This is more than £625 per month on average and so cannot be reclaimed.

VAT schemes

VAT schemes exist in order to simplify the workings of the VAT system. The annual accounting scheme and the cash accounting scheme have already been described (see above). Other schemes include:

(a) the retail schemes

(b) the margin scheme for second-hand goods

(c) the flat-rate scheme for farmers and the flat-rate scheme for small businesses.

Retail schemes

Retailers are those who supply goods and services directly to the public. A retailer's sales will often consist of a very large number of relatively small transactions and in these circumstances it would sometimes be difficult and expensive to keep detailed records of each transaction for VAT purposes. In response to this problem, retail schemes have been devised which enable retailers to calculate their output tax in a fairly straightforward way. The standard retail schemes (*which are available only to retailers with a taxable turnover of up to £100 million a year*) are as follows:

(a) **Point of Sale Scheme**. This scheme is the only standard retail scheme available to retailers who make supplies at just one positive rate of tax (i.e. all standard-rated or all lower-rated). The scheme is also available to retailers who make supplies at two or more rates, so long as they can distinguish at the point of sale between supplies made at each rate (usually by having a till which can accumulate separate daily totals for supplies at each rate or by having separate tills).

Retailers operating this scheme keep a record of their daily gross takings (DGT) for supplies at each rate. Output tax is then calculated by multiplying DGT by 7/47 (standard rate) or 1/21 (lower rate).

(b) **Apportionment Scheme 1**. This scheme is available to retailers with an annual taxable turnover of £1 million or less who make supplies at more than one rate of tax. The scheme covers only the supply of goods bought for resale. It cannot be used in relation to supplies of services or supplies of self-made or self-grown goods. For a retailer operating this scheme, the computation of output tax for a tax period involves the following steps:

Step 1 Calculate total DGT for the period.

Step 2 Calculate the VAT-inclusive cost (S) of goods bought in the period for resale at the standard rate.

Step 3 Calculate the VAT-inclusive cost (L) of goods bought in the period for resale at the lower rate.

Step 4 Calculate the VAT-inclusive cost (A) of all goods bought in the period for resale (at any rate).

Step 5 Output tax on sales at the standard rate = Total DGT × S/A × 7/47.

Step 6 Output tax on sales at the lower rate = Total DGT × L/A × 1/21.

This computation is performed again at the end of each year, taking into account takings and purchases for the whole year. Any difference between the result of this computation and the total of the amounts which were computed during the year must be accounted for to HM Revenue and Customs.

(c) **Apportionment Scheme 2**. This scheme is available to retailers who make supplies at more than one rate of tax. It can be used for supplies of goods bought for resale and for supplies of self-made or self-grown goods. It cannot be used for supplies of services. The computation of output tax for a tax period (for retailers making quarterly returns) normally proceeds as follows:

Step 1 Calculate total DGT for the period.

Step 2 Calculate the total (S) of the expected selling prices, including VAT, of standard-rated goods received, made or grown for retail sale in the current tax period and in the three previous periods.

Step 3 Calculate the total (L) of the expected selling prices, including VAT, of lower-rated goods received, made or grown for retail sale in the current tax period and in the three previous periods.

Step 4 Calculate the total (A) of the expected selling prices, including VAT, of all goods (standard, lower and zero-rated) received, made or grown for retail sale in the current tax period and in the three previous periods.

Step 5 Output tax on sales at the standard rate = Total DGT × S/A × 7/47.

Step 6 Output tax on sales at the lower rate = Total DGT × L/A × 1/21.

The computation for the first three tax periods in which the scheme is used is slightly more complex, since an adjustment is required for the expected selling prices of opening stock on the date that the retailer started using the scheme.

For a retailer making monthly returns, each monthly computation will involve the expected selling prices of the previous eleven tax periods (rather than the previous three) and the computation for the first eleven tax periods in which the scheme is used will involve a stock adjustment.

(d) **Direct Calculation Scheme 1**. This scheme is available to retailers with an annual taxable turnover of £1 million or less who make supplies at more than one rate of tax. The scheme works by calculating the expected selling prices of the retailer's "minority goods". These are defined as those goods which are supplied at the rate (or rates) of tax which:

(i) forms the smallest proportion of retail supplies (where goods are supplied at two rates of VAT) or

(ii) form the two smaller proportions of retail supplies (where goods are supplied at three rates of VAT).

The scheme can be used for supplies of goods bought for resale and for supplies of self-made or self-grown goods. Supplies of services cannot be included unless they are taxable at a different rate from the minority goods. If a retailer's minority goods are zero-rated and/or lower-rated, the computation of output tax for a tax period involves the following steps:

Step 1 Calculate total DGT for the period.

Step 2 Calculate the total (Z) of the expected selling prices of zero-rated goods received, made or grown for retail sale in the period.

Step 3 Calculate the total (L) of the expected selling prices of lower-rated goods received, made or grown for retail sale in the period.

Step 4 The standard-rated element of takings (S) = Total DGT - Z - L.

Step 5 Output tax on sales at the standard rate = S × 7/47.

Step 6 Output tax on sales at the lower rate = L × 1/21.

If, on the other hand, a retailer's minority goods are standard rated and/or lower-rated, the computation of output tax for a tax period is as follows:

Step 1 Calculate total DGT for the period. (Although this figure is not used in the calculation it must still be calculated and entered on the retailer's VAT return.)

Step 2 Calculate the total (S) of the expected selling prices of standard-rated goods received, made or grown for retail sale in the period.

Step 3 Calculate the total (L) of the expected selling prices of lower-rated goods received, made or grown for retail sale in the period.

Step 4 Output tax on sales at the standard rate = S × 7/47.

Step 5 Output tax on sales at the lower rate = L × 1/21.

(e) **Direct Calculation Scheme 2**. This scheme works in a very similar way to Direct Calculation Scheme 1 but requires an annual stock adjustment. The £1 million turnover limit does not apply to this scheme.

Retailers with an annual taxable turnover exceeding £100 million cannot use any of the standard schemes listed above. If such retailers wish to use a retail scheme they must negotiate an individual "bespoke retail scheme" with HM Revenue and Customs.

It should be noted that the growing use of information technology by large retailers and by many small retailers means that it is now much easier to record individual sales than it was when VAT was introduced in 1973. This means that the original rationale for the retail schemes has been diminished over the years. Accordingly, retailers may not use any of these schemes unless permitted to do so. HMRC permission will be granted only if a retailer cannot reasonably be expected to account for VAT in the normal way, so that the use of a retail scheme is strictly necessary.

Margin scheme for second-hand goods

In general, VAT is charged on the full value of goods sold by a taxable person, regardless of whether those goods are new or second-hand. However, subject to certain conditions, a taxable person selling second-hand goods may choose to sell them through the "margin scheme" and charge VAT only on his or her profit margin. The scheme operates as follows:

(a) VAT is charged only on the seller's profit margin (i.e. the difference between the purchase price and the selling price).

(b) The seller's profit margin is deemed to be VAT-inclusive, so that the amount of tax due is calculated by multiplying this margin by the VAT fraction.

(c) Any expenses incurred by the seller (e.g. the costs of restoration, repairs, spare parts etc.) are ignored when establishing the amount of the profit margin.

(d) No tax invoice is issued.

(e) The buyer of the goods cannot reclaim the input tax suffered, even if he or she is a taxable person.

The margin scheme is intended mainly for use by those who deal in second-hand goods. The main conditions which must be satisfied for the scheme to be used are that the goods concerned are second-hand and that they were acquired either:

(a) on a supply on which no tax was chargeable (e.g. the goods were acquired from a non-taxable person), or

(b) on a supply from someone who also sold the goods under the margin scheme.

EXAMPLE 3

A dealer in second-hand antiques buys an antique table from a member of the public for £2,000, spends a further £500 on restoration work and then sells the table for £5,000. Compute the output tax which must be accounted for on the sale.

Solution

The dealer's margin is £3,000, ignoring the restoration costs. The output tax due is therefore £3,000 x 7/47 = £446.81.

Flat-rate scheme for farmers

In general, a farmer making taxable supplies which exceed the registration threshold is liable to register for VAT in the normal way. Similarly, a farmer whose taxable supplies are below the threshold may register voluntarily. Since farmers make mainly zero-rated supplies, a farmer who is registered will usually receive regular repayments of input tax, at the expense of maintaining the necessary VAT records.

An alternative to registration is the "flat-rate scheme for farmers". This scheme is available to farmers regardless of the size of their taxable turnover and is intended to reduce the administrative costs associated with VAT registration. The scheme operates as follows:

(a) A farmer who is a member of the scheme does not register for VAT. This reduces administrative costs but deprives the farmer of the opportunity to reclaim input tax.

(b) In compensation, the farmer is allowed to add a flat-rate addition of 4% to his or her selling prices and to retain this addition.

(c) From the point of view of a taxable person buying goods from a flat-rate farmer, the flat-rate addition is treated as input tax and may be reclaimed, subject to the usual rules.

A farmer may not join this scheme if the total of the flat-rate additions which would be charged if the farmer were a member of the scheme exceeds the total amount of input tax which the farmer would otherwise be entitled to reclaim by £3,000 p.a. or more.

Flat-rate scheme for small businesses

An eligible business which is registered for VAT may opt to join the flat-rate scheme (FRS) for small businesses. This scheme enables a small business to calculate its VAT liability as a flat-rate percentage of total turnover and so avoids the need to keep detailed records of input tax and output tax. The FRS operates as follows:

(a) Output tax is charged to customers at the normal rate for the supply. Similarly, input tax is paid to suppliers at the normal rate. However, the output tax charged to customers is not paid over to HM Revenue and Customs and (in general) input tax is not recoverable.

(b) In each tax period, a flat-rate percentage is applied to the VAT-inclusive turnover for the period (including the value of any exempt supplies). The result of this calculation is the amount of VAT payable to HMRC for the period.

(c) The applicable flat-rate percentage ranges from 2% to 13.5%, depending on the trade sector in which the business operates.

(d) Input tax on the purchase of capital assets costing at least £2,000 (including VAT) can be reclaimed in the usual way, in which case output tax must be accounted for in the usual way on the eventual disposal of the asset.

(e) The FRS can be used in conjunction with the annual accounting scheme. It *cannot* be used in conjunction with the cash accounting scheme, the retail schemes or the margin scheme for second-hand goods. However, the FRS offers an optional cash-based turnover method and an optional retailer's turnover method.

The FRS is available to small businesses with a taxable turnover which is not expected to exceed £150,000 in the next 12 months and with a total turnover (including exempt and non-business income) which is not expected to exceed £187,500 in the next 12 months. A business must leave the scheme if total turnover exceeds £225,000 in a year unless total turnover for the next 12 months is not expected to exceed £187,500.

Administration of VAT

Overall responsibility for the VAT system rests with the Commissioners for Revenue and Customs. The collection of VAT is dealt with by the VAT Central Unit in Southend. The main functions of this unit are:

(a) to maintain registration records
(b) to issue VAT return forms to registered persons and to receive completed returns
(c) to collect VAT due from registered persons and to make repayments of tax where necessary.

There is also a network of local VAT offices which deal with local VAT administration and which may make "control visits" to registered persons in their area. The purpose of a control visit is to check the accuracy of the registered person's VAT returns and to ensure that the VAT system is being operated correctly.

The merger of the Inland Revenue and HM Customs and Excise may result in PAYE and VAT visits being combined.

VAT assessments

VAT is very largely a self-assessed tax and, in the normal course of events, it is not necessary to raise formal tax assessments. However, HM Revenue and Customs may issue such an assessment if a taxable person has failed to make a VAT return or has made an incorrect or incomplete return.

In normal circumstances, assessments may not be raised any later than three years after the end of the tax period to which they relate, but this time limit is extended to twenty years if the taxable person has behaved dishonestly or fraudulently. Any claim for a refund of overpaid tax must also be made within three years.

Appeals

A person who disagrees with a VAT decision made by HMRC may, within 30 days of the date of the document containing the disputed decision, appeal to a VAT tribunal or ask a local VAT office to reconsider the decision. Note that:

(a) Appeals to a tribunal are permitted in relation to a wide variety of matters, but certain matters may not be the subject of an appeal.

(b) A VAT tribunal may award costs to the successful party.

(c) If either HMRC or the person concerned is dissatisfied with a tribunal decision, a dispute on a point of law may be referred to the High Court and beyond.

(d) If the local VAT office is asked to reconsider a decision, it may either confirm the decision (in which case the person concerned has 21 days in which to lodge an appeal with a VAT tribunal) or revise the decision (in which case the person concerned may still wish to appeal to a tribunal and may do so within 30 days).

Avoidance schemes

As from 1 August 2004, businesses with a taxable turnover of £600,000 or more are required to notify HM Revenue and Customs if they make use of certain VAT avoidance schemes listed on a statutory register. Similarly, businesses with a taxable turnover exceeding £10 million are required to notify HMRC if they make use of schemes which bear certain hallmarks of VAT avoidance.

Penalties, surcharges and interest

A wide variety of penalties may be exacted for non-compliance with VAT regulations. The main penalties are as follows:

(a) **Criminal fraud**. A person who attempts to evade VAT in such a way that his or her conduct amounts to criminal fraud may, on a "summary" conviction obtained before a magistrate, be imprisoned for up to six months and/or fined up to £5,000 or three times the amount of tax evaded, whichever is the greater. If the conviction is "on indictment" (obtained before a jury), the maximum term of imprisonment is seven years and there is no limit to the size of any fine.

(b) **Conduct involving dishonesty**. A person who attempts to evade VAT in such a way that his or her conduct involves dishonesty is liable to a maximum penalty of up to 100% of the amount of tax evaded.

(c) **Misdeclaration**. If a VAT return is made which understates the VAT payable (or overstates the VAT repayable) and the amount of tax which would have been lost if the inaccuracy had not been detected is at least:

    (i) 30% of the "gross amount of tax" (the total of input tax and output tax) for the period concerned, or

    (ii) £1,000,000

    whichever is the lower, a penalty may be exacted of up to 15% of the tax which would have been lost.

(d) **Repeated misdeclaration**. HM Revenue and Customs may issue a penalty liability notice to a taxable person if that person has made a "material inaccuracy" in a VAT return. A material inaccuracy is defined as one which, if undiscovered, would have resulted in a loss of tax equal to at least 10% of the gross amount of tax for the period in question or £500,000, whichever is the lower. If the person concerned then makes at least two further material inaccuracies during the penalty period specified in the notice, a penalty may be exacted of up to 15% of the tax which would have been lost.

(e) **Late registration**. A taxable person who fails to notify HMRC of liability to register, or makes late notification, is liable to a penalty. The penalty is calculated as a percentage of the amount of tax due between the date on which registration should have occurred and the date on which notification is eventually made. The percentage is 5% for a delay of up to nine months, 10% for a delay of between nine and 18 months and 15% for a longer delay. The minimum penalty is £50 in all cases.

(f) **Breaches of regulations**. A taxable person who fails to comply with sundry VAT regulations will receive a written warning from HMRC. If non-compliance is continued, the person is liable on a first offence to a penalty of £5 per day until the breach is remedied. The penalty rises to £10 per day on a second offence within a period of two years and to £15 per day on a third or subsequent offence. The maximum penalty which may be exacted is equal to 100 times the daily rate and the minimum penalty is £50.

(g) **Default surcharge**. If a taxable person submits a late VAT return or makes a late payment of the VAT due, then a default has occurred and HMRC will issue a surcharge liability notice specifying a surcharge period. If within this period the person concerned makes a further default, a default surcharge is levied, calculated as the greater of £30 and a percentage of the tax paid late. The surcharge percentage is 2% for the first default within the surcharge period, 5% for the second default, 10% for the third default and 15% for the fourth and any subsequent default. A surcharge period comes to an end only when no defaults have occurred for a continuous 12-month period.

    Automatic late payment penalties for businesses with a turnover not exceeding £150,000 per year have now been removed. Such businesses are initially offered help and advice if they are late with their VAT payments.

In general, penalties may be mitigated (i.e. reduced or not charged at all) if the taxable person has a reasonable excuse for his or her conduct. Penalties may also be mitigated if the person concerned has voluntarily disclosed any non-compliance and has co-operated fully with HM Revenue and Customs.

Interest

"Default interest" is charged on VAT which has been assessed (see above) or which could have been assessed but for the fact that payment was made before an assessment was raised. Such interest runs from the date on which the tax should have been paid to the date of payment. Conversely, if a taxable person makes an overpayment of VAT as a result of an error on the part of HM Revenue and Customs, the person is paid interest on the amount of tax which is subsequently refunded.

Default interest is not charged if the taxable person discloses errors in previous tax returns and the total amount of those errors is £2,000 or less. In these circumstances, the required adjustment can be included in the next VAT return.

Repayment supplement

If a taxable person is entitled to a repayment of VAT for a tax period, this repayment is increased by a "repayment supplement" of 5% (or £50, if greater) so long as:

(a) the return for the relevant tax period is submitted on time, and

(b) the amount stated to be repayable in the return is correct (or differs from the correct figure by no more than 5% or £250, whichever is the greater), and

(c) HMRC fails to issue written instructions for the repayment to be made within 30 days from the *later* of the date on which the return was received and the end of the tax period to which it relates.

Summary

- VAT is normally accounted for quarterly to HM Revenue and Customs but monthly and annual accounting schemes exist.
- The date on which a supply is deemed to occur is known as the "tax point".
- A taxable person may join the cash accounting scheme if certain conditions are satisfied. Members of this scheme account for VAT according to the dates on which payments are received from customers and made to suppliers.
- The input tax suffered in relation to certain types of supply (e.g. business entertaining) is not recoverable.
- A person making a mixture of taxable supplies and exempt supplies is "partially exempt" and may reclaim only part of the input tax suffered.
- Special VAT schemes exist in relation to retailers, small businesses, farmers and second-hand goods.
- The VAT system is administered by HM Revenue and Customs and penalties may be exacted for non-compliance with VAT regulations.

Exercises

30.1 List the required contents of a valid VAT invoice.

30.2 Describe the main features of:

(a) the cash accounting scheme

(b) the annual accounting scheme.

30.3 Calculate the output tax which must be accounted for or the input tax which may be reclaimed by a taxable person in respect of each of the transactions below. All of the amounts shown exclude any VAT which may be applicable.

(a) the purchase of a book for £18.95

(b) the sale for £3,000 of a motor car which had been bought originally for £4,000 (the input tax paid when acquiring the car could not be reclaimed)

(c) the sale of a used commercial building for £200,000.

30.4 Sebastian is self-employed. He drives a 3,000cc petrol-engined car and charges the cost of all the petrol used to his business bank account. In the quarter to 31 March 2006 he drives 3,800 miles on business and 1,400 miles for private purposes. The VAT-inclusive cost of all the petrol bought in the quarter is £792. How should Sebastian deal with petrol in his VAT return for the quarter?

***30.5** During the quarter to 31 August 2005, a taxable person makes the following supplies:

	£
Standard-rated supplies (including VAT)	319,600
Zero-rated supplies	88,000
Exempt supplies	440,000

Input tax for the quarter is £118,000, attributed as follows:

	%
Attributed to taxable supplies	35
Attributed to exempt supplies	40
Unattributed	25

Compute the VAT provisionally payable to or reclaimable from HMRC for the quarter.

***30.6** Tracey is a sole trader. She has the following transactions during the quarter to 30 November 2005 (all amounts shown are VAT-exclusive):

	£
Sales to UK customers:	
Standard-rated	39,400
Zero-rated	12,600
Exports:	
To non-EU members	8,600
To EU members (all customers are VAT registered)	17,300
Purchases:	
Standard-rated	25,800
Zero-rated	6,200
Expenses:	
Wages and salaries	22,450
Car repairs	120
Insurances	260
Entertaining foreign customers	420
Other expenses (all standard-rated)	9,700
Capital transactions:	
Purchase of new plant and machinery	8,000
Purchase of motor van	12,000

Tracey drives a 1,800cc diesel-engined car and charges the cost of all the petrol used, whether for business or private motoring, to her business bank account. Calculate the amount of VAT due for the quarter.

Chapter 31

Inheritance tax

Introduction

This chapter provides a basic introduction to Inheritance tax (IHT). An IHT liability can arise in a number of ways but the events which most commonly trigger such a liability are the transfer of assets on the death of their owner and the gift of assets during the lifetime of their owner.

IHT was introduced in 1986 to replace Capital Transfer Tax. Current IHT legislation is to be found in the Inheritance Tax Act 1984 (originally the Capital Transfer Tax Act 1984) as amended by subsequent Finance Acts.

Chargeable transfers of value

The main situation in which a charge to IHT may arise is when a *transfer of value* of *chargeable property* is made by a *chargeable person*.

Transfers of value

A transfer of value occurs when a person (the "transferor") makes a "disposition" such that his or her estate is lower in value than it was before the disposition occurred. The value of a transfer for IHT purposes is equal to the reduction in the value of the transferor's estate. If the transferor also pays the IHT in relation to the transfer, this further reduces the value of the estate, so that the total value of the transfer is then equal to the amount of the disposition plus the associated IHT.

A disposition is any disposal of property or of an interest in property. The term includes disposals made during the lifetime of the transferor ("lifetime transfers") as well as disposals caused by the death of the transferor. However, certain dispositions are *not* regarded as transfers of value for IHT purposes. The most important exemptions are:

(a) dispositions without gratuitous intent (e.g. genuine commercial transactions which give rise to a loss and therefore a reduction in the value of the transferor's estate)

(b) dispositions made for the maintenance of the transferor's family, including spouses, children and dependant relatives

(c) gratuitous dispositions which constitute allowable expenditure for the purposes of income tax and corporation tax (e.g. payments made by an employer into a pension fund for the benefit of employees)

(d) dispositions caused by the fact that the transferor has been killed whilst on active service.

Chargeable property

All property is chargeable property unless specifically excluded from charge. The main exclusions are:

(a) property which is situated outside the UK and which is owned by a person who is domiciled outside the UK (i.e. a person whose permanent home is situated outside the UK)

(b) reversionary interests in a trust or settlement unless acquired for a consideration (see later in this chapter).

Chargeable persons

An individual who is domiciled in the UK (i.e. an individual whose permanent home is in the UK) is a chargeable person and is liable to IHT in relation to all of his or her chargeable property, wherever in the world that property is situated. An individual who is not domiciled in the UK is liable to IHT only in relation to property situated in the UK. Note the following points:

(a) Husbands and wives are assessed to IHT independently.

(b) A partnership is not a chargeable person. The assets of a partnership are owned by the partners and each partner is liable to IHT in relation to his or her share of those assets.

(c) A company is not a chargeable person and cannot incur an IHT liability. But the participators of a close company (see Chapter 27) may incur an IHT liability in relation to transfers of value made by that company.

(d) The life tenants of an interest in possession trust (see later in this chapter) are regarded for IHT purposes as owning the assets of the trust, divided between them in proportion to their interests. The trust itself is not a chargeable person.

Exempt transfers

Certain transfers are wholly exempt from IHT. In other cases, an exemption may serve to reduce the value of a transfer for IHT purposes. The main exemptions are:

(a) business and agricultural property reliefs (see later in this chapter)

(b) exemptions for transfers made to certain transferees (see below)

(c) exemptions available to the transferor (see below).

If more than one type of exemption applies to a given transfer, the exemptions should be applied in the order given above.

Exemptions for transfers made to certain transferees

The following transfers are wholly exempt from IHT whether made on death or during the lifetime of the transferor:

(a) transfers to the transferor's spouse (i.e. husband or wife)

(b) as from 5 December 2005, transfers to the transferor's same-sex civil partner (if the couple have entered into a legally-recognised civil partnership)

(c) transfers to charities, community amateur sports clubs or political parties

(d) transfers made for national purposes to certain national bodies (e.g. museums, libraries, art galleries etc.)

(e) transfers of eligible property made for the public benefit to a non-profit making body, so long as this body undertakes to maintain and preserve the property and provide reasonable public access to it.

In the case of transfers between spouses, there is no requirement that the husband and wife should live together, only that the marriage should be valid under UK law. This exemption ceases when the marriage is dissolved by a decree absolute.

Exemptions available to the transferor

The following exemptions are available in relation to lifetime transfers only:

(a) **Small gifts**. Gifts to individuals with a value of up to £250 per transferee per tax year (6 April to 5 April) are wholly exempt from IHT. This exemption cannot be used to exempt part of a gift which has a value exceeding £250.

(b) **Normal expenditure out of income**. Transfers which consist of "normal expenditure out of income" (e.g. birthday and Christmas presents) are wholly exempt from IHT. In order for a transfer to benefit from this exemption, HM Revenue and Customs must believe that the transfer:

    (i) is part of the normal expenditure of the transferor, and

    (ii) is made out of income rather than capital, and

(iii) leaves the transferor sufficient income to maintain his or her usual standard of living.

(c) **Gifts in consideration of marriage**. Gifts made by a transferor to a bride or bridegroom in consideration of their marriage are exempt from IHT up to the following limits:

(i) £5,000 if made by a parent of the bride or groom

(ii) £2,500 if made by the grandparent or remoter ancestor of the bride or groom

(iii) £2,500 if made by the bride to the groom or vice versa

(iv) £1,000 in any other case.

The above exemptions are per transferor per marriage and can be used to exempt part of the value of larger gifts.

(d) **Annual exemption**. The first £3,000 of lifetime transfers made in any tax year is exempt from IHT. Note that:

(i) If the total of the lifetime transfers made in a tax year exceeds £3,000, the exemption is set against the year's transfers in chronological order.

(ii) Any unused part of the annual exemption may be carried forward to the following tax year (but no further) and set against the excess of that year's lifetime transfers over that year's annual exemption.

(iii) It is HM Revenue and Customs practice to set the annual exemption against potentially exempt transfers (see below) as well as chargeable lifetime transfers, even though potentially exempt transfers may never become chargeable to inheritance tax. There is some doubt as to whether this practice is statutorily correct but it has been followed in this book.

EXAMPLE 1

Tania makes no transfers during 2003/04. Her only transfers during 2004/05 and 2005/06 are as follows:

		£
2004/05		
June 2004	Gift to her son on his marriage	6,000
October 2004	Gift to her granddaughter	4,500
January 2005	Gift to Oxfam	10,000
March 2005	Gift to a friend	100
2005/06		
July 2005	Gift to her nephew	1,000
August 2005	Gift to her cousin	3,500

Calculate the value of each of the above transfers after deduction of all the relevant exemptions. None of the gifts are regarded as normal expenditure out of income.

Solution

(AE = Annual exemption)

	Value before AE	*AE for current year*	*AE for previous year*	*Value after AE*
	£	£	£	£
2004/05				
Gift to son on marriage (£6,000 - £5,000)	1,000	1,000	-	-
Gift to granddaughter	4,500	2,000	2,500	-
Gift to charity (exempt)	-	-	-	-
Gift to friend (exempt as a small gift)	-	-	-	-
	5,500	3,000	2,500	-
2005/06				
Gift to nephew	1,000	1,000		-
Gift to cousin	3,500	2,000		1,500
	4,500	3,000		1,500

Note:

£500 of the 2003/04 annual exemption remains unused but cannot be carried forward beyond 2004/05. The 2004/05 and 2005/06 annual exemptions are fully utilised.

Potentially exempt transfers (PETs)

If a lifetime transfer has not been wholly exempted from IHT as a result of the various exemptions described above, the transfer will be either a "chargeable lifetime transfer" or a "potentially exempt transfer". A chargeable lifetime transfer is charged to IHT immediately. A potentially exempt transfer (PET) is charged to IHT only if the transferor dies within seven years of the date of the transfer. A potentially exempt transfer is a lifetime transfer which is made by an individual to any of the following:

(a) another individual

(b) a trust with an interest in possession

(c) an accumulation and maintenance trust

(d) a trust which is for the benefit of a person who is physically or mentally handicapped.

Most lifetime transfers are in fact PETs. The main example of a chargeable lifetime transfer is a transfer made to a discretionary trust.

Types of trust

The above definition of a PET makes reference to various types of trust. These were introduced briefly in Chapter 6 but are explained again below:

(a) A trust (or settlement) is an arrangement whereby property is held by persons known as trustees for the benefit of other persons known as beneficiaries.

(b) If one or more persons are entitled to the lifetime use of the trust property or to the income generated by the trust property, those persons are "life tenants" and the trust is a "trust with an interest in possession". A person whose interest will not take effect until some future event occurs (e.g. the death of a life tenant) is said to have a "reversionary interest".

(c) A trust with no interest in possession is known as a "discretionary trust". The trustees of such a trust have the discretion to distribute as much or as little of the trust income to the beneficiaries as they see fit.

(d) An accumulation and maintenance trust is a special instance of a discretionary trust, where the trustees may choose whether to accumulate the trust income or to pay it out for the maintenance of the beneficiaries, who must be under 25 years old.

EXAMPLE 2

Consider each of the following transfers (assuming in each case that the annual exemption for both the current year and the previous year have been set against earlier transfers) and classify each one as either an exempt transfer, a PET or a chargeable lifetime transfer.

(a) a gift of £10,000 made by a husband to his wife

(b) a gift of £20,000 made by a mother to her son on his marriage

(c) a gift of £50,000 made to a trust with an interest in possession

(d) a gift of £100,000 made to a discretionary trust.

Solution

(a) wholly exempt (transfers between spouses are not chargeable)

(b) exempt £5,000 (made in consideration of marriage); PET £15,000

(c) PET

(d) chargeable lifetime transfer.

IHT payable on chargeable lifetime transfers

The amount of IHT payable on a chargeable lifetime transfer depends upon:

(a) the value of the transfer (less any relevant exemptions), which must be grossed-up if the tax is paid by the transferor

(b) the rates of IHT in force on the date of the transfer

(c) the total (including the current transfer) of the gross chargeable lifetime transfers made during the seven years ending on the date of the current transfer.

Grossing-up

IHT is chargeable on the *gross* value of a transfer. This is the reduction in the value of the transferor's estate which the transfer has caused. If the transferee pays the tax due on a transfer, the gross value of the transfer is simply the amount received by the transferee (less any exemptions). However, if the tax due is paid by the transferor, the amount received by the transferee (less exemptions) is only the net value of the transfer and this must be grossed-up at the appropriate rates to find the gross value.

In general, any capital gains tax payable by the transferor in relation to the transfer is ignored when calculating the reduction in value of the transferor's estate.

Rates of IHT applicable to chargeable lifetime transfers

The rates of IHT applicable to chargeable lifetime transfers made on or after 6 April 2005 are as follows:

Gross chargeable lifetime transfers for the seven years to date	*Rate of tax*	*Grossing-up fraction*
first £275,000	0%	nil
remainder after the first £275,000	20%	100/80

The rates of tax have been 0% and 20% for many years but the threshold beyond which 20% tax is payable is usually increased in each tax year. Recent values of the threshold have been:

Date of transfer	£
6 April 1998 to 5 April 1999	223,000
6 April 1999 to 5 April 2000	231,000
6 April 2000 to 5 April 2001	234,000
6 April 2001 to 5 April 2002	242,000
6 April 2002 to 5 April 2003	250,000
6 April 2003 to 5 April 2004	255,000
6 April 2004 to 5 April 2005	263,000

It has been announced that the IHT threshold will rise to £285,000 for tax year 2006/07 and to £300,000 for 2007/08.

For each transfer, the calculation of the tax due involves the following steps:

(a) The total gross value of previous chargeable lifetime transfers made during the seven years to date is brought forward.

(b) If the total brought forward has utilised the whole of the 0% band, tax is due at 20% on the gross value of the current transfer.

(c) If the total brought forward has not utilised the whole of the 0% band, the balance of the 0% band is set against the current transfer. If this does not absorb the whole of the transfer, tax is due at 20% on the gross value of the remainder.

EXAMPLE 3

On 1 July 2005, Violet makes a chargeable lifetime transfer (after deduction of relevant exemptions) of £48,000. Her only previous chargeable lifetime transfer was made in 2001 and had a gross value of £233,000. Calculate the IHT due if:

(a) the transferee agrees to pay the tax due
(b) the tax due is paid by Violet.

Solution

The total of transfers brought forward is £233,000, leaving £42,000 of the nil band to set against the current transfer.

(a) If the transferee pays the tax, the gross value of the transfer is £48,000 and the IHT due is £42,000 @ 0% + £6,000 @ 20% = £1,200.

(b) If Violet pays the tax, the net value of the transfer is £48,000. The gross value and the tax due are calculated as follows:

	Net	*Gross*	*Tax*
	£	£	£
£42,000 grossed up @ 0%	42,000	42,000	0
£6,000 grossed up @ 20%	6,000	7,500	1,500
Totals	48,000	49,500	1,500

The gross value of the transfer is £49,500 and the tax due is £1,500. The total of gross transfers for the seven years to 1 July 2005 is now £282,500.

IHT payable on death

The IHT payable on death consists of:

(a) additional tax on any chargeable lifetime transfers made by the deceased person during the seven years ending on the date of death

(b) tax on any PETs made by the deceased person during the seven years ending on the date of death

(c) tax on the estate of the deceased person as at the date of death, to the extent that the transfers made on death are not exempt from IHT.

Tax on chargeable lifetime transfers and PETs

The tax payable on death in respect of the chargeable lifetime transfers and PETs made in the seven years ending on the date of death is calculated as follows:

(a) The transfers are considered in chronological order with no distinction made between chargeable lifetime transfers and PETs.

(b) The gross value of each chargeable lifetime transfer remains as previously calculated. The gross value of a PET is the amount received by the transferee, less any relevant exemptions.

(c) Tax is recalculated on the gross value of each transfer using the IHT bands and rates in force *on the date of death* and taking into account any other chargeable transfers made in the seven years ending on the date of the transfer. The tax rates used are those applicable to transfers on death, *not* those used for chargeable lifetime transfers. For deaths occurring on or after 6 April 2005 the applicable rates are as follows:

Gross chargeable transfers for the seven years to date	*Rate of tax*
first £275,000	0%
remainder after the first £275,000	40%

(d) The tax calculated at (c) for each transfer may then be reduced by *taper relief*, depending upon the number of years which have elapsed between the date of the transfer and the date of death. Taper relief is given as follows:

Period between transfer and death	*Percentage tax reduction*
3 years or less	0%
Over 3 but not more than 4 years	20%
Over 4 but not more than 5 years	40%
Over 5 but not more than 6 years	60%
Over 6 but not more than 7 years	80%

(e) Finally, for each transfer, any tax paid during the lifetime of the transferor is subtracted, leaving a balance of tax due on that transfer. This tax liability is the responsibility of the transferee. If the lifetime tax paid in relation to a transfer exceeds the liability on death, no further tax is due on that transfer but no repayment is given.

EXAMPLE 4

Wilson dies on 20 December 2005, having made only the following transfers during his lifetime:

		£
6 June 1995	Gift to daughter	50,000
4 May 2001	Gift to discretionary trust	443,000
11 June 2002	Gift to son on marriage	50,000

Calculate the IHT payable during Wilson's lifetime (if any) in relation to each of the above transfers, assuming that Wilson paid this tax himself. Also calculate the further IHT payable (if any) on Wilson's death.

Solution

The value of each gift after deduction of exemptions is as follows:

		Value before AE	*AE for current year*	*AE for previous year*	*Value after AE*
		£	£	£	£
1995/96	Daughter	50,000	3,000	3,000	44,000
2001/02	Discretionary trust	443,000	3,000	3,000	437,000
2002/03	Son (£50,000 - £5,000)	45,000	3,000	-	42,000

Lifetime tax liability

The gifts to Wilson's son and daughter were PETs and gave rise to no immediate tax liability but the gift to the discretionary trust was a chargeable lifetime transfer. There were no other such transfers during the seven years to date so the whole of the 0% band (£242,000 at that time) was set against the gift. The tax due was £48,750, calculated as follows:

	Net	*Gross*	*Tax*
	£	£	£
£242,000 grossed up @ 0%	242,000	242,000	0
£195,000 grossed up @ 20%	195,000	243,750	48,750
Totals	437,000	485,750	48,750

Tax liability on death

The June 1995 PET is more than seven years old at the time of Wilson's death. This PET is exempt from tax and can be completely ignored for IHT purposes. The tax due on the other two transfers is calculated as follows:

(i) *Transfer made on 4 May 2001*

The gross value of this transfer is £485,750 and there were no other chargeable transfers in the seven years to date (5 May 1994 to 4 May 2001). The tax due at the death rates applicable on 20 December 2005 is:

	£
£275,000 @ 0%	0
£210,750 @ 40%	84,300
	84,300
Less: Taper relief (4-5 years) @ 40%	33,720
	50,580
Less: Lifetime tax paid	48,750
IHT payable by transferee	1,830

(ii) *Transfer made on 11 June 2002*

The gross value of this transfer is £42,000. Previous gross chargeable transfers in the seven years to date (12 June 1995 to 11 June 2002) were £485,750, completely absorbing the 0% band. The tax due at the death rates applicable on 20 December 2005 is:

	£
£42,000 @ 40%	16,800
Less: Taper relief (3-4 years) @ 20%	3,360
	13,440
Less: Lifetime tax paid	0
IHT payable by transferee	13,440

Tax on the deceased person's estate

IHT on the deceased person's estate (to the extent that the transfers made on death are not exempt from IHT) is calculated using the rates of tax applicable on death. The calculation proceeds as follows:

(a) First, the 0% band is reduced by the total of gross chargeable transfers made in the seven years ending on the date of death, including any PETs made during that period.

(b) The remainder of the 0% band (if any) is then set against the value of the estate and tax at 40% is calculated on the balance.

(c) The tax due is divided by the value of the estate and the result (expressed as a percentage) is the "estate rate" i.e. the average rate of tax borne by the estate.

EXAMPLE 5

Toby dies on 2 March 2006, leaving an estate valued at £400,000. None of the transfers made on death are exempt from IHT. Calculate the IHT due on the estate if the total of the gross chargeable transfers made by Toby in the seven years up to his death was:

(a) Nil (b) £95,000 (c) £285,000.

Solution

(a) £275,000 @ 0% + £125,000 @ 40% = £50,000. (Estate rate 12.5%).

(b) £180,000 @ 0% + £220,000 @ 40% = £88,000. (Estate rate 22%).

(c) £400,000 @ 40% = £160,000. (Estate rate 40%).

Quick succession relief

Quick succession relief (QSR) is available when property which is transferred on death was transferred to the deceased person within the previous five years and was charged to IHT at that time. The tax (if any) payable in relation to the transfer made on death is reduced by an amount which depends upon the value of the earlier transfer and the amount of IHT paid on that transfer. The relief is calculated as:

$$\frac{\text{net value of earlier transfer}}{\text{gross value of earlier transfer}} \times \text{IHT paid on earlier transfer} \times \text{QSR\%}$$

The QSR percentage depends upon the date of the earlier transfer, as follows:

Period between earlier transfer and death	*QSR percentage*
1 year or less	100%
Over 1 but not more than 2 years	80%
Over 2 but not more than 3 years	60%
Over 3 but not more than 4 years	40%
Over 4 but not more than 5 years	20%

Valuation

As stated at the beginning of this chapter, the value of a transfer for IHT purposes is equal to the reduction in value of the transferor's estate as a result of that transfer. In general, this is equivalent to the open market value of the transferred assets on the date of the transfer but it should not be assumed that this will always be the case. For instance, if the transferor disposes of:

(a) a single item from a matching set of such items, or

(b) a small number of shares in a company, sufficient to convert a majority shareholding into a minority shareholding

it is likely that the true reduction in value of the transferor's estate (and therefore the value of the transfer for IHT purposes) will exceed the market value of the transferred assets. This caveat aside, determining the market value of the transferred assets may in itself cause difficulty and special valuation rules are sometimes required. The most important of these rules are described below.

Listed shares

Shares which are listed on a recognised stock exchange (referred to as "listed shares" or "quoted shares") are valued at the *lower* of:

(a) the lower of the two prices quoted for those shares on the day of the transfer, plus one-quarter of the difference between these two prices (the "quarter-up" rule)

(b) the average of the highest and lowest prices at which bargains have been marked on that day (if any).

If listed shares are transferred on a non-working day (for which prices are unavailable) the shares are valued as if transferred on the last working day before the date of the transfer or the first working day after it, whichever gives the lower figure.

Units in a unit trust are valued at the bid price (i.e. the buying price quoted by the trust manager) for the day of the transfer. If this is a non-working day, the bid price for the last working day before the date of the transfer is used.

EXAMPLE 6

On 1 June 2005, Shirley gives 5,000 shares in Listed plc to her daughter. The shares are quoted at 189 - 197 on that day, with bargains marked at 190, 192 and 196 (all quoted prices are in pence). Calculate the market value of the shares for IHT purposes.

Solution

The quarter-up rule gives 189 + 1/4 x (197 - 189) = 191. The average of the highest and lowest marked bargains is 193, so the shares are valued at 191p and the transfer has a market value of 5,000 x £1.91 = £9,550.

Overseas property

Property situated outside the UK is valued in the appropriate foreign currency. This value is then converted into sterling, using the exchange rate for the day of the transfer which gives the lowest sterling value.

Related property

When calculating the value of a transfer for IHT purposes, the existence of any "related property" may be taken into account. Related property consists of property which:

(a) is owned by the transferor's spouse or (as from 5 December 2005) by his or her same-sex civil partner, or

(b) is owned (or has been owned within the previous five years) by a charity, political party etc. as a result of an exempt transfer made by either spouse or partner.

Under the related property rules, the property being transferred and the related property are valued together (as a whole) and then part of that value is apportioned to the property being transferred. These rules are intended to prevent taxpayers from avoiding IHT by fragmenting the ownership of an asset and will only be used if the valuation given by the related property rules is greater than the valuation that would have been calculated normally.

EXAMPLE 7

Roy owns 3,500 ordinary shares in R Ltd, an unlisted company which has an issued share capital of 10,000 ordinary shares. Roy's wife owns a further 1,600 shares. Shareholdings in R Ltd are valued as follows:

	£		£
500 shares	5,000	4,600 shares	64,400
3,000 shares	33,000	5,100 shares	96,900
3,500 shares	43,750		

Roy now transfers 500 of his shares to a discretionary trust. Calculate the value of this transfer for IHT purposes.

Solution

Ignoring related property, Roy's estate has reduced in value by £10,750 (£43,750 - £33,000) and this would normally be the value of the transfer. But taking related property into account, the value of the transfer is calculated as follows:

	£
Value of Roy's holding before the transfer (£96,900 x 3,500/5,100)	66,500
Value of Roy's holding after the transfer (£64,400 x 3,000/4,600)	42,000
Value of the transfer	24,500

Since £24,500 exceeds £10,750, the value of the transfer is £24,500.

Business property relief

Business property relief of either 100% or 50% is available in relation to a transfer which meets *all* of the following conditions:

(a) the property transferred consists of "relevant business property"

(b) the business concerned is a "qualifying business" (non-profit making businesses and investment businesses do not qualify)

(c) the property has been owned by the transferor for at least two years, or has replaced other relevant business property, such that the combined period of ownership of both the original and replacement property is at least two years out of the five years preceding the date of the transfer.

The main categories of relevant business property, together with the applicable rates of relief, are as follows:

		Rate of relief
(a)	Property consisting of a business or an interest in a business (e.g. a share in a partnership)	100%
(b)	Securities in an unlisted company which (either by themselves or with other such securities or unlisted shares) gave the transferor control of the company immediately before the transfer	100%
(c)	Shares in an unlisted company	100%
(d)	Shares transferred from a controlling holding in a listed company	50%
(e)	Land, buildings, plant and machinery which, immediately before the transfer, were used for business purposes by a partnership in which the transferor was a partner or by a company of which he/she had control	50%
(f)	Land, buildings, plant and machinery which, immediately before the transfer, were used in the transferor's business and owned by a trust of which the transferor was a life tenant.	50%

No relief is given in relation to "excepted assets". These are assets which have not been used for business purposes throughout the two years prior to the transfer (or since they were acquired, if within the last two years) and which are not required for the future use of the business.

Agricultural property relief

Agricultural property relief of either 100% or 50% is available in relation to a transfer of agricultural property so long as that property has been either:

(a) occupied by the transferor and used for agricultural purposes throughout the two years preceding the transfer, or

(b) owned by the transferor throughout the seven years preceding the transfer and occupied by the transferor or someone else for agricultural purposes throughout those seven years.

For this purpose, agricultural property consists mainly of agricultural land and pasture, woodlands and associated buildings. Land managed according to the terms of certain wildlife habitat schemes (together with associated buildings) is also eligible for agricultural property relief. The rates of relief are:

(a) 100% if, immediately before the transfer, the transferor enjoys vacant possession of the property or the right to obtain it within the following 12 months (extended by extra-statutory concession to 24 months in certain cases)

(b) Otherwise, 100% if the property is let on a tenancy starting after 31 August 1995 and 50% if the property is let on a tenancy starting before 1 September 1995.

These rates apply only to the "agricultural value" of the property. This is the value that the property would have if it could only ever be used for agricultural purposes. No relief is available in respect of any extra value that the property might have by virtue of its development potential. If a property qualifies for both business property relief and agricultural property relief, agricultural property relief is given first.

Administration of IHT

Inheritance tax is administered by the Capital Taxes Office (CTO) of HM Revenue and Customs. For chargeable lifetime transfers and transfers caused by the death of the transferor, an "account" must be delivered to this office, giving details of the transfers made and their value. Details of this procedure are as follows:

(a) **Chargeable lifetime transfers**. The transferor must deliver an account to the CTO within 12 months of the end of the month in which the transfer occurred. There is no requirement to deliver an account if the transfer is exempt or potentially exempt, or if the total value of transfers for the tax year to date does not exceed £10,000 and the total for the seven years to date does not exceed £40,000.

(b) **Death**. The personal representatives of a deceased person must deliver an account to the CTO within 12 months of the end of the month in which the death occurred. However, if the deceased person was domiciled in the UK there is no requirement to deliver an account so long as:

   (i) the gross value of the estate does not exceed £240,000, and

   (ii) no more than £75,000 of the estate is situated outside the UK, and

   (iii) any trust assets in which the deceased person had an interest in possession were held in a single trust and do not exceed £100,000 in value, and

   (iv) there have been no chargeable lifetime transfers (or PETs) made within the seven years to date, other than transfers consisting of cash, listed shares, listed securities or land and buildings (and contents) with a total gross value not exceeding £100,000.

   If the deceased person was domiciled outside the UK and had never been domiciled in the UK, an account is not required so long as the value of UK assets transferred on death does not exceed £100,000 and these assets consist solely of cash, listed shares or listed securities.

When a transfer gives rise to an IHT liability, the CTO issues a notice showing the value of the transfer for IHT purposes and the amount of IHT payable. Appeals in writing, stating the grounds for the appeal, may be lodged within 30 days of the date of the notice. Such appeals are normally heard in the first instance by the Special Commissioners but may progress to the courts.

Payment of IHT

The IHT relating to a transfer is usually payable six months after the end of the month in which the transfer (or death) occurred. However, the tax on chargeable lifetime transfers made in roughly the first half of the tax year (6 April to 30 September) is not payable until 30 April in the following tax year.

It is notable that the tax on a transfer is usually due for payment well before the end of the 12-month period within which an account of the transfer must be delivered to the CTO. Since interest is charged on tax paid late, there is an incentive to deliver the account (and pay the tax due) on or before the due date of payment.

Summary

- The main occasion on which IHT is charged is when a transfer of value of chargeable property is made by a chargeable person. A transfer may be a lifetime transfer or a transfer made on death.
- The value of a transfer is equal to the reduction in value of the transferor's estate as a result of the transfer. The value of a transfer for IHT purposes may be reduced by business property relief and/or agricultural property relief.
- Transfers made to certain transferees (e.g. spouses, civil partners, charities, and political parties) are exempt from IHT.
- Lifetime transfers comprising small gifts, gifts made out of income and gifts made on consideration of marriage are wholly or partly exempt from IHT. The first £3,000 of lifetime transfers made in any tax year is exempt from IHT.
- A potentially exempt transfer (PET) is not chargeable to IHT unless the transferor dies within seven years.
- The IHT on a transfer is normally payable six months after the end of the month in which the transfer took place.

Exercises

31.1 Phoebe made the following transfers during 2005/06:

		£
12 April 2005	Gift to grandson	50
17 May 2005	Gift to her nephew on his marriage	3,000
3 August 2005	Gift to her husband	25,000
31 October 2005	Gift to a discretionary trust	10,000
1 January 2006	Gift to the Labour Party	5,000

None of the gifts are regarded as normal expenditure out of income. Phoebe made no transfers at all during 2004/05. Calculate the value of each of her 2005/06 transfers after deduction of all the available exemptions.

31.2 Classify each of the following lifetime transfers as either exempt, potentially exempt, or chargeable:

(a) a gift to an accumulation and maintenance trust

(b) a gift to the transferor's favourite charity

(c) a gift to a discretionary trust

(d) a gift to the transferor's grandfather

(e) a gift to a trust with an interest in possession.

31.3 On 5 December 2005, Nicholas makes a gift of £80,000 (after deduction of all relevant exemptions) to a discretionary trust. His only previous chargeable lifetime transfers were in June 1996 (gross chargeable value £200,000) and July 2000 (gross chargeable value £231,000). Calculate the IHT payable and state the due date of payment:

(a) if the trustees pay the tax (b) if Nicholas pays the tax.

31.4 On 31 August 2000, Martha gave £500,000 to her daughter as a wedding present. On 1 June 2004 she gave a further £500,000 to a discretionary trust. Martha died on 1 January 2006, having made only these two transfers during her life.

(a) Calculate any lifetime tax due on each of the above transfers and state the due date of payment, assuming that Martha paid this tax herself.

(b) Calculate any further tax due on Martha's death in relation to these transfers and state the due date of payment.

31.5 On 29 June 2005, Hyacinth makes a transfer consisting of 1,000 shares in a listed company. The shares are quoted at 572 - 588 on that day, with bargains marked at 572, 577 and 578. Calculate the market value of the transfer for IHT purposes.

***31.6** On 12 November 1995, Hazel made a gross chargeable transfer to a discretionary trust of £216,000. On 1 April 2001 she gave £300,000 to her grandson. These were her only transfers. She died on 17 December 2005. Calculate the tax payable by her grandson as a result of Hazel's death.

***31.7** Tony died on 11 July 2005, leaving an estate valued at £500,000. None of the transfers made on his death were exempt from IHT. He had made the following transfers during his lifetime:

		£
3 May 1997	Gift to discretionary trust (tax paid by trustees)	100,000
1 July 1998	Gift to daughter	250,000
1 August 1998	Gift to son	250,000
10 June 2002	Gift to discretionary trust (tax paid by Tony)	450,000

Calculate the tax payable as a result of Tony's death.

Chapter 32

Overseas aspects of taxation

Introduction

The main purpose of this final chapter is to consider the way in which the UK tax system deals with the overseas income and gains of UK resident individuals and companies. The treatment of non-residents with income or gains arising in the UK is also briefly considered.

The chapter begins by explaining the factors which affect an individual's UK tax status and then continues with a brief review of the overseas aspects of income tax, capital gains tax and inheritance tax. The UK tax status of companies and overseas aspects of corporation tax are dealt with towards the end of the chapter.

Residence, ordinary residence and domicile

The extent to which an individual is chargeable to UK tax depends entirely upon that individual's *residence*, *ordinary residence* and *domicile*. These key concepts are explained below. It should be noted that an individual's nationality is usually *not* an important factor when determining that individual's UK tax status.

Residence

The term "residence" is not clearly defined in statute law and therefore the meaning of the term has evolved from case law. The main circumstances in which an individual is normally deemed to be UK resident are as follows:

(a) An individual who is physically present in the UK for at least 183 days during a tax year (excluding days of arrival or departure) is deemed to be resident in the UK for the whole of that tax year.

(b) An individual who is in the habit of making regular visits to the UK averaging at least 91 days per tax year (excluding days spent in the UK because of circumstances beyond the individual's control, such as illness) is usually regarded as UK resident. Two situations are possible:

(i) An ex-resident who has now left the UK but who makes regular visits as described above is deemed to be UK resident for the whole of each tax year during which the visits continue.

(ii) An individual who was not previously a UK resident but who begins making regular visits as described above is normally deemed to be UK resident with effect from the fifth year of the visits. However, if it is clear from the outset that the visits are going to be regular, the individual may be regarded as UK resident with effect from the first year of the visits.

It is important to appreciate that the concept of UK residence normally applies to *whole* tax years. An individual is deemed to be UK resident for the whole of a tax year or for none of it and it is not usually possible to apportion a tax year into periods of residence and non-residence. The significance of this will become clear when the tax implications of residence and non-residence are described (see below). However, such apportionment is permitted in the following cases:

(a) in the year of arrival, if an individual takes up permanent residence in the UK or comes to stay in the UK for at least two years

(b) in the year of departure, if an individual leaves the UK in order to take up permanent residence abroad or to live abroad for at least three years

(c) in the years of departure and return, if an individual leaves the UK in order to take up employment abroad under a contract of employment for at least a whole tax year (in which case the individual concerned is normally regarded as being non-resident throughout the period of the contract, so long as UK visits during that period do not exceed 183 days in any one tax year or 91 days per year on average).

If a tax year is apportioned into periods of residence and non-residence, personal allowances are available in full for that year.

Ordinary residence

The term "ordinary residence" is also without a statutory definition. In general terms, an individual is ordinarily resident in the UK if he or she is habitually UK resident (i.e. resident year after year). In a given tax year, it is quite possible to be resident but not ordinarily resident, or vice versa.

An individual who is ordinarily resident in the UK but who is temporarily abroad during a particular tax year (i.e. not present for at least 183 days but not absent for the entire tax year) is deemed to be resident in the UK for the whole of that tax year.

EXAMPLE 1

(a) Pierre, who has lived in France for the whole of his life, arrives in the UK on 1 May 2005 and remains until 31 March 2006, when he returns permanently to France. What is his UK residence status for 2005/06?

(b) Peter, who has lived in the UK for the whole of his life, leaves the UK on 1 May 2005 and returns permanently on 31 March 2006. What is his UK residence status for 2005/06?

(c) Petra, who has lived in the UK for the whole of her life, leaves the UK on 1 April 2005 and returns permanently on 30 April 2006. She makes no visits to the UK during her time abroad. What is her UK residence status for 2005/06?

Solution

(a) Pierre is *resident* in 2005/06 (spending at least 183 days in the UK during the year) but he is *not ordinarily resident.*

(b) Peter does not spend at least 183 days in the UK during 2005/06. However, he does spend at least some time in the UK during the year and he is *ordinarily resident.* Therefore he is also *resident* for the year.

(c) Petra is *ordinarily resident.* However, she is absent from the UK for the whole of 2005/06 and therefore she is *not resident* for that year.

Domicile

An individual's domicile is the country in which the individual has his or her permanent home. It is not possible to have more than one domicile at a time.

Individuals acquire a "domicile of origin" on birth. This is usually the domicile of the father or other person on whom the individual is dependent and is not necessarily the country of birth. Having reached the age of 16, an individual may then change domicile and acquire a "domicile of choice", but such a domicile can only be acquired by settling in the chosen country.

If an individual acquires a domicile of choice, that domicile is also acquired by anyone under the age of 16 who is dependent on that individual. A domicile acquired in this way is known as a "domicile of dependency".

Income tax - general rules

The general rules governing an individual's liability to UK income tax are as follows:

(a) Individuals who are *resident* in the UK for a tax year are liable to pay UK income tax on all of their income for that year, including both UK income and overseas income. Note that:

   (i) Overseas employment income is taxed in accordance with the rules of ITEPA 2003 (see below). Overseas trading income, property income and investment income are taxed by ITTOIA 2005 (see below).

   (ii) ITTOIA 2005 provides that the "relevant foreign income" of a UK resident who is not domiciled in the UK or who is not ordinarily resident in the UK may be taxed only to the extent that the income is remitted to the UK, so long as the taxpayer concerned makes a claim to this effect. This is known as the "remittance basis". The term "relevant foreign income" covers most of the forms of overseas income to which ITTOIA 2005 applies.

   (iii) Personal allowances may be claimed by UK residents.

(b) Individuals who are *not resident* in the UK are liable to pay UK income tax on their UK income only. Note that:

   (i) The property income of non-residents is usually payable after deduction of basic rate income tax by the letting agent or tenant.

   (ii) Personal allowances may be claimed by certain non-residents, principally those who are citizens of either the European Economic Area or the Commonwealth (see Chapter 3).

(c) If a tax year is apportioned into periods of residence and non-residence, the above rules apply to the two periods as if they were separate tax years.

These general rules are subject to a number of exceptions, depending upon the type of income involved (see below).

Unremittable income

A UK resident who would normally be liable to income tax on income arising from an overseas source may make a claim to the effect that the income is "unremittable". Such a claim may be made if the income cannot be remitted to the UK because of:

(a) the laws of the country in which the income arises, or

(b) the executive actions of the government of that country, or

(c) the impossibility of obtaining foreign currency in that country which could be transferred to the UK.

Th effect of the claim is that the income is not taxed in the year in which it arises but is taxed instead in the year in which it ceases to be unremittable (if that occurs).

Double taxation relief (DTR)

The rules given above are likely to lead to a number of situations in which income is taxed twice. For example, the overseas income of a UK resident will be taxed in the UK and might also be taxed in the country in which the income arises, depending upon that country's taxation laws. Similarly, the UK income of a non-resident will be taxed in the UK and might also be taxed overseas. In order to avoid this situation, the UK has made "double taxation treaties" with many overseas countries. Typically, such a treaty might provide that certain forms of income should be exempt from income tax in the country of origin (or charged at a reduced rate) if receivable by a non-resident.

Unilateral double tax relief

Unless overridden by a double taxation treaty with the country from which a UK resident receives overseas income, the UK tax system provides "unilateral double tax relief" for any foreign tax which has been suffered. Overseas income received net of foreign tax is grossed-up and charged to UK income tax in the usual way, but the taxpayer is then given tax relief equal to the *lower* of:

(a) the amount of foreign tax suffered (the "withholding tax") and

(b) the amount of UK tax due on the overseas income.

The amount of UK tax due on the overseas income is equal to the difference between the tax due on the taxpayer's total income (including overseas income) and the tax which would be due if the overseas income were ignored. If the foreign tax suffered exceeds the UK tax due, part of the foreign tax suffered will be unrelieved.

Unilateral relief is available only if the taxpayer has taken all reasonable steps to minimise the amount of the foreign tax liability.

EXAMPLE 2

Vicky's income for 2005/06 consists of her salary from UK employment of £37,550 and rents from overseas property (net of 30% withholding tax) of £3,500. Vicky is UK resident in 2005/06. Calculate her UK income tax liability for the year.

Solution

	£
Employment income	37,550
Property income (£3,500 x 100/70)	5,000
	42,550
Less: Personal allowance	4,895
Taxable income	37,655

		£
Income tax		
2,090	@ 10%	209.00
30,310	@ 22%	6,668.20
5,255	@ 40%	2,102.00
37,655		8,979.20
Less: Double tax relief, lower of:		
(a) foreign tax (£1,500)		1,500.00
(b) UK tax on foreign income (40% x £5,000)		
UK tax liability		7,479.20

Income from employment

Income from employment is taxed according to detailed rules contained in the Income Tax (Earnings and Pensions) Act 2003. Broadly, the extent to which an individual's income from employment is taxable depends upon the individual's residence status and whether the duties of the employment are performed in the UK or overseas. The rules are briefly summarised in the following table:

Residence status	*Duties performed wholly or partly in the UK*		*Duties performed wholly outside the UK*
	UK duties	*Non-UK duties*	
Resident and ordinarily resident	Taxable on the receipts basis	Taxable on the receipts basis	Taxable (see below)
Resident but not ordinarily resident	Taxable on the receipts basis	Taxable on the remittance basis	Taxable on the remittance basis
Not resident	Taxable on the receipts basis	Not taxable	Not taxable

If an individual is both resident and ordinarily resident in the UK, earnings from duties performed wholly outside the UK are taxable on the receipts basis unless derived from a non-resident employer by an individual who is not UK domiciled. In this case the earnings (which are referred to as "chargeable overseas earnings") are taxable on the remittance basis.

Note that the income tax on *foreign pensions* received by a UK resident is calculated on only 90% of the amount arising unless the remittance basis applies, in which case the whole of the amount remitted to the UK is taxable.

The 100% deduction for seafarers

Individuals who are resident, ordinarily resident and domiciled in the UK are normally charged to income tax on all of their income from employment, whether their duties are performed in the UK or abroad. However, in the case of *individuals employed as seafarers*, if the duties are performed wholly or partly outside the UK throughout a continuous qualifying period of 365 days or more, a 100% deduction is given against all of the earnings for that period (including earnings relating to any work performed in the UK). In effect, the earnings attributable to such a qualifying period are entirely exempt from UK income tax. Note that:

(a) The income which is attributable to a qualifying period is the income *earned* in that period, not the income received in the period.

(b) A qualifying period begins when an individual leaves the UK to work abroad as a seafarer and the period is treated as continuous even if the individual returns to the UK from time to time, so long as:

   (i) no visit in the UK during the period lasts for more than 183 days, and

   (ii) on each day of return to the UK, the total number of days present in the UK since the qualifying period began is no more than one-half of the total length of the period so far.

   If condition (i) is broken, the qualifying period ends immediately before the start of the offending UK visit. If condition (ii) is broken, the qualifying period ends immediately before the start of the most recent UK visit.

(c) For this purpose, an individual is deemed to be present in the UK on a given day if he or she is in the UK at midnight on that day. Therefore, a day of arrival in the UK counts as a day present in the UK, but a day of departure does not.

EXAMPLE 3

Robin is domiciled in the UK and has lived in the UK all his life. On 1 June 2005 he leaves to work as a seafarer and does not visit the UK again until he returns on 31 July 2006.

(a) What is his residence status in 2005/06?

(b) To what extent are his earnings as a seafarer subject to UK income tax?

Solution

(a) Robin is ordinarily resident in the UK and spends some time in the UK during 2005/06. Therefore he is resident for the year.

(b) As Robin is domiciled, resident and ordinarily resident in the UK he is normally taxed on all of his earnings from employment, no matter where in the world his duties are performed. But the period from 1 June 2005 to 31 July 2006 is a qualifying period of at least 365 days. Therefore Robin's earnings as a seafarer during this period are not subject to UK tax.

Travelling and subsistence expenses

If the duties of an employment are performed abroad and the employee is resident and ordinarily resident in the UK and the earnings from the employment are not classed as chargeable overseas earnings (see above), then the following expenses may be deducted from the employee's earnings for tax purposes:

(a) where duties are performed wholly abroad:

  (i) the costs of travelling abroad at the start of the employment and travelling back to the UK at the end of it

  (ii) the costs of overseas board and lodging paid for or reimbursed by the employer (and assessable as earnings)

(b) where duties are performed partly in the UK and partly abroad, travelling and subsistence expenses paid for or reimbursed by the employer (and assessable as earnings) relating to:

  (i) travel by the employee between the UK and the overseas place of work

  (ii) travel by the employee's spouse and minor children, if the employee is working abroad for a continuous period of 60 days or more, but limited to two return journeys per person per tax year.

Similar deductions to those described at (b) above are available to non-UK domiciled individuals who are working in the UK but these deductions are available for only five years, beginning with the date of arrival in the UK.

Trading income

The extent to which the profits of a trade, profession or vocation are charged to UK income tax depends upon whether or not the owner of the business is UK resident and whether the business is carried on in the UK or overseas. The rules are as follows:

(a) Trading profits arising to a UK resident are charged to income tax wherever in the world the trade is carried on. Therefore UK residents are taxed on the profits of businesses which are carried on wholly or partly overseas.

(b) If a business is carried on wholly overseas, then income arising from that business ranks as "relevant foreign income" (see above). Therefore a UK resident who is not domiciled in the UK or who is not ordinarily resident in the UK may claim that the income concerned should be taxed on the remittance basis.

(c) Trading losses arising from a business carried on wholly overseas may be relieved under Sections 385 and 388 of ICTA 1988 in the usual way (see Chapter 11). But relief under Sections 380 and 381 is available only against overseas income which is not charged on the remittance basis and which consists of:

(i) trading profits arising from a business which is carried on wholly overseas

(ii) employment income ranking as "chargeable overseas earnings" (see above)

(iii) overseas pensions.

(d) Trading profits arising to a non-UK resident are charged to income tax only if the trade is carried on wholly or partly in the UK. In the case of a trade which is carried on only partly in the UK, the profits which are charged to income tax are the profits arising from the UK part of the trade.

Travelling and subsistence expenses

If a trade is carried on wholly overseas and the owner of the business is absent from the UK wholly and exclusively for business purposes, then the expenses listed below are allowable deductions when computing trading profits (so long as those profits are not taxed on the remittance basis):

(a) expenses incurred by the trader in travelling between the UK and the location of the overseas business

(b) overseas board and lodging expenses

(c) expenses relating to travel by the proprietor's spouse and minor children, if the proprietor is abroad for a continuous period of 60 days or more, but limited to two return journeys per person per tax year.

Income from property and investments

Income from property and income from savings and investments are charged to UK income tax according to the following rules:

(a) Income from property situated in the UK is taxable whether or not the person to whom the income arises is UK resident. Income from property situated overseas is taxable only if the person to whom the income arises is UK resident.

(b) Savings and investment income from a UK source is generally taxable whether or not the person to whom the income arises is UK resident. However, interest on UK Government securities is exempt from UK income tax if the recipient is *not ordinarily resident* in the UK. Savings and investment income from an overseas source is taxable only if the person to whom the income arises is UK resident.

(c) Overseas property income and overseas savings and investment income generally rank as "relevant foreign income" (see above). Therefore a UK resident who is not domiciled in the UK or who is not ordinarily resident in the UK may claim that these forms of income should be taxed on the remittance basis. However, overseas savings and investment income which is taxed on the remittance basis is taxed as if it were non-savings income (see Chapter 2) and so cannot benefit from the lower rate (20%) or the dividend lower and upper rates (10% and 32.5%).

Capital gains tax - general rules

The general rules which govern an individual's liability to UK capital gains tax (CGT) are as follows:

(a) Individuals who are resident or ordinarily resident in the UK for a given tax year are liable to CGT in relation to all disposals of chargeable assets which occur in that year, no matter where in the world the assets are situated. Double taxation relief may be available.

(b) Individuals who are neither resident nor ordinarily resident in the UK are not liable to CGT at all, even in relation to disposals of assets situated in the UK.

There are three main exceptions to these general rules:

(a) A non-UK domiciled individual who is resident or ordinarily resident in the UK is fully liable to CGT on the disposal of assets situated in the UK but is liable to CGT on the remittance basis only in relation to disposals abroad.

(b) An individual who is neither resident nor ordinarily resident in the UK but who carries on a business in the UK is chargeable to CGT in relation to disposals of business assets situated in the UK.

(c) Individuals who acquire assets before temporarily leaving the UK (for up to five tax years) and then dispose of those assets whilst abroad remain chargeable to CGT in relation to these disposals. Gains arising in the tax year of departure are taxed in that year. Later gains are taxed in the year in which residence resumes.

A claim may be made to defer a CGT assessment relating to a disposal of overseas assets if it can be shown that the gain in question cannot be remitted to the UK. The conditions which must be satisfied in order that such a claim should be successful are the same as the equivalent conditions for income tax (see above). The taxpayer must show that the gain cannot be remitted to the UK because of either:

(a) the laws of the country in which the gain arises, or

(b) the executive actions of the government of that country, or

(c) the impossibility of obtaining foreign currency in that country.

Such a claim must be made by 31 January in the sixth year of assessment following the year in which the gain arises. If the conditions preventing remittance of the gain to the UK subsequently cease to exist, the gain becomes chargeable in the year in which this occurs.

Inheritance tax - general rules

An individual who is domiciled in the UK is liable to inheritance tax (IHT) in relation to all of his or her chargeable property, wherever in the world that property is situated. An individual who is not domiciled in the UK is liable to IHT only in relation to property situated in the UK. The definition of "domicile" for IHT purposes is broader than the general definition given earlier in this chapter. An individual is treated as domiciled in the UK on the date of a transfer if that individual:

(a) was domiciled in the UK at any time within the previous three years, or

(b) was UK resident for at least 17 of the 20 tax years ending with the tax year in which the transfer takes place.

In general, transfers between spouses are exempt from IHT (see Chapter 31). However, transfers made by a UK-domiciled spouse to a spouse who is not UK-domiciled are exempt only up to a cumulative total of £55,000. As from 5 December 2005, this rule applies equally to same-sex civil partners who have entered into a legally-recognised civil partnership.

Corporation tax - general rules

A company's liability to UK corporation tax depends upon whether or not it is resident in the UK. A company is regarded as resident in the UK if it is incorporated in the UK or if its central management and control is situated in the UK. The general rules which govern a company's liability to UK corporation tax are as follows:

(a) A UK resident company is chargeable to UK corporation tax on all of its profits, no matter where in the world those profits are earned. The overseas income and gains of UK resident companies are taxed as follows:

  (i) The profits of a trade conducted through a permanent establishment situated overseas but controlled in the UK (e.g. an overseas branch) are taxed under Schedule D Case I. Trading losses may be relieved as usual and group relief is generally available. However, the losses of an overseas establishment may be surrendered to another UK resident company in the same group only to the extent that those losses are not relievable in the overseas country.

  (ii) The profits of a trade conducted through a permanent establishment situated and controlled overseas are taxed under Schedule D Case V. Trading losses may be relieved only against other Case V income.

  (iii) Income from foreign investments is taxed under either Schedule D Case III (foreign securities) or Case V (foreign possessions). Dividends received from non-UK resident companies are not franked investment income.

(iv) The gains arising on the disposal of overseas assets are chargeable gains and form part of the company's chargeable profits.

(b) A non-UK resident company is chargeable to UK corporation tax only if it has a permanent establishment situated in the UK. If so, the company is taxed on:

(i) the trading profits of the UK establishment

(ii) income from property in the possession of the UK establishment

(iii) gains arising from the disposal of assets used by the UK establishment.

The trading losses of a UK establishment of a non-UK resident company may generally be set against any other profits of the establishment or may be carried forward against the establishment's future trading profits. The establishment may also surrender its losses to UK resident companies in the same group, so long as those losses are not relievable in the overseas country. Similarly, the establishment may claim losses surrendered by other UK resident group companies. Also, assets transferred between such an establishment and a UK resident group company are transferred on a no-gain, no-loss basis, so long as the assets concerned remain within the charge to UK corporation tax.

A non-UK resident company is not generally entitled to the starting rate or small companies rate of corporation tax or to marginal relief. However, this rule will not apply if it is overridden by the double taxation treaty (if any) between the UK and the country in which the non-UK company is resident.

Overseas subsidiaries

The profits of a non-UK resident subsidiary of a UK resident parent company may be subject to overseas tax but are not generally subject to UK tax unless the subsidiary is treated as a controlled foreign company (see later in this chapter). The UK resident parent company is of course liable to corporation tax on any income received from the overseas subsidiary. As explained in Chapter 28, groups of companies usually enjoy a number of corporation tax reliefs, including (subject to certain conditions):

(a) the transfer of trading losses and certain other items between group members

(b) the transfer of chargeable assets between group members on a no-gain, no-loss basis.

However, these reliefs are generally available only to UK resident companies and do not apply to an overseas subsidiary. An overseas subsidiary *does* count as an associated company for small company relief purposes.

Company migration

A UK resident company may wish to "migrate" overseas in order to escape paying UK corporation tax on its worldwide profits. This is only possible for companies which are incorporated outside the UK and involves moving the central management and control of the company from the UK to an overseas location. A company wishing to take this step must:

(a) notify HM Revenue and Customs of its intentions, specifying the date on which it intends to become non-resident, and

(b) provide HMRC with a statement of all the tax payable up to that date, specifying the arrangements which will be made to ensure that this tax is paid.

On the date that a company becomes non-resident it is deemed to make a disposal of all its assets at their market value on that date. This deemed disposal is likely to result in a sizeable chargeable gain, which is sometimes referred to as the "exit charge". However, this charge is not made in full in the following circumstances:

(a) If a company retains a permanent establishment in the UK, the deemed disposal does not include assets which are situated in the UK and which are used for trade purposes by that establishment.

(b) If the company in question is, immediately on becoming non-resident, a 75% subsidiary of a UK resident company (the "principal company") the gains arising in connection with the deemed disposal of the company's *foreign* assets may be postponed, so long as both companies make an election in writing to that effect. The postponed gains will crystallise if:

    (i) within the following six years, any of the foreign assets are disposed of, or

    (ii) at any time, the company concerned ceases to be a 75% subsidiary of the principal company, or

    (iii) at any time, the principal company ceases to be UK resident.

    Any gains which crystallise are chargeable on the principal company.

Transfer pricing

A UK resident company might try to reduce its tax liability by transferring goods at an artificially low price to an overseas subsidiary. This would have the effect of lowering the UK company's profits (which are liable to UK tax) and increasing the subsidiary's profits (which are not liable to UK tax).

However, this tax avoidance manoeuvre is blocked by "transfer pricing" legislation which requires that a true market price should be substituted for the transfer price in these circumstances and that the UK company should make the necessary adjustment when completing its self-assessment tax return (see Chapter 28). Small and medium-sized companies are generally exempt from the transfer pricing legislation.

Controlled foreign companies (CFCs)

A UK resident company which wishes to operate overseas may operate through an overseas permanent establishment (e.g. an overseas branch) or through a separate non-UK resident company which is under the control of the UK company.

Since the profits of a non-UK resident company are not generally chargeable to UK corporation tax, it would seem to be beneficial for a UK company to adopt the second of these alternatives, especially if the operation is carried on in a country with low tax rates. The overseas profits would not be subject to UK tax at all and could be accumulated in the overseas company. Admittedly, any dividends paid to the UK company would be taxed under Schedule D Case V but such dividends might be put off indefinitely or at least paid some time after the accounting year to which they relate, so delaying the Case V liability.

As an anti-avoidance measure, the profits of a *controlled foreign company* (CFC) are apportioned between its shareholders for tax purposes and CFC profits apportioned to a UK resident company are charged to corporation tax. This tax is calculated at the average rate payable by the UK company for the accounting period in which the CFC's accounting period ends. Double taxation relief (see below) is available. However, no assessment is raised on a UK company to which less than 25% of a CFC's profits are apportioned. A CFC is a company which:

(a) is resident overseas but is under UK control, and

(b) is subject to a level of taxation in the country in which it is resident which is less than 75% of the corresponding UK tax which would be due if the company were UK resident, or

(c) is resident in one of a number of countries which (in effect) allow companies to choose their own "designer rate" of tax as a means of side-stepping the CFC rules.

The definition of "control" for this purpose normally means that the overseas company must be more than 50% controlled from the UK. However, an overseas company will also be treated as a CFC if it is at least 40% controlled by a UK company and at least 40% (but not more than 55%) controlled by a foreign company. The profits of a CFC for an accounting period are usually *not* apportioned between its shareholders if any of the following conditions are satisfied for that period:

(a) The CFC adopts an "acceptable distribution policy", distributing at least 90% of its taxable profits within 18 months of the end of the accounting period.

(b) The profits of the CFC for the period do not exceed £50,000 per annum.

(c) The CFC has a public quotation, at least 35% of its ordinary share capital is held by the public and its shares have been dealt in on a recognised stock exchange.

(d) The CFC is engaged in certain exempt activities.

(e) HM Revenue and Customs is convinced that the main reason for setting up the CFC was not to achieve a reduction in UK tax.

Double taxation relief for companies

A UK resident company which receives income from overseas is generally entitled to unilateral double taxation relief (unless this is overridden by the terms of a double taxation treaty). Unilateral relief takes the form of a tax credit equal to the *lower* of the amount of foreign tax suffered and the amount of UK tax which is payable on the foreign income. Any excess foreign tax is unrelieved, but it may be possible to carry the excess back or forward to other accounting periods (see below).

EXAMPLE 4

In the year to 31 March 2006, a UK resident company had UK trading profits of £5,200,000 and received overseas dividends (net of 35% withholding tax) of £130,000. Compute the corporation tax liability for the year.

Solution

	UK	*Overseas*	*Total*
	£	£	£
Sch D Case I	5,200,000		5,200,000
Sch D Case V £130,000 x 100/65		200,000	200,000
Chargeable profits	5,200,000	200,000	5,400,000
Corporation tax @ 30%	1,560,000	60,000	1,620,000
Less: Unilateral DTR		(60,000)	(60,000)
Corporation tax due	1,560,000	-	1,560,000

Note:

The unilateral relief given is restricted to the UK tax due on the overseas income. The remaining £10,000 (£70,000 - £60,000) of foreign tax paid is unrelieved.

Unrelieved foreign tax

Unrelieved foreign tax arising in connection with certain types of overseas income is known as eligible unrelieved foreign tax (EUFT). EUFT may be carried back to accounting periods beginning not more than three years before the period in which the EUFT arises or may be carried forward without time limit. Note that:

(a) When EUFT arising in respect of a source of income is carried back or forward, it is treated as if it were foreign tax paid in respect of that same source of income in the accounting period to which it is carried back or forward.

(b) The carry-back and carry-forward provisions relate only to foreign tax on the profits of an overseas establishment and foreign tax on dividends. In the case of dividends, the rules extend to underlying tax (see below) as well as to direct tax.

Underlying DTR

If a UK resident company owns at least 10% of the voting power of an overseas company from which it receives a dividend, then an additional form of unilateral relief, known as "underlying double tax relief", is available. The idea of underlying DTR is to give relief for the foreign tax suffered on the profits out of which the dividend has been paid. Underlying relief is calculated by the formula:

$$\frac{D}{P} \times T$$

where: D = the gross dividend received

P = the profit available for distribution as shown in the accounts for the accounting period to which the dividend relates

T = the overseas tax actually paid on the profits of that period.

EXAMPLE 5

A UK resident company receives a dividend from an overseas company (in which it holds 15% of the voting power) of £10,500, net of 30% withholding tax. The profit and loss account of the overseas company for the year to which the dividend relates is as follows:

	£
Profit before tax	400,000
Less: Provision for taxation liability	150,000
Profits after tax	250,000
Dividends	100,000
Retained profits c/f	150,000

The actual tax liability of the overseas company is finally agreed at £160,000. Compute the maximum unilateral double tax relief available in respect of the £10,500 dividend.

Solution

(i) D = £10,500 x 100/70 = £15,000. P = £250,000. T = £160,000

(ii) Withholding tax = £4,500

(iii) Underlying tax = $\frac{D}{P} \times T = \frac{£15{,}000}{£250{,}000} \times £160{,}000 = £9{,}600$

(iv) Maximum unilateral DTR = £4,500 + £9,600 = £14,100. The gross dividend is £24,600 (net £10,500 + tax £14,100).

Unilateral expense relief

A company may waive the right to claim unilateral "credit relief" (where DTR takes the form of a tax credit) and opt for unilateral "expense relief". In this case, the company is assessed on the *net* foreign income, so that the foreign tax is treated as if it were an expense. Expense relief may be attractive if (for example) a company makes a claim under Section 393A(1)(a) to set a trading loss against its total profits, so that it has no corporation tax liability on the foreign income and so cannot obtain any credit relief.

EXAMPLE 6

A UK resident company has a trading loss for the year to 31 March 2006 of £50,000. During the year, the company received a dividend from an overseas company of £12,000, net of 40% withholding tax. Show the corporation tax computation for the year if:

(a) unilateral credit relief is claimed (underlying relief is not available), or

(b) unilateral expense relief is claimed.

Note: The company will be claiming loss relief under S393A(1)(a).

Solution

		Credit relief	*Expense relief*
		£	£
Schedule D Case I		0	0
Schedule D Case V:			
Gross dividend	20,000	20,000	
Less: Foreign tax	8,000		12,000
		20,000	12,000
Less: S393A(1)(a) relief		(20,000)	(12,000)
Chargeable profits		0	0
Corporation tax liability		0	0
Unrelieved trading losses		30,000	38,000
Unrelieved foreign tax		8,000	nil

Notes:

(i) No unilateral credit relief is available since the overseas dividend is absorbed by the S393A(1)(a) claim, leaving a UK tax liability of £nil.

(ii) The choice of credit relief gives £8,000 of unrelieved foreign tax. This can be carried forward and treated as foreign tax paid in respect of dividends received from the same foreign company in future years. However, if dividends from that company continue to be received net of 40% tax (and UK tax rates remain at no more than 30%) it is unlikely that there will be any scope for relieving the £8,000 in future years.

(iii) The choice of expense relief increases by £8,000 the trading losses available for carry-back under S393A(1)(b) or carry-forward under S393(1).

Interaction of charges, loss reliefs and DTR

As explained in Chapters 23 and 26, a company's chargeable profits are reduced by the amount of any charges paid in the accounting period and by the amount of any loss relief claimed under S393A(1). Normally, it is sufficient simply to subtract the charges and loss reliefs from total income without allocating these deductions to particular sources of income. However, if unilateral double tax relief is claimed, such an allocation must be made so that the amount of UK tax payable on the foreign income can then be computed.

Clearly, if any charges or losses are deemed to be set against the foreign income, this will have the effect of reducing the UK tax due on that foreign income and so reducing the maximum unilateral DTR available. Therefore charges and losses should be set first against UK income, then against foreign income. If a company has more than one source of foreign income, charges and losses should be set against foreign income which has suffered low rates of foreign tax in preference to foreign income which has suffered high rates of foreign tax.

Mixer companies

At one time, companies could reduce their tax liability on dividends received from low-tax countries by the use of so-called "mixer companies". Dividends receivable by a UK parent company from a number of overseas subsidiaries would be channelled through an overseas mixer company, which would then pay a single dividend to the UK parent. This practice allowed dividends received from low-tax countries to be mixed with dividends received from high-tax countries, so generating an average rate of underlying tax more or less equal to the UK corporation tax rate. In this way, the UK company would be able to use what would have been unrelieved foreign tax on dividends received from high-tax countries to reduce its UK corporation tax liability on dividends received from low-tax countries.

As from 31 March 2001, however, the underlying foreign tax on dividends received by a mixer company from its overseas subsidiaries is regarded as having been paid at a capped rate not exceeding the main UK rate of corporation tax (currently 30%). This means that the practice described above is no longer effective.

DTR and relief of surplus ACT

If a company has surplus ACT brought forward from before 6 April 1999, the amount of that ACT which can be relieved in an accounting period is governed by the shadow ACT regulations (see Chapter 25). These regulations stipulate that the maximum ACT set-off for an accounting period is equal to the ACT which would be payable on a franked payment equal to the chargeable profits for that period. If double tax relief is claimed, the maximum offset is further restricted to the amount of corporation tax payable on each source of income after DTR has been deducted.

EXAMPLE 7

In the year to 31 March 2006, a UK resident company has UK trading profits of £4,800,000 and receives overseas dividends (net of 45% withholding tax) of £2,750,000. Charges of £1,000,000 (gross) are paid in the year. The company also has unrelieved surplus ACT brought forward from before 6 April 1999. Compute the corporation tax liability for the year and the maximum ACT set-off.

Solution

	UK	*Overseas*	*Total*
	£	£	£
Schedule D Case I	4,800,000		4,800,000
Schedule D Case V			
£2,750,000 x 100/55		5,000,000	5,000,000
	4,800,000	5,000,000	9,800,000
Less: Charges	1,000,000	-	1,000,000
Chargeable profits	3,800,000	5,000,000	8,800,000
Corporation tax @ 30%	1,140,000	1,500,000	2,640,000
Less: Unilateral DTR		(1,500,000)	(1,500,000)
Corporation tax liability	1,140,000	-	1,140,000
Maximum ACT set-off	760,000	-	760,000

Notes:

(i) The charges are set against the UK income so as to maximise double tax relief on the overseas income.

(ii) DTR is limited to the UK tax due on the overseas income. Foreign tax paid is £2,250,000, of which £750,000 is unrelieved.

(iii) ACT set-off is restricted in the usual way but is also restricted to the corporation tax liability on each source of income after deduction of DTR. For the UK income, the first of these restrictions gives a maximum set-off of £760,000 (20% of £3,800,000). For the overseas income, the second restriction gives a maximum set-off of £nil.

(iv) As usual, the shadow ACT arising on any dividends paid in the year will use up some or all of the maximum ACT set-off and so reduce the scope for relieving surplus ACT brought forward from before 6 April 1999.

Summary

- An individual's liability to UK tax depends upon that individual's residence, ordinary residence and domicile.
- Individuals who are resident in the UK for a tax year are liable to UK income tax on their worldwide income for that year. Non-residents are liable to tax on their UK income only.
- Double taxation relief may be available if income is subject to both UK tax and overseas tax.
- The extent to which an individual's income from employment is taxable depends upon the individual's residence status and whether the duties of the employment are performed in the UK or overseas.
- Trading profits arising to a UK resident are charged to income tax wherever in the world the trade is carried on. Trading profits arising to a non-resident are charged to income tax only if the trade is carried on wholly or partly in the UK.
- Income from UK property and investments is taxable whether or not the person to whom the income arises is UK resident. Income from overseas property and investments is taxable only if the person to whom the income arises is UK resident.
- Individuals who are resident or ordinarily resident in the UK for a tax year are liable to UK CGT on their disposals throughout the world in that year.
- Individuals who are domiciled in the UK are liable to UK IHT. The definition of "domicile" for IHT purposes is broader than the general definition.
- UK resident companies are liable to UK corporation tax on their worldwide profits. A non-UK resident company is liable to UK corporation tax only if it has a permanent establishment situated in the UK.
- The profits of a controlled foreign company may be apportioned between the controlling UK companies and assessed to UK corporation tax.
- Double tax relief for companies may take the form of credit relief, underlying tax relief or expense relief.

Exercises

32.1 Jean-Paul is a Canadian citizen. He owns a house in Canada and regards Canada as his home but he lives in London for nearly all of tax year 2005/06. His income for the year is derived from the following sources:

(a) a part-time employment with a UK company (the duties of which are performed entirely in London)

(b) a second part-time employment with a Belgian company (the duties of which are performed entirely in Brussels, which he visits on one day each month)

(c) dividends from stocks and shares held in Canada

(d) interest on UK Government securities.

To what extent is any of his income chargeable to UK income tax?

32.2 Amy is domiciled in the UK and has lived in the UK all her life. On 1 January 2004 she leaves to work in Australia for three years. Explain her UK income tax status for tax years 2003/04 to 2006/07 inclusive.

32.3 Cara is a UK resident. She receives a pension of £10,000 per annum from the Italian company for whom she used to work when she lived in Italy. Explain how the UK income tax system will treat this pension if Cara is:

(a) domiciled in the UK

(b) domiciled in Italy.

32.4 How would a UK resident company proceed if it wished to "migrate" overseas? Why might this be a desirable step?

32.5 Explain the term "controlled foreign company" (CFC). In what circumstances are the profits of a CFC chargeable to UK corporation tax?

32.6 Brits Ltd is a UK resident company and has a trading profit of £2,120,000 for the year ended 31 March 2006. During the year, the company received a dividend from a wholly-owned overseas subsidiary of £57,400 (net of 18% withholding tax). The overseas company is liable to 50% overseas tax on all of its profits. Compute the corporation tax liability of Brits Ltd for the year.

***32.7** Donald is domiciled, resident and ordinarily resident in the UK. He has the following income in 2005/06:

	£
UK trading profits	31,595
UK bank interest (net amount)	1,600
Income from foreign property (net of 45% withholding tax)	2,200

Donald claims only the personal allowance. Compute his income tax payable for 2005/06.

***32.8** X Ltd is a UK resident company with nineteen subsidiaries, one of which is situated abroad. In the year to 31 March 2006, X Ltd had the following results:

	£
UK trading profits	720,000
UK dividends received	40,000
UK chargeable gains	120,000
Dividend from overseas subsidiary (net of 30% withholding tax)	8,400
Charges paid (gross amount)	80,000

X Ltd owns 60% of the ordinary share capital of the overseas subsidiary (which does not rank as a controlled foreign company). The summarised profit and loss account of this subsidiary for the year to 31 March 2006 is as follows:

	£
Profit before tax	75,000
Less: Provision for taxation liability	25,000
Profits after tax	50,000
Dividends	20,000
Retained profits c/f	30,000

Calculate the corporation tax liability of X Ltd for the year. Also, given that X Ltd has a substantial amount of surplus ACT brought forward from before 6 April 1999, calculate the maximum ACT set-off for the year.

Review questions (Set D)

D 1 You have received a letter from the managing director of Wakem & Co. Ltd, a company making wholly standard rated supplies. Extracts from the letter are as follows:

"During the course of the last quarter, sales have been very good. In particular, we sold £30,000 worth of goods to St. Oggs Inc, an American company, and we also sold £20,000 worth of goods to Rappit Ltd in Scotland. Mr Jakin, the managing director of Rappit Ltd, drove a hard bargain and to secure the order we had to allow a 5% discount for prompt settlement. As we closed down the box manufacturing line, we sold off the machinery and made a useful £15,000. The electrical equipment remaining has been hired to Mudport Ltd for £1,000 per month. One piece of bad news is that Garum Furs plc has gone into liquidation owing us £14,000, though there is a possibility of recovering part of that amount in the liquidation."

Required:

Explain the significance for VAT purposes of the events described in this letter. *(AAT)*

D 2 A Ltd is the holding company for a group of five companies. The relationships between the companies in the group are shown in the diagram below:

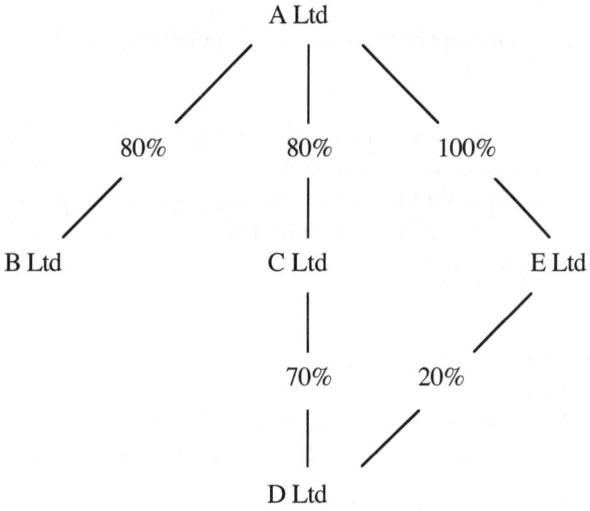

All of the companies are UK resident except for E Ltd which is resident in a country where the rate of tax is 5%. For the purposes of this question, E Ltd can be regarded as a

Controlled Foreign Company. All of the companies have an accounting year ended 31 March 2006 and their incomes/(losses) for the year were as follows:

	Schedule D Case I	*Bank interest*
	£	£
A Ltd	90,000	-
B Ltd	100,000	15,000
C Ltd	(90,000)	12,000
D Ltd	(5,000)	-
E Ltd	15,000	-

You are required:

(a) To identify the companies which are treated as associated companies.

(b) To identify the companies which form a group (or groups) for group relief purposes.

(c) To compute the corporation tax liability of each company, assuming that the most efficient use is made by the group of any trading losses. Assume also that none of the companies paid or received any dividends during the year.

(d) To advise the board of any steps it should take to minimise next year's corporation tax liabilities, given that E Ltd will have chargeable profits of £60,000. *(CIMA)*

D3 Your company has a number of branches and subsidiaries trading outside the UK. The board is about to offer contracts to employees resident in the UK and working in UK locations which will allow them to transfer to foreign locations on a temporary basis, with all of their duties being performed outside the UK. There are two contracts being offered - one lasting nine months and one lasting eighteen months.

You are required:

To draft a report to the board on the taxation implications, for the employees, of each of the possible contracts. *(CIMA)*

D4 M Ltd, a UK resident trading company, owns 6% of the share capital of Z Inc and 8% of the share capital of X S.A. Neither of these companies is resident in the UK for tax purposes. In addition, M Ltd has a controlling interest in two UK resident companies - N Ltd and O Ltd. The following information relates to M Ltd's 12-month accounting period ended 31 March 2006:

	£	£
INCOME		
Schedule D Case I trading profits		500,000
Schedule D Case V:		
Dividend from Z Inc, after deduction of 30% withholding tax	35,000	
Dividend from X S.A., after deduction of 5% withholding tax	38,000	73,000
CHARGE PAID (gross amount)		10,000

M Ltd also has a substantial amount of unrelieved surplus ACT brought forward from before 6 April 1999.

You are required:

To compute the corporation tax liability of M Ltd for the above period, showing clearly the relief for double taxation. Also calculate the maximum ACT set-off for the period.

(CIMA)

***D5** David Deans started trading as a painter and decorator on 1 July 2005. He has notified you of his turnover each month which, up to November 2005, has been as follows:

	£
July 2005	5,000
August 2005	6,000
September 2005	7,000
October 2005	8,200
November 2005	9,000

In anticipation of a meeting with Mr Deans, you have received a letter from him, of which the following is an extract:

"In preparation for our meeting, I have some further information for you and some questions which I hope you will be able to answer for me. I anticipate that my turnover is likely to be £12,000 in December 2005 and £13,500 in January 2006. It must be reaching the time at which I need to be registered for VAT. Could you give me some idea of when this might be and whether I could delay it in order to improve my cash flow?

Since starting business I have purchased substantial quantities of stock. Will I be able to recover any of the VAT I have paid?

In June next year, I intend to buy a new van and a new car for the business. Their cost, including VAT, will be £14,000 and £8,000 respectively. I assume that I will be able to recover the VAT on both items. The van will be used wholly for business and the car for both business and private use. The firm will pay for all the petrol used by both vehicles.

As yet, I have not suffered any bad debts but as the business expands there is always the risk that they might arise. Are there any special VAT arrangements to deal with them?"

Required:

Draft notes in preparation for the meeting with Mr Deans, responding to the queries which he has raised.

(AAT)

***D6** Mrs Lammle, who is registered for VAT, has traded as a manufacturer of standard-rated items since 1 January 1992. She has decided to retire on 31 May 2005, her 65th birthday, and you are asked to finalise her tax position up to that date. You are provided with the following information:

(i) Mrs Lammle's first accounts covered the period to 31 May 1993. Since then, she has prepared accounts annually to 31 May. Adjusted profits for the year to 31 May 1997 were £45,000.

(ii) The last accounts will be for the year to 31 May 2005. Interim accounts have been prepared to 28 February 2005, revealing the following:

	£
Sales	100,200
Cost of sales	24,700
Gross profit	75,500
Expenses	29,000
Net profit	46,500

All of the above figures are net of VAT and contain no disallowable items.

(iii) For the last three months to 31 May 2005 (which is also the last VAT quarter), you have extracted the following figures from the accounting records:

	£
Sales:	
To UK customers	30,652
To overseas customers	8,000
Materials purchased:	
Standard-rated	4,087
Zero-rated	2,000
Exempt	800
Expenses:	
General (all standard-rated)	6,130
Wages	7,000
Hire of machinery	613
Business bank charges	500
Entertaining overseas clients	400

All of the above include VAT if appropriate. There was no stock at 1 March 2005 and there is no outstanding stock left at 31 May 2005. All of the general expenses are allowable for income tax purposes.

(iv) The tax written down value of the plant and machinery carried forward after capital allowances had been calculated for the year to 31 May 2004 was:

	£
Plant and machinery pool	12,375
Expensive car (with no private use)	5,250

No plant and machinery was acquired during the year to 31 May 2005.

(v) The business was sold as a going concern to a major competitor on 31 May 2005 (RPI 191.5). The items sold were:

	£
Freehold shop	200,000
Freehold workshop	130,000
Goodwill	180,000
Plant (no item worth more than £6,000)	25,000
Car	6,000

The shop and workshop were acquired on 1 January 1992 (RPI 135.6) for £30,000 and £27,000 respectively. The RPI for April 1998 was 162.6.

Required:

(a) Calculate the VAT due for the quarter to 31 May 2005.

(b) Calculate the final adjusted profit for the year to 31 May 2005, after deduction of capital allowances.

(c) Calculate Mrs Lammle's trading income for 2005/06.

(d) Calculate the chargeable gain (before taper relief) arising on the disposal of the business. *(AAT)*

***D7** The group structure below shows holdings in ordinary shares in other companies. All of the companies are UK resident except for O Inc which is foreign resident.

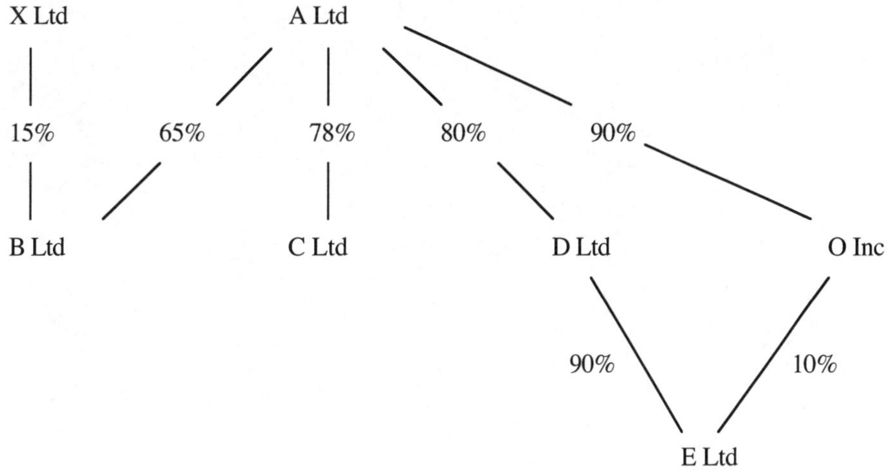

The results for each of the above companies for the accounting year ended 31 March 2006 are as follows:

		£			£
X Ltd	Loss	(40,000)	D Ltd	Profit	35,000
B Ltd	Profit	60,000	O Inc	Loss	(30,000)
A Ltd	Profit	103,000	E Ltd	Loss	(2,000)
C Ltd	Loss	(70,000)			

You are required:

(a) To identify the associated companies for starting rate and small company rate purposes and to state the upper and lower thresholds for each of the companies shown.

(b) To identify any groups and consortia in the above structure qualifying for group relief.

(c) To compute the corporation tax liability of each company, assuming that loss relief has been claimed in the most efficient manner.

(d) To advise the directors of A Ltd on the weakness, from a tax point of view, of the existing structure. *(CIMA)*

***D8** You are the chief accountant of Z Ltd, a UK resident company, whose activities to date have been confined wholly to the UK. The company is about to acquire three UK resident subsidiaries and the members of the newly-formed group will engage, for the first time, in import and export activities (all with non-EU countries).

You are required:

To draft a brief report to the board on the VAT implications of the above changes. *(CIMA)*

Part 5

ANSWERS

Answers to exercises

Chapter 2

2.1

(a) 2,090 @ 10% + 10,600 @ 22% = £2,541.00.

(b) 2,090 @ 10% + 30,310 @ 22% + 7,700 @ 40% = £9,957.20.

(c) 2,090 @ 10% + 30,310 @ 22% + 33,703 @ 40% = £20,358.40.

2.2

(a)

	Total	*Non-savings*	*Savings*
	£	£	£
Business profits	20,360	20,360	
Bank interest £720 × 100/80	900		900
Statutory total income	21,260	20,360	900
Less: Personal allowance	4,895	4,895	
Taxable income	16,365	15,465	900

Income tax due

Starting rate band	: Non-savings	2,090	@ 10%	209.00
Basic rate band	: Non-savings	13,375	@ 22%	2,942.50
	: Savings	900	@ 20%	180.00
		16,365		
Tax borne				3,331.50
Less: Tax deducted at source				180.00
Tax payable				3,151.50

(b)

	Total	*Non-savings*	*Savings*
	£	£	£
Business profits	25,030	25,030	
Building society interest £8,000 × 100/80	10,000		10,000
Bank interest £2,300 × 100/80	2,875		2,875
Statutory total income	37,905	25,030	12,875
Less: Personal allowance	4,895	4,895	
Taxable income	33,010	20,135	12,875

Income tax due				
Starting rate band	: Non-savings	2,090	@ 10%	209.00
Basic rate band	: Non-savings	18,045	@ 22%	3,969.90
	: Savings	12,265	@ 20%	2,453.00
Higher rate	: Savings	610	@ 40%	244.00
		33,010		
Tax borne				6,875.90
Less: Tax deducted at source				2,575.00
Tax payable				4,300.90

(c)

	Total (all savings income)
	£
Building society interest £30,520 × 100/80	38,150
Statutory total income	38,150
Less: Personal allowance	4,895
Taxable income	33,255

Income tax due				
Starting rate band	: Savings	2,090	@ 10%	209.00
Basic rate band	: Savings	30,310	@ 20%	6,062.00
Higher rate	: Savings	855	@ 40%	342.00
		33,255		
Tax borne				6,613.00
Less: Tax deducted at source				7,400.00
Tax refund due				(787.00)

2.3

	Total	*Non-savings*	*Savings*	*Dividends*
	£	£	£	£
Employment income	22,175	22,175		
Income from property	14,730	14,730		
Bank interest £160 × 100/80	200		200	
UK dividends £225 + tax credit £25	250			250
Statutory total income	37,355	36,905	200	250
Less: Personal allowance	4,895	4,895		
Taxable income	32,460	32,010	200	250

Income tax due

Starting rate band	: Non-savings	2,090	@ 10%	209.00
Basic rate band	: Non-savings	29,920	@ 22%	6,582.40
	: Savings	200	@ 20%	40.00
	: Dividends	190	@ 10%	19.00
Higher rate	: Dividends	60	@ 32.5%	19.50
		32,460		
Tax borne				6,869.90
Less: Tax credits on dividends				25.00
Tax payable				6,844.90
Less: Tax deducted at source				40.00
Tax payable				6,804.90

Note: Stephanie would also be given credit for any PAYE tax paid.

2.4

	Total	*Non-savings*	*Savings*
	£	£	£
Retirement pension	4,285	4,285	
Bank interest £416 × 100/80	520		520
Statutory total income	4,805	4,285	520
Less: Personal allowance	4,805	4,285	520
Taxable income	0	0	0

£90 of the personal allowance (£4,895 - £4,805) is unused. Tax borne is £nil and Ernest is entitled to repayment of the £104.00 of tax deducted at source. If he received dividends of £468, dividend income of £520 (£468 + £52) would replace the bank interest. Tax borne would still be £nil but he would not be able to claim payment of the £52 tax credit.

Chapter 3

3.1

(a) This taxpayer is in the 65-74 age group and is entitled to a PA of £7,090 for the year.

(b) This taxpayer is over 75 and has an STI which exceeds the limit by £1,000, giving a PA of £6,720 (£7,220 - 1/2 × £1,000).

(c) This taxpayer reaches the age of 65 during tax year 2005/06 and has an STI which exceeds the income limit by £4,600. This would give a PA of £4,790 (£7,090 - 1/2 × £4,600) but the allowance is never reduced to less than the PA for those aged under 65 so the taxpayer will claim £4,895.

3.2

(a) The husband is over 75 and therefore receives a PA of £7,220. His wife is over 65 but her STI exceeds the limit by £300, giving her a PA of £6,940 (£7,090 - 1/2 × £300). The MCA is £5,975 (which is not reduced, since the husband's STI does not exceed the income limit).

(b) The husband is over 65 but his STI exceeds the limit by £700, giving him a PA of £6,740 (£7,090 - 1/2 × £700). His wife is over 65 and is entitled to a PA of £7,090 (of which £590 is unused). An MCA of £5,905 is also available. This is not reduced at all since the reduction required because of the husband's STI has already been made in full against his PA.

(c) The husband is over 65 but his STI exceeds the limit by £4,560. Therefore he must lose a total of £2,280 in allowances. His own PA is first reduced from £7,090 to the minimum of £4,895 (a reduction of £2,195). The remaining £85 is deducted from the MCA of £5,905 giving an MCA of £5,820. His wife is under 65 and is therefore entitled to a PA of £4,895.

3.3

					(a) £	(b) £	(c) £
HUSBAND							
Statutory total income					13,720	6,800	7,555
Less: Personal allowance					7,220	6,800	7,220
Taxable income					6,500	0	335
Income tax							
	(a)	(b)	(c)				
	2,090	0	335	@ 10%	209.00	0.00	33.50
	4,410	0	0	@ 22%	970.20	0.00	0.00
	6,500	0	335		1,179.20	0.00	33.50
Less: MCA £5,975 @ 10%					597.50		
MCA £5,975 × 8/12 @ 10% = £398.33 (all transferred to wife)						0.00	
MCA £5,975 @ 10% = £597.50 (£564.00 transferred to wife)							33.50
Tax borne					581.70	0.00	0.00
WIFE							
Statutory total income					15,020	12,445	14,885
Less: Personal allowance					7,220	7,220	7,220
Taxable income					7,800	5,225	7,665
Income tax							
	(a)	(b)	(c)				
	2,090	2,090	2,090	@ 10%	209.00	209.00	209.00
	5,710	3,135	5,575	@ 22%	1,256.20	689.70	1,226.50
	7,800	5,225	7,665		1,465.20	898.70	1,435.50
Less: MCA transferred from husband						(398.33)	(564.00)
Tax borne					1,465.20	500.37	871.50

3.4

(a) No MCA is available if both taxpayers were born on or after 6 April 1935.

(b) The MCA is reduced to £5,905 × 2/12 = £984.

(c) The husband is the higher earner and his income is £1,100 over the limit. He cannot claim age-related PA so the MCA of £5,905 is reduced by £550 (1/2 × £1,100), giving £5,355. This is further reduced to £5,355 × 4/12 = £1,785.

3.5

	Total	Non-savings	Savings
	£	£	£
Retirement pension	6,200	6,200	
Bank interest £912 × 100/80	1,140		1,140
Statutory total income	7,340	6,200	1,140
Less: Personal allowance	7,220	6,200	1,020
Taxable income	120	0	120

Income tax due

120 @ 10%	12.00
Less: Tax deducted at source	228.00
Refund due	(216.00)

3.6

(a) PA £4,895, Blind person's allowance £1,610.

(b) PA £4,895.

(c) PA £4,895 (which is mostly unused).

3.7

	Richard	Patricia
	£	£
Business profits	19,530	
UK dividends £1,800 + £200		2,000
Less: Personal allowance	4,895	2,000
Taxable income	14,635	0

Income tax

Richard	Patricia			
2,090	0	@ 10%	209.00	0.00
12,545	0	@ 22%	2,759.90	0.00
14,635	0		2,968.90	0.00
Less: MCA £5,890 @ 10%			589.00	
Tax borne			2,379.90	0.00
Less: Tax credits on dividends				0.00
Tax payable			2,379.90	0.00

Notes:

(i) Patricia was born before 6 April 1935. MCA is £5,890 (£5,905 - 1/2 × £30).

(ii) Patricia is entitled to a PA of £7,090 but can use only £2,000 of this. The remainder is lost and she cannot claim payment of the £200 tax credits on dividends.

Chapter 4

4.1

	£
Income	19,460
Less: Charges £195 × 100/78	250
Statutory total income	19,210
Less: Personal allowance	4,895
Taxable income	14,315
Income tax	
2,090 @ 10%	209.00
12,225 @ 22%	2,689.50
14,315	
Tax borne	2,898.50
Add: Tax deducted from charge	55.00
Tax liability	2,953.50

4.2

	(a) £	(b) £
Income	41,400	41,400
Less: Charges £1,248 × 100/78	1,600	
Statutory total income	39,800	41,400
Less: Personal allowance	4,895	4,895
Taxable income	34,905	36,505

Income tax

(a)	(b)		(a) £	(b) £
2,090	2,090	@ 10%	209.00	209.00
30,310	30,310	@ 22%	6,668.20	6,668.20
2,505	4,105	@ 40%	1,002.00	1,642.00
34,905	36,505			
Tax borne			7,879.20	8,519.20
Add: Tax deducted from charge			352.00	
Tax liability			8,231.20	8,519.20

Paul's tax liability is reduced by £288 if he pays the charge. The cost of the charge to him is therefore only £960 (payment £1,248 less reduction in tax liability £288). In effect, the gross charge of £1,600 is reduced by tax relief at 40% (£640), leaving £960 as the cost to Paul.

4.3

	£
Income	4,885
Less: Charges £19.50 × 100/78	25
Statutory total income	4,860
Less: Personal allowance (restricted)	4,860
Taxable income	nil
Income tax	
Tax borne	0.00
Add: Tax deducted from charge	5.50
Tax liability	5.50

4.4

(a) 23% (b) marginal rate (c) 10% (d) marginal rate.

4.5

(a) The donation is deemed to be made net of 22% income tax. Charities are not liable to income tax so the charity concerned recovers a further £264 (£936 × 22/78) from HMRC, making the donation worth £1,200 in total.

(b) If the taxpayer does not pay income tax for 2005/06 of at least £264, his or her income tax liability for the year will be increased to exactly £264.

(c) The taxpayer's basic rate band for 2005/06 is extended by £1,200. If the taxpayer pays income tax at the higher rate, this extension will have the effect of moving up to £1,200 of income from the higher rate to the basic rate, resulting in a tax saving of up to £216 (18% × £1,200).

4.6

		£
Business profits		20,500
Less: Personal allowance		6,765
Taxable income		13,735
Income tax		
2,090	@ 10%	209.00
11,645	@ 22%	2,561.90
13,735		
Tax liability		2,770.90

Notes:

(i) The grossed-up donation is £350 (£273 × 100/78) and the tax deemed deducted is £77.

(ii) For the purpose of computing age-related allowances, STI is reduced by £350 to £20,150. This is £650 over the income limit, so the personal allowance is £6,765 (£7,090 - 1/2 × £650).

(iii) Raj pays income tax of far more than £77 so there is nothing more to be done.

4.7

			Total	*Non-savings*	*Dividends*
			£	£	£
Employment income			35,875	35,875	
UK dividends £2,880 + tax credit £320			3,200		3,200
Statutory total income			39,075	35,875	3,200
Less: Personal allowance			4,895	4,895	
Taxable income			34,180	30,980	3,200

Income tax due

Starting rate band	: Non-savings	2,090	@ 10%	209.00
Basic rate band	: Non-savings	28,890	@ 22%	6,355.80
	: Dividends	1,820	@ 10%	182.00
Higher rate	: Dividends	1,380	@ 32.5%	448.50
		34,180		
Tax liability				7,195.30
Less: Tax credits on dividends				320.00
Tax payable				6,875.30

Notes:

(i) The basic rate band is extended by a grossed-up donation of £400 (£312 × 100/78) to £30,710 (£30,310 + £400).

(ii) Geoffrey is not entitled to MCA (he and his wife are too young).

(iii) Tax paid under PAYE would also be deducted.

Chapter 5

5.1

The property income assessable in 2005/06 (i.e. the income accrued for the year) is £8,200 (£8,000 × 9/12 + £8,800 × 3/12). The amount actually received is not relevant.

5.2

		£	£	£
Rents received £120 × 48				5,760
Less: Expenses allowed in full:				
Advertising			35	
Repairs to furniture			50	
Apportioned expenses:				
Council tax		400		
Gardener's wages		520		
Insurance		230		
	$\frac{48}{52}$ ×	1,150	1,062	
Wear and tear (see below)			539	1,686
Property income				4,074

Note:

The wear and tear allowance is 10% of (£5,760 - (£400 × 48/52)) = £539.

5.3

(a) Premiums received in relation to the granting of long leases (i.e. leases of more than 50 years) are not assessable to income tax.

(b) £12,000 less (49 × 2% of £12,000) = £240.

(c) £12,000 less (19 × 2% of £12,000) = £7,440.

5.4

The income tax assessment on Jasper's landlord is £12,300, i.e. £15,000 less (9 × 2% of £15,000). Therefore Jasper will be allowed an annual deduction from his trading profits of £1,230 for each of the 10 years of the lease.

5.5

All three flats pass the 140-day test. However, Flat 1 does not pass the 70-day test and so will not be regarded as a furnished holiday let unless it can be averaged with one or more of the other flats. Possible averaging claims are:

(a) Average Flat 1 with Flat 2. This is no use since the average number of days let is only 68.

(b) Average Flat 1 with Flat 3. This is no use since the average number of days let is only 69.

(c) Average Flat 1 with Flat 2 and Flat 3. This is beneficial since the average number of days let is 70.

Chapter 6

6.1

	Total	Savings	Dividends
	£	£	£
BSI £10,508 × 100/80	13,135	13,135	
UK dividends £27,468 + tax credit £3,052	30,520		30,520
Statutory total income	43,655	13,135	30,520
Less: Personal allowance	4,895	4,895	
Taxable income	38,760	8,240	30,520

Income tax due

Starting rate band	: Savings	2,090	@ 10%	209.00
Basic rate band	: Savings	6,150	@ 20%	1,230.00
	: Dividends	24,160	@ 10%	2,416.00
Higher rate	: Dividends	6,360	@ 32.5%	2,067.00
		38,760		
Tax borne				5,922.00
Less: Tax deducted at source and tax credits				5,679.00
Tax payable				243.00

6.2

	Total	Non-savings	Savings	Dividends
	£	£	£	£
Retirement pension	6,606	6,606		
Bank interest £384 × 100/80	480		480	
UK dividends £585 + tax credit £65	650			650
Statutory total income	7,736	6,606	480	650
Less: Personal allowance	7,220	6,606	480	134
Taxable income	516	0	0	516

Income tax is due of £51.60 (£516 @ 10%), less tax credit on dividends of £51.60, leaving a tax liability of zero. Anne cannot claim payment of the remaining £13.40 of the tax credits but she is entitled to a refund of the £96 tax deducted at source from her bank interest.

Note:

The ISA interest is exempt from tax.

6.3

See text.

6.4

See text.

6.5

			Total	*Non-savings*	*Savings*
			£	£	£
Retirement pension			14,970	14,970	
NSB interest (£8 + £52)			60		60
BSI £3,784 × 100/80			4,730		4,730
Statutory total income			19,760	14,970	4,790
Less: Personal allowance			6,960	6,960	
Taxable income			12,800	8,010	4,790
Income tax due					
Starting rate band	: Non-savings	2,090	@ 10%	209.00	
Basic rate band	: Non-savings	5,920	@ 22%	1,302.40	
	: Savings	4,790	@ 20%	958.00	
		12,800			
Tax borne				2,469.40	
Less: Tax deducted at source				946.00	
Tax payable				1,523.40	

Notes:

(a) The first £70 of the NSB ordinary account interest is exempt from income tax.

(b) Bernice reaches her 65th birthday during 2005/06 and is therefore entitled to the personal allowance of £7,090 for the year. However, her STI exceeds the income limit by £260, so the allowance is reduced by £130 to £6,960.

(c) Any PAYE tax deducted from the pension will be subtracted when calculating tax payable.

Chapter 7

7.1

See text.

7.2

The basis of assessment for employment income is the receipts basis. The assessable income for 2005/06 is therefore £19,850 (£17,500 + £2,350).

7.3

(a) 15p per day would be exempt. The remaining £1.85 per day would be taxable.

(b) Free meals in the company canteen are exempt if available to all employees.

(c) Removal expenses of up to £8,000 are exempt if reasonable and incurred on first taking up an appointment or transferring to a new location.

(d) Long-service awards made in cash are taxable.

(e) A gift made in a personal capacity (rather than for services rendered) is exempt so long as it is reasonable in amount.

(f) The mileage allowance is exempt since it is less than the standard figure of 40p per mile for the first 10,000 miles. The employee has an allowable expense of £250 (2,500 @ 10p).

7.4

(a) Not generally allowable since not incurred in performing the duties of the employment. But see the text of Chapter 7 for exceptions to this rule in the case of site-based employees, employees undertaking business journeys from home and employees who are seconded to a temporary place of work.

(b) Allowable so long as necessarily incurred.

(c) Allowable if relevant to the employment.

(d) Allowable.

(e) Not allowable, even if worn only at the office. A suit provides warmth and decency and is therefore not purchased exclusively for the purposes of the employment.

(f) Not allowable unless reimbursed or paid out of a specific entertaining allowance. The expenses must also be wholly, exclusively and necessarily incurred.

7.5

For the purpose of deciding Kim's classification it is necessary to take into account all of her earnings (valued as if she were a P11D employee) and to ignore expenses other than superannuation contributions. This gives total earnings of £9,450 (95% of £7,000 + £1,000 + £1,800) which exceeds £8,500 so Kim is a P11D employee.

7.6

The applicable percentage is 30% (15% + 12% + 3%) so the assessable car benefit is £5,640 (30% of £18,800. There is a further assessable fuel benefit of £4,320 (30% of £14,400).

7.7

The first £28,250 (£30,000 - £1,750) of compensation is exempt from tax.

(a) £12,000 is less than £28,250 and is therefore exempt from tax.

(b) £29,000 exceeds £28,250 so the excess of £750 is taxable.

Chapter 8

8.1

Subject matter; length of ownership; frequency of transactions; supplementary work; reason for sale; motive.

8.2

Expenditure must be incurred wholly and exclusively for the purposes of the trade.

8.3

(a) allowable so long as the salary is commensurate with the work done

(b) not allowable when computing trading profits, but relieved under the Gift Aid rules

(c) not allowable (capital expenditure)

(d) allowable so long as the diaries carry a prominent advertisement for the business

(e) allowable

(f) not allowable (fails the duality test)

(g) not allowable (related to capital expenditure)

(h) probably allowable as a trade subscription

(i) not allowable (food, drink or tobacco)

(j) allowable (relates directly to trading).

8.4

(a) add £45 (b) add £15 (c) no adjustment required.

8.5

(a) The allowable amount each year is given by:

$$£5{,}670 \times \frac{£12{,}000 + 1/2(£21{,}000 - £12{,}000)}{£21{,}000} = £4{,}455$$

The amount to be added back each year is therefore £1,215 (£5,670 - £4,455).

(b) The allowable amount each year is given by:

$$\frac{£15{,}000 - (14 \times 2\% \times £15{,}000)}{15} = £720.$$

The amount to be added back each year is therefore £280 (£1,000 - £720).

8.6

	£	£
Net profit for the year		6,960
<u>Add</u>: *Disallowed expenditure*:		
Proprietor's salary	10,400	
Cost of new heating system	3,800	
Telephone (1/4 of £880)	220	
Motor expenses (1/5 of £3,250)	650	
Entertaining	520	
General provision for bad debts	200	
Loss on sale of fixed asset	70	
Depreciation	2,500	18,360
		25,320
<u>Less</u>: *Non-trading income*:		
Rents receivable	1,200	
Bank interest receivable	80	
Profit on sale of fixed assets	310	1,590
Trading profit (before capital allowances)		23,730

Chapter 9

9.1

(a) 2005/06 (b) 2005/06 (c) 2007/08 (d) 2006/07

9.2

(a)	2003/04	Actual	1/7/03 to 5/4/04
	2004/05	12 months to a/c date in year 2	y/e 30/6/04
	2005/06	CYB	y/e 30/6/05
	2006/07	CYB	y/e 30/6/06

There is an overlap period between 1 July 2003 and 5 April 2004.

(b)	2003/04	Actual	1/7/03 to 5/4/04
	2004/05	Actual	6/4/04 to 5/4/05
	2005/06	12 months to a/c date in year 3	1/5/04 to 30/4/05
	2006/07	CYB	y/e 30/4/06

There is an overlap period between 1 May 2004 and 5 April 2005.

(c)	2003/04	Actual	1/7/03 to 5/4/04
	2004/05	First 12 months	1/7/03 to 30/6/04
	2005/06	CYB	y/e 30/4/05
	2006/07	CYB	y/e 30/4/06

There is an overlap period between 1 July 2003 and 5 April 2004. There is another overlap period between 1 May 2004 and 30 June 2004.

9.3

				£
2004/05	Actual	1/1/05 to 5/4/05	£27,300 × 3/18	4,550
2005/06	Actual	6/4/05 to 5/4/06	£27,300 × 12/18	18,200
2006/07	12 months to a/c date in year 3	1/7/05 to 30/6/06	£27,300 × 12/18	18,200

Overlap period is 1/7/05 to 5/4/06 (9 months). Overlap profits are 9/18 × £27,300 = £13,650.

9.4

(a)	2003/04	CYB	y/e 31/1/04
	2004/05	CYB	y/e 31/1/05
	2005/06	End of previous basis period to date of cessation	1/2/05 to 31/5/05
(b)	2003/04	CYB	y/e 31/1/04
	2004/05	CYB	y/e 31/1/05
	2005/06	End of previous basis period to date of cessation	1/2/05 to 31/3/06
(c)	2004/05	CYB	y/e 31/1/05
	2005/06	12 months to normal a/c date	1/2/05 to 31/1/06
	2006/07	End of previous basis period to date of cessation	1/2/06 to 30/4/06

9.5

The assessment for 1996/97 (the transitional year) would be based upon the 24 months to 31 July 1996. Therefore transitional overlap relief relates to the period from 1 August 1996 to 5 April 1997 (8 months). The relief is £15,900 × 8/12 = £10,600.

The basis period for 2005/06 is the year to 31 July 2005, so trading income for 2005/06 is £600 (£11,200 - £10,600).

Chapter 10

10.1

		Pool	Expensive car		Allowances
		£	£		£
1/6/04 - 30/6/05					
Additions not qualifying for FYA			15,000		
WDA (restricted, £3,000 × 13/12)			3,250	× 60% =	1,950
Additions qualifying for 50% FYA	14,400				
FYA @ 50%	7,200	7,200			7,200
WDV c/f		7,200	11,750		
Total allowances					9,150

The adjusted trading profit is now £32,630 (£41,780 - £9,150). Trading income for the first two tax years is as follows:

Year	*Basis period*	*Workings*	*Trading income*
			£
2004/05	1/6/04 to 5/4/05	£32,630 × 10/13	25,100
2005/06	1/7/04 to 30/6/05	£32,630 × 12/13	30,120

There is a nine-month overlap period from 1 July 2004 to 5 April 2005. The overlap profits are £32,630 × 9/13 = £22,590.

10.2

		Pool	Allowances
		£	£
y/e 31/3/06			
WDV b/f		10,300	
Additions not qualifying for FYA		8,000	
		18,300	
Disposals (£3,000 + £4,000)		(7,000)	
		11,300	
WDA @ 25%		2,825	2,825
		8,475	
Additions qualifying for 40% FYA	1,000		
FYA @ 40%	400	600	400
WDV c/f		9,075	
Total allowances			3,225

10.3

Norma's first period of account covers 20 months and must be divided into two chargeable periods for capital allowances purposes. These are 1 November 2002 to 31 October 2003 and 1 November 2003 to 30 June 2004. The capital allowances computation is as follows:

		Pool	*Car bought 12/10/03 (40% private)*	*Car bought 31/3/05 (40% private)*	*Allowances*
		£	£	£	£
1/11/02 - 31/10/03					
Additions (no FYA)			8,800		
WDA @ 25%			2,200 × 60%		1,320
Additions	27,400				
FYA @ 40%	10,960	16,440			10,960
		16,440	6,600		
1/11/03 - 30/6/04					
Additions (no FYA)		7,200			
		23,640			
Disposals		(1,750)			
		21,890			
WDA @ 25% × 8/12		3,648	1,100 × 60%		4,308
		18,242			
Additions	4,600				
FYA @ 40%	1,840	2,760			1,840
		21,002	5,500		
Total allowances					18,428
y/e 30/6/05					
Additions (no FYA)				14,100	
Disposals		(1,500)	(6,300)		
		19,502			
Balancing charge			(800) × 60%		(480)
WDA @ 25%		4,876			4,876
		14,626			
WDA (restricted)				3,000 × 60%	1,800
Additions	9,200				
FYA @ 50%	4,600	4,600			4,600
WDV c/f		19,226		11,100	
Total allowances					10,796

Profits after deduction of capital allowances are £37,772 (£56,200 - £18,428) for the period from 1 November 2002 to 30 June 2004 and £49,104 (£59,900 - £10,796) for the year to 30 June 2005. Trading income for the first four tax years as follows:

Year	*Basis period*	*Workings*	*Trading income*
			£
2002/03	1/11/02 to 5/4/03	£37,772 × 5/20	9,443
2003/04	6/4/03 to 5/4/04	£37,772 × 12/20	22,663
2004/05	1/7/03 to 30/6/04	£37,772 × 12/20	22,663
2005/06	y/e 30/6/05		49,104

The overlap period is the nine months from 1 July 2003 to 5 April 2004. Overlap profits are 9/20 × £37,772 = £16,997.

10.4

	Factory	*Allowances*
	£	£
y/e 30/6/04		
Cost	57,500	
WDA @ 4% of £57,500	2,300	2,300
WDV c/f	55,200	
y/e 30/6/05		
WDA @ 4% of £57,500	2,300	2,300
WDV c/f	52,900	

Note:

Subtracting the cost of the land (which does not attract IBAs) from the total cost of the factory leaves £80,000. The cost of the offices is more than 25% of £80,000 and so IBAs are available only on the cost excluding offices, i.e. £57,500.

10.5

(a)

	Building	*Allowances*
	£	£
y/e 31/12/98,99,00,01,02,03 & 04		
Cost	45,000	
WDA @ 4% of £45,000 for 7 years	12,600	12,600
WDV c/f	32,400	
y/e 31/12/05		
Disposal value	30,000	
Balancing allowance	2,400	2,400

Note:

The building was not in use on 31 December 1997 and therefore no IBAs are available for the year to 31 December 1997. The tax life of the building begins on 1 January 1998.

(b) The residue of expenditure is £30,000 (£32,400 - £2,400). The tax life of the building ends on 31 December 2022, giving an unexpired life of 17 years 6 months on the date of the second-hand purchase by Maria. Maria may claim an annual WDA of £30,000/17.5 = £1,714.

Note that Maria's first period of account (1 May 2005 - 30 November 2005) is only seven months long, so she will receive IBAs for that period of only £1,714 × 7/12 = £1,000.

10.6

(a) Giles' allowances are:

		£
year to 31/3/05	£30,000 × 4%	1,200
year to 31/3/06	£30,000 × 4% × 6/12	600

Pam's allowances are:

1/5/05 to 31/12/05	£30,000 × 4% × 3/12	300
y/e 31/12/06 etc.	£30,000 × 4%	1,200

Note:

Pam will continue to receive WDAs of £1,200 per annum until the barn's WDV reaches zero.

(b) Giles' allowances in y/e 31 March 2005 are £1,200, reducing the WDV of the building to £28,800. The building is sold for £35,000, but the disposal value is restricted to the original cost of £30,000, giving a balancing charge of £1,200 in y/e 31 March 2006.

The tax life of the building began on 1 April 2004 (the first day of the chargeable period in which ABAs were first given) and ends on 31 March 2029, giving an unexpired life of 23 years and 6 months on the date of the second-hand purchase by Pam (23.5 years). The residue of expenditure is £30,000 (£28,800 + £1,200). Therefore Pam's annual WDA is calculated at £30,000/23.5 = £1,277. But Pam's first period of account is only eight months long, so she will receive ABAs for that period of only £1,277 × 8/12 = £851.

Chapter 11

11.1

(a) £nil.

(b) The loss will be carried forward indefinitely under S385 and set against the first available profits of the same trade.

(c) The loss may be set against the STI of 2005/06 and/or 2004/05.

11.2

	2002/03	*2003/04*	*2004/05*	*2005/06*
	£	£	£	£
Trading income	-	4,710	6,210	14,810
Less: S385 relief	-	(4,710)	(6,210)	(7,940)
	-	-	-	6,870
Other income	5,000	5,000	5,000	5,000
Total income	5,000	5,000	5,000	11,870

11.3

(a)

Year	*Basis period*	*Workings*	*Trading income*
			£
2003/04	1/1/04 to 5/4/04	(£12,720 - £2,460) × 3/12	2,565
2004/05	y/e 31/12/04	£12,720 - £2,460	10,260
2005/06	y/e 31/12/05		nil

(b) The trading loss of 2005/06 is £9,800 (£8,480 + £1,320). A Section 380 claim could be made for 2005/06 or for 2004/05 or for both of these years:

(i) A claim for 2005/06 is pointless since there is no income in that year.

(ii) A claim for 2004/05 would reduce total income for that year to £460 (£10,260 - £9,800) and so eliminate the income tax liability for the year. The personal allowance would be largely wasted.

(iii) A claim for both years is pointless since a claim in 2005/06 is pointless.

The 2004/05 claim would be less wasteful if Marcus declined to claim any capital allowances in either of the first two years of trading. Trading income for 2004/05 would become £12,720 and the 2005/06 loss would become £8,480. Claiming Section 380 relief in 2004/05 would then leave income of £4,240 for the year, which would absorb most of the personal allowance.

11.4

The losses eligible for Section 381 relief are:

Year	*Basis period*	*Workings*	*Trading loss*	*Years for S381 claim*
			£	
2003/04	1/10/03 to 5/4/04	£(26,850) × 6/15	(10,740)	00/01-02/03
2004/05	1/1/04 to 31/12/04	£(26,850) × 12/15 - overlap		
		£(26,850) × 3/15	(16,110)	01/02-03/04
2005/06	y/e 31/12/05		(25,660)	02/03-04/05

If all possible Section 381 claims are made, total income is:

		2000/01	*2001/02*	*2002/03*	*2003/04*
		£	£	£	£
Trading income		-	-	-	nil
Other income		15,100	15,250	16,400	8,450
		15,100	15,250	16,400	8,450
Less: Section 381 relief:	2003/04 loss	(10,740)			
	2004/05 loss		(15,250)	(860)	
	2005/06 loss			(15,540)	(8,450)
Total income (after loss reliefs)		4,360	-	-	-

Notes:

(a) Personal allowances are totally wasted in 2001/02 to 2003/04.

(b) The loss incurred in 2005/06 has been only partly relieved. The remaining £1,670 of the loss (£25,660 - £15,540 - £8,450) is eligible for S381 relief in 2004/05 but there is no income in this year against which to set the loss. The loss will be carried forward under S385.

Chapter 12

12.1

	Nickleby	Copperfield	Drood	Total
	£	£	£	£
1/1/05 - 31/3/05				
(£18,300 × 3/12 = £4,575)	1,525	1,525	1,525	4,575
1/4/05 - 31/12/05				
(£18,300 × 9/12 = £13,725)	2,745	5,490	5,490	13,725
Allocation of profit for the year	4,270	7,015	7,015	18,300

12.2

	Pickwick	Snodgrass	Tupman	Total
	£	£	£	£
Interest on capital	720	1,200	600	2,520
Salaries	8,000	-	8,000	16,000
Remainder (shared equally)	(1,340)	(1,340)	(1,340)	(4,020)
	7,380	(140)	7,260	14,500
Notional loss divided 7,380:7,260	(71)	140	(69)	-
Allocation of profit for the year	7,309	-	7,191	14,500

12.3

The allocation of profit for each period of account is:

	Dodson	Fogg	Jackson	Total
	£	£	£	£
y/e 30/6/03 (shared equally)	8,500	8,500	-	17,000
y/e 30/6/04 (shared 5:4:1)	11,000	8,800	2,200	22,000
y/e 30/6/05 (shared 5:4:1)	14,500	11,600	2,900	29,000

Each partner's trading income is:

Dodson

Year	Basis period	Workings	Trading income
			£
2002/03	1/7/02 to 5/4/03	£8,500 × 9/12	6,375
2003/04	y/e 30/6/03		8,500
2004/05	y/e 30/6/04		11,000
2005/06	y/e 30/6/05		14,500

Fogg

Year	Basis period	Workings	Trading income
			£
2002/03	1/7/02 to 5/4/03	£8,500 × 9/12	6,375
2003/04	y/e 30/6/03		8,500
2004/05	y/e 30/6/04		8,800
2005/06	y/e 30/6/05		11,600

Jackson

Year	*Basis period*	*Workings*	*Trading income*
			£
2003/04	1/7/03 to 5/4/04	£2,200 × 9/12	1,650
2004/05	y/e 30/6/04		2,200
2005/06	y/e 30/6/05		2,900

Note:

Dodson and Fogg each have overlap profits of £6,375. Jackson has overlap profits of £1,650.

12.4

(a) The trading profit of £23,490 for the year to 30 September 2004 is allocated Wardle £16,443, Jingle £4,698, Trotter £2,349. The trading profit of £27,310 for the year to 30 September 2005 is allocated Wardle £19,117, Jingle £5,462, Trotter £2,731. Each partner's trading income is:

	Wardle	*Jingle*	*Trotter*
	£	£	£
2003/04 (6/12 × y/e 30/9/04)	8,222	2,349	1,174
2004/05 (y/e 30/9/04)	16,443	4,698	2,349
2005/06 (y/e 30/9/05)	19,117	5,462	2,731

(b) The untaxed interest of £2,000 for the year to 30 September 2004 is allocated Wardle £1,400, Jingle £400, Trotter £200. The untaxed interest of £2,200 for the year to 30 September 2005 is allocated Wardle £1,540, Jingle £440, Trotter £220. Each partner's untaxed interest is:

	Wardle	*Jingle*	*Trotter*
	£	£	£
2003/04 (6/12 × y/e 30/9/04)	700	200	100
2004/05 (y/e 30/9/04)	1,400	400	200
2005/06 (y/e 30/9/05)	1,540	440	220

(c) The taxed interest of £1,250 (gross) for the year to 30 September 2004 is allocated Wardle £875, Jingle £250, Trotter £125. The taxed interest of £1,360 (gross) for the year to 30 September 2005 is allocated Wardle £952, Jingle £272, Trotter £136. The gross amount on which each partner is charged to tax in 2004/05 (assuming time-apportionment between tax years) is:

	£
Wardle (£875 × 6/12 + £952 × 6/12)	914
Jingle (£250 × 6/12 + £272 × 6/12)	261
Trotter (£125 × 6/12 + £136 × 6/12)	131

Chapter 13

13.1

See text.

13.2

(a) 15% of £20,000 = £3,000.

(b) 15% of £105,600 = £15,840.

13.3

See text.

13.4

		£	£
Trading income			22,450
Less:	Loss relief	1,200	
	Excess of trade charges over unearned income (£250 - £0)	250	1,450
Net relevant earnings for 2005/06			21,000

Karen was aged 60 at the start of 2005/06 so her allowable percentage is 35%. The maximum allowable personal pension premium (gross) which Karen could pay in 2005/06 is £7,350 (35% of £21,000).

13.5

Damon reaches his 51st birthday on 10 July 2004, so the allowable percentage of NRE is 17.5% in 2003/04 and 2004/05 and 20% in 2005/06.

In 2003/04, 17.5% of NRE is £3,010. The premiums paid of £2,500 are allowed in full and there is £510 of unused relief to carry forward.

In 2004/05, 17.5% of NRE is £3,220. The premiums paid of £2,600 are allowed in full and there is £620 of unused relief to carry forward.

In 2005/06, 20% of NRE is £1,120, so there are excess premiums of £1,480 in the year. The unused relief of £400 from 1998/99 is now too old to be used but £1,130 of the excess premiums can be relieved by using the unused relief from 2003/04 and 2004/05 (£510 + £620). The remaining £350 of excess premiums (£1,480 - £1,130) cannot be relieved in any way.

Chapter 14

14.1

(a) No POAs are required because the 2004/05 liability (less tax deducted at source) was less than £500. A balancing payment of £440 (£1,750 - £1,250 - £60) is payable on 31 January 2007.

(b) The amount paid by deduction at source in 2004/05 (£4,390) was not more than 80% of the total liability for the year and the remainder (£2,340) was not less than £500. Therefore POAs are required for 2005/06. A first POA of £1,170 (one-half of £2,340) is due on 31 January 2006 and a second POA of £1,170 is due on 31 July 2006.

A balancing *repayment* of £605 (£6,580 - £4,810 - £35 - £2,340) will be due on 31 January 2007. Marie could have made a claim to pay reduced POAs for 2005/06 if she had known that the POAs based on her 2004/05 liability were likely to be excessive.

(c) No POAs are required because more than 80% of the 2004/05 liability was satisfied by deduction at source. A balancing payment of £3,600 (£16,110 - £12,370 - £140) is payable on 31 January 2007.

14.2

(a) Dorothy's balancing payment was not more than 28 days late so no surcharges are payable.

(b) The first POA of £12,000 was paid 27 days late, the second POA of £12,000 was paid 43 days late and the balancing payment of £4,000 was paid 21 days late. The interest payable is as follows:

	£
£12,000 × 7.5% × 27/366	66.39
£12,000 × 7.5% × 43/366	105.74
£4,000 × 7.5% × 21/366	17.21
	189.34

14.3

(a) Jabran notified HMRC of his chargeability to tax within the permitted six months and so incurs no penalty in relation to this notification.

(b) His completed tax return was due to be submitted to HMRC within three months of the issue date. He submitted the return late (but not more than six months late) and so incurs a fixed penalty of £100.

(c) The balancing payment was due three months after the issue date of the tax return. His payment was more than 28 days late and therefore he incurs a 5% surcharge.

(d) Interest is payable on the tax paid late and interest is payable on the surcharge if it is not paid within 30 days of the date of its imposition.

Chapter 15

15.1

(a) Primary : 11% × (£98 - £94) = £0.44
Secondary : 12.8% × (£98 - £94) = £0.51

(b) Primary : 11% × (£208 - £94) = £12.54
Secondary : 12.8% × (£208 - £94) = £14.59

(c) Primary : 11% × (£630 - £94) + 1% × (£665 - £630) = £59.31
Secondary : 12.8% × (£665 - £94) = £73.09

(d) Primary : nil (earnings do not exceed the primary threshold)
Secondary : nil (earnings do not exceed the secondary threshold)

(e) Primary : 11% × (£495 - £408) = £9.57
Secondary : 12.8% × (£495 - £408) = £11.14

(f) Primary : 11% × (£2,730 - £408) + 1% × (£2,894 - £2730) = £257.06
Secondary : 12.8% × (£2,894 - £408) = £318.21.

15.2

(a) Primary : 9.4% × (£98 - £94) = £0.38
Secondary : 9.3% × (£98 - £94) = £0.37

(b) Primary : 9.4% × (£208 - £94) = £10.72
Secondary : 9.3% × (£208 - £94) = £10.60

(c) Primary : 9.4% × (£630 - £94) + 1% × (£665 - £630) = £50.73
Secondary : 9.3% × (£630 - £94) + 12.8% × (£665 - £630) = £54.33

(d) Primary : nil (earnings do not exceed the primary threshold)
Secondary : nil (earnings do not exceed the secondary threshold)

(e) Primary : 9.4% × (£495 - £408) = £8.18
Secondary : 9.3% × (£495 - £408) = £8.09

(f) Primary : 9.4% × (£2,730 - £408) + 1% × (£2,894 - £2,730) = £219.91
Secondary : 9.3% × (£2,730 - £408) + 12.8% × (£2,894 - £2,730) = £236.94.

15.3

Mark's profit for Class 2 purposes in 2005/06 is £5,633 (£6,890 × 8/12 + £3,120 × 4/12). This exceeds the small earnings exception limit so Mark is liable to pay Class 2 contributions of £2.10 per week. His profit for Class 4 purposes in 2005/06 is £8,080 so Class 4 contributions of £254.80 are payable (8% × (£8,080 - £4,895)).

Chapter 16

16.1

(a) Companies are not chargeable persons, so the sale will not give rise to a CGT liability.

(b) Disposals between husband and wife who are living together are deemed to occur at a disposal value such that neither a gain nor a loss arises. Therefore there will be no CGT liability on the gift.

(c) Gifts to charities are exempt from CGT.

(d) Charities are not chargeable persons and therefore disposals by charities do not give rise to a CGT liability.

(e) The sale is made in the course of trade. Therefore the profit arising will be a trading profit which is subject to income tax, not CGT.

(f) The partnership is not a chargeable person but the partners are. Any CGT liability arising on the disposal of the leasehold property will be divided between them.

16.2

(a) Shares and securities are chargeable assets (apart from gilt-edged securities and certain corporate bonds).

(b) Gilt-edged securities are not chargeable assets.

(c) A table is a chattel. Chattels disposed of for more than £6,000 are chargeable assets.

(d) A chair is a chattel. Chattels disposed of for £6,000 or less are not chargeable assets.

(e) A taxpayer's principal private residence is not a chargeable asset.

(f) Motor cars are not chargeable assets.

16.3

(a) Net losses are £2,500. The annual exemption is lost and the CGT assessment is £nil.

(b) Net losses are £1,000. The annual exemption is lost and the CGT assessment is £nil.

(c) Net gains are £3,650. The unused part of the annual exemption (£4,850) is lost and the CGT assessment is £nil.

(d) Net gains are £9,950. The annual exemption of £8,500 is fully used and the CGT assessment is £1,450.

16.4

Taxable income is £28,675 (£33,570 - £4,895), using the whole of the 10% band and £26,585 of the 22% band. This leaves £3,725 (£30,310 - £26,585) of the 22% band remaining. Therefore CGT is payable at 20% on the first £3,725 and 40% on the remaining £1,675, giving a CGT liability of £1,415.

16.5

(a) Net gains are £6,600. £1,900 of the annual exemption is lost and the CGT assessment is £nil. The losses brought forward of £4,800 remain unrelieved and are carried forward to 2006/07.

(b) Net gains are £9,100. This exceeds the annual exemption by £600, so £600 of the losses brought forward are relieved and the CGT assessment is £nil. The remaining £4,200 of the losses brought forward are carried forward to 2006/07.

(c) Net gains are £14,500. This exceeds the annual exemption by £6,000, so all of the losses brought forward are relieved and the CGT assessment is £1,200 (£14,500 - £4,800 - £8,500). There are no unrelieved losses to carry forward.

16.6

Net losses in 2005/06 are £14,200. The annual exemption is lost and the CGT assessment for the year is £nil. The net losses may be offset against the net gains of 2004/05, 2003/04 and 2002/03, in that order, to the extent that those net gains exceed the annual exemption. Relief is £nil in 2004/05, £2,800 (£10,700 - £7,900) in 2003/04 and £6,500 (£14,200 - £7,700) in 2002/03. Total relief is £9,300. The remaining £4,900 of net losses in 2005/06 cannot be relieved at all.

16.7

31 January 2007.

Chapter 17

17.1

		£
Sale proceeds		172,000
Less: Incidental costs of disposal		8,600
		163,400
Less: Acquisition cost	35,000	
Enhancement expenditure	3,000	38,000
Unindexed gain		125,400
Less: Indexation allowance:		
(i) on acquisition cost $\frac{162.6 - 103.3}{103.3} = 0.574 \times £35{,}000$	20,090	
(ii) on enhancement expenditure $\frac{162.6 - 103.7}{103.7} = 0.568 \times £3{,}000$	1,704	21,794
Chargeable gain (before taper relief)		103,606

(The repainting costs do not rank as enhancement expenditure).

17.2

	(a)	(b)	(c)
	£	£	£
Sale proceeds	4,950	4,350	5,780
Less: Deemed acquisition cost	4,500	4,500	4,500
Unindexed gain or loss	450	(150)	1,280
Less: Indexation allowance			
$\frac{162.6 - 135.6}{135.6} = 0.199 \times £4{,}500 = £896$	450	nil	896
Chargeable gain (before taper relief) or allowable loss	nil	(150)	384

Notes:

(i) In case (a) indexation allowance is restricted to £450 to avoid converting a gain into a loss.

(ii) In case (b) there is an unindexed loss. Therefore the indexation allowance is restricted to £nil.

If the asset was acquired in 2001, no indexation allowance is available. Therefore the chargeable gain (or allowable loss) is equal to the unindexed gain (or loss) in each case.

17.3

	Total	*Gain A (85%)*	*Gain B (50%)*	*Gain C (25%)*	*Gain C (60%)*
	£	£	£	£	£
Chargeable gains	41,000	17,000	4,000	6,000	14,000
Less: Allowable losses	22,000	17,000			5,000
	19,000	nil	4,000	6,000	9,000
Less: Taper relief	10,100	nil	2,000	4,500	3,600
Tapered gains	8,900	nil	2,000	1,500	5,400
Less: Annual exemption	8,500				
CGT assessment	400				

Gain C is divided into a business gain of £6,000 (3/10ths of £20,000) and a non-business gain of £14,000 (7/10ths of £20,000). Both gains have a qualifying holding period of more than 10 years.

17.4

	£
Sale proceeds (June 2001)	100,000
Less: Incidental costs of disposal	5,000
	95,000
Less: Part cost:	
$\frac{£100{,}000}{£100{,}000 + £500{,}000} \times £240{,}000$	(40,000)
Part incidental costs of acquisition:	
$\frac{£100{,}000}{£100{,}000 + £500{,}000} \times £12{,}000$	(2,000)
Unindexed gain c/f	53,000

		£
Unindexed gain b/f		53,000
Less: Indexation allowance		
$\frac{162.6 - 134.1}{134.1}$	= 0.213 × £42,000	8,946
Chargeable gain (before taper relief)		44,054

	£
Sale proceeds (January 2006)	520,000
Less: Remainder of cost (£240,000 - £40,000)	(200,000)
Remainder of costs of acquisition (£12,000 - £2,000)	(10,000)
Unindexed gain	310,000
Less: Indexation allowance	
$\frac{162.6 - 134.1}{134.1}$ = 0.213 × £210,000	44,730
Chargeable gain (before taper relief)	265,270

17.5

(a)

	Original cost	*Rebasing*
	£	£
Sale proceeds	37,500	37,500
Less: Original cost	12,500	
Market value 31/3/82		10,000
Unindexed gain	25,000	27,500
Less: Indexation allowance		
$\frac{162.6 - 79.44}{79.44}$ = 1.047 × £12,500	13,088	13,088
Chargeable gain (before taper relief)	11,912	14,412

The rebasing calculation gives the higher gain, so rebasing does not apply and the chargeable gain (before taper relief) is £11,912.

(b)

	Original cost	*Rebasing*
	£	£
Sale proceeds	37,500	37,500
Less: Original cost	12,500	
Market value 31/3/82		15,000
Unindexed gain	25,000	22,500
Less: Indexation allowance		
$\frac{162.6 - 79.44}{79.44}$ = 1.047 × £15,000	15,705	15,705
Chargeable gain (before taper relief)	9,295	6,795

The rebasing calculation gives the lower gain, so rebasing applies and the chargeable gain (before taper relief) is £6,795.

17.6

(a)

	£
Deemed disposal proceeds	80
Less: Acquisition cost	6,000
Allowable loss	(5,920)

No indexation allowance is available since the asset was acquired on or after 1 April 1998 and (in any case) indexation allowance cannot be used to increase an unindexed loss.

(b)

	£
Disposal proceeds	120
Less: Deemed acquisition cost (November 2005)	80
Chargeable gain (before taper relief)	40

No indexation allowance is available in relation to expenditure incurred (or deemed to be incurred) on or after 1 April 1998.

17.7

(a)

	Original cost	*Rebasing*
	£	£
Sale proceeds	8,450	8,450
Less: Original cost	100	
Market value 31/3/82		7,000
Unindexed gain	8,350	1,450
Less: Indexation allowance		
$\frac{162.6 - 79.44}{79.44} = 1.047 \times £7,000$	7,329	1,450
Chargeable gain (before taper relief)	1,021	nil

One calculation gives a gain and the other gives a nil result. So the situation is "no gain, no loss".

(b)

	Original cost	*Rebasing*
	£	£
Sale proceeds	8,450	8,450
Less: Original cost	100	
Market value 31/3/82		12,500
Unindexed gain or loss	8,350	(4,050)
Less: Indexation allowance		
$\frac{162.6 - 79.44}{79.44} = 1.047 \times £12,500 = £13,088$	8,350	nil
Allowable loss	nil	(4,050)

One calculation gives a loss and the other gives a nil result. So the situation is "no gain, no loss".

Chapter 18

18.1

(a) Wasting chattel. (b) Chattel. (c) Wasting chattel.
(d) Wasting asset. (e) Wasting chattel. (f) Chattel.

18.2

		£
Sale proceeds		7,200
Less: Incidental disposal costs		200
		7,000
Less: Acquisition cost		2,000
Unindexed gain		5,000
Less: Indexation allowance		
$\frac{162.6 - 115.5}{115.5}$	= 0.408 × £2,000	816
Chargeable gain (before taper relief)		4,184

However, the gain is restricted to (£7,200 - £6,000) × 5/3 = £2,000.

18.3

	£
Deemed sale proceeds	6,000
Less: Acquisition cost	50,000
Unindexed loss	(44,000)
Less: Indexation allowance	nil
Allowable loss	(44,000)

18.4

		£
Sale proceeds		25,000
Less: Part cost:		
$\frac{£25{,}000}{£25{,}000 + £85{,}000}$	× 38,500	8,750
Unindexed gain		16,250
Less: Indexation allowance		
$\frac{162.6 - 141.3}{141.3}$	= 0.151 × £8,750	1,321
Chargeable gain (before taper relief)		14,929

The maximum gain is (£110,000 - £6,000) × 5/3 × 25/110 = £39,394. The actual gain is far less than this so the chargeable gain (before taper relief) is £14,929.

18.5

	(a)	(b)
	£	£
Sale proceeds	65,000	35,000
Less: Acquisition cost	50,000	50,000
	15,000	(15,000)
Less: Available capital allowances	0	15,000
Chargeable gain (before taper relief) or allowable loss	15,000	0

Note:

Indexation allowance is not available in relation to expenditure incurred on or after 1 April 1998.

18.6

	£
Sale proceeds	8,000
Less: Unexpired portion of cost $\frac{3}{5} \times £10,000$	6,000
Chargeable gain (before taper relief)	2,000

Note:

Indexation allowance is not available in relation to expenditure incurred on or after 1 April 1998.

18.7

When the lease was acquired it had a 30-year life (Sch 8 percentage 87.330%). On 31 March 1982 there were 28 years 5 months remaining (Sch 8 percentage 85.053 + (1.173 × 5/12) = 85.542%). When the lease was assigned there were 5 years remaining (Sch 8 percentage 26.722%). Therefore the computation is as follows:

	Original cost	*Rebasing*
	£	£
Sale proceeds	20,000	20,000
Less: Unexpired portion of cost		
$\frac{26.722}{87.330} \times £12,500$	3,825	
Unexpired portion of MV 31/3/82		
$\frac{26.722}{85.542} \times £15,000$		4,686
Unindexed gain	16,175	15,314
Less: Indexation allowance		
$\frac{162.6 - 79.44}{79.44} = 1.047 \times £4,686$	4,906	4,906
Chargeable gain (before taper relief)	11,269	10,408

The rebasing calculation gives the lower gain, so rebasing applies and the gain is £10,408.

Chapter 19

19.1

(a)	20 October 2004	200	(bought on same day)
	17 October 1999	50	(bought after 5 April 1998)
(b)	1 December 2004	150	(bought after 5 April 1998)
	17 October 1999	50	(bought after 5 April 1998)
	23 February 1990	250	(S104 holding)
	4 August 1981	50	(1982 holding)
(c)	4 August 1981	950	(1982 holding)
	10 September 1962	250	(pre-6 April 1965)

19.2

	No of shares	*Cost*	*Indexed cost*
		£	£
Bought 29 June 1982	1,000	3,000	3,000
Bought 5 May 1984	1,000	3,500	3,500
Add: Indexation to April 1985			
(a) $\frac{94.78 - 81.85}{81.85} = 0.158$			
$0.158 \times £3,000$			474
(b) $\frac{94.78 - 88.97}{88.97} = 0.065$			
$0.065 \times £3,500$			228
S104 holding at 5 April 1985	2,000	6,500	7,202
Add: Indexation to August 1987			
$\frac{102.1 - 94.78}{94.78} \times £7,202$			556
Bought 13 August 1987	1,350	6,500	6,500
S104 holding at 13 August 1987	3,350	13,000	14,258
Add: Indexation to September 1990			
$\frac{129.3 - 102.1}{102.1} \times £14,258$			3,798
Bought 7 September 1990	2,650	14,150	14,150
S104 holding at 7 September 1990	6,000	27,150	32,206
Add: Indexation to October 1995			
$\frac{149.8 - 129.3}{129.3} \times £32,206$			5,106
Bought 4 October 1995	2,000	22,500	22,500
S104 holding at 4 October 1995	8,000	49,650	59,812

19.3

S104 holding at 4 October 1995	8,000	49,650	59,812
Add: Indexation to April 1998			
$\frac{162.6 - 149.8}{149.8} \times £59,812$			5,111
			64,923
Sold June 2005 (2,000/8,000ths)	(2,000)	(12,413)	(16,231)
S104 holding c/f	6,000	37,237	48,692

	(a)	(b)	(c)
	£	£	£
Sale proceeds	14,000	12,000	17,000
Less: Cost	12,413	12,413	12,413
Unindexed gain or loss	1,587	(413)	4,587
Less: Indexation allowance (£16,231 - £12,413 = £3,818)	1,587	nil	3,818
Chargeable gain (before taper relief) or allowable loss	nil	(413)	769

19.4

The 1982 holding is as follows:

	No of shares	*Cost*	*MV 31/3/82*
		£	£
Acquired 5 August 1978	300	2,400	3,000
Acquired 12 May 1980	200	1,700	2,000
Acquired 11 July 1981	250	2,000	2,500
	750	6,100	7,500
Sold August 2005 (150/750ths)	(150)	(1,220)	(1,500)
1982 holding c/f	600	4,880	6,000

The calculation of the gain arising on the disposal is as follows:

	Original cost	*Rebasing*
	£	£
Sale proceeds	3,500	3,500
Less: Original cost	1,220	
Market value 31/3/82		1,500
Unindexed gain	2,280	2,000
Less: Indexation allowance		
$\frac{162.6 - 79.44}{79.44} = 1.047 \times £1,500$	1,571	1,571
Chargeable gain (before taper relief)	709	429

The rebasing calculation gives the lower gain, so rebasing applies and the gain is £429.

19.5

S104 holding:

	No of shares	*Cost*	*Indexed cost*
		£	£
Bought 21 June 1990	10,000	9,000	9,000
Add: Indexation to March 1993			
$\frac{139.3 - 126.7}{126.7} \times £9{,}000$			895
			9,895
Bought 3 March 1993	10,000	11,000	11,000
S104 holding at 3 March 1993	20,000	20,000	20,895
Add: Indexation to April 1998			
$\frac{162.6 - 139.3}{139.3} \times £20{,}895$			3,495
			24,390
Sold December 2005	(20,000)	(20,000)	(24,390)
S104 holding c/f	nil	nil	nil

The gain arising on the disposal of the S104 holding is:

	£
Sale proceeds (20,000 @ £1.25)	25,000
Less: Cost	20,000
Unindexed gain	5,000
Less: Indexation allowance (£24,390 - £20,000)	4,390
Chargeable gain (before taper relief)	610

The qualifying holding period is eight years (including the bonus year).

1982 holding:

	No of shares	*Cost*	*MV 31/3/82*
		£	£
Bought 28 December 1980	10,000	5,000	6,000
Sold December 2005 (5,000/10,000ths)	(5,000)	(2,500)	(3,000)
1982 holding c/f	5,000	2,500	3,000

The gain arising on the disposal from the 1982 holding is:

	Original cost	*Rebasing*
	£	£
Sale proceeds (5,000 @ £1.25)	6,250	6,250
Less: Original cost	2,500	
Market value 31/3/82		3,000
Unindexed gain c/f	3,750	3,250

	Original cost	Rebasing
	£	£
Unindexed gain b/f	3,750	3,250
Less: Indexation allowance		
$\frac{162.6 - 79.44}{79.44}$ = 1.047 × £3,000	3,141	3,141
Chargeable gain (before taper relief)	609	109

Rebasing applies and the gain is £109. The qualifying holding period is eight years.

19.6

The 1982 holding is as follows:

	No of shares	Cost	MV 31/3/82
		£	£
Acquired 17 February 1963 (@ £9)	500	4,500	7,500
Acquired 8 January 1980	700	8,500	10,500
	1,200	13,000	18,000
Sold September 2005 (1,000/1,200ths)	(1,000)	(10,833)	(15,000)
1982 holding c/f	200	2,167	3,000

The gain arising on the disposal is:

	Original cost	Rebasing
	£	£
Sale proceeds (1,000 @ £40)	40,000	40,000
Less: Original cost	10,833	
Market value 31/3/82 (1,000 @ £15)		15,000
Unindexed gain	29,167	25,000
Less: Indexation allowance		
$\frac{162.6 - 79.44}{79.44}$ = 1.047 × £15,000	15,705	15,705
Chargeable gain (before taper relief)	13,462	9,295

Rebasing applies and the gain is £9,295. The qualifying holding period is seven years.

19.7

1982 holding:

	No of shares	Cost	MV 31/3/82
		£	£
Acquired 8 January 1980	700	8,500	10,500
Sold September 2005	(700)	(8,500)	(10,500)
1982 holding c/f	nil	nil	nil

The gain arising on the disposal of the 1982 holding is:

	Original cost	Rebasing
	£	£
Sale proceeds (700 @ £40)	28,000	28,000
Less: Original cost	8,500	
Market value 31/3/82 (700 @ £15)		10,500
Unindexed gain	19,500	17,500
Less: Indexation allowance		
$\frac{162.6 - 79.44}{79.44} = 1.047 \times £10{,}500$	10,994	10,994
Chargeable gain (before taper relief)	8,506	6,506

Rebasing applies and the gain is £6,506. The qualifying holding period is seven years.

Pre-6 April 1965 shares:

	Original cost	MV 6/4/65
	£	£
Sale proceeds (300 @ £40)	12,000	12,000
Less: Original cost (£4,000 × 300/500)	2,400	
Market value 6/4/65 (300 @ £9)		2,700
Unindexed gain	9,600	9,300
Less: Indexation allowance		
$\frac{162.6 - 79.44}{79.44} = 1.047 \times £4{,}500$ (300 @ £15)	4,712	4,712
Chargeable gain (before taper relief)	4,888	4,588

The lower gain is £4,588, which is then compared with the gain produced by rebasing:

	Rebasing
	£
Sale proceeds	12,000
Less: Market value 31/3/82 (300 @ £15)	4,500
Unindexed gain	7,500
Less: Indexation allowance	4,712
Chargeable gain (before taper relief)	2,788

This is lower than £4,588 so rebasing applies and the gain is £2,788. The qualifying holding period is seven years.

Chapter 20

20.1

25 bonus shares are attached to the 100 shares acquired on 9 October 2003 (which do not join any pool). The remaining 200 bonus shares join the 1982 holding and the S104 holding, as follows:

1982 holding:

	No of shares	*Cost*	*MV 31/3/82*
		£	£
Acquired 17 February 1980	600	900	1,020
Bonus issue January 2006 (1 for 4)	150	nil	nil
1982 holding c/f	750	900	1,020

In effect, the market value at 31/3/82 is now reduced to 4/5ths of £1.70 = £1.36 per share.

S104 holding:

	No of shares	*Cost*	*Indexed cost*
		£	£
Acquired 13 November 1988	200	400	400
Add: Indexation to April 1998 $\frac{162.6 - 110.0}{110.0} \times £400$			191
			591
Bonus issue January 2006 (1 for 4)	50	nil	nil
S104 holding c/f	250	400	591

20.2

The first 125 shares of the disposal are matched with the shares acquired on 9 October 2003. These shares cost £300 and they are sold for £500, giving a chargeable gain (before taper relief) of £200. The remaining 300 shares are matched with the S104 holding and the 1982 holding, as follows:

S104 holding (250 shares sold):

	No of shares	*Cost*	*Indexed cost*
		£	£
S104 holding b/f	250	400	591
Sold February 2006	(250)	(400)	(591)
S104 holding c/f	nil	nil	nil

The gain arising on the disposal of the S104 holding is:

	£
Sale proceeds (250 @ £4)	1,000
Less: Cost + indexation allowance	591
Chargeable gain (before taper relief)	409

1982 holding (50 shares sold):

	No of shares	Cost	MV 31/3/82
		£	£
b/f	750	900	1,020
Sold February 2006 (50/750ths)	(50)	(60)	(68)
1982 holding c/f	700	840	952

The gain arising on the disposal from the 1982 holding is:

	Original cost	Rebasing
	£	£
Sale proceeds (50 @ £4)	200	200
Less: Original cost	60	
MV 31/3/82		68
Unindexed gain	140	132
Less: Indexation allowance		
$\frac{162.6 - 79.44}{79.44} = 1.047 \times £68$	71	71
Chargeable gain (before taper relief)	69	61

The rebasing calculation gives the lower gain, so rebasing applies and the gain is £61. In summary, William has a chargeable gain of £200 with a qualifying holding period of two years and chargeable gains of £470 (£409 + £61) with a qualifying holding period of seven years (plus the bonus year if the shares are a non-business asset).

20.3

1982 holding:

	No of shares	Cost (original)	Cost (rights)	MV 31/3/82
		£	£	£
Acquired 30 September 1979	2,000	1,200		1,500
Rights issue January 1998 (1 for 8)	250		250	
1982 holding c/f	2,250	1,200	250	1,500

S104 holding:

	No of shares	Cost	Indexed cost
		£	£
Acquired 1 December 1992	3,000	3,600	3,600
Add: Indexation to January 1998			
$\frac{159.5 - 139.2}{139.2} \times £3,600$			525
			4,125
Rights issue January 1998 (1 for 8)	375	375	375
S104 holding c/f	3,375	3,975	4,500

20.4

S104 holding:

	No of shares	*Cost*	*Indexed cost*
		£	£
b/f at January 1998	3,375	3,975	4,500
Add: Indexation to April 1998			
$\frac{162.6 - 159.5}{159.5} \times £4,500$			87
			4,587
Sold March 2006	(3,375)	(3,975)	(4,587)
S104 holding c/f	nil	nil	nil

The gain arising on the disposal of the S104 holding is:

	£
Sale proceeds (3,375 @ £1.80)	6,075
Less: Cost	3,975
Unindexed gain	2,100
Less: Indexation allowance (£4,587 - £3,975)	612
Chargeable gain (before taper relief)	1,488

1982 holding:

	No of shares	*Cost (original)*	*Cost (rights)*	*MV 31/3/82*
		£	£	£
b/f	2,250	1,200	250	1,500
Sold March 2006	(2,250)	(1,200)	(250)	(1,500)
1982 holding c/f	nil	nil	nil	nil

The gain arising on the disposal of the 1982 holding is:

	Original cost	*Rebasing*
	£	£
Sale proceeds (2,250 @ £1.80)	4,050	4,050
Less: Cost up to 31/3/82	(1,200)	
Market value 31/3/82		(1,500)
Cost January 1998	(250)	(250)
Unindexed gain c/f	2,600	2,300

		Original cost	*Rebasing*
		£	£
Unindexed gain b/f		2,600	2,300
Less: Indexation allowance:			
$\frac{162.6 - 79.44}{79.44}$	= 1.047 × £1,500	(1,571)	(1,571)
$\frac{162.6 - 159.5}{159.5}$	= 0.019 × £250	(5)	(5)
Chargeable gain (before taper relief)		1,024	724

Rebasing gives the lower gain, so the gain is £724. The total chargeable gain on the entire disposal is £2,212 (£1,488 + £724) with a qualifying holding period of seven years (plus the bonus year if the shares are a non-business asset).

20.5

The value of the part disposed of is £6,000 (6,000 @ £1) and the value of the part remaining is £12,000 (6,000 @ £2) so there has been a 6,000/18,000 (1/3rd) part disposal. The S104 holding is as follows:

	No of shares	*Cost*	*Indexed cost*
		£	£
Bought November 1997	6,000	30,000	30,000
Add: Indexation to April 1998			
$\frac{162.6 - 159.6}{159.6} \times £30,000$			564
			30,564
Distribution May 2005 (1/3rd)	-	(10,000)	(10,188)
S104 holding c/f	6,000	20,000	20,376

The computation of the allowable loss is:

	£
Disposal proceeds	6,000
Less: Part cost	(10,000)
Unindexed loss	(4,000)
Less: Indexation allowance (£10,188 - £10,000)	nil
Allowable loss	(4,000)

20.6

The value of Yolande's shares immediately prior to the sale of rights was £600. £25 is less than 5% of £600, so the sale of rights ranks as a small capital distribution. Assuming that this distribution is not treated as a disposal, the S104 holding is as follows:

	No of shares	Cost	Indexed cost
		£	£
Bought January 1998	300	360	360
Add: Indexation to April 1998			
$\frac{162.6 - 159.5}{159.5} \times £360$			7
			367
Distribution March 2004	-	(25)	(25)
	300	335	342
Sold November 2005	(300)	(335)	(342)
S104 holding c/f	nil	nil	nil

The gain arising on the disposal is:

	£
Sale proceeds	780
Less: Cost	335
Unindexed gain	445
Less: Indexation allowance (£342 - £335)	7
Chargeable gain (before taper relief)	438

20.7

Walter received 19,200 shares worth £82,560, plus £6,000 in cash, a total of £88,560. The amount received in cash is more than 5% of the total and exceeds £3,000. Therefore this does not rank as a small capital distribution and the situation must be treated as a part disposal.

The shares in Oval plc were acquired after 5 April 1998. They are not pooled and no indexation allowance is available on their disposal. The shares cost £70,200 (12,000 × £5.85). The gain on the part disposal is as follows:

	£
Disposal proceeds	6,000
Less: Part cost:	
$\frac{£6,000}{£6,000 + £82,560} \times £70,200$	4,756
Chargeable gain (before taper relief)	1,244

The qualifying holding period is three years. Walter now owns 19,200 shares in Round plc (deemed to have been acquired in April 2002) with a cost of £65,444 (£70,200 - £4,756).

Chapter 21

21.1

So long as Mohammed actually resides in both properties he may choose which is to be regarded as his PPR. Whichever property he bought and lived in first was automatically regarded as his PPR. After he bought the second property (and began residing in it) he could, if he wished, elect that this property should become his PPR for CGT purposes. He would do this if he thought that the gain arising on the disposal of the second property would exceed the gain arising on the disposal of the first property. The election would have to be made within two years of the date from which it is to take effect.

21.2

	Original cost	*Rebasing*
	£	£
Sale proceeds	163,000	163,000
Less: Original cost	18,000	
Market value 31/3/82		21,000
Unindexed gain	145,000	142,000
Less: Indexation allowance		
$\frac{162.6 - 79.44}{79.44} = 1.047 \times £21,000$	21,987	21,987
Chargeable gain (before PPR exemption)	123,013	120,013

The rebasing calculation gives the lower gain, so rebasing applies and the chargeable gain (before considering the PPR exemption) is £120,013. Considering each of the three cases individually:

(a) The house is not a chargeable asset and therefore the disposal is exempt from CGT. The gain is £nil.

(b) After 31 March 1982, Melanie owned the house for 23 years and 7 months (283 months) and was absent for 48 months. There is no indication that the absence was work-related and this absence exceeds the permissible maximum "absence for any reason" by 12 months. Therefore the PPR exemption is £120,013 × 271/283 = £114,924 and the chargeable gain (before taper relief) is £120,013 × 12/283 = £5,089.

(c) Letting relief is available and is the lowest of £5,089, £114,924 and £40,000, which is £5,089. This reduces the chargeable gain to £nil.

21.3

	£
Sale proceeds	172,000
Less: Acquisition cost	55,000
Unindexed gain	117,000
Less: Indexation allowance	
$\frac{162.6 - 95.92}{95.92} = 0.695 \times £55,000$	38,225
Chargeable gain (before PPR exemption)	78,775

Rupert's period of ownership (a total of 244 months) is broken down as follows:

(i)	1 November 1985 to 31 October 1989	48 months	Actual residence
(ii)	1 November 1989 to 31 October 1990	12 months	Working abroad
(iii)	1 November 1990 to 31 January 1993	27 months	Actual residence
(iv)	1 February 1993 to 30 April 1997	51 months	Working in UK
(v)	1 May 1997 to 31 May 1997	1 month	Actual residence
(vi)	1 June 1997 to 1 March 2006	105 months	Living with friend

Periods (i), (iii) and (v) are exempt (actual residence) and period (ii) is exempt (working abroad). Period (iv) exceeds the four-year maximum allowable for working in the UK but the remaining 3 months of this period are exempt as part of the 36 months allowed for any reason. The last 36 months of ownership are exempt but the remaining 69 months of period (vi) cannot be exempt since they are not followed by a period of actual residence. The chargeable gain is:

	£
Total gain (as above)	78,775
Less: PPR exemption:	
£78,775 × 175/244	56,498
	22,277
Less: Letting relief (lowest of £22,277, £56,498 and £40,000)	22,277
Chargeable gain	nil

21.4

	£
Sale proceeds	155,000
Less: Acquisition cost	37,500
Unindexed gain	117,500
Less: Indexation allowance	
$\frac{162.6 - 97.82}{97.82}$ = 0.662 × £37,500	24,825
Chargeable gain (before PPR exemption)	92,675

Samantha owned the house for a total of 19 years (228 months). For 6 years (72 months) the house was used partly for business purposes. The computation of the chargeable gain is as follows:

	£	£
Total gain (as above)		92,675
Less: PPR exemption:		
£92,675 × 156/228	63,409	
£92,675 × 72/228 × 4/5	23,413	86,822
Chargeable gain (before taper relief)		5,853

Chapter 22

22.1

The allowable expenditure in relation to the porcelain is £9,850 (£10,000 incurred March 1996, plus £3,850 incurred March 2003, less £4,000 received July 2003). The computation of the gain arising in March 2006 is:

		£
Sale proceeds		23,500
Less: Allowable expenditure		9,850
Unindexed gain		13,650
Less: Indexation allowance on original cost:		
$\frac{162.6 - 151.5}{151.5}$	$= 0.073 \times £10{,}000$	730
Chargeable gain (before taper relief)		12,920

No indexation allowance is available in relation to the restoration expenditure, since this was incurred on or after 1 April 1998. Similarly, there is no need to make a negative indexation adjustment in relation to the compensation, since this was received on or after 1 April 1998.

22.2

The gain arising on the loss of the original necklace would have been:

		£
Disposal proceeds		19,000
Less: Acquisition cost		13,500
Unindexed gain		5,500
Less: Indexation allowance		
$\frac{142.1 - 103.7}{103.7}$	$= 0.370 \times £13{,}500$	4,995
Chargeable gain		505

The allowable cost of the new necklace is reduced to £18,995 (£19,500 - £505). The gain arising on its disposal is as follows:

		£
Disposal proceeds		24,000
Less: Deemed acquisition cost		18,995
Unindexed gain		5,005
Less: Indexation allowance		
$\frac{162.6 - 142.1}{142.1}$	$= 0.144 \times £18{,}995$	2,735
Chargeable gain (before taper relief)		2,270

22.3

The gain on the disposal of the original building is computed as follows:

		£
Sale proceeds		174,300
Less: Acquisition cost		50,000
Unindexed gain		124,300
Less: Indexation allowance		
$\frac{162.6 - 129.3}{129.3}$	= 0.258 × £50,000	12,900
Chargeable gain (before taper relief)		111,400

(a) £2,500 of the sale proceeds have been retained. Therefore £2,500 of the gain is immediately chargeable. The remaining £108,900 may be rolled-over against the cost of the new building, reducing its allowable cost to £62,900 (£171,800 - £108,900).

(b) £111,600 of the sale proceeds have been retained. This exceeds the gain. Therefore the whole gain is immediately chargeable and no part of the gain may be rolled-over. The allowable cost of the new building is the full £62,700.

(c) The entire sale proceeds have been spent on a replacement building. Therefore none of the gain is immediately chargeable and the entire gain may be rolled-over against the cost of the new building, reducing its allowable cost to £65,400 (£176,800 - £111,400).

22.4

The gains which could be held-over were those relating to chargeable business assets. These were the freehold (£23,500) and the goodwill (£40,000) totalling £63,500. Listed investments do not rank as a chargeable business asset, so the gain of £10,600 was immediately chargeable.

22.5

The amount of the held-over gain is computed as follows:

			£
Disposal value			215,000
Less: Acquisition cost		91,500	
Enhancement expenditure		34,500	126,000
Unindexed gain			89,000
Less: Indexation allowance			
$\frac{162.6 - 149.1}{149.1}$	= 0.091 × £91,500		8,327
Held-over gain			80,673

The son's deemed acquisition cost is £134,327 (£215,000 - £80,673). If he had paid his mother £150,000 for the premises, the held-over gain would be reduced by £24,000 (£150,000 - £126,000) to £56,673 and his deemed acquisition cost would be £158,327 (£215,000 - £56,673).

Chapter 23

23.1

(a) The year to 30 November 2005 is an accounting period.

(b) The period from 1 October 2004 to 31 July 2005 does not exceed 12 months and is an accounting period.

(c) The period from 1 January 2006 to 31 January 2006 does not exceed 12 months and is an accounting period.

(d) The 33 months to 31 August 2005 is divided into three accounting periods. These are the 12 months to 30 November 2003, the 12 months to 30 November 2004 and the 9 months to 31 August 2005.

(e) The 18 months to 30 September 2005 is divided into two accounting periods. These are the 12 months to 31 March 2005 and the 6 months to 30 September 2005.

23.2

(a) (i) Assuming that the debentures were acquired for non-trading purposes, the debenture interest receivable is income from a non-trading loan relationship and is assessable under Schedule D Case III. The gross amount of debenture interest accrued during the accounting period is chargeable to corporation tax.

(ii) The income tax of £2,160 (£8,640 × 20/80) deducted at source from the debenture interest paid must be accounted for to HM Revenue and Customs, but the gross interest accrued during the accounting period is allowed either as a trading expense in the company's Schedule D Case I computation or as a debit when computing the net credit or debit arising from non-trading loan relationships (depending on whether or not the loan is for trade purposes).

(b) Both items would normally be shown gross in the company's profit and loss account.

23.3

The gross amount of interest accrued for the accounting period is a credit on a non-trading loan relationship (assuming that the securities were acquired for non-trading purposes) and will be aggregated with other debits and credits arising on non-trading loan relationships. Net credits are assessed under Schedule D Case III. Net debits may be relieved in various ways (see text).

23.4

The 17 months to 30 June 2005 will be divided into two accounting periods. These are the 12 months to 31 January 2005 and the 5 months to 30 June 2005. The chargeable profits for each accounting period are as follows:

	12 months to 31/1/05	5 months to 30/6/05
	£	£
Trading income (time apportioned)	300,000	125,000
Debenture interest receivable	3,600	2,000
Income from property (time apportioned)	6,360	2,650
Chargeable gains	28,700	49,760
	338,660	179,410
Less: Charges on income	12,000	-
Chargeable profits	326,660	179,410

Notes:

(a) The debenture interest receivable is allocated on the accruals basis. Interest accrues at £400 per month. In the first accounting period, interest is due for the 9 months from 1/5/04 to 31/1/05. In the second accounting period, interest is due for the 5 months from 1/2/05 to 30/6/05.

(b) The chargeable gains are allocated according to the dates of the disposals. Even though the two disposals are on consecutive days, they fall into different accounting periods.

(c) The charges on income are allocated according to the date of payment.

23.5

The chargeable profits for the year to 31 March 2006 are as follows:

	£
Schedule D Case I (trading income)	1,561,400
Schedule D Case III (income from non-trading loans) (£19,820 + £44,670 + £23,980)	88,470
Chargeable gains	531,000
	2,180,870
Less: Charges on income	9,000
Chargeable profits	2,171,870

Chapter 24

24.1

FY2004	1 July 2004 to 31 March 2005	£30,000 × 9/12 = £22,500
FY2005	1 April 2005 to 30 June 2005	£30,000 × 3/12 = £7,500

24.2

(a) Profits are £287,500 (£267,000 + (£18,450 + £2,050)). This is less than the small companies rate lower limit of £300,000 but greater than the starting rate upper limit of £50,000. The small company rate applies and the corporation tax liability is £50,730 (19% × £267,000).

(b) Profits are £1,505,000 (£1,450,000 + (£49,500 + £5,500)). This exceeds the FY2005 small companies rate upper limit of £1,500,000. Therefore the full rate applies and the corporation tax liability is £435,000 (30% × £1,450,000).

(c) Profits and chargeable profits are both £10,000,000. Profits exceed the small companies rate upper limit for FY2005 so the full rate applies and the corporation tax liability is £3,000,000 (30% × £10,000,000).

(d) Profits and chargeable profits are both £1,000. Profits do not exceed the FY2005 starting rate lower limit of £10,000. Therefore the starting rate applies and the corporation tax liability is £nil (0% × £1,000). The company has paid no dividends to individual shareholders during the accounting period so the non-corporate distribution rate does not apply.

24.3

The company's profits are £577,000 (£536,000 + (£36,900 + £4,100)), a figure which lies between the small companies rate lower and upper limits for FY2005. The chargeable profits (£536,000) are taxed at the full rate and marginal relief is available. The computation is:

	£
Corporation tax on £536,000 @ 30%	160,800.00
Less: Marginal relief:	
$\frac{11}{400} \times (£1,500,000 - £577,000) \times \frac{£536,000}{£577,000}$	23,578.89
Corporation tax liability	137,221.11

24.4

(a) Company X has chargeable profits of £875,983 and profits of £908,783 (£875,983 + £32,800) for this accounting period which falls partly into FY2004 and partly into FY2005. Since corporation tax rates and limits are the same in both of these financial years, there is no need to apportion between the two FYs when computing the tax liability (except that separate figures would be required for each FY when completing the company's CT600 return). The computation is as follows:

	£
Corporation tax on £875,983 @ 30%	262,794.90
Less: Marginal relief:	
$\frac{11}{400} \times (£1,500,000 - £908,783) \times \frac{£875,983}{£908,783}$	15,671.60
Corporation tax liability	247,123.30

The strictly correct calculation (splitting the liability between the two financial years) is:

FY2004 (1 month)	£	£
Corporation tax on £72,999 @ 30%	21,899.70	
Less: Marginal relief:		
$\frac{11}{400} \times (£125,000 - £75,732) \times \frac{£72,999}{£75,732}$	1,305.98	20,593.72
FY2005 (11 months)		
Corporation tax on £802,984 @ 30%	240,895.20	
Less: Marginal relief:		
$\frac{11}{400} \times (£1,375,000 - £833,051) \times \frac{£802,984}{£833,051}$	14,365.62	226,529.58
Corporation tax liability		247,123.30

(b) Company Y has chargeable profits and profits of £12,500 for this six-month accounting period which falls wholly within FY2005. The starting rate lower and upper limits are scaled down to £5,000 and £25,000 respectively for a six-month period and the company's profits lie between these scaled-down limits. Therefore corporation tax is due at 19% less marginal relief. The computation is as follows:

	£
Corporation tax on £12,500 @ 19%	2,375.00
Less: Marginal relief:	
$\frac{19}{400} \times (£25{,}000 - £12{,}500)$	593.75
Corporation tax liability	1,781.25

Since the company has paid no dividends to individual shareholders during the accounting period, the non-corporate distribution rate does not apply.

(c) Company Z has chargeable profits and profits of £28,000 for this accounting period which coincides with FY2005. If there were no dividends to individual shareholders, the computation would be:

	£
Corporation tax on £28,000 @ 19%	5,320.00
Less: Marginal relief:	
$\frac{19}{400} \times (£50{,}000 - £28{,}000)$	1,045.00
Corporation tax liability	4,275.00

This gives an underlying rate of approximately 15.27%. Tax must be charged at 19% (at least) on the profits of £8,000 used to pay dividends to individual shareholders, so the tax liability is £8,000 @ 19% + £20,000 @ 15.27% = £4,573.57.

24.5

The due date of payment is 1 June 2005 (nine months and one day after 31 August 2004). The final payment of £4,650 was made on 3 October 2005, i.e. 124 days late. The interest due is:

$$£4{,}650 \times 7.5\% \times \frac{124}{366} = £118.16.$$

Chapter 25

25.1

(a) payment made net of lower rate income tax

(b) income received gross

(c) income received net of basic rate income tax

(d) payment made gross

(e) income received gross.

25.2

Return period	*Tax deducted*	*Tax suffered*	*Tax deducted less tax suffered*	*Cumulative*	*Income tax payable (repayable)*
	£	£	£	£	£
1/4/05 - 30/6/05	4,000	2,200	1,800	1,800	1,800
1/10/05 - 31/12/05	4,000		4,000	5,800	4,000
1/1/06 - 31/3/06		1,300	(1,300)	4,500	(1,300)
	8,000	3,500	4,500		4,500

25.3

The income tax returns for the year are as follows:

Return period	*Tax deducted*	*Tax suffered*	*Tax deducted less tax suffered*	*Cumulative*	*Income tax payable (repayable)*
	£	£	£	£	£
1/4/05 - 30/6/05		7,000	(7,000)	(7,000)	0
1/7/05 - 30/9/05	9,000		9,000	2,000	2,000
1/1/06 - 31/3/06		7,000	(7,000)	(5,000)	(2,000)
	9,000	14,000	(5,000)		0

The company requires an income tax repayment of £5,000. This is made by means of a reduction in the corporation tax liability for the year, as follows:

	£
Corporation tax liability for the year (19% of £240,000)	45,600
Less: Income tax repayable	5,000
Corporation tax payable 1 January 2007	40,600

25.4

(a) See text.

(b) See text.

Chapter 26

26.1

	y/e 31/5/03	*y/e 31/5/04*	*y/e 31/5/05*
	£	£	£
Schedule D Case I	-	23,800	40,300
Less: S393(1) relief	-	23,800	8,400
	-	0	31,900
Less: Non-trade charges	-	-	600
Chargeable profits	0	0	31,300
Trading losses c/f	32,200	8,400	-
Non-trade charges unrelieved	400	500	-

26.2

	£
Schedule D Case I	-
Schedule A	210,200
Chargeable gains	45,540
	255,740
Less: S393A(1)(a) relief	232,300
	23,440
Less: Non-trade charges	23,440
Chargeable profits	0
Non-trade charges unrelieved	560

26.3

The correct answer is (c). Under S393A(1)(a), trading losses may be relieved against total profits (including capital gains) of the accounting period in which the loss was incurred.

26.4

	y/e 31/1/04	y/e 31/1/05	y/e 31/1/06
	£	£	£
Schedule D Case I	22,700	73,600	-
Capital gains	-	-	48,700
	22,700	73,600	48,700
Less: S393A(1)(a) relief	-	-	48,700
	22,700	73,600	0
Less: S393A(1)(b) relief	-	73,600	-
	22,700	0	0
Less: Non-trade charges	1,000	-	-
Chargeable profits	21,700	0	0
Trade losses c/f	-	-	33,400
Non-trade charges unrelieved	-	1,000	1,000

Note:

Losses of £122,300 (£48,700 + £73,600) are relieved, leaving losses to carry forward of £33,400.

26.5

The main effects of a S393A(1)(b) claim are as follows:

(a) Chargeable profits for the year to 31 March 2005 are reduced to £200,000 and the company pays corporation tax at the FY2004 small companies rate of 19%. Without the claim, the company would pay corporation tax at the full rate, less marginal relief.

(b) The maximum ACT set-off for the year to 31 March 2005 is reduced to 20% of £200,000 = £40,000. This reduces the scope for relief of the surplus ACT brought forward from before 6 April 1999.

(c) The corporation tax refund due for the year to 31 March 2005 carries interest dating from 1 January 2006 (or the date on which the tax was originally paid, if later).

Chapter 27

27.1

(a), (d) and (e) are associates, (b) and (c) are not.

27.2

The top five shareholders are Sejanus (with Apicata) 1,020 shares, Claudius (with Livia) 590 shares, Agrippa 300 shares, Cleopatra 300 shares and Tiberius 200 shares, totalling 2,410 shares. So the company is not under the control of five or fewer shareholders.

Sejanus is ranked as a director (since he is a manager and, with his wife, owns 20.4% of the share capital). So the directors are Sejanus (with Apicata) 1,020 shares, Claudius (with Livia) 590 shares, Agrippa 300 shares, Cleopatra 300 shares, Tiberius 200 shares and Gaius 200 shares, totalling 2,610 shares. The company is under the control of its participator-directors and is therefore a close company.

27.3

(a) The director owns more than 5% of the company's share capital so the loan is taxable. The company must pay tax of £3,000 (25% of £12,000) by 1 January 2007 (unless the loan is repaid before then). Once paid, this tax is not refundable until nine months and one day after the end of the accounting period in which the loan is repaid or written off. The director will be subject to income tax on loan interest calculated at the official rate. If the loan is eventually written off (wholly or partly) the director will be taxed on the amount written off.

(b) The director will be subject to income tax on a benefit in kind of £1,800. But if the ticket had been given to a shareholder who was not a director or other employee earning at least £8,500 per annum, it would have been treated as a distribution. The cost of the ticket would have been disallowed in the company's accounts and the shareholder would have been charged to income tax as if he or she had received a dividend of £1,800 (tax credit £200).

Chapter 28

28.1

(a) They are associated companies and therefore they share the starting rate and small companies rate upper and lower limits.

(b) The transfer pricing legislation applies to transactions carried out at artificial prices between group companies, though small and medium-sized companies are generally exempt from this legislation.

(c) They also form a 75% group so trading losses and other items may be surrendered by a group member to any other group member.

(d) Chargeable assets are transferred between the three companies on a no-gain, no-loss basis.

28.2

	£	£
Trading profits	220,000	
Bank deposit interest	6,000	
Income from property	4,000	
Charges	(17,000)	
Chargeable profits	213,000	
FII (£27,000 + £3,000)	30,000	
Profits	243,000	
Small companies rate lower limit (£300,000 × 1/3)	100,000	
Small companies rate upper limit (£1,500,000 × 1/3)	500,000	
Corporation tax on £213,000 @ 30%		63,900.00
Less: Marginal relief: $\frac{11}{400} \times (£500,000 - £243,000) \times \frac{£213,000}{£243,000}$		6,194.97
Corporation tax due		57,705.03

Note:
Small companies rate limits are shared between Alpha Ltd, Beta Ltd and the other active subsidiary.

28.3

Base Ltd has current year trading losses of £90,000 and excess charges of £1,000, giving a total of £91,000. But Apex Ltd has chargeable profits of only £73,000 (£120,000 - £42,000 + £7,000 - £12,000) so the maximum group relief that may be claimed is £73,000.

28.4

A1 Ltd owns at least 75% of A2 Ltd and A2 Ltd owns at least 75% of A3 Ltd, of which A1 Ltd (indirectly) owns more than 50%. Therefore A1 Ltd, A2 Ltd and A3 Ltd form a capital gains group. A2 Ltd does not own at least 75% of A4 Ltd, so A4 Ltd is not a member of the group, even though A1 Ltd does (indirectly) own more than 50% of its ordinary share capital.

28.5

The amount of PP Ltd's loss which is available for group relief is £84,000 (£96,000 less a potential S393A(1)(a) claim of £12,000). This is shared between the consortium members as follows:

	QQ Ltd	*RR Ltd*	*SS Ltd*
	£	£	£
Share of PP Ltd's available loss	26,880	29,400	19,320
Chargeable profits	59,000	47,000	14,000
Maximum group relief claim	26,880	29,400	14,000

Chapter 29

29.1

(a) The value of the supply is £340, VAT charged is 17.5% of £340 = £59.50 and the consideration for the supply is £399.50.

(b) The value of the supply is £333.20 (£340, less 2%), VAT charged is 17.5% of £333.20 = £58.31 and the consideration for the supply is £391.51.

(c) VAT chargeable remains at £58.31 but the consideration for the supply is £398.31.

29.2

(a) Lorna must register since her taxable turnover exceeds the registration threshold.

(b) Mike must register since his aggregate taxable turnover exceeds the registration threshold.

(c) No-one need register. The partnership of "Pat and Phil" is not the same person as "Phil" so the turnover of the two businesses is not aggregated.

(d) The taxable "person" in this case is the company (not the shareholders) and therefore the company must register.

29.3

(a) She is not a taxable person, may not register for VAT and cannot reclaim input tax.

(b) She is a taxable person and must register for VAT. She must account for output tax and may reclaim input tax.

(c) She is a taxable person and must register for VAT unless granted an exemption by HMRC. If she registers she may reclaim input tax. If she is granted exemption she will not be able to reclaim input tax but she will avoid the administrative burden associated with VAT registration.

29.4

See text.

Chapter 30

30.1

See text.

30.2

See text.

30.3

(a) Books are zero-rated. No input tax has been paid and so none may be reclaimed.

(b) No output tax is chargeable if a second-hand car is sold for less than its original purchase price, so long as input tax paid when acquiring the car was not deductible.

(c) The supply of a used commercial building is exempt unless the seller elects for the "option to tax". If this is the case, output tax of £200,000 @ 17.5% = £35,000 must be accounted for.

30.4

Input tax reclaimed is £792 × 7/47 = £117.96. Output tax must be accounted for of £68.06 (scale figure).

Chapter 31

31.1

	Value before AE	*AE for 2005/06*	*AE for 2004/05*	*Value after AE*
	£	£	£	£
Gift to grandson (exempt as a small gift)	-	-	-	-
Gift on marriage (£3,000 - £1,000)	2,000	2,000	-	-
Gift to husband (spouse exemption)	-	-	-	-
Gift to discretionary trust	10,000	1,000	3,000	6,000
Gift to Labour Party (exempt)	-	-	-	-
	12,000	3,000	3,000	6,000

31.2

(a) PET (b) exempt (c) chargeable (d) PET (e) PET.

31.3

The total of transfers brought forward in the seven years to date is £231,000, leaving £44,000 of the nil band to set against the current transfer.

(a) If the trustees pay the tax, the gross value of the transfer is £80,000 and the IHT due is £44,000 @ 0% + £36,000 @ 20% = £7,200, payable on 30 June 2006.

(b) If Nicholas pays the tax, the net value of the transfer is £80,000. The gross value and the tax due are as follows:

	Net	*Gross*	*Tax*
	£	£	£
£44,000 grossed up @ 0%	44,000	44,000	0
£36,000 grossed up @ 20%	36,000	45,000	9,000
Totals	80,000	89,000	9,000

The tax due is £9,000, payable on 30 June 2006.

31.4

The value of each gift after deduction of exemptions is as follows:

		Value before AE	*AE for current year*	*AE for previous year*	*Value after AE*
		£	£	£	£
2000/01	Daughter (£500,000 - £5,000)	495,000	3,000	3,000	489,000
2004/05	Discretionary trust	500,000	3,000	3,000	494,000

Lifetime tax liability

The gift to Martha's daughter was a PET, so no lifetime tax was payable. The lifetime tax on the gift to the discretionary trust was £57,750, payable on 30 April 2005 and calculated as follows:

	Net	*Gross*	*Tax*
	£	£	£
£263,000 grossed up @ 0%	263,000	263,000	0
£231,000 grossed up @ 20%	231,000	288,750	57,750
Totals	494,000	551,750	57,750

Tax liability on death

(i) *Transfer made on 31 August 2000*

The gross value of this transfer is £489,000 and there were no other chargeable transfers in the seven years ending on the date of the transfer. Tax due at death rates applicable on 1 January 2006:

	£
£275,000 @ 0%	0
£214,000 @ 40%	85,600
	85,600
Less: Taper relief (5-6 years) @ 60%	51,360
	34,240
Less: Lifetime tax paid	0
IHT payable by daughter on 31 July 2006	34,240

(ii) *Transfer made on 1 June 2004*

The gross value of this transfer is £551,750 and previous gross chargeable transfers in the seven years ending on the date of the transfer (2 June 1997 to 1 June 2004) were £489,000, which used the whole of the 0% band. Tax due at death rates applicable on 1 January 2006:

	£
£551,750 @ 40%	220,700
Less: Taper relief (0-3 years) @ 0%	0
	220,700
Less: Lifetime tax paid	57,750
IHT payable by trustees on 31 July 2006	162,950

31.5

The quarter-up rule gives 572 + 1/4 × (588 - 572) = 576. The average of the highest and lowest marked bargains is 575, so the shares are valued at 575p and the transfer has a market value of 1,000 × £5.75 = £5,750.

Chapter 32

32.1

Jean-Paul is a UK resident during 2005/06 but he is neither ordinarily resident nor domiciled in the UK. His UK income tax position is as follows:

(a) The earnings from his UK employment are fully taxable.

(b) The earnings from his Belgian employment are taxable but only on the remittance basis. This would be the case even if he were ordinarily resident in the UK (the "chargeable overseas earnings" rule).

(c) The dividends on the Canadian shares are taxable on the remittance basis (if Jean-Paul makes a claim to this effect).

(d) The interest on UK Government securities is exempt from UK income tax since Jean-Paul is not ordinarily resident in the UK.

(e) He may claim personal allowances for 2005/06.

32.2

Normally, a person is regarded as being either resident for the whole of a tax year or non-resident for the whole of that year, but a person who leaves the UK to take up employment abroad for at least an entire tax year (as Amy has done) is regarded as resident for the part of the tax year before the date of departure and non-resident thereafter. Amy's situation is therefore as follows:

(a) In 2003/04 she is resident until 31 December 2003 and non-resident from 1 January 2004. She will receive full personal allowances for 2003/04 to set against her income for that year. Her income for UK tax purposes after 31 December 2003 will consist only of any income arising in the UK (e.g. rents from letting her house whilst away). Her Australian salary will not be subject to UK tax.

(b) In 2004/05 and 2005/06 she is non-resident. Her Australian salary will not be subject to UK tax and she will be taxed only on her UK income, if any. As a citizen of the European Economic Area, she is entitled to personal allowances.

(c) In 2006/07 she is resident from 1 January 2007. She will receive full personal allowances for 2006/07 to set against her income for the year. Her income for UK tax purposes before 1 January 2007 consists only of her UK income. Once again, her Australian salary will not be subject to UK tax.

However, if Amy visits the UK for 183 days or more in any one tax year she will be resident for that year and her worldwide income will be subject to UK income tax. Similarly, she will be regarded as resident if she visits the UK for 91 days or more per annum.

32.3

(a) 90% of the pension is subject to UK income tax.

(b) 100% of the amount of the pension remitted to the UK is subject to UK income tax (if Cara makes a claim to the effect that the remittance basis should apply).

32.4

See text.

32.5

See text.

32.6

	UK	*Overseas*	*Total*
	£	£	£
Schedule D Case I	2,120,000		2,120,000
Schedule D Case V			
(£57,400 × 100/82 × 100/50)		140,000	140,000
Chargeable profits	2,120,000	140,000	2,260,000
Corporation tax @ 30%	636,000	42,000	678,000
Less: Unilateral DTR		(42,000)	(42,000)
Corporation tax due	636,000	-	636,000

Notes:

(i) Underlying tax relief is available since Brits Ltd owns at least 10% of the voting power of the overseas company.

(ii) The unilateral relief given is restricted to the UK tax due on the foreign income. The remaining £40,600 (£82,600 - £42,000) of foreign tax paid is unrelieved.

Answers to review questions

Set A

Question A1

(a)

	£
Car (35% of £19,500)	6,825
Fuel (35% of £14,400)	5,040
Loan (5% of £5,250)	262
LVs (200 @ £4.85)	970
Nursery fees	3,286
	16,383

(b) (i) Consider a car with a lower emission rating. The car on offer has an emission rating which gives the highest possible tax charge. Each 5g/km reduction would save income tax on £339.

(ii) If the £400 contribution is made towards running costs of the car such as maintenance, insurance etc. (not towards private fuel) it will reduce the taxable car benefit.

(iii) Reduce the loan to £5,000, so that no taxable benefit arises.

(iv) Take the canteen meals instead of LVs. No taxable benefit will arise.

(v) Transfer the son to the in-house nursery. No taxable benefit will arise. Alternatively, up to £50 per week of childcare can be received tax-free if the employer contracts with an approved childminder or provides vouchers for paying an approved childminder.

(c)

	Mr Tulliver				*Mrs Tulliver*		
	Total	*Non-savings*	*Savings*	*Divs*	*Total*	*Non-savings*	*Savings*
	£	£	£	£	£	£	£
Salary	50,000	50,000			14,000	14,000	
Less: Pension cont.					840	840	
					13,160	13,160	
Benefit package	16,383	16,383					
BSI (× 100/80)	8,000		8,000		2,990		2,990
UK divs £4,680 + £520	5,200			5,200			
	79,583	66,383	8,000	5,200	16,150	13,160	2,990
Less: PA	4,895	4,895			4,895	4,895	
Taxable income	74,688	61,488	8,000	5,200	11,255	8,265	2,990

Income tax

Mr T	*Mrs T*			
2,090	2,090	@ 10%	209.00	209.00
30,310	6,175	@ 22%	6,668.20	1,358.50
	2,990	@ 20%		598.00
37,088		@ 40%	14,835.20	
5,200		@ 32.5%	1,690.00	
74,688	11,255			
Tax borne			23,402.40	2,165.50

Tax could be saved by switching investments from Mr T to Mrs T, using the rest of her basic rate band (where savings income would be taxed at only 20% and dividends at only 10%).

Question A2

	Total	*Non-savings*	*Savings*	*Dividends*
	£	£	£	£
Employment income	12,720	12,720		
Property income	3,680	3,680		
Annuity £25 × 12	300		300	
UK divs £6,750 + tax credit £750	7,500			7,500
Statutory total income	24,200	16,400	300	7,500
Less: Personal allowance	4,895	4,895		
Taxable income	19,305	11,505	300	7,500

Income tax due

Starting rate band	: Non-savings	2,090	@ 10%	209.00
Basic rate band	: Non-savings	9,415	@ 22%	2,071.30
	: Savings	300	@ 20%	60.00
	: Dividends	7,500	@ 10%	750.00
		19,305		
				3,090.30
Less: MCA £5,950 @ 10%				595.00
Tax borne				2,495.30
Less: Tax credits on dividends				750.00
Tax payable				1,745.30
Less: Tax deducted at source (£300 @ 20%)				60.00
Tax payable				1,685.30

Notes:

1. Rents received are £5,000. Insurance is £370 (9/12 × £360 + 3/12 × £400). The wear and tear allowance is £450 (10% × (£5,000 - £200 - £300)) so total expenses are £1,320 (£370 + £200 + £300 + £450). Property income is £3,680 (£5,000 - £1,320).

2. STI exceeds the limit for age-related allowances by £4,700 so allowances are reduced by £2,350 (£4,700 × 1/2). £2,325 is deducted from the personal allowance of £7,220, bringing it down to the lowest possible figure of £4,895. The remaining £25 is deducted from the MCA of £5,975, giving £5,950.

Question A3

(a) (i) 30 September following the end of the tax year to which the return relates.

(ii) 31 January following the end of the tax year to which the return relates.

(b) (i) 31 January 2006 (POA1), 31 July 2006 (POA2), 31 January 2007 (Balancing payment).

(ii) The two payments on account are generally each equal to 50% of the preceding year's tax liability. The balancing payment (or repayment) is equal to the final liability for the year less the two payments on account.

(c) (i) £100 if the return is not submitted by 31 January following the end of the tax year and a further £100 if the return is not submitted by the following 31 July.

(ii) If a fixed penalty has been imposed for late submission of a return and it then transpires that the tax liability for the year is less than this penalty, the penalty will be reduced to the amount of the liability.

(iii) HM Revenue and Customs may ask the Commissioners for permission to charge a further penalty of up to £60 per day until the return is submitted.

Question A4

(i) *Mr de Praet*

	2004/05	*2005/06*
	£	£
Trading income	20,000	nil
Income from property	5,000	5,000
	25,000	5,000
Less: S380 relief	25,000	5,000
Statutory total income	nil	nil

Mr de Praet's personal allowance is lost in both years. Tax savings are achieved at starting rate and basic rate. If the loss had been carried forward under S385, there would have been no loss of personal allowances and tax savings would have been achieved at the higher rate.

(ii) An FYA of £7,360 (50% × £14,720) is available in the year to 30 June 2005. This increases the loss to £17,360. A Section 380 claim for 2004/05 will reduce total income to £640 (£18,000 - £17,360), so wasting personal allowances.

It would be better to restrict the capital allowances claim to £3,255. This reduces the S380 claim to £13,255, leaving total income of £4,745 which exactly absorbs the 2004/05 personal allowance. The unclaimed capital allowances increase the WDV carried forward and so result in higher capital allowances in future years.

Question A5

If the transactions are of a trading nature, then the profits made by the partnership of Bernard and Gerald will be charged to income tax as trading income in years 2005/06 and 2006/07. The "badges of trade" will be used to decide whether they are trading, as follows:

(a) *Subject matter*. It appears that the subject matter of the transaction is of a type normally associated with a trading venture, rather than of a type more normally associated with investments or personal consumption.

(b) *Frequency of transactions*. There was only one purchase but there were several sales. The fact that sales were made to a number of different garden centres gives the impression of trading.

(c) *Length of ownership*. This was a fairly short-term venture. Most of the barrels had been sold within six months and this again gives the impression of trading.

(d) *Supplementary work*. The barrels were sawn in half and Bernard and Gerald canvassed garden centres in the hope of finding customers. These activities constitute supplementary work and support the view that they were trading.

(e) *Motive*. It seems clear that the barrels were bought with only one view in mind - resale at a profit. This is a clear indicator of trading.

(f) *Acquisition*. The barrels were not inherited or gifted. They were purchased by Bernard and Gerald. This and all the other badges of trade combine to support the view that they were trading.

Set B

Question B1

(i)

	£
Sale proceeds	13,000
Less: Auctioneer's commission (8%)	1,040
	11,960
Less: Acquisition cost	500
Unindexed gain	11,460
Less: Indexation allowance	
0.574 × £500	287
Chargeable gain (before taper relief)	11,173

The maximum gain is 5/3 × £7,000 = £11,667, so the chargeable gain (before taper relief) remains at £11,173. The qualifying holding period is eight years (seven years plus the bonus year).

(ii)

	£
Sale proceeds	900,000
Less: Acquisition cost	300,000
Unindexed gain	600,000
Less: Indexation allowance	
0.889 × £300,000	266,700
Chargeable gain (before taper relief)	333,300

£200,000 of the sale proceeds were not reinvested in the new factory. Therefore £200,000 of the gain is immediately chargeable. The qualifying holding period for this gain (assuming that the old factory was a business asset) is seven years. The rolled-over gain is £133,300.

The base cost of the new factory is £566,700 (£700,000 - £133,300). When this factory is disposed of its qualifying holding period will run from March 2006.

Question B2

(i) The disposal is matched first with the 1,000 shares bought in the following 30 days. These shares were sold for £4,600 and bought for £4,400, giving a chargeable gain of £200. This gain is not eligible for taper relief.

The disposal is then matched with the 2,000 shares bought after 5 April 1998. These shares were sold for £9,200 and bought for £5,000, giving a chargeable gain of £4,200. The qualifying holding period for this gain is five years.

Finally, the disposal is matched with 2,000 of the shares in the Section 104 holding. This holding is as follows:

	No of shares	*Cost*	*Indexed cost*
		£	£
Bought 18 August 1995	3,000	6,000	6,000
Add: Indexation to April 1998			
0.085 × £6,000			510
			6,510
Sold 13 March 2006	2,000	4,000	4,340
c/f	1,000	2,000	2,170

Sale proceeds are £9,200, so the chargeable gain is £4,860 (£9,200 - £4,340). The qualifying holding period for this gain is seven years (plus the bonus year if the shares rank as a non-business asset).

(ii) Sally's CGT assessment for 2005/06 is £1,700, calculated as follows:

	Total	Gain 1 (85%)	Gain 2 (100%)
		£	£
Chargeable gains	30,000	20,000	10,000
Less: Allowable losses for the year	6,000		6,000
	24,000	20,000	4,000
Less: Allowable losses b/f	12,000	8,000	4,000
	12,000	12,000	0
Less: Taper relief	1,800	1,800	0
	10,200	10,200	0
Less: Annual exemption	8,500		
CGT assessment	1,700		

Question B3

(i) The gain on the disposal of the building is:

	£
Sale proceeds	250,000
Less: Acquisition cost	100,000
Unindexed gain	150,000
Less: Indexation allowance	
$\frac{162.6 - 144.2}{144.2} = 0.128 \times £100,000$	12,800
	137,200
Less: "Held-over" gain	127,200
Chargeable gain (before taper relief)	10,000

The immediately chargeable gain is the amount not re-invested (£250,000 - £240,000).

(ii) The "held-over" gain of £127,200 is deferred until the earliest of:

a. disposal of the plant

b. the date that the plant ceases to be used in Ranek's business

c. December 2014 (10 years after the acquisition of the plant).

Question B4

(a) Marlene has net gains of £4,000. These are covered by £4,000 of the annual exemption, leaving a CGT assessment of £nil. The remaining £4,500 of the annual exemption is wasted. There are no losses carried forward.

(b) Moira has net gains of £12,000. Losses brought forward of £3,500 are subtracted from these gains, leaving £8,500. This is covered by the annual exemption, leaving a CGT assessment of £nil. Losses carried forward are £4,500 (£8,000 - £3,500).

(c) Marina has net gains of £3,000. These are covered by £3,000 of the annual exemption, leaving a CGT assessment of £nil. The remaining £5,500 of the annual exemption is wasted. The losses brought forward of £8,000 are carried forward to next year.

(d) Melissa has net gains of £4,000. These are covered by £4,000 of the annual exemption, leaving a CGT assessment of £nil. The remaining £4,500 of the annual exemption is wasted. The losses brought forward of £4,000 are carried forward to next year.

Question B5

(a) *Disposal of flat*

	Original cost	*Rebasing*
	£	£
Sale proceeds	71,000	71,000
Less: Incidental costs of disposal	2,000	2,000
	69,000	69,000
Less: Part cost:		
$\frac{£71,000}{£71,000 + £65,000} \times £29,000$	(15,140)	
Part market value 31/3/82:		
$\frac{£71,000}{£71,000 + £65,000} \times £40,000$		(20,882)
Part conversion costs:		
$\frac{£71,000}{£71,000 + £65,000} \times £18,000$	(9,397)	(9,397)
Unindexed gain	44,463	38,721
Less: Indexation allowance		
$\frac{162.6 - 79.44}{79.44} = 1.047 \times £20,882$	(21,863)	(21,863)
$\frac{162.6 - 90.11}{90.11} = 0.804 \times £9,397$	(7,555)	(7,555)
Chargeable gain (before taper relief)	15,045	9,303

The chargeable gain before taper relief is £9,303. The qualifying holding period is eight years (seven years plus the bonus year) so that the tapered gain is 70% × £9,303 = £6,512.

Disposal of ICI shares

S104 holding:

	No of shares	*Cost*	*Indexed cost*
		£	£
Bought December 1983	20,000	60,000	60,000
Add: Indexation to April 1985 $\frac{94.78 - 86.89}{86.89} = 0.091 \times £60,000$			5,460
			65,460
Add: Indexation to April 1998 $\frac{162.6 - 94.78}{94.78} \times £65,460$			46,840
All sold December 2005	20,000	60,000	112,300

The chargeable gain before taper relief is £37,700 (£150,000 - £112,300) and the tapered gain is 70% × £37,700 = £26,390. The total tapered gains are £32,902 (£6,512 + £26,390). After deducting the 2005/06 annual exemption of £8,500, chargeable gains for the year are £24,402. CGT due is (£32,400 - £23,000) @ 20% + £15,002 @ 40% = £7,880.80.

(b) Mr More should transfer the shares to Mrs More (at no gain, no loss). If she then disposes of them and realises the gain of £37,700, this will be entirely covered by losses brought forward, taper relief and her annual exemption, so saving a substantial amount of CGT.

Set C

Question C1

(a) The accounting periods are the year to 31 March 2005 and the six months to 30 September 2005.

(b)

	y/e 31/3/05	*6 months to 30/9/05*
	£	£
Trading profits (time apportioned)	260,000	130,000
Less: Capital allowances:		
50% × £120,000	60,000	
25% × £60,000 × 6/12		7,500
Schedule D Case I	200,000	122,500
Schedule A	20,000	10,000
Schedule D Case III:		
£2,000 + £2,000 + £1,000	5,000	
£12,000 - £1,000 + £4,000		15,000
Chargeable gains		10,000
	225,000	157,500
Less: Charges on income	5,000	5,000
Chargeable profits	220,000	152,500
Corporation tax @ 19%	41,800.00	
Corporation tax @ 30%		45,750.00
Less: 11/400 × (£750,000 - £152,500)		16,431.25
Corporation tax liability	41,800.00	29,318.75

SCR lower and upper limits for the second accounting period are £150,000 (£300,000 × 6/12) and £750,000 (£1,500,000 × 6/12) respectively.

Question C2

Quarterly accounting for income tax

Return period	*Tax deducted*	*Tax suffered*	*Tax deducted less tax suffered*	*Cumulative*	*Income tax payable (repayable)*
	£	£	£	£	£
1/4/05 - 30/6/05	-	7,040	(7,040)	(7,040)	-
1/7/05 - 30/9/05	9,000	4,400	4,600	(2,440)	-
1/10/05 - 31/12/05	10,400	-	10,400	7,960	7,960
1/1/06 - 31/3/06	-	6,160	(6,160)	1,800	(6,160)
	19,400	17,600	1,800		1,800

£7,960 is payable on 14 January 2006, but £6,160 of this is due to be repaid in April 2006.

Question C3

(a) *Poynton Producers Ltd*

	£
Cost 1 April 1998	150,000
WDA for accounting period to 30/9/98 (4%)	6,000
	144,000
WDA for accounting period to 30/9/99	6,000
	138,000
Notional WDAs for two accounting periods to 30/9/01	12,000
	126,000
WDA for accounting periods to 30/9/02, 03 and 04	18,000
WDV at 30/9/04	108,000

(b) The net cost of the building is £10,000 (£150,000 - £140,000). The period of ownership is seven years and the period of industrial use is five years and seven months (5.583 years), so the adjusted net cost is £7,976 (£10,000 × 5.583/7). The allowances actually given are £30,000, so the balancing charge is £22,024 (£30,000 - £7,976).

(c) The residue of expenditure after the sale is £130,024 (£108,000 + £22,024) and the remaining tax life of the building is 18 years. Sale Switches Ltd may claim an annual WDA of £7,224 (£130,024 × 1/18) for each of its 18 accounting periods to 31 December 2022.

Question C4

(a) The company has two alternatives. One alternative is to carry the loss back under S393A(1)(b) and set it against the total profits (before charges) of the year to 31 July 2004. The other is to carry the loss forward under S393(1) and set it against the trading profits of the year to 31 January 2006.

(b) The main deciding factor is the marginal rate of corporation tax payable in the period in which loss relief is given. The marginal rate for the year to 31 July 2004 is 19%. The marginal rate for the year to 31 January 2006 is 32.75%.

Therefore the better alternative is to carry the loss forward and save tax at 32.75%. The non-trade charges of £750 are unrelieved.

Question C5

(a)

	£
Trading profits	170,000
Less: Capital allowances	32,000
Schedule D Case I	138,000
Schedule A	46,000
Capital gains £6,400 - £1,400	5,000
	189,000
Less: Charges on income	20,000
Chargeable profits	169,000
FII (£14,400 + £1,600)	16,000
Profits	185,000
Corporation tax at 19% due 1 January 2007	32,110

(b) If the company has one subsidiary, the limits for the small companies rate are divided by two. The lower limit becomes £150,000 and the upper limit becomes £750,000. Corporation tax is due as follows:

	£
£169,000 @ 30%	50,700.00
Less: $\frac{11}{400} \times (£750{,}000 - £185{,}000) \times \frac{£169{,}000}{£185{,}000}$	14,193.71
Corporation tax due 1 January 2007	36,506.29

Set D

Question D1

(i) The sale to St Oggs Inc is an export to a non-EU country and is zero-rated, even though the goods in question are normally standard-rated. HMRC may require documentary evidence that the goods have actually been exported.

(ii) Scotland is not outside the UK so the sale to Rappit Ltd is not an export and the supply is standard-rated. The value of the supply is £19,000 (£20,000 less 5%) and the related output tax is £3,325 (17.5% of £19,000). This is the case whether or not Rappit Ltd takes advantage of the discount offered.

(iii) The sale of the machinery is a taxable supply of goods, even though the machinery was a fixed asset rather than stock in trade.

(iv) The hire of electrical equipment is a taxable supply of services.

(v) Unless Wakem & Co. Ltd operates the cash accounting scheme, output tax relating to supplies of goods to Garum Furs plc will have been paid over to HMRC at the end of the quarters in which the supplies took place. This VAT can be recovered from HMRC so long as at least six months have elapsed since the date of supply and Wakem & Co. Ltd has written off the debt in its books. If part-payment is eventually received from the liquidator, part of the recovered VAT will be repayable to HMRC.

Question D2

(a) A Ltd controls B Ltd, C Ltd, D Ltd and E Ltd, so all five companies are associated companies.

(b) A Ltd controls 75% or more of B Ltd, C Ltd and D Ltd so these four companies form a 75% group for group relief purposes. E Ltd is not UK resident and so cannot belong to the group.

(c) The profits of E Ltd (a CFC) do not exceed £50,000, so there is no allocation of E Ltd's profits to A Ltd. The profits of £15,000 are not chargeable to UK corporation tax at all.

Both A Ltd and B Ltd will pay tax at the marginal rate of 32.75% unless their chargeable profits are reduced to the small companies rate lower limit of £60,000 (£300,000 × 1/5). Therefore the first priority when dealing with the losses of C Ltd and D Ltd is to use them to reduce the profits of A Ltd and B Ltd to £60,000 each. This absorbs £85,000 of losses. C Ltd's profits (before deducting any loss relief) are £12,000 and the starting rate upper limit is £10,000 (£50,000 × 1/5). If the remaining £10,000 of losses is set against C Ltd's Schedule D Case III income, this will save tax at 19% on £2,000 and at 23.75% on £8,000. The corporation tax liability of each company is as follows:

	A Ltd	*B Ltd*	*C Ltd*	*D Ltd*	*E Ltd*
	£	£	£	£	£
Schedule D Case I	90,000	100,000	-	-	-
Schedule D Case III	-	15,000	12,000	-	-
	90,000	115,000	12,000	-	-
Less: Group relief	30,000	55,000	-	-	-
S393A(1)(a)	-	-	10,000	-	-
Chargeable profits	60,000	60,000	2,000	-	-
Tax @ 19%/0%	11,400	11,400	0	-	-

(d) If E Ltd has profits exceeding £50,000, as seems likely next year, these profits will be allocated to A Ltd (since E Ltd is a CFC) and assessed to UK corporation tax. This can be avoided if E Ltd adopts an "acceptable distribution policy", which will involve paying at least 90% of its profits to A Ltd. This 90% would then be subject to UK corporation tax but the remaining 10% would escape UK tax.

Question D3

The report should make the following points:

(a) Employees on a nine-month contract will not be absent from the UK for a whole tax year and so, for tax purposes, these employees will be both resident and ordinarily resident in the UK throughout the nine months. Their earnings whilst working abroad will be fully assessable to UK income tax.

(b) Employees on an 18-month contract which includes an entire tax year will be treated as non-resident for the duration of the contract. Their earnings from duties performed overseas (and any other foreign income) will not be subject to UK income tax. As non-residents, they will also not be liable to UK capital gains tax. They will, however, be liable to UK income tax on any income arising in the UK (e.g. rents from letting their homes whilst working abroad).

(c) Employees on an 18-month contract which does not include an entire tax year will be treated as both resident and ordinarily resident in the UK throughout the 18 months. Their overseas earnings will therefore be assessed to income tax. A 100% deduction will be available if they are employed as seafarers and have a qualifying period of at least 365 days.

Question D4

	UK income	*Income from Z Inc*	*Income from X S.A.*	*Total*
	£	£	£	£
Schedule D Case I	500,000	-	-	500,000
Schedule D Case V	-	50,000	40,000	90,000
	500,000	50,000	40,000	590,000
Less: Charges	10,000	-	-	10,000
Chargeable profits	490,000	50,000	40,000	580,000

M Ltd, N Ltd and O Ltd are associated companies, so the starting rate and small companies rate limits are divided between them. Each company has an SCR upper limit of £500,000 and an SCR lower limit of £100,000. M Ltd's chargeable profits are £580,000, so tax is due at 30%.

	UK income	*Income from Z Inc*	*Income from X S.A.*	*Total*
	£	£	£	£
Corporation tax at 30%	147,000	15,000	12,000	174,000
Less: DTR	-	15,000	2,000	17,000
Corporation tax liability	147,000	0	10,000	157,000
Maximum ACT set-off	98,000	0	8,000	106,000

Notes:

(i) Maximum ACT set-off is:

- UK income, 20% of £490,000 = £98,000
- Income from Z Inc, 20% of £50,000 = £10,000, restricted to £nil
- Income from X S.A., 20% of £40,000 = £8,000.

(ii) The shadow ACT arising on any dividends paid in the year by M Ltd will of course use up some or all of the maximum ACT set-off of £106,000, so reducing the scope for relieving surplus ACT brought forward from before 6 April 1999.

Index